ships

Books by Enzo Angelucci:
AIRPLANES
AUTOMOBILES, with Alberto Bellucci
SHIPS, with Attilio Cucari

ships

enzo angelucci & attilio cucari

GREENWICH HOUSE
Distributed by Crown Publishers, Inc.
New York

This 1983 edition is published by Greenwich House,
a division of Arlington House, Inc.,
distributed by Crown Publishers, Inc.

Originally published in Italian under the title *Le Navi*

Printed and bound in Italy by Arnoldo Mondadori Editore, Milan

Library of Congress Cataloging in Publication Data

Angelucci, Enzo.
　Ships.
　Translation of: Le navi.
　Includes index.
　1. Ships—History.　2. Navigation—History.　3. Naval
art and science—History.　I. Cucari, Attilio, 1931–
II. Title.
VM15.A6513　1983　　　387.2　　　82-21116
ISBN: 0-517-407337

h g f e d c b a

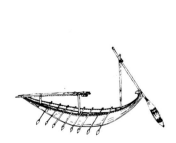

contents

introduction

On a gray expanse of water, constantly swept by violent winds, a man paces his narrow cabin, torn by impatience and hope. Outside, in the dismal night of the southernmost point of the American continent, lies a wild, inhospitable land. The small ship—hardly 110 tons—that has brought him the farthest south that man has ever reached [after countless adventures] is called the *Trinidad*, and the man she has brought to the mouth of the strait that will be called after him is Ferdinand Magellan. The symbolism of this scene is the triumph of one man's determination to conquer the desperation and fear which sweep over him with the terrible winds of that region. It is also a symbol of a resolute faith and a stubborn desire to discover new lands, the same desire that led Hanno the Carthaginian to explore the coast of Africa, and Piteo the Greek to icy Thule, the inhospitable land of the Arctic and Erik the Red to Greenland. It was this that also led Drake, Bougainville, Cook, La Pérouse, and James Clark Ross to take to the seas in a constant struggle of man against himself.

The image of Horatio Nelson fallen on the *Victory's* deck at Trafalgar, mortally wounded by an unknown French sharpshooter positioned in the tops of the *Redoutable*, marks another stage in the history of man and the sea, the most memorable moment in the history of the great sailing warships, their decks painted red to blend with the blood of sailors.

In the course of history, from the Greeks to the present day, dominating the seas has been the means to assert political, military, or commercial superiority. At Salamis, the victory over Xerxes' Persian fleet led to the birth of our present civilization; the defeat of the "Invincible Armada" in the Channel and the North Sea brought Elizabethan England three centuries of uninterrupted supremacy on the seas. At Tsushima the East won its first great victory over the West; the Battle of Jutland revealed the supremacy of battle cruisers, and Midway marked the triumph of naval air tactics. Today the large nuclear aircraft carriers and submarines have an almost limitless autonomy over the seas.

Exploration, commerce, war: these are the main aspects of man's history and progress on the seas and therefore of the history of ships.

The authors have tried to bring this history to life in this volume, which is not meant to be merely a technical work. It is an attempt to satisfy, through information and illustrations, the curiosity of all those who are transported back in time by the dramatic impact of the Tall Ships of 1976 or the harmonious lines of an ocean going vessel, those who are astounded by the amazing technical advances of today or who recognize in the reality or the image of the ship a sign of the greatness of the human mind.

This work is dedicated to all those who have faced the centuries-old struggle against the forces of nature, widening the horizons of knowledge, marking the gradual evolution of the individual, and allowing him to escape from the restrictions of the tribe to become a citizen of the world. It is intended as a tribute to men of the past and of today, daring warriors, intrepid captains, and anonymous sailors; to all of those who have spent their lives on the sea, in the heat of battle or at unknown tasks; to the dedication and industry of men who, during the difficult march of civilization, have been able to transform the prehistoric raft into the perfect ship of today. Last [but not least] this book is dedicated to those who in small boats, driven only by strong winds, dare to defy the silence and constant dangers of the oceans, in search of the intimate satisfaction of a victory without spectators.

To men, therefore, then to the sea and the ships, to all the protagonists of an epic—which is far from finished.

The Authors

The Tree Trunk to the Sail

When man built his first boat is a question that cannot be answered with any certainty. All we really know is that the boat already existed in historical times, and we can only reconstruct its evolution in prehistoric times. There is some fairly reliable evidence to lead us back in time in our search for man's first boats, back to the 8th millennium B.C. Only a great leap of the imagination can take us further back than that, but our imagination must be guided by the evidence and, above all, by common sense.

Imagine primitive man living on the ani-

Animal skins, sewn together and waterproofed, were undoubtedly used both as containers and for floating. This technique is still used in boat construction by some primitive peoples.

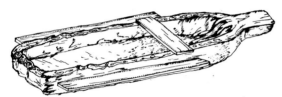

The dugout was made more stable by two rudimentary balancing fins added to its sides.

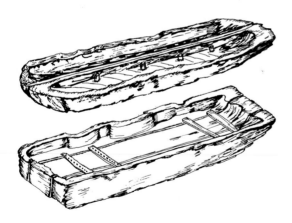

Primitive boats. The first (above) is made of two hollowed-out logs joined together; the second, by joining together three or more planks with crossbars. The seams between the planks were calked with moss and mud.

A canoe still built in Finland. A poplar trunk is dug out and then steamed until it becomes pliable. It is then widened and ribbed.

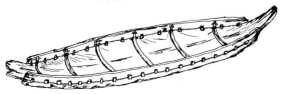

mals he hunted and on the fruits and vegetables he gathered. He knew water and had learned to respect it. The world he lived in was full of danger, and he probably had more than one occasion to ease the pain of a wound by washing it, on a riverbank or on the shore of a lake. It may have been on some such occasion that he first noticed a tree trunk floating idly on the water. It certainly did not occur to him that the trunk was to bring about a fundamental change in the life of his species, nor could he realize the full implications of his first discovery that the floating trunk could bear his weight.

Of course, we have no way of knowing how or when this discovery came about, nor is there any reason to assume that prehistoric man did not know how to swim and that he clutched at the floating tree trunk to keep from drowning. It may have been an altogether casual discovery without any practical consequences, and a long time may have passed before anyone else tried to sit astride another floating trunk. Nevertheless someone eventually realized that the current would carry him significant distances with relatively little physical effort on his part. Also, many animals that threatened man on dry land never ventured into the water. It does not seem too far fetched to suggest that these two attractions — ease of movement and safety from attack — drew man to water as a precious ally, as well as something with

The Prehistoric Boat

The **tree trunk** *may have been man's first means of water transport.*

The **cufa** *of the Tigris and Euphrates rivers, a round boat with a softwood frame and a covering of hides.*

THE ADVENTURE BEGINS

We can attempt to reconstruct the prehistoric development of boats by studying boats used today by primitive peoples.

Boatbuilding techniques of primitive peoples seem to have remained unchanged for thousands of years, and one is often surprised by the remarkable similarity of boats used in areas thousands of miles apart. We can be fairly sure, however, that boats not unlike those illustrated on these pages were developed in the early stages of man's great adventure on the waters of the world.

The Welsh **coracle**, *with its skin-covered frame, is similar to the cufa of Iraq.*

which to quench his thirst and wash his wounds.

It is no easy matter to keep one's balance astride a tree trunk, and it is hard to direct its movement. Eventually man devised solutions to these problems as well. When he lashed two trunks together, he had built his first raft and was no longer in danger of rolling off; and he could propel his raft through shallow, stagnant water with a long pole.

Thanks to the stability of the raft and the control provided by the pole, man ventured farther and farther from shore. He must have reached a point where his primitive rudder no longer touched bottom. But just moving the pole back and forth in the water still gave him some control of his raft. It must have cost this first boatman a great deal of energy to get back to shallow water, but he had discovered that his long pole could propel the raft even without touching bottom. Perhaps this first experience in deeper water led

man to devise his first oar or paddle. He carried shorter and wider pieces of wood onto the raft and used them, instead of the pole, when he went out into deep water. He could cover long distances in less time than he could on land, and by paddling his raft, early man could transport his belongings from place to place as well.

We shall probably never know whether or not man's first water transport was a log or a raft, an inflated animal skin or a bundle of reeds. But we do know that water transport developed long before man discovered an equally practical system of land transport. That is to say, it was a long time after the beginning of water transport that man invented the wheel.

In a few paragraphs we have made an imaginary reconstruction of the possible origin of the first real boat. We have given a hypothetical summary of thousands of years of man's prehistory. But we are still thousands of years from the boats and ships of

The Prehistoric Boat

The first step forward in achieving stability on the water was probably made by binding several trunks together.

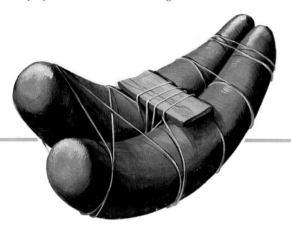

Man then made a more solid support for himself by tying crosspieces to the bound trunks.

In the Strait of Magellan, the natives used boats made of inflated sea lion skins tied together.

A typical single-trunk dugout with a paddle. The prow and stern are clearly distinguished.

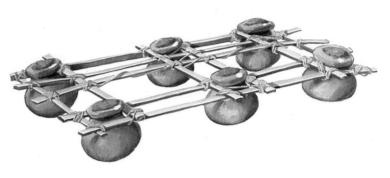

A vessel made of six large pots linked together by thin strips of wood.

historical times. We can reasonably infer the development of boats in this long period from the boats that are still in use among the so-called primitive peoples of today. We may assume that the boats these peoples use are similar to those developed during periods for which archaeological finds and historical documents are lacking. Boats made from a single trunk, hollowed out for lightness and greater thrust in the water, are used in densely forested areas of the world. The dugout probably marked the first real advance in the evolution of paddle-driven boats. The next step was to streamline the dugout by shaping its front end to enable it to cut through the water with a minimum of friction. Thus prow

Two dugouts joined together by crossbeams. This vessel can accommodate four rowers. These double dugouts provide good balance and fairly good speed.

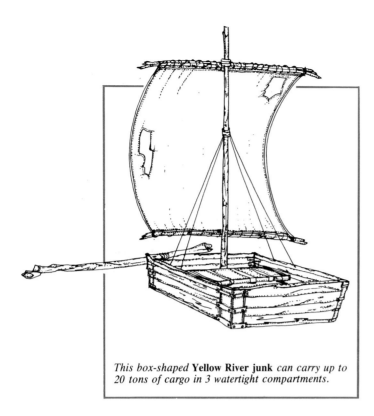

*This box-shaped **Yellow River junk** can carry up to 20 tons of cargo in 3 watertight compartments.*

and stern were first distinguished. The one-piece pirogues used by some Amazon tribes are veritable masterpieces of hydrodynamic streamlining.

Some primitive peoples used only the bark of the tree. The tree trunk was stripped, not hollowed out, and the bark was stretched over frames. These canoes were lighter and faster than dugouts.

In other areas, where thick-trunked trees were scarce, canoes were built of pieces of wood lashed together with clay calking to

keep the water out. Rushes and papyrus plants have also been used in boatbuilding. Strong, lightweight papyrus canoes are still used today on Lake Chad in Africa. Dozens of other examples of primitive boats in use today could be added to this catalog, but what is most relevant to our purposes is this: among ethnological peoples in various areas of the world, where comparable raw materials are available, the kinds of boats used are very similar indeed. For instance, the *cufa* of the Tigris is remarkably like the Welsh *coracle* in form and structure, and the South American balsa dugouts bear a striking technical resemblance to the papyrus boats of ancient Egypt.

Like primitive peoples today, prehistoric dwellers on lakebanks and riverbanks went out in small boats, but there were others who navigated the open sea, perhaps a millennium before man developed agriculture and stock raising. More than 9,000 years ago there were sailors in Greece who explored the Aegean Islands: obsidian artifacts discovered in a cave in the Peloponnesus could have come only from the island of Milos, and therefore they must have been transported by sea. Anyone familiar with the Melteni, the fierce north wind that blows over that stretch of the Aegean, can imagine what skilled sailors those unknown obsidian carriers must have been; and one may infer that they must have had hardy vessels. Although we are sure that sea traffic existed at the time, we know nothing at all about the nature of the watercraft involved. Thor Heyerdahl's *Kon*

*This **kola maran** (flying catamaran) is made tapered towards the bow into a kind of stempost: this lets boats go quite fast under sail.*

A rice boat of the Irrawaddy River, Burma. The hull is formed by steaming and shaping softwood logs, a technique similar to that used by the Vikings for their longships.

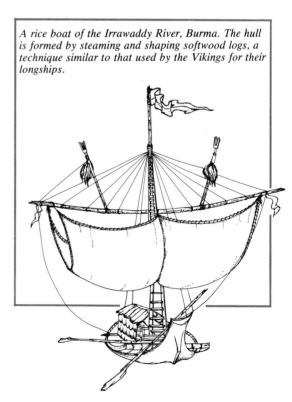

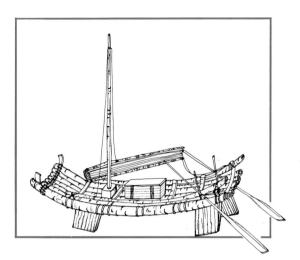

*This **Formosa raft** is constructed of large bamboo canes, which give the hull an ideal shape for standing up to waves and breakers. The planks below the water-line are centerboards that are lowered when the raft is under sail.*

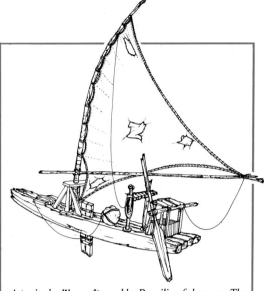

*A typical **sailing raft** used by Brazilian fishermen. The hull is made of large logs held together by wooden pins. Note the primitive stone anchor. This boat too has a sliding keel.*

Tiki expedition showed that skilled sailors could face the open seas on a well-designed raft.

We have more knowledge, however, about the river navigation that was so important in the development of the Egyptian and Meso-potamian civilizations. Evidence of these ancient civilizations suggests that the boat was a very important instrument in spreading civilization.

The oldest sailing vessel of which we have any evidence comes from southern Mesopo-tamia, where a clay model of one was found dating from the middle of the 4th millennium B.C. It has been suggested that this boat was covered with skins, for it is decidedly oval in shape. This vessel was quite different from Mesopotamian boats of the second half of the 4th millennium, which had a high prow and stern, so high that they were often bent back and held taut by cables. The markings on clay tablets suggest that these boats were built of reed bundles tied together.

Egyptian boats of the same period (early 4th millennium B.C.) had crescent-shaped hulls and were much longer and lower. The basic construction material was papyrus, which was bound together in tight bunches to form lightweight and quite strong vessels. The rowers used paddles and sat in the prow, while a pair of paddles in the stern were used for steering. The Nile boats that we can reconstruct from carvings and pictographs had two roofed pavilions set toward the

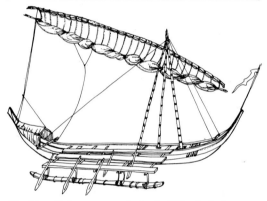

*The New Guinea **caracor** had a hull like that of some North Sea boats. The rowers sit on the outrigger, and there is a three-legged mast.*

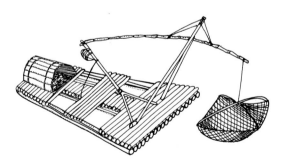

*A bamboo raft called a **salamba**, still used by fisher-men in the Malay Archipelago.*

*A New Zealand **war canoe**. Canoes are built up to 70 feet long and can carry up to 80 men.*

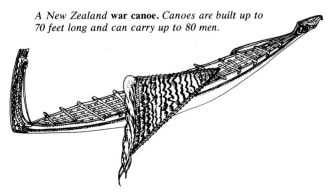

middle of the vessel at an almost standard distance. This could mean that the boats were used to carry important public figures. But this is mere inference, since the evidence that has come down to us is not always easy to interpret. Suffice it to say that some archaeologists believe that what are depicted are not boats at all, but palisades, or fortifications. Thus all the illustrations of prehistoric boats are the result of archaeological deduction and a certain amount of bold guesswork.

We have spoken of Egypt and Mesopotamia, but what was happening in other parts of the world? Archaeological research has not yet come up with an answer to our question; what took place in the seas of the Far East, for example, is still shrouded in darkness. We can only guess that the great rivers of China were equally active and that highly perfected sailing junks were devel-

*The hull of the **Irish curragh** has a skeleton of branches over which oxhides are sewn. It is light, easy to handle, and quite seaworthy.*

An Egyptian papyrus boat. *This very light craft sometimes had a rudimentary two-legged mast that carried a sail of woven reeds.*

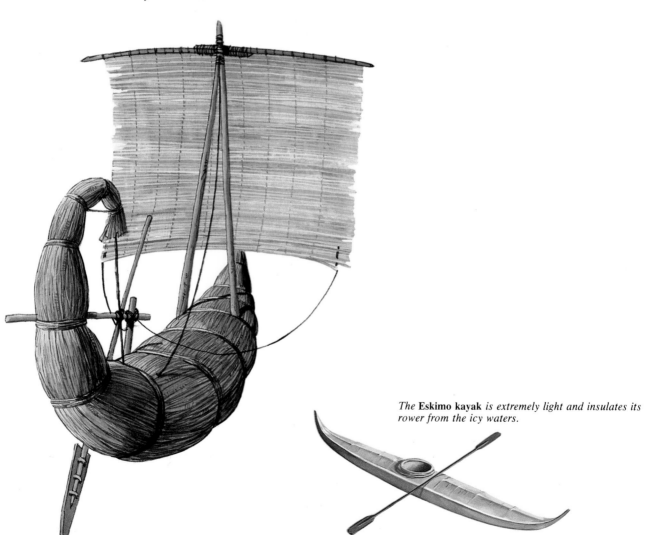

*The **Eskimo kayak** is extremely light and insulates its rower from the icy waters.*

oped at a very early date. But this is merely a hypothesis suggested by the shape of the boats used today by peoples who have remained attached to traditions thousands of years old. Thus we realize just how precious those ancient pictographs are. They give us some idea, at least, of boat development through the ages.

*An **Indonesian double outrigger canoe** with two outriggers and a square sail. It is still widely used in the Celebes Archipelago and can reach good speeds with either sail or paddle.*

Some South American tribes used boats of reed bunches bound together. This boat is still used on Lake Titicaca.

*A typical North American **Indian canoe**. It has a wooden framework covered with sewn hides.*

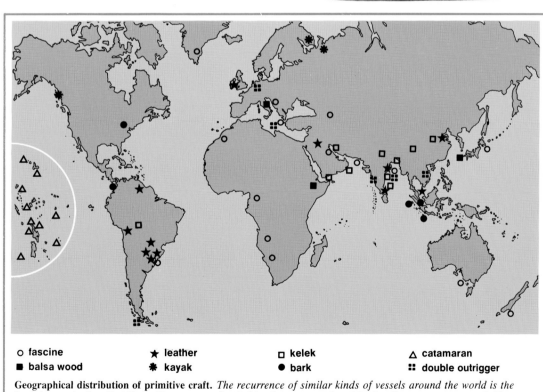

○ fascine	★ leather	☐ kelek	△ catamaran
■ balsa wood	✳ kayak	● bark	⠸⠸ double outrigger

Geographical distribution of primitive craft. *The recurrence of similar kinds of vessels around the world is the best demonstration that "primitive men, confronted by the same need and having the same means available, react in a similar way."*

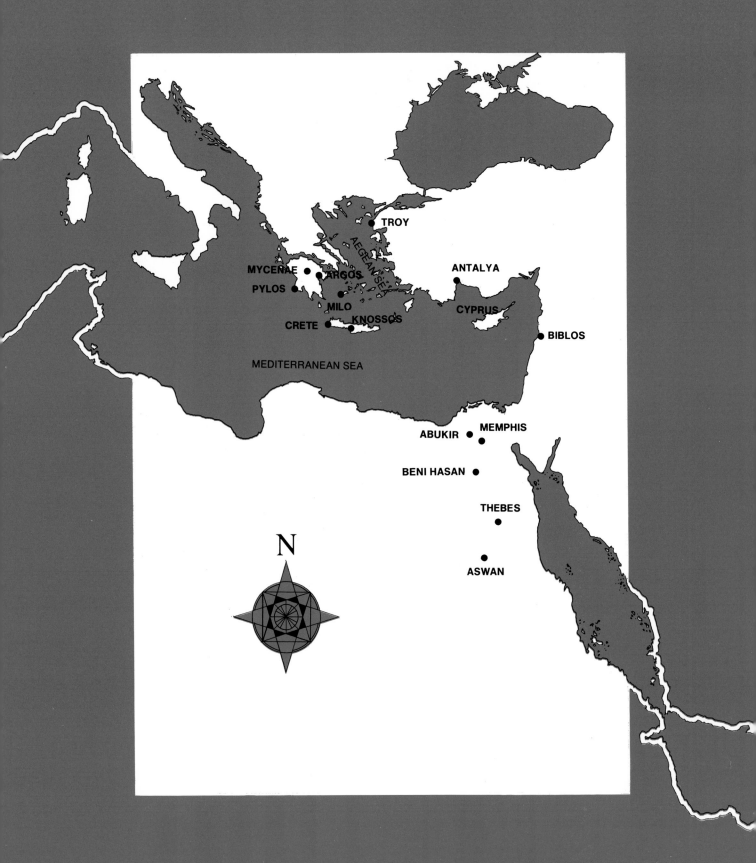

TROY

ANTALYA

MYCENAE

ARGOS

PYLOS

MILO

CYPRUS

CRETE   KNOSSOS

AEGEAN SEA

BIBLOS

MEDITERRANEAN SEA

ABUKIR   MEMPHIS

BENI HASAN

THEBES

N

ASWAN

In the 3d millennium B.C. adventurous navigators were already making the crossing between Egypt and Crete.

The Kingdom of the Oar

The prehistoric evolution of the boat can be imaginatively reconstructed only with the help of the few archaeological remains and by comparative inferences from boats used by present-day ethnological peoples. The situation is not much different when we turn to boats in the protohistoric and early historic periods. But studies in this field have undergone an important evolution in the past fifteen years or so. In addition to the interpretation of written documents and images, there have been more substantial archaeological finds. Modern techniques of underwater research have brought up evidence of Greek and Roman ships. The Nordic peoples have left important traces, thanks to their habit of burying entire ships near the tombs of their chieftains. Burial ships have been found in an excellent state of preservation. Marine archaeology is still a young science, and its full possibilities are probably as yet untapped. The first remains of a Bronze Age ship came to light in the Mediterranean only in 1960. Great progress has been made since then, and new data make it possible to confirm or modify theories developed from the interpretation of written documents, which have sometimes proved to be less than reli-

able in the light of concrete archaeological finds.

For the sake of clarity, we will consider one by one the histories of those peoples who distinguished themselves in the art of navigation from the 4th millennium B.C. This treatment will make it more evident that the evolution of boats throughout the world has been influenced decisively by environmental factors as well as by the evolution of civilization in general.

The first Egyptian boats were made of bunches of papyrus bound tightly together. While many surviving bas-reliefs demonstrate that this construction technique was used for thousands of years, we do not know

*This may well be history's first **pleasure boat**. It belonged to the Egyptian nobleman Mektire, in whose tomb many very accurate miniature vessels were found. This wooden model reminds us of the earlier boats made of papyrus.*

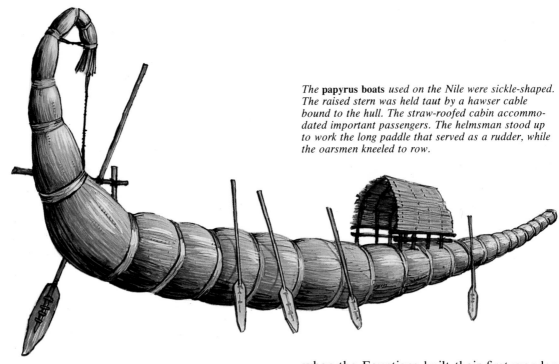

*The **papyrus boats** used on the Nile were sickle-shaped. The raised stern was held taut by a hawser cable bound to the hull. The straw-roofed cabin accommodated important passengers. The helmsman stood up to work the long paddle that served as a rudder, while the oarsmen kneeled to row.*

when the Egyptians built their first wooden boat. We can guess, though, that the sailors of the 4th millennium B.C. found that papyrus boats were fine for river navigation and for paddle propulsion, but far from adequate when the boat ventured beyond the Nile Delta or when there was a large cargo to transport. The problem was not merely the strength of the boat but also the means of propulsion. For paddle power is limited. A real oar requires fulcrum support to achieve leverage and get the most out of muscle power. Papyrus boats could not, by their very nature, provide a fulcrum. Wooden boats could.

The first Egyptian engravings of wooden boats date from about 2800 B.C., the beginning of the Old Kingdom in Egypt. There are hieroglyphics that document an expedition sent to Syria by Pharaoh Sahure early in the

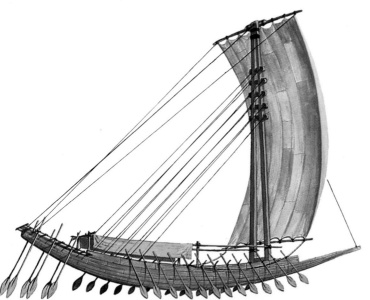

*The first large **Egyptian wooden boats** were probably built around 2800 B.C. They were constructed of very light wooden planks and had neither bracing ribs nor keel.*

Pharaoh Sahure sent such ships to Syria to bring back a cargo of valuable timber. The two-legged mast could be lowered, and a thick, taut cable bound prow to stern and reinforced the hull.

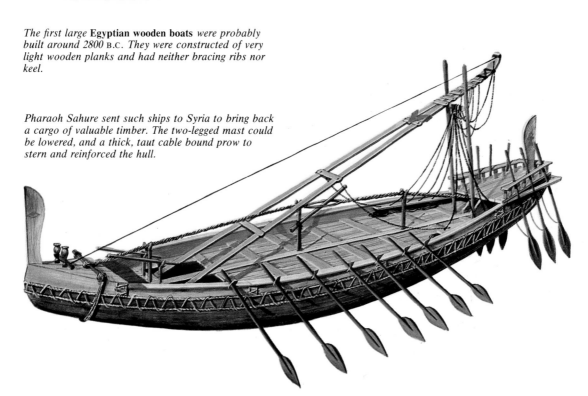

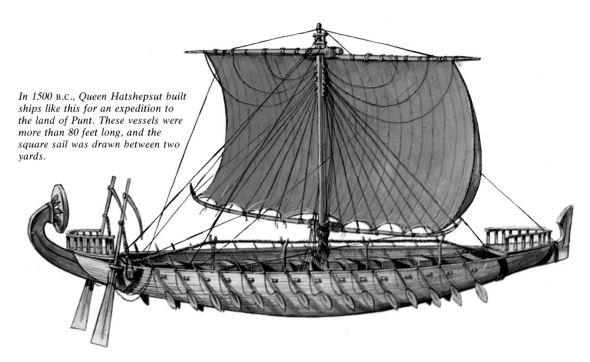

In 1500 B.C., Queen Hatshepsut built ships like this for an expedition to the land of Punt. These vessels were more than 80 feet long, and the square sail was drawn between two yards.

3d millennium to obtain rare wood. Bas-reliefs give us a fairly accurate idea of the features of the first Egyptian wooden boats, which may have been built as early as 3400 B.C. Large trees did not grow in Egypt, but an ingenious building technique was developed to build large boats from small planks of sycamore and acacia. These first wooden boats had neither ribs nor keel, but the hull was solid nevertheless, thanks to the careful joining of the small planks, either with pegs or with perfect notches. The resulting flat-bottomed structure was held firm by the pressure of the water and by its own tension, on the same principle as a stone arch. The very weight and tension of its members give it solidity. It is clear that the construction of such boats involved some highly refined naval engineering.

Later, the boats were strengthened with a

rudimentary keel and wooden deck beams that often protruded from the hull. A thick hawser cable ran from prow to stern, resting on props and under steady tension provided by a rod twisted into the cable weave. This cable, running the full length of the boat, made up for the lack of a more sophisticated keel and prevented the midsection of the boat from collapsing under pressure. The mast was two-legged so as to distribute the weight and sail pressure more evenly over the rather frail hull. The mast on Pharaoh Sahure's boats could be dismantled to make rowing easier when there was no wind. The sail was probably used only in a stern wind on these boats of the 3d millennium B.C., although surviving documents suggest that even then they could flatten in sail to make full use of side winds.

More precise information has survived

A naval battle fought in 1200 B.C. saw Egyptian ships triumph over the "Peoples of the Sea." The ships of Ramses III were the first to carry a crow's-nest and a single rudder.

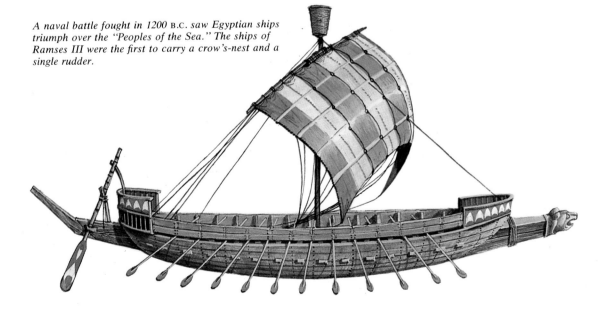

20

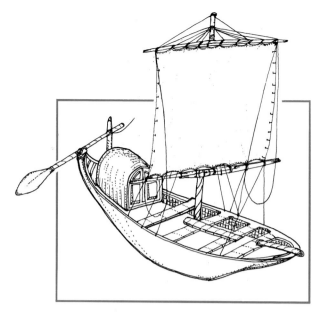

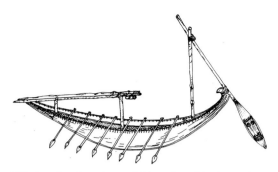

This is a drawing of a model boat found in the tomb of Mektire. The counterweighted mast could be lowered.

This drawing is taken from a wooden model found in the tomb of Mektire. This is the first known example of an Egyptian boat with a central rudder over the stern.

from the period after 2000 B.C., and particularly important remains were found in the tomb of a nobleman named Mektire, who was buried at the beginning of the 2d millennium. These remains include a number of extremely fine model ships; four of these models, painted yellow, represent wooden sailboats. The originals of these models must have been about 40 feet long, and for the first time the thick hawser cable has been replaced by a strong beam from stern to prow. Ten pairs of frames branch off from this beam, with movable planks between them that can be considered the first-known example of *dunnage*. The sail has become much wider and lower, and the mast is no longer two-legged. It has stays and shrouds, and can be lowered. The pair of paddles that served as a rudder have been replaced by one long paddle set over the stern. A ship of this kind was manned by a crew of about 20 sailors.

One of the models found in the tomb of Mektire can be considered history's first pleasure boat: bow and stern have raised platforms, and the general form of the boat is

*An **Egyptian ceremonial ship**, from about 1800 B.C. The hull was wood, but the long shape is reminiscent of papyrus vessels.*

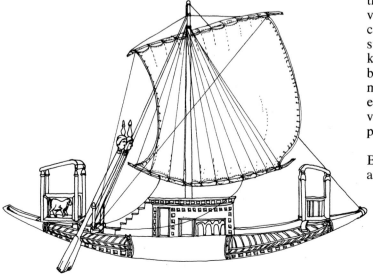

reminiscent of the older papyrus boats. It, too, is steered by a pair of paddles, but it is made of wood.

Mektire's tomb also contained models of papyrus boats, demonstrating that wooden boats were constructed along with papyrus boats. The originals of Mektire's papyrus models were steered by two men with paddles. The models in the tomb were set side by side with a fishing net between them.

In the first half of the 3d millennium B.C. the Egyptians undertook an immense task: the digging of a canal from the Red Sea to the eastern branch of the Nile, thus making a direct connection from the Red Sea to the Mediterranean. The project was probably completed during the reign of Sesostris III (1887–1849 B.C.) and opened new horizons for the maritime exploits of the Egyptians.

The most important period in ancient Egypt's maritime history began in the reign of Queen Hatshepsut, about 1500 B.C. Her large merchant fleet went on an expedition to the land of Punt (perhaps Somaliland) to obtain gold, myrrh, ivory, and ebony, as well as monkeys and greyhounds. A highly detailed series of bas-reliefs in the temple in the valley of Der-el-Bahari depicts the boats that took part in that expedition. The hulls of these boats seem to have been built around a very strong keel. The fact that a hawser cable runs from stern to prow, however, suggests that ribs did not branch out from the keel. The reliefs show projecting deck beams, which provided transverse reinforcement. The one-piece mast stood almost in the exact center of the vessel and supported a very wide, low sail, large enough to provide propulsion even with light winds.

The bas-reliefs of the temple at Der-el-Bahari, near Thebes, also bear witness to another colossal undertaking during the reign

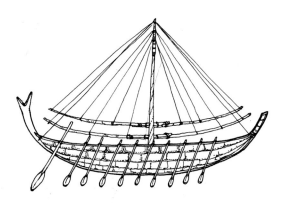

An **Egyptian ship** *from 1700 B.C., built of wood. A taut hawser between prow and stern reinforces the hull, which has no keel or ribs.*

Incised drawings of ships from the year 2000 B.C. have been found on the islands of the Aegean Sea. They show strong Egyptian influence, both in the shape of the hull and in the fittings.

of Hatshepsut. She had two huge obelisks carved at the quarries of Assuan, each of which was about 100 feet high and weighed 350 tons. An enormous boat was built to carry the obelisks down the Nile to Karnak. The boat was a veritable giant. (Suffice it to say that each of the 4 steering controls set in the stern weighed about 5 tons.) It took 27 smaller vessels, each manned by 30 oarsmen, to pull the huge transport. What with oarsmen, helmsmen, and overseers, more than 1,000 men must have been employed in hauling the obelisks upriver, not to mention the enormous number of slaves involved in loading and unloading the "cargo."

Ramses III, the last great Egyptian Pharaoh, developed a military fleet to ward off a concerted attack by Mediterranean raiders. The main characteristics of the ships Ramses III built can be deduced from a 12th-century B.C. relief of a naval battle. The Egyptian ships, clearly based on foreign models, were very low craft with a raised edge around the hull to protect the rowers. A sentinel in a crow's-nest at the top of the mast gave instructions to the men, and for the first time in Egypt we see sails shortened without the yards being lowered. This made maneuvering much faster. The sea victory of Ramses III may have been the last great naval exploit of a people whose history was bound more closely, by its natural environment, to river than to sea navigation. Egyptian power declined under the successors to Ramses III, and technical innovations in shipbuilding also ended. But, even at the height of its development, the typical Egyptian vessel was a river boat.

In discussing the evolution of boats in prehistoric times, we mentioned that there was evidence of full-scale navigation between the islands of the Aegean Sea as far

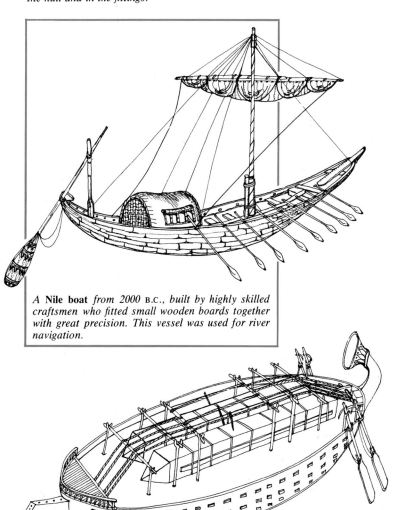

A **Nile boat** *from 2000 B.C., built by highly skilled craftsmen who fitted small wooden boards together with great precision. This vessel was used for river navigation.*

This was the largest **Nile boat** *built at the time of the Pharaohs. It was built to transport two huge obelisks and weighed a total of 700 tons.*

A clay model from Crete is the source of this drawing of a Bronze Age **canoe.**

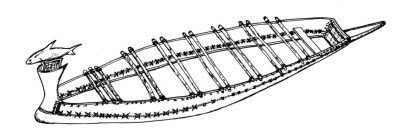

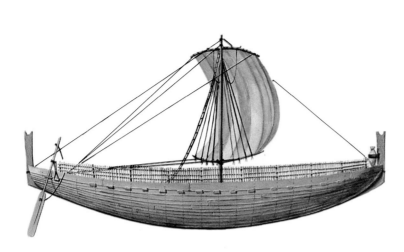

A 7th-century B.C. **Etruscan bireme**. *It closely resembles the Greek bireme, especially in the shape of its hull.*

A **Phoenician cargo ship** *of the 2d century* B.C. *The hull was very strong, despite the absence of keel and ribs. The square sail was hoisted with a yard.*

A Judaean cargo ship of the 14th century B.C. *The rounded hull is typical of merchant vessels of the time. The only means of propulsion seems to be the square sail, but it is probable that oars were also used, at least for maneuvering in port.*

back as the 8th millennium B.C., but we know next to nothing about the maritime history of the Aegean peoples. The excavation of objects that must have been carried by sea demonstrates that maritime traffic must have been fairly important. A clay-model boat dating from the early Aegean Bronze Age (3d millennium B.C.), found in Crete, is evidence of the kind of ships that Aegean sailors launched on a sea that could often be quite rough. They were long canoe-shaped vessels. They may have been built of oak with crossbeam reinforcement, and the prow was almost vertical.

Incised Cretan jewels dating from about 2200–2000 B.C. portray sailing ships with a high, almost vertical stempost, and a raised stern that probably helped the boats float higher in the water. The prow of the ships of that age suggests that the Cretans understood that vessels could be kept on course more easily if the keel was lengthened.

A **Roman cargo ship** *of the 3d century* A.D. *The rounded and deeper hull made cargo stowage more practical.*

*A **Greek merchant ship** of the 7th century B.C. The scanty information we have suggests that these ships had no decks but simply a gangway over the cargo area.*

Maritime commerce in the Mediterranean increased in the late Bronze Age. For many years scholars credited the Aegeans with the main role in this development of seafaring trade. The evidence for this theory came from the many finds of Minoan and Mycenean pottery all around the shores of the Mediterranean. It seemed likely that the sea transport of copper must also have been in the control of the Achaeans, and some written documents seemed to confirm this theory. The case for pottery was clear. Its style indicated its provenance. But copper was transported in ingots and was worked into objects only after delivery. Thus the location of worked metal finds provides no indication of source or carrier.

Recent research, however, has shown that the Phoenicians played an outstanding role in commerce and navigation at the time. The first evidence of this fact came to light in some tomb paintings found in Egypt and dating from between 1500 and 1200 B.C. They clearly refer to copper ingots carried by Syrian ships.

But the most convincing proof of Phoenician maritime activity is provided by the discovery of a Canaanite ship in Lycia, near Cape Chelidonia. In 1960, Peter Throckmorton and George Bass organized an expedition to recover and study the remains of that ship. Its hull had been practically destroyed by the sea, but much of the cargo was recovered. It consisted of a complete supply of material for metalworking, including ingots of copper, bronze, and tin, and a complete set of tools for working metals.

On the basis of this evidence and further studies still being carried out, it is clear that Phoenician merchant sailors played a major role in maritime trade in the late Bronze Age. Unfortunately, very little is known about their ships. Our idea of them comes from the art of other peoples, such as the Egyptians, Assyrians, and Greeks. Wall paintings from the Egyptian tomb at Drah Abou'l Neggah, dated from about 1500 B.C., show that the Phoenician merchant ships resembled Egyptian vessels of the same period, although the absence of the hawser cable suggests that they had a stronger hull. This is a likely hypothesis, because Syria was rich in large forests. The mast was set almost in the middle of the ship, and a protective rail ran from stern to bow.

A bas-relief on a sarcophagus at Sidon shows that by the 1st century B.C. Phoenician merchant ships had taken on that rounded form that was to mark all transport vessels for many centuries.

Not only were the Phoenicians able merchants but they also developed a powerful military fleet. Indeed, the first documented military bireme is Phoenician. Galleys with two banks of oars can be seen in Assyrian bas-reliefs dated from about 70 B.C. The

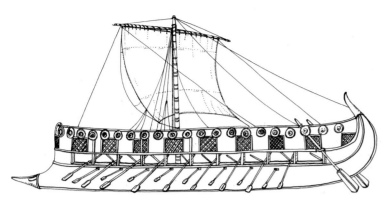

*A **Phoenician bireme** of the 8th century B.C. It was a long warship with two banks of oars and a combat deck set above the thwarts of the oarsmen.*

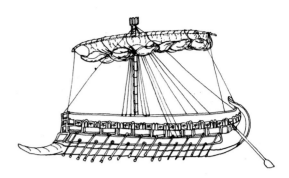

*Another reconstruction: a **Phoenician warship**. One constant element was the combat deck set above the oarsmen. This ship also had a crow's-nest.*

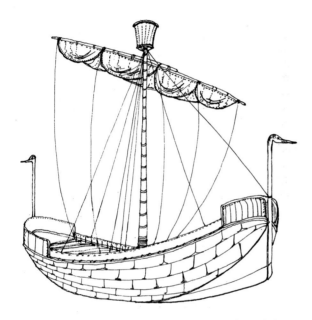

A ship depicted in a tomb at Medinet Habu as belonging to the "Peoples of the Sea." The bow and stern are alike. The sail is square, and the mast is topped by a crow's-nest.

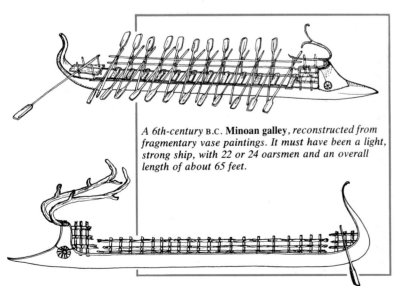

*A 6th-century B.C. **Minoan galley**, reconstructed from fragmentary vase paintings. It must have been a light, strong ship, with 22 or 24 oarsmen and an overall length of about 65 feet.*

prows of these ships had a horn-shaped ram, and a long, narrow combat deck ran above the oarsmen's benches. The hull was very narrow, probably carved from a single trunk, and could therefore achieve impressive impact when rammed against another ship.

There is little reliable documentation about Phoenician construction techniques, though it is clear that this people must have produced superb sailors and vessels. Archaeological research may discover more about the ships that, as Herodotus tells us, the Phoenicians sailed around the continent of Africa at the end of the 7th century B.C., setting out eastward from the Arabian Gulf and reaching Egypt again through the Strait of Gibraltar.

About the middle of the 2d millennium B.C. Cretan-Mycenaean civilization came to an abrupt end, perhaps as a result of a cataclysm that invested the entire Aegean area. The next culture to come to the fore in this area was Achaean, and it too was a maritime civilization. We know little or nothing of the ships in which the legendary Argonauts set out on their quest for the Golden Fleece, and there are only scraps of information about the ships that carried the Achaeans to the Trojan War. All we know is that these ships may have had only one bank of oars. The information we can deduce from Greek bowls and vases datable from 600 B.C. is also sketchy. At any rate, one can guess that cargo ships of the period had a stumpy prow very much like that of some present-day Sicilian and Maltese fishing boats. The stern, instead, was higher and more tapered, with two long steering rudders. Propulsion was provided almost exclusively by a square sail, while the oars were used for maneuvering and in case of calm.

An important contribution to our knowledge of Greek merchant ships of the 4th

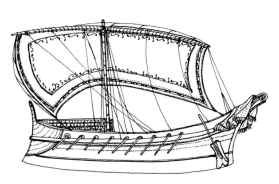

The mythical Greek heroes who set out to find the Golden Fleece may have sailed a ship like this. Nine pairs of oars served for port maneuvering and for propulsion when the sea was becalmed.

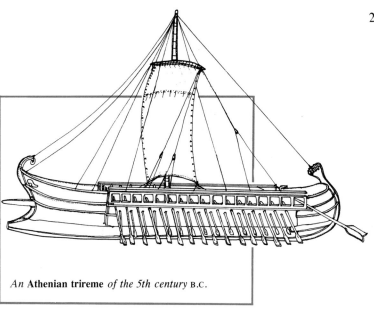

*An **Athenian trireme** of the 5th century B.C.*

century B.C. was made in the years 1967–1969, with the discovery and study of the so-called *Kyrenian* ship. The discovery was made by a group of archaeologists led by Michel Katzev. The ship had been completely buried by the sand, and part of the hull was well preserved. The vessel was about 52 feet long, with a transom stern, while the prow (of which only a small section survived) seemed to be more tapered and projecting than those of ships depicted on the vases of the 6th and 5th centuries B.C. The ship was built entirely of pinewood, and the building technique was as follows: first the keel was laid; then the outer shell was raised by fitting the pine planks together with pins set into notches; and finally, the framework was fastened to the plans by copper nails hammered in from outside. Thus the frame had a strengthening and not a bearing function. The outside of the hull was completely covered with lead sheeting fastened by copper nails. This "armor" served to protect the wood from the destructive action of marine

organisms. Rolls of lead sheeting were found on board the ship, together with tools for repairing damaged sections of the "armor."

The mast was set toward the prow on a sturdy base. The positioning of the mast suggests that a gaff sail was used rather than a square one.

Greek artists seem not to have been interested in depicting merchant ships, but many representations of military vessels survive. These are clearly different in shape from those used for commerce. A war vessel had to meet some specific demands: speed, light weight, and a strong keel. Light weight was obtained through the use of firwood for the hull. But fir did not stand up well at sea, and ships had to be towed to shore for repairs quite often. The keel had to be strong for two reasons: to stand up to the shock of being rammed by enemy ships, and to survive damage and abrasion when it was hauled overland.

The sail was raised only on long trips, while the oarsmen supplied the needed thrust

Greek ships controlled the Mediterranean for a long time. Fitted with a large square sail for long voyages, they had a very long hull, strong enough to stand up to the tremendous strain of ramming.

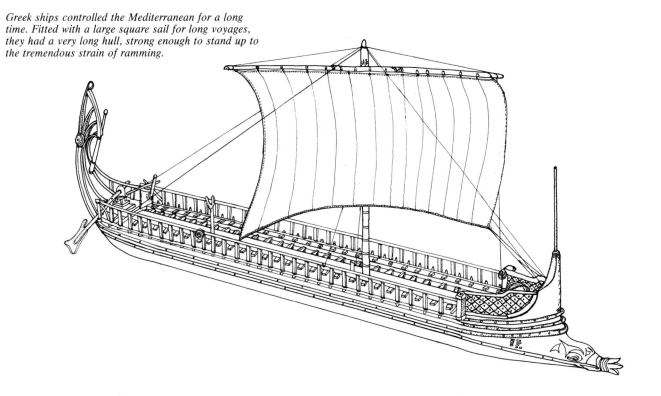

26

*Artists of the 1st century
B.C. depicted Phoenician
biremes in bas-reliefs.
They were very fast and
solid vessels, but their
low sides made them un-
practical in high seas.*

in battle, when ramming the enemy required speed and precision. The first warships of this type were the *biremes*, clear depictions of which appear in vase paintings of the 7th and 6th centuries B.C. Greek shipbuilders must have been under constant pressure to build stronger and faster vessels. They eventually developed the *trireme*, a warship with three banks of oars; it was less maneuverable than the bireme but certainly able to provide greater ramming impact. Ramming was a basic feature of the naval strategy of the time. Such ships were the leading actors at the Battle of Salamis (480 B.C.), where 310 Greek triremes under the command of Themistocles defeated the 1,207 ships of Xerxes' Persian fleet.

Several ancient writers mention the *quad-riremes* and *quinqueremes* built by the Greeks of Syracuse. For a long time scholars, with the support of naval experts, doubted that such ships could ever have been built. But a recent theory, and a more reliable one

in the present authors' opinion, suggests that the quadriremes and quinqueremes mentioned by ancient historians were not ships with four or five superimposed banks of oars but wider ships that could accommodate additional oarsmen. Thus parallel rows of oarsmen were not stationed one above the other. There was room for more rowers, and they had longer oars. It is probable that there were never more than three superimposed banks of oars; the additional banks of rowers sat next to, rather than above, the others. There is recent evidence that seems to support this interpretation, and it suggests that ancient historians knew what they were talking about.

The people that lived along the Italian coast of the Tyrrhenian Sea, in what is now Tuscany and upper Latium, certainly had great familiarity with the sea. There is evidence of intense maritime activity in that area as far back as the 7th century B.C., and Etruscan remains from the period have been

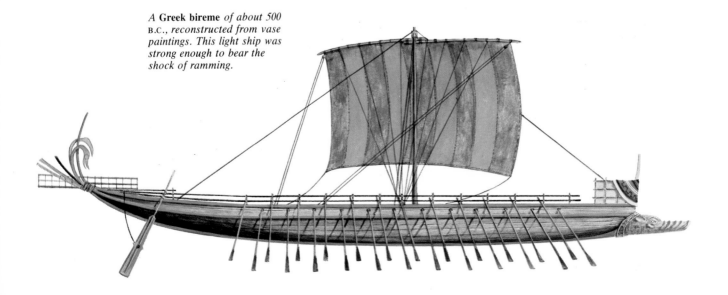

*A **Greek bireme** of about 500
B.C., reconstructed from vase
paintings. This light ship was
strong enough to bear the
shock of ramming.*

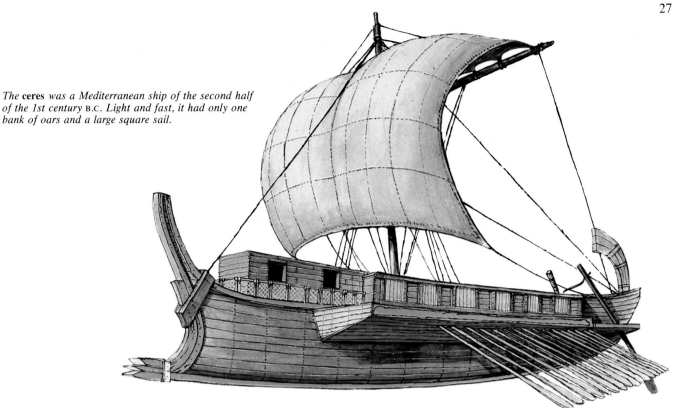

*The **ceres** was a Mediterranean ship of the second half of the 1st century B.C. Light and fast, it had only one bank of oars and a large square sail.*

found on practically all the shores of the Mediterranean. But trade was not the only maritime activity of the Etruscans. They were well known to other Mediterranean peoples for their pirate ships—fast vessels, probably biremes, that raided all over the Mediterranean basin. A vase dated from 670 B.C. shows an Etruscan ship with two raised platforms, one at the bow and the other at the stern, and a rostrum that is not merely an extension of the prow but makes a sharp angle with it. There are still very few documents to help reconstruct Etruscan naval history. All that we can be certain of is that the Etruscans were feared by other Mediterranean peoples. And we can guess that perhaps the men who designed and manned the first Roman warships were Etruscan by birth.

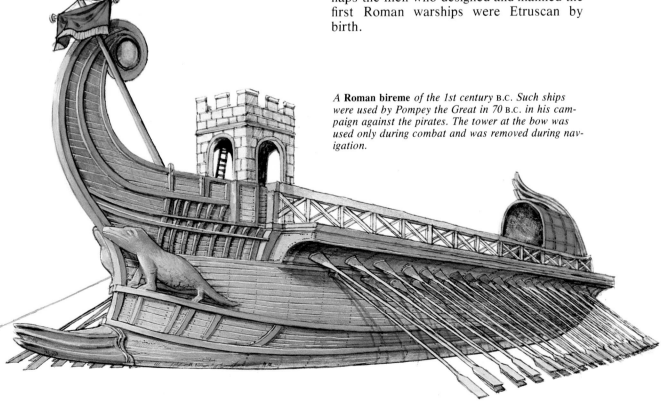

*A **Roman bireme** of the 1st century B.C. Such ships were used by Pompey the Great in 70 B.C. in his campaign against the pirates. The tower at the bow was used only during combat and was removed during navigation.*

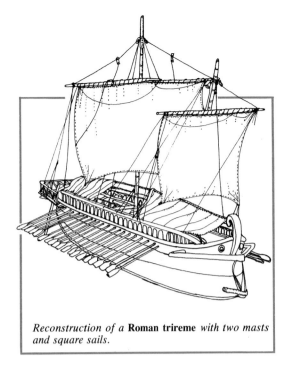

Reconstruction of a **Roman trireme** *with two masts and square sails.*

Although some early Romans were famous navigators, Rome did not pay special attention to the sea until the whole Italian peninsula had been subjected to its power. Only then did Rome consider the defense of its coasts and begin to extend its dominion to the other shores of the Mediterranean. The first Roman fleet was built in the 4th century B.C. and consisted of about 20 ships, which were probably modeled on the older Greek or Etruscan triremes. In other words, it was a very modest fleet developed from types that were considered outmoded by the older naval powers. When a clash with Carthage became inevitable, Rome had to develop a

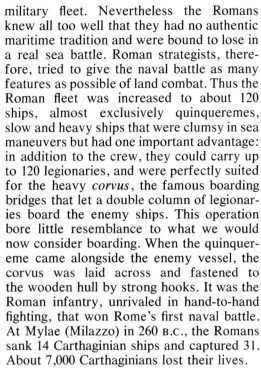

military fleet. Nevertheless the Romans knew all too well that they had no authentic maritime tradition and were bound to lose in a real sea battle. Roman strategists, therefore, tried to give the naval battle as many features as possible of land combat. Thus the Roman fleet was increased to about 120 ships, almost exclusively quinqueremes, slow and heavy ships that were clumsy in sea maneuvers but had one important advantage: in addition to the crew, they could carry up to 120 legionaries, and were perfectly suited for the heavy *corvus*, the famous boarding bridges that let a double column of legionaries board the enemy ships. This operation bore little resemblance to what we would now consider boarding. When the quinquereme came alongside the enemy vessel, the corvus was laid across and fastened to the wooden hull by strong hooks. It was the Roman infantry, unrivaled in hand-to-hand fighting, that won Rome's first naval battle. At Mylae (Milazzo) in 260 B.C., the Romans sank 14 Carthaginian ships and captured 31. About 7,000 Carthaginians lost their lives.

Some scholars maintain that the ships that took part in that battle were not Roman-built and that even the crews may have ben foreign. If they are right, it is possible that these "foreigners" were Etruscans, a people that had been subjected to Rome.

There are few archaeological remains to indicate the nature of Roman warships. One can suggest, however, that the Romans made good use of the experience of the maritime peoples they conquered. Thus the Romans adopted the Illyrian *liburna*, a fast vessel designed for the calm waters of the islands of the archipelagoes. The Romans gave the *liburna* a modified bireme form.

There were two unique archaeological finds that provided extremely important evidence of Roman naval construction methods and capabilities. Two ships were found at the bottom of Lake Nemi in the Alban Hills, about 19 miles from Rome. The existence of these ships had been known for centuries, and many unsuccessful efforts had been made to find them. In 1927 a decision was taken to drain the lake and bring up the

Toward the end of the 2d century B.C., *the Roman fleet was equipped with* **liburnae**, *fast and light biremes.*

Reconstruction of the hull of a **Roman quinquereme.** *There were not five superimposed banks of oars. The name may refer to the number of men who rowed at the same oar, or to the number of oars set on the same bank.*

A **Carthaginian cargo ship***. It had two masts with large square sails and one bank of oars, which were used in emergencies or for maneuvering.*

vessels. The work went on for five years, and in 1932 the fairly well preserved remains of two very large hulls were brought to dry land. One measured 71.3 × 20 meters (234 × 66 feet), the other 73 × 24 meters (239 × 79 feet). We do not know why such large ships were sunk in a body of water as small as Lake Nemi. Many theories have been advanced, but none of them can be proved. We can only note the skill with which these two ships, undoubtedly propelled by a large number of oarsmen, were built. The two ships were destroyed by fire during World War II.

Roman skill in shipbuilding was also put at the service of the commercial fleet. Merchant ships played a large part in the spread of Roman culture, and quite a few reliable images of their form have survived. One of the most important is a bas-relief found at Ostia, near Rome, and dated from the 2d century A.D. The ship is rounded in shape, and the hull becomes wider toward the stern. There are two long steering oars on the sides of the stern, and there are two sails; one a mainsail; the other, a much smaller sprit-sail, at the bow. This vessel was a medium-sized cargo ship not unlike those built 200 years earlier.

The largest Roman cargo ships were the grain ships, the *frumentariae*. Reliefs from Pompeii and descriptions left by writers of the 2d century A.D. suggest that one of these ships was about 165 feet long and 50 feet wide. The sails were fairly complex and included a mainsail, a topsail, and the *artemon*, a (bow) sprit-sail. On the authority of surviving documents, it seems certain that the Roman merchant fleet was the most important in the Mediterranean for several centuries.

Modern underwater archaeological research will undoubtedly be able to tell us much more about those ships and give us a more detailed picture of maritime trade in the Mediterranean basin.

The **Roman frumentariae***, or grain ships, were very large. This one, reconstructed from a relief found at Pompeii, was probably more than 165 feet long and about 50 feet across.*

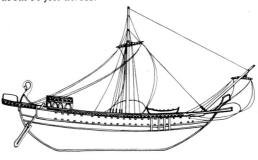

A **Judaean cargo ship** *of the 3d century* A.D. *It had an elongated hull and was steered by two side oars.*

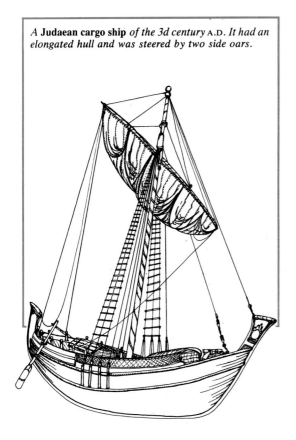

A sarcophagus from Sidon is the basis for this reconstruction of a **Roman cargo ship***, with a rounded and rather squat hull.*

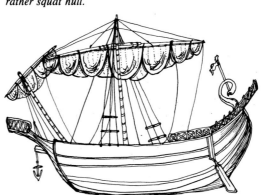

The Trireme

THE ROSTRUM GOES TO WAR

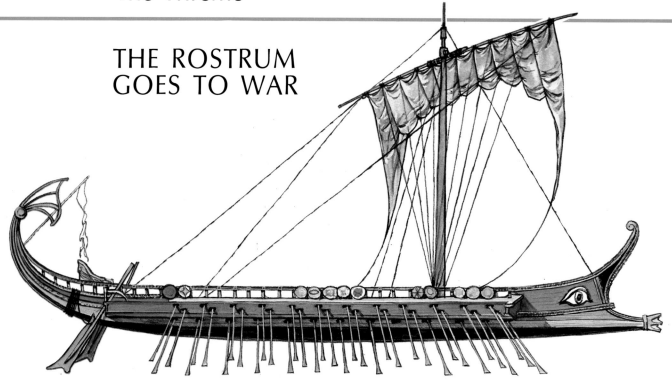

*A **Greek trireme**. The mast could be lowered in battle for greater speed. The rostrum was incorporated in the hull as an extension of the keel itself.*

The facts in our possession about what was considered antiquity's best planned and most efficient ship are few and controversial. We cannot even be sure that the trireme was developed from the fast and maneuverable bireme to increase the power of the only weapon (until the appearance of the cannon) that could sink a ship, the bow ram. This kind of *long ship* first appeared about 500 B.C. and played an important role in the naval history of Athens, Phoenicia, Corinth, Egypt, and Rome.

The Greek war trireme was a narrow vessel about 120 feet long and about 20 feet wide, with up to 170 oarsmen divided into 3 groups: 62 on the upper bank, 44 on the middle one, and 44 on the lower oars. The trireme, like the bireme or the Mycenean ship, had only one mast and one square or rectangular sail. In addition to the rowers, who came from the poorer classes of society, the ship carried a trained crew to handle the sails and warriors for combat.

The placement of oars and rowers has long been a matter of contention. We do know that the oars were short in proportion to the overall length of the ship: those of the upper bank measured about 14 feet in length, while those of the middle and lower banks were about 10 feet and 7 feet long, respectively. In the opinion of some scholars, even oars in the same bank were not all of equal length, but decreased in length like the fingers of a hand. We know a bit more about the fighting tactics of the Greek trireme. There were two basic maneuvers. The first, *diekoplous*, consisted of forcing a path through the enemy ship formation, breaking oars on the way, and then swinging around quickly to attack the immobilized fleet from the rear. The second attack method was the *periplous*, a fast turn around the enemy's flank to get into position for an attack from behind.

A variety of fighting ships, some highly original in form, were developed from the trireme. They have attracted the attention of naval scholars, but because of the lack of documentation the frequently interesting conclusions of such studies cannot be considered authoritative. We know, for instance, that Dionysus, tyrant of Syracuse, had *quadriremes* and that during the wars following the death of Alexander the Great (323 B.C.), quinqueremes and even hexaremes and heptaremes were built. The names almost certainly do not refer to the number of banks of oars, but to the number of oarsmen who worked each single oar. That would mean that those fighting ships had three banks of oars at most and that ramming power was enhanced by increasing the number of rowers. We also know that the Carthaginians used quinqueremes during the First Punic War (264–241 B.C.). The Romans began that war without any fleet worthy of the name, but thanks to their talent for organization, they readied 100 quinqueremes and 20 triremes in 60 days. The triremes determined the outcome of the Battle of Mylae (Milazzo), in 260 B.C., thanks partly to the use of the *corvus*, an adjustable gangplank or boarding bridge that could be used on either side of the trireme. It had a hooked beak at the end (hence the name *corvus*, "crow"). It was thrown across the enemy ship so that combat troops could board the enemy vessel.

The Trireme

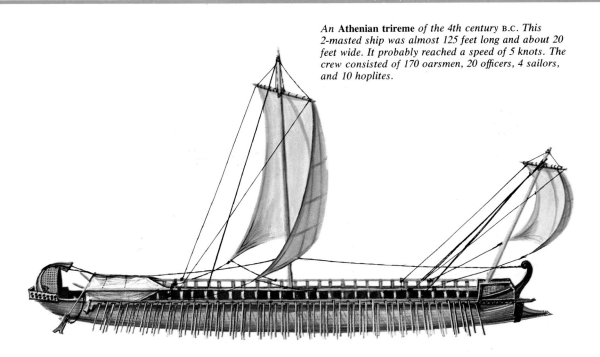

*An **Athenian trireme** of the 4th century* B.C. *This 2-masted ship was almost 125 feet long and about 20 feet wide. It probably reached a speed of 5 knots. The crew consisted of 170 oarsmen, 20 officers, 4 sailors, and 10 hoplites.*

The Roman military establishment developed a war fleet with bases throughout the Mediterranean, along the Rhine and the Danube, on the Red Sea, and even on the English Channel; and the trireme was the basic ship of this fleet.

When the great empire of Rome declined, the fleet declined along with it, and the last Roman triremes formed the nucleus of the Byzantine fleet in the East.

*A **Roman trireme**, with its corvus-hooked gangplank for grappling enemy ships. Infantrymen used the gangplank for boarding enemy ships. Thanks to this tactical innovation, the Romans, who had no particular naval ability, managed to gain control of the seas.*

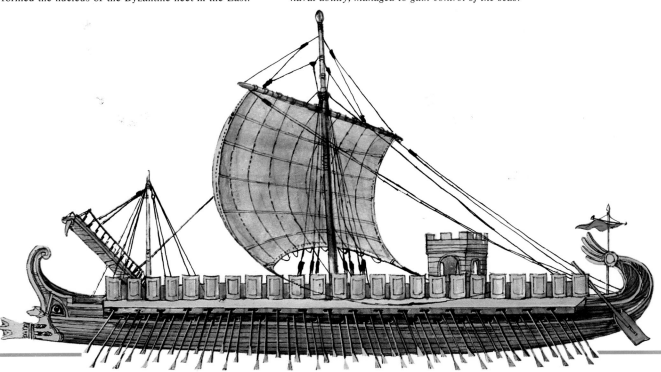

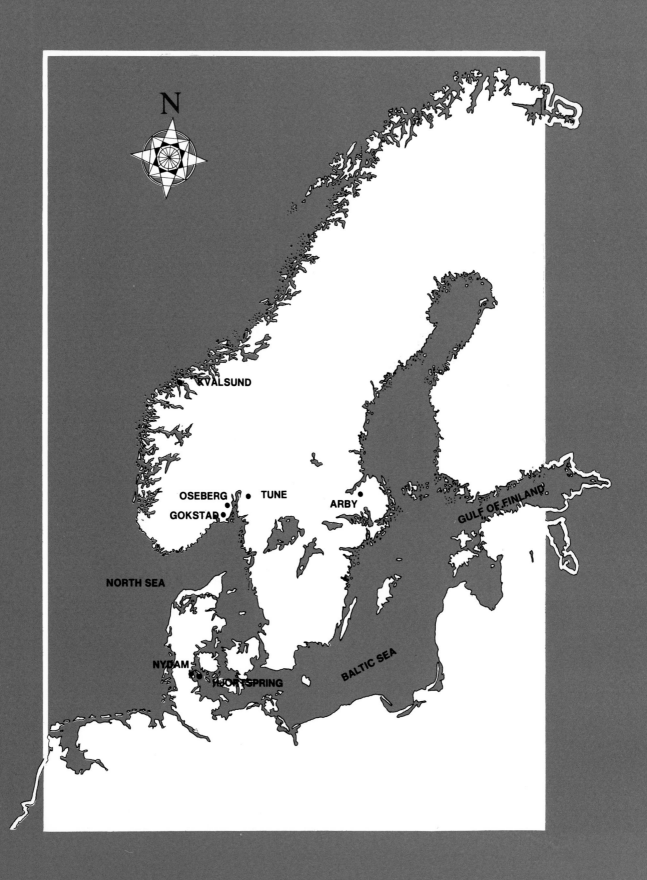

N

KVALSUND

OSEBERG • TUNE

GOKSTAD •

ARBY

GULF OF FINLAND

NORTH SEA

NYDAM

HJORTSPRING

BALTIC SEA

Central-southern Scandinavia, showing the major discovery sites of naval archaeology.

The North Sea

In recent years underwater archaeology has greatly increased our knowledge of the maritime history of the Mediterranean. One might even say that the only concrete facts in our possession have come from the bottom of the sea, or, in the case of the two Nemi ships, from the bottom of a lake.

As for the seas of northern Europe, underwater archaeology has played a less important role. Our main source of information has been provided by an old Nordic custom, that of burying chiefs with their dearest possessions (often including a ship). Also, from time to time, Nordic people made votive offerings in the form of ships filled with weapons and ornaments. Thus the most important excavations for vessels have been made on dry land and have often resulted in the discovery of remains that are perfectly preserved. Thousands of one-piece dugouts have been found. Many of them, however, are not carved from a single trunk. They were made of two or three large pieces of wood shaped under steam, a method that guaranteed greater stability. From the very beginning, the Nordic peoples showed great ability in building boats; and their dugouts and canoes were well proportioned for seas that could often be rough.

Dugout canoes must have been used for a very long time—throughout the Bronze Age. At the same time there was a slow but steady development that produced larger and lighter boats. Many Bronze Age sandstone engravings depict boats. These incisions are not easy to interpret, and some scholars have thought they represent sleds. Generally, however, they seem to show long narrow boats made of animal skins sewn over a softwood frame. The great skill in sewing

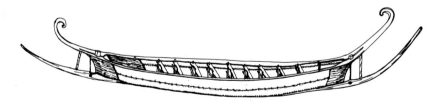

The **Hjotspring boat** *was built of wood in a style reminiscent of sewn-hide boats. It was more than 40 feet long and about 6 feet wide.*

animal hides is confirmed by the oldest-known Nordic wooden boat. It is the Hjotspring boat, and it seems to mark the peak of a boatbuilding technique developed from hide boats. At the same time, it is a forerunner of the more highly refined Viking ships.

The Hjotspring boat was found in southern Denmark in 1921. It was probably a

*The **Kvalsund ship** was found in Norway in 1920 along with another much like it. The larger of the two was about 60 feet long and some 10 feet wide. It carried a square sail and 10 pairs of oars. It was probably used for long trips, although it was not well suited for deep-sea navigation.*

*The **Sutton Hoo ship** was reconstructed from the impression it left in the sand of a burial mound. It was about 80 feet long, clinker-planked, and deckless. No trace of a mast was found.*
▼

*The **knorr** was the principal Viking cargo ship. Little is known about this vessel, but it may have had a deck and clinker planking.*
▼

votive offering, and its date of construction can be set about 200 B.C. It is about 40 feet long, and its supporting structure is a long bottom board bent at both ends. This board is also curved up at the sides to model the hull. The planks are of limewood and are tied together. Several crosspieces of thin hazelwood branches reinforce the hull. The bow and stern are exactly alike, a feature that was to be typical of later Viking boats.

The Hjotspring boat straddles two long periods in the evolution of Scandinavian shipbuilding technique. This conclusion is based on archaeological finds. The first datable Nordic vessel after the Hjotspring boat is the so-called Nydam ship, which was built at least 600 years later. There is no longer any

trace of the hide-covered boat, and the ship documents the building techniques that made it possible for the Vikings to carry out their astonishing exploits on almost all the seas of the world.

The Nydam ship is about 75 feet long and more than 9 feet wide. It is built entirely of oak. Each of the 5 rows of planking on both sides is made of one board, cut with astonishing precision and ability. The planking was done in the so-called clinker method. The planks are fastened together by iron nails, and there is no trace of the bindings that were to reappear in the keels of later Viking ships. The Nydam ship was most certainly a fighting ship, although we may hazard a guess that it followed and perhaps extended the building methods used in nonmilitary vessels of the time. It was probably in ships like this one that the Nordic peoples made their first incursions on the coasts of Britain. The Sutton Hoo ship found in England demonstrates the strong influence of Scandinavia on British shipbuilding techniques.

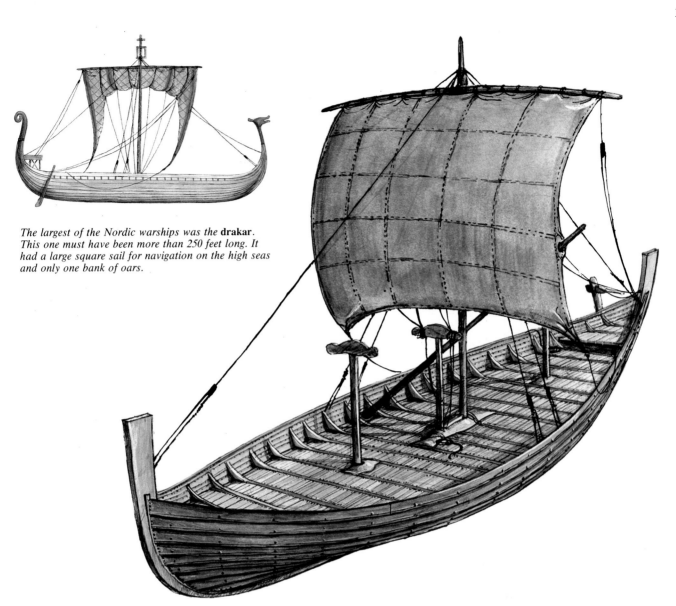

The largest of the Nordic warships was the **drakar**. This one must have been more than 250 feet long. It had a large square sail for navigation on the high seas and only one bank of oars.

The **Gokstad ship** was about 70 feet long and more than 15 feet wide. Built of oak, it had 16 rows of planking on each side, was propelled by 32 oars, and had an efficient square sail that let it sail even against the wind.

Reconstruction of a **Scandinavian drakar**. The prow and stern were identical except for decoration. The warriors hung their shields over the edge during navigation.

The story of the discovery of the Sutton Hoo ship is worth recounting. In 1938, excavations began on some burial mounds at Sutton Hoo in Suffolk. In some of these mounds, votive offerings had been placed inside a boat. Unfortunately, grave robbers had destroyed almost all traces of the ships. When the largest mound was excavated in 1939, several rows of rivets were found. It was clear at once that the wooden parts of the ship had decayed, but a precise and well-preserved impression of the ship had been left in the sand of the burial mound. Excavation required great care as well as fine weather, because the site was out-of-doors, and the slightest shower would have destroyed the precious cast forever. It was established that the ship was more than 80 feet long, had no deck, and the planking was in overlapping clinker style. The keel was reinforced by 26 ribs set in place after the entire hull had been built. Although no trace of masts or a place to set them at the bottom of the hull was found, it is possible that the ship had some kind of sail, since sails were used throughout the area during the 7th century. The rich grave goods indicate that this was an early Anglo-Saxon king's grave.

When we speak of the northern seas, we almost inevitably think of the Vikings. The Viking era began about A.D. 800, more than 100 years after the date ascribed to the Sutton Hoo ship. The popular view of the Viking as a savage dressed in animal skins and wearing a pair of horns on his helmet is a serious distortion of the truth. His was a hardy race, living by raiding, it is true; but the Vikings were certainly not savages. The sagas written by Viking poets are of great cultural value, and most of the major ships carried a bard on board to sing the deeds of sailor-warriors. We are able to reconstruct many aspects of their culture from their written documents. But our sources of information about the maritime history of the Vikings are not restricted to their sagas, which most certainly gave free rein to the imagination. The archaeological remains of Viking ships are among the most complete and best preserved vessels that have survived from that era, thanks to the fact that they were found, not at the bottom of the sea, but in the burial mounds of important personages. As we noted above, the Vikings used to bury the dead man with all he held dearest—his ship; his weapons; and his favorite woman, who joined him in death. In the sagas this funeral rite, cruel but rich in meaning, is described with exceptional skill and great emotional depth. The sacrifice of the woman was almost always followed by the burning of the ship, so that very few ships have been preserved. Two of these, however, are extremely important, the Oseberg and Gokstad ships.

*The **umiak** is a large open boat used by the Eskimos for transporting goods. Sewn sealskins are stretched over a wooden frame. In the summer large umiaks are used for whaling, and a square sail of reindeer skins may be mounted. Some umiaks are up to 30 feet in length.*

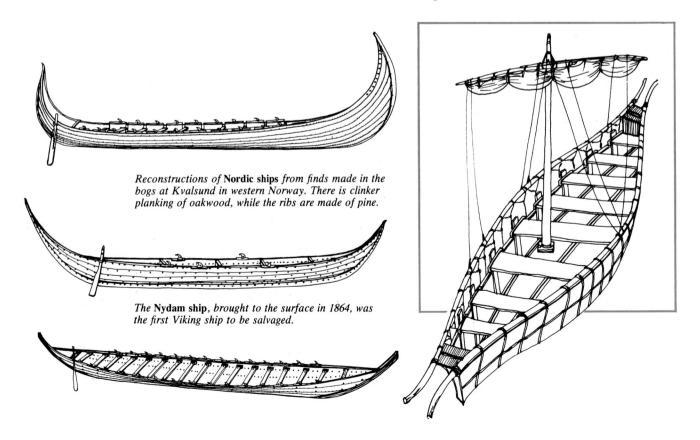

*Reconstructions of **Nordic ships** from finds made in the bogs at Kvalsund in western Norway. There is clinker planking of oakwood, while the ribs are made of pine.*

*The **Nydam ship**, brought to the surface in 1864, was the first Viking ship to be salvaged.*

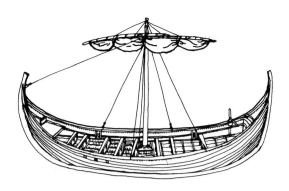

*Various Nordic ships were found at Skuldelev; among them was this **smaller merchant ship** dating from the end of the 10th century.*

*A dragon's head is set on the prow of this 15th-century **Nordic sailing ship**.*

The Oseberg ship, built around A.D. 800, is about 70 feet long and has a maximum width of more than 15 feet. All its timbers have survived in a perfect state of preservation, because the burial mound was covered with clods of peat, which sealed it off completely from the air. Each side of the ship has 12 rows of planking arranged in clinker fashion. This ship is the first example of an unusual building technique. The topside rows of planking, those above the waterline, are nailed together and then solidly riveted to the ribs. The rows of planking below the waterline are fastened to the ribs only by elastic bindings, and the ribs themselves are simply laid against the keel.

In practical terms, this means that the hull is very unstable and far from watertight. The planks are movable, and a great deal of water can enter through the seams. There has been much discussion of this feature, which weakened the hull. But the Vikings knew all too well how to nail planks to create a strong, rigid structure. The only plausible explana-

tion pays homage to the Vikings' knowledge of the sea and of their own ships. That is, a non-rigid keel can achieve two results: it is less subject to mechanical strains, and it is far more hydrodynamic. A non-rigid bottom, able to bend to the pressure of the sea, can make a ship much faster. The disadvantage is that the boat leaks. But it was not all that great a disadvantage, for the ship's very low sides insured that part of the crew would be kept busy bailing out the water that poured in over the sides. It made very little difference, then, if a few more gallons of water came up from below! Bails exactly like those we use today were employed for this purpose. Bailing was so continual and so essential a function that one saga tells of a ship on which six men bailed and seven rowed.

The Gokstad ship has the same maximum width as the Oseberg ship, but is about 6 feet longer. It is also much heavier and much stronger, reinforcing the belief that it must have been used on the high seas. Built of oak, with 16 rows of planking on each side,

The seal of Richard II shows a ship with a central rudder mounted at the stern. This is one of the new features that distinguished late-14th- and early-15th-century sailing vessels.

Toward the middle of the 13th century, castle decks were built fore and aft on sailing ships. Here they begin to blend in better with the hull.

This ship found in Kalmar Bay in Sweden closely resembles the round ships of the Mediterranean. The oak hull is clinker-built. It is 15 feet wide and 40 feet long.

*A typical **Hanseatic cog** built around 1300. It was about 100 feet long and some 20 feet wide. The single mast carried a square sail with an overall surface of approximately 2,000 square feet.*

*A one-masted **cargo ship** of the 15th century. Ships of this kind were still widely used after the appearance of the more maneuverable carracks.*

*The **Hanseatic cog**, a merchant ship plying the sea lanes between the Baltic and North Sea ports of the Hanseatic League.*

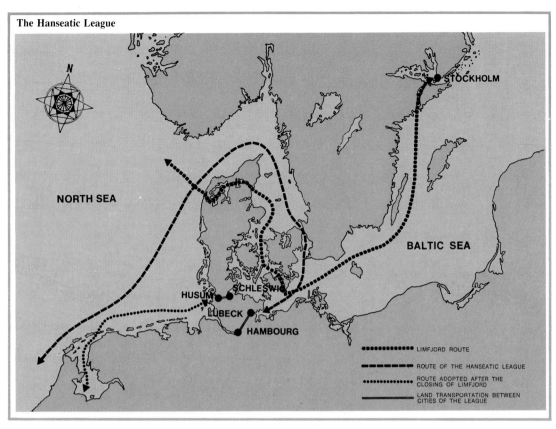

The Hanseatic League

When the Limfjord Canal silted up, two overland routes were opened up between the Baltic Sea and the North Sea, one from Hamburg to Lübeck and one from Hedeby to Hollingstedt.

the Gokstad ship had 32 oars and an efficient sail rig that let it navigate even with adverse winds.

It was in ships like these that the Nordic peoples carried out their incredible voyages across the seas. The Normans reached Ireland as early as the 8th century A.D. and Russia a century later. They pushed into the interior along the Dnieper and reached the Black Sea.

Their experience in deep-sea navigation led the Nordic peoples to build bigger and stronger ships. The length was measured in units of length corresponding to the distance separating one oarsman from another. This distance was about 3 feet, and we know of ships 32 units long, down to King Canute's famous *Great Dragon*, which is reputed to have been more than 250 feet long. These warships were called *drakars* and were the prime instrument of the most sensational Viking sea exploits.

In A.D. 98 Eric the Red was banished from Iceland for three years. He set out to sea and

discovered a new land, which he called Greenland. He settled there, and it was from Greenland that his sons, Leif and Thorwald, crossed over to America, where they are believed to have explored the coast from Labrador to Massachusetts. Legend would have it that they penetrated into the interior along the Mississippi River.

But while one group of Northmen was tackling the ocean, another was drawn to the seas of the south. The first to feel the effects was France, as early as the Age of Charlemagne. In the 9th century, the Vikings, or Normans, entered France. They hauled their ships onto dry land and carried them on carts for great distances. They pillaged Rouen and Paris and finally were granted the territory of the lower Seine by Charles the Simple. Normandy took its name from them, and from that shore they invaded Britain. In 1066, William the Conqueror got together a fleet of 3,000 ships, 700 of which were warships.

As new areas were invaded or merely contacted by the Normans, merchant fleets

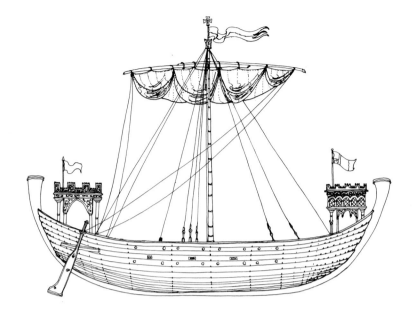

developed. One of the most traveled routes ran between the North Sea and the Baltic. Countless shoals, broad and dangerous, made it a dangerous route, and hundreds of ships came to grief. This perilous stretch of sea was often avoided by the use of a natural canal known as the Limfjord. When this canal became impracticable, there was a great increase in land transport.

Certain coastal cities became almost obligatory stopping points on this route and prospered accordingly. Some of them, like Lübeck, were founded at that time. Lübeck and Hamburg realized the importance of

The seal of the city of Winchelsea from the year 1300 documents an early transformation of the drakar. A large square sail has completely replaced the oars, and a castle has been added at prow and stern.

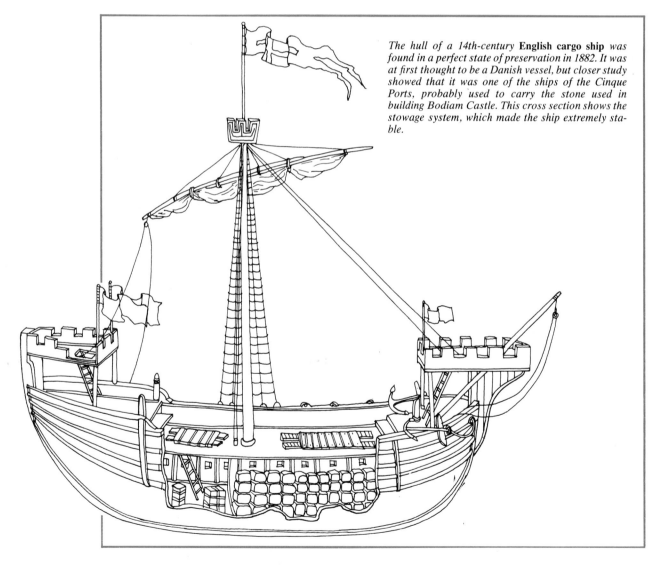

*The hull of a 14th-century **English cargo ship** was found in a perfect state of preservation in 1882. It was at first thought to be a Danish vessel, but closer study showed that it was one of the ships of the Cinque Ports, probably used to carry the stone used in building Bodiam Castle. This cross section shows the stowage system, which made the ship extremely stable.*

*A small **Mediterranean merchant ship** of the 14th century, about 30 feet long, with a lateen sail. There is a double side rudder.*

and sailing them under a common flag. The ships turned out by these ports had a quarter-deck and a forecastle that extended out beyond the ends of the hull. Though not really part of the hull, these raised areas were more rationally developed than the first castles installed on the cogs. One such ship is pictured on the seal of the city of Dover; it has a rudder that is still of the Viking type, that is to say, fastened on the starboard side. This bears further witness to the immense influence the Vikings had throughout the north and to their primary place in naval history.

defending these maritime routes and formed an alliance that led to the founding of the Hanseatic League in 1241. All the more important German cities of the coast joined the league, which increased in political and economic importance. The security of the league fostered civil shipbuilding, another important source of these cities' economic wealth. It was at this time that the cog came to the fore, a merchant ship that dominated maritime trade in northern Europe for centuries. The Hanseatic cog had overlapping clinker planking on its high sides. The cog had smoother lines than did contemporaneous Mediterranean merchant vessels. The cog drew a lot of draft, but its cargo capacity and its relatively high speed made it so important economically that new cities and ports were built along the coast.

While the Baltic cities joined in the Hanseatic League, maritime transport in England also took on ever greater importance, and there too the larger coastal cities came to the fore. Dover, Hythe, Romney, Hastings, and Sandwich on the southeast coast formed a kind of league called the Cinque Ports. These cities were granted important benefits in return for building sizable number of ships

The ship depicted on a seal of Dover, about 1305, shows a top on the mast; the raised platforms at bow and stern are the beginnings of the forecastle and sterncastle.

*A **Scandinavian cargo ship** from the late Middle Ages. It has three masts and a broad sail surface, which is not sufficiently articulated for maximum flexibility.*

The Viking Ships

THE SEARCH FOR ULTIMA THULE

The Greeks and Romans called the northernmost regions of Europe Thule. The Greek explorer and geographer Pytheas of Massalia described Thule, about 300 B.C., as an island about six days journey north of Britain. Scholars have variously identified Thule as Iceland, Norway, or Jutland. The Romans used the term "Ultima Thule" to designate the edge of the world. The Viking ships that carried Scandinavian peoples around the northern seas were the product of a slow evolution. At the height of Viking expansion, the Northmen had the finest ships of their time.

In his *Germania*, the Roman historian Tacitus described the vessels used at that period by the Suiones, the ancient inhabitants of Scandinavia: "The shape of their ships is remarkable in that both ends have a prow and can be used for landing. These men do not handle sails, nor do they fasten the oars along the sides; they simply shift them around according to their needs." We can get a fairly accurate and detailed picture of the later Viking *long ship* from descriptions in the Icelandic sagas, and from images on runic stones and on woven fabrics (the famous Bayeux tapestry). And there are well-preserved archaeological finds (including ships found at Nydam, Kvalsund, Tunö, and Gokstad).

The Viking long ship was up to 120 feet long and 20 feet wide. Built of oakwood, it was propelled by oars and by a large single rectangular sail. Bow and stern were exactly alike. The mast stood about 40 feet tall in the center of the ship, solidly inserted into a strong step. It carried a rectangular woolen sail, which was reinforced by a net of rope or leather that served to keep the fabric from being stretched out of shape and made it easier to strike. The rudder was a large oar placed to starboard. Simply by lifting the rudder, the ship could be pushed off from the shore in the direction from which it had come. This rudder also acted as a leeboard, increasing lateral resistance and making the boat more manageable. When the rudder was drawn aboard, the ship's draft decreased and it could get closer to shore and even run aground. At the beam, the ship's side was about 5 feet high. Oakwood was used for the keel, and pine for the mast and deck. The internal framework was generally made up of 17 frames. Sixteen or more planks were bound with pine-root cords on each side. The seams between these planks were calked with a 3-strand cable of cattlehair. On both sides of the ship, 16 small openings for the oars were made in the fourteenth plank from the bottom; these holes had covers and could be closed. The round Viking shields, about 3 feet in diameter, were hung over the sides when the ship was in port. The bow was often ornamented with a serpent- or dragon-headed prow.

These were the ships that the Northmen sailed on their forays in the North Atlantic. Without maps and compasses, highly ingenious methods were developed to assure safe navigation: close attention was paid to the type of marine life seen en route, to the color of the water, to the types of winds, and to the depth of the sea bottom, which was measured with a plumb line. The northern sagas say that wide use was also made of land birds, which were released during the voyage and then followed to land.

The Viking ship was a perfect vessel for facing long Atlantic voyages. In 1893, a faithful reproduction of the Gokstad ship, under the command of Captain Magnus Andersen, crossed the Atlantic to North America in 28 days, demonstrating not only the exceptional sailing capacity of the Viking vessels, but also their remarkable speed: Andersen's ship covered well over 100 miles a day.

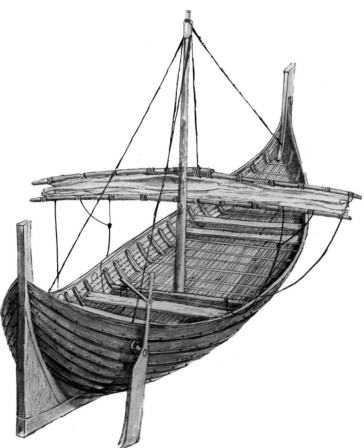

Reconstructions made from contemporary engravings show that some transport vessels had bow and stern pieces set almost at a right angle to the keel. These cutting edges reduced friction and increased speed. The hull was broad with low sides.

The Viking Ships

*The famous **Oseberg ship** is one of the most interesting archaeological finds. The hull has been rebuilt and restored and is now in the Oslo Museum. It is about 70 feet long and built of oak, with 12 rows of planking on each side.*

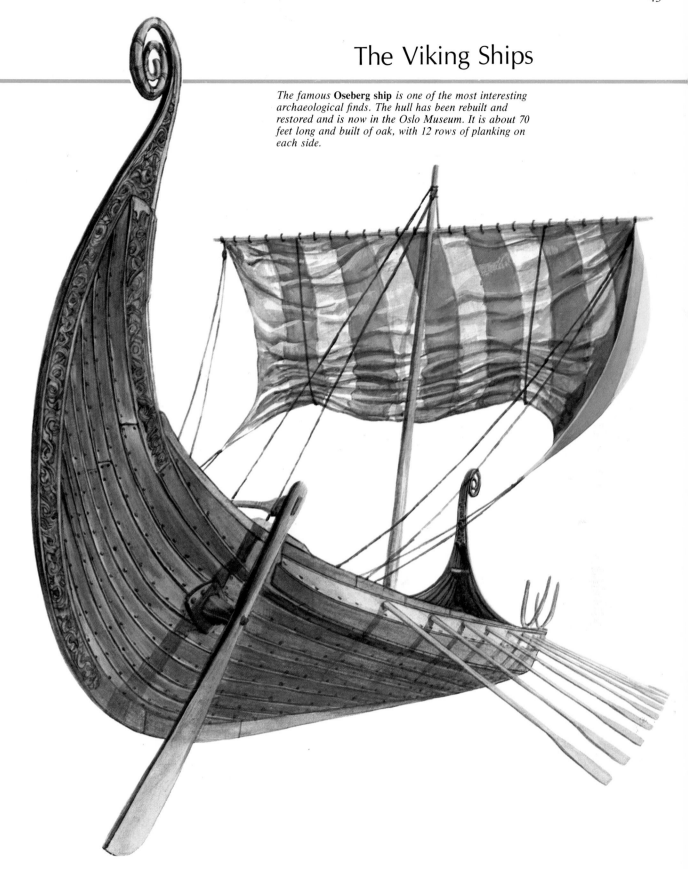

FRANKS

LOMBARDS

AVARS

SLAVS

VISIGOTHS

RAVENNE
ANCONA
ROME

BYZANTIUM

LARISSA

CARTHAGE

YASSI ADA

RHODES

CYPRUS

ALEXANDRIA

NILE

N

The Byzantine Empire at the end of Justinian's reign.

The Shipyards of the Mediterranean

In the 3d century A.D., the western provinces of the Roman Empire were shaken by a series of grave events, and the result was a shift of economic and political activity to the east. In 330 the emperor Constantine founded a new capital on the European shores of the Bosporus, where the ancient Greek city of Byzantium had once stood. The new city, Constantinople, was an entrepôt for eastern and western trade. The site was easily defended as long as sea routes and the Dardanelles were well protected. Despite this obvious necessity, the new empire did not build a real fleet for almost a century. Meanwhile Germans, Visigoths, and Ostrogoths established permanent settlements in the western Mediterranean. The Vandals conquered Carthage in 439 and organized a large fleet, soon becoming masters of the entire western Mediterranean area.

In the year 468, the empire in the East decided to face the new masters of Carthage on the seas, but the Byzantine fleet was too weak and was destroyed. In the century that followed a new fleet was built, a stronger one that could regain control of the Mediterranean. The emperor Justinian (527–565) knew, though, that his naval forces were still no match for those of his enemies. Justinian stirred up a revolt in Sardinia, forcing the Vandal fleet to sail there and put down the rebels. The Byzantine ships thus met almost no resistance when they attacked and conquered Carthage. The primary vessel of this and other sea exploits was the dromon. The Greek word *dromon* means "runner" and captures the main quality of these ships—speed. Unfortunately, no substantial information as to the appearance and performance of the dromon has come down to us. It was probably a bireme with from 100 to 200 men aboard. The few depictions of the dromon all have one thing in common: two curved wings that rise near the stern. These may have been extensions of the railing that ran outside the planking, and in some cases seem to have been linked by spars that must have supported the yard of the lateen sail when it was lowered. Another interesting feature was the rostrum, no longer set at the waterline, but raised up as if it were an extension of the deck and not of the keel.

The Byzantine fleet that conquered the Vandals in 533 was made up of 500 cargo ships and 92 dromons. The cargo ships carried about 10,000 foot soldiers and 6,000

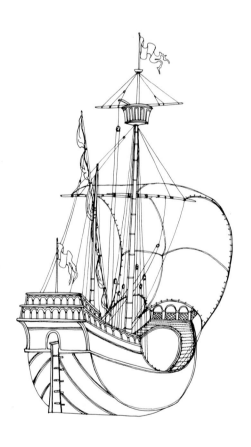

*A 13th-century **Venetian buzzo**, from a painting by Carpaccio. The large square sail has a yard for a topsail. The mast at the bow carried a lateen sail.*

cavalrymen aboard. The Vandals had about 120 warships in their ranks. The decisive battle against the Ostrogoths in Italy was fought near Ancona in 551, when 47 Ostrogoth ships faced Byzantine fleet of 50 ships. In the same period Justinian defeated the Visigoths.

Justinian realized that his empire required military and commercial control of the seas. He strengthened the fleet and a whole series of land and sea services to control distant provinces that were hard to reach by land. Small fleets were thus created to operate in restricted zones and had the task of escorting large convoys and policing the seas. Small military ports were probably established at strategic points, and land bases were defended by troops transported by sea. These small communities followed the architectural style of the capital, and soon churches were built of prefabricated sections prepared by Byzantine stonecutters and shipped by sea to the new settlements. An interesting 6th-century shipwreck was discovered with a cargo of architectural marbles.

The 7th century saw the emergence of a new historical force that kept the Byzantine Empire in alarm for a long time and affected the existence of many Mediterranean countries. In 641, the Arabs conquered Alexandria. Four years later the Byzantines recovered the city. The Arabs, who had no naval tradition, soon learned the lesson. They built

The dromon replaced the trireme in naval battles. The Greek name means "runner." This fast boat probably had a trimaran shape.

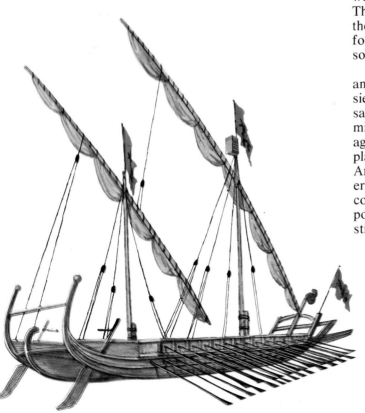

A typical Mediterranean Arab boat of the 9th century. It was used for carrying goods and was one of the first boats to forgo oars for propulsion.

a strong fleet and did what the Romans had done centuries earlier against the Carthaginians when forced to fight on the sea with no naval experience to guide them. In 655 an Arab fleet of 200 ships faced a Byzantine force of almost 1,000 vessels. The Arabs won, thanks to a brilliant strategic move. They bound several ships together so that the enemy vessels could not penetrate their formations and transformed the battle into something resembling a land battle.

The Arab fleet soon controlled the seas and in 673 sailed up the Bosporus and besieged Constantinople itself. The capital was saved only by the use of an inflammable mixture called Greek fire, which was hurled against the enemy ships from a bronze-plated leather tube. In the meantime, the Arabs had turned their attention to the western part of the Mediterranean. Byzantium could no longer defend its Mediterranean position by force of arms, but its fleet was still powerful enough to protect limited trad-

47

ing between the eastern Mediterranean and Byzantine possessions in Italy.

Byzantine maritime trade in the Arab-controlled zones was all but stopped. The Arabs conquered Crete in 826 with only 40 ships, and used it as the base for their conquest of Byzantine possessions in the West. Practically all of southern Italy fell into their hands. The exclusion of Byzantium from the western Mediterranean lasted for almost a century. Then, in 960, a new Byzantine fleet with 2,000 warships and almost 1,500 cargo ships recaptured Crete and soon reestablished its hegemony on the seas.

These centuries were marked by a series of sea and land invasions of the Italian peninsula. It was in this period that effective local defenses were developed with the emergence of independent communities. In the Veneto region, people took refuge from the invaders on the islands of the lagoon, where Venice was later to become an important sea power. In the south, the steep mountains along the Amalfi coast favored local defense. In the space of a few decades, various city-states and maritime republics were born.

The first to appear was Pisa. By the early

Reconstruction of a 13th-century merchant ship, after a mosaic in Ravenna. The castle aft is partly formed by a curve in the hull, while the forecastle forms a covered deck area.

This drawing of a carrack is based on a model on display for centuries in the church of Mataró, north of Barcelona on the coast of Spain. The mast on the forecastle was probably added later and probably was not part of the ship's original outfitting.

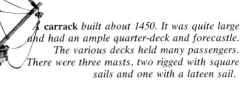

A carrack built about 1450. It was quite large and had an ample quarter-deck and forecastle. The various decks held many passengers. There were three masts, two rigged with square sails and one with a lateen sail.

48

The **chelandion** *was a very fast warship with two banks of oars. Very little is known about it, and this reconstruction is largely hypothetical.*

Carracks *were basically cargo vessels. Some of them, however, were outfitted with a small battery of cannon, like this late-15th-century example.*

years of the 7th century that city had a powerful fleet of its own. It maintained its independence against its rivals in the Tyrrhenian Sea. The new republics (Amalfi, Pisa, Venice, and Genoa) owed their success to control of the sea lanes, which were avoided by the land-bound barbarians. The maritime republics established excellent trade relations with the main trade centers of the Mediterranean. They demonstrated great political acumen when they established close contact, first with the Byzantine emperors, and then with the Islamic rulers who dominated the Mediterranean. Some of the mari-

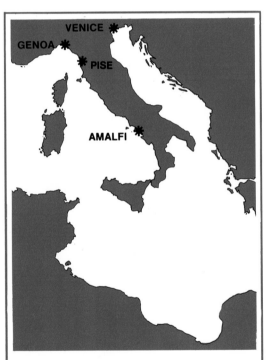

The Italian maritime republics. Coastal peoples and refugees from the barbarian invasions that marked the end of the Roman civilization in the Western Empire developed veritable city-states that soon boasted a flourishing trade with other nations overseas. Close ties with Constantinople and the Islamic world, the needs of the Crusades, and the profitable East-West trade increased their power on the seas and led to armed conflict and their eventual decline.

A **Venetian merchant ship,** *from a model preserved in the Arsenal in Venice. Its tubby lines caused it to be nicknamed the* **barca pantofola** *(slipper boat).*

time republics enjoyed considerable prosperity at the time of the Crusades.

The Christian kings who proclaimed them were filled with holy zeal, but often knew little or nothing about the art of navigation. So they turned to the maritime republics, asking them to guarantee the transportation of the crusaders to the Holy Land. Irreverent though it may seem, the Crusades were one of history's biggest shipping rentals. At first the maritime cities simply supplied shipping for pay. Later it became clear that direct participation in the Crusades could be more profitable in terms of prestige, power, and useful alliances. To give an idea of the amount of transport involved, suffice it to say that during the Fourth Crusade, Venice agreed to provide shipping for the bulk of the forces—4,500 knights and horses, 9,000 equerries, and 20,000 foot soldiers.

The sea passage was far from comfortable for the crusaders. A special area was set aside for the horses, which were embarked through large hatches just above the waterline. Once on board, they had to be accommodated in such a way as not to be injured. Since they could neither stand all the time nor lie down, they were supported by straps that kept them on their feet even when the ship rolled heavily. Many were injured by the straps, and the animals' muscles were often so affected that they had to be taught to walk all over again. But if the horses were uncomfortable, the less important passengers had nothing to thank the shipowners

A **warship**, *after a fresco by Pace di Faenza, a pupil of Giotto, in Imola. Pace worked with Giotto in Padua, and it is clear that this vessel is a Venetian ship.*

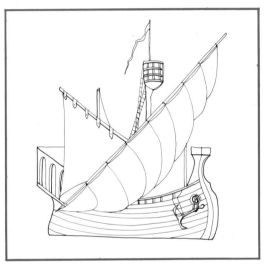

A northern **cog**, *after a painting by Bernardino Licino (16th century) in the Ducal Palace in Venice.*

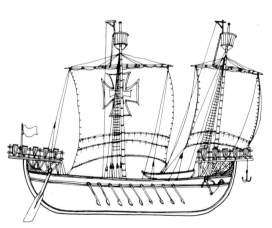

A 12th-century ship used for carrying soldiers during the Crusades. It has two masts with tops for sailing the high seas and a row of oars for maneuvering and for propulsion during calms.

for: many were quartered on a level right underneath the horses.

If the maritime republics had shown the same ability in allying themselves with one another that they revealed in dealings with foreigners, they might well have dominated the waters of the Mediterranean for many decades. Unfortunately, their relations were always strained, and many wars were waged as a result. New ships appeared in this period. The most important was undoubtedly the *galley*, which will be described later. Here we should like to describe some of the minor warships, which were also important. Many different kinds of ships were built to satisfy various needs. The minor rowing

This reconstruction is based on the oldest-known depiction of a European ship with a stern rudder. It is from a bas-relief in Winchester Cathedral.

*A **Danish cog**, with its hull built along the lines of Viking ships. The sterncastle fills the area behind the mast but is still not an integral part of the hull structure.*

*A 15th-century **carrack**. The ship is completely equipped with sails, and one can see the play of the canvas as the ship runs before the wind.*

This drawing is based on a 14th-century model of a Dutch merchant ship.

galleys basically served to transport soldiers on short journeys, as well as for exploration and coastal defense. The *galliot* was a ship with no more than 20 oars, each rowed by one man, and with one or 2 lateen sails. The *brigantine* had no deck and soon became a deep-sea sailing ship. Then there was the *saettia*, which could reach high speeds with its very long oars. About the 13th century, small service ships came into being and later developed into veritable war barks, through modification and enlargement. Such was the *frigate*, originally a cutter assigned to the larger galleys, with a single lateen sail and eight or ten oarsmen. It was later used on its own as an exploration boat. The *felucca* too was a service boat at the start, with a deck and one lateen sail, and with six or eight oars; but it soon became a fast boat for coastal defense.

The maritime republics did not limit themselves to producing warships. They did a great deal to increase knowledge of navigation and developed highly refined techniques for taking bearings at sea. It is no accident

*An **Arab Sambook** rigged with lateen sails on two masts. This fast boat could face any type of wind. It is still built today, as it has been for centuries.*

*The **Bucentaur**, the ceremonial ship of the Venetian doges. It was used for the symbolic Wedding of Venice and the Sea, a rite performed annually on Ascension Day. The rite was initiated in the early 12th century. The Bucentaur was a solid ship with very high sides, 2 decks, and 21 oars per side.*

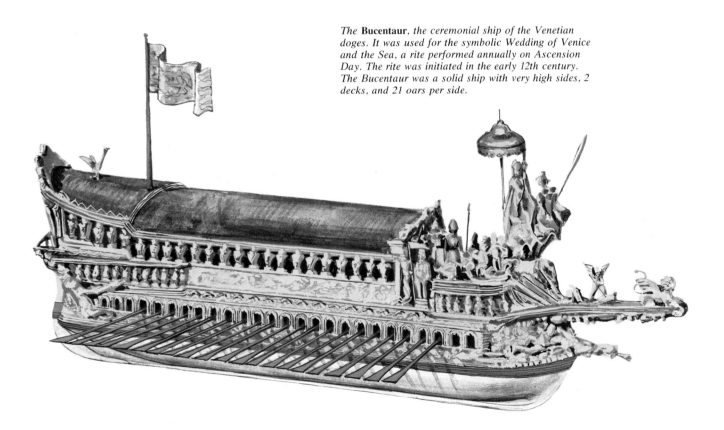

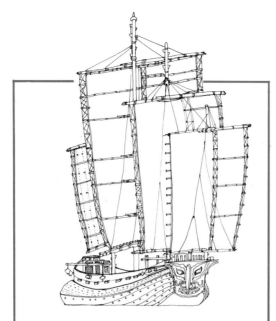

*During his travels, Marco Polo must have seen many vessels unlike the European types he knew. He may have seen the **Chinese junk**, a very large boat with square sails stiffened by a system of bamboo rods.*

that the legendary Flavio Gioia, said to have invented the compass in 1302, was reputed to have been an Amalfitan. There is evidence that the compass was already known in China and in northern Europe, but it is very likely that Amalfitans were among the first to use it in the Mediterranean.

Another distinguished citizen of a maritime republic of this period, and this one not fictitious, was Venice's Marco Polo, who traveled by sea and land to Cathay and brought back to the West a unique account of the life and customs of the peoples of the East.

The maritime republics devoted much energy to the development of merchant shipping. Attempts were made to enlarge and adapt rowing galleys for cargo service, but merchant shipping continued to be the domain of rounder ships propelled almost exclusively by sail. During preparations for the Eighth Crusade, Louis IX ordered 120 transports to be built, with the following dimensions: overall length, 84 feet; length at waterline, 57 feet; beam, 20 feet: height of the sides, 6.25 meters (20.6 feet).

Contacts between northern and Mediterranean mariners resulted in the development of a new vessel that resembled the cog in general form but was built with flush, rather than clinker, planking. It had a large and more easily handled square sail, and a mizzenmast was later added for a lateen sail. This was the first step in the development of sails that got under way in the 15th century. Northern experience with square sails was assimilated to Mediterranean practice with the lateen sail. Both had advantages and disadvantages. The square sail is certainly more adapted for navigation on the high seas with strong stern winds, while the lateen is superior near the coast and especially when the wind changes direction frequently, as often happens in the Mediterranean. The fusion of these two types of sail gave birth to the *carràck*, so called from the Arabic word for "merchant ship." It evolved rapidly and soon developed into three-, four-, and even five-masted ships. The mainmast and the smaller foremast had square sails, while the mizzenmast was rigged with a lateen sail, as was the fourth mast, the *bonaventura.* To the square mainsail there were added topsails to make changing sails easier and increase the ship's maneuverability. Very few details about the carrack are known. The most important testimony comes from the model of a carrack which was displayed in a church in Mataró, Spain, for many centuries. It shows the typical characteristics of the Mediterranean carrack: there are two masts; a rounded stern; and curved, overlapping planking under the forecastle. The beams protrude from the sides, a detail already noted in drawings of the time, but one which scholars disagreed about.

It was not long before carracks were built with three masts. The balancing function of the lateen sail in the stern could be reinforced by another sail in the bow; so the foresail was added, with the sole function of making the ship more maneuverable. One might argue that this was the high point in the carrack's development. The carrack was the first great step forward in the development of sailing vessels that was to see the appearance in following centuries of such important ships as the caravel and the galleon, ships that were to carry man across the oceans to new worlds.

Venetian cog.

Arabs still sail as they did in the past. *Almost nothing is known about mediaeval Arab vessels, but it is assumed that they were similar to several types still used today.*

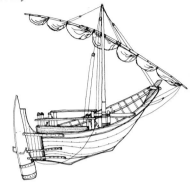

The **zaruk**, *a small merchant boat rigged with one mast and a lateen sail. It is mainly used for coastal trade.*

The **badan** *closely resembles the zaruk, but is more elongated in shape and has a sharper prow.*

The **Baghla** *is a cargo ship clearly based on European vessels and reminiscent of the caravel.*

A **sambook**, *perhaps the most typical boat used in the Red Sea. It is fast and easy to handle, the ideal boat for sailing close to dangerous coral reefs.*

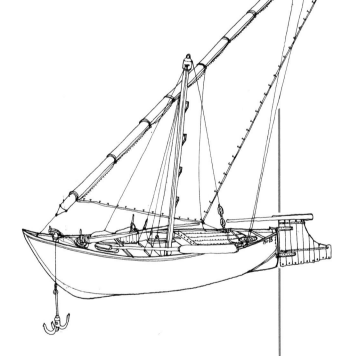

A **fishing boat** *used in the Suez Canal. It has a lateen sail and is built much along the lines of the earliest Arab boats to use such a sail.*

LIFE AT THE OAR

The galley was the classic fighting ship from the Middle Ages to the end of the 17th century. It was a long, narrow ship, driven by oars and furnished with one or two lateen-sail masts and a ram at the prow. The galley form is very old; the "long ships" of Mycenaean times, the Greek and Roman biremes and triremes, and the Byzantine dromon can all be considered galleys. Emperor Leo of Byzantium, in the 9th century A.D., was the first to apply the name "galley" to a ship that resembled the fighting dromon, with only one bank of oars and ideal for reconnoitering. Toward the end of the 1st millennium A.D. the lateen sail appeared, a milestone in the history of civilization, which allowed a ship to close-haul and thus freed it from the centuries-old slavery of having to sail only in the direction toward which the wind blew. Galleys with lateen sails could be seen from the Mediterranean to the North Sea, with their narrow hulls—with low board and moderate draft—from which rose a rectangular framework supported by strong transverse brackets projecting outside the rail.

The oars protruded in pairs (later in threes), set in oarlocks placed on the same horizontal plane; the rowers' thwarts were set in herringbone fashion, with the acute angle pointing toward the stern, along a central aisle, or "gangway," that connected the forecastle with the stern, where the captain's quarters were located. The ram was a framework protruding from the prow, well above the waterline; its purpose was not so much to sink an enemy ship as to break its oars and form a kind of boarding bridge. In 1400, a second mast, the foremast, set on the forecastle in the bow, was added to the single mast of the galley; and some galleys even had a third, or mizzenmast, toward the stern, all with the lateen sail.

Toward the year 1450, two improvements appeared: the central rudder set at the stern and worked by a tiller replaced the lateral rudder; a cannon was installed in the bow, and lighter guns were set on swivels along the bulwarks.

The galley was the standard combat ship of the maritime republics, and in Venice, in 1534, a new system of rowing was adopted, with several men working the same oar. Larger galleys sometimes had as many as five or seven men on one oar. It was this type of galley which fought at Lepanto and which, with only minor variations, continued to be used by the Venetians and the Knights of Malta until 1797. A model called the galleass also saw service at Lepanto.

The hull of the galley was built to obtain maximum speed under the thrust of the oars. This type of ship had rather low sides and was easy to handle, but it was not well suited for rough seas.

It was designed to combine the speed and easy handling of the galley with the power and solidity of the galleon, but this ship was a disappointment. The oar-thrust was inadequate for the squat keel (four times as heavy as the galley type), and the galleass had to be towed when the wind fell.

Although the galley was preeminently a Mediterranean ship, it was also adopted by the English and the French. The Baltic was the last stronghold of the northern galleys; and Russians, Swedes, and Danes used them in the shallow, island-studded waters of the coasts. Peter the Great's Russian galleys were smaller variations of the Mediterranean type, equipped with just one lateen sail mast and driven by 36 oars set in a single bank. The last sea battle in which galleys were used took place in 1808, during the Russo-Swedish War.

The galley was probably developed in the Greek islands, perhaps in Crete. It may be the only fighting ship that despite variations in size and armament has preserved its general character and appearance practically unaltered throughout its history, a history that extends over more than 3,000 years.

The *Celeuma* was a chanty sung by Mediterranean sailors and oarsmen in time with their stroke. One man sang the first half of each line as a solo and the *O* was the signal for the oarsmen to take the stroke and repeat the line in chorus:

> O Dio—ayunta noy
> O que somo—servi toy
> O voleamo—ben servir
> O la fede—mantenir
> O la fede—de cristiano
> O malmenta—lo pagano
> sconfondi—u sarrahin
> torchi y mori—gran mastin
> O filioli—debrahin
> O non credono—queben sia
> O non credono—la fe santa
> en la santa—fe di Roma
> O di Roma—està el perdòn
> O San Pedro—grán varòn
> O San Pablo—son compañòn
> O que ruege—O Dios por nos
> O por nosostros—navegantes
> en este mundo—semo tantes
> O ponente—digo levante
> O levante—se leva el sol
> O ponente—resplendor
> fantineta—viva lli amor
> O joven home—gauditor

God aid us / who are your servants / we would serve you well / preserve the faith, the Christian faith / thrash the pagan / confusion on the Saracen / throttle and kill the dogs / sons of debrahin / they do not believe good though it is / they do not believe the holy faith / the holy faith of Rome / from Rome comes pardon / Saint Peter great helmsman / Saint Paul his companion / who rule God be with us / and with ours sailing / in this world we are so many / westward I say and eastward / eastward the sun rises / westward it glows / maiden long live love / young man rejoice

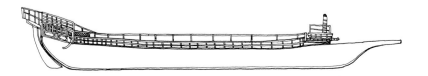

The Galley

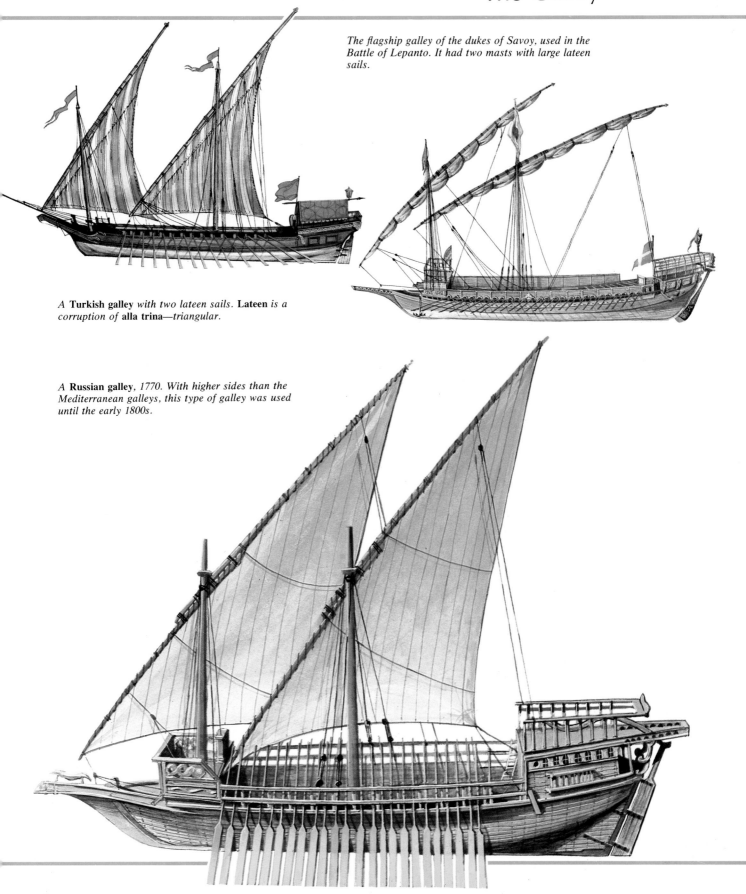

The flagship galley of the dukes of Savoy, used in the Battle of Lepanto. It had two masts with large lateen sails.

A **Turkish galley** *with two lateen sails.* **Lateen** *is a corruption of* **alla trina**—*triangular.*

A **Russian galley**, *1770. With higher sides than the Mediterranean galleys, this type of galley was used until the early 1800s.*

The Conquest of the Oceans

Even in ancient times, Mediterranean ships had passed through the Strait of Gibraltar, the mythical Pillars of Hercules which marked the passage to the ocean. In the Middle Ages Normans entered the Mediterranean through the strait. In the 14th century, the seaports of Portugal were flourishing, and it was not unusual to find hundreds of Italian ships at anchor there, mainly Genoese and Venetian, the most active and best equipped of the day. At the same time, the northern seas from Flanders to the Baltic were dominated by the intense trade of the fleets of the Hansa, the commercial league of Germanic cities, and Italian and French trade associations also developed.

Portugal had freed itself from Moorish rule, and after long wars with Castile, the country began to look westward to the unlimited horizon of the ocean. At first Portuguese shipping was dominated by Italian navigators, but Portugal soon came to rely on its own resources, although Italian sailors were always well received. It was not long before Portugal was ready for the great Atlantic adventure.

The driving force behind Portuguese exploration of the Atlantic was the infante Prince Henry (1394–1460). Although he is known to history as Henry the Navigator, he never actually took part in the expeditions he organized. But it is thanks to his constancy and interest that Portugal was to play a major role on the ocean. Henry was the second son

La Grande Hermine—*The 118-ton caravel was Jacques Cartier's flagship on his expedition along the coast of Canada and the Saint Lawrence River in 1535.*

of John I, king of Portugal; he had the mind of a scholar and the soul of a mystic, combined with a vigorous character and a zeal worthy of a missionary. The contemporary chronicles of Gomes Eanes de Zurara describe the Lusitanian prince's various aims: to gather knowledge about unknown lands; to spread the Christian religion and reduce the power of the Arab Moslems; to import

Sâo Gabriel—*The carrack in which Vasco da Gama doubled the Cape of Good Hope and reached the coast of India in 1497.*

Near Sagres, in the vicinity of Cape Saint Vincent, Henry established a center for nautical information, the Villa do Infante. There navigators, geographers, astronomers, and mathematicians assembled over the years. A vast collection of maps and books gathered from all over Europe included, of course, that *Book of Wonders* dictated a century and a half earlier by Marco Polo. This volume was a gift to Henry from the doge of Venice.

For 12 years Portuguese expeditions failed to pass Cape Bojador. The trade winds beyond the cape tend to drive ships away from land and toward the open sea. It was only in 1434 that Gil Eannes and Alfonso Gonçalves Baldaia managed to double the difficult cape in two *nâos*, or carracks, giving the lie to the legend that the sea beyond Bojador was so hot that the water turned to pitch. Eannes was received in triumph when he returned home. One of the most serious obstacles to Henry's program had finally been overcome. Two years later, Baldaia alone went beyond the Río de Oro and reached Pedra da Galè. Nuño Tristão reached Cape Blanco in 1441, two years before the expedition led by Lancelot Pesanha, who was probably a descendant of the Genoese Emmanuel Pessagna, *almirante* of King Denis's war fleet in 1317.

the products of those unknown lands; and to reach by sea the kingdom of the mythical Prester John, the Christian king of Abyssinia, and obtain his help in the struggle against the Moslems. In other words, to sail around the southern end of Africa along the route taken by the Phoenician sailors that the Egyptian King Neco sent out from Egypt, according to Herodotus.

Portuguese caravel—*Faster and more graceful than the carrack, with three masts rigged with lateen sails.*

Spanish caravel—*With lateen sails. A typical example of the 15th-century two-masted caravel.*

Tristào fortified the island of Arguin on the bay of the same name, and then discovered the mouth of the Senegal River. New Portuguese discoveries then followed rapidly: in 1445, Antonio de Noli, from Genoa, discovered the Cape Verde Islands; Dionisio Dias sailed to the cape of that name; and in 1446, Alvaro Fernandes reached the coast of Sierra Leone.

In 1455, a Venetian, Alvise Cà da Mosto (1432–1488), who entered the service of Henry the Navigator after having sailed and traded all along the coasts of the Mediterranean and North Atlantic, touched Madeira and the Canaries, doubled Cape Blanco and Cape Verde, and tried to sail up the Gambia River, but was driven back by the arrows of the angry natives. Another Italian navigator in Henry's service was Antoniotto Usodimare of Genoa (1416–1461). He went to Portugal in 1451 (probably because of financial difficulties) and brought with him the one caravel left of his merchant fleet. A year later, three caravels set sail with Usodimare and Cà da Mosto. They sighted the island of Buena Vista, in the Cape Verde Archipelago, and tried to go up the Gambia River once more. This second attempt also failed, because of a fever that killed many of the men.

Henry the Navigator ended his active and glorious life in 1460. His plans were carried forward with renewed vigor by his nephew, Ferdinand, whose caravels reached Cape Saint Catherine, well below the equator and the point where the African coast turned due south. The expedition of Diego Cam (or Câo) reached the Congo River and the coast of what is now Angola in 1482, almost at latitude 22 degrees, with two caravels.

Instruments, supplies, weapons and goods carried on Magellan's ships
24 nautical charts on parchment
6 compasses
21 wooden quadrants
7 astrolabes
35 compass needles
18 hourglasses
Food supplies consisting of biscuits, wine, olive oil, anchovies, dried pork, cheese, and sugar.
One thousand lances, 360 dozen arrows, 125 swords, 10 dozen javelins, 95 dozen darts, and 60 crossbows.
Among the goods for barter: cloth, caps, handkerchiefs, combs, mirrors, brass basins, knives, scissors, fishhooks, 500 pounds of glass trinkets, and 20,000 bells of three different types.

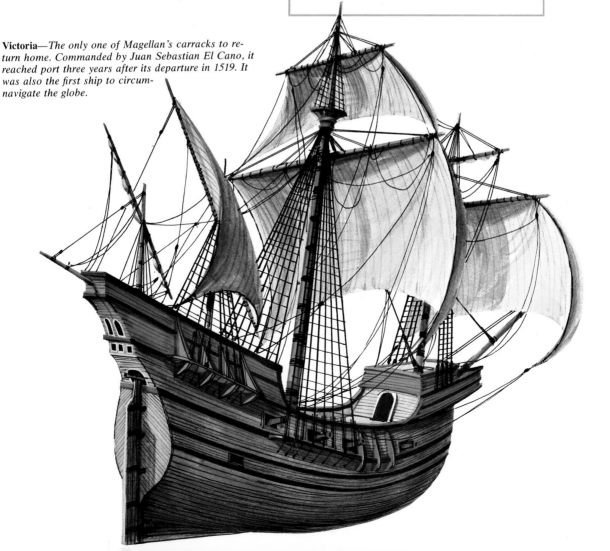

Victoria—*The only one of Magellan's carracks to return home. Commanded by Juan Sebastian El Cano, it reached port three years after its departure in 1519. It was also the first ship to circumnavigate the globe.*

60

Mediterranean caravel—*With mixed sail rigging and four masts; the foremast had two square sails. This is a 16th-century example.*

Venetian carrack—*From the Arabic word* qaraqir, *plural of* qurqūr, *"merchant ship." It had a bulging round hull, and square sails on the foremast and mainmast, bowsprit and spritsail.*

The African coast headed south and east. By circumnavigating the entire African continent, one could sail to Asia, and the Indies, the source of such vast and varied wealth. With this aim in mind, in 1456 Henry had obtained from Pope Calixtus III a grant ceding to Portugal spiritual supremacy over all lands discovered and yet to be discovered *usque ad Indos,* "as far as the Indies." Efforts were renewed after Henry's death. King John II, who succeeded Afonso V on the throne of Portugal, sent an expedition with three caravels (or two caravels and a galley) under the command of Bartholomeu Dias (1450–1500) to follow the route of Diego Cam. (Cam had died of hardship and fatigue at Walvis Bay, but the surviving crew managed to get back to Portugal, and their accounts aroused new interest in African exploration.) The small expedition set out in 1487 and soon reached what was later to be called the bay of Saint Helena. From that point the coast stretched far off to the south. Dias courageously headed out of sight of land and crossed the open sea for 15 days. A tremendous storm came up, and the ships were at the mercy of the elements for days. When the sea finally calmed, Dias turned his prow to the east, expecting to sight land. He did not and so turned north again. When he saw land once more, it stood to the west, and Dias realized that he had gone around the southern tip of Africa. Worn out by the terrible voyage, and with his supply ship lost, Dias decided to head for home. Coasting toward the west, he sighted the tip of Africa, the cape that divided the Atlantic Ocean from the Indian Ocean; and, in memory of the tremendous storm he had weathered, he named it Cape of Storms. King John later changed the name to the Cape of Good Hope.

The news that a Genoese captain in the service of Spain had crossed the Atlantic in 1492 and reached the famous Indies by an entirely different route did not stifle Portuguese ambitions, although the Spaniards now challenged Portugal's papal authority over the newly discovered lands. Pope Alexander VI Borgia (who was born in Spain) issued a bull in 1493 granting Spain control of all lands already discovered and yet to be discovered west of a line from pole to pole 100 miles west of the Azores and the Cape Verde Islands. The Portuguese protested, and the line was moved to 370 miles west of the Azores (the Tordesillas treaty, June 7, 1494).

King John died in 1495, before what was to be the decisive expedition set sail. On July 8, 1497, favored by northern trade winds, Vasco da Gama (1469–1524), a young and able captain of noble lineage, left Lisbon with four ships: the *Sâo Gabriel* (118 tons), the *Sâo Raphael* (98 tons); and the *Berrìo* (50 tons); and a supply carrack—all rigged and equipped by the Florentine house of Servigi.

The four ships got supplies of water and fresh food at the Cape Verde Islands and left there on August 3. They did not follow the coast but took a direct route (the one fol-

Santa Catalina—*The carrack of Pedro de Mendoza (1487–1537), commander of the expedition of 12 ships and 800 men sent by Charles V to occupy the Rio de la Plata.*

Mary Fortuna—*A 16th-century English carrack. One of the first ships to carry artillery pieces.*

lowed by all the sailing ships of later centuries). Three months and three days later, they anchored in the bay of Saint Helena, already touched by Dias, only 100 miles from the Cape of Good Hope. The Cape of Good Hope was doubled on November 22, despite contrary winds and currents. On December 25, the expedition anchored at a place it called Terra Natalis (modern Natal) and reached the mouth of the Zambesi on January 22, 1498.

The crew rested there for a month, and then Vasco da Gama headed for the Indies, with an Arab pilot aboard, the famous Ahmed ben-Madjid, the finest eastern naval expert of the 15th century. Favored by the southern monsoon, the expedition had a quiet crossing of the Indian Ocean and sighted the Malabar coast on May 18, 1498. The ships anchored in the bay of Calicut, the major commercial center of the day. Vasco da Gama was given a warm greeting by Prince Samuddrin, lord of the city, but was later violently threatened by the Arab merchants who controlled the city's economy. He decided to leave, but only after having filled his ships with the highly prized spices of the East, a cargo that more than paid for the cost of the expedition. The Portuguese ships left the Indian coast on October 5 and, after three months of often difficult navigation, sighted Africa once more.

Having lost 3 ships and 100 men (including his brother Paulo), Vasco da Gama entered the port of Lisbon in mid-September 1499, to receive a hero's welcome.

Manuel I, the successor of John II, named Vasco Almirante do Mar das Indias, made him Count of Vidigueira and awarded him a pension of 300,000 crusados a year. The way to the Indies had been opened to travel and to the creation of a Portuguese colonial empire. Portugal was anxious to pluck the fruit that had been maturing for almost a century and assure herself the monopoly of the rich trade with Asia before Spain could establish her claim. It was still believed that Columbus had reached the eastern shores of Asia. The conquest of the seas lost its idealistic motivation and became a phenomenon of colonial expansion.

Not long after Vasco's return, a large squadron left Portugal under the command of Pedro Alvares Cabràl (1460–1526) with 1,500 men on board 13 ships, one of which was captained by Dias. In sailing down the Atlantic, Cabràl kept well out to sea, and after a long tack sighted the coast of Brazil. He thought it was an island and did not know that it had been discovered a year earlier by Amerigo Vespucci. Nevertheless Cabràl took possession of the new land for the Portuguese crown and called it Terra Sanctae Crucis. He sent a ship back to Portugal to announce his discovery and set off for the Cape of Good Hope, where he met with a furious storm. Four ships were destroyed, including the one commanded by the famous Bartholomeu Dias. The death of Dias was later to be celebrated by Camoëns in his national epic, *The Lusiads*.

Genoese carrack—*Although the galley was still considered the ideal military ship, even the Republic of Genoa adopted the carrack in the 16th century.*

62

Cabràl headed for the Indian Ocean, discovered the island of Madagascar, touched Ceylon, and founded the first Portuguese trading colony in Calicut and a second one at Cochin, also on the Malabar coast. Leaving a few ships to protect these first bases in India, Cabràl headed back to Portugal in 1501 with a rich cargo of spices, mostly pepper.

By now Portuguese expeditions to Asia had all the air of veritable military operations. The ships went out as war squadrons and no longer stayed quietly at anchor in ports already conquered. They continued to extend Portuguese power and dominion and loaded their ships with precious goods.

The golden age of Portuguese discoveries and explorations was coming to an end. Portugal established a vast colonial empire that included most of the islands of southern Asia. From that time on, its history is part of the history of European colonialism. In the meantime, other areas of the world had also been discovered by European navigators. New lands and peoples became known. A decisive turning point had been reached in European history, with consequences that are still being felt in our own time.

Royal galley—*The last type of galley, created by the French and armed with light artillery in the bow. About 140 feet long, it was built until 1720. The lightness of the hull, which assured high speed, made it extremely vulnerable to cannon shot. There were luxurious lodgings for the ship's officers and the captain in the stern, while the crew lived on the decks as best it could.*

The attempts to reach Asia, reputed to be a land of fabulous riches, continued for about a century before the dream became a reality. Princes and kings, mathematicians and shipbuilders, astronomers and navigators, for generation after generation worked toward that goal; but that achievement was overshadowed by one man—Christopher Columbus. Setting out across the Atlantic, a totally new route for navigation, he reached a new land in a couple of months. Indeed, he thought he had reached India. But when it was understood that he had actually discovered a new continent, the existence of which had never been dreamed of, his fame was only enhanced. An era in man's history had ended, and a new one had begun.

Despite rival claims, it is now certain that Columbus was born in Genoa sometime between August and October 1451, that he was the son of Domenico Colombo and Susanna Fontanarossa, and that he had three brothers and sisters. On his way to England in 1476, on a mission for the shipowners Spinola and Di Negro, the carrack Columbus was sailing in was attacked by corsairs in the pay of the king of France, under the command of the Gascon Guillaume de Casenove. The ship went down, and it seems that Columbus had to swim to shore in Portugal. If this is true, it was a fateful adventure, for he later married Dona Felipa Moniz of Portugal and sent for his brother Bartolomeo. Columbus was certainly infected by the sea fever that was sweeping Portugal.

Royal French galleass—*First half of the 18th century. An example of the longevity and extensive use of this kind of military vessel.*

John II had come to the throne of Portugal in 1481, and it was to him that Columbus explained his plan and asked for financial aid, but Columbus's project was given short shrift. A widower with a small son, Columbus left Portugal for Spain. Ferdinand and Isabella, the rulers of Castile, were unifying the various regions of Spain and deferred the Genoese navigator to a board of scholars in Salamanca in 1486.

The interview was not very successful, and Columbus went back to Portugal. It was at the court of Lisbon that he heard from Bartholomeu Dias himself, of the Portuguese discovery of the Cape of Good Hope. Columbus realized that with the opening of the African route to the Indies, the king of Portugal would have no further need of his services, and again he went to Spain.

It was the year 1489, and Spain was en-

Matthew—*An English 50-ton carrack, in which John Cabot explored the coast of Newfoundland and discovered Cape Breton Island. It had a crew of 18 men.*

Venetian galleass—*The first warship with cannons that shot through portholes instead of from the open deck. It appeared during the Battle of Lepanto (1571).*

Turkish galley—*With one mast, propelled by a single row of oars on each side.*

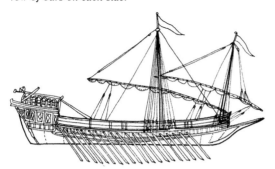

Genoese galley—*One of the galleys of Gian Andrea Doria's squadron.*

Galley of the Duchy of Parma—*It served at Lepanto in the Holy League fleet organized by Pope Pius V.*

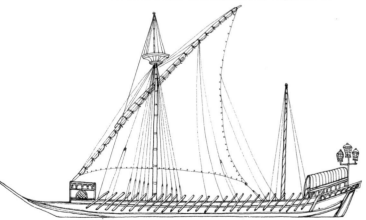

Beatrice—*A 17th-century Genoese half-galley.*

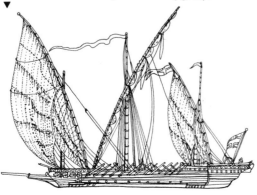

gaged in the last phase of the struggle against the Moors. Despite noble supporters at court, Columbus still failed to obtain a royal audience and spent two years in poverty in the Ràbida monastery near Palos. Time worked in his favor. Granada, the last Moorish stronghold on Spanish soil, fell on January 2, 1492, and the unification of the Spanish nation was completed. The rulers could turn to works of peace and progress. And Columbus's project was listened to with benevolence and finally accepted. Preparations for departure were fast and decisive. On April 17, 1492, the "Capitulations" were signed, and Columbus received the title of High Admiral of the Ocean Sea, the office of viceroy of all the new lands, and a tenth of their income and other financial benefits. The city of Palos furnished two fully equipped caravels in payment for past debts. These ships were the *Pinta* of Gomez Rascòn and Cristobàl Quintero, and the *Niña* of Juan Nino. The Pinzòn brothers, from a family that had been sailors and shipbuilders in Palos for generations, were persuaded to take part in the expedition. The third ship, the *Gallega* of Juan de la Cosa, was hired by Columbus himself and renamed *Santa Maria*. On August 3, 1492, the three ships sailed off to the west.

The voyage of Christopher Columbus is part of mankind's cultural heritage, and this is not the place to retrace its steps in detail. Suffice it to mention the discovery of Cuba and Haiti; the desertion of the *Pinta*, later recovered; the loss of the *Santa Maria*, wrecked on the reefs in calm waters on the night of December 24; and the construction of the Navidad fort, the first Spanish colony overseas. The two surviving caravels set out for home on January 16, 1493, heading north-

◄**Turkish galley**—*The type of galley used by Amurat Dragut, commander of the rear-guard reserves at the Battle of Lepanto.*

Bombard-galleass—*This ship, built in the Arsenal shipyards in Venice, turned out to be decisive for the outcome of the Battle of Lepanto, although it had to be towed to the place where it was to be used because of its enormous weight. It had 36 cannons and 64 stone mortars and could carry up to 1,200 soldiers.*

east to take advantage of favorable winds. They ran into a storm, and the two ships were separated. The *Niña*, with Columbus on board, reached the Azores; from there, after another storm that tore its sails away, it touched land at Belèm, at the mouth of the Tagus, in Portugal. Columbus was received with all honors by John II of Portugal, and continued on to Spain. On Friday, March 13, 1493, his caravel anchored in the little port of Palos, from which it had set out seven months before. In the meantime, the *Pinta* too had managed to get to shore, in Galicia.

Rivers of ink have been poured out down the centuries in celebration of Columbus's exploit, recounting the story of the three fragile ships, barely 100 feet long; the disappointment in the Sargasso Sea; the threatened mutiny of the crew; the bitter frustration at the end, when they found not the rich subjects of the Great Khan described by Marco Polo, but primitive natives, half-naked and frightened; the determination of the Genoese navigator; and the terror of the men who had followed him into a world of unknown dangers. When astronaut Neil Armstrong first set foot on the moon, his achievement was compared with that of Columbus. The astronauts made their fantastic voyage with the aid of a highly developed, technically advanced organization, with the whole world watching; but no one was there in 1492 to measure the heartbeats of a man alone among hostile sailors, sustained only by his faith in himself, facing unknown seas, heading toward a goal indicated only vaguely (and erroneously) on the charts of a Florentine map maker. A man alone, forsaking the safer coastal lanes, challenged the open sea with its fearful mysteries. If the trip to the moon represents the triumph of science,

The Galley

Galleys were divided into royal, flagships, master, simple, large, thin, and *bastardelle* types, according to their size and importance. Many smaller ships were derived from the galley: half-galleys, galliots, brigs, fuste, and saettie.

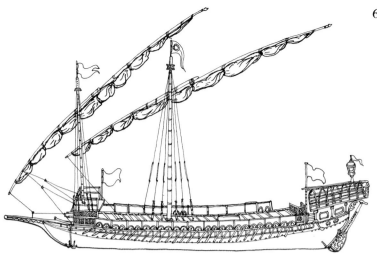

Galley of the Duchy of Urbino—*The Duke of Urbino's 12 galleys fought bravely at Lepanto.*

Venetian galley—*One of those that took part in the Battle of Lepanto.*

Galley of the Order of Malta.

Papal galley—*At Lepanto, the galleys of Pius V were under the command of Marcantonio Colonna.*

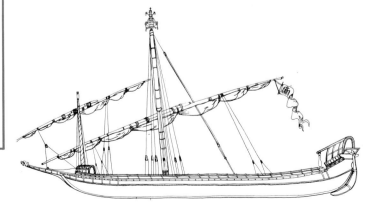

Columbus's voyage represents the triumph of humanism.

The gradual conquest of the seas was given a sudden violent thrust forward by Columbus's success. Various nations redoubled their efforts on the seas, navigators stretched their courage, and Atlantic exploration began in earnest. The Atlantic Ocean was no longer a terrifying mystery but a challenge and an invitation. One man to take up the gauntlet was Amerigo Vespucci (1454–1512), a man of vast culture. Vespucci went to Seville as a commercial agent. He settled there in 1492 and worked for Giannotto Berardi, who represented the great Medici family of Florence. It was in Spain that Vespucci met Christopher Columbus, on the eve of his first voyage. The organization of Columbus's second expedition was later entrusted to Berardi, and Vespucci had meanwhile become Berardi's partner. A non-official expedition was organized by Bishop Fonseca, on the basis of a report and a map sent back to Spain by Columbus during his third voyage. Thus Vespucci set

La Grande Françoise—*One of the last great carracks, built in France in 1535. It was the rival of the English* Great Harry *and was so enormous that it never succeeded in leaving the port of Le Havre.*

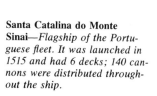

Santa Catalina do Monte Sinai—*Flagship of the Portuguese fleet. It was launched in 1515 and had 6 decks; 140 cannons were distributed throughout the ship.*

out from Cadiz on May 16, 1499, with three or four caravels, commanded by Alonso de Ojeda. Vespucci shared with Juan de la Cosa the task of map maker and cosmographer, but evidently he had other responsibilities as well. The ships separated after reaching the shores of Guiana. Ojeda's headed for Haiti, while Vespucci, with one or two ships sailed south, reaching the mouths of the Parà and Amazon rivers. In his ship's boats Vespucci went about 60 miles up the Amazon. He continued down the coast as far as what is now Cape Sâo Roque. He was the first European to reach Brazil. He returned to Cadiz about the middle of June 1500, convinced that he had sailed along the coast of Asia. He believed that if one continued along the coast, one would certainly find a passage leading to those Indian seas that Vasco da Gama had reached by another route.

It is worth mentioning again that in the very year Vespucci returned to Spain the Portuguese navigator Alvares Cabràl, heading for the Indies via the Cape of Good Hope, touched the coast of Brazil, which he took for a large island. Since this new land seemed to lie east of the line established in the Treaty of Tordesillas, it was argued that the new land belonged to the Portuguese crown. The task of ascertaining the truth of this hypothesis (which proved to be correct, making Brazil a Portuguese possession) was entrusted unofficially to Vespucci by the king of Portugal. On May 13, 1501, he set sail from Cadiz and this time went farther south, reaching the bay of Rio de Janeiro and the immense estuary of the Rio de la Plata. The voyage was a peaceful one, and Vespucci returned to Lisbon in the middle of October 1502, having made several important discoveries in the fields of mathematics and nautical astronomy. This time he became convinced that the long and continuing coastline he had followed was something completely different from the Asia he had formerly believed it to be. Although the expression "new world" had already been used by Bartolomeo Colombo, the great navigator's brother, it was officially adopted for the first time by Vespucci. And in a map drawn in

Gabriel—*The 16th-century, 25-ton English carrack in which Martin Frobisher explored the coasts of Greenland and Labrador in 1576.*

68

The Elizabethan galleon Triumph—*The largest English vessel to fight against the ships of the Spanish Armada.*

French galleon—*1592. With two decks and an elegant prow in the form of a rostrum.*

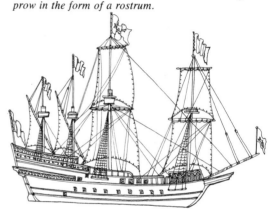

Haabet—*1589. One of the first Dutch galleons, an improved type that evolved from the carrack, which it replaced as both a military and a commercial vessel.*

1507, the German cosmographer Martin Waldseemüller called the continental mass south of the Caribbean America. It was still generally believed that Asia lay north of the lands discovered by Christopher Columbus.

The idea that there was a southern passage to the Indies and that it could be reached by sailing along the coasts that Vespucci and those who followed in his wake had so thoroughly explored gradually took on substance, especially after the expedition led by Vasco Nuñez de Balboa. He crossed the *cordillera* that separates the Gulf of Darien from the Pacific Ocean in 1513, after a bold and bloody trip. He looked at the Pacific stretching southward as far as the eye could see. He called it the Southern Sea. Vespucci's observations that the Atlantic coastline he had followed gently sloped toward the southeast led to the conclusion that the two coasts had to meet at some point, perhaps not far from the point reached by Vespucci

himself, and that this would open the long-sought passage to the Indies. This passage was finally discovered in 1520 by Ferdinand Magellan on a voyage that remains one of the high points in the history of maritime exploration.

Magellan (in Portuguese, Fernâo de Magalhâes) was born in Oporto about 1480; his name first appears among the members of the expedition organized by Francisco de Almeida in 1505 to strengthen the new Portuguese colonies set up in the Indies. Magellan was wounded in the Battle of Cannanore (on March 16, 1506) against the 200 ships of Prince Samorin, ruler of Calicut. He took part in the expedition of Lopez de Sequira in 1509, which culminated in a daring attempt to gain control of Malacca. On this occasion Magellan saved the life of Francisco Serrâo, who became his lifelong friend and whose letters from the Moluccas, or Spice Islands, contributed so much to the decision to un-

Dutch galleon—*1597. Low and easy to maneuver in shallow water.*

San Martin—*1588. A Spanish galleon in the Portuguese squadron; it was a 1000-ton vessel armed with 48 cannons.*

dertake his historic and adventurous voyage. Back in Portugal, Magellan talked with navigators and cosmographers, and met the astronomer Rui Faleiro, with whom he consulted nautical charts and travel reports filed in the secret archives of the state. In the autumn of 1517, Magellan went to Spain. Magellan and Faleiro renounced their Portuguese nationality and submitted to King Charles I, the future Emperor Charles V, Magellan's long-cherished scheme for sailing to the Spice Islands by way of the New World and then through the passage that most certainly existed. Unexpected support came from Cardinal Fonseca, Columbus's former enemy. After many delays and much uncertainty, complicated by diplomatic obstacles raised by King Manuel of Portugal, agreement was finally reached. A "treaty" was signed on March 22, 1518. Magellan spent the next year preparing his fleet. At dawn on September 20, 1519, five ships left the port of Sanlúcar de Barrameda for what was to be one of the most exciting and dramatic voyages in the history of navigation.

The *San Antonio* (118 tons) was commanded by Juan de Cartagena, Cardinal Fonseca's cousin; Gaspar de Quesada was captain of the *Concepciòn* (90 tons); Luis de Mendoza had the *Victoria* (85 tons); and Joâo Serrâo commanded the *Santiago* (75 tons). Magellan's flag was hoisted on the 110-ton *Trinidad*. Each of these ships was to meet a different fate. The crew consisted of about 250 men, including about 20 Italians, mostly from Liguria. Antonio Pigafetta of Vicenza (1491–1534), one of their number, left the fullest account of the great voyage.

The long trip south along the African coast in search of favorable winds for the Atlantic crossing provoked the first clash between Magellan and Juan da Cartagena, who was replaced as captain of the *San Antonio*. The Antarctic winter halted the expedition at Puerto San Juliàn, the southernmost point of South America reached by Vespucci, and it was decided to wait for spring. It was here that the Spanish captains mutinied against Magellan. He regained control of the situation through a strategem. When spring came,

St. Michael—*An English galleon built in 1569 and armed with 98 cannons, one of the most powerful of its time and the last example of the large warships that preceded the ship of the line.*

Henry Grace à Dieu—*1514. Also known as the* Great Harry, *it was the most impressive carrack of its century, built for Henry VIII of England. It had 21 bronze cannons and 130 smaller artillery pieces of iron. It was rebuilt in 1540 and finally destroyed by fire in 1552, without ever having fired a shot.*

the ships were ready to start off again. In the meantime, friendly contact had been made with the natives, who timidly approached the foreigners. The natives were very large. It would seem that Magellan was particularly impressed by the size of their feet, for he called them *Patagones*, the "bigfooted." Although the race is now on the way to extinction, the area is still called Patagonia.

The weather improved, and Joâo Serrâo's *Santiago* was sent out on reconnaissance. It was wrecked on the shoals of the bay of Santa Cruz, and the crew barely managed to struggle back to the winter camp alive. On October 18, 1520, the ships headed south again; doubled the cape, which was called Once Mil Virgenes (an allusion to Saint Ursula's companions): and, on October 21,

Great Michael—*1511. An intermediate phase between the large carrack and the new type of ship, the galleon. A painted cloth was hung between the mainmast and the foremast to protect the crew from enemy fire.*

The Composition of the Spanish Fleet at the Battle of Gravelines

"The Invincible Armada"—25 galleons; 4 galleasses; 4 Portuguese galleys; 40 armed merchant ships; 23 transport hookers; and 34 smaller vessels (*zabras, fragatas,* and *patajes* that could also be oardriven), for a total of 130 ships.

The main ships: *San Martin*—980 tons, 48 cannons, 177 sailors, and 300 soldiers; *San Juan de Portugal*—1,029 tons, 50 cannons; *Grangrina*—960 tons, 38 cannons; *Santa Ana*—931 tons, 30 cannons.

Crews and fighting men: 7,000 sailors, 18,000 soldiers.

Artillery: 40-pound cannons, 32-pound half-cannons, and large-caliber stone mortars (for a total of 2,500 pieces).

Total tonnage: 61,023 tons.

Ark Royal—*The first English ship to bear this name, built in 1587 by Richard Chapman for Sir Walter Raleigh. This 800-ton vessel had 50 cannons and a crew of 425 men; it was Lord Howard's flagship during the naval operations against the "Invincible Armada."*

72

Grand—*A French vessel with 90 cannons. It led the French rear guard at the Battle of Beachy Head (1690).*

Royal Charles—*Flagship of the duke of York at the Battle of Lowestoft in 1665.*

Fire ship—*A ship of any kind that is set for demolition and launched in flames against the enemy.*

entered a broad bay which was explored by the *San Antonio* and the *Concepcion* and which seemed to stretch off the west. On October 25, Magellan, with all his ships, entered the strait that he named Todos los Santos, but which was later to bear his name.

The general opinion was that the small fleet should go forward. But the pilot of the *San Antonio*, Estevâo Gomez, disagreed; and a few days later, as they were underway once more, he put the captain of his ship in chains and headed for Spain, where he arrived on May 6 of the following year and accused Magellan of high treason and murder. The three remaining ships continued on their way, and the name Tierra del Fuego was given to the land on which every night they saw fires burning. Finally, on November 28, 1520, the last cape, the "*Cabo deseado*," was doubled and they entered the waters of the Southern Sea. The bows were then turned to the northwest, following the indications Serrâo had made in the Moluccas, and Magellan hoped to reach those islands in a short time.

Such was not the case, though. For three months the crew, decimated by scurvy and reduced to eating boiled leather, with sawdust and some putrid drops of water, bobbed on the Pacific, the name given to the great ocean because of its frequent calms. At last, on March 17, after a lifesaving stop at what are now the Mariana Islands (and which Magellan named the Thieves' Islands after an unpleasant experience with the natives), they reached two small islands in the Philippines, and the crew was able to recover its strength after such great hardships.

But Magellan's destiny was spinning out. After establishing cordial relations with Humabon, master of the island of Sebu and rich in gold (for which the Europeans traded iron), Magellan and 60 of his men crossed to the nearby islet of Mactan to display the might of the crown of Spain to the inhabitants and to their king, Silapulapu, who had rebelled against Humabon. The small expedition was met by thousands of savages, while the boats which carried the firearms were still far from shore. Magellan fought alone against the fury of the natives, trying to cover his companions' retreat. He was wounded in the leg by an arrow and then slaughtered by the angry throng. With Magellan dead, the expedition suffered even

Sant'Antonio—*A Genoese vessel used by the papal squadron that freed the island of Corfu.*

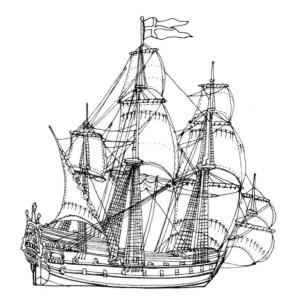

Prinzess Maria—*A Dutch vessel with 90 cannons.*

further losses during a banquet offered by the king of Sebu, who hoped to capture the remaining ships.

There was no alternative: they had to head for home. The *Concepciòn* was burned, because there were not enough men to handle her, while the *Trinidad* and the *Victoria* began the long voyage home, stopping in the Moluccas at Tidore. Magellan's old friend Serrâo had died only a few weeks earlier. The local king gave the tired men a kind welcome and had the ships filled with gifts and spices. A leak in the keel of the *Trinidad* kept the two ships from leaving in convoy; so only the *Victoria*, commanded by Juan Sebastiàn de Elcano, with Pigafetta aboard, set sail for the Cape of Good Hope, thus completing the circumnavigation of the globe. On September 6, 1522, 18 of the men who had left Spain 3 years before returned to the port of Sanlucar de Barrameda. The *Trinidad* had left the Moluccas after the *Victoria* but was forced back by violent storms. It was then captured by the Portuguese, who imprisoned the crew.

Magellan's achievement is on a par with those of Columbus and Vespucci. Although he did not complete the circumnavigation of the globe, the bold conception of an east-west crossing was his, together with the conviction that there must be a passage to the Southern Sea.

Thanks to the courage and ability of these three great navigators and those who followed in their wake, the 15th and 16th cen-

turies marked man's first mastery of the oceans and a major step forward in his knowledge of the planet we inhabit. While Spain and Portugal were struggling to establish routes to the Indies, east and west, European waters were the scene of battles and strife arising from the policies of the new world powers. England, France, Spain, and Portugal, later joined by the new nation of Holland, were constantly at war with one another; their alliances turned into rivalry with the same ease with which they were created, and they often became allies again

(cont'd on p. 76)

Dauphin Royal—*1658. Flagship of French Admiral Chateâu-Renault at the Battle of Beach Head (1690), against the Anglo-Dutch fleet.*

The Caravel

A NEW WORLD IN 33 DAYS

Niña—*One of Columbus's caravels. During his first voyage, he modified the rigging, replacing the lateen sails with more efficient square sails on the foremast and mainmast. It had a tonnage of 52 tons, and was about 70 feet long, and 20 feet wide, with a draft of about 5 feet. With Columbus as captain, it covered at least 25,000 miles during three of the great navigator's four voyages.*

The word "caravel" appears for the first time in the 14th century and is used to designate a small sailing ship with a round bow and a square stern, which sailed in the western Mediterranean and beyond the Straits of Gibraltar, along the coast of Portugal.

The caravel was first used for fishing and coastal transport and then became famous in the period of oceanic discovery. We know very little about the technical characteristics of this very special type of vessel. It was carvel-built, a typically Mediterranean method in which the planks were laid with the seams touching, but not overlapping, as in the north. It normally had a single deck (lacking on some of the small-

er ships) and displaced from about 25 to 60 tons; the rudder was suspended in the center of the square stern, and the ship had 2 or 3 masts with lateen sails. There was no foremast as such. The mainmast functioned as foremast, although it stood almost in the center of the ship. At times a fourth mast stood at the bow, with square rigging.

The construction formula defining the proportions of the hull—*tres, dos y as*— has been interpreted in various ways, and at any rate was not always followed to the letter by builders; this affects the accuracy of modern caravel reconstructions, both full-sized and to scale, and explains the rather obvious differences between them.

The hypothesis has been broached that the caravel was invented by Prince Henry the Navigator (1394–1460) and his naval architects at the famous school of ocean navigation at Sagres, near Cape Saint Vincent. One thing is sure: in prints and paintings, the early caravel is always shown with Portuguese flags. What-

Pinta—*One of Columbus's caravels, owned by Gomez Rascon and Cristòbal Quintero. It was a* redunda *caravel, that is, it had square sails on the mainmast and foremast. There was a crew of 25 men, under the command of Martìn Alonso Pinzòn.*

The Caravel

ever the truth may be, the Portuguese perfected the hull of the most widely used local type of fishing and coastal-trade boat, modifying it to suit the needs of long ocean voyages and making it a medium-sized ship, halfway between the mercantile sailing ship completely rigged with square sails (the round ship) and the long, low galley, a warship basically powered by the muscles of its oarsmen.

The triangular lateen sail made it faster to windward, and the not too heavy hull made it easy to maneuver, both with sails and with oars. Its shallow draft made it less likely to be damaged by currents and reefs, and it was useful for navigation in the mouths of little-known (or completely unknown) rivers. The largest caravels—which reached 150 tons—had a deck and could hold cannon. They had a poop deck; a forecastle; and smaller boats aboard, set on the deck. When a storm arose, the sailors could probably reef and hoist smaller sails on the yards.

The Portuguese jealously kept secret the building details of these ships, which may explain why we know so little about them today. Most of our information refers not so much to the typical Portuguese caravels of the 15th century as to those used by the Spaniards in the area of Cadiz. The ships Gil Eannes led past Cape Bojador in 1434 were caravels; it was in three caravels that Antão Gonçalves and Nuño Tristào reached Cape Blanc, at latitude 21 degrees north, in 1441; and two caravels, under the command of Bartholomeu Dias, went around the Cape of Good Hope and up the eastern coast of Africa, to Cape Recife, opening up the fabulous spice route to commerce. It was with two *carabelas redondas* (that is, rigged with square sails), the *Niña* and the *Piñta*—the *Santa Maria* was probably a *nao*, a carrack—that Christopher Columbus touched the coast of the unknown American continent. And in 1497 Vasco da Gama's ships reached Calicut, India. The third ship of the expedition, the *Berrio*, of only 50 tons, was a caravel.

The caravel survived until the second half of the 17th century, when the demands and length of ocean travel made its size inadequate. Its influence and nautical characteristics survived in the merchant schooners of the 19th century and, in our own time, in the Arab dhows of the Red Sea and the Persian Gulf.

Santa Maria—*The flagship of Columbus and his largest vessel. It was a carrack (*nao *in Spanish) of between 100 and 250 tons, and it was originally called* La Gallega. *It ran aground in a strong wind on Christmas Day, 1492, off the coast of Hispaniola.*

Mediterranean merchant galleon—*16th century. A high-seas sailing ship.*

Danish hooker—*17th century. A typical northern merchant ship.*

to crush the power of the Ottoman Empire, which in the second half of the 16th century controlled the Near East and Egypt in North Africa, and even extended as far as Hungary, in the heart of Europe.

Although the Mediterranean declined to the rank of a secondary sea (and remained such until the opening of the Suez Canal), there was still much commercial activity. The fast ships of the Barbary pirates, encouraged by the Ottoman Empire, were a scourge to the trade of Genoa and Venice with the East. After the Moors were expelled from Spain at the end of the 15th century, the sailors of the Maghrib, the Barbary Coast, carried out ruthless raids along the coasts of Spain and Italy and devastated convoys that passed

Dutch pinnace—*17th century. A merchant and fighting ship, derived from, but larger than, the* fluyut. *It was the great trading vessel of the northern seas, forerunner of the large ships of the East India Company.*

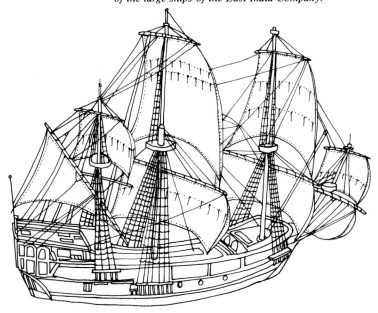

through the Strait of Gibraltar. Two Greek-born brothers named Barbarossa founded the Barbary states of Tunis and Algiers. The last dey of Algiers, Dragut, "the sword of Islam," religiously fanatic and rapacious, was killed during the Turkish fleet's siege of the island of Malta.

The galley, the fast ship that had dominated naval warfare for many centuries, played a leading role in the last and greatest naval encounter of the postmedieval age of the oar, the Battle of Lepanto. The Turks were dominant throughout the Mediterranean. Venice maintained a wary neutrality, trying to protect her last trade routes with the East and keep Spanish power at bay. Spain, engaged in hostilities with France and England, could not deal with the Turks by herself. And the "unholy alliance" established in 1533 between Francis I and Suleiman the Magnificent made the Mediterranean situation even more serious. Pope Pius V was alarmed by the dangerous and fragile balance of power and succeeded in organizing a Christian League against the Turks. A pact was signed in Rome on May 24, 1571, by the pope, the king of Spain, Venice, Emanuel Filibert of Savoy, the grand duke of Tuscany, the duke of Urbino, the duke of Parma, the Republic of Genoa, and the Order of Malta. Command of the league's fleet was entrusted to Don John of Austria (1547–1578), the illegitimate son of Emperor Charles V and Barbara Blomberg. The left wing was commanded by Agostino Barbarigo, general controller of the galleys of Venice, while the twelve pontifical galleys in the fleet were at the orders of the Roman Prince Marcantonio Colonna, who fought heroically against the Turkish flagship commanded by Ali Pasha. The league's fleet included 208 galleys, 6 galleasses, and 24 tenders, with a total of 12,920 seamen, 42,500 oarsmen, 28,000 soldiers, and 1,815 cannons. The Turkish fleet, commanded by Ali Pasha, included 210 large galleys, 63 galiots, 13,000 seamen, 41,000 oarsmen, 34,000 soldiers, and 750 cannons. On the morning of October 7, 1571, the two fleets were face to face in the waters of the Echinades Islands at the mouth of the gulf of Patras; and the ensuing battle was given the name of those islands by the chroniclers of the time. Only later was it called the Battle of Lepanto, from the place on the gulf of Patras where the Turkish fleet assembled.

The Christian ships were in the following formation: in the center were the 61 galleys of Don John of Austria; to the right were the Genoese galleys commanded by Gian Andrea Doria; and to the left, as already noted, the ships of Agostino Barbarigo; while the rear guard of thirty galleys was made up of the Spanish Marquis of Santa Cruz's Neapolitan reserves.

The Turkish forces saw the bey of Algiers, Uluc Ali, with the Algerian galleys, opposite Doria, while the bey of Alexandria, Mehmet Choraq, called Scirocco, faced Barbarigo; the pirate Amurat Dragut commanded the reserve ships.

A westerly wind came up toward midday, favoring the galleys of the league, and battle was joined. The first ships to enter combat were the Venetian galleys, designed by Francesco Bressan and equipped with powerful artillery. The battle developed in the center and on the left wing of the Christian formation, where Barbarigo saw victory assured, despite a mortal wound. The battle ended about five in the afternoon. The Turks lost about 40,000 men, including Ali Pasha and all the other commanders, except Ulugh Ali. Eighty galleys and 27 galliots were destroyed, while 17 galleys and 13 galliots were captured, along with 8,000 men. Fifteen of the league's galleys were sunk, with 7,656 dead and 7,784 wounded; among the latter was a Spaniard who had fought on one of Gian Andrea Doria's ships, Miguel de Cervantes, who was to write the most famous novel in Spanish literature.

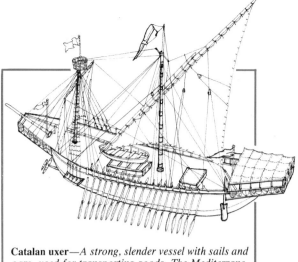

Catalan uxer—*A strong, slender vessel with sails and oars, used for transporting goods. The Mediterranean heir of the Cinque Ports cogs.*

Some of the outstanding participants in the Battle of Lepanto had practiced piracy for their homelands. And in northern Europe as well, men who had practiced piracy often made decisive contributions to the formation of national navies.

The word "privateer" was applied to privately owned ships commissioned by the state to attack enemy ships, but piracy must have been practiced since the start of navigation. The means used by the various pirates, corsairs, buccaneers, and freebooters were different, but what they had in common was the seizure of booty by violence. They worked the major trading routes, the English Channel, the Strait of Gibraltar, and the Caribbean Sea. The English and French crowns had tried to control piracy, but it was only under the great Elizabeth I of England, in the 16th century, that piracy was somewhat controlled by commissioning some of

Brandenburg flute—*Typical merchant ship of the North Sea area, sometimes lightly armed for protection against attack from the corsairs of the English Channel.*

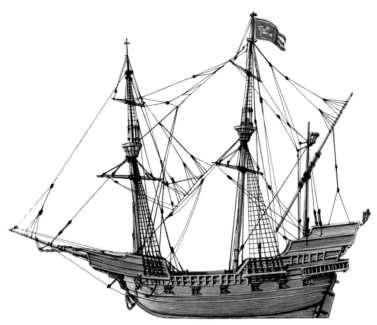

Venetian galleon—*18th century. A transport and military ship of the Venetian Republic, smaller and more agile than its Spanish and English cousins.*

their leaders as privateers. And some of them became officers at the time of the invasion of the Spanish Armada. But privateering, or piracy, if one prefers, was given a particular flavor, as "a new way to pay old debts," by an Englishman named Sir Francis Drake, who saw action on almost all the seas of the world as a corsair, navigator, and explorer. He ended his brilliant career as a national hero.

Francis Drake, born about 1540, was related to the Hawkins family, the famous Plymouth shipbuilders, and it was on one of their ships, the *Judith*, that he first crossed the seas to sell African slaves to the Spanish colonies in America. Drake, little more than twenty-five, began his career as a corsair and became one of the most successful raiders on the Spanish Main. It was during a daring raid on Panama in 1572 that Drake first glimpsed the Pacific Ocean and promised himself that one day he would "sail an English ship in those seas." Between 1577

Spanish galleon—*18th century. Used mainly in the Atlantic by the Spaniards to carry gold and precious goods from the American colonies, and the choice prey of pirates, corsairs, and buccaneers in the West Indies. It often sailed in convoys, protected by a strongly armed escort.*

and 1580 Drake carried out the first English circumnavigation of the world.

In December 1577, he set out with 5 ships and a crew of 164 men on the most famous voyage in English naval history, under sealed orders from the queen. He passed through the Strait of Magellan and entered the broad Pacific, where a storm drove his ship south as far as latitude 57°. He discovered that beyond the Strait of Magellan, the New World did not continue as compact dry land, but dwindled into a complex archipelago of islands off the Chilean coast. Drake continued his voyage through the Pacific and carried out what may have been the main purpose of his mission: raiding Spanish ships and ports on the western coast of South America. His expedition made a profit of 400 percent over its expenses.

Attacking and looting, Francis Drake sailed beyond the land that Balboa had called New Spain, hoping to find a western entrance to the Northwest Passage that would take him directly back into the Atlantic. He conducted a life of piracy and exploration at the same time. His *Golden Hind* touched the coast of what is now California, at the same time that his fellow countryman, Martin Frobisher, was busy on the Atlantic coast looking for the Northwest Passage between the Atlantic and the Pacific.

It was probably from San Francisco Bay that Drake's galleon, the *Golden Hind*, set out across the Pacific and headed for the Spice Islands. Despite illness and fatigue, Drake's men reached Ternate, in the Moluccas. With six tons of cloves in the hold, Drake's ship headed back toward England. On September 26, 1580, he anchored at Plymouth. Wealth and honors awaited Drake, who was knighted by the queen and officially became a member of Her Majesty's Navy. When Philip II's fleet appeared off the English coast in 1588, Drake took part in the great battle as vice admiral. The battle lasted almost a week and ended with the destruction of the "Invincible Armada."

In 1595, a second expedition against the Spanish West Indies was organized, but this time things did not function as well as on the first. Cities that had been easily sacked were now strongly defended, and a Spanish war fleet patrolled the Caribbean. Drake, worn out by worry and fever, died on January 27, 1596, and was buried at sea.

Golden Hind—*1577. Originally known as the* Pelican. *The flagship of Sir Francis Drake during his legendary voyage around the world during which, among other exploits, he captured the famous "treasure galleon" of Panama. It was a 98-ton vessel.*

Although the coat of arms that went with his knighthood bore the legend *Tu primo circumdedisti me, divino auxilio,* Drake was simply the first Englishman to circumnavigate the earth. A brilliant and courageous leader at sea, Drake was one of the best mariners of his time. He made a major contribution to the early development of the Royal Navy, and certainly earned his place among the great navigators of the 16th century.

80

English pirates had a field day in the Caribbean, which Spain claimed as part of its empire. At the same time, they gave support to the English colony founded in North America by Sir Walter Raleigh, which became an important base for the raiders of the Spanish Main. The reign of Elizabeth I (1558–1603) saw enormous growth in maritime commerce, and important trading companies were granted privileges and concessions by the crown. The Muscovy Company was established as early as 1555 for the fur trade with Russia; and the Levant Company, founded in 1584, was the original basis on which the powerful East India Company was developed.

The spark that set off the war between Protestant Queen Elizabeth of England and Catholic King Philip II of Spain was the execution of Catholic Mary Stuart, queen of Scotland, in 1587. On July 31, 1588, a Spanish fleet of 130 ships, about half of them fighting galleons, appeared off Plymouth under the command of the inexperienced duke of Medina Sidonia, who had replaced the marquis of Santa Cruz after the latter's death earlier that year. The aim of the Spanish Armada was to rendezvous with the duke of Parma's Netherlands troops and then land in England at Margate. The English fleet, commanded by Lord Admiral Charles Howard of Effingham, had courageous and experienced captains, including Sir Francis Drake, Hawkins, and Frobisher, but was somewhat inferior to the Spanish in the number of front-line ships available. In what may be considered the first modern naval battle, there was no hand-to-hand fighting and no boarding. For the first time artillery fire from ships was the decisive factor in sea warfare. Medina Sidonia's fleet was drawn up in

roughly square formation, with the transport ships in the center. The English had faster ships and were more flexible in maneuvers. The struggle lasted almost a week. The Armada sailed up the Channel toward Calais, which it reached without great difficulty on August 6. But the troops of the duke of Parma, blocked in Flanders by the English and by Dutch rebels, failed to rendezvous with the Spanish fleet.

On the night of August 7, the English launched half a dozen fire ships down wind towards the Spanish fleet, which was anchored off Calais. The Spanish ships panicked and broke their formation. Then the English attacked. The decisive battle was engaged off Gravelines on August 8. At least three Spanish ships were destroyed—probably more—and the others withdrew. Bad weather forced the Spaniards to head north; their fleet proceeded to circle Scotland and return home. With their masts and sails damaged, a shortage of food and water, the retreat was disastrous. Some 20 ships ended up on the Irish reefs, and perhaps 35 vanished in fog and storms. About half of the Spanish Armada got back to the port of Santander with what was left of the crews. Aside from the political consequences, this encounter was to have important influence on naval strategy during the following decades. Later fighting ships would be armed with cannon that had longer range than the Spanish and more power than the English; they would carry larger stocks of food supplies and ammunition to give them greater endurance. Hulls would be designed for increased steadiness, and additional sails would increase speed and facilitate closehauling. The Spanish navy learned a great deal from the experience, and in later battles

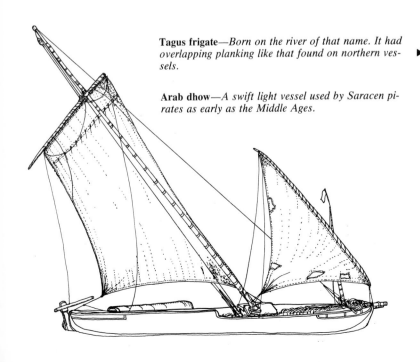

Tagus frigate—*Born on the river of that name. It had overlapping planking like that found on northern vessels.*

Arab dhow—*A swift light vessel used by Saracen pirates as early as the Middle Ages.*

Portuguese moliceiro—*A boat used to carry wood along the Tagus River.*

Muleta—*A Portuguese fishing boat that combined the building techniques of three maritime peoples: the Normans, the Arabs, and the Dutch.*

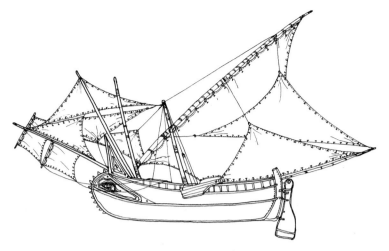

English admirals would taste the bitterness of defeat at Spanish hands.

In the 16th century the Low Countries rebelled against Spain, exasperated by Philip II's anti-Protestant religious policy and heavy taxation. William I ("the Silent"), Prince of Orange, tried unsuccessfully all his life to unite the Netherlands. While the Dutch were unable to defeat the powerful Spanish infantry, they were superb seaman and managed to put together the largest war-and-trading fleet that Europe had ever seen. The port of Amsterdam became an active commercial center, and in 1602 the Dutch created their own flourishing and official East India Company. Dutch ships dealt hard blows to the Spanish galleons returning to their homeland laden with gold and spices from America and the Indies. Piter van der Does (1562–1599), the most famous Dutch admiral of the age, was busy raiding in the Channel and as far as the Spanish naval base of La Coruña and the Canary Islands and Gomera (1599). A few years later Willem Cornelius Schouten (1567–1625) and Jakob Lemaire doubled the southern point of the Tierra del Fuego on January 24, 1616, during an expedition to Java, and gave the name

Cape Hoorn, in honor of his native city, to the "fierce guardian of the gloomy gate of the Southern Seas."

The Dutch East India Company, with an initial capital of 6.5 million florins, managed to drive the Portuguese and the Spanish from the Moluccas and from Malabar. The company established colonies and trading posts on the coasts of Sumatra and Ceylon; and in 1595, thanks to Frederick Houtman (1571–1627) and his brother Cornelius, at Bantam, on the southern coast of Java. By the end of the 16th century, the sea routes of both the North and South Atlantic were being crossed by Spaniards, Portuguese, Dutchmen, Frenchmen, and Englishmen; those of the Pacific, opened up by Magellan, saw Spanish galleons from the Philippines carry their precious cargoes to Acapulco and to the Central American Isthmus of Panama for transshipment by land to the Atlantic to be loaded on ships for Spain. The Portuguese

Portuguese rabelo—*A small boat with a gaff sail, used for carrying wine on inland waterways.*

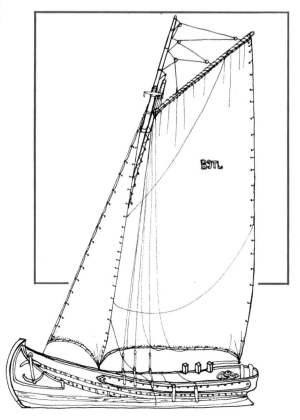

Dutch fluyut—*The most important merchant ship of the 17th century, it played a leading role in the commercial and mercantile expansion of the people of Flanders.*

imported African slaves for their sugar plantations in Brazil, while France and England established colonies in North America. Several commercial routes were established in the Atlantic and the Pacific. The Old World and the New World grew closer to each other, and many old rivalries were intensified.

During the 16th century the warship evolved toward the ship of the line, of which the three-decked three-master was to be the finest achievement until the arrival of steam. Our rapid summary of the 15th and 16th centuries reflected the great advance made in the knowledge of the seas and oceans. This progress went hand in hand with the evolution of the sailing vessel and the development of navigational sciences. In the 16th century Copernicus demonstrated that the earth's motion was heliocentric, and Galileo was to confirm this experimentally a century later. The circle of Henry the Navigator methodically studies the problems of navigation. Ptolemy's *Geography* had been translated into Latin early in the 15th century, and the astrolabe, an ancient instrument for measuring the altitude of celestial bodies, was

perfected. Astronomical tables were compiled and perfected, and in the 16th century the Flemish geographer Gerhardus Mercator (1512–1594) devised a system of flat projection of the earth's surface. Magnificent nautical charts were prepared—veritable works of art, with detailed notes, warnings, and instructions. Magellan was able to sound the ocean depths without touching bottom. The compass was installed in a tin binnacle, suspended by gimbals, or rings, to keep the instrument free from the ship's movements. The first artillery pieces were used on board ship in the middle of the 14th century, and they were improved and made more powerful in the next two centuries. Sails and rigging increased in size, along with the greater dimensions of the hull. In other words, the sailing ship had begun its great process of evolution.

It was in the sailing ship that man set out to conquer his *ultima Thule.* As Victor Hugo once said, if the sea is the symbol of the power of the Lord, the ship is the symbol of the ingenuity of man.

Saint Louis—*1626. Ordered from Dutch shipbuilders by Cardinal Richelieu, "the father of the French navy," and armed with 60 cannons, it was one of those wooden fortresses that replaced the galleon. The central deck was protected from enemy artillery by a wooden grill, and the ever more complex and improved sails let the ship be maneuvered more quickly and efficiently.*

Xebec—*A distant descendant of the Byzantine dromon, the* shabbac *of 17th-century Algerian corsairs was more like a yacht, with its elegant lines and rich decoration. Its many cannons and fierce crew made it a formidable vessel.*

The Golden Age of the Sail

By the end of the 16th century, the commercial and mercantile prospects opened up by the voyages of Vasco da Gama, Columbus, and Magellan had become a solid reality. Portugal's colonial empire extended down the African coast from Guinea to the Cape of Good Hope and over to Mozambique; in the Indian Ocean, it included the ports of Goa, Diu, and Cochin; the large island of Ceylond; Malacca and the Indonesian archipelagoes; and touched China and Japan by way of the trading center of Macao. It was deported Marranos, converted Jews who were still viewed with suspicion by the Inquisition, who introduced the cultivation of sugar cane in Brazil, along with that of other tropical crops such as cocoa and coffee, while important deposits of gold and diamonds were discovered in that country.

This colonial expansion was accompanied by the activities of Catholic missionaries, who did much to spread knowledge of the new lands and their customs. If Portugal had worried more about the mercantile side of its colonial development and less about its religious aspects (the hope of mass conversion was the main motive behind Henry the Navigator's great plan for expansion), the Portuguese might well have had much greater commercial success in the Far East than they actually did. The Portuguese colonial empire at this period, restricted by the policies of Philip II of Spain, felt the repercussions of the blows inflicted by the Dutch on the Spanish crown. The voyages of Columbus and Magellan had opened the way to Central and South America, as well as to part of North America, with Florida and California. And in the Pacific, Spain dominated the Philippine archipelago, with its great trading port, Manila.

France had small trading settlements in Canada, thanks to Samuel de Champlain (1608), and later in the Antilles (the islands of San Domingo, Martinique, and Guadalupe). England, despite the serious political, social, and religious crisis that followed the death of Elizabeth I (1603), was extending its naval and commercial influence to other continents, in fierce competition with the Spanish and Portuguese and the Dutch. The Virginia colony, whose first settlers were decimated by the climate and the Indians, became a rich and profitable possession when the first tobacco plantations were created there, and their product began to be exported throughout Europe.

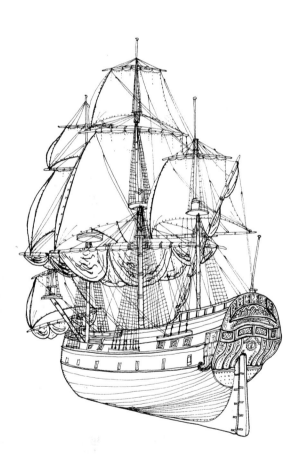

D'bataviase Eeuw—*One of the large Dutch merchant ships of the East India Company.*

Geertruyd—*Built in 1717 for the Dutch East India Company, it was about 130 feet long, and had a crew of 180 men and a cargo tonnage of 100 tons.*

Santissima Madre—*A third-rate Spanish vessel, launched in 1778. The third-rate vessel was an ideal warship because of its combination of armament and maneuverability.*

Mayflower—*The galleon on which the Pilgrim Fathers traveled from England to the coast of North America and founded the Plymouth Colony in Massachusetts. The trip was subsidized by a group of English merchants, who invested 7,000 pounds sterling in the voyage. The* Mayflower *had 2 decks; 102 men, women and children were packed into it. In September 1620, the small galleon sailed from England and reached the coast of America on November 20, after an adventurous voyage.*

The colonial economic system—and especially that of the Spanish-Portuguese—was based on a rigid monopoly that permitted the subjects of the mother country to have access only to the colonies. One tenet of mercantilism, the dominant economic doctrine of the time, held that the wealth of a nation was basically calculated on the amount of gold and silver it possessed. To pay for a long series of exhausting wars, the Spanish ruling class made lavish use of the wealth drawn from its empire; a river of gold and silver thus flowed incessantly from the colonies to the motherland, carried by large galleons. This boundless wealth did not remain in Spain, though. It ended up in the hands of foreign merchants, mainly Genoese, through whose agents almost all the supplies needed by Spain had to be imported. In fact, the Castilian aristocracy disdained the idea of being involved in industry and commerce and confined itself to furnishing the leaders of the army, maintaining a corrupt and dishonest bureaucracy, a cancer gnawing at the empire, and providing for an ever more powerful and autocratic clergy. The major European powers competed for almost two centuries for colonial possessions, and ships played a decisive role in this military and commercial rivalry.

Philip II of Spain died in 1598 and was succeeded by his incompetent son, Philip III (who reigned from 1598 to 1621). Philip III also inherited the ruinous war against England and Holland, and an enormous financial deficit, caused mainly by the militaristic and religiously fanatical Spanish aristocracy. The enormous Spanish-Portuguese colonial empire, which made Spain Europe's most powerful state in the early 1600s, was closed to the other Atlantic nations. The Dutch had been scornfully called "the beggars of the

Prince—*An English warship of 1670, designed by shipwright Phineas Pett. It was 130 feet long and 45 feet wide. The 17th century saw the development of the ship of the line, with 3 decks and cannon batteries on each one. In the British navy, the building and outfitting of the large ship of the line was regulated by special rules and regulations that fixed the general measurements of the ship down to the last detail.*

Le Mirage—*A French first rate of 1659. The bowsprit has been lengthened to carry the jib boom.*

Scotch merchant vessel—*17th century. Like the frigate, and armed with one artillery battery; tonnage between 700 and 1,178 tons.*

sea"; but when they achieved national unity, Holland proved a formidable enemy of the Spanish colossus, and the rivalry was political, commercial, and religious. In little more than 50 years, Dutch merchants and navigators managed to create a strictly commercial colonial empire, that is, one devoid of those warlike and missionary ideals that marked the Spanish and Portuguese conquests. The East India Company, founded in 1602, operated in the seas of India, Malaysia, and China. The Dutch replaced the Portuguese in trade with Cochin, Ceylon, and Malacca; the Dutch also set up trading posts on Java and the neighboring islands and established huge plantations. In 1619 the Dutch founded Batavia, the capital of their new empire. Dutch ships carried colonists to Africa to found settlements, forts, and commercial centers on the Gulf of Guinea and at the Cape of Good Hope. There the Transvaal Republic was established by Dutch Calvinist farmers, the Boers.

The Dutch West India Company was founded in 1621 and operated mainly in the American zone, first through smuggling and piracy, at the expense of the Spanish and Portuguese. The Dutch West India Company then set up commercial ports in the Antilles, Curacao, and Surinam. In North America, at the mouth of the Hudson River, in 1624 the Dutch founded New Amsterdam, the original nucleus of what was to become New York. About the middle of the 17th century, Holland reached the peak of its economic prosperity and initiated new types of group undertakings, among them a maritime insurance organization. The Bank of Amsterdam was considered the most powerful in Europe, and the India companies, which had their own military forces and war fleet, paid an annual dividend of 50 percent to their shareholders. About 15,000 to 16,000 of the approximately 20,000 European ships at the time were Dutch. In a few years, Holland had become the richest, most civilized, and

Dutch yacht—*First used on the Dutch canals; it was used as a coastal vessel in the 17th century.*

Dutch yacht—*Note the two leeboards on the sides which provided lateral resistance in shallow water as well as on the high seas.*

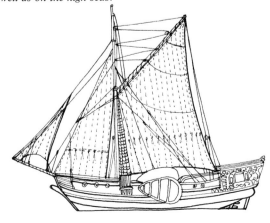

most energetic nation in Europe. The 100-ton *fluyut*, the typical merchant sailing ship, was, together with the popular transport ship, a commercial ship to all effects, but it also carried cannon. Although less heavily armed than warships, it could defend itself at all times. This can be seen in the models of the East Indiaman (a very fast, frigate-type sailing ship used by the India companies) in the Dutch naval museum in Rotterdam, a ship that for centuries controlled Dutch trade routes.

The development and success of Dutch commercial activity inevitably coincided with the growth of Holland's military fleet, for which a new type of warship was created, less tough than English and French vessels, but faster, easier to handle, and extremely seaworthy. The Dutch ship of the line, derived from the 15th-century galleon, had lower superstructures and very little decoration, since the latter was easily destroyed by a good broadside. Rudder control was improved by the adoption of a vertical and articulated countertiller that let the helmsman steer directly from the upper deck, with a full and unhindered view of the sails. The lower gun battery was raised to a height of about four feet above the waterline, so that water no longer poured through the cannon ports when the ship was heeling over during combat. The hull was plated with sheets of lead (later with a lighter metal, copper) for protection and endurance. Military and commercial shipbuilding led the Dutch to set up trade relations with the Baltic nations, the leading producers of material for naval construction, such as wood, hemp for sails and rigging, and pitch and tar.

Throughout most of the 17th century, Dutch ships fought proudly and stubbornly against other European powers—Spain chiefly, and England—whose economic interests and political ambitions were chal-

Buccaneer ship—*For two centuries the Caribbean Sea was the scene of the piracy of the "Brothers of the Coast" and the buccaneers.*

lenged by the younger nation. As Spanish power declined, a political and strategic void was created and the Dutch tried to fill it. England was torn by domestic conflicts and had neglected its international naval interests for a time. This led to three Dutch wars (1651–1654; 1666–1668; 1672–1674) which were fought predominantly at sea. The Dutch were among the age's finest sailors, sons of a new nation that fought boldly for its place in the economic, social, industrial, and cultural evolution that was to change the course of history a century later.

In the 17th century England went through a profound social, ideological, and constitutional crisis, and she did not take active part in the Thirty Years' War (1618–1648). With the death of Elizabeth I, the Tudor line came to an end. She was succeeded by James I, Mary Stuart's son. His successor, Charles I, an absolutist, clashed with Parliament, which he had tried unsuccessfully to dissolve. The

Cacafuego—*A 17th-century Spanish* bombarda, *a sturdy vessel and with a solid bow platform on which a bomb mortar was mounted.*

Le Tonnant—*A French corsair ship of 1793. Privateering was officially abolished by the Congress of Paris in 1856.*

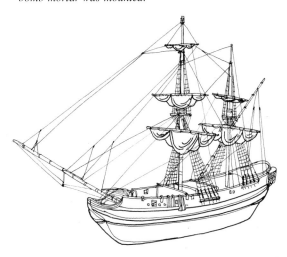

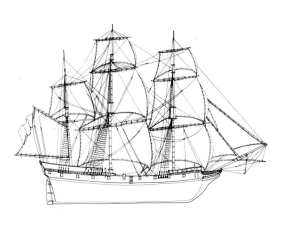

Sovereign of the Seas—*Designed by Phineas Pett and launched in 1637. It was 170 feet long and 48 feet at the beam. The ship carried 102 cannons on its 3 decks and cost 66,000 pounds sterling to build. It had a displacement of 1,541 tons. In 1652, it was turned into a 2-decker to make it more stable and was renamed* Royal Sovereign. *It flew Lord Torrington's flag at Beachy Head.*

violent civil war that ensued was fought between Royalists and Parliamentarians, Catholics and Protestants.

Parliament entrusted its forces to Oliver Cromwell. Cromwell had been a farmer and member of the House of Commons, and he had no specific training as a soldier. Nevertheless he proved to be an outstanding leader in the Civil War. In 1649 Charles I was beheaded, and in 1653 Cromwell became Lord Protector of the Commonwealth. What is of particular interest here is that his naval policy was a great stimulus to merchant shipping. The Commonwealth fleet was increased to protect the expansion of British trade, and a first step toward that goal was the Navigation Act of 1651, which struck at Dutch naval domination by prohibiting the landing in England of foreign goods not carried in English ships or in those of the nations from which they were sent. The Dutch, who earned large profits from carry-

ing merchandise for third parties, found their commercial interests seriously damaged. The conflict soon led to the first Dutch War.

The three men chiefly responsible for the development of a powerful French military fleet in the 17th century were Cardinal Richelieu, head of Louis XIII's government; Jean Baptiste Colbert, Louis XIV's minister; and Le Tellier de Louvois, secretary of war and untiring organizer of the Sun King's military and maritime power. Other European nations, such as Sweden, Russia, Denmark, and Spain, also took part in the naval-armament race. The fighting ship of the line was born; it was destined to dominate naval warfare for two centuries. The various types were classified by tonnage, number of cannon, and types of sail. These ratings, modified by modern shipbuilding techniques, are still used in classifying military vessels according to operational functions. The rating system was adopted throughout Europe, and in little

Aemilia—A Dutch first rate, built in 1630. The flagship of the famous Marten Tromp at the Battle of the Downs, September–October 1639, between the Dutch and Spanish fleets. That action was Spanish Minister Olivares's last attempt to destroy Dutch naval power in the waters of the North Sea.

more than fifty years all the great naval powers had formed efficient and well-organized national fleets. A century earlier, in England, Sir John Hawkins—for ten years First Treasurer and then Comptroller of the Navy—had imposed advanced ideas and modernization that made him the promoter of the concept of the ship of the line. The term first appeared in the British Admiralty's *Fighting Instructions* in 1653; the "line" was considered the optimum fighting formation provided that all the ships in it could maintain the same speed, were equally maneuverable, and were sufficiently armed so that no ship would have to face an enemy with greater firing power. This principle inspired the construction of series of vessels that automatically defined the categories of ships. Battle-line ships belonged to the first three rates. Convoy escort ships and exploration ships were fourth-rate. The fifth-rate ships also included exploration ships and commu-

nications vessels. Coast-guard cutters were sixth-rate. Many of the European and non-European fleets adopted the military ratings established by the British Admiralty, with certain variations as regarded armament. Ships of the line increased in size until they reached some 2,000 tons in the 18th century. At the end of the 17th century, the finest warships were those built in French shipyards; they were faster and more stable at sea, thanks to a concept of flexibility that made each new vessel slightly larger in size than its predecessor and incorporated any improvements that had appeared. In England, one of the pioneers of new naval building techniques was Sir Anthony Deane, mainly responsible for the construction of warships with large holds with a six-month supply of provisions and ammunition reserves, instead of the earlier ten-weeks supply. These new ships were extremely self-sufficient.

92

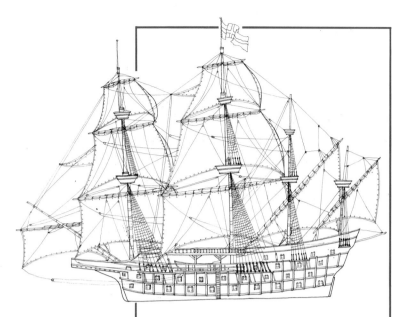

San Matteo—*One of the last galleons. It belonged to the Genoese fleet and was used for trade with the East. It had 60 cannons on its 2 gun decks, on the quarter-deck, and on the forecastle.*

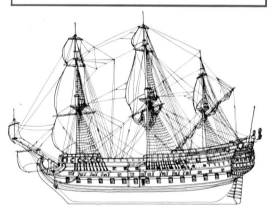

San Felipe—*One of the most elaborate and impressive Spanish warships, built in 1690 and armed with 110 artillery pieces of various calibers.*

Vanguard—*A 95-gun English first-rate ship of the line, Nelson's flagship at the Battle of Aboukir.*

Ottoman warship—*The classification of warships differed from fleet to fleet. Here we see a second-rate ship of the line with 80 cannons.*

Ships' artillery also underwent a radical change. Between 1670 and 1700, the old cannon, richly decorated with seals, blazons and Latin inscriptions, was replaced with all-iron pieces that looked and performed strictly like weapons of war. Late in the 17th century Commander Denox noted that the cannon had become so powerful that the fate of a naval battle depended on it. The warship had become a floating gun-carriage, and fighting tactics were aimed at creating the best conditions of use and fire for the cannon. The next century saw a large-caliber but fairly light cannon, the carronade, appear on board light ships used for surveillance and interfleet contact; it was serviced by only three men and could fire a shot every three minutes, either balls or grapeshot. The carronade also armed merchant ships well into the 19th century. The carronade was the last of the smoothbore guns, that is, with an unrifled barrel. Apart from cannon, warships carried mortars; hand bombs (large terracotta containers filled with grapeshot and powder); small revolving cannons; and muskets and pistols for the crew. In the mid-18th century, naval foot soldiers were embarked for close combat.

The artillery on board large ships was placed on various decks, along the sides of the ship, and the cannon mouths protruded from hatches with special covers. For reasons of stability, the heavier pieces were installed in the lowest battery. The cannon was mounted on a wooden gun carriage with wheels, and recoiled with each shot; to reduce the recoil effect, the gun carriage was

Agamemnon—*The third-rate English ship of the line commanded by Horatio Nelson from 1793 to 1796.*

Soleil Royal—*This first-rate French warship carried over 100 guns. As Tourville's flagship, it lay at the center of the formation at the Battle of Beachy Head.*

fastened to the ship's side by cables. These cables might snap in bad weather, with disastrous consequences for the crew. The gunners worked under difficult conditions: the average gun deck was less than six feet high, and the only light came in through the cannon hatches. With each shot, acrid smoke filled the cramped space, and the air became unbreathable. Salt was strewn on the battery floor to prevent slipping, and a net stretched along the sides was supposed to protect the men from splinters of wood that

flew all over when the hull was shattered by enemy shot. The small space was further cramped by piles of cannonballs and grapeshot and tubs of cold water for cooling the bore of the barrels. The gunners could not man the batteries on both sides of the ship at the same time. (The great danger of the age was being attacked simultaneously on both sides.) After 150 shots, the cannon bore could no longer be used, and the piece had to be sent back to the foundry for repair. Top range for a large-caliber cannon was 2,500–

Russian warship—*Flagship of the Baltic Sea squadron, armed with 74 cannons. Russia slowly reorganized its entire fleet.*

English warship—*Final expression of the large ship of the line. Built in 1840 and armed with 120 cannons on its 3 decks.*

La Couronne—*The first warship completely French in design, construction, outfitting, and crew; one of the largest ships ever to sail the seas until then. Launched in 1638, it had a tonnage of 984 tons, a crew of 660 men, and 72 cannons on 2 decks; the keel was 130 feet long, and the beam was 50 feet long.*

Swedish ship of the line—*First-rate ship armed with 120 cannons. Until the first half of the 19th century, the sail-equipped warship was, with the frigate, the fulcrum of all military fleets.*

3,000 feet, but good results could be obtained only at half that distance. Firing range was calculated by eye, and the naval gunner remained for centuries an "artist" with no scientific or mathematical knowledge. English gunners were considered the best: they shot "full at the ship," aiming to wipe out the enemy's firing power. The French, instead, fired cannonballs bound together with a chain or an iron bar to dismast enemy vessels. (The invention of these so-called angels, or chained cannonballs, is attributed to Dutch Admiral Cornelius de Witt.) But the buoyancy of those warships was remarkable, and they were rarely sunk by artillery fire.

Ships' masts were also improved. About 1620, the mizzenmast was outfitted with square sails instead of with the traditional lateen sail, or else was hung with both. The bonaventure mast disappeared, and each mast carried the same number of sails. To increase the ship's maneuverability, a small square sail was put at the far end of the bowsprit. This sail, along with the spritsail, was later replaced by the more practical triangular staysail, which took its name from the fact that it was put on the stays, that is, on the cables that braced the masts longitudinally from bow to stern. From the second half of the 18th century on, the various riggings of the sails were simplified. The long yard of the mizzenmast lateen sail was replaced by a gaff and then by the spanker, two horizontal yards that supported the upper and lower parts of the sail and made it easier to manage. Jibs, triangular staysails, appeared on the bowsprit, which was lengthened and reinforced and a fourth sail was added to taller masts. The tiller at the helm gave way to the wheel, which was more efficient and easier to use.

In 1690 the French navy was able to reap the rewards of Colbert's efforts to build a large and powerful fleet. Off Beachy Head, on the Sussex coast southwest of Eastbourne, the battleships of Admiral Tourville clashed with an Anglo-Dutch fleet commanded by Lord Torrington. The French supported the claims of the deposed James II against William III. Some 75 French warships were present at the Battle of Beachy Head, together with frigates and other smaller vessels. There were 27,000 men present and 4,200 artillery pieces. The Anglo-Dutch fleet consisted of 62 warships with 19,000 men and 4,100 guns. The French vanguard was led by Admiral Château-Renault, aboard the 104-cannon *Dauphin Royal*; the *Soleil Royal* was in the center carrying the flag of Tourville himself; and the rear guard was under the command of Count d'Estrées, aboard the 90-gun *Grand*. The vanguard of the allied fleet was made up of Dutch ships led by the 90-cannon *Prinzess Maria*, carrying Admiral Evertzen; the center was made up exclusively of English vessels, including the 100-cannon *Royal Sovereign* carrying Lord Torrington; and the rear guard, also English, was commanded by Dutch Admiral Vanderkulen.

The large number of ships involved made this one of the great battles of all time. The French quickly won the advantage, since they were more astute in maneuvering, and their attack line managed to cut off and surround the Dutch vanguard. The French sank or captured 16 enemy ships. The rest of the allied fleet withdrew from combat and managed to sail to safety. At the time France had one of the most powerful and best organized fleets in Europe, matched only by that of Great Britain. The French navy boasted many exceptional figures, sailors and men at arms who combined strategic ability with a perfect knowledge of their ships and the seas on which they fought. Suffice it to mention Abraham Duquesne (or Du Quesne, 1610–1688), who distinguished himself on the Swedish side at the Battle of Fermen against the combined fleets of Holland and Denmark. It was Duquesne who defeated the great De Ruyter at the Battle of Augusta.

The English colonies of North America were also exposed to the French. There were French settlements in Canada as well as in Louisiana. The various European wars between France and England (the War of the League of Augsburg, 1688–1697; the War of the Austrian Succession, 1740–1748; the Seven Years' War, 1756–1763) had repercussions in America. After the Peace of Paris in 1763, long-dormant reasons for conflict between the American colonies and England again came to the fore. The American Revolutionary War (1775–1783) was fought partly at sea. It was only after George Washington's victory over General Burgoyne at Saratoga, in October 1777, that France, Holland,

Vasa—*A 64-cannon Swedish galleon built for King Gustav Adolph II during the Thirty Years' War (1618–1648). About 170 feet long and 38 feet at the beam, it displaced 1,279 tons and had a tonnage of 1,053. There were 3 decks, forty-eight 24-pound cannons in the 2 batteries, 133 sailors, and 300 soldiers. The Vasa was launched in 1627 and set out on its maiden voyage on August 10, 1628. Taking advantage of a south-southwest wind, it had covered little more than a mile when, at the entrance to the port of Stockholm, it was hit by a squall. Water poured into the open cannon ports of the lower battery, and the huge vessel sank in a short time. It settled upright on the sea floor. Attempts to recover the ship began at once but were unsuccessful. Only 300 years later, in 1957, did a serious effort to raise the hull begin, thanks to the determination of a Swedish scholar named Anders Franzén. On April 24, 1961, the Vasa was raised to the surface, remarkably well preserved. After special treatment to keep the wood of the hull from disintegrating on contact with the air, the ship was installed in the Vasa Museum in Stockholm, protected by a shell of glass and cement.*

and Spain decided to intervene in favor of the newborn American nation. England's great fleet had to face a long and wearying military campaign against the new nation on the other side of the Atlantic, which was aided by some of the best European sailors. The U.S. Navy's first commodore was John Barry (1745–1803), born in Ireland but brought to America by his family when he was only eleven. He commanded the frigate *Effingham* at the end of 1776 and fought well during the siege of Philadelphia, carrying out bold and able night raids against enemy shipping on the Delaware River. He later commanded the 36-gun *Alliance*, considered to be the finest American warship of the day.

France sent Théodat Estaing du Saillans (1729–1794) to the aid of the Americans. He left Toulon on April 13, 1777, with twelve ships, raising his vice admiral's flag on the *Languedos*, a 60-cannon vessel. His men took part in the capture of Newport. With 13 more vessels to strengthen his small fleet, Estaing appeared off the island of Grenada on July 2, 1779, and captured the English garrison there. The 21 ships of English Admiral Byron, who had come to defend that English base, withdrew. Estaing was wounded during the unsuccessful American attack on Savannah and returned to France. He later supported the French Revolution and became Admiral of France. But his aristocratic lineage and his testimony in favor of Marie Antoinette led him to the guillotine on April 28, 1794.

In April 1782, the French and the English clashed off the island of Dominica. The rival fleets were commanded by Adm. Paul de Grasse (1722–1788) and Adm. George Rodney. (A year earlier De Grasse had captured the island of Tobago; taken part in the siege of Yorktown; and, on September 5, led his 24 ships of the line against an English formation of 19 vessels commanded by Adm. Thomas Graves, in the Battle of Chesapeake Bay.) The battle of Dominica, or to be more exact, of Saints Passages, saw Rodney's 37 ships beat the De Grasse's 30. De Grasse was captured on board his flagship, the 74-cannon *Ville de Paris*. One of the men aboard Rodney's ship was Samuel Hood (1724–1816), who was later to take part in the siege of Toulon against the French revolutionary artillery, commanded by a young and brilliant

Snow—*A hermaphrodite brig that appeared for the first time in the Swedish fleet in 1669, serving as an escort vessel.*

La Flore—*A 40-cannon French frigate; 30 of the guns were set in one deck battery. In the 18th century, the frigate became the most useful and highly regarded ship.*

Charles—*A French frigate galley of 1776, with both sails and oars, used against the Barbary pirates.*

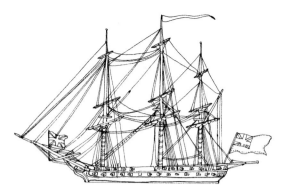

Albemarle—*Captured by the British in 1781 and so named, this 50-gun frigate was larger than most British-built ships of this rating.*

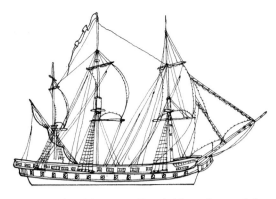

Muiron—*The 18th-century French frigate that carried Napoleon from Egypt back to France in 1799.*

officer named Napoleon Bonaparte. Hood had an enthusiastic admirer in Horatio Nelson, under whom he served in the Napoleonic Wars.

In 1776, the American Congress issued many privateering certificates to New England sailors to support the few fighting ships the rebel colonies could muster. When hostilities ended, 323 corsair vessels were on the seas. Their crews were to provide some of the first officers of the American navy. The most famous naval hero of the American Revolution was John Paul Jones. In 1779 his *Bonhomme Richard*, an old East Indiaman, halfway between warship and armed merchantman, engaged in a famous combat with the British frigate *Serapis* off Flamborough Head. Jones later wrote that "no action before was ever, in all respects, so bloody, so severe and so lasting." Jones is considered the father of the American navy. When the war ended, he became rear admiral of the Russian fleet of Catherine the Great, and he died in Paris. His remains were brought back a century later to the United States and now rest in the chapel of the Naval Academy at Annapolis.

A famous U.S. naval hero was Stephen

Decatur (1779–1820), who won particular distinction in the war against the North African pirates of Tripoli. In command of the schooner *Enterprise*, he captured the Tripoli ketch *Mastico*, set it on fire, and launched it against the American frigate *Philadelphia*, which had been captured by the enemy and anchored in the port of Tripoli. During the War of 1812, Decatur, commanding the *United States*, captured the English frigate *Macedonian*. Three years later he commanded the frigate *President* and, on the night of January 14, 1815, managed to take advantage of a terrible storm to slip past the English blockade of New York. The next day he was attacked by an English squadron of five ships and was wounded and forced to surrender, after having inflicted serious damage on the British frigate *Endymion*. In 1815, he led a squadron against the Barbary States in the Mediterranean and captured the Algerian frigate *Meshouda* and the brigantine *Estedio*. Decatur, one of America's most illustrious naval figures, was killed in a duel by Comdr. James Barron on March 22, 1820.

Two outstanding figures in the early history of the U.S. Navy were David Porter and Edward Preble, commander of the first

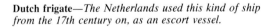

Dutch frigate—*The Netherlands used this kind of ship from the 17th century on, as an escort vessel.*

Lutine—*A French frigate launched in 1785 and captured by the English in 1793. It sank on the night of October 9, 1799, while carrying a million pounds sterling worth of goods and money from Yarmouth to Germany. The gold of the* Lutine *has been vainly sought for since that night.*

English frigate—*18th century. One of the first examples of this kind of ship with rather squat hull and high quarter-deck and forecastle.*

Bounty—*This famous English frigate was launched in 1787. It was the scene of the famous mutiny. Under the command of William Bligh and with a crew of 46 men, it sailed from England for Tahiti in 1789 to carry a cargo of breadfruit trees to the West Indies. On the return voyage, the crew, led by Second Mate Christian Fletcher, mutinied and set Captain Bligh and 17 others adrift in a small boat. The mutineers returned to Tahiti, where 14 of them landed and settled, while the rest reached Pitcairn's Island, where an American ship accidentally discovered their descendants years later. After 40 days of hardship and hunger, Bligh reached Timor and managed to get back to England. The mutineers who had settled on Tahiti were captured by the frigate* **Pandora** *and returned to England for court-martial.*

American naval squadron to appear in the Mediterranean (1803).

Some of the outstanding ships that Americans sailed in the War of 1812 were small frigates, such as the *General Armstrong* and the *Yankee*, and the *Chasseur*, with only 16 cannons. The American frigate was an extremely efficient vessel, superior to European frigates. The ship's official strategy provided that it should always be able to withdraw if attacked by a larger number, that it should not get involved in combat except on its own terms, and that it should be able to join combat with two-battery ships. The frigate *Constitution*, designed by Joshua Humphreys (1751–1838) and launched in 1797, was as solidly built as a ship of the line; it usually carried more than 50 cannons.

The victory of the American rebels on land and sea had important moral and political repercussions in Europe. A revolutionary movement had succeeded in resisting a monarchy. The enlightened ideals and liberal principles in the name of which the war had been fought came out of the struggle solidly reinforced. The enterprise and skill of American sailors laid the basis for what was to become, in the course of less than two centuries, the world's largest and most powerful fleet.

In the period we are so rapidly examining, the Mediterranean became the theater of important naval events, including those of the Napoleonic era. These events were to

have an influence that went well beyond the conflicts in which they occurred. The Venetian fleet had declined, but it was still able to demonstrate its traditional naval valor. Once again it clashed with its eternal adversary, the Ottoman Empire. Venice allied itself with Austria during the two wars waged against the Turks between 1688 and 1718, and Francesco Morosini, the courageous defender of Crete, was one of Venice's last great men of the sea. In February 1695, the Venetian Antonio Zeno lost 1,600 men and 8 ships at Chios to Turkish Adm. Hussein Pasha (1648–1701). Hussein clashed with the Venetians once again in September 1697. This battle, in which the Venetians were led by Contarini, took place near Tenedos and later off Cape Martello. In the following year, Hussein (the first to make use of fire ships in the Mediterranean) again fought the Venetian fleet off Mytilene, but the outcome was not decisive. Both the great Venetian Republic and the centuries-old Ottoman Empire had begun their decline. For Venice, these long wars led to general insecurity on the seas, and by 1722 what had been considered one of the most powerful fleets in the world was reduced to 49 deep-sea transport vessels, 26 fighting ships with more than 50 cannons, and 80 smaller ships. The last naval battle in which the ships of the "Serenissima" took part was the expedition against the Barbary pirates of Tunis in 1786. The last surviving ships of a great fleet could do nothing to defend the Republic when Napoleon's troops destroyed the Arsenal between December 26 and 31, 1797, and, with the Treaty of Campoformio, Venice was handed over to Austria.

The main struggle waged by the declining Turkish fleet was with the Russian navy of Catherine the Great. Her chief adviser, Grigori Aleksandrovich Potëmkin, was a highly gifted commander and organizer. He created the first Russian naval military shipyard at Nikolaev, and the first naval base for the fleet at Sevastopol. In 1770 a Russian squadron commanded by Admiral Orlov left the Baltic, was supplied and reinforced at Leghorn, and then occupied Corno and Navarino. On July 15 of that year, it clashed with a Turkish fleet near Chios. The Turks were led by Hassan Passa and had 15 warships, 4 frigates, and 8 galleys. The Turkish admiral

Boudeuse—*The corvette in which Louis Antoine de Bougainville crossed the Pacific in 1766, discovering the island of Tahiti.*

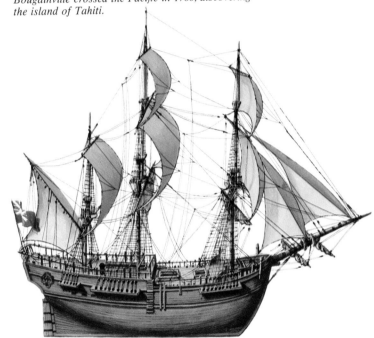

Endeavour—*The bark used by James Cook on his first voyage of exploration in the South Seas. It was about 100 feet long.*

Mediterranean polacre—*A small merchant ship with its foremast sharply inclined toward the bow.*

Languedoc—*A second-rate, 80-cannon French vessel that took part in the American Revolutionary War.*

Orlgosktovet—*A 17th-century Danish corvette. The corvette gradually took over the functions of the frigate.*

Diligente—*A French corvette of 1803. It was smaller than the frigate, with 20 guns in a single deck battery.*

Astrolabe—*The 18th-century French corvette in which Dumont d'Urville made his voyage of discovery, which lasted 26 months.*

was forced to retreat and took refuge in the port of Cesme, on the Turkish coast opposite Chios, but the Russians boldly attacked with fire ships and red-hot cannonballs and destroyed the entire Ottoman fleet, capturing a warship and four galleys, the only ones to escape the fire. Hassan barely managed to flee to safety after losing 7,000 men.

War broke out again in 1788. A squadron of 80 Turkish ships, including warships, frigates, and galleys appeared at the mouth of the Dnieper, on the Black Sea. Potëmkin, supreme commander of land and sea forces, sent 5 ships of the line and 5 frigates from the Sevastopol base to counter the action of Hassan Passa. Command of these 10 large ships was entrusted to the American John Paul Jones, then rear admiral of the Russian fleet, while Prince Nassau-Siegen commanded a fleet of smaller vessels with galleys, gunboats, and floating batteries, as well as 80 Cossack boats with one cannon each. This oar-driven fleet had a total of 400 guns.

Nassau-Siegen's fleet met the Turks in battle three times—on June 18, 28, and 29, 1788—sinking four 64-cannon warships, five 40-cannon frigates, one xebec, a brigantine, and other small vessels.

This was one of the Turkish fleet's last naval battles. The Turkish fleet had become obsolescent in comparison with the maritime progress made by other 18th-century fleets.

In the meantime, the "scourge of Christianity" (as the Barbary pirates of Tunis and Algiers were called) continued to flourish. A leading figure in the struggle against them was Antonio Barceló (1717–1793), one of the rare examples in the Spanish navy of a simple sailor who rose to be a lieutenant general. Barceló was clever enough to fight the pirates with their own weapons, that is, by using fast xebecs armed with light artillery pieces. He commanded the expedition against Algiers in 1775. In 1779, he led the Franco-Spanish fleet at the siege of Gibraltar. This was the first time that ironclad

Spanish xebec—*Low-keeled for coastal navigation; derived from the boats of the Barbary pirates.*

Mediterranean polacre—*A square-rigged merchant ship, with one-shaft masts for making the best use of the wind.*

gunboats were used. Despite the 1816 bombardment of Algiers by an Anglo-Dutch fleet under Lord Exmouth, Barbary piracy in the Mediterranean was was not halted until 1830, when French troops occupied Algeria.

The traditional rivals France and England were the leading figures in naval warfare at the end of the 18th century. There was the struggle of the French revolutionary forces against Austria, Prussia, and the Kingdom of Sardinia in 1792. Then, in the years that followed there was the great clash that found the First European Coalition (England, Prussia, Austria, Spain, Holland, and the Kingdom of Sardinia) united against Napoleon. French ships of the line (*les vaisseaux du roi*) were considered the most advanced of the age, and had proved their worth on more than one occasion.

Earlier in the century there had been the Seven Years' War (1756–1763), when France, Austria, and Russia were arrayed against Frederick II, the young king of Prussia, supported by England. A French squadron of 10 ships of the line and five 50-gun frigates left the Toulon naval base, passed through the Strait of Gibraltar, and began operations in the North Atlantic. Admiral de La Clue's flagship was the *Océan*. On August 18 and 19, 1759, the French ships met in battle with the squadron of English Vice Adm. Boscawen (13 ships of the line and 2 frigates), which had left Gibraltar on the seventeenth of that month to intercept the enemy. During the night, five of De La Clue's ships, without specific orders, left the fleet and entered the port of Cadiz, while the English joined battle with the remaining ships. The English flagship, the *Namur*, fought with the *Océan* and lost its mizzenmast and its topsail yards. The French withdrew under cover of darkness, but the English caught up with them on the morning of the nineteenth. The French ships *Océan*, *Redoutable*, *Téméraire*, and *Modeste* were outside the bay of Lagos on the Portuguese coast. The *Océan* ran aground on a sandbank and lost its masts. It was forced to surrender to the *America*, a 36-cannon English frigate. The *Warspite* easily captured the *Téméraire*, while the *Modeste* surrendered after a bitter struggle. The *Redoutable* was seriously damaged and abandoned by its crew after being set on fire. Bailli de Souffren, who later became one of the most famous French admirals, was captured for the second time in his life on board the *Océan*.

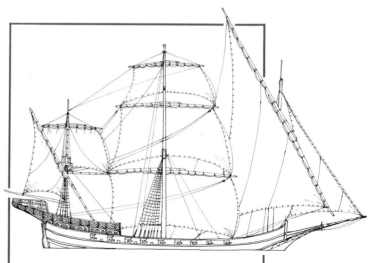

Polacre xebec—*A variant of the xebec. From the middle of the 18th century on, the mainmast carried the square sail of the polacre.*

Dutch bootship—*Derived from the* fluyut, *but smaller, it was used as a whaler by the Dutch in the 18th century.*

Berlin—*A Brandenburg frigate of 1674, developed from the heavier and slower ship of the line.*

The Battle of the First of June, fought in 1794 in the waters of Brittany, saw 51 fighting ships (25 English vessels commanded by Admiral Howe and 26 French ships from the base at Brest led by Admiral Villaret-Joyeuse) join in a fierce battle. The English were trying to stop a convoy of 130 cargo ships carrying grain from the American colonies to the French provinces. Villaret maneuvered for five days, and the convoy safely reached the coast of France.

The Battle of Camperdown took place on October 12, 1797, off the Dutch coast near the village of Kamperduin, and saw the 18 warships of English Admiral Duncan combating the 20 of Dutch Admiral de Winter. The Dutch, the most recent adherents to the cause of the French Revolution, had a large and formidable fleet, but it had been in harbor for months. The Dutch were unable to match the greater seamanship of the English ships, which had been almost constantly at sea for many months and had superior artillery. Duncan's ships broke through the enemy line, and each ship faced off against another. Eleven Dutch ships were captured. De Winter surrendered. Duncan declined to accept his sword and said, "I would much

rather take a brave man's hand than his sword." Since the battle took place close to the Dutch coast, thousands of people watched it from the shore. Camperdown was the third English naval victory in the campaign against the French, after Howe's success in the Battle of the First of June and that of Jervis over the Spanish fleet on February 14, 1797. But Napoleon's great naval adversary was Horatio Nelson (1758–1805), the most brilliant admiral in modern history. Bold and impetuous, witty, vain, conservative, a realist who could not resist flattery, he was a true "superman with all the human weaknesses." His life was a series of exceptional events, from the time when he was barely twelve and embarked on the *Raisonnable*, commanded by his maternal uncle Maurice Suckling, to the Arctic expedition of the *Carcass*. A midshipman at fifteen and lieutenant at eighteen, he then became commander of the brigantine *Badger*. In 1780 he took part in operations against Nicaragua as captain of the frigate *Hinchinbrooke* and a year later commanded the frigate *Albemarle*. After some misadventures and a long period away from the sea, he obtained command, in 1793, of the *Agamemnon*, a third-rate ship of

the line with 64 cannons, and thus began the most glorious and most discussed period of his career.

In the Mediterranean, he took part in the defense of Toulon, the last stronghold of the French royalists. Then, still under the command of Lord Hood, he went to Corsica, where he lost an eye in a rock-and-sand landslide. As commander of the *Captain*, he took part, on February 14, 1797, in the Battle

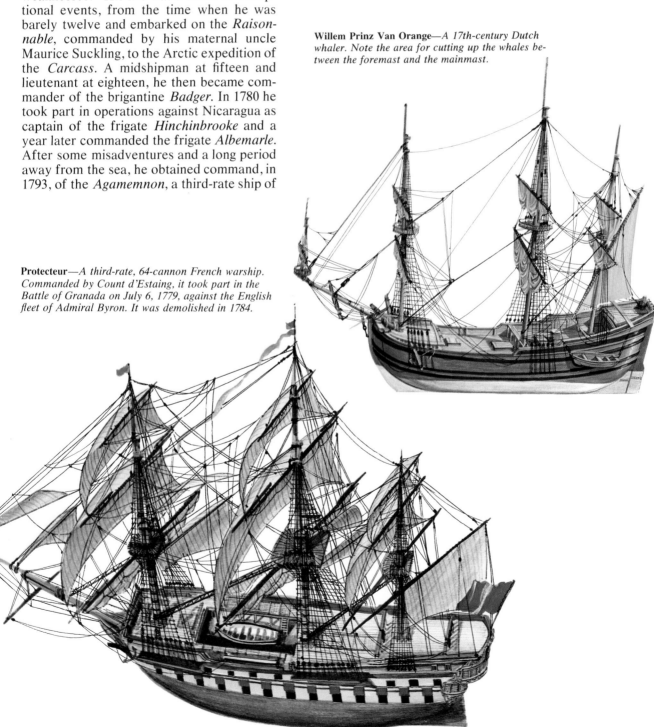

Willem Prinz Van Orange—*A 17th-century Dutch whaler. Note the area for cutting up the whales between the foremast and the mainmast.*

Protecteur—*A third-rate, 64-cannon French warship. Commanded by Count d'Estaing, it took part in the Battle of Granada on July 6, 1779, against the English fleet of Admiral Byron. It was demolished in 1784.*

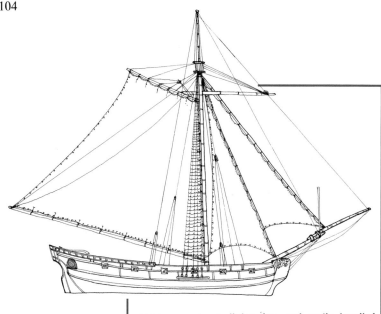

Aldebaran—*A small but fast and easily handled cutter. The English cutter was derived from the Dutch pleasure boat and was used in the middle of the 18th century by British customs officers and smugglers.*

of Cape Saint Vincent, during which he single-handedly attacked 5 French ships that were trying to block the action being carried out by the 15 ships of Admiral Jervis, who had succeeded Hood in the Mediterranean command. Nelson was made a rear admiral. At the Battle of the Nile, his flagship was the *Vanguard*. With the 13 ships in his squadron (*Culloden, Goliath, Minotaur, Defence, Bellerophon, Majestic, Zealous, Swiftsure, Theseus, Audacious, Orion,* and *Alexander*—all 2-decked vessels with 74 cannons—and *Leander*, with 50 cannons), Nelson defeated the French on August 1, 1798, in the bay of Aboukir, a dozen miles northwest of Alexandria. The engagement is still considered one

of the most instructive sea battles for students of naval strategy. This single battle destroyed French naval supremacy in the Mediterranean.

The French fleet that carried Napoleon to Egypt left Toulon on May 9, 1798, taking advantage of a strong mistral that had upset the English blockage of that port. Nelson followed the French fleet for a long time and finally caught up with it on August 1, off Aboukir Island. French Adm. Brueys d'Aigaïlliers had arrayed his ships close to the coast, with the cannon set to fire only toward the open sea, since he was sure that the enemy could not get between him and the shore. But Nelson quickly sized up the situation. He managed to break the French line and get ships in on the landward side of the French ships. His action was completely successful, and the French vessels, hampered by an adverse wind that prevented any favorable maneuver, were struck by the British from both the landward and seaward sides.

The French flagship, the *Orient*, a new and impressive 3-decker with 120 guns, was shattered by British guns. A fire broke out and the ship exploded. Brueys was not among the survivors who got off the *Orient* at the last moment. After a few hours of battle, two-thirds of the French fleet had been destroyed, including two 80-gun warships, the *Franklin* and the *Tonnant*; eight 74-gun vessels; and two 40-gun frigates. Only the *Guillaume Tell* and the *Généreux*, with two frigates, managed to escape to Malta, under the command of Villeneuve. Aboukir marked the end of France's Egyptian adventure and

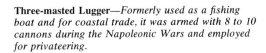

Three-masted Lugger—*Formerly used as a fishing boat and for coastal trade, it was armed with 8 to 10 cannons during the Napoleonic Wars and employed for privateering.*

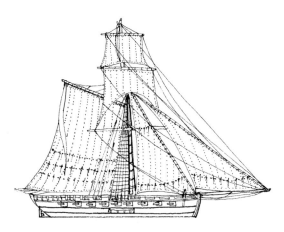

Dutch cutter—*Derived from the fast and lightly armed yacht, it was used for surveillance during the 18th century.*

was a superb victory for Nelson, one of the most overwhelming victories in the annals of naval warfare.

Nelson was wounded in the head during the fighting (it was his third wound, after the loss of an eye in Corsica and the shattering of his right elbow during the attack on Santa Cruz de Tenerife in 1797), but went on to Naples to support the wavering power of the Bourbons. There began the most troubled and controversial period of his life and his attachment to Emma Hamilton, wife of the British envoy to the kingdom of Naples. When hostilities broke out in 1803, Nelson went back to sea as commander of the famous *Victory*, a 3-decker with 120 cannons. On board this ship, after various operations off Naples, Sardinia, the coast of Tuscany, and Genoa, Nelson clashed once again, and for the last time, with his traditional adversary, the French ship of the line. It was on board the *Victory* that Nelson took part in the Battle of Trafalgar.

Few battles have had such profound and decisive consequences. The third European Coalition (England, Austria, Prussia, Sweden, and the Kingdom of Naples) again tried to stem the irresistible advance of Napoleon's immense army through Europe. A French plan to invade England had been prepared, and the Grande Armée was to be ferried across from Boulogne to Britain. But first the powerful English fleet had to be lured far from the field of operations to the Antilles, where Franco-Spanish ships were to make their presence credible by attacking the English colonies, thus causing the transfer of British naval forces to that distant area. Once that was accomplished, the French fleet would return as quickly and quietly as possible to Europe, hastening to the English Channel. In 1805 Adm. Jean Baptiste Silvestre de Villeneuve (1763–1806) sailed from Toulon with 11 ships of the line, 7 frigates, and 2 brigantines and at Cadiz joined up with another 14 Spanish vessels commanded by Gravina. This fleet then proceeded to Fort Royal in Martinique, where it was reinforced by four more ships of the line and a Spanish frigate, plus another three ships from Rochefort. Nelson followed the French ships and reached the Barbados on June 9. After wiping out Fort Diamant, Villeneuve was convinced that the plan of luring

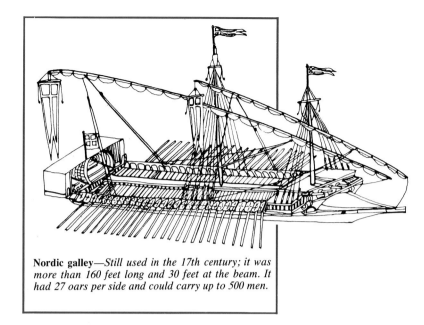

Nordic galley—*Still used in the 17th century; it was more than 160 feet long and 30 feet at the beam. It had 27 oars per side and could carry up to 500 men.*

the great English admiral away from European waters had succeeded, and hastened back to Europe. But instead of going straight to the Channel, to protect the expeditionary corps Napoleon had marshaled in Boulogne, he lost time in trying to assemble the squadrons scattered in other Atlantic ports. At first Nelson seemed to have fallen into the trap, but he became suspicious when the two enemy fleets failed to attack. He quickly headed for the western approaches to the Channel, the only possible direction from which immediate danger for England might strike.

On August 25 the British ships were in European waters once again. Meanwhile Villeneuve gave up his plan of joining up

Centurion—*An English warship of 1739. Under Commodore Anson, it captured the famous Acapulco galleon, which was carrying a precious cargo of silver from Manila.*

Victory—*A first-rate warship, pride of the British navy and Nelson's flagship at Trafalgar. Launched at Chatham on May 7, 1765, it was armed with 120 cannons and had a double-sheathed oak hull. The keel timber was 148 feet long. It is now in drydock in the port of Portsmouth, restored as it was at the time of the Battle of Trafalgar (October 21, 1805), and is used as a naval museum. Horatio Nelson, commander of the English fleet, was mortally wounded by a musketshot on the quarter-deck of this ship.*

Figurehead *of the* Victory, *with the royal coat of arms.*

with the naval forces of Admiral Ganteaume and sailing to Boulogne. He took refuge at Cadiz instead. Nelson then divided his 34 ships into two groups: one of them blocked Ganteaume at Brest; the other, commanded by Nelson himself, appeared before Cadiz. Villeneuve heard that Napoleon was about to strip him of his command because of his dilatory behavior, and he decided to show the world that he was not afraid to die. At dawn on October 21, 1805, Nelson's 24 ships attacked the Franco-Spanish ships just as they were about to turn about off Cape Trafalgar and head back to the port of Cadiz, which they had left in an attempt to force the enemy blockade. The English warships attacked according to an original plan of Nelson's. The ships advanced in two parallel columns perpendicular to the long row of enemy ships, divided them into three sections, and then attacked at close quarters.

The first column was led by Nelson himself, in full uniform with decorations, while the second was commanded by Cuthbert Collingwood (1750–1810) whose vice admiral's flag was raised on the *Royal Sovereign*. Once again Nelson's strategy achieved outstanding results. Perhaps the recollection of what had happened at Aboukir seven years before had a paralyzing effect on Villeneuve. When the hard-fought battle ended, the Franco-Spanish fleet no longer existed as a fighting force. And England's great naval hero lost his life in this battle. Nelson was struck down by musket fire from the *Redoutable*. He died in the arms of Thomas Hardy, flag captain of the *Victory*. A coffin made from the wood of the mainmast of the *Orient*, which had blown up at Aboukir, received the remains of the great British admiral. The Battle of Trafalgar crushed the

Redoutable—*A French warship with 3 decks and 74 cannons. A musketeer in its crow's-nest shot the bullet that mortally wounded Horatio Nelson at Trafalgar. Commanded by the brave Captain Lucas, it sank that very day, during the epic battle.*

French navy and all but destroyed the Spanish navy. Britain was to rule the sea unchallenged for more than a century.

The end of the Napoleonic Wars coincided with the final decline of the ship of the line, an expression of the grace and power of sailing fleets and one of the most beautiful creations of mankind. The last time these great fighting ships fired their guns was during the War of Greek Independence. The Aegean Islands and mainland Greece rebelled against Turkish domination in 1821. The fighting was marked by unparalleled ferocity. In July 1827 the Treaty of London established that Great Britain, France, and Russia would use their joint influence to impose an armistice that could lead to peace

Valmy—*The last and largest warship of the French navy, launched in 1847. The 3 masts were almost 200 feet high. It had a triple battery of 120 cannons. The* Valmy *was used for many years as a training ship.*

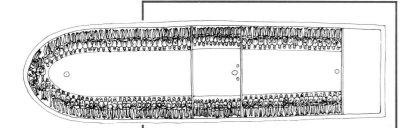

The slave ship—Robert Walsh, first mate on board the *North Star*, an English frigate of 1829, described what he saw on board the *Isabelle*, a slave ship captured in the South Atlantic. The cargo of the ship consisted of 505 men and women. The crew had thrown 55 overboard during the 17 days of navigation, and the rest were penned under grilled hatches between decks. They sat between each other's legs, so tightly packed that they were unable to stretch out by day or night—and this was considered one of the better slave ships. The slaves were usually kept in areas about 3 feet high, and at times only half that, according to Walsh. Slaves were often chained at foot and neck.

negotiations. To that end, the Turkish-Egyptian fleet commanded by Ibrahim Pasha was held in check in the bay of Navarino, a port in the Peloponnesus, by an allied squadron under the command of Vice Adm. Sir Edward Codrington. On the morning of October 20, 1827, as the allied ships advanced in two columns under a light breeze, to anchor within the bay where they were to winter, a rifle shot fired from a Turkish ship touched off a violent battle. When it ended, the Turks had lost one battleship, three 64-gun frigates, 9 smaller frigates, 22 corvettes, 10 brigantines, 1 schooner, 5 fire ships, and almost 4,000 men.

The large ship of the line, which had ruled the seas for 300 years, began its dignified decline, surviving as an anachronism in the British navy until 1880.

Like the military ship of the line, the merchant sailing ship of the era was also derived from the galleon, and closely resembled the warship in its lines. Those designed and built for the long voyages to America and the East, beyond the Cape of Good Hope, were owned by shipping companies and never by private individuals. The most famous trading company of the day, the

Venetian galliot—*A smaller version of the galley, but with only one or two oarsmen per bank. The armament too was reduced, with two or four light cannons.*

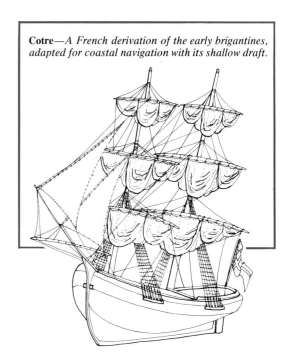

Cotre—*A French derivation of the early brigantines, adapted for coastal navigation with its shallow draft.*

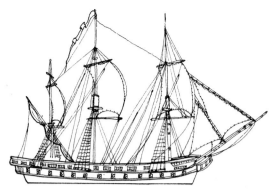

Rodney—*A third-rate English warship with 74 cannons.*

Duc de Duras—*An 18th-century French warship owned by the East India Company.*

Honorable John Company, an English group for commerce with the East Indies, owned well-armed sailing ships with large and well-trained crews. These ships carried goods and passengers to and from the vast empire in India that 18th-century England had gradually built up from the first bases at Madras, Calcutta, and Bombay. Thanks to the abilities of Robert Clive, agent of the East India Company, England had managed to gain control of Bengal and other neighboring states in just a few years. Because of the almost constant state of hostility between England and France, Indies merchantmen were always subject to attack. These encounters could be brutal, like the battle on June 21, 1805, between the East Indiaman *Warren Hastings* (1,181 tons and 44 guns) and the French frigate *La Piemontaise*. It took the French ship 5 hours to defeat the merchant ship.

The shipping companies of other nations—Holland, Denmark, and Sweden, for example—also had monopoly markets, like the various French companies, until the

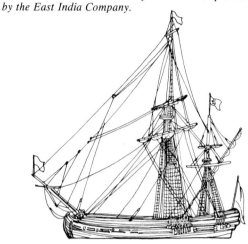

18th-century British bombsloop—*On a vessel of this class, HMS* Carcass, *Horatio Nelson, just turned fifteen, took part in an Arctic expedition in 1773; during this trip there took place the famous incident when the young cockswain tried to kill a polar bear with the butt of his musket.*

Dutch merchant ship—*In the 1700s, the Dutch organized a close network of coastal trade routes with the nations of northern Europe, using their own fast and easily handled transport vessels.*

Pomone—*An 18th-century French frigate. It was one of the largest ships of this type, with 2 decks and 50 cannons, and was extremely fast.*

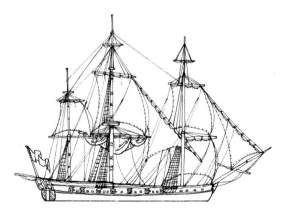

Swallow—*An English transport ship launched in 1782 and used for trade with the East and the Indies.*

end of the Napoleonic era, when new concepts of economic liberalism changed political and mercantile policy. The captains of the great oceanic sailing ships were esteemed and revered as the elite of the maritime world. They were entitled to an honor guard and a 13-gun salute when they arrived in port, and the wealth they accumulated during their voyages (they had the right to load 50 tons of goods on the outgoing and 20 on the return voyage, to sell for their personal profit) was often remarkable. The last great sailing ship of the East Indies was probably the *Elisabeth*, which made its last return trip in 1834, the year in which the British East India Company ended its long and profitable career in business.

Many other types of sailing ships carried on commercial activity in the Mediterranean and were privately owned. Among them were the xebecs, already noted in their military form, the Genoese *pinco*, the *bombarda*, the polacre, the Maltese *speronara*, the Greek *scapho*, and the Turkish *moana*, with one lateen-sail mast. Another ship had made its appearance late in the 17th century. This was the felucca, of Arab origin, a low-sided ship with two masts slightly inclined toward the bow, and rigged with lateen sails. It was common throughout the Mediterranean. About 1796, the naval chronicles of the Genoese *Mercantile Courier* announced the arrival in port of the felucca *Concezione*, of 29 tons, coming from Sardinia with a cargo of 430 barrels of preserved tuna, and the *Amabile Livetta*, with 550 sacks of Indian corn.

Whale hunting had a long and profitable history. It was practiced as early as the 12th century, if not earlier, by French and Spanish fishermen from the Bay of Biscay. The banks of Newfoundland were for years the richest hunting ground for whales, and early in the 17th century, during voyages in search of the Northeast and Northwest passages, whales were sighted off the Bear and Spitsbergen islands. The first English Muscovy Company ship set sail in 1610, carrying the famous Basque harpooners who taught the English the art of catching and killing the huge mammals. It was soon followed by the ships of a Dutch syndicate set up in 1622, which located its general headquarters on the Spitsbergens. This led to the creation of the

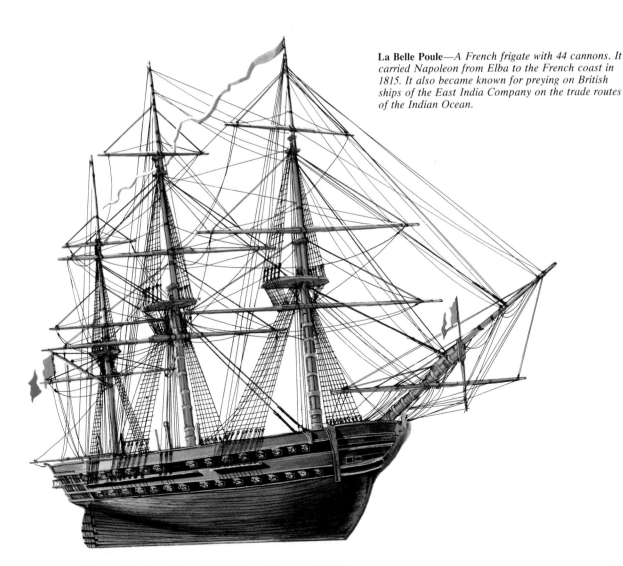

La Belle Poule—*A French frigate with 44 cannons. It carried Napoleon from Elba to the French coast in 1815. It also became known for preying on British ships of the East India Company on the trade routes of the Indian Ocean.*

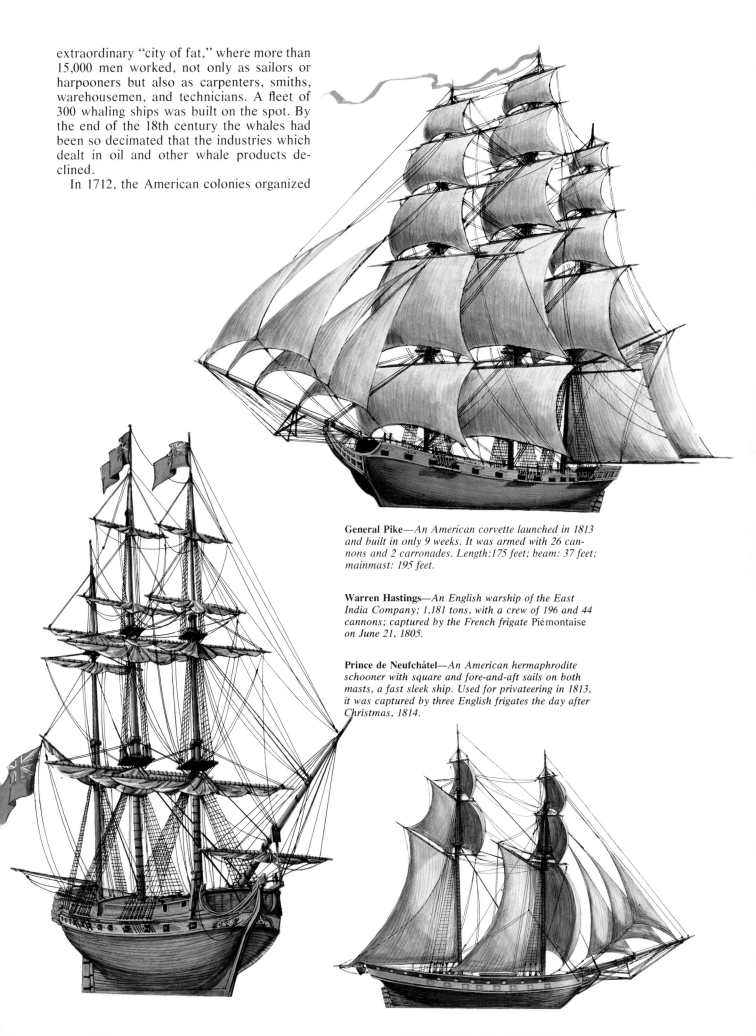

extraordinary "city of fat," where more than 15,000 men worked, not only as sailors or harpooners but also as carpenters, smiths, warehousemen, and technicians. A fleet of 300 whaling ships was built on the spot. By the end of the 18th century the whales had been so decimated that the industries which dealt in oil and other whale products declined.

In 1712, the American colonies organized

General Pike—*An American corvette launched in 1813 and built in only 9 weeks. It was armed with 26 cannons and 2 carronades. Length:175 feet; beam: 37 feet; mainmast: 195 feet.*

Warren Hastings—*An English warship of the East India Company; 1,181 tons, with a crew of 196 and 44 cannons; captured by the French frigate* Piémontaise *on June 21, 1805.*

Prince de Neufchâtel—*An American hermaphrodite schooner with square and fore-and-aft sails on both masts, a fast sleek ship. Used for privateering in 1813, it was captured by three English frigates the day after Christmas, 1814.*

Lougre—*Like the lugger, and armed in the 18th century with 2 cannons.*

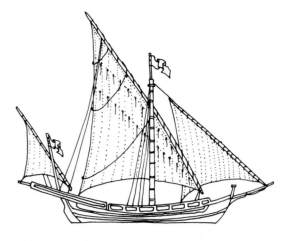

Mediterranean tartan—*For fishing or cargo, about 40 feet long.*

Genoese pinco—*A sailing ship of about 300 tons, widely used in the 18th and 19th centuries.*

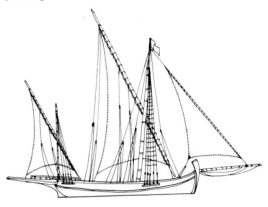

Spanish felucca—*A small 18th-century merchant vessel, occasionally used for combat.*

Chasse-Marée—*Used by the French corsairs on the Channel; armed with 10 cannons and a crew of from 40 to75 men.*

Greek Trakandini—*Synthesis of the sail fittings of the northern seas and the Mediterranean.*

Dutch Kof—*A practical and tough coastal-trade sailing ship, forerunner, in its rigging, of the topsail schooner.*

Turkish boat—*An all-purpose vessel of the Bosporus.*

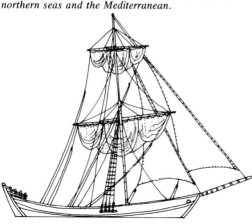

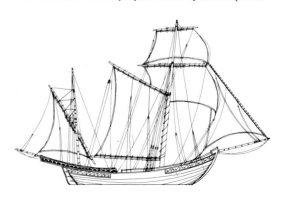

large-scale sperm-whale hunting, with large-decked ships of about 30 tons; the smaller whaleboats set out from these whalers to track down and kill the cetaceans. For about a century, from the mid-1700s, American whalers regularly left the ports of New England to hunt whales in the Atlantic, as far north as Baffin Bay; along the west coast of America and the eastern coast of Japan; and in the Pacific and Indian oceans and the seas of Australia and New Zealand.

The 19th century especially, in Europe and America, was an exceptionally flourishing period for merchant sailing ships, which withstood the competitions of steam and the propeller. The sailing ship reached its technical peak in the 20th century and was then overtaken by the progress made in little more than 100 years by an industrial revolution that changed the face of the planet.

The brigantine first appeared in the era of oar-driven vessels as a sailing variant of the galley. Subsequently it became a high-seas ship of about 150 tons, with 2 square-sailed masts (foremast and mainmast), a bowsprit with jibs, and a spanker with gaff and booms. It underwent many changes, especially in its rigging; and variant forms appeared, including the bark (with 3 or more masts), the 2-masted hermaphrodite brig (with a square-sailed foremast, and a mainmast with just a spanker and gaff topsail), and a topsail hermaphrodite brig (which had not only a spanker but also topsails on its mainmast).

Another variant of the brigantine was the fast and easily handled brick, a merchant ship often armed with 14 or 16 guns, with 2 square-sailed masts as well as a spritsail on the bowsprit, in imitation of 15th- and 16th-century vessels. The bark was the typical Italian sailing ship in the years between 1860 and 1900; it had an average length of about 150 fleet, 3 masts, and a tonnage of between

Brigantine—*It appeared at the end of the 17th century. It had two square-sailed masts and was rather small.*

Hermaphrodite brig—*A gaff was added to the mainmast.*

Hermaphrodite brig—*A further evolution made during the 18th century. It had square sails on the foremast and fore-and-aft sails on the mainmast.*

Finnish Jagt

Thames barge of England   **English ketch**

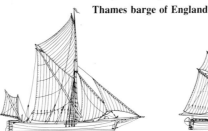

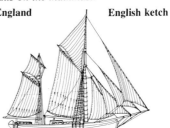

400 and 1,000 tons. Until 1870 this type of sailing ship carried enormous numbers of emigrants to Argentina, Uruguay, Chile, and Peru.

On January 20, 1875, in Rangoon, Burma, some 20 Italian barks loaded their holds with rice for Europe. That same year, one of the largest Italian passenger-carrier sailing ships, the 1,689-ton *Cosmos*, sailed from Genoa to Callao, Peru, in 83 days, carrying 650 emigrants on second deck and 40 first-class passengers in the stern cabins. The captain was Filippo Frassinetti. The Italian commercial sailing ship carried the Sardinian and Neapolitan flags to all the seas of the earth. Toward the end of the century, the Italian bark, the last of which reached 2,165 tons, could be seen in all the ports and on all the routes of the world, from California to Ceylon, from the Atlantic to Java.

The *cutter*, a typical northern European ship, had only one mast and was fast and maneuverable; it was used by smugglers and customs officers alike until 1860. It also served as a pilot boat leading large ships to anchorage in river ports and estuaries. It was also employed, perhaps for the first time in naval history, in regular postal service between Southampton and the Channel Islands.

The ketch, popular in European waters between 1700 and 1900, was a fishing boat of between 45 and 90 tons. It was the first vessel driven by sails to have a steam engine mounted on it (in England) to shift the fishing nets. The ketch was carefully built and very robust and had two masts with fore-

Constitution—*An American frigate launched in 1797. It was one of six ships built to defend United States merchant ships sailing in the Mediterranean from attack by Barbary pirates. It was commanded by William Baimbridge, who had surrendered his frigate* Philadelphia *to the Barbary pirates on an earlier occasion. The* Constitution *waged a historic battle on December 29, 1812, off Bahia on the coast of Brazil, with the British frigate* Java, *a 49-cannon ship, sinking it after a furious exchange of broadsides. Baimbridge was wounded by a musket ball, but went on directing the battle to the end, then doing all he could to save the shipwrecked Englishmen and their captain, Henry Lambert. This battle—in which the Americans used rifles along with the outdated smooth-bore musket—cost the English 60 dead and 170 wounded. The* Constitution *remained in service until 1881 and is now preserved in the Boston Navy Yard.*

E. W. Morrison—*A 560-ton American Great Lakes schooner, graceful and strong, with fore-and-aft sails.*

Armistad—*An American topsail schooner of 1839, 75 feet long, used to carry slaves from Cuba to the United States. It became famous in the annals of the Negro slave trade because of the revolt that broke out aboard: the slaves rebelled, killed the captain, and then forced the crew to change course and head for Africa.*

Brick—*A fast and easily handled sailing ship armed with 14 or 16 cannons and used by the American navy in the 18th century.*

and-aft sails and jibs. It had a long life and still survives as a sporting yacht. The *Good Intent*, built in Plymouth in 1790, was still in use in 1928.

The schooner had two square-rigged masts, the mainmast usually being the taller. Experience with the lateen sail, from which the fore-and-aft sail evolved, had shown that one could "point higher" more successfully with the fore-and-aft sail than with square sails, and the adoption of the staysail along with the latter on the large 18th-century ships of the line were proof of the fact. But it was in the United States, in the last three decades of the 18th century, that the schooner with the most refined features and best keel shape was born.

The end of the 19th century was also a

prosperous period for merchant sailing ships, with three, four, or even five masts, and with mixed sails. They carried grain, wood, coal, and other goods that the development of trade and the needs of the new industrial technology required. But their fate was sealed; and the irony of history was that just when sailing vessels were faster and more efficient than ever before, they were challenged and eventually replaced by steam. The great sailing ship, "one of the most powerful means of civilization available to man," may often have been an instrument of death, but it also helped man discover the true dimensions of his world. The sea joins more than it separates, and the large sailing ship contributed to the circulation of ideas as much as it did to the exchange of goods.

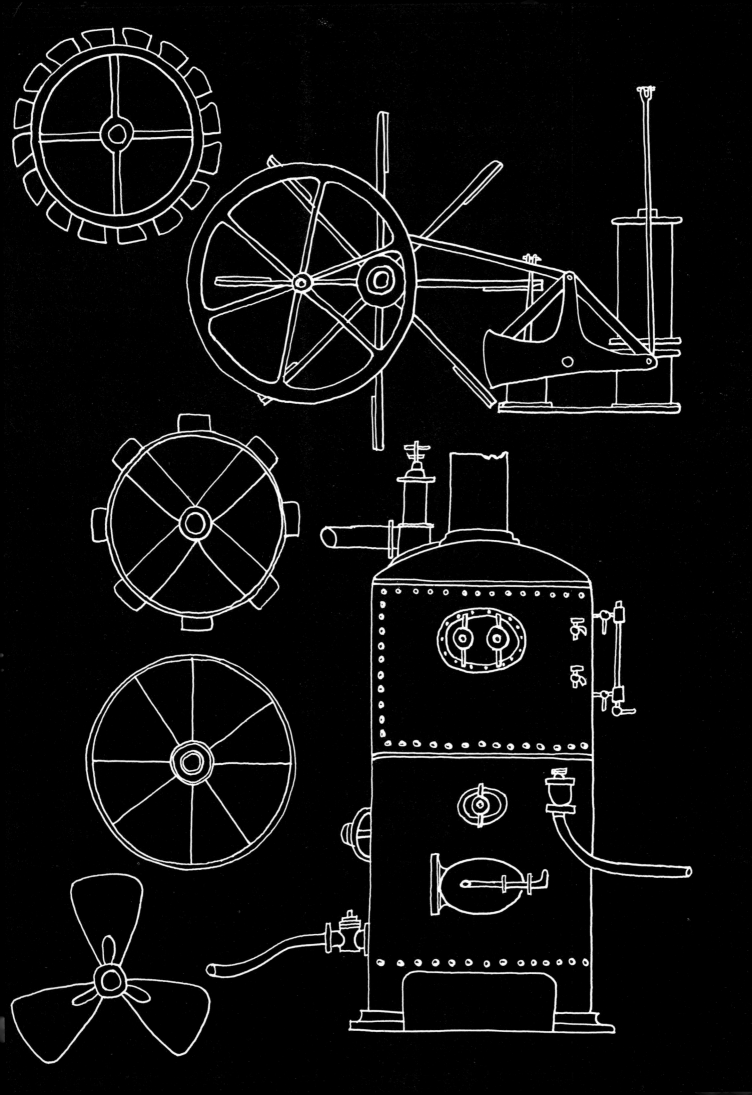

The Steam Revolution

The 19th century was a crucial one in the long history of the ship. For centuries the oar and the sail had been the only means of propulsion at sea. The oar required muscular force to drive a vessel. Wind power created a paradoxical situation. Better and better ships were built with highly complex rigging, but man could not go in the direction he wished without paying a high price in fatigue, sacrifice, and worry. It was therefore both logical and necessary that man should try to free himself from the slavery of the oar, and from the unreliability of the wind, by creating something that could give him mechanical propulsion.

It has been ascertained that in 263 B.C., Roman Consul Appius Claudius had naval experiments carried out with ships moved by hand-driven paddle wheels; and in the 1st century B.C., Vitruvius, in his treatise on architecture, proposed ships with paddle wheels turned by men or by animals such as oxen or horses. Leonardo da Vinci also studied the problem and designed boats with pedal-worked wheels. We also know of some experiments made in China around the year 1200, in some of which man-powered wheels were installed on warships. A wheel-driven ship was almost certainly tested by Blasco Garay in Barcelona in 1543. But these ingenious experiments all relied on muscle power. A more powerful source of energy was needed. Toward the end of the 17th century, a French physicist named Denis Papin invented a device that led to the development of the boiler. He tried to harness the power of steam and in 1707 managed to travel along the Fulda from Kassel to Weser in a small boat on which he had mounted his boiler.

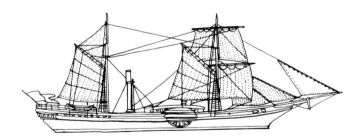

Arciduca Ludovico—*The first steamship of the Austrian Lloyd Triestino Company used on the Middle East route (1837).*

Castor—*One of the first French steamboats (1830).*

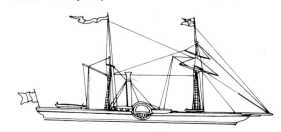

The paddle wheels, however, were turned by man power. An English inventor named Thomas Newcomen developed an "atmospheric engine" in the early years of the 18th century.

In this engine, the steam went into a vertical cylinder with a pressure slightly

Hull tugboat—*Built in England by Jonathan Hull in 1736 and equipped with Newcomen's atmospheric engine.*

Fitch's boat—*In 1787, a boat built by Connecticut watchmaker John Fitch together with Johann Voigt, went up the Delaware River at a speed of 8 knots; a one-cylinder engine like that invented by James Watt moved 6 paddles on each side.*

Pyroscaphe—*In 1783, Frenchman Claude Jouffroy went up the Saône River in his* Pyroscaphe, *driven by a double-acting steam engine that operated two side blades.*

Charlotte Dundas—*Built in 1802 by William Symington, it succeeded in towing two 70-ton barges 19 miles in 6 hours, along the Forth-Clyde Canal, with a one-cylinder, 558-mm (22-in.) steam engine.*

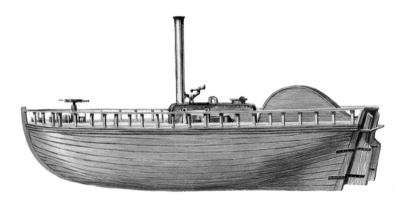

higher than atmospheric pressure. The cylinder was not raised by steam pressure but by a counterweight. When the piston that stood above the cylinder reached its top dead center, steam injection was interrupted by a valve and a sprinkling of cold water caused condensation. The resulting vacuum let atmospheric pressure cause the piston to make an active stroke, at the end of which a new cycle began.

James Watt was a builder of mathematical instruments at the University of Glasgow. He patented a new steam engine in 1769, in which the piston was moved by steam pressure and condensation took place in a container separated from the driving cylinder, that is, in the condenser. Watt went into partnership with Matthew Boulton of Birmingham and produced pumping engines. Watt later adapted his engine to drive all sorts of machines.

In the meantime Watt's idea that the expansion of steam, and not atmospheric pressure, should drive the piston inspired a mining engineer named Richard Trevithick, who built the first steam locomotive in 1804. But the new source of energy was still harnessed to land.

The first man to achieve practical success in the field of steam navigation was a Frenchman, Marquis Claude François de Jouffroy d'Abbans. After a partial failure in 1778 with a steamboat 43 feet long, the Parisian engineer built a paddle-wheel boat 148.5 feet long, with a displacement of 182 tons; this vessel, called the *Pyroscaphe*, went up the Saône near Lyon for fifteen minutes, and can thus be considered the first successful steamboat. The paddle wheels of the *Pyroscaphe* were worked by a double-acting horizontal engine through a gear rack taken from a drawing by Leonardo da Vinci.

In the United States significant developments were being made in steam navigation. In 1787 a merchant named James Rumsey drove a steamboat 4 miles up the Potomac River with a power pump. In the same year John Fitch (1743–1798) and the German Johann Voigt went upstream on the Delaware River in a boat they had invented, moved by a steam engine that worked 12 paddles, 6 per side. Two years later, Fitch and Voight improved their boat, which

Clermont—*Built by Fulton in New York in 1806. Displacement: 100 tons; copper boiler with 0.35 (5 psi) atmospheres; one-cylinder, 700-mm (27-in.) steam engine. In 1807 it reached a speed of 4.5 knots.*

reached a speed of 8 knots (a record for the period). They set up a regular passenger service between Philadelphia and Trenton, a distance of about 30 miles. But the river journey took longer than the coach journey between the two cities, and Fitch's enterprise soon collapsed.

Another step forward was made in Scotland by William Symington (1763–1831), with the financial backing of Patrick Miller. Symington built an atmospheric engine like that created by Newcomen and mounted it on a 2-hulled boat, with 2 paddle wheels set between the hulls. This boat went along the Forth-Clyde Canal at a speed of 7 knots; but in adapting a separate condenser to his engine, Symington had infringed on Watt's

patent, and the threat of court action led Miller to give up the experiment. The stubborn Scotsman found a new backer, and when Watt's patent expired quickly built another steamboat that was given the name of the daughter of his new patron, Lord Dundas. During testing in March 1802, the *Charlotte Dundas* towed 2 barges of 70 tons each for 6 hours against a strong wind, for 19½ miles. But Symington's towboat was thought to be dangerous for the banks of the canal on which it was to navigate. Meanwhile Lord Dundas died, and William Symington's project was abandoned.

The American Robert Fulton was to bring the efforts of the pioneers of steam navigation to fruition. Fulton, born on a small

Comet—*The first European steam-driven cargo ship, built in 1812 from plans by Henry Bell. It served the passenger line between Glasgow and Helensburg on the Clyde, at a speed of 6.5 knots; tickets cost 3 and 4 shillings.*

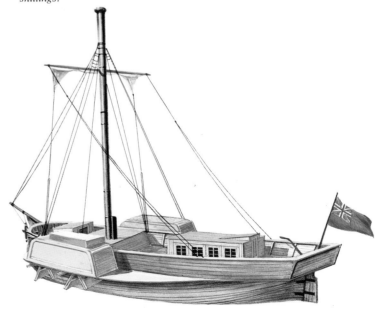

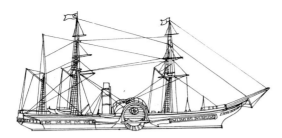

Britannia—*The first Cunard Line steamship. Gross tonnage: 2,050 tons. Launched in 1840, it carried the first mails by steam from Liverpool to Boston in July, 1840.*

Washington—*French Line's steamship used on the New York–Le Havre run. Length: 105 meters (115 yards); speed: 12 knots; number of passengers: 400.*

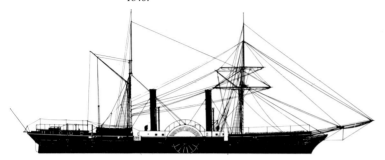

Governolo—*A fine wooden paddle-wheel ship, built in Britain in 1848–1849 for the Sardinian navy.*

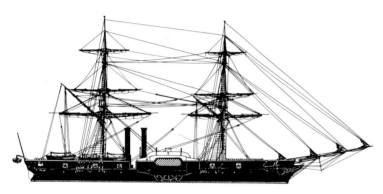

Tuckery—*A second-class steam frigate with paddle wheels, bought from England in 1860 by the Sicilian Provisional Government.*

Pennsylvania farm in 1765, studied art, although his main bent was for mechanical invention. His mind was filled with ideas and projects; one of these, the building of the submarine (the *Nautilus*), took him to Paris, where he met the American ambassador, Robert Livingston, a steam enthusiast. With Livingston's encouragement and financial aid, Fulton built a small steamboat that went up the Seine, but at the very slow speed of less than 3 knots. This did not discourage Fulton. He studied Symington's *Charlotte Dundas* closely, as well as the Watt and Boulton workshops in England. He went back to New York in 1806 and, with Livingston's help, put his studies to practical use. He ordered a 100-ton flat-bottomed hull to be built, with elegant lines. A copper boiler of 0.35 (5 psi) atmospheres was installed, together with a 700-mm (27-in.) cylinder engine, supplied by Watt and Boulton, and 2 paddle wheels (one for each side) with a diameter of 15 feet each. In 1807 this steamboat reached a speed of more than 4.5 knots during testing and was put in regular passenger service between New York and Albany. It was rebuilt during the winter and began passenger service again in the spring under the name *Clermont*, a name famous in the annals of navigation as that of the first boat to supply commercial service using steam. But Fulton did not limit himself to the *Clermont*. He was sure by then that steam navigation had a great future and built larger and better boats, the most important being the *Chancellor Livingston*, which eventually reached a speed of 9.25 knots on the New York–Albany run. That was 1817, two years after Fulton's death, but the steamboat had already proved itself commercially viable for river navigation in the United States.

Principessa Clotilde—*A first-class corvette, with propeller and lower-deck battery, built in Genoa between 1861 and 1864. It was at Lissa with the squadron of wooden-hulled ships in 1866. Withdrawn in 1875.*

Alabama—*A Confederate ship launched in 1862.*

Florida—*Privateer of the Confederacy, launched in 1860. It was torpedoed by a northern vessel at Bahia.*

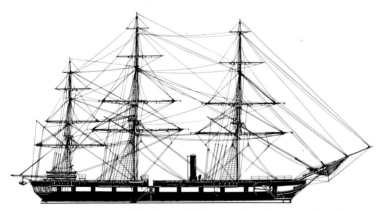

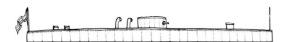

Monitor—*Ironclad ship of the American navy, built by John Ericsson in 1862.*

Merrimack—*The Confederates overhauled this Union steam frigate in 1861 and renamed it the* Virginia.

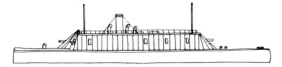

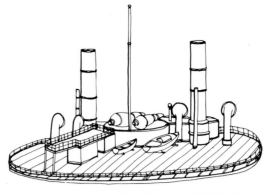

Novgorod—*Circular in shape, 31 meters (102 feet) in diameter, with two 300-mm (11.8-in.) guns; put into service by the Russian navy in 1873.*

In Europe, meanwhile, another man was making practical use of the principle of steam navigation: Henry Bell, a Scot who was born in Torphichen in 1767. He became interested in the steam engine, studied the *Charlotte Dundas,* and kept in close touch with both Symington and Fulton. But Bell had difficulty finding a backer and had to accumulate enough money of his own before commissioning a Glasgow shipyard to build a vessel on which he mounted an engine and boiler of the Watt type. This vessel had two paddle wheels. The *Comet,* as Bell's boat was called, began regular passenger service on the Clyde between Glasgow and Helensburg in the summer of 1812. The *Comet* reached a speed of 6.5 knots, and tickets cost 3 and 4 shillings. The passenger service was not a commercial success, and Bell soon went out of business.

Before turning to the later developments of steam navigation, it might be useful to summarize the principles on which the first steam engines worked. The piston rod was connected at one end to a rocker arm pivoted in the center, and at the other to a crankshaft. The engine drove wheels with fixed paddles (later replaced by movable paddles) held vertical during immersion by a series of rods worked by a cam. As long as the engine had to turn only the large wheels, it did its task to perfection. The steam-engine plant was made up of a steam generator and the driving engine, which transformed heat into mechanical force. For almost a century, the boiler actually hindered the evolution of the steam engine; for while the engines themselves rapidly increased in power, it was hard to build big enough boilers to develop the pressure the engines needed. The first boilers were hemispheric. Watt's wagon boil-

er developed only 0.35 (5 psi) atmospheres of pressure. It had the form of a mixtilinear parallelopiped, with the combustion chamber and external smoke flues in fireproof masonry.

In 1803, Trevithick placed the furnace and smoke flue inside a locomotive boiler. A step forward was made with the invention of the fire-tube boiler, an improved version of which is still used on railroad locomotives. It was invented by the Frenchman Marc Seguin in 1827–1828. The next advance was the Scotch boiler, while the triple-expansion engine, built by A. C. Kirk in 1874, came into use only in 1881, when a boiler was developed that could supply sufficient steam for it. Rectangular Scotch boilers for pressures never over 2.5 (37 psi) atmospheres were used almost until the end of the 19th century. The cylindrical Scotch boiler raised that pressure to 9 (132 psi) atmospheres, and the improved Proudhon-Capus and Howden-Johnson version of it ruled unchallenged until 1930, when it was replaced by the

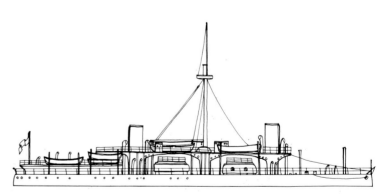

Duilio—*Designed by B. Brin in 1873. The armor at the center of the ship was 550-mm (21.6 in.) thick, and there were two 100-ton Armstrong guns; two 7,710-hp engines permitted a speed of 15 knots.*

Dante Alighieri—*The first Italian battleship of the* Dreadnought *class, launched in 1913.*

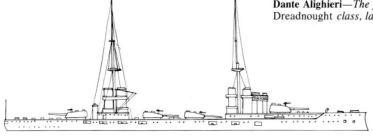

122

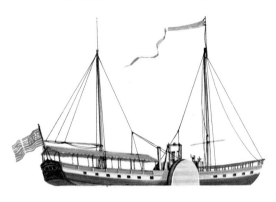

Phoenix—*The first steamship to face the seas between New York and Philadelphia. Designed and built by John Stevens in 1808.*

Savannah—*An American steam- and sailing-ship, and the first with detachable paddle wheels. In 1819, it crossed the Atlantic from Savannah to Liverpool in 27 ¹/₂ days, of which 85 hours were by steam and the rest under sail.*

watertube boiler. The first watertube boiler, invented by Stevens in 1804, was based on the principle of the transmission of heat through tubes containing the water to evaporate, which were surrounded by the products of combustion. In the second half of the 19th century, this boiler was installed on large warships and supplied pressures varying from 13 to 20 (191–294 psi) atmospheres. This type was later improved, and a lighter model with small tubes was developed. It was ideal for smaller ships. The boilers of Yarrow and Thornycroft, the French Normads, and the German Schultz and Wagner, provided pressures up to 58 (852 psi) atmospheres. In addition to the watertube boiler, other kinds were produced, with accelerated and forced circulation and very high pressures: serpentine, including the Sul-

zer and the Benson; indirect heating, like the Loeffer; intermediate heating, like the Lamont; and supercharged combustion under pressure, like the Velox. The adoption of the superheater, of forced ventilation and of economizers, made these boilers even more efficient and economical. Important progress was made with the use of oil-firing, which was introduced in the 1890s. It made precise regulation of the fire possible, eliminated the hot smoky atmosphere that coal fire produced in boiler rooms, and did away with the tragic figure of the ship stoker. Modern boilers furnish steam up to 60 to 70 (882 to 1,028 psi) atmospheres at 510 degrees C (932 degrees F), and with unitary power up to 40,000 hp.

The vertical steam engine came to the fore. It acted directly on the driving shaft

Sirius—*A 703-ton steamship with paddle wheels, and an engine of 320 hp, rented to the British and American Company. It sailed from Cork on April 4, 1838, and reached New York on April 22, after a crossing of 18 days and 10 hours at an average speed of 6.5 knots.*

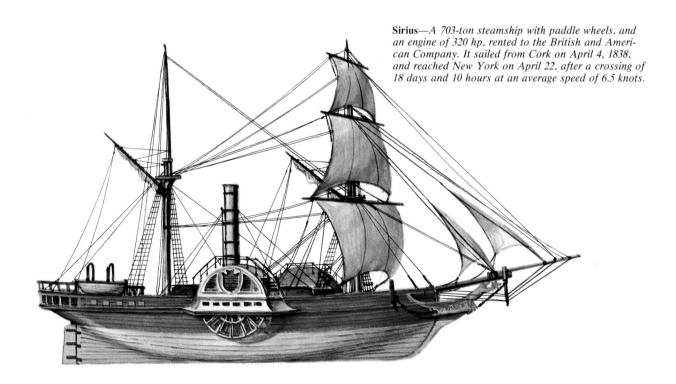

and on the crankshaft placed under the cylinders. The use of the three-cylinder engine for high, medium, and low pressure permitted fuller use of steam expansion: the principle of Kirk's triple-expansion engine.

Now we must take a step back, to the period when the *Comet* was carrying its passengers up and down the Clyde. Although the business did not make Henry Bell wealthy, it opened the way for a number of other commercial enterprises. The steamship still went along the rivers and occasionally along the coast, but that was only the beginning. In the years that followed the *Clermont* and the *Comet*, many river-boat companies were formed. The General Steam Navigation Company was founded in 1824, and is today the world's oldest steam navigation firm. The United States and England were soon keen competitors in steam navigation. England already had a great steel industry and a long maritime tradition. The *Comet* engine served as the prototype for the adoption of two rocker arms set below instead of the single upper rocker arm in the Watt and Newcomen engines.

In 1819 the American ship *Savannah* crossed the Atlantic from Savannah to Liverpool in 27½ days, but it carried only enough pinewood to keep the engine going for 85 hours. This was indeed the first Atlantic crossing in which steam power was used; but it was still not a steam crossing, for the *Savannah* was a sailing ship with an auxiliary steam engine and detachable paddle wheels.

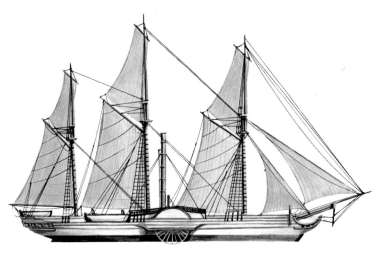

James Watt—*The largest steamship in service between London and Leith at the turn of the century. It was 43.18 meters (142 feet) long and 7.77 meters (25.5 feet) wide; the diameter of the wheels was 5.49 meters (18 feet).*

Aaron Manby—*Launched in 1820. The first steamship with an iron hull. Speed between 8 and 9 knots.*

Great Western—*The first steamship put into transatlantic service. Tonnage: 1,319 tons; length: 71.90 meters (212 feet). It sailed from Bristol with 7 passengers and reached New York 15 days and 5 hours later, at an average speed of 8.75 knots.*

Great Britain—*The first iron-hull transatlantic liner with propeller propulsion, designed by I. Brunel. Length: 98.72 meters (324 feet); beam: 14.68 meters (48 feet); tonnage: 4,545 tons. Six auxiliary masts.*

124

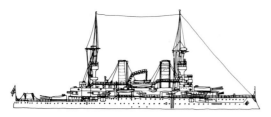

Kaiser Barbarossa—*Launched in 1901, as part of Admiral von Tirpitz's program for strengthening the German navy.*

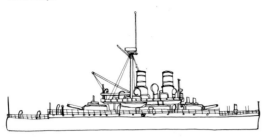

Devastation—*The first English battleship with all-mechanical propulsion, launched in 1873. Displacement: 9,536 tons; speed: 13 knots.*

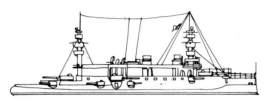

Charles Martel—*A typical example of the gigantic French battleship of the period (1893). The armor plate was 450-mm (16 in.) thick at the waterline and 356-mm (14.75 in.) thick on the turrets.*

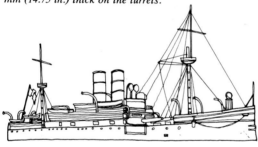

Maine—*An armored American warship, also classed as a cruiser.*

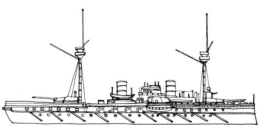

Pelayo—*A Spanish ship of the line (1897). Displacement: 9,950 tons; length: 110 meters (330 feet); speed: 16 knots; two 320-mm (12.6-in.), two 280-mm (11-in.), and nine 117-mm (1-pounder) guns.*

Most of the crossing was under sail. A more important crossing was the one made by the steam and sailing-ship *Enterprise* in 1825, from London to Calcutta. A distance of 11,450 miles was covered in 103 days, and steam power was used on 69 days. But even the most advanced steam engines had too low a power/weight ratio, and they consumed too much fuel. The chief reason for limited efficiency was, of course, the low steam pressure that worked the engine. Even using material such as forged iron instead of copper, it was hard to build boilers that could safely sustain pressures above 0.35–0.50 (5–7.3 psi) atmospheres. During the first half of the 19th century, steamboats were profitable only on rivers, along the coast, or for short trips on the open sea. Sailing ships were still faster and more economical on the ocean. Moreover the sailing ship had a great deal more cargo space, since it did not have the encumbrance of huge boilers, engines, and coal piles.

It was not long, though, before regular transatlantic service got underway, thanks to the enterprise and boldness of an English engineer named Isambard K. Brunel (1806–1859). As Engineer to the Great Western Railway Company, he was responsible for linking London with Bristol and Plymouth by his broad-gauge railroad and for solving all the architectural and engineering problems involved—design of stations, bridges and viaducts. Brunel linked his name to the building of three famous transatlantic liners: the *Great Western* (1838), the *Great Britain* (1845), and the *Great Eastern* (1858).

The first of the three was built for the Great Western Steamship Company of Bristol, of which Brunel was one of the founders in 1836. The *Great Western*, a wooden steamship with paddle wheels, was launched in 1837. It was driven by 2 engines generating a total of 750 hp. The ship was 236 feet long and 36 feet deep. Its maiden voyage to New York, with 111 passengers aboard, took less than 16 days.

In the meantime the British and American Steam Navigation Company, founded in London in 1835, had ordered a 1,968-ton ship from a Clyde shipyard. It was unable to make its first voyage to New York because of a delay in the delivery of the engines. The directors of the British and American were determined to be the first to set up a transat-

Merchant Ships

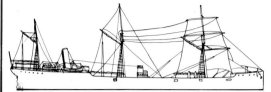

Gluckaüff—*The world's first tanker, built in England in 1885. Tonnage: 2,307 tons. Propeller propulsion with an auxiliary sail.*

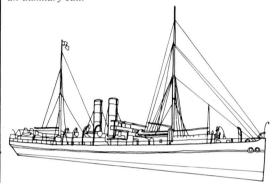

Ballaarat—*Launched in 1882; another example of naval longevity, it remained in service until 1904, after having covered the southern routes as a passenger and cargo ship. Displacement: 4,677 tons; speed: 14 knots.*

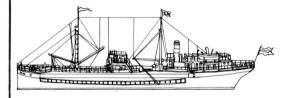

Vulcanus—*A Dutch ship and the world's first oil-tanker, with diesel engines in the stern. Launched in 1910 to serve on the Borneo route.*

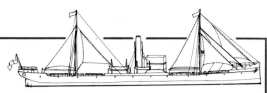

Cockerill—*Built in Belgium in 1901, the first example of the many small cargo steamships that slowly replaced the sailing ship. Displacement: 2,441 tons; length: 88 meters (289 feet); beam: 13.7 meters (45 feet).*

Bowes—*1852, a collier in service between London and Tyne. Displacement: 437 tons; speed: 9 knots.*

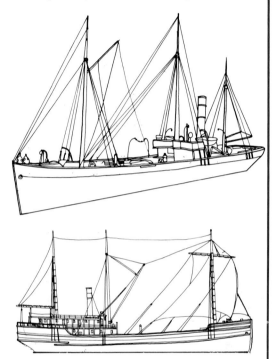

Willapa—*A sequoia schooner, used for carrying lumber. Firwood hull. Length: 54.3 meters (178.5 feet); beam: 12.2 meters (40 feet); tonnage: 752 tons.*

lantic passenger service, so they rented the 703-ton paddle-wheel steamship *Sirius*, which was supposed to start regular service between England and Ireland. On April 4, 1838, the *Sirius*, packed to the rails with passengers, cargo, mail, and 400 tons of coal, left Cork for New York. Four days later, the *Great Western* sailed from Bristol in the wake of the *Sirius*. The *Sirius* had less power (320 hp) than the *Great Western* but managed to make the crossing in 18 days and 10 hours, at an average speed of 6.5 knots. Just as the enthusiasm of the New Yorkers was dying down, the *Great Western* entered the port

12 hours later, after a crossing of 15 days and 5 hours at an average speed of 8.75 knots. In the history of navigation, the *Sirius* is considered to be the first ship to have crossed the Atlantic Ocean under the steady use of steam; and the *Great Western*, the first real transatlantic liner.

But Brunel did not stop with the *Great Western*. The second ship the English engineer put into service for the Great Western Company was another step forward in the building of large transatlantic ships. This ship, the *Great Britain*, was built of iron and had a screw propeller. This type of propul-

Great Eastern—I. Brunel's last creation, built of iron in 1858. Length: 210.92 meters (680 feet); gross tonnage: 23,424 tons. Moved by propellers and wheels, and also outfitted with auxiliary sails. It was built to carry 5,000 passengers. It was a commercial failure and earned money for its owners only while laying transatlantic communication cables, from 1866 to 1874.

Alecto—An English paddle-wheel frigate, tested by the British Admiralty in 1845 to see if propeller propulsion was superior to that of paddle wheels.

Rattler—Alecto's 888-ton sister-ship with propeller propulsion. On April 3, 1845, it had a tug of war with the Alecto (paddle-wheel propulsion). The Rattler won, towing the Alecto at a speed of 2.5 knots. This experiment demonstrated the superiority of the screw propeller to the paddle wheel.

sion had already been successfully applied, and it was after observing demonstration tests of a propeller-driven steamship, the *Archimedes*, which used a propeller patented by Francis Petitt Smith, that Brunel decided to replace the paddle wheels designed for the *Great Britain* with a large, 6-bladed propeller. The building of the new transatlantic liner met with a host of difficulties. There was no English shipyard large enough to accommodate the 324-foot hull. A solution was finally found, and the *Great Britain* was launched in 1845, 6 years after construction had begun. It made its first transatlantic crossing in July, 1846, but it was an extremely slow voyage. The engines did not live up to expectations. Then one of the propeller blades broke, and the voyage had to be completed under sail. In September 1846, the ship ran aground off the Irish coast and was blocked there for 18 months. It was then transferred to the Australian route, and finally ended its days as a coal pontoon in the Falkland Islands. In 1970, it was reclaimed, restored, and towed to Bristol to become a floating naval museum. The structure Brunel designed was exceptionally resistant.

Probably Brunel's most remarkable achievement was the *Great Eastern*, the ship that cost its builder his life. Brunel's last project was ordered by the Eastern Navigation Company. The hull was far too advanced for the technological level and the social and economic conditions of the time. The ship was almost 700 feet long, with a gross tonnage of 18,914 tons. It was launched in 1858, after all kinds of difficulties had been

Normandie—*The first French transatlantic liner to bear this name was launched in 1885 for the Compagnie Générale Transatlantique. Propeller-driven, with a complete set of auxiliary sails.*

City of New York—*A 10,334-ton vessel built, with its sister ship, the* City of Chicago, *for the American Inman Line. It was the first twin-screw transatlantic liner.*

Oceanic—*A revolutionary passenger ship of 1871, the first to provide modern cabins for passenger comfort. Length: 128 meters (140 yards); beam: 12.20 meters (40 feet); draft: 9.14 meters (30 feet).*

overcome. Brunel died on September 15, 1859, worn out by fatigue, a few months before it went into service on the North American route. Between 1860 and 1863, the enormous liner made nine Atlantic crossings. Although the ship was built to accommodate 5,000 passengers, there were only 36 on the maiden voyage of 11 days from Southampton to New York. One of them was Jules Verne, who described his experience in a tale called "A Floating City." The running of the *Great Western* as a passenger liner turned out to be a financial disaster. It was later used in laying the Atlantic cable. The ship was demolished in the years between 1888 and 1891. The skeleton of a worker was found in a hollow wall space, and according to a naval superstition, that explained the bad luck that had dogged the ship from the start. In any case, the *Great Eastern* represented the fullest expression of Brunel's talent. The ship's length was surpassed only by the *Oceanic*'s in 1899, and its gross tonnage by the *Baltic*'s in 1904.

In mentioning the construction of the *Great Britain*, it was noted that the hull of the world's first propeller-driven transatlantic liner was made of iron, but that was not a first. The great progress made in iron metallurgy and the shortage of wood for building,

especially in England, made iron highly desirable for naval construction, despite skepticism from some quarters. The first-known iron vessel was a small ship built in Yorkshire, England, in 1777, and was used to carry passengers on the Foss River. From the beginning it was clear that iron hulls offered greater strength, more space, and lighter weight than wood.

Iron had long been used to reinforce wooden hulls, and iron ribs had replaced wood. All doubts concerning the resistance of iron plating were laid to rest in 1838, when the iron steamship *Gary Owen* was the only ship to survive a violent storm in the English Channel that had driven several other ships to destruction on the coast. The creation of underwater antifouling paints resolved the problem of corrosion. The observations and practical applications of Matthew Flinders, the explorer of the Australian seas, and of George B. Airy eliminated the magnetic disturbance of the compass caused by the iron hull. The first steamship with an all-iron hull was the *Aaron Manby*, which went into service in 1820 as a passenger ship between England and the French coast. It inaugurated a regular, state-subsidized postal service that gave mercantile navigation a financial boost and encouraged further steam developments.

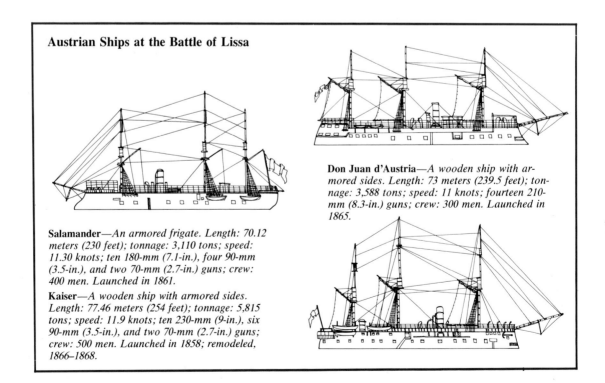

Austrian Ships at the Battle of Lissa

Salamander—*An armored frigate. Length: 70.12 meters (230 feet); tonnage: 3,110 tons; speed: 11.30 knots; ten 180-mm (7.1-in.), four 90-mm (3.5-in.), and two 70-mm (2.7-in.) guns; crew: 400 men. Launched in 1861.*

Kaiser—*A wooden ship with armored sides. Length: 77.46 meters (254 feet); tonnage: 5,815 tons; speed: 11.9 knots; ten 230-mm (9-in.), six 90-mm (3.5-in.), and two 70-mm (2.7-in.) guns; crew: 500 men. Launched in 1858; remodeled, 1866–1868.*

Don Juan d'Austria—*A wooden ship with armored sides. Length: 73 meters (239.5 feet); tonnage: 3,588 tons; speed: 11 knots; fourteen 210-mm (8.3-in.) guns; crew: 300 men. Launched in 1865.*

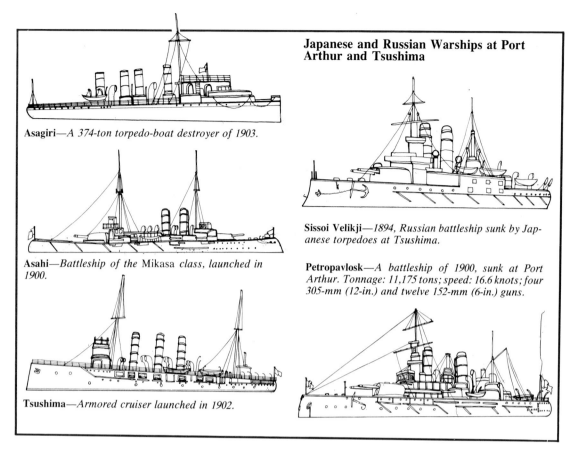

Japanese and Russian Warships at Port Arthur and Tsushima

Asagiri—A 374-ton torpedo-boat destroyer of 1903.

Asahi—Battleship of the Mikasa class, launched in 1900.

Tsushima—Armored cruiser launched in 1902.

Sissoi Velikji—1894, Russian battleship sunk by Japanese torpedoes at Tsushima.

Petropavlosk—A battleship of 1900, sunk at Port Arthur. Tonnage: 11,175 tons; speed: 16.6 knots; four 305-mm (12-in.) and twelve 152-mm (6-in.) guns.

The decisive innovation that put steam navigation ahead of the great sailing ships was the introduction of the screw propeller in place of the large and fragile paddle wheels. The paddle wheel's fragility and its limited power of propulsion had made maritime nations reluctant to install the steam engine on board their warships. There was also some concern that an iron hull would prove more vulnerable to cannon fire than a solid wood one. In 1738 the Swiss scientist Daniel Bernouilli published his *Hydrodynamica* on the statics and motion of fluids. His work had enormous practical consequences for navigation and, in particular, for the use of a propeller in water. Bushnell in 1775 and Fulton in 1800 tried to install a propeller on their submarines, but the first practical results were due to the experiments made by Giuseppe Ressel of Trieste, a government forestry employee who applied a single-blade propeller to the brigantine *Civetta* in 1826. Ten years later, the Englishman F. Petitt Smith patented a wooden propeller of corkscrew shape, but the ship on which it was installed had an accident that broke off half the length of the propeller. The speed of the ship increased at once, and thus was born the modern screw propeller.

Skepticism was finally overcome in 1845, when the British Admiralty organized a remarkable tug of war between two ships of

Kniaz Potëmkin Tavricevski—A first-class battleship of the Russian Imperial Navy, launched in October 1900. Length: 113.08 meters (371 feet); beam: 22.05 meters (74 feet); draft: 8.53 meters (28 feet); displacement: 12,548 tons; speed: 18 knots; four 305-mm (12-in.), sixteen 152-mm (6-in.), and twelve 75-mm (3-in.) guns; 4 torpedo tubes; armor plate thickness: from 227-mm (9-in.) to 152-mm (6-in.). The Potëmkin is famous for the mutiny that broke out among the crew on June 25, 1905. The revolt began because of the inedible food served to the crew.

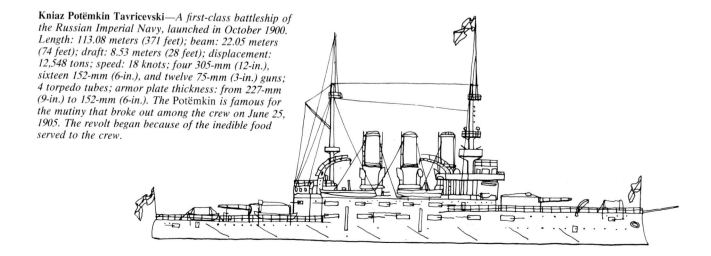

Mississippi—An 1850 river boat with paddle wheels, typical of those used on the 2,000 miles of the Mississippi River. Service between New Orleans and Natchez was inaugurated in 1812. By 1822, there were 35 boats of between 40 and 450 tons plying the Mississippi.

Massachusetts—A North American passenger and cargo steamship launched in 1877 and used on the New York–Boston run. It had paddle-wheel propulsion and could carry 350 passengers.

equal displacement and power: the *Alecto* with paddle wheels, and the *Rattler* with a propeller. A cable was stretched between the sterns of the two ships, and the engines were given full steam ahead. The *Rattler* towed the *Alecto* at a speed of 2.5 knots, even with the *Alecto*'s wheels turning at full power. This was the decisive test, and the years ahead saw the screw propeller drive the paddle wheel off the scene. Steam was officially adopted by the major navies of the world, although the steam engine was sometimes merely an auxiliary on the classic sailing ship of the line. The first vessels of this type were built in England: the *Ajax*, the *Horatio*, and the *Nelson*, older ships modified to accommodate the new means of propulsion. The first ship of the line expressly designed for propeller propulsion was the English 90-gun

Agamemnon. The next step forward was made in the Crimean War, fought between Russia and a coalition of England, France, Turkey, and Piedmont (1853–1855). On November 30, 1853, a Turkish naval squadron was attacked by Russian naval forces in the bay of Sinop. All the Turkish ships were made of wood and were completely destroyed by Russian fire power. This episode marked the end of wooden hulls for warships. Thanks to naval architect Dupuy de Lôme, the French navy entered the new era with the launching of the *Gloire* in 1859, a one-battery wooden frigate with its sides protected by half-inch iron plates. The same year the British Admiralty made its entry with the *Warrior*, the world's first all-iron warship, which served as a model for all the navies of the world. It was still fitted with sails, but between the mainmast and the foremast could be seen the two smokestacks of the boilers. The propellers, driven by a 5,470-hp steam engine, reached a speed of 14.35 knots. This might be considered the world's first modern battleship, although the term was first applied officially in 1868, to the British ship *Ocean*. The *Ocean* was the first ship on which the guns were concentrated in a central area and not arrayed in the classic battery line along the sides of the ship.

Naval armament underwent revolutionary changes. Increased use was made of rifled-bore cannons, which permitted more precise firing. Breech-loading replaced barrel-loading; less gunpowder was used; and the projectile was hermetically enclosed in the barrel. About 1880 the breech-loading cannon was adopted by most navies. Cannon were no longer mounted on wooden carriages but on solid iron frames, which were later replaced by the gun turret. As more and more ships were armor-plated, heavier guns had to be developed. Eventually designers and builders introduced motors to raise, aim, and load the guns.

The end of the 19th century saw the appearance of small, fast-firing guns and the introduction of brass shell cases containing both the projectile and the propelling powder charge. Ships' arsenals were rounded out by machine guns—Nordenfeldts, Gardners, and Maxims—often with multiple barrels. Pro-

Karteria—The first steamship involved in naval combat. Launched in the United States in 1826, it was offered to the Greeks in their rebellion against the Ottoman Empire. The ship was armed with 8 guns of rather small caliber.

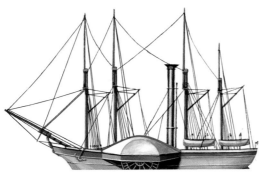

jectiles also changed radically: the old round cannonball gave way to long cylindrical shells with heads tapering to a point. The introduction of smokeless gunpowder aided combat by keeping the air of the battle zone fairly clear.

Fire ships, used until the 18th century, were replaced by more brutal and deadly weapons. Torpedoes first appeared during the American Civil War and were steadily improved. They were launched from dry land and were detonated by contact or simply by the passing of a ship at a certain distance from the explosive.

Willcox and Anderson in Great Britain made an important contribution to the success of steamships. Their mail boats outclassed the postal sailing ships operated by the British Admiralty. In 1839 Samuel Cunard of Halifax obtained a government contract to set up regular steam passenger service between Liverpool, Boston, and Halifax. The Cunard Line to North America was an immediate success, and the idea was quickly imitated by others, including the American Collins line.

It is worth mentioning that the 19th century and the early 20th was a time of mass emigration from Europe to America. The overwhelming majority of immigrants to America were poor people, and steerage accommodation offered few comforts. In *Martin Chuzzlewit* Charles Dickens describes one such crossing and the hopes of its passengers. After the long and uncomfortable crossing, the passengers are relieved simply to go ashore. One character remarks: "And, this . . . is the Land of Liberty, is it? Very well. I'm agreeable. Any land will do for me, after so much water!"

A few decades later, larger transatlantic ships existed with luxurious accommodations for first-class passengers and a minimum of comfort for the immigrants in steerage. Between 1856 and 1864, France and Germany also entered the market for transatlantic traffic, and an award was established for the ship that made the fastest crossing between Europe and North America. The official regulations of the North Atlantic Blue Ribbon Challenge Trophy were laid down only in 1935, but by that time the Blue Ribbon already had more than a century of history behind it, most of it written by fast British-built ships. Fine German transatlan-

Napoleon—*A propeller warship with 92 guns, launched in 1850 for the French navy. Designed by Stanislas Dupuy de Lôme, it surpassed in speed (14 knots) and power all comparable ships of its time.*

Gloire—*An 1859 French navy frigate, considered to be the world's first armored ship. Displacement: 5,528 tons; length: 78 meters (256 feet); speed: 13.5 knots; 36 rifled, breech-loading guns, six of 240-mm (9.4-in.) and twenty-four of 160-mm (6.3-in.). Armored with iron plates from the deck down to 2 meters (6.6 feet) below the waterline.*

Warrior—*The English answer to the first French battleship, all-iron and launched in 1861. Displacement: 9,210 tons; speed: 14.35 knots; a battery of thirty-four 178-mm (7-in.) guns. Armored with 114-mm (4.5-in.) iron plates, but only in the central part of the hull.*

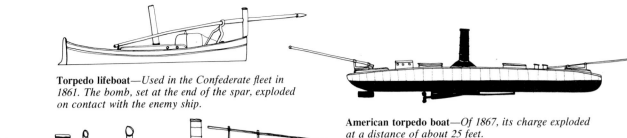

Torpedo lifeboat—*Used in the Confederate fleet in 1861. The bomb, set at the end of the spar, exploded on contact with the enemy ship.*

American torpedo boat—*Of 1867, its charge exploded at a distance of about 25 feet.*

Torpedo-boat launch—*Steam-powered and armed with a torpedo on the boom. From the American Civil War.*

American torpedo boat—*Of 1865, theoretically able to carry out two attacks.*

tic liners appeared at the end of the century, such as the *Kaiser Wilhelm der Grosse* of the Norddeutscher Lloyd, which covered the distance from the Isle of Wight to Sandy Hook in 5 days and 20 hours at an average speed of 22.29 knots. This record was broken in the summer of 1900 by the *Deutschland* of the Hamburg-American Line. Albert Ballin, the director of Hamburg-American, was the first to use ships on winter cruises when Atlantic traffic slowed down.

These impressive passenger ships engaged in a kind of speed race on the North Atlantic routes. These fast crossings were made possible by an engine that transformed steam-produced energy directly into rotary motion. This was the turbine engine. The globe of Hero of Alexandria, designed 2,000 years ago, was a kind of forerunner of this engine. The 1629 engine of Giovanni Branca, a jet of steam that worked a bladed wheel, was considered a joke; and the turbine of the Swedish inventor Laval had rotors that moved so fast (30,000 rpm) that the energy it generated could not be transmitted to the shafts, which turned much more slowly. The experiments of Zoelly and Curtiss anticipated the first turbine engine, the work of Sir Charles Par-

sons in 1894. The new engine was installed on his steam-yacht *Turbina*. The yacht reached a speed of 34 knots, incredibly fast for the time, driving 3 groups of 3 propellers each. The engine was demonstrated at the 1897 British Naval Review at Spithead. The new engine was adopted at once by the British navy, which mounted it first on the torpedo-boat destroyer *Viper* in 1898.

The steam turbine eliminated all the obstacles to propulsion power and made possible the gigantic passenger ships that dominated transatlantic commerical navigation between the end of the last century and the first decades of the 1900s. The first of these new liners were Cunard liners, the *Lusitania* and the *Mauretania*. There were luxury accommodations in first-class, and second- and third-class were comfortable. Below decks the stokers sweated. "King" coal, the supreme source of power, reigned in the suffocating and smoke-filled furnace room.

The *Mauretania* kept the Blue Ribbon for 22 years, despite the efforts of its two direct rivals, White Star liners both of them, the *Olympic* (about 900 feet long, with a displacement of 64,957 tons), and the ill-fated *Titanic*. On the night of April 14, 1912, racing

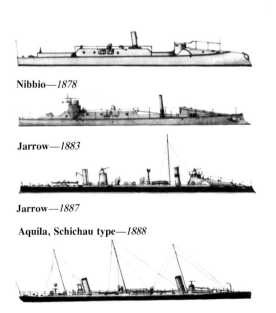

Nibbio—*1878*

Jarrow—*1883*

Jarrow—*1887*

Aquila, Schichau type—*1888*

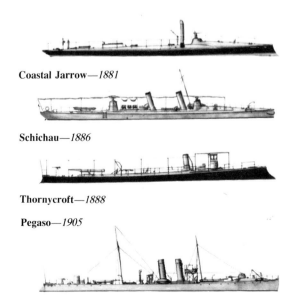

Coastal Jarrow—*1881*

Schichau—*1886*

Thornycroft—*1888*

Pegaso—*1905*

over a transatlantic course that was shorter but dangerous, in an effort to win the Blue Ribbon, the *Titanic* struck an iceberg and sank. Germany put into service the *Imperator* (over 900 feet long; gross tonnage, 51,148 tons). It was launched in 1912, with the imperial eagle at the tip of its prow and the motto *Mein Feld ist die Welt*. The *Imperator* was lost during a storm. A year later the *Vaterland* made its appearance on the North Atlantic route (950 feet long; 53,424 tons). The last of that period's great German transatlantic liners was the *Bismarck*, which never hoisted the German flag. It was acquired by the White Star Line and rechristened the *Majestic*, and for many years it was the world's largest ship.

The last great liner to enter service before World War I was Cunard's *Aquitania*, perhaps that company's finest ship and certainly one of its most durable. It was scrapped in 1950, after 36 years of uninterrupted service. Between 1880 and 1890, commercial steamships totally replaced the last "western ocean packets," the large, fast sailing ships that crossed the Atlantic in 15 to 18 days.

We left the world's navies viewing the launching of the *Warrior* with cautious interest. The history of the evolution of the fighting ship is the story of a continuing duel between cannon and armor, and of the men behind that duel—men of the sea, soldiers, builders, and technical experts. A date can even be assigned to the start of that duel: March 8–9, 1862, when the first clash between ironclad vessels took place. It was during the American Civil War, at Hampton Roads off Norfolk, Virginia. The Confederates had put back into shape the steam frigate *Merrimack*, furnishing it with an improvised armor plating mostly made of iron tracks, in an attempt to break the Union's naval blockade. The *Merrimack* rammed the *Cumberland*, a 30-gun sloop; captured the 50-gun *Congress*; and inflicted serious damage on the frigate *Minnesota*. But the next day it found itself face to face with a Union vessel, the *Monitor*, designed and built by John Ericsson. The *Monitor* was the first vessel to carry its engines below the waterline. The deck was at water-level, and only the pilothouse, the smokestack, and a revolving turret containing two large guns were

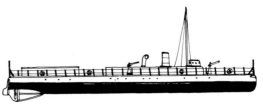

French torpedo boat—*From the late 1800s. Speed: 23 knots. With torpedo tubes.*

Lightning—*An English torpedo boat of 1876, 25.6 meters (84 feet) long and with a speed of 18 knots, able to launch a torpedo from a tube at the bow.*

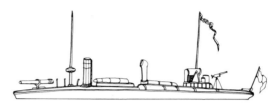

Russian torpedo boat—*1890. The torpedo was self-propelled and launched from a special tube at the bow.*

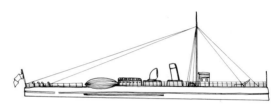

French torpedo boat—*1898. With 2 torpedo tubes, a fixed one in the bow and a revolving one in the stern.*

Audacieux—*Deep-sea torpedo boat, 1901: 185 tons; 30 knots; 3 torpedo tubes; two 3-pounders.*

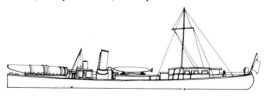

Lancier—*Deep-sea torpedo boat, with a maximum speed of 26 knots, and armed with three torpedo tubes.*

Spica—*Italian torpedo boat of 1905.*

Havock—*The first English torpedo-boat destroyer, built at the end of the 19th century. Length: 55 meters (180 feet); beam: 5.60 meters (18.5 feet); 260 tons; speed: 26 knots; 3 torpedo tubes and 4 small-caliber guns.*

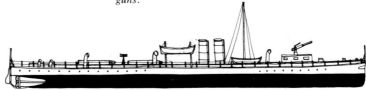

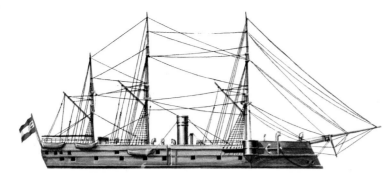

Ferdinand Max—*Tegetthoff's flagship at the Battle of Lissa, where it rammed and sank the battleship* Re d'Italia. *The wooden hull was armored on the sides. Displacement: 5,059 tons; length: 79.97 meters (262 feet); speed: 10.3 knots; fourteen 180-mm (7.1-in.), four 90-mm (3.5-in.), and two 70-mm (2.7-in.) guns; crew: 482 men. Launched in 1865.*

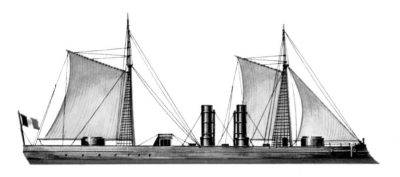

Affondatore—*An armored Italian ramming vessel, at Lissa. The hull was protected by armor plate 12.7 cm (5-in.) thick. The ship was modernized in 1883. Displacement: 4,307 tons; length: 89.6 meters (294 feet); speed: 12 knots; two 254-mm (10-in.) guns and an iron ram; 309 crewmen. Launched in 1865.*

above water. The clash between these two mastodons lasted all morning but was indecisive. Neither the armor of the *Monitor* nor the tracks of the *Merrimack* had suffered serious damage. There were no dead among the crews, just a few wounded, including the captains of the new vessels, Buchanan of the *Merrimack* and Worden of the *Monitor*. Another naval episode that had repercussions on the construction of battleships was the clash between the Italian and Austrian fleets near the island of Lissa on July 20, 1866. The underarmed Italian fleet was hastily rearmed when war with Austria seemed inevitable. The Italian operational fleet was made up of 3 squadrons. The first, under the commander in chief, Adm. Carlo Pellion di Persano, was composed of 6 large ironclad ships. It had to face 27 Austrian vessels, of which 7 were ironclad, under the command of thirty-nine-year-old Adm. Wilhelm von Tegetthoff. Admiral Persano could have put off occupying the island of Lissa, which was of great strategic importance in the framework of naval operations in the Adriatic, but he put out to sea without waiting for the second squadron, which was composed of unarmored wooden ships commanded by Admiral Albini. Persano faced an Austrian fleet that outnumbered his own and was superior in training and morale. The *Re d'Italia*, Persano's flagship, was rammed by the *Ferdinand Max*, Tegetthoff's flagship, and sank in a few minutes, with a loss of 612 men. This was the last battle in which the ram was used as an offensive weapon and the first in which fleets of ironclad battleships met face to face.

By the time of the Russo-Japanese War (1904–1905) ironclad battleships formed the heart of world navies. Port Arthur, a Russian naval base situated at the tip of the small Chinese Kuantung Peninsula, was the setting of the early part of the war. This was the first

Re d'Italia—*The Italian armored frigate rammed and sunk by the* Ferdinand Max *during the Battle of Lissa. Displacement: 5,610 tons; length: 84 meters (275.6 feet); speed: 12 knots; two 200-mm (3.9-in.), thirty 160-mm (6.3-in.), and four 72-mm (3-in.) guns; crew: 650 men. Launched in 1863.*

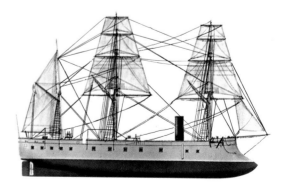

Palestro—*Ironclad gunboat, built by the La Seyne shipyards. It was commanded by Commander Cappellini and was in the thick of the Battle of Lissa, where it caught fire and blew up, killing almost the entire crew. Four 203-mm (8-in.) and one 165-mm (6.5-in.) guns; speed: 8 knots.*

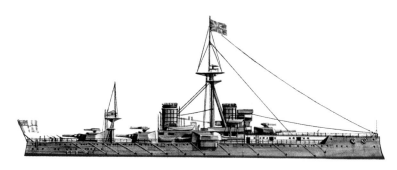

Dreadnought—*The prototype of all other battleships built before World War II. The world's first combat ship with turbine engines. It was launched in England in 1906. Displacement: 17,900 tons; length: 160 meters (175 yards); speed: 21 knots; ten 305-mm (12-in.) guns and 24 of smaller caliber; crew: 800 men.*

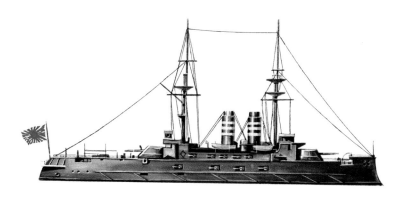

Mikasa—*Togo's flagship at the Battle of Tsushima (May 27–28, 1905) during the Russo-Japanese War. Displacement: 15,200 tons; length: 125 meters (137 yards); speed: 18.5 knots; four 305-mm (12-in.), fourteen 152-mm (6-in.) and 32 smaller-caliber guns; crew: 770 men. Launched in 1899.*

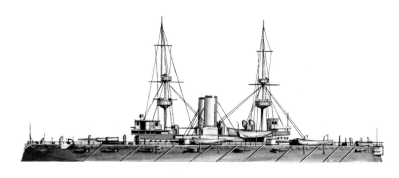

Royal Sovereign—*1892. Steel-hulled British battleship. Displacement: 14,150 tons. Length: 380 feet. Four 13.5-in. and thirty-eight lighter guns.*

time that Japan entered on the world political scene as a vital force that could no longer be ignored. The commander in chief of the Japanese fleet, Admiral Togo, based his strategy on fast and determined action, made possible by the great mobility of his ships. At dawn on February 8, 1904, when the war had just begun, Japanese destroyers attacked the Russian ships anchored in the outer harbor of Port Arthur and quickly put three of the largest ones out of action. After two attempts to block the entrance to the Russian base by sinking some old cargo ships, the Japanese mined the waters off the base. That was the night of April 12–13, 1904. The siege lasted until January 2, 1905, when Port Arthur surrendered, with the remaining Russian ships. In the meantime, the Russian government had prepared a second fleet, and on October 15, 1904, it sailed from Libava, on the Gulf of Finland. It was no mean feat to transfer all those ships from the Baltic Sea to the Yellow Sea. The long and difficult voyage, under the command of Admiral Rozdestsvenskij, emphasized the defects of hasty preparation and training. A third squadron, made up of older ships commanded by Admiral Njebogatov, headed out to sea and finally joined the rest of the fleet in the middle of May 1905, off Indonesia. Port Arthur had already fallen, and Rozdestsvenskij's mission was futile. One of the most destructive naval battles in history was waged in the waters of Tsushima from 1:30 P.M., May 27, until 9:30 A.M., May 28, 1905. Admiral Togo took advantage of rough seas and a strong wind to make a determined attack and won the day. Four Russian battleships, including the *Suvorov*, the commander in chief's own ship, went to the bottom, as did six vessels in Njebogatov's squadron. That squadron's flagship, the *Imperator Nicolaj I*, surrendered with the commander of the third squad. The *Admiral Ushako* was

Castelfidardo—*Launched in 1863; a steam frigate with mixed propulsion, overhauled between 1870 and 1880. Displacement: 4,183 tons; speed: 13 knots; twenty-two 160-mm (6.3-in.) and four 72-mm (3-in.) guns. It took part in the Battle of Lissa in 1866.*

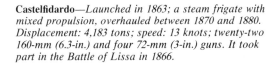
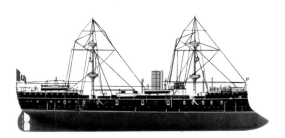

Terrible—*An ironclad floating battery launched by the La Seyne shipyards in 1860 for the Sardinian Royal Navy. It was the first ship to enter the port of Civitavecchia after the city surrendered to Piedmontes troops.*

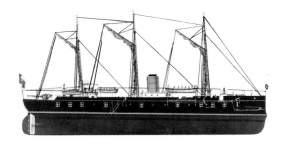

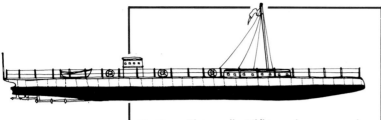

Turbina—*The small, 44½-ton pleasure vessel on which Charles Parsons (1854–1931) mounted his 980-hp, 2,200-rpm turbine for the first time in 1894, making use of Laval's experience. In 1897, with the "reaction" turbine built by Parsons, the boat attained a record speed of 34.5 knots.*

Viper—*The first torpedo-boat destroyer with a steam-turbine engine, built by the Hawthorn Leslie shipyards in England in 1900; 363 tons; speed: 37 knots.*

sunk by its own crew to keep it from falling into the hands of the enemy; and five other ships, including two old ironclad coast-guard vessels, hoisted the white flag. Not one large Japanese ship went down, and the only vessel seriously damaged was a light cruiser. The decisive factor in the battle was the rapid maneuverability of the ultramodern Japanese battleships *Mikasa*, *Shikishima*, *Fuji*, and *Asahi*, as well as the faster firing speed of their guns.

Cannon power was to be the decisive factor in any clash between battleships. The "cult of the big bang"—the 12-inch gun with a range of more than 20,000 feet—became the major theme in designing the new battleships, along with high speed and strong armor plating. These elements found their finest fruit in the *Dreadnought*, an ironclad battleship built in England in 1906, under the direction of Lord Fisher. The *Dreadnought* immediately made earlier ironclads obsolete, including the impressive Italian *Duilio* and *Dandolo*, built by Benedetto Brin in 1876; the French *Martel*; and the German battleships of the *Kaiser* class built between 1890 and 1900 on orders from Admiral von Tirpitz. The *Dreadnought*, with its practically noiseless turbine engines driven by oil-fired boilers, its armor plate almost a foot thick at crucial points, its ten 12-inch guns and a displacement of 17,912 tons, opened a completely new era in warship construction. The British example was quickly followed by the Germans, Italians, Russians, and French, among others. With the launching of the *Texas* (1912) and the *New York* (1914), with their more than 27,000 tons and distinctive steel trestle masts, the Americans, too, began producing gigantic battleships. Less heavily armored vessels were also built. They were armed with large-caliber guns and were

Fuel-oil boilers *were first used on board the Russian destroyer* Viborg, *in 1897, and soon cut down the running cost of ships.*

called battle cruisers. The first of these ships was the *Invincible*, launched in 1908. England and Germany used this type of ship during the two world wars, chiefly in the North Sea.

The arrival of steam and the propeller, one of the aspects of the industrial revolution that, along with colonial expansion, characterized the 19th century, also marked the inevitable decline of the glorious sailing ship, both military and commercial. In this realm, one last exciting achievement was made in America, the creation of the typical 19th-century sailing ship, the famous clipper ship. It had a long, low hull and tapered bow and stern. Its highly sophisticated rigging made it extremely fast. The clipper became famous throughout the world. It was the last attempt to create an economical alternative to the new steamships, and there were moments when it seemed that the modern sailing ship might outclass steam competition. On certain trade routes, the cargo steamship, despite improved and economical engines, was outclassed by the sailing ship. The sailing ship had no fuel expense. From 1890 on, the large sailing ships fought their last battle with the propeller on the routes to California, Peru, Chile, and Australia. The English and American clippers, used mainly for the fast transport of tea from China to Europe, were followed by the western ocean packets, basically passenger craft; the colonial or wool clippers, which plied the Australian route; and finally the gigantic carriers, swan song of the sail, with six or even seven masts. These noble efforts proved futile, even though the use of iron and later steel in the construction of sailing ships reduced their weight, provided more cargo space, and made construction more economical. Steam navigation had won the day. The centuries-old history of the sailing ship really ends with the 19th century, its memory kept green by a few sailing ships now preserved as museums or as training ships.

In the second half of the 19th century, the last great commercial sailing ships had a final moment of glory. On October 23, 1848, a man named James Marshall saw the first gold nugget gleaming in a California stream. This started one of the great migratory movements of modern times; a mass of adventurers, dreamers, speculators, and men with

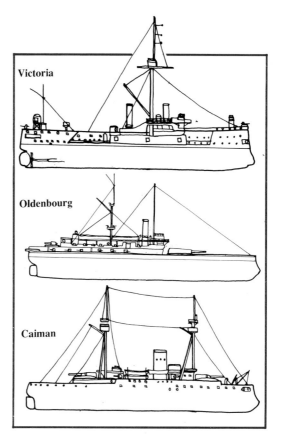

Cruisers—*The modern cruiser appeared between 1880 and 1890. It was armed with breech-loading guns and improved engines. It was built of steel, with a great reduction in weight and an increase in speed. In 1887, the Royal Navy reclassified all its outdated vessels as cruisers, a measure quickly adopted by all other navies.*

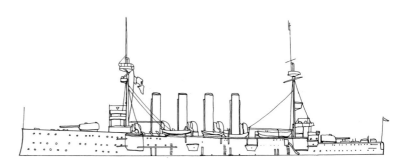

Cressy—*The first of a series of 6 armored cruisers, launched in Great Britain on December 4, 1899. It reached a speed of 20 knots and had a displacement of 11,810 tons.*

Lepanto—*Forerunner of the battle cruiser, launched in 1883 by the Cantiere Orlando in Livorno; designed by B. Brin and almost without armor; 13,678 tons; speed: 18 knots; four 431-mm (17-in.) guns paired amidships, eight of 152-mm (6-in.), and various anti-torpedo pieces. It could embark an entire army division. Withdrawn from service in 1914.*

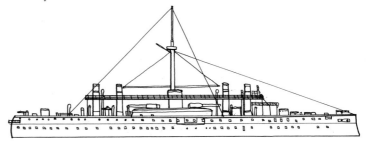

nothing to lose rushed from Europe to the new Eldorado. These gold seekers were carried along the long and dangerous Cape Horn route by sailing ships, to land at San Francisco, then a small village. In 1853 sailing ships carried English coal to India and China. In 1870 the nickel of New Caledonia gave the majestic sailing ships a chance to continue their often successful struggle with the steamship. The year 1875 was marked by the great current of emigration toward Australia, and in 1876 sailing ships filled their holds with barrels of American oil. These ships were still economically advantageous in 1890, with fast speed, reduced building costs, and smaller crews, thanks to new riggings and winches.

There was a steady increase in the tonnage of ocean-going sailing ships, above all in northern Europe. In 1895 the commercial sailing fleet of the Western nations reached a total of about 10 million tons. The early displacement of 2,460 tons rose to the 4,430 tons of the 4-masters. After a final building effort during the last 20 years of the century, 5,000 sailing vessels flew the British flag, 1,200 the French, almost as many that of Sweden, about 1,000 the German flag, and about 2,000 the Norwegian flag. But steam soon made the "white-winged birds" extinct.

Thomas W. Lawson—*A 7-masted merchant schooner of 5,218 tons, built to carry coal. With 4,000 square meters (4,784 square yards) of sails. Length: 123 meters (134.5 yards); beam: 15 meters (49 feet).*

James Baines—*A famous wool clipper that bore the name of its builder. It sailed on the Australia route. During its maiden voyage, in 1852, it went from London to Melbourne in 68 days; 2,275 tons; length: 88 meters (289 feet); beam: 13.6 meters (45 feet).*

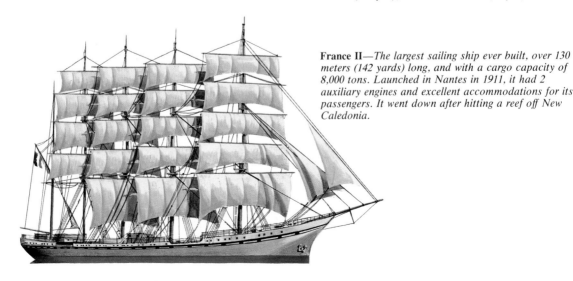

France II—*The largest sailing ship ever built, over 130 meters (142 yards) long, and with a cargo capacity of 8,000 tons. Launched in Nantes in 1911, it had 2 auxiliary engines and excellent accommodations for its passengers. It went down after hitting a reef off New Caledonia.*

Star of India—*A fast "colonial clipper," it carried goods and passengers to the English colonies in Asia, Indonesia, New Zealand, and Australia. With a composite hull.*

Lightning—*One of the most famous clippers, 1,468 tons. Length: 85 meters (279 feet); beam: 13.4 meters (44 feet). Launched in 1854 by the Mackay shipyards in Boston, it unfurled a sail surface of 1,200 square meters (1,435 square yards) to the wind, which under optimum conditions let it reach a speed of 18 knots.*

The Sail

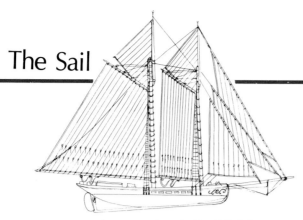

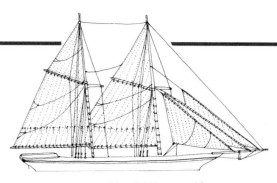

Elsie—*An elegant schooner launched in 1910. It has a round bow and was used for fishing on the Newfoundland banks.*

Schooner—*Between 100 and 300 tons, with two masts and square sails, still sails today as a pleasure craft.*

THE WIND IS CAGED

The oldest-known image of a boat with a sail is painted on an Egyptian vase from the Predynastic period and probably dates from 4000 B.C. The square sail was the most common means of marine propulsion for thousands of years. It took the wind only on the stern side and could leave the shore easily when bad weather prevented easy landing. All the maritime peoples of the Mediterranean, including the Greeks and Romans, used the square sail. In northern Europe it was at first made of handwoven wool, reinforced with netting bound to its front surface to keep the wind from tearing it. On their larger ships, the Vikings used cloth sails that could be pulled taut and make better use of the propulsive power of the wind. With such sails and with oars, the bold Scandinavian navigators made long voyages in European waters and on the Atlantic. By the late Middle Ages, ships had two and even three masts, and late in the 15th century another square sail was added to the mainmast. It was smaller than the

main sail, and crewmen rigged it on a kind of protected platform at the top of the mast. The second sail of the mainmast came to be called the main topsail, while the men who handled it took the name of topmen.

By the mid-1500s, ships were larger, and so were their sails. A large, three-masted ship of that time was "rigged"—technically speaking—with six sails: two on the mainmast, two on the foremast, and one on the mizzenmast. The sixth sail, the spritsail, was set at the bowsprit, the mast that protruded almost horizontally from the bow, and aided in tacking, or changing the ship's direction. By this time the mizzenmast sail was no longer square but triangular. The triangular lateen sail probably appeared around the 9th century in the Mediterranean Sea. It may have been introduced by the Arabs. It was the chief sail of the Mediterranean until the 13th century, when ships began to carry square and lateen sails together.

There was a kind of exchange between Mediterranean and Northern Europe, and the rigging of ever larger sailing ships became more complex. While the square sail favored navigation with stern winds, the lateen sail let the vessel close-haul or "point up" the wind, that is, sail at a closer angle to the direction from which the wind blew. The lateen sail was thus the first fore-and-aft sail and until the mid-18th century was internationally used as the mizzenmast sail.

1 *lower spanker;* 2 *upper spanker;* 3 *gaff topsail;* 4 *jigger staysail;* 5 *jigger topmast staysail;* 6 *jigger topgallant staysail;* 7 *mizzen sail;* 8 *mizzen lower topsail;* 9 *mizzen upper topsail;* 10 *mizzen lower topgallant sail;* 11 *mizzen upper topgallant sail;* 12 *mizzen royal;* 13 *mizzen topmast staysail;* 14 *mizzen topgallant staysail;* 15 *mizzen royal staysail;* 16 *mainsail main course;* 17 *main lower topsail;* 18 *main upper topsail;* 19 *main lower topgallant sail;* 20 *main upper topgallant sail;* 21 *main royal;* 22 *main topmast staysail;* 23 *main topgallant staysail;* 24 *main royal staysail;* 25 *foresail fore course;* 26 *fore lower topsail;* 27 *fore upper topsail;* 28 *fore lower topgallant sail;* 29 *fore upper topgallant sail;* 30 *fore royal;* 31 *fore topmast staysail;* 32 *inner jib;* 33 *outer jib;* 34 *flying jib.*

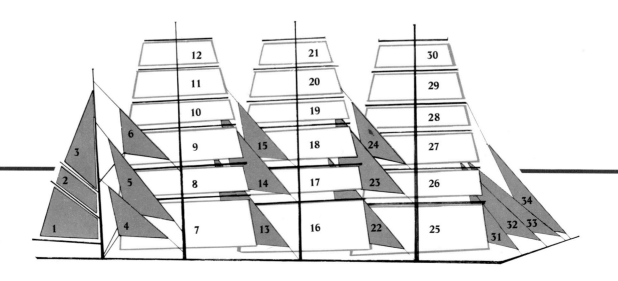

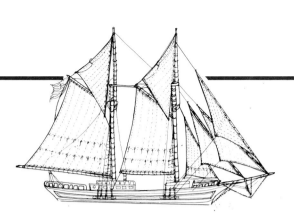

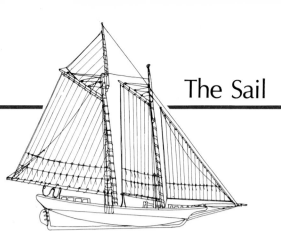

E. W. Morrison—*A fore-and-aft schooner with its classic rig, very efficient and easy to handle.*

Romp—*1847, a fishing schooner of the Newfoundland banks, built much like a clipper.*

The jib was a Dutch innovation. This triangular sail was hoisted on a shaft that extended from the bowsprit and was called the jib boom. This sail soon proved its worth, and early in the 18th century replaced the square bowsprit sails (the spritsail, and a smaller sail that had been early in the 17th century). Triangular sails called staysails appeared between one mast and another; the masts had increased in size and could thus support three and sometimes even four square sails. A fifth sail appeared after the Napoleonic era, and the square-sail rig reached its highest peak with the American and English clipper ships, to continue with the last great sailing ships made of iron and steel. In the middle of the 17th century, the mizzenmast lateen sail became the spanker, still a fore-and-aft sail but trapezoidal in shape and bound to the mast by two gaffs, or spars, that supported it horizontally top and bottom.

Apart from the jibs and the spanker, other fore-and-aft sails also appeared, especially on smaller vessels: rectangular spritsails hung from a diagonal spar that went from the base of the mast to the stern apex of the sails; and lugsails sustained by an oblique yard.

The spanker came to the fore during the 19th century, especially on board the large commercial sailing vessels of that period, like the schooners with three, four, and up to seven masts. As the sail was perfect-

ed, so was the rigging—all the cables, hooks, and pulleys expressly created for sailing ships, and each with its own technical name. While the sailor's task was always very hard, it was made easier by capstans and transmission systems. Indeed many of the last great sailing ships were able to make long voyages with a relatively small crew. Steel replaced plant fibers such as hemp and abaca for the rigging, and sailmaking was improved.

As pleasure sailing increased in popularity, pleasure craft everywhere adopted spankers and jibs, rounded out with other fore-and-aft sails. Nowadays the mainsail of cruise and regatta yachts is the Marconi spinnaker, so called because the mast that supports it, with its many cables, or shrouds, generally resembles a large radio antenna. Tall and triangular, and without a gaff—the upper supporting spar that acts as a link with the mast bearing only a spanker—the Marconi spinnaker is derived from the sail used by the Bermuda fishermen two centuries ago.

John B. Prescott—*A 5-masted schooner with a mixed rig, built to compete with the steamboat.*

Helen Barnet Gring—*A 4-masted schooner for coastal navigation, with a crew of only 16 men.*

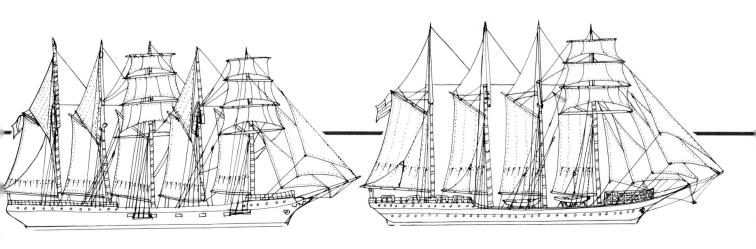

The Clipper Ship

FASTER THAN EVER

The verb "to clip" supplied the name for the final and most perfect stage in the evolution of the sailing ship—the clipper. It was born in the United States in the first decades of the 19th century, and it was later improved and brought to its technical peak in England. The clipper was a sailing ship with a very slender hull and very high masts, which made it extremely fast. There were always three masts, all with square sails, and up to 24 sails with a spanker, 6 stay sails, and 3 jibs.

The tea clippers—especially the British clippers—were famous for their speed, a factor which depended on a number of characteristics: the line of the hull, the quality and stowage of the cargo, the cleanliness of the outside of the hull below the waterline, the character and ability of the captain, the qualities of the officers, and the training and number of the crew.

With a light breeze, or even without wind and in the equatorial calms of the Atlantic, the clipper could advance silently at 5 or 6 knots, while with a strong breeze or moderate wind it could reach 12 to 14 knots, maintaining a very high daily average.

The American clippers were often built of unseasoned wood, while the British clippers, most of them constructed in the Aberdeen and Clyde shipyards, were made of well-seasoned timber, often of teak. The deckline sagged moderately, which gave the ship a graceful line, and there was a short forecastle and a small bridge house at the stern. The North American clippers had rigging systems that required a small crew. They were very large ships (almost always with a tonnage of more than 980 tons), and most were built in the shipyards of New England or New Orleans.

The clippers were usually owned by shipowners of the traditional type, who refused to organize into companies but were closely attached to their ships. Nevertheless it was the captain who really lived the life of his ship, stretching the limits of legality to win the annual "tea race" from China to England. Sailors on a clipper ship had to know what they were doing and be ready for action. Above all, a clipper sailor needed a strong physique, since the race back from China made exorbitant physical demands.

Passenger clippers, known as packets, had the same origin as the North American tea clippers and the same weakness. They were short-lived, because they were built of unseasoned wood that could not long survive the stress of fast sailing. The era of the ocean packets that connected America and northern Europe was a short one, about half a century, but these ships were the liners of their time. The packets had a first-class always set in the stern, a second-class in the center of the vessel, and a third-class in the bow, with steerage space for emigrants.

The colonial clippers were fast sailing ships of wood structure or wood and iron. Built in Great Britain up until 1890, they provided fast service to Australia, New Zealand, and Tasmania.

The only clipper ship which has survived, as a kind of monument, is the *Cutty Sark*, one of the last really fast sailing ships to be built in Great Britain. It was launched in 1869 and was used first as a tea clipper and then as a wool carrier. It was bought by English Capt. Wilfred Dowman in 1922 for use as a boys' training-ship and taken over in 1952 by the Cutty Sark Preservation Society. It is now a floating maritime museum on the Thames, at Greenwich, near London.

William Laurence—*The famous North American tea clipper, built in Maitland; its exceptional speed was due to its vast sail surface and the many bow jibs.*

The Clipper Ship

Cutty Sark—*The only surviving clipper, a relic of the past. It was launched on November 26, 1869, in the Scott and Linton shipyard at Dumbarton; designed by H. Linton as a tea clipper. It was used on the Australian wool route for more than ten years, with Richard Woodget as captain. But steam drove clippers off these routes. In 1895 the Cutty Sark's owner sold the ship to the Lisbon shipowner Ferreira, who used it for transatlantic voyages. It was bought for Great Britain in 1922 and became a naval monument and museum.*

Flying Cloud—*A 1,795-ton clipper ship built in New England. It left New York on June 6, 1851, and sailed around Cape Horn to San Francisco in 89 days and 21 hours.*

Essex—*A British vessel owned by the East India Company. It was launched in 1751 and had more sail than any other ship of its time: 63 sails, with 21 on the mainmast alone.*

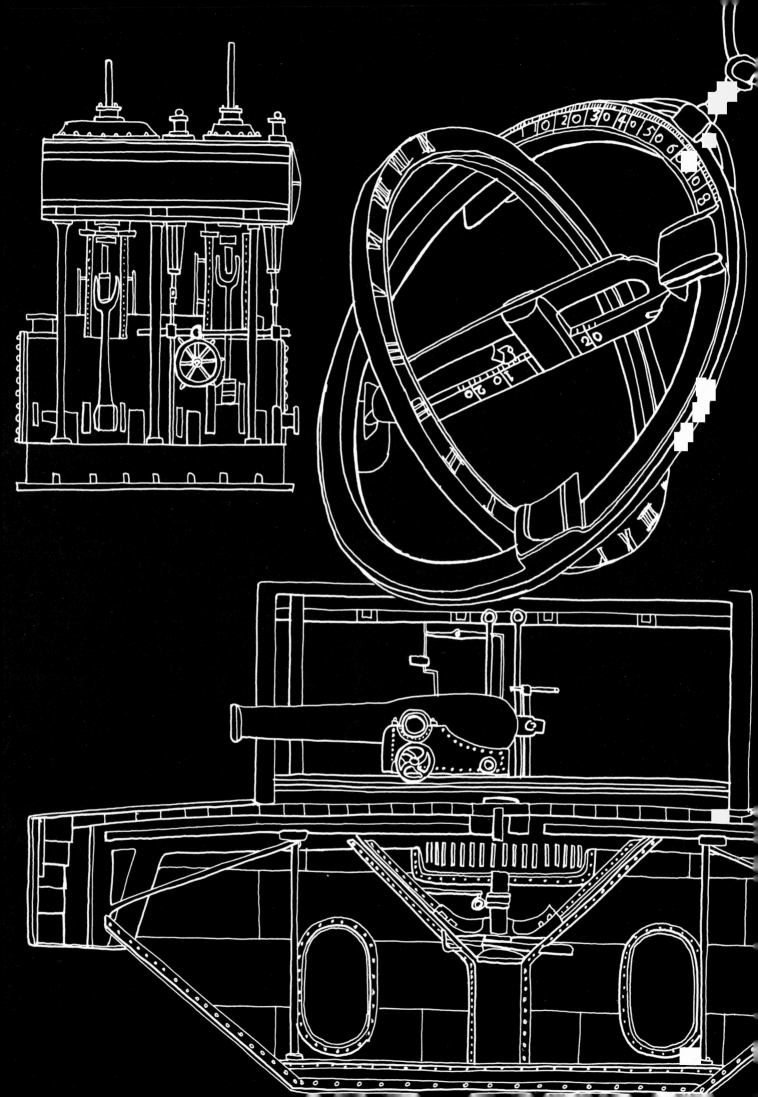

World War I

The industrial revolution had a profound effect on the evolution and technical development of the ship.

In 1861 French engineer Alphonse Beau de Rochas outlined the principles of an engine that did not use steam and coal, but instead was to use the new fuels that had come onto the world's industrial scene: oil, with its derivatives, gasoline and naphtha, or fuel oil. Beau de Rochas's internal-combustion engine was based on four conditions: (1) maximum cylinder volume and minimum coaling surface; (2) maximum speed of expansion; (3) maximum expansion ratio; (4) maximum ignition pressure.

The principle of the four-stroke internal-combustion engine was established. The Italians Barsanti and Matteucci had built engines of this type in 1854, and in 1860 the Frenchman Lenoir had tried to develop an illuminating-gas engine for industrial purposes. The Abbeé de Hautefeuille, in 1678, and Denis Papin, in 1688, had already attempted this with the use of gunpowder.

German engineers Otto and Langen created an atmospheric engine of the Barsanti and Matteucci type in 1867 and then, in 1876, applied Beau de Rochas's principles to an engine that can be considered the prototype of the modern internal-combustion engine and that was adopted on a large scale. The first fuel used was illuminating gas; then came the "poor" gas produced by the incomplete oxidation of coal, and finally gasoline.

Around the turn of this century, the internal-combustion engine was installed in submarines. It was much smaller than the steam engine, and the saving of space was considerable. The first European vessel to

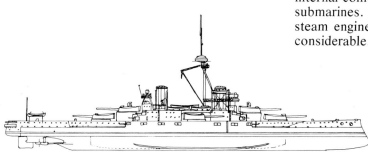

São Paulo—*A Brazilian battleship built by British shipyards and launched in 1907. A typical example of the large and impressive battleship used during World War I.*

Good Hope—*A cruiser of the* Drake *class, launched in England in 1901. Displacement: 14,100 tons; speed: 24 knots; two 233-mm (9.2-in.) guns; sixteen of 152-mm (6-in.); 15 smaller guns; crew: 900 men. It was sunk in the Battle of Coronel.*

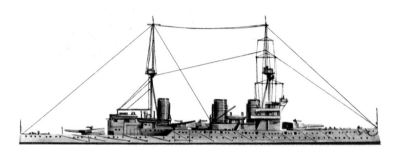

Invincible—*Launched for the British fleet in 1907, this ship represented something truly new. Displacement: 17,400 tons; length: 171.3 meters (187 yards); speed: 26.5 knots; four propellers; eight 305-mm (12-in.) and sixteen 4-inch guns.*

use the new means of propulsion was the Italian submarine *Delfino*, built in 1895 to plans by Gen. Giacinto Pullino of the naval engineers. The internal-combustion engine was then used on fast military vessels and pleasure boats. A further development was the work of German engineer Rudolf Diesel (1858–1913). In his engine, the ignition of the highly compressed fuel took place inside the cylinder itself. (In the gasoline engine, air and fuel are mixed in a carburetor before the fuel is inducted into the cylinder.) The diesel engine had a two-stroke cycle, with slow combustion and steady pressure. It is the working cycle (and the form of ignition) that distinguishes the two kinds of internal-combustion engines, those based on the Beau de Rochas-Otto principle, and those of Diesel. A host of improvements were made subsequently, from the four-stroke, compressed-air engine to the two-stroke, double-acting engine with a fuel pump, and the modern supercharged exhaust-gas engine. The *Selandia* was the world's first ship

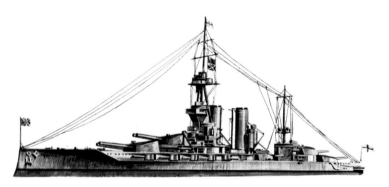

Iron Duke—*One of the most powerful British battleships, put into service in 1914. Displacement: 25,000 tons; length: 186 meters (203 yards); speed: 21 knots; ten 342-mm (13.5-in.) and twelve 152-mm (6-in.) guns; 4 torpedo tubes; crew: 950 men. Admiral Jellicoe's flagship at the Battle of Jutland.*

Lion—*British battle cruiser of 1910. It flew Admiral Beatty's flag at the Battle of Jutland. Displacement: 26,350 tons; length: 204 meters (223 yards); speed: 26 knots; eight 242-mm (13.5-in.) and sixteen 100-mm (4-in.) guns; 2 torpedo tubes; crew: 1,000 men.*

to use an internal-combustion engine, inaugurating a new era in the history of navigation with its maiden voyage on February 12, 1912. When World War I broke out, warships and merchant ships seemed to be highly perfected instruments that could play a decisive role because of their varied forms and adaptability to different functions. Increasingly complex methods and tactics were adopted in naval warfare, thanks to the development of armor and artillery and optical-sighting and range-finding devices. The larger naval artillery pieces could fire simultaneously against the enemy, through a general centralized aiming-and-firing system. The range of these guns was as much as nine miles and more. The traditional conventions of naval warfare were overturned with the appearance of such new combat vessels as the torpedo boat and the torpedo-boat destroyer, which could be hurled against the enemy while the huge battleships maneuvered into new firing positions. Light combat ships gave additional protection to the battle

fleet by rapid scouting and quick sighting of the enemy. A new kind of combat, even at night, engaged torpedo boats, scout cruisers, and light cruisers.

But the heart of the fleet was always the battleship, even though it was only used in larger-scale clashes. Around 1915–1916 the British Admiralty put into service the finest fighting ships of the time: the *Queen Elizabeth*, the *Barham*, the *Malaya*, the *Valiant*, and the *Warspite*. They were armed with 15-inch guns mounted in 3 armored turrets. This arrangement of artillery was first made by Italian shipbuilders in the construction of the 18,400-ton *Dante Alighieri*. The British battleships, with a speed of 25 knots and a displacement of about 31,000 tons, remained in service for almost a quarter of a century; three of them—the *Barham*, the *Queen Elizabeth*, and the *Valiant*—were sunk only in 1941, during World War II.

The cruiser also played an important part in the fleet. Following the lead of the Royal Navy, this classification was assigned to

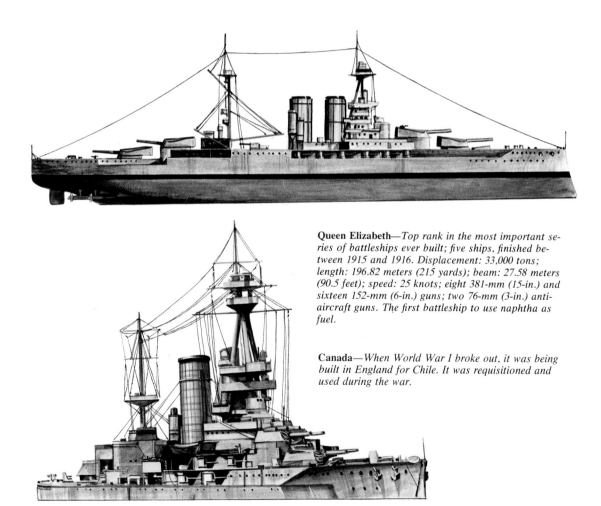

Queen Elizabeth—*Top rank in the most important series of battleships ever built; five ships, finished between 1915 and 1916. Displacement: 33,000 tons; length: 196.82 meters (215 yards); beam: 27.58 meters (90.5 feet); speed: 25 knots; eight 381-mm (15-in.) and sixteen 152-mm (6-in.) guns; two 76-mm (3-in.) anti-aircraft guns. The first battleship to use naphtha as fuel.*

Canada—*When World War I broke out, it was being built in England for Chile. It was requisitioned and used during the war.*

148

Tsukuba—*Japanese armored cruiser of 1905: 15,000 tons; speed: 21 knots.*

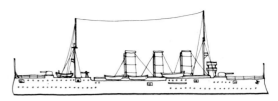

Königsberg—*German cruiser of 1905. Displacement: 3,390 tons; speed: 24 knots.*

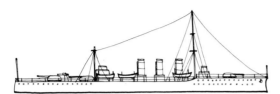

Galatea—*British cruiser of 1914. Displacement: 3,520 tons; length: 125 meters (137 yards); speed: 29 knots; two 152-mm (6-in.) and six 102-mm (4-in.) guns.*

Seydlitz—*German battle cruiser (enlarged* Moltke *class launched 1911). Part of Hipper's squadron at Jutland.*

outdated vessels as well, such as the frigate and the corvette. The creation of the *Dreadnought* had a decisive effect on the development of the cruiser as well. When the new battleships were built, following the lead of the British, it became clear that if the cruiser were to carry out its assigned tasks, it had to be able to move at a speed at least 20 percent faster than that of the slow battleship. The obvious solution was the turbine engine, which reduced the weight of the ship and increased its speed. The German and the English kept their outdated armored cruisers in service but began producing a kind of light cruiser, or scout cruiser. The Germans concentrated on the building of very fast ships, the basic weapon of which was the fast-firing 4.1-inch gun. Great Britain, instead, devoted greater attention to the weight of the shell, relying on the already tested 6-inch gun. In 1916–1917 Germany also developed more efficient weapons for its cruisers and installed them even on older models. In 1912 the English had begun using oil-firing combustion on their ships. The elimination of boilers and steam and the consequent reduction in weight made it possible to armor-plate cruisers of less than 4,000 tons, including ships of the *Arethusa* class (1914; 3,512 tons; three 6-inch guns; four 4-inch guns; two antiaircraft 3-inch guns, or one 4-inch gun; eight 21-inch torpedo tubes; speed of 29 knots), which were plated with 3-inch-thick

armor that could stand up to 4-inch shells. The cruisers *Quarto* and *Nino Bixio*, with mixed combustion, are of the same period and are excellent examples of the building techniques of the Italians, who were famous for turning out fast ships.

After the Japanese victory at the Battle of Tsushima (1905), the cruiser was assigned an important role in modern naval strategy. Eventually it was as powerfully armed as the battleship, but it was faster and more maneuverable. Ultimately it was used as an attack vessel on its own.

So was born the battle cruiser. It was Lord Fisher, First Lord of the Admiralty, who gave the British navy the battle cruisers that were soon to win fame in sea warfare. Such a ship was the *Inflexible*, of 17,250 tons (armed with 305-mm [12-in.] cannons, protected by armor 152-mm [7-in.] thick, with a speed of 25 to 26 knots), which was soon followed by ships of the *Lion* and *Renown* class. Comparable ships were the German *Von der Tann* (1908–1910; 19,400 tons; eight 280-mm [11-in.] guns; a speed of 27.4 knots) and *Derfflinger*, of 28,000 tons.

When World War I broke out, in August 1914, the German cruiser squadron in Asia did serious damage to British merchant shipping in that region. The exploits of the cruiser *Emden* (1909; 4,200 tons; coal-burning with reciprocating engines; a speed of 24 knots) is still remembered for private war

Leipzig—*German light cruiser of 1905.*

Nürnberg—*German light cruiser of 1906.*

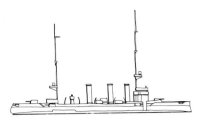

Emden—*A cruiser of the German navy; it made a famous raiding voyage in the Indian Ocean.*

Prinzregent Luitpold—*German battleship of the* Kaiser *class, launched in 1913.*

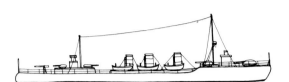

Tatsuta—*Japanese cruiser of 1918. Displacement: 3,504 tons; length: 120.8 meters (132 yards); speed: 33 knots; crew: 332 men.*

Collingwood—*British battleship of the* Saint Vincent *class, launched in 1918. It survived the Battle of Jutland.*

against English, French, and Russian bases. The *Emden* was finally intercepted and sunk by the cruiser *Sydney*, the most heavily armed Australian ship of the time (5,511 tons), as it was landing men to destroy radio installations on the Cocos-Keeling Islands in the Pacific.

The concept of fast attack resulted in the torpedo-boat destroyer, a very fast warship. The first English ships of this type were the *Rattlesnake* and *Gossamer*, built in 1886, and almost contemporary were the Italian *Folgore* and *Saetta*. But the first ship to which the name was applied and the first to enter active service in intercepting and hunting down fast torpedo boats was the British *Havock*, launched in 1893. Its maximum speed was 27 knots. The use of the Parsons

turbine increased the speed of the torpedo-boat destroyer. The *Viper* (370 tons), the first British destroyer to adopt the turbine engine, reached 36.6 knots during speed tests in 1900.

After the year 1900, the major navies got busy building faster and larger destroyers, but every knot over 30 knots required an inordinate increase in power and was extremely expensive.

During World War I, the destroyer defended large battleships against attack by torpedo boats and enemy destroyers and attacked enemy battleships. Destroyers and cruisers were used as an attack and surveillance force and as minelayers and minesweepers. When submarine warfare acquired strategic importance in 1917, destroyers were given another

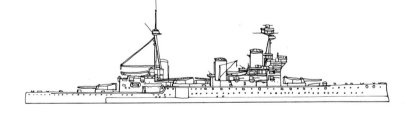

Inflexible—*Battle cruiser that sank with its sister ship, the* Invincible, *during the Battle of the Flakland Islands. Displacement: 18,454 tons; length: 174 meters (190 yards); speed: 26 knots; eight 305-mm (12-in.) and sixteen 100-mm (4-in.) guns; 5 torpedo tubes; crew: 800 men.*

Dresden—*German light cruiser of 1907.*

Glasgow—*British light cruiser of 1909.*

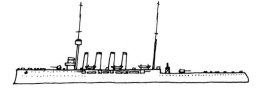

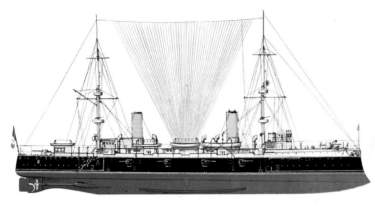

Carlo Alberto—*Italian armored cruiser launched in 1896 and designed by E. Masdea. Displacement: 6,715 tons; speed: 19 knots; twelve 152-mm (6-in.), six 120-mm (4.7-in.), two 75-mm (3-in.), and other lighter guns; 4 torpedo tubes. Marconi carried out his wireless telegraphy experiments on this vessel. In 1918, it was turned into a troopship and renamed Zenson.*

Napoli—*Italian armored cruiser designed by Colonel Cuniberti and launched at Castellammare di Stabia in 1905. Displacement: 12,625 tons; speed: 22 knots; two 305-mm (12-in.) and twelve 205-mm (8-in.) guns; 20 anti-torpedo guns; 2 torpedo tubes.*

San Giorgio—*Italian armored cruiser designed by Edoardo Masdea and built at Castellammare di Stabia in 1908. Displacement: 9,830 tons; four 154-mm (6-in.), eight 190-mm (7.5-in.), and eighteen 76-mm (12-pdr) guns. During World War I, it took part in naval actions in the Adriatic.*

Giuseppe Garibaldi—*Italian armored cruiser built by the Ansaldo shipyards in Genoa in 1901. Displacement: 7,400 tons; speed: 20 knots; one 254-mm (10-in.), two 203-mm (8-in.), fourteen 152-mm (6-in.), ten 76-mm (12-pdr), and six 47-mm (3-pdr) guns; 4 torpedo tubes. It was sunk by the German submarine U-4 off the Dalmation coast during World War I.*

tactical role. They created an antisubmarine screen to protect both the war fleet and cargo convoys.

The natural adversary of the destroyer was the torpedo boat, a small, fast vessel designed for surprise attack and coastal defense. Its first weapon was the submarine mine, towed or launched, and then the torpedo. The torpedo boat was the successor of the fireboat, any small vessel filled with inflammable material and rammed against the wooden hulls of the enemy's ships. The torpedo was extremely popular at the end of the 19th century, especially in France. The appearance of the faster and more powerful destroyer seemed to make the torpedo boat obsolete, but its armament and tactical use were modernized, and the torpedo boat continued to function as a small assault craft in the form of submarine-mine ships, escort vessels, and gunboats.

When World War I broke out, the navies involved in hostilities developed a new vessel based on the torpedo boat, with a powerful internal-combustion engine. This vessel was used for antisubmarine defense and coastal patrol. The Adriatic coast of Italy had no natural defenses, and Austrian submarines and light naval forces represented a serious menace. In March 1916, after various attempts had been made, 16 new Italian vessels entered service. They were called Motoscafi Antisommergibile (MAS), or antisubmarine motorboats, and were about 50 feet long. There were 2 versions: the 11.4-ton gunboat, armed with a 47/40-mm (18/15-in.) gun, two 6.5-mm (0.25-in.) Colt machine guns, and 4 or 6 torpedoes for launching and one for towing; and the 12.3-ton torpedo boat, armed with two 356-mm (14-in.) torpedoes, later replaced by a 450-mm (18-in.) type, and 2 or 3 Colt machine guns. These early versions of a vessel that was to win distinction during the war owed much to the similar ships built in 1905 by the Yarrow and Thorneycroft shipyards. The agile and powerful motor torpedo boats for antisubmarine

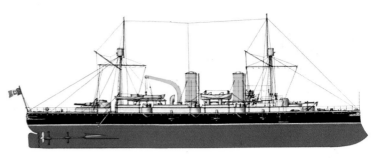

Giovanni Bausan—*Italian ramming torpedo boat, built 1885 by Armstrong, England. Displacement: 3,330 tons; speed: 17 knots; two 254-mm (10-in.), four 152-mm (6-in.) and four 57-mm (6-pdr) guns; 3 torpedo tubes.*

Montebello—*Italian torpedo-boat cruiser, designed by B. Brin and launched La Spezia in 1888. Displacement: 860 tons; four 57-mm (6-pdr); 3 torpedo tubes.*

warfare soon attracted the attention of military experts all over the world. MAS boats commanded by Costanzo Ciano performed several daring exploits. On December 10, 1917, two MAS boats commanded by Luigi Rizzo and Andrea Ferrarini entered the port of Trieste and sank the Austrian battleship *Wien.* On February 10, 1918, three MAS boats with Ciano, Rizzo, Ferrarini, and the writer Gabriele d'Annunzio aboard, entered the bay of Bakar, near Fiume, and sank another Austrian ship. On June 10 of the same year, Luigi Rizzo and Aonzo sank the Austrian battleship *Santo Stefano* off the Dalmatian coast, eluding the battleship's escort of smaller ships. On November 1, 1918, Paolucci and Rossetti broke through the barriers set up in the port of Pola and sank another important Austrian vessel, the dreadnought *Viribus Unitis.*

German submarines launched their first offensives between February 22, 1915, and April 24, 1916, putting an end to the debate between the supporters of the capital ship (the large warship) and those who supported the theory, dear to the French, of a fleet's *pouissière navale,* that is, attack power made up of torpedo boats and destroyers. The submarine was a more serious threat to slow cargo ships, with rudimentary armament, than to powerful warships. The submarine was still too slow and clumsy to make successful attacks on the big, heavily armed fighting ships. Moreover the tactics of the submarine violated international shipping conventions. The German government, concerned over the international political repercussions of submarine warfare, limited submarine warfare. The sinking of the transatlantic liner *Lusitania* (June 5, 1915), the steamship *Arabic* (August 30, 1915), and the *Sussex* (April 24, 1916) had aroused indignation throughout the world. Henceforth attacks on passenger ships and the shipping of neutral nations were forbidden. Attacks on the cargo vessels of the Allies (Britain, France, Russia, Turkey, and Italy) were to be *(cont'd. on p. 155)*

Benedetto Brin—*Battleship launched in 1901. Displacement: 32,427 tons; speed: 20 knots; four 305-mm (12-in.), four 203-mm (8-in.) and twelve 152-mm (6-in.) guns, as well as smaller-caliber guns.*

Ammiraglio di Saint Bon—*Italian armored cruiser launched at Venice in 1897. Displacement: 9,800 tons; speed: 18 knots; four 254-mm (10-in.), eight 152-mm (6-in.), and eight 120-mm (4.7-in.) guns, as well as smaller-caliber guns; 4 torpedo tubes.*

Andrea Doria—*Italian battleship of 1913. Displacement: 22,700 tons; speed: 22 knots; thirteen 305-mm (12-in.) and sixteen 152-mm (6-in.) guns, as well as smaller anti-torpedo-boat guns; 3 torpedo tubes.*

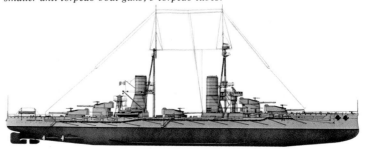

The Submarine

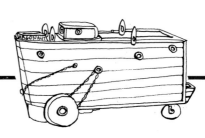

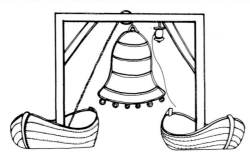

Catalan Bell—*This wooden vessel, reinforced with iron staves, was used in the 17th century to recover underwater wreckage.*

FROM BELL TO PERISCOPE

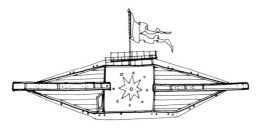

The De Son Boat—*Never tested. Built in Rotterdam in 1653.*

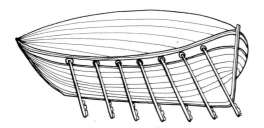

Borelli's Machine—*Designed in 1680, it was supposed to move by oar power, but was never built.*

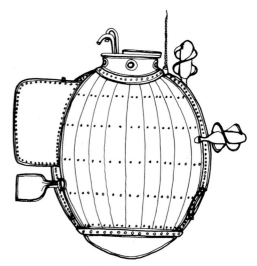

Turtle—*Built in 1775 by Bushnell, the* Turtle *was used by American Sergeant Lee to mine the British frigate Eagle.*

Along with the evolution of construction technique, the triumph of engine propulsion, and the new and revolutionary conception of commercial and fighting ships, the 19th century was also marked by the introduction of submarine navigation. Leonardo da Vinci was the first to consider underwater navigation. In 1620 the Dutchman Cornelius van Drebbel built a wooden submarine moved by oars, the forerunner of the modern submarine. The submarine used by Sgt. Ezra Lee in 1775, during the American Revolution, was a genuine underwater vessel. David Bushnell's *American Turtle* had an internal variable-level water tank that let it alter its weight. Bushnell mounted a drill on the *Turtle* and tried to bore a hole in the hull of the frigate *Eagle*. In the early 1800s, Robert Fulton submerged in his *Nautilus* for an hour, and later for 6 hours, at a depth of 25 feet, but the new vessel was considered an unfair combat weapon by the naval authorities of the time, and was rejected.

Sixty years later, the Americans again took up the idea of the submarine as a means of underwater warfare. During the Civil War, the Confederates built the *David*, with a cylindrical hull 60 feet long, driven

by a propeller turned by 8 men. The *David* was sunk 5 times in action and salvaged each time. In 1864, it finally managed to sink the northern corvette *Housatonic*, of 1,240 tons, with a bow torpedo.

After 1860 submarines driven by steam engines for surface navigation and by electric engines for underwater navigation were built in Europe. Later submarines were equipped with the new piston engine invented in 1897 by German engineer Rudolf Diesel.

In the 1890s, Gustave Zedé in France built the *Gymnote*, Giacinto Pullino in Italy built the *Delfino*, and John Holland in America built the *Plunger*, the first really efficient examples of what is now considered one of the most important ships in any modern navy. Submarine tonnage increased; and so did offensive power, speed, and range. The submarine played a major role in World War I. Advanced vessels appeared with a double hull, the inner one cylindrical and tough, the outer one flared and light in weight. They had a displacement varying from 300 to 900 tons, a speed of about 16 knots, and a range from 2,000 to 5,000 miles. They were equipped with improved technical devices, such as the

Aquapede—*Designed and built by Alvary Templo in 1896 and driven by a pedal system.*

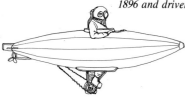

El Ictineo—*The first modern submarine, built by the Spaniard Monturiol in 1862 and powered by a steam engine.*

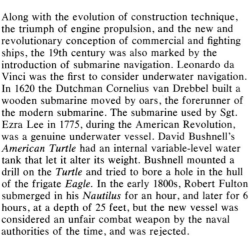

The Submarine

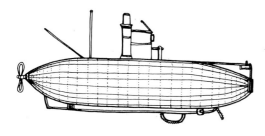

Nautilus—*Built by Robert Fulton in 1801, it had an auxiliary sail for surface navigation.*

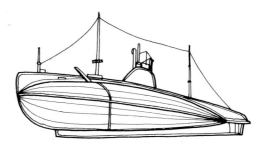

B-1—*Designed by J. Holland, the father of the modern submarine, the B-1 was built in 1907. Tonnage: 147 tons; speed: 8.5 knots.*

Leonardo da Vinci—*A modern submarine with conventional propulsion. Submersion displacement: 2,387 tons. Ten 533-mm (21-in.) torpedo tubes.*

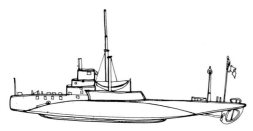

Argonaut—*An American design of 1898. It was to move over the sea bottom on its wheels.*

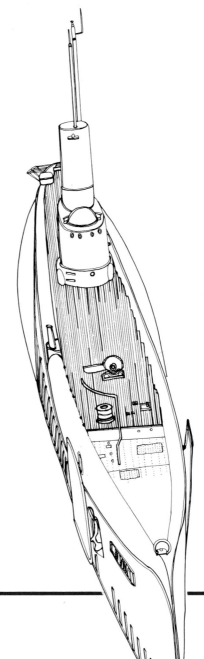

Delfino—*The first Italian submarine, with a Fiat gasoline engine. It was built in 1903.*

small-diameter attack periscope and the gyrocompass.

The submarine is essentially a military vessel. The average-size submarine with conventional propulsion has 2 diesel engines of 2,000 to 25,000 hp each, with a maximum surface speed of about 18 knots. Electric engines, mounted on the same tail shafts as the diesel, are used for navigation in submersion and provide a top speed of 8 to 10 knots per hour. The control tower has 2 periscopes, one for observation and one for attack. On the bow side of the tower there is a 76- to 102-mm (3- to 4-in.) artillery piece and sometimes even twin antiaircraft machine guns. At both bow and stern there are from 4 to 6 torpedo-launching tubes, equipped with as many as 16 torpedoes.

Valves, rudders, engine exhaust-ports, ballast tanks, and trim tanks are controlled by a single oil-pressure system. The controls are centralized and can be handled by one man. In the center of the bulkheads are two large vertical tubes (Bernardis escape chambers) with two watertight doors and a door opening on the deck. If the submarine is unable to surface, the crew can be evacuated two by two, wearing closed-cycle oxygen masks.

U-boat 46—*A German World War I submarine.*

Giulio Cesare—*Italian battleship launched in 1911 at the Ansaldo shipyards in Genoa. Displacement: 28,800 tons; waterline length: 186.4 meters (204 yards); speed: 28 knots; thirteen 320-mm (12-in.), eighteen 120-mm (4.7-in.), fourteen 100-mm (3-in.), and lighter weapons.*

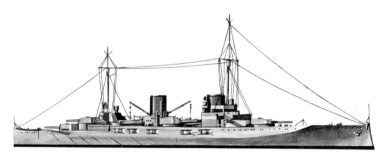

Goeben—*German battle cruiser of 1911. It fought against French squadrons in the Mediterranean during World War I; when the war ended, it went to the Turks. Displacement: 22,640 tons; length: 183 meters (200 yards); speed: 27 knots; ten 280-mm (11-in.) and twelve 152-mm (5.9-in.) guns; 3 torpedo tubes; crew: 1,107 men.*

Varese—*Italian armored cruiser of 1899. Displacement: 7,350 tons; length: 363 feet; beam: 59 feet. Armament: one 10-inch, two 8-inch, fourteen 6-inch and other lighter weapons. Speed: 20 knots. Complement: 524.*

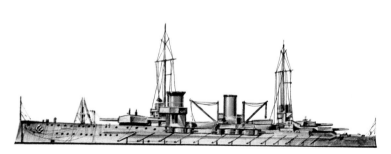

Moltke—*German battle cruiser of 1910, Von Hipper's flagship at the Battle of Jutland, the most important naval battle of World War I. The* Moltke, *sister ship of the* Goeben, *was badly damaged at Jutland.*

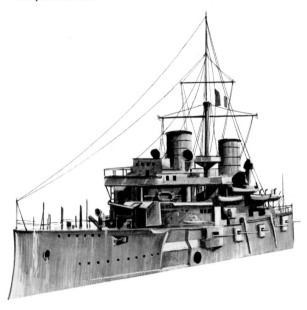

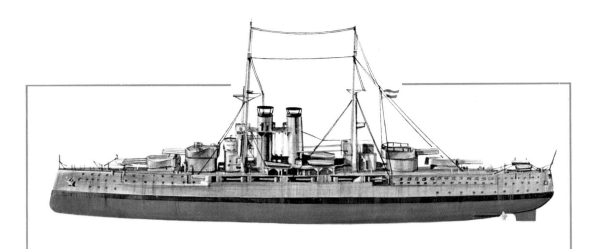

Szent Istran—*During the 1914–1918 war, the Austro-Hungarian navy suffered two serious losses at the hands of the Italian MAS, the antisubmarine motorboats. At dawn on June 10, 1918, as it took part with its sister ship, the* Tegetthoff, *in naval action against the Italian barrage in the canal of Otranto, the Austrian battleship* Szent Istran *(displacement: 20,000 tons; length: 159 meters [174 yards]; speed: 21 knots; twelve 305-mm [12-in.], twelve 149-mm [6-in.], and 20 smaller guns; 4 torpedo tubes; crew: 1,000 men) was hit by 2 torpedoes fired by the MAS 15, under the command of Luigi Rizzo; it then overturned and sank.*

effected in strict accordance with the rules of international maritime law. These rules did not apply to military vessels, and German U-boats caused great consternation after the sinking of the English scout cruiser *Pathfinder* and three other British cruisers, the *La Hogue*, the *Aboukir*, and the *Cressy*. These three vessels were all torpedoed on the same day by Commander Weddingen's submarine *U-21*. Early in the war there were 811 submarines under construction in German ship-

yards, although only 338 actually saw action. German U-boats also attacked naval supply lines along the Arctic route that the Allied navies used to furnish the Russian army with arms and ammunition. The Allied blockade stopped the supply of raw materials for the German war industry. So Germany developed cargo submarines, including the 2,500-ton *Deutschland* and *Bremen*, both of which made several voyages to South America. But the land war was not going so well for the

Scharnhorst—*German armored cruiser, Von Spee's flagship in the battles of Coronel and the Falklands. Displacement: 11,417 tons; speed: 22.5 knots; length: 130 meters (148 yards); eight 208-mm (8.2-in.), six 152-mm (5.9-in.), and 20 smaller guns; crew: 765 men.*

Derfflinger—*German battle cruiser of 1913. Displacement: 26,180 tons; speed: 26.5 knots; length: 194 meters (689 feet); eight 305-mm (12-in.), twelve 152-mm (5.9-in.), and twelve 4.1-inch guns; 4 torpedo tubes; crew: 1,214 men. When the Battle of Jutland ended, this ship was little more than a floating hull.*

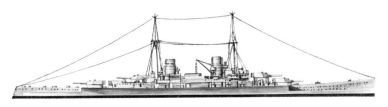

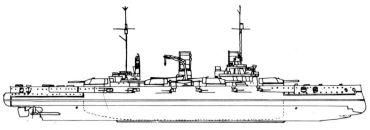

Westfalen—German battleship of the Nassau class, put into service in 1907. It took part in the Battle of Jutland. On August 19, 1916, it was torpedoed by the British submarine E-23 but was not too badly damaged.

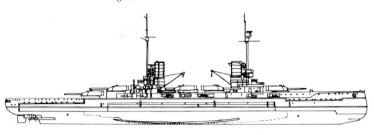

Friedrich der Grosse—German battleship of the Kaiser class, launched in 1910. Speed: 22 knots. At Jutland, it was hit by two British broadsides but not badly damaged. It was sunk by its crew at Scapa Flow in 1918.

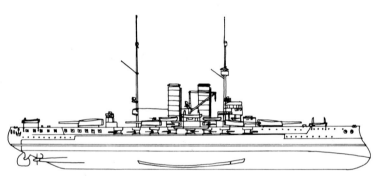

Erzherzog Franz Ferdinand—Austro-Hungarian battleship of the Radetzky class, launched in 1912. It took part in the bombardment of Ancona in May 1915.

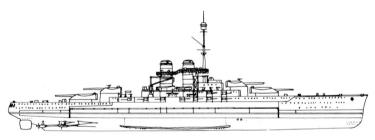

Ersatz Monach—Austro-Hungarian cruiser, launched in 1914. Because of the war, it was left unfinished, and its heavy guns (355 mm [14 in.]) were used on land on the Italian front.

Utah—A North American battleship of the Florida class, launched in 1911 and part of the Atlantic Fleet. It ended its career as a target ship.

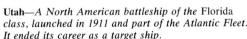

Germans, and on January 9, 1917, Chancellor Bethmann-Hollweg removed the restrictions on submarine warfare.

The year 1917 marked the start of an all-out submarine offensive, which continued till the end of the war. The German navy torpedoed Allied ships and any neutral vessels that had anything to do with the Allies.

The Allies built very few submarines and even fewer minelayers. Germany launched some 116 minelayers, with a range of 4,600 miles and a supply of 36 torpedoes mounted in vertical tubes. The British class K submarines, large steam-powered vessels that were hard to maneuver and slow in submersing, were not successful in combat. Nor was the class M monitor submarine more impressive, with an armored tower and one 305-mm (12-in.) gun. But British ships built to hunt down enemy submarines underwater proved to be highly successful. The Allies did all they could to combat the German submarine threat, which became extremely critical in 1917. Supply convoys were escorted by antisubmarine ships. The Allies built depth charges and bomb-launching ships and developed hydrophones that could pick up sound waves of submarines in submersion. Antitorpedo and submarine nets were laid down at harbor entrances and even around ships. Camouflage was used, and zigzagging became a standard maneuver. The attacking submarine had a hard time torpedoing ships on a zigzag course. Ships were adapted or specially built to track down submarines:

Connecticut—Of the class of the same name, put into service in 1906, a standard American battleship.

patrol ships; fast motorboats; camouflaged cargo ships (the Q ships which appeared in the summer of 1915 were famous); and sailing ships camouflaging heavy armament that included even torpedo tubes. Many camouflaged ships flew flags of neutral countries. When a German submarine approached to make the inspection authorized by international law, the camouflaged ship would run up its true colors and fire on the submarine. When the United States entered the war, it became clear that the German underwater offensive was a failure. From 1914 until the 1918 armistice, the German navy lost 198 submarines, 178 of them sunk at sea, 14 lost in evacuated bases, and 6 interned in foreign ports.

Submarine warfare was a new feature of naval combat, but it played a decisive role during World War I. The battleships also had a chance to show their mettle, and new weapons and strategy were introduced. Three episodes may illustrate the functions of the battleship during World War I.

On November 1, 1914, off Coronel on the coast of Chile, a German squadron commanded by Admiral von Spee clashed with a British naval force under Rear Adm. Sir Christopher Cradock. When Japan declared war on Germany, Von Spee had to evacuate Far Eastern waters, and he headed for South America. The Germans had two powerfully armed ships, the battle cruisers *Scharnhorst* and *Gneisenau* under Von Spee's command. Cradock had older ships manned by naval

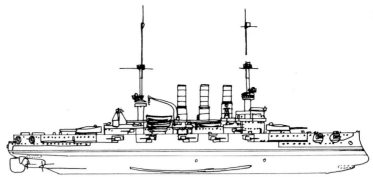

Schlesien—*Of the* Deutschland *class, launched in 1906; it took part in the Battle of Jutland.*

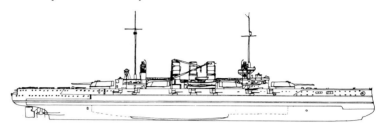

Helgoland—*German battleship of the class of the same name, launched in 1909.*

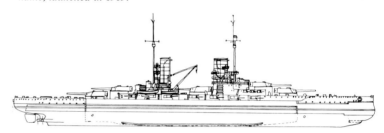

König—*German battleship that gave its name to a class made up of 4 ships. At Jutland, it was hit by 4 English shells. In October 1917 it sank the Russian battleship* Slava *during a naval battle off the islands of the Baltic Sea.*

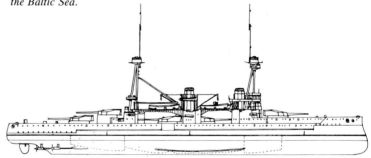

Neptune—*British battleship, launched in 1911. It took* ▶ *part in the Battle of Jutland on May 31, 1916.*

Bellerophon—*Battleship of the* Téméraire *class, launched in 1909. On May 26, 1911, it collided with the* Inflexible. ▼

Regina Elena—*A pre-*Dreadnought *battleship of the Italian navy.*

Canopus—*British pre-* Dreadnought. *Guardship at Port Stanley in 1914 (it took no part in the Battle of the Falklands). It saw service in 1915 at the Dardanelles.*

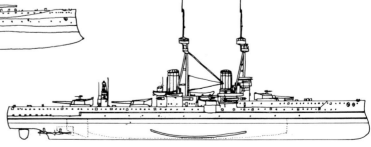

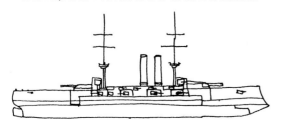

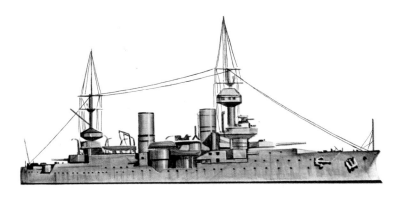

Bouvet—*French battleship launched in 1896; it took part, with English ships, in the attempt to force an entrance into the strait of the Dardanelles, held by the Turks, allies of the Germans. The ship hit a mine and 670 men lost their lives. Displacement: 12,012 tons; length: 120 meters (131 yards); speed: 17 knots; two 305-mm (12-in.), two 274-mm (10.8-in.), and 46 smaller guns; 4 torpedo tubes.*

Delaware—*One of the first American battleships to be modeled on the British* Dreadnought *in 1909.*

Italian MAS—*A fast antisubmarine motorboat, almost noiseless because of its electric engines. Displacement: 20 tons; speed: 28 knots; 2 torpedo tubes; antisubmarine bombs. During the war, Italy used 244 MAS boats in all; 178 were in construction when the armistice was signed.*

reserves. The *Canopus*, the battleship on which the British fleet relied for its firing power, was a very slow and outdated vessel. The German guns opened fire at 7:50 A.M. on November 1 and immediately demonstrated their superior destructive power.

The English cruiser *Good Hope* was hit repeatedly and finally went down. A second cruiser, the *Monmouth*, was seriously damaged in the encounter and was sunk during a second German attack. The cruiser *Glasgow* and the armed vessel *Otranto* were lost, while the German squadron suffered only light damage. The gates of the Atlantic now lay open before it.

In England, news of the defeat inflicted by the German fleet in the Pacific had a devastating effect. Another fleet was quickly dispatched to the South Atlantic. The backbone of this force were the modern battle cruisers *Invincible* and *Inflexible*. This squadron was commanded by Adm. Sir Doveton Sturdee. Allied forces caught up with Von Spee off the Falkland Islands, about 400 miles east of the Atlantic end of the Strait of Magellan. This time the British won the day. The two German cruisers *Scharnhorst* and *Gneisenau*

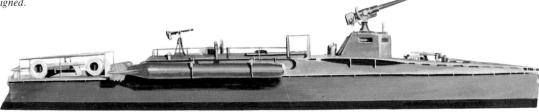

Italian MAS—*An antitorpedo boat created by the Società Veneziana Automobili Navali (12.3 tons). Two 356-mm (14-in.) torpedoes, later replaced by 450-mm (17.7-in.) torpedoes; 2 to 3 Colt machine guns; 4 torpedo tubes.*

were sunk at 4:17 P.M. and 6:02 P.M., respectively. Only one German ship, the *Dresden*, managed to get away.

The most important naval battle took place off the coast of the Jutland Bank, between Helgoland and Cuxhaven, on May 31, 1916. For the first time in naval history, there was a direct clash between great battleships. Let us try to reconstruct an imaginary log of this battle, one of the most decisive in the war. It was partly as a result of the Battle of Jutland that Germany concentrated on submarine warfare and indiscriminately fired on enemy and neutral ships. It was because of these attacks that the United States entered the war in 1917.

May 30, 1916: The German High Seas Fleet left its bases in the north hoping to lure part of the British fleet into a trap. The British Grand Fleet left its base at Scapa Flow and the Battle Cruiser Fleet sailed out of Rosyth in the Firth of Forth. The fleet of battle cruisers was commanded by Vice Adm. Sir David Beatty. The Grand Fleet was commanded by Adm. Sir John Jellicoe.

May 31, 1916—2:28 P.M.: Beatty's fleet headed toward the Skagerrak to rendezvous with Jellicoe's fleet. The light cruiser *Gala-tea*, scouting on the east flank of the formation, sighted the enemy. When Hipper sighted the English he turned south hoping to lure them toward Admiral Scheer's High Seas Fleet. The two cruiser fleets opened fire in a running battle. Beatty's force outnumbered Hipper's six to five. The German cruiser *Von der Tann* blew up the British *Indefatigable*.

The British battleship squadron caught up with Beatty's cruisers and opened fire on Hipper's ships. The battle cruiser *Queen Mary* engaged in battle with the cruisers *Derfflinger* and *Seydlitz* and was sunk. Meanwhile the German ships had been seriously damaged by the 15-inch guns of the fast battleships, and Hipper withdrew from the battle.

Then the cruiser *Southampton*, on reconnaissance, sighted the German battle fleet that was advancing north to support Hipper's cruisers. Beatty turned back to get out of range of Scheer's fleet, which consisted of 16 dreadnoughts and 6 other battleships. Scheer did not realize that he had fallen into a trap. Pursuing Beatty's ships, he was heading straight for the waiting Grand Fleet.

Combat visibility was almost zero, because of haze and gunsmoke. Beatty, on

Italian submarine—*The Italian submarines used in World War I were of a type created by Cesare Laurenti, with a composite hull. Another type was created by General Ferrati, with a displacement of between 32 and 40 tons. Maximum range: 128 miles; 2 torpedo tubes.*

British submarine—*The first British submarines were the experimental* Holland *type. This is an example of class M of the interwar years. The largest submarines in the world, they could carry a 305-mm (12-in.) gun or a small hangar with a seaplane.*

German U-boat—*The most efficient fighting ship used in World War I. Surface displacement: 1,142 tons; length: 83.5 meters (274 feet); beam: 7.5 meters (24.6 feet); surface speed: 17.5 knots; submersion speed: 7 knots; 6 torpedo tubes.*

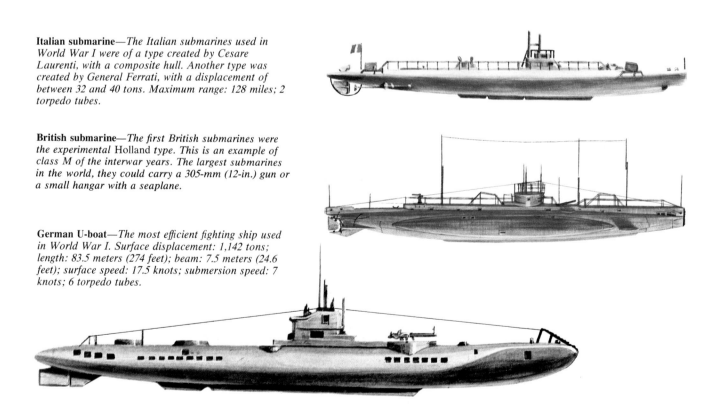

160

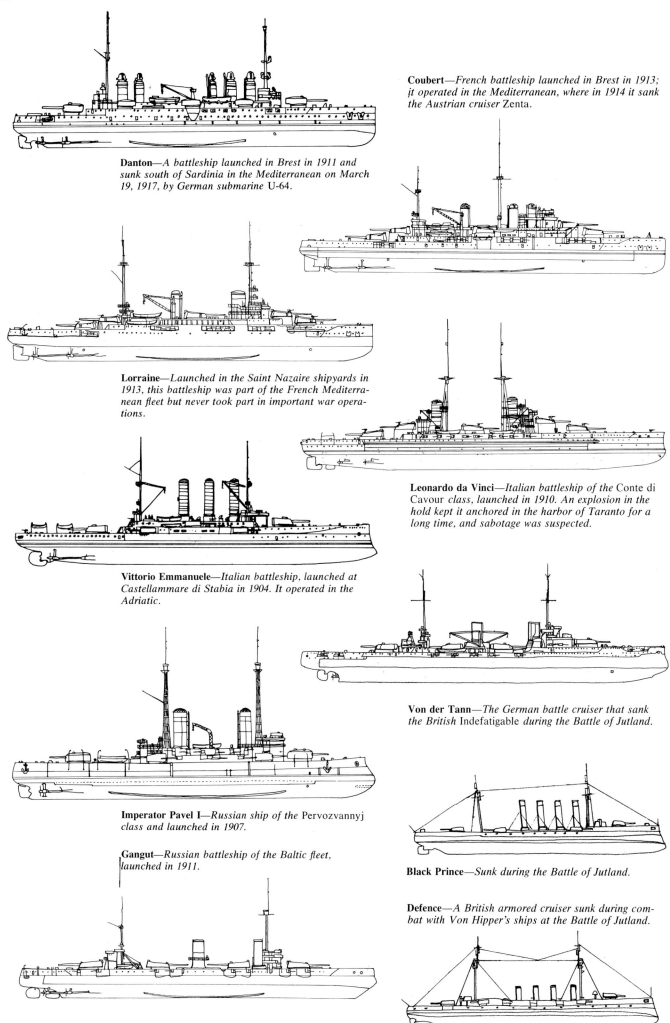

Danton—*A battleship launched in Brest in 1911 and sunk south of Sardinia in the Mediterranean on March 19, 1917, by German submarine U-64.*

Coubert—*French battleship launched in Brest in 1913; it operated in the Mediterranean, where in 1914 it sank the Austrian cruiser* Zenta.

Lorraine—*Launched in the Saint Nazaire shipyards in 1913, this battleship was part of the French Mediterranean fleet but never took part in important war operations.*

Leonardo da Vinci—*Italian battleship of the* Conte di Cavour *class, launched in 1910. An explosion in the hold kept it anchored in the harbor of Taranto for a long time, and sabotage was suspected.*

Vittorio Emmanuele—*Italian battleship, launched at Castellammare di Stabia in 1904. It operated in the Adriatic.*

Von der Tann—*The German battle cruiser that sank the British* Indefatigable *during the Battle of Jutland.*

Imperator Pavel I—*Russian ship of the* Pervozvannyj *class and launched in 1907.*

Gangut—*Russian battleship of the Baltic fleet, launched in 1911.*

Black Prince—*Sunk during the Battle of Jutland.*

Defence—*A British armored cruiser sunk during combat with Von Hipper's ships at the Battle of Jutland.*

board the *Lion*, lead his remaining cruisers to the fore along with 3 cruisers from Jellicoe's fleet. Contact with Hipper's ships was resumed, and the artillery duel recommenced. The British armored cruiser *Defence* was hit by the guns of the German battle cruisers and blew up.

A broadside from the *Derfflinger* cut in two the battle cruiser *Invincible*.

The German armored cruisers, followed by the battleships, emerged from the fog and found themselves face to face with the waiting fleet of Jellicoe. A tremendous hail of projectiles fell on the first German ships. Scheer realized he was outnumbered and reversed his course. Bad visibility kept Jellicoe from following this maneuver. Two German destroyers attacked and damaged the battleship *Marlborough*, hitting it with torpedoes that forced it to slow down to a speed of barely 17 knots.

Scheer tried to outmaneuver the British, but again he came face to face with them.

The German ships were seriously damaged by the English guns. The cruiser *Lützow* left the battle line and later was scuttled. Scheer withdrew and ordered his battle cruisers and destroyers to charge the enemy and cover his

retreat. Scheer headed for his home bases, while Jellicoe arranged his fleet for night navigation. But Jellicoe's fleet was still between the Germans and their bases. So the Germans decided to try to break through the British fleet. The German battleship *Pommern* and a cruiser were sunk, while the English lost the armored cruiser *Black Prince*.

The final balance sheet of the Battle of Jutland was as follows:

Britain—3 armored cruisers, 3 battle cruisers, and 8 destroyers sunk, a total of 113,208 tons; 6,097 officers and men killed in battle.

Germany—One battle cruiser, one battleship, 4 light cruisers, and 5 destroyers sunk, a total of 60,213 tons; 2,551 officers and men killed in battle.

British losses in both men and ships were greater than those of the Germans, but the German fleet had lost its power to continue war operations.

Thanks to Scheer's nautical skill, the German ships avoided total destruction at the hands of the larger British forces. But after the Battle of Jutland, Germany was strategically confined to the North Sea and the Baltic, and its surface fleet was much weakened.

The Battle of Jutland
May 31, 1916

Britain—Commander of the Grand Fleet, Adm. Sir John Jellicoe; commander of the battle cruiser fleet, Sir David Beatty. Battleships: **28**; battle cruisers: **9**; armored cruisers: **8**; light cruisers: **22**; destroyers: **78**; seaplane carriers: **1**.

Germany—Commander of the High Seas Fleet, Admiral Reinhard Scheer; commander of the Cruiser Fleet, Vice Adm. Franz von Hipper. Battleships and armored cruisers: **22**; battle cruisers: **5**; cruisers: **11**; destroyers: **61**.

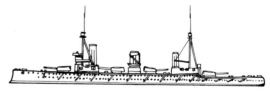

Indefatigable—*British battle cruiser of 1911.*

Tiger—*British armored cruiser of 1914. Displacement: 30,000 tons; length: 196 meters (214 yards); speed: 28 knots; eight 320-mm (13.5-in.) and twelve 152-mm (6 in.) guns; 4 torpedo tubes; crew: 1,185 men.*

King George V—*British battleship launched in 1911. It survived the Battle of Jutland.*

Queen Mary—*Armored cruiser of the Home Fleet, launched in 1912. Sunk by the* Derfflinger *and the* Seydlitz, *with a loss of 1,278 men. Of the* Lion *class.*

Agincourt—*Battleship begun for the Brazilian government with the name* Rio de Janeiro, *then given to Turkey in a half-finished state, and shortly thereafter, in 1914, put back into the Home Fleet with its new name.*

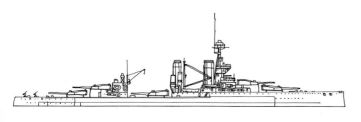

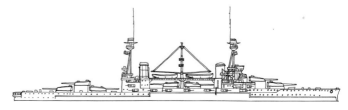

FLAGS

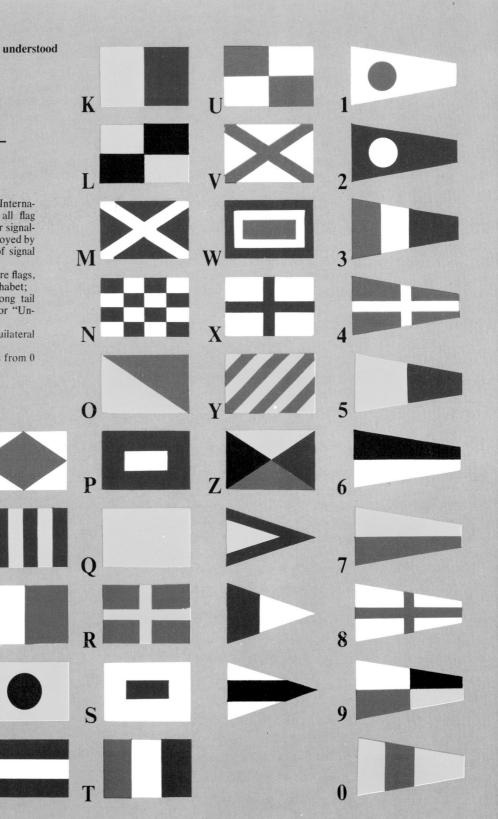

understood

THE INTERNATIONAL CODE

Used to send visual signs numbered by the International Code of Signals which regulates all flag signaling. Flags are still commonly used for signaling by warships, but are less generally employed by the merchant marine. The complete set of signal flags comprises:
—2 broad pennants (A and B) and 24 square flags, one for each letter of the international alphabet;
—1 pennant with the end of its very long tail chopped off, the International code flag for "Understood";
—3 pennants shaped like isosceles or equilateral triangles, for double letters;
—10 numerical pennants, for the numbers from 0 to 9.

COMMUNICATION BY COLOR

Other signal flags, which are not in the International Code, exist and are used by seafarers throughout the world as visual communications. They comprise a numerical series from 0 to 9 of flags rather than pennants and 27 other signal flags and pennants each with its precise meaning. By such means it is possible to send long messages between ships in conventional code. Furthermore, certain flags are used as identification signals by warships.

In yachting, flags from the International Code are used to identify the various classes competing in a regatta and others can be hoisted when required to indicate the number of minutes left before the start of a particular race.

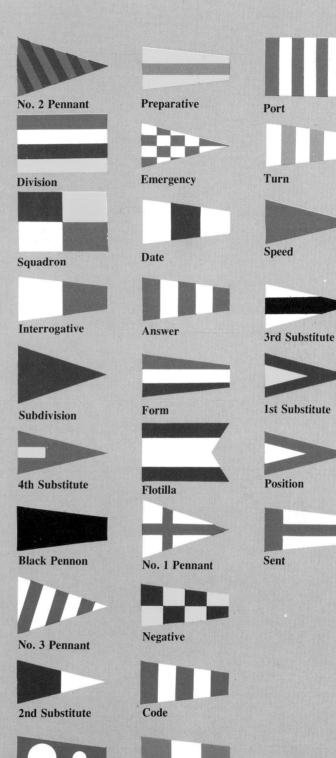

The Merchant Marine

German submarines wreaked havoc on merchant shipping during World War I, but maritime commerce flourished again when hostilities ended. The freighter, or cargo ship, first powered by steam and then by diesel engines, had finally replaced the last great commercial sailing ships, although there were a few survivors. In 1921 sailing ships from Nantes were still carrying grain on the Australian routes, while in England, Stewart & Co. and Sir William Garthwaite's Marine Corporation managed to keep going until 1928–1929. The last of Garthwaite's ten sailing ships, the four-masted *Gartpool*, was lost at sea in November 1929 off Cape Verde. In 1921 Denmark launched its last five-master with an auxiliary engine at the Ramage & Ferguson shipyards in Leith. It was called the *Kobenhaven*, and it too was lost at sea: on December 14, 1928, en route from the Rio de la Plata to Australia. The German sailing ship cargo fleet was completely destroyed during the war, but Erich Ferdinand Laeisz maintained a line of sailing vessels for transporting phosphates from Chile until 1931. Finnish Capt. Gustav Erikson had 17 sailing ships carrying grain on the Australian route until 1940. His crews were generally non-professional and consisted of young men looking for adventure at sea or naval cadets.

The opening of the Suez Canal in 1869 had shortened the route to India by thousands of miles, while the inauguration of the Panama Canal in 1914 shortened the Pacific trade routes.

In the years between 1920 and 1935, two types of commercial traffic emerged, that conducted by regular shipping lines, and that carried by the tramp steamers.

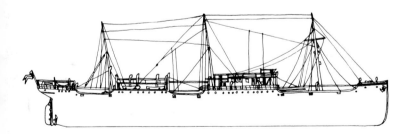

Selandia—*The first motor-driven diesel ship. It was built in Copenhagen in 1912 and had two 4-cycle diesel engines of 1,250 hp each. It could carry 24 passengers on its route to Bangkok. The vessel sank in 1942, when it was flying the Finnish flag and had been renamed Tornador.*

The regular cargo ship usually carried a few passengers as well. If there were more than 12 passengers, it was considered a passenger ship. More valuable goods and perishable goods were generally entrusted to the regular shipping line. These ships usually had

Lusitania—*A magnificent but not very robust British transatlantic liner of 37,340 tons (gross). It was 230.8 meters (216 yards) long and 26.82 meters (88 feet) wide, with a speed of 27.4 knots. It was torpedoed off the coast of Ireland by a German submarine (U-20) at 2:10 P.M. on May 7, 1915, as it was ending its crossing from New York with 1,951 passengers on board, including 128 American citizens. Twenty-two minutes after being torpedoed, the* Lusitania *capsized and went to the bottom. A total of 1,198 people died, including 94 children and the commander of the ship, Captain Turner. It was the most serious of the incidents that finally led the United States to intervene in the war against Germany.*

Titanic—*A large British transatlantic liner launched in 1911. It belonged to the White Star Line and set off on its maiden voyage on April 10, 1912, on the Southampton–New York route, with 1,316 passengers and a crew of 820 men. At 11:40 P.M. on April 14, it collided with an iceberg that opened a 300-foot hole in its hull. It sank in two hours, and about 1,500 people lost their lives. Tonnage: 46,329 tons; length: 270 meters (295 yards); speed: 25 knots.*

Mauretania—*One of the forerunners of the giant ships of more than 30,000 tons, this liner was built by the Cunard Line with the help of the British government, and put into service in 1907. It had four turbines with a total of 75,000 hp fed by 25 boilers working 4 propellers at about 180 rpm. Speed: 26 knots. This ship held the Blue Riband for the fastest eastbound North Atlantic crossing for 22 years, after winning it in 1907 with an average speed of 23.69 knots. Length: 232.2 meters (254 yards); beam: 26.8 meters (88 feet); gross tonnage: 31,983 tons.*

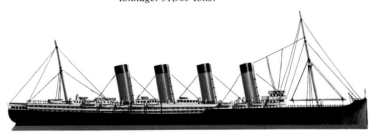

6 cargo compartments. These ships normally followed established sailing schedules and routes and passed more time in port than at sea, given the great amount of time needed for loading and the complexity of the stowing. (Goods had to be stowed according to destination.)

The tramp steamer was traditionally smaller and slower than a regular freighter, and cheaper as well. It often carried raw materials. The tramp did not have a fixed schedule. It moved from port to port and loaded any cargo available. The tramps carried cereals, coal, sugar, lumber, phosphates, steel, and scrap iron from one port to another. They were rented either for part of a trip or for the entire voyage, depending on the market. The holds and cargo equipment were like those of the freighter lines, and some companies used their ships as regular carriers or as tramps as the need arose, sometimes carrying passengers on the trip out and cereals on the way back.

Bulk carriers became important between the two wars and carried mineral products from faraway production areas. The first cargo carried by the bulk carriers was oil. The first oil tanker, the *Gluckaüff*, had been launched in 1885 in Newcastle-upon-Tyne. Until 1908 the hull of the oil tanker was made with transverse armature, but later longitudinal elements were employed. More tankers were built as the demand for oil and its derivatives increased. The tanker owed much of its success to the diesel engine. The first diesels were installed in 1910 on the *Vulcanus*, a German tanker owned by Shell. In 1939 the total net tonnage of oil tankers was 11,403,520 tons, equal to about 16.9 percent of world shipping tonnage.

The growth of commercial and passenger shipping was matched by the increased efficiency and capacity of the ports they depended on. The ports of New York, London, Amsterdam, Marseilles, and Genoa were extremely busy, thanks in part to the progressive development of railroad and highway transport. New systems, such as cargo-discharge pressure pipelines, cableways, and funiculars, were created to handle the enormous amount of goods carried to the docks of the world's most important commercial ports.

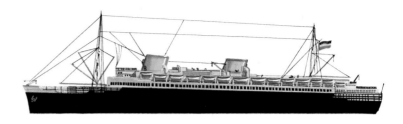

Bremen—*Launched in 1928 for the Norddeutscher Lloyd Company of Bremen, it won the Blue Riband on its maiden voyage, taking the famous trophy from the British liner* Mauretania, *which had held it since 1907. In 1934, it covered the distance between Cherbourg and New York in 4 days, 15 hours, and 27 minutes. Displacement: 51,656 tons; length: 281 meters (307 yards); 4 turbine engines; crew: 950 men; 2,500 passengers.*

Giulio Cesare—*Built for the Compagnia Italia for use on the South American route, and transferred to the North Atlantic. One of the first large passenger ships launched after World War I. Its passenger accommodations were very refined and highly functional, even in tourist class. Displacement: 21,657 tons; length: 190 meters (208 yards); speed: 21 knots; 2 steam turbines. Launched in 1921.*

Aquitania—*One of the longest-lived of the great European transatlantic liners. Launched in Scotland in 1914, it was turned into a troopship after a few trips on the Southampton–New York route. Right after the war, flying the colors of the Cunard Line, it resumed passenger service and made 422 crossings in 35 years of service. It ended its career in 1950, after having covered an estimated 3 million miles and carried 1,200,000 passengers. Tonnage: 45,647 tons; length: 263 meters (288 yards); beam: 30 meters (97 feet).*

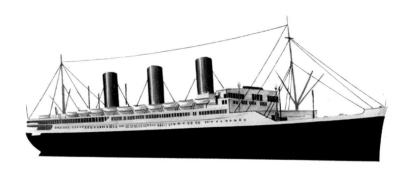

Ile de France—*Flagship of the Compagnie Générale Transatlantique launched by the Saint Nazaire shipyards in 1926. It was one of the most luxurious liners of its time. It made its fastest crossing on the Le Havre–Southampton–New York run at an average speed of 23.5 knots. Displacement: 42,763 tons; length: 229 meters (250 yards); 4 steam turbines; crew: 700 men; 1,500 passengers.*

168

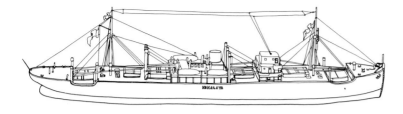

Himalaya—Cargo motor ship of the Fujiyama *class, launched for Lloyd Triestino in 1928. Speed: 13 knots; displacement: 8,110 tons.*

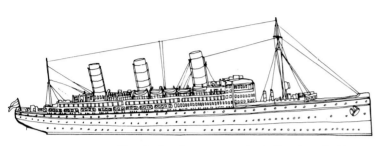

Vaterland—*German transatlantic liner launched in 1913. It covered the Hamburg–New York route. Displacement: 55,115 tons.*

Cracovia—*The first passenger-cargo ship with turbine propulsion, launched in 1918.*

The period between the wars was also the golden age of the transatlantic liner. Liner construction had been interrupted by the 1914–1918 war, but after 1920 shipyards all over the world were busy launching the great passenger ships that were to remain unequalled for style and comfort.

The first transatlantic liner launched after the war was the French ship *Paris* (34,029 tons), owned by the Compagnie Générale Transatlantique. The Norddeutscher Lloyd Company launched the *Columbus*, the last large passenger ship to be powered by a triple-expansion boiler rather than a turbine. The United States remodeled the German *Vaterland*, which had been used as a troopship during the war. It was rechristened the *Leviathan* and went into service in 1923. The use of oil fuel reduced both the number and the discomfort of engine-room personnel and in some cases increased speed. For example, the *Mauretania* crossed the Atlantic in 1924 at an average speed of 26.25 knots, faster than its top speed using coal.

Things went very well indeed for the great transatlantic navigation companies until 1924, when America introduced laws restricting immigration. The great liners could no longer count on immigrants to fill their decks and had to rely on cabin passengers who traveled for business or pleasure. Italy produced some fine passenger ships in this period, including the 30,329-ton *Roma*, launched in 1926, and the 1927 *Augustus*, the largest motorship built at the time. In the same period, the *Ile de France* was launched at the French Penhoët shipyards, and was considered the ultimate in luxury, with its gourmet cooking and elaborate furnishings, including famous paintings.

The race for the "larger than ever" knew no end. Norddeutscher Lloyd in Germany put the 50,840-ton *Bremen* into service shortly before the launching of the 48,960-ton *Europa*, and both ships took part in the Blue Riband competition in 1929.

Saint Dunstan—*A 5,661-ton tramp, 122 meters (133 yards) long; speed: 11 knots. Typical of the cargo boats turned out in Great Britain between 1920 and 1935.*

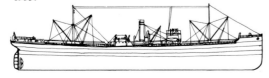

Scotia—*One of the oldest ferryboats, built in Canada in 1915. Displacement: 3,607 tons; speed: 12 knots; 239 passengers.*

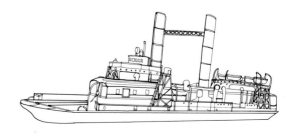

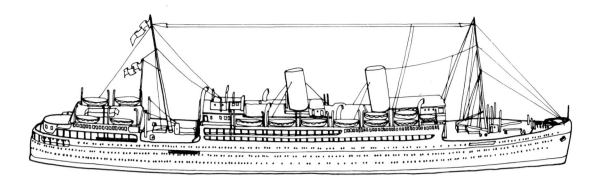

The largest Italian transatlantic liner, the *Rex*, also competed for the prize. Built by the Ansaldo shipyards in Genoa-Sestri and launched in 1932, the *Rex* had a gross tonnage of 50,255 tons and drew 13 meters (42.6 feet) with a full load. It could carry 2,000 passengers in three classes. The 4-propeller engine machinery (12 water-tube boilers and 4 turbine engines with gears) generated a total of 123,890 hp. Each passenger had 2,472 cubic feet at his disposal, 27 percent more than on any earlier transatlantic liner. In August 1933, it left Gibraltar and covered the 3,181 miles to New York in 4 days, 13 hours, and 58 minutes at an average speed of 28.92 knots, and won the famous Blue Riband.

The economic crisis that followed the 1929 stock market crash also had repercussions on world shipbuilding, especially in France and England, where programs were underway to turn out the largest ships yet built. Hundreds of ships were laid up, and such famous transatlantic liners as the *Mauretania*, the *Olympic*, the *Berengaria*, and the *Majestic* were scrapped. France suspended work on the *Normandie* (gross tonnage, 81,491 tons), with turboelectric engines, the largest ship ever built in that country. In Britain, only the merger of two rival companies, the Cunard Line and the White Star Line, and a government guarantee permitted the completion of ship no. 534, built by the John Brown shipyards on the Clyde, a yard that had turned out such famous giants as the *Lusitania* and the *Aquitania*. The new, 79,695-ton British transatlantic liner was launched in 1938 and called the *Queen Mary*. This immense vessel was hailed as the sym-

Conte Biancamano—*An Italian ship launched in 1928 for the North Atlantic route. Displacement: 23,842 tons; length: 195 meters (213 yards); speed: 20 knots; crew: 532 men; 1,708 passengers.*

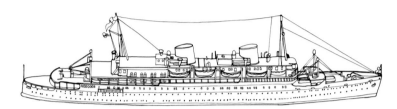

Victoria—*A British motor ship launched in 1931 for service to the Far East. It sank in the gulf of Syrtis in 1942. Displacement: 12,861 tons; length: 165 meters (180 yards); 900 passengers.*

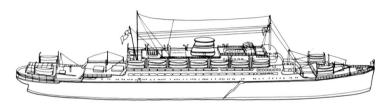

Vulcania—*A 24,496-ton Italian transatlantic liner launched in 1928 for the Trieste–New York route. Sister ship of the Saturnia, it was refitted with Fiat engines in 1935 and could reach a speed of 23 knots. Length: 195 meters (213 yards); 1,500 passengers.*

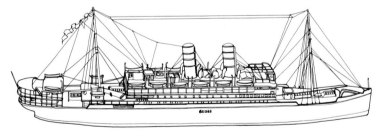

Ganges—*A British passenger steamship launched in 1911. Displacement: 12,368 tons; speed: 18 knots; 1,526 passengers.*

Jan Pieterszoom Coen—*A Dutch passenger-cargo transatlantic liner, launched in 1915 for the East Indies route. Displacement: 11,140 tons; length: 153.4 meters (168 yards); 400 passengers.*

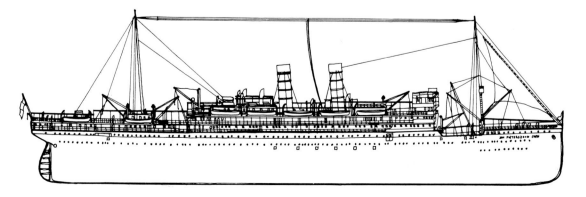

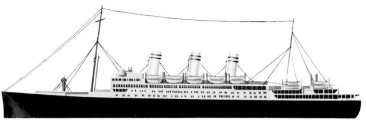

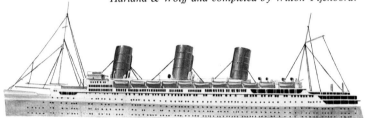

Statendam—*This luxurious transatlantic liner of the Holland-American Line was launched in 1919 and reached New York for the first time on the 300th anniversary of the arrival of the first Dutch ship in America. Displacement: 29,511 tons; length: 200 meters (219 yards); 6 turbine engines; speed: 18 knots; crew: 600 men; 1,670 passengers. Laid down by Harland & Wolff and completed by Wilton–Fijenoord.*

Empress of Britain—*Built by the John Brown shipyards in 1931 for the Canadian Pacific Railway. In 1932, it crossed the Atlantic 12 times in 12 weeks, beating the regular service record. In 1939 it was used as a troopship and in 1940 was set on fire in a German air attack. Displacement: 42,348 tons; length: 228 meters (249 yards); speed: 24 knots; crew: 700 men; 1,155 passengers.*

Rex—*In 1932, the year of its launching, it was the world's fourth largest transatlantic liner for tonnage. On September 27, 1932, it made its maiden voyage on the Genoa–New York route for the Italia Flotte Riunite group. It won the Blue Riband on that same route on August 16, 1933, taking the trophy from the* Bremen *with a journey from Gibraltar to New York made in 4 days, 13 hours, and 58 minutes, at an average speed of 28.92 knots. Displacement: 51,062 tons; length: 263 meters (287.6 yards); speed: 28 knots; 2,032 passengers.*

Conte di Savoia—*A few months after the launching of the Rex, in 1932, the Italia Flotte Riunite put this large, 48,502-ton transatlantic liner into service on the North American route. It made the crossing in six and a half days. Length: 258 meters (282 yards); speed: 28 knots; 2,012 passengers.*

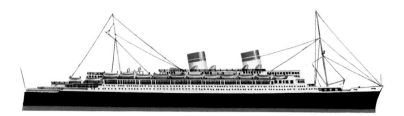

bol of national economic recovery. In the same period the Dutch launched the 35,714-ton *New Amsterdam*, the last of the great liners to make its appearance on the North Atlantic routes.

Life on board these great floating hotels presented certain ironies. Passengers were offered incredibly luxurious accommodations with every comfort, but the voyage between Europe and America was a very short one and often plagued by bad weather. The passenger was attracted by the prospect of superb food and pleasant shipboard amusement, but he was often compelled to spend most of the crossing seasick in his cabin.

In speaking of transatlantic liners, we have often mentioned the comfort and modern innovations that even a short stay on board could offer. One of these was the wireless telegraph, invented by Guglielmo Marconi.

Marconi began experimenting with wireless communication in 1894, but the Italian government's refusal to provide him with the financial aid he requested led him to move to England. There, in 1896, he demonstrated his equipment by transmitting a message across the Bristol Channel, a distance of about 9 miles. When he returned to Italy, he set up his first coastal station at La Spezia and carried out tests on board Italian warships, transmitting up to a distance of 12 miles. The first ship equipped with wireless telegraph was the United States cargo vessel *Saint Paul*. But Marconi's most spectacular experiment was carried out on board the *Electra*, when in 1930 by radio control across the ocean he turned on the lights of the World's Fair at Sydney, Australia.

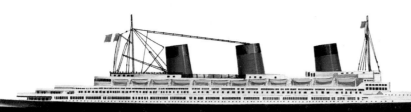

Normandie—*The largest transatlantic liner built before World War II. On its maiden voyage, in May 1935, on the Le Havre–New York route, it took the Blue Riband from the* Rex, *with a crossing of 4 days, 3 hours, and 28 minutes, at an average speed of 29.68 knots. This she improved upon still further on her eastward passage, averaging 30.31 knots. Displacement: 82,792 tons; length: 309 meters (338 yards); speed: 30 knots; crew: 1,300 men; 2,000 passengers.*

Queen Mary—*One of the largest and most luxurious transatlantic liners and the Cunard Line's flagship until the* Queen Elizabeth *entered service; it was begun in the John Brown shipyards in 1930. Her maiden voyage was in 1936. It took the Blue Riband from the* Normandie *in August 1938 averaging 30.99 knots westward and 31.69 knots eastward. Displacement: 81,237 tons; length: 305 meters (333 yards); speed: 30 knots; crew: 1,100 men, 2,139 passengers.*

Morse Code

In all methods of transmission which utilize Morse Code, a key closes a circuit (telegraphic, radio, or light) for a longer (dash) or shorter (dot) interval, thereby forming letter by letter, word by word, the message to be transmitted. The dot is considered as a unit of duration in relation to which all other units are measured: the dash has a duration of three dots; the interval between one signal and another lasts one dot; that between letters lasts three dots; and the interval between words is five dots long.

a	= .—		q	= ——.—
ä	= .—.—		r	= .—.
à	= .——.—		s	= ...
ъ	= —...		t	= —
c	= —.—.		u	= ..—
ç	= —.—..		ù	= ..——
d	= —..		v	= ...—
e	= .		w	= .——
è	= ..—..		x	= —..—
f	= ..—.		y	= —.——
g	= ——.		z	= ——..
h	=		1	= .————
i	= ..		2	= ..———
j	= .———		3	= ...——
k	= —.—		4	= ....—
l	= .—..		5	= .....
m	= ——		6	= —....
n	= —.		7	= ——...
ñ	= ——.——		8	= ———..
o	= ———		9	= ————.
ò	= ———.		0	= —————
p	= .——.			

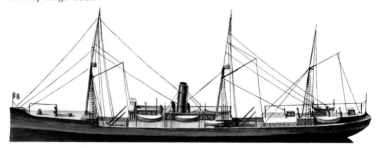

Iberia—*A cargo steamship launched by a Spanish shipyard in 1881. Tonnage: 1,310 tons; length: 77.58 meters (254.6 feet); beam: 10.98 meters (36 feet); draft: 5.92 meters (19.5 feet); the flush deck is typical of this kind of cargo boat.*

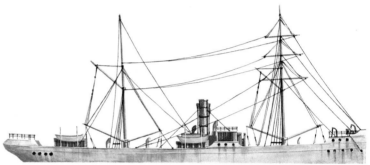

Berenice—*The classic 3-masted steamship, with a straight stem, launched in 1893. Displacement: 3,529 tons; speed: 12.32 knots; crew: 48 men; 62 passengers.*

Tzar Ferdinando—*A Bulgarian passenger-cargo steamship, launched in 1914 by the Orlando shipyards in Livorno. Displacement: 3,149 tons.*

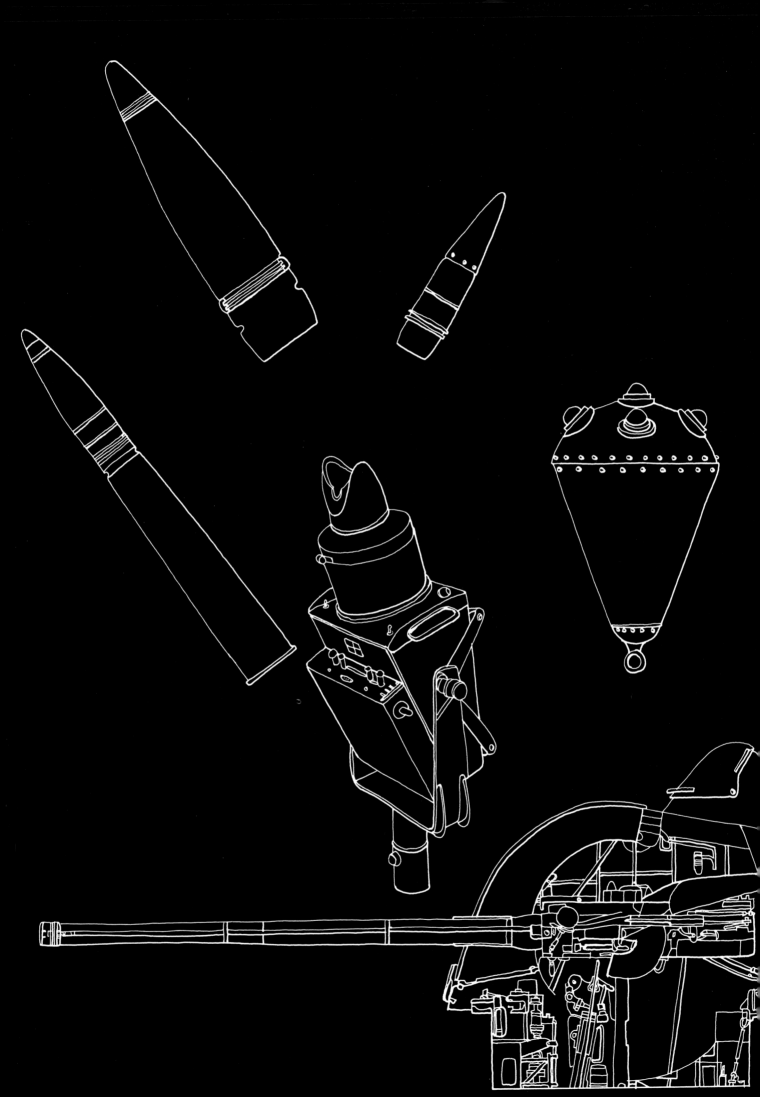

War on the Seas Again

When World War I ended, all of mankind sincerely hoped that a long peace was at hand. This hope was encouraged by agreements set up between the five great powers to limit rearmament. On November 12, 1921, the first international naval conference met in Washington, with Great Britain, France, the United States, Japan, and Italy present. After more than three months of negotiations, Great Britain, the United States, and Japan agreed not to build new battleships for a period of ten years, after which they would be able to produce battleships with a maximum displacement of 34,447 tons and with the following tonnage: Great Britain and the United States, 516,705 tons, equal to 15 ships; Japan, 310,023 tons, equal to 9 ships. Italy and France promised not to start building new warships for a period of 5 years, after which time they could build military vessels for a total of 172,235 tons, or 5 ships for each nation. Cruisers, on the other hand, could be freely built as long as their tonnage was less than 9,842 tons and their heaviest armament was limited to 203-mm (8-in.) cannons; that is, to cruisers of the *Washington* class.

The second naval conference, held in London in 1930, allowed the United States and Great Britain an overall tonnage for cruisers of 324,786 tons, while the limit was set at 233,255 tons for Japan. Limits were also set to the development of a submarine fleet, but France and Italy felt that they were discriminated against and claimed freedom of action. At the same they pledged to observe the date of 1933 as the final limit of the naval holiday. For the Great Powers, the period of suspension in battleship construction was limited to 1936.

The atmosphere of the third naval conference (London, 1935–1936) was far different. In 1934 Japan had denounced the Washington agreements, and a year later Hitler's Germany rejected the limitations imposed on its navy by the Treaty of Versailles. Italy was subject to sanctions applied by France and Britain because of its colonial action in Ethiopia. The third conference was a failure and added to international tension. Hitler had launched his political and military challenge in Europe, and the clouds of war were massing over the world.

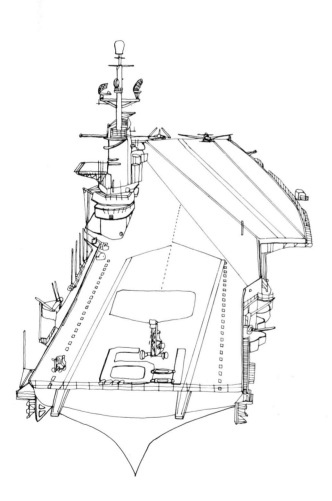

The **aircraft carrier** *can be considered the most important warship of World War II.*

Repulse—*It operated mainly in the Atlantic. After being transferred to Force G in the Indian Ocean, it was sunk along with the* Prince of Wales *during an attack by Japanese torpedo bombers, on December 10, 1941.*

The battleship was still the fulcrum of the world's navies, despite its vulnerability to air and submarine attack. Its use was as limited in World War II as in World War I. Although the battleship had been all but replaced by the aircraft carrier, the Americans and Japanese put gigantic battleships into action toward the end of the war. These were the finest battleships that had ever been built. The Japanese vessels *Yamato* and *Musashi*, with almost 70,000 tons of displacement, nine 457-mm (18-in.) guns and heavy armor, were considered unsinkable. But it is unlikely that an unsinkable ship will ever be built. Even the toughest Japanese battleships had to give way before an airplane attack. The smaller *Iowa* and *New Jersey* of the American navy were launched in 1943, when the war was half over. These were the only battleships to come through the great conflict in triumph.

The cruiser played a fundamental tactical and strategic part in World War II. Japanese and American cruisers were implacable enemies in the battle zones of the Pacific. They provided antiaircraft cover, with a greater firing potential than the battleship. The cruiser also provided artillery cover during landing operations.

The destroyer had not been included in the restrictions imposed on larger ships by the treaties of Washington and London. Destroyers got bigger and bigger. When war broke out, these vessels were present in the major world navies. Britain had 179 in service; Germany, 22; France, 30; and the United States, 215.

The name "corvette" was revived after half a century of oblivion and applied to ships that protected merchant traffic on the sea during wartime. It was applied to a very simply built vessel, small and with light tonnage and low speed. The corvette made an important contribution to the war effort, thanks above all to the self-sacrifice of its crew. Another name was revived from the glorious days of sailing ships—the frigate. The first modern frigates appeared in 1943 in British shipyards. They backed up the lightly armed corvettes.

Experience in World War I had demonstrated that the submarine was the most efficient means of waging war on mercantile traffic. Naval ports and bases were camouflaged against surface and air attack, while the submarine threat led to the laying of nets and booms across their entrances. Protective barriers were set up even around single ships; and convoy escort ships were equipped with the echo-detecting goniometer, or sonar, based on the supersonic waves that bounced off a submerged hull. Surfaced submarines could be detected by radar (radio detecting and ranging), an instrument based on the emission of high-frequency radio waves, developed in Britain. Radar had a chance to demonstrate its worth on March 28, 1941, on board the British battleship *Valiant*. Radar soundings located Italian cruisers at night at a distance of some 20 miles off Cape Matapan. Submarines quickly adopted new tactics and instruments to try to neutralize the action of enemy detection-techniques. Electromagnetic-wave detectors and special antiradar paints were introduced. German submarines carried small gyroplanes that rose 20 or 30 feet into the air to see whether enemy shipping was in the vicinity.

Between 1941 and 1943 antisubmarine devices proved their worth. Radar equipment was often installed on "merchant aircraft carriers." Allied ships carried mortars that could fire a salvo of 24 depth charges from the bow. Together with the traditional depth charge, this weapon could inflict terrible damage on undersea vessels. The Germans assigned submarine warfare a primary role from the beginning of the war. In 1944 they put into action ships of the *XXI* type, with powerful storage batteries for electric engines that were more powerful than diesel engines. These German submarines were much faster in attack and in retreat. They were also faster in diving. The snorkel (a tube 25 to 35 feet long), with its tip above the surface of the water, extended the air-intake and -exhaust pipes. Thus the submarine could move 35 to 45 feet below the surface at high speed and keep its electric storage batteries charged.

Nevertheless, by the end of the war the submarine was in decline, and antisub defense, including larger convoy escorts of warships and planes, the use of decoy ships, zigzag navigation, smokescreens, radar and sonar, depth bombs and torpedoes, could provide a solid barrier against the submarine.

The other outstanding ship of World War I was the aircraft carrier. It eventually became the hub of the fighting fleet. Its development and continued improvement led to the formation of a new and complex type of naval unit, the famous American task force. The task force appeared in the Pacific sector at the time of Pearl Harbor and consisted of groups of aircraft carriers and such surface vessels as battleships, cruisers, and destroy-

Prince of Wales—*During the hunt for the* Bismarck, *it hit the German battleship with two 356-mm (14-in.) shells, despite the fact that it had been hit itself by four 380-mm (15-in.) and three 203-mm (8-in.) shells. It operated in the Mediterranean theater and then at Singapore, after November 1941. It was sunk by Japanese torpedo bombers as it headed toward Kuantan in Malaysia to block the Japanese invasion of Southeast Asia.*

Hood—*Launched in 1918 and modernized before the war, pride of the British navy. It encountered the German battleship* Bismarck *in the North Atlantic in May 1941. On May 24 it was blown up by the* Bismarck's *fifth salvo.*

Warspite—*The most famous battleship in the British fleet, flagship of the Mediterranean Fleet commanded by Admiral Cunningham. It took part in the battle of Punta Stilo, where one of its shells hit the Italian ship Giulio Cesare. After operating in the Eastern Fleet off Ceylon, it returned to the Mediterranean (the landing at Salerno) and the North Atlantic. It was wrecked in 1947 and scrapped in situ.*

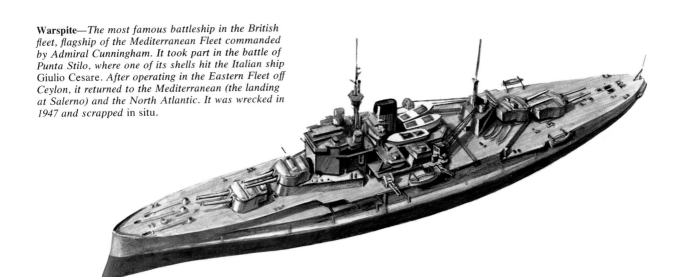

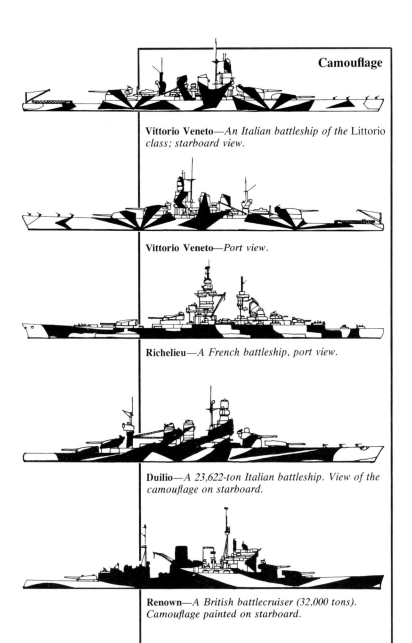

Camouflage

Vittorio Veneto—*An Italian battleship of the* Littorio *class; starboard view.*

Vittorio Veneto—*Port view.*

Richelieu—*A French battleship, port view.*

Duilio—*A 23,622-ton Italian battleship. View of the camouflage on starboard.*

Renown—*A British battlecruiser (32,000 tons). Camouflage painted on starboard.*

Camouflage painting on ships was introduced during World War I to make them less identifiable during enemy attack. Bands and patches of color were applied in such a way as to break the lines of the hull and superstructure, confusing the observer as to its course and speed. The colors most commonly used were gray, black, yellow, blue, green, and white.

ers. Naval aviation took the place of traditional long-range artillery, as in the actions at Taranto (November 11, 1941), Pearl Harbor (December 7, 1941), and Cape Matapan (March 1941); in the sinking of the German battleship *Bismarck* (May 1941); in the Battle of the Coral Sea (May 1942); and above all at the Battle of Midway (June 1942), where the aircraft carrier made one of its most convincing claims to supremacy. As the speed and power of aircraft increased, special mechanisms for landing and taking off during navigation were installed on the armored decks of the carriers. Helicopters were carried on ships as supply, rescue, and antisubmarine aircraft.

A special offensive was waged by the Italian navy against British bases in the Mediterranean, with naval assault vessels like the *barchini*, fast one-man motorboats with an explosive charge at the bow, designed by Aimone di Savoia-Aosta, and the slow torpedoes (SCL), or "pigs," piloted by one man with a second as crew, which carried the bomb right under the keels of ships in enemy ports.

Queen Elizabeth—*The oldest class of British battleships, made up of 5 ships with a displacement of 30,600 tons. It was launched in Portsmouth in 1913 and modernized in 1940.*

Nelson—*With the* Rodney, *it made up a powerfully armed class of battleship, built by Cammell Laird and Armstrong respectively between 1922 and 1927.*

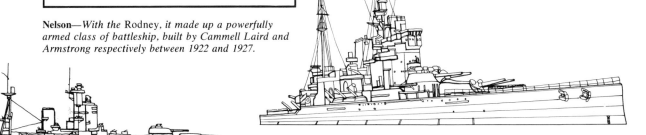

Great Britain

Hopes for peace and the apparent agreement reached by the Great Powers on naval disarmament led Britain to reduce naval expenditure after 1922. Only large battleships, the *Rodney*, 32,971 tons, and its sister ship, the *Nelson*, were put into construction. The British navy had 13 other battleships, which had been built before 1918 and were subsequently modernized.

After 1936 five ships of 34,447 tons each were put into construction for the British battleship fleet. They were still being built when World War II broke out and went into service in 1941-1942.

Along with Japan and the United States, Great Britain was one of the nations that fully realized the strategic importance of the aircraft carrier in any large-scale war operation. The Naval Air Service went on duty in the opening months of World War I with operations aimed at land objectives and also against ships, as in the Dardanelles. Britain produced the first design for a ship planned exclusively for naval aviation (although the Japanese were the first to make such a ship operational), the *Hermes*, with a displacement of 10,678 tons. It was built just after the transatlantic liner *Argus* of 14,222 tons, which was turned into an aircraft carrier and equipped with a flight deck 190 meters (208 yards) long and 21 (69 feet) wide. The Washington Naval Conference's decision to sus-

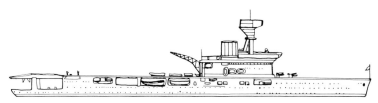

Hermes—*The prototype of British aircraft carriers, begun at Newcastle in 1918 and completed at Devonport in 1920. The deck is clear from bow to stern. Sunk on April 9, 1942, in the Indian Ocean by Japanese aircraft.*

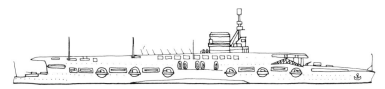

Courageous—*One of the first British aircraft carriers to be sunk by a German submarine, on September 17, 1939. Its sister ship, Glorious, was sunk by German surface craft off Narvick in 1940.*

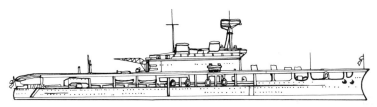

Eagle—*One of the oldest British aircraft carriers, launched in 1920. It was a former Chilean battleship called* Almirante Cochrane, *and was sunk in the Mediterranean by German submarines on August 11, 1942.*

pend the construction of large warships was partly due to the new strategic theory of "bomb as against armor," which considered the future of the battleship endangered by the airplane, its most powerful enemy.

When World War II broke out, Great Britain had 7 aircraft carriers, mostly remodelings of other types of ships, such as the *Furious* of 22,450 tons, designed as a heavy cruiser; and the *Eagle*, an ex-battleship built for the Chilean navy with the name *Almirante Cochrane* and modified after launching. The *Argus* itself was taken from an earlier project for a transatlantic liner and sister ship of the Italian *Conte Rosso*. The most efficient British aircraft carrier in service as of September 3, 1939, was the *Ark Royal*, a 21,652-ton vessel that could carry 60 planes.

Duke of York—*One of the five ships of the* King George V *class; 40 percent of its displacement of 35,000 tons was due to its armor plate.*

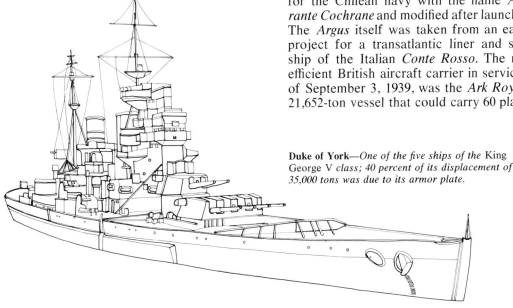

King George V—*It entered the Home Fleet in October 1940 and was the flagship during the hunt for the* Bismarck. *In the Mediterranean it supported the landing in Sicily, and in the Pacific it took part in the operations on Okinawa. It was one of the ships that anchored in Tokyo Bay at the end of the war. Withdrawn from service in 1957.*

It was sunk by a German U-boat in the Mediterranean on November 31, 1941. Six more carriers of 22,637 tons each were being built, with armored flight decks. Among them was the *Illustrious*, which went into action early in 1940 and, thanks to the armor on its deck, was able to resist both the attacks of the German Stukas in the channel of Sicily and the suicide missions of the Japanese Kamikazes.

At the beginning of the war, British aircraft carriers were not very lucky. The *Courageous* was sunk by a German submarine in the first few months of the conflict; and in April 1940, during the evacuation of British troops from Norway, the *Glorious* was sunk by two German warships. Nevertheless British aircraft carriers played a decisive role in European operations, and the torpedo planes that took off from their flight decks often stopped or slowed down the navigation of large enemy battleships. A "Fairy Albacore" from the aircraft carrier *Formidable* immobilized the Italian cruiser *Pola* during the Battle of Cape Matapan (March 1941); and a "Fairy Swordfish" from the *Ark Royal* ruined the steering mechanism of the German battleship *Bismarck*, which was then sunk by advancing ships from the Home Fleet.

In 1930, during the inconclusive naval conference in London, the tonnage of heavy and light cruisers was established. The British navy was assigned an overall figure of 193,-200 tons; and to fit the largest possible number of ships into this tonnage, British shipyards turned out vessels of the *Arethusa* class (1934–1936), of only 5,200 tons, with six 152-mm (6-in.) guns and light armor. The later *Southampton* class reached 9,400 tons,

Revenge—*Entered service in the Home Fleet in 1916; during the search for the* Bismarck *it remained in reserve. In 1942 it went to the Indian Ocean; it was withdrawn in 1943.*

Rodney—*Of the* Nelson *class, put into service in 1927. One of the most active British battleships during the war. Its third salvo finished the* Bismarck, *which had already been damaged by British air attack. It served for a long time in the Mediterranean, taking part in almost all of the major naval operations in that zone, and also supported the landing in Normandy. The* Rodney *was scrapped in 1948.*

Indomitable—*The fourth aircraft carrier of the* Illustrious *class, launched in 1940. Assigned to the Mediterranean and the defense of Malta, it had armored hangars for the planes and powerful antiaircraft armament.*

a displacement greater than the 7,874 tons designated as the maximum for light cruisers by the 1936 naval conference. The expensive heavy cruiser of the *Washington* type had its British counterpart in the *York* (8,250 tons) and the *Exeter* (8,390 tons), both armed with six 203-mm (8-in.) guns. At the start of the war, the British had a total of 49 heavy and light cruisers, while 10 light cruisers of the *Dido* class (5,450 tons, ten 133-mm [5.3-in.] guns); 5 of the *Fiji* class (8,000 tons, twelve 152-mm [6-in.] guns); 2 of the *Fiji* class (8,000 tons, twelve 152-mm [6-in.] guns); and 6 more *Dido* class (5,770 tons, ten 133-mm [5.3-in.] guns) were waiting to be completed and put into service.

At the same time, new ships joined the destroyers already in service; 16 ships of the *Lightning* class, of 1,920 tons, with six 120-mm (4.3-in.) cannons, eight 533-mm (21-in.) torpedoes, and a speed of 36 knots, brought the British destroyer fleet up to 179 ships. In 1945, during the last phase of the war, the battle class got larger in size, with a displacement of 2,400 tons. Britain also had 69 submarines in combat against the German U-boats and in defense of Atlantic convoys. There were also "pocket submarines," which distinguished themselves in the sinking of the German battleship *Tirpitz* and in other offensive actions.

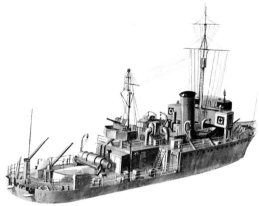

British minesweeper—*Of the* Bangor *class, and part of the fleet of 287 minesweepers that took part in Operation Neptune, the crossing of the Channel before the landing in Normandy (Operation Overlord), to eliminate the German minefields.*

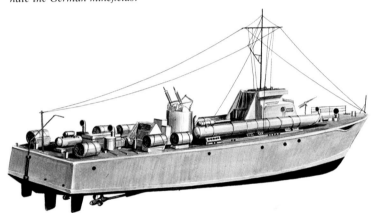

M.T. B/4—*A British torpedo boat that took part in* Operations Cerberus, *in February 1942, when* Scharnhorst *and* Prinz Eugen *made their dash up the English Channel.*

"X" boat—*A pocket submarine designed for special operations in difficult waters.*

Chariot—*A torpedo guided by two men, derived from the Italian "pigs" that had sunk the British battleships* Valiant *and* Queen Elizabeth *in the Mediterranean. Like the Italian torpedo, it had to be towed fairly close to the target.*

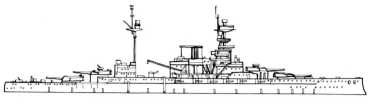

Malaya—*A British battleship of the* Queen Elizabeth *class, modernized in 1928–1929.*

Repulse—*Completed in 1915 and modernized in 1922, it was sunk by Japanese planes off Malaysia on December 10, 1941.*

Ramillies—*A British battleship of the* Royal Sovereign *class, launched in 1916 and modernized in 1932.*

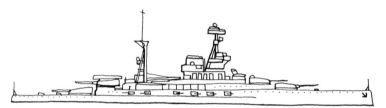

Resolution—*A battleship of the same class. Served in the Home Fleet, on Atlantic convoys, and in the Far East.*

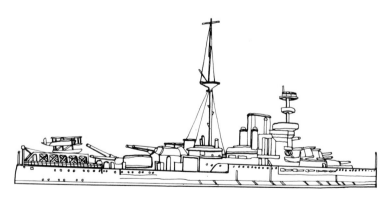

Valiant—*A ship of the* Queen Elizabeth *class, modernized in 1937. It served with the Mediterranean fleet for a long time.*

The British navy had to bear the burden of a naval war that grew steadily fiercer. Much of the merit for the fact that the retreat from Dunkirk in June 1940 did not turn into total defeat is due to the British sailors who carried 300,000 men of the defeated British Expeditionary Corps across the Channel to safety.

When France fell, British ships had to face the Italian and German fleets alone. They blocked the concentration of large German battleships in the Atlantic, where many submarine groups were already in action. An outstanding operation resulted in the sinking of the German battleship *Bismarck*. On May 23, 1941, the British cruisers *Norfolk* and *Suffolk* sighted the *Bismarck* (commanded by Admiral Lütjens) and the heavy cruiser *Prinz Eugen* as they entered the Denmark Channel. They communicated the information to Vice Admiral Holland on board the battle cruiser *Hood*, which had sailed from Scapa Flow the previous day with the *Prince of Wales*. The next day, the German and British ships entered into ballistic contact. The *Hood* was hit and blew up after only eight minutes of combat. The *Bismarck* left the *Prinz Eugen* and headed toward France. On May 26 an attack by Swordfish planes from the aircraft carrier *Ark Royal* paralyzed the German battleship. On the following day the British battleships *Rodney* and *King George* attacked, and the torpedoes of the cruiser *Dorsetshire* finished off the *Bismarck*, which sank at 10:40 A.M.

In the Mediterranean British ships frustrated Italian plans to invade Malta and harried supply lines between Italy and North Africa. The British lost two of their finest battleships in the war with Japan. The intervention of the United States in the war in 1941 was a great relief to the sorely tried British fleet, which was present in November 1942 at the landing in Morocco; in July 1943 at the invasion of Sicily; and on June 6, 1944, at Normandy.

The Royal Navy's losses during the war were high in both men and ships. When the conflict ended British shipyards had 4 new battleships, 29 aircraft carriers, and a number of smaller vessels in construction.

181

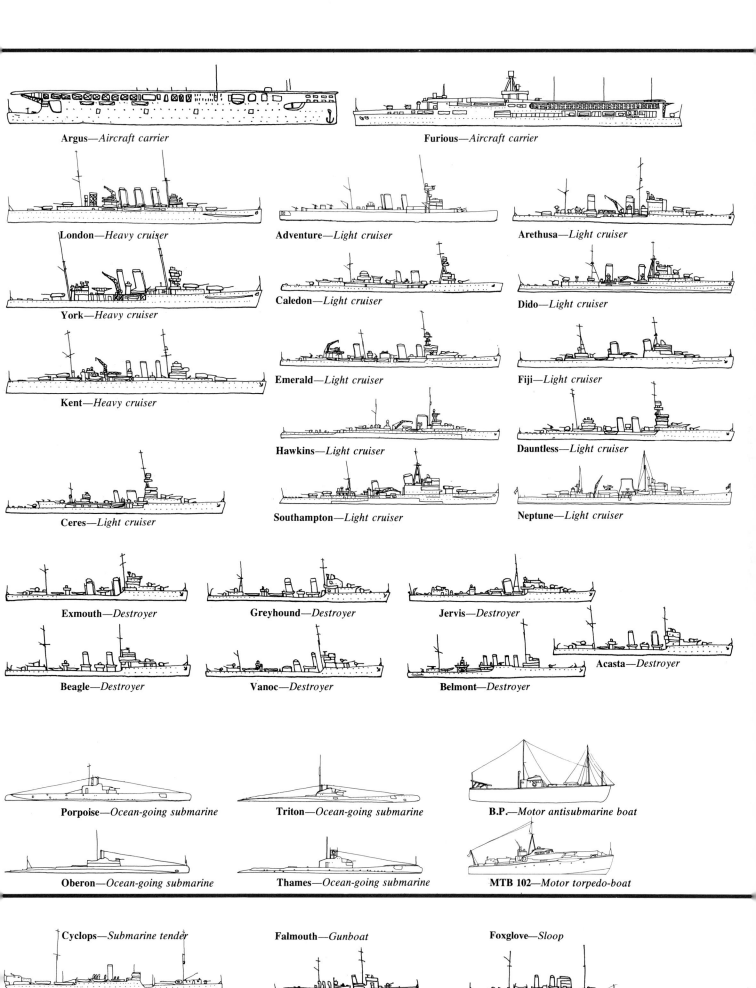

Argus—*Aircraft carrier*

Furious—*Aircraft carrier*

London—*Heavy cruiser*

Adventure—*Light cruiser*

Arethusa—*Light cruiser*

York—*Heavy cruiser*

Caledon—*Light cruiser*

Dido—*Light cruiser*

Kent—*Heavy cruiser*

Emerald—*Light cruiser*

Fiji—*Light cruiser*

Hawkins—*Light cruiser*

Dauntless—*Light cruiser*

Ceres—*Light cruiser*

Southampton—*Light cruiser*

Neptune—*Light cruiser*

Exmouth—*Destroyer*

Greyhound—*Destroyer*

Jervis—*Destroyer*

Acasta—*Destroyer*

Beagle—*Destroyer*

Vanoc—*Destroyer*

Belmont—*Destroyer*

Porpoise—*Ocean-going submarine*

Triton—*Ocean-going submarine*

B.P.—*Motor antisubmarine boat*

Oberon—*Ocean-going submarine*

Thames—*Ocean-going submarine*

MTB 102—*Motor torpedo-boat*

Cyclops—*Submarine tender*

Falmouth—*Gunboat*

Foxglove—*Sloop*

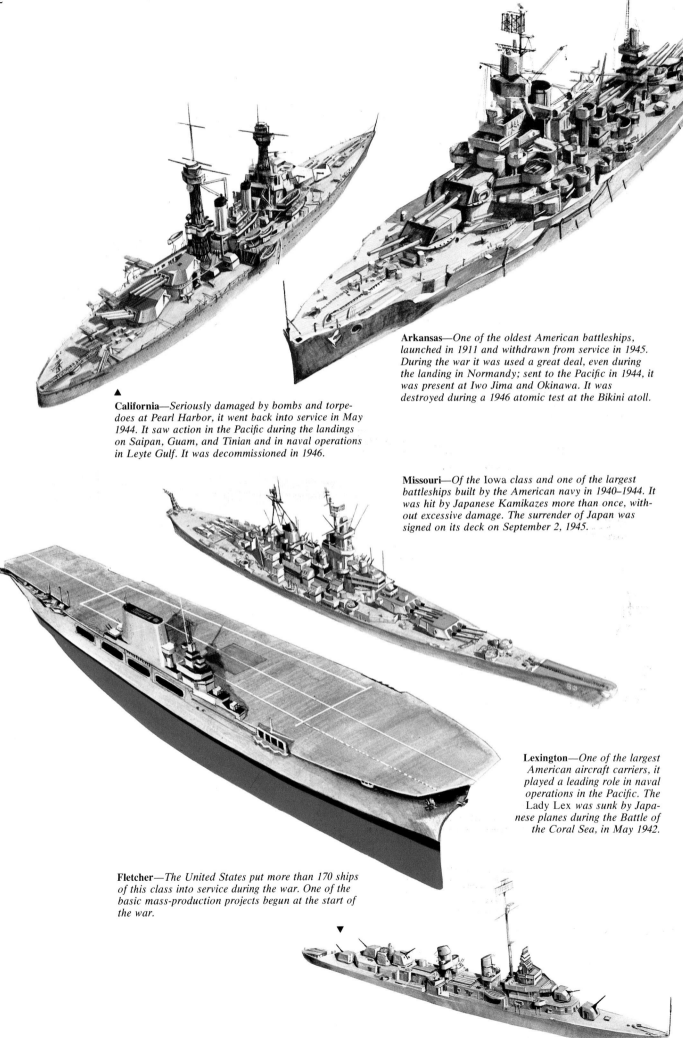

California—Seriously damaged by bombs and torpedoes at Pearl Harbor, it went back into service in May 1944. It saw action in the Pacific during the landings on Saipan, Guam, and Tinian and in naval operations in Leyte Gulf. It was decommissioned in 1946.

Arkansas—One of the oldest American battleships, launched in 1911 and withdrawn from service in 1945. During the war it was used a great deal, even during the landing in Normandy; sent to the Pacific in 1944, it was present at Iwo Jima and Okinawa. It was destroyed during a 1946 atomic test at the Bikini atoll.

Missouri—Of the Iowa class and one of the largest battleships built by the American navy in 1940–1944. It was hit by Japanese Kamikazes more than once, without excessive damage. The surrender of Japan was signed on its deck on September 2, 1945.

Lexington—One of the largest American aircraft carriers, it played a leading role in naval operations in the Pacific. The Lady Lex was sunk by Japanese planes during the Battle of the Coral Sea, in May 1942.

Fletcher—The United States put more than 170 ships of this class into service during the war. One of the basic mass-production projects begun at the start of the war.

The United States of America

American public opinion was at first contrary to intervention in the conflict that was already raging in Europe. But when the Japanese bombed Pearl Harbor the United States declared war. On December 7, 1941, the U.S. Pacific Fleet was destroyed, one of the fleets that had been developed under the Two Oceans Bill. The law of June 14, 1940, authorized an 11 percent increase in the tonnage of aircraft carriers, cruisers, and submarines, and provided for the purchase or construction of a total of 73,815 tons of auxiliary vessels. The total tonnage of the United States fleet was raised to 1,697,319 tons. Developments in the European war led the Americans to create two independent fleets, one for each ocean, and the Senate Naval Affairs Committee recommended another 70 percent increase in naval fighting forces. When war was declared on Japan and on the Axis, the United States had an unprecedented program of strengthening its naval power. On September 9, 1940, the Senate proposal became law, and the new ships were begun. To contain Japanese expansion in the Pacific, America could count on only the few vessels that had survived the Pearl Harbor disaster in fighting condition: 3 aircraft carriers, 3 cruisers, 13 destroyers, and 29 submarines.

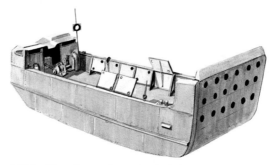

LCM—*"Landing craft, mechanized." It could hold 100 soldiers, or a tank, or a truck weighing up to 16 tons. Speed: 7.5 knots. Armed with two 8-mm machine guns.*

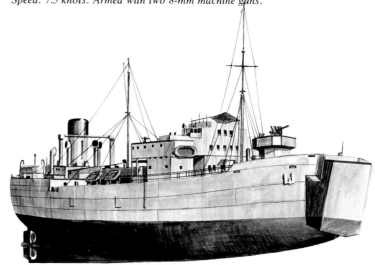

LST—*"Landing ship tank." A landing craft used during operations on the coast of Madagascar (May-November 1940). It could hold twenty-two 25-ton tanks or thirty-three 33-ton trucks.*

Boise—*Took part in the Battle of Guadalcanal in August 1942. It belonged to the* Brooklyn *class of light cruisers and was badly damaged in the Battle of Cape Esperance.*

Elco—*Antisubmarine vessel and one of the main types of American torpedo boats, particularly effective in narrow channels between groups of islands.*

Gato—*A submarine of the class of the same name, the class that standardized American submarines and made possible their mass production. American underseas ships fought the Japanese in the Pacific for control of supply routes.*

Pennsylvania—*Battleship*

Minneapolis—*Heavy cruiser*

Mississippi—*Battleship*

Augusta—*Heavy cruiser*

Maryland—*Battleship*

Chester—*Heavy cruiser*

Nevada—*Battleship*

Portland—*Heavy cruiser*

Savannah—*Light cruiser*

Pensacola—*Heavy cruiser*

Atlanta—*Light cruiser*

Concord—*Heavy cruiser*

"Flush-Deck" Class—*Destroyer*

Farragut Class—*Destroyer*

Porter Class—*Destroyer*

Sims Class—*Destroyer*

Mahan Class—*Destroyer*

Craven Class—*Destroyer*

R Class—*Coastal submarine*

O Class—*Coastal submarine*

PT 12—*Submarine chaser*

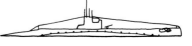

185

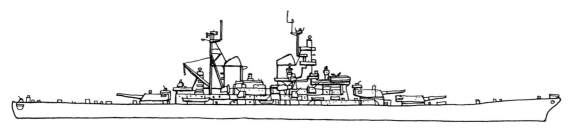

Iowa—*This American battleship survived the war. Completed in 1943, it was the first ship to carry helicopters as an integral part of its armament.*

United States naval authorities believed wholeheartedly in the future of the aircraft carrier. The first ships of this type were created by transforming two ships originally intended to be battle cruisers, the *Saratoga* and the *Lexington*, which carried 79 and 90 planes, respectively, and had a speed of 34 knots. These ships cost a great deal to build—45 million dollars; and 15 million dollars more was spent to modernize them in 1939. After World War II began, the vast program of naval building proceeded very rapidly, partly because of the extensive use of prefabricated parts. During the war, American industry turned out 20 aircraft carriers of the *Essex* class (26,672 tons); 9 light ones of the *Independence* class (10,826 tons); 19 escort carriers of the *Bairoko Commencement Bay* class (11,220 tons); 50 of the *Casablanca* class (7,677 tons); and 36 of the *Bogue* class (9,645 tons), 26 of which were loaned to Great Britain. This powerful fleet, with its immense striking power, gradually turned back the Japanese advance in the Pacific. The phases of this defeat can be

summed up in a few names—the Coral Sea, Midway, the Mariana Islands, and Leyte Gulf. In February 1945 the American Pacific Fleet lying off the coast of Japan included 11 heavy and 5 light aircraft carriers, carrying more than 1,200 planes; 8 battleships; 17 cruisers; and more than 80 destroyers. Statistics show that the Pacific Fleet's aircraft carriers destroyed 12,000 Japanese planes, 168 fighting and auxiliary ships, and 359 cargo ships. Never in the history of the ship had one type of war vessel waged such

Idaho—*Completed in 1919 and modernized in 1935, it was one of the oldest battleships in the American navy.*

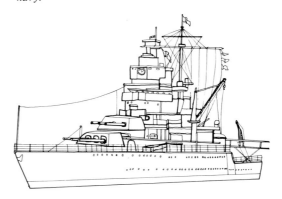

Texas—*With the* New York, *it was the first battleship class launched by the Americans in 1914. Modernizing in 1926 removed the steel-framework tower.*

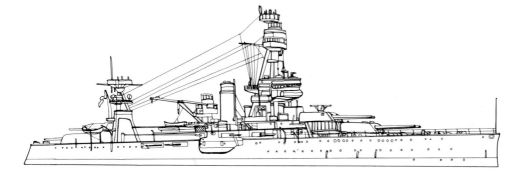

186

Saratoga—*Laid down, like its sister ship, the Lexington, in 1916; it was converted from a battle cruiser into an aircraft carrier in 1922.*

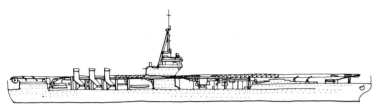

Ranger—*The first American ship to be designed as an aircraft carrier, 1934.*

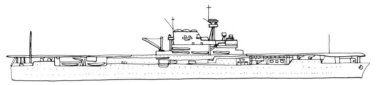

Enterprise—*The newest aircraft carrier in the American fleet at the time of Pearl Harbor.*

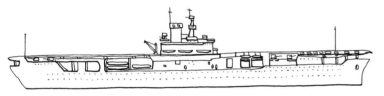

Wasp—*One of the smaller aircraft carriers in the American navy, sunk during the Battle of Guadalcanal, on September 15, 1942.*

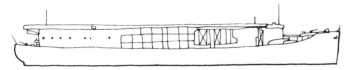

Long Island—*An escort-carrier converted from a cargo ship of the Standard C3 type.*

destruction. When the war ended, the American aircraft carrier fleet totaled 102 ships.

Before war broke out, three new classes of cruisers had been begun. The 13,385-ton *Baltimore* type, armed with nine 203-mm (8-in.) guns, were the protagonists of surface fleet battles, perhaps even more important strategically and tactically than the battleships.

There were very many destroyers by the end of the war, and together with torpedo boats, they came to a total of 745 vessels.

The United States' submarine fleet (which reached 205 at the end of the war) did a great deal of damage to Japanese cargo and supply ships.

American naval power played a leading role in the landing at Normandy, the prelude to the invasion of Europe and the final defeat of Germany. At dawn on June 6, 1944, 4,000 troopships, protected by 6 battleships and by dozens of cruisers and destroyers (including British and Free French ships) and preceded by 200 minesweepers, appeared off the coast of German-occupied Normandy and landed 250,000 men in the space of 24 hours.

Operation Overlord and the dropping of the two atomic bombs on Hiroshima and Nagasaki put an end to a war that had involved 56 nations in its various phases and caused the death of about 50 million people.

Liberty—*The American solution to the problem of replacement of merchant ships sunk by U-boats. The Liberty, conceived in the Kaiser yards, was built of prefabricated sections which could be assembled in five days.*

▼

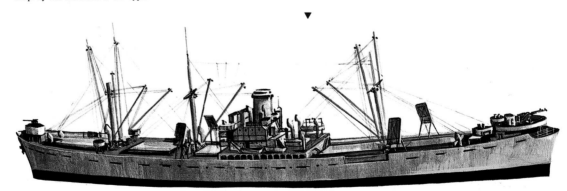

France

On September 3, 1939, the day war was declared, the French navy had only two modern warships, the *Dunkerque* and the *Strasbourg*, both excellent vessels of the battleship type.

Five battleships (the *Courbet*, *Paris*, *Bretagne*, *Provence*, and *Lorraine*), with a displacement of 22,189 tons, dated back to the World War I period. They had been built between 1910 and 1915 and were modernized in the 1930s. The French fleet had one aircraft carrier, the *Béarn*, with a displacement of 21,796 tons, built in 1920 and modernized in 1935. It was one of the first carriers to have a totally clear flight deck, 183 meters (200 yards) long and 27 meters (89 feet) wide, because the smokestack, mast, and bridge were placed on a platform protruding from the starboard side of the ship. Two other aircraft carriers were being built when war broke out but were never finished. According to the agreements signed at the naval conferences, France was able to begin construction of four large (35,000-ton) ships only in 1936. One of these was the *Richelieu*. Work was suspended when France fell, and it was not launched until 1945. The *Richelieu* was 242 meters (264.6 yards) long and had eight 381-mm (15-in.) cannons, many smaller guns, 3 planes, and maximum speed of 31.5 knots.

The *Richelieu's* side armor had the highest ratio ever of weight of armor to displacement for any warship in history. The ship was used during the final naval operations against Japan. The French navy, which had been the first to adopt the armored cruiser, in 1890, observed the restrictions established during the first naval conference in Washington, on February 6, 1922. This conference put the standard displacement of the new cruiser

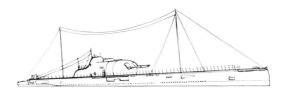

Surcouf—*Built between 1927 and 1934, it belonged to the class of French cruiser-submarines. Armed with two fixed 203-mm (8-in.) guns, it also carried a reconnaissance plane set in a small hangar.*

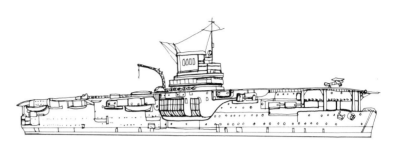

Béarn—*A battleship turned into an aircraft carrier by the French navy in 1923, modernized in 1935. Smokestack, mast, and bridge were placed on a platform that protruded from starboard so that the flight deck could be completely clear.*

Strasbourg—*A battleship of the* Dunkerque *class, the first on which large-caliber guns were mounted in quadruple turrets arranged like those on the British Nelson, that is, with the main weapons concentrated in the bow. It was sunk by its crew at Toulon.*

Richelieu—*When France fell, this ship was still in construction at Brest. It managed to escape to Dakar, Senegal. On July 8, 1940, it was hit by British torpedo planes, and its keel settled on the low sea bottom. In 1942 it was incorporated into the Allied Fleet, refitted, and sent to the Pacific, where it operated until the end of the war. It was laid up in 1960.*

Dunkerque—*Launched in 1942, this was the French answer to the German pocket battleship. It was at Mers-el-Kebir when the French fleet that had taken refuge there after the armistice was bombed by British ships. It was finally sunk by its own crew at Toulon on November 27, 1942.*

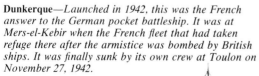

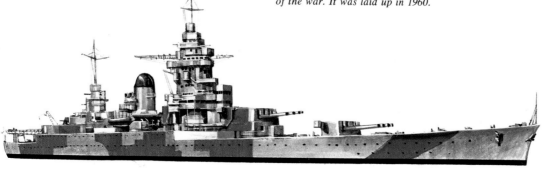

Tourville—*A French heavy cruiser, completed in 1928 under the terms of the Washington Treaty.*

Suffren—*A French cruiser completed in 1930.*

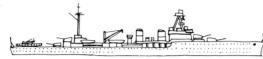

Duguay-Trouin—*A French light cruiser put into service in 1926.*

La Galissonière—*Completed in 1935, sunk by its crew at Toulon.*

types at 10,160 tons. To remain within these limits, French heavy cruisers had to sacrifice armor protection. Typical examples of this building compromise were the *Tourville* and later the *Algérie* class (1932). The London Naval Conference of 1930 tried to remedy this weakness, and the result was a distinction between heavy cruisers (still bound to the 9,842-ton limit) and light ones, with guns of a caliber not exceeding 155 mm (6 in.). The excellent vessels of the *La Galissonière* class (1933) belonged to this last category.

Destroyers were not restricted by the naval conferences. When World War II started, the French navy had 59 destroyers, 8 of them of the *Mogador* class, as well as several survivors of World War I. French submarines, 86 in number in 1939, did not see much action, but the cruiser-submarine de-

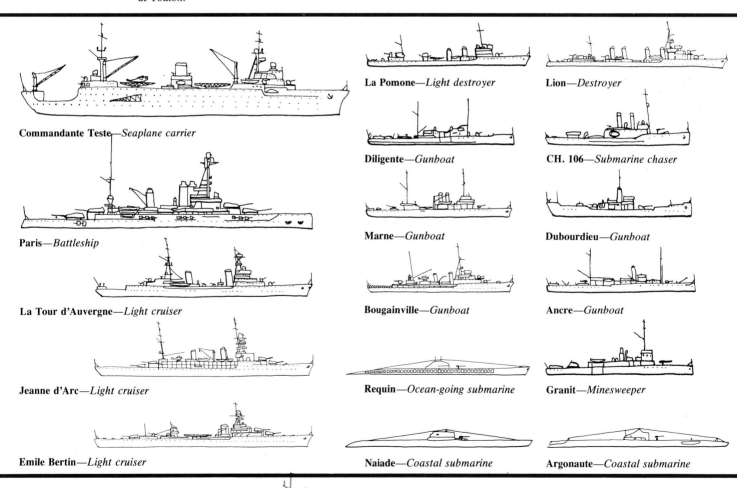

Commandante Teste—*Seaplane carrier*

Paris—*Battleship*

La Tour d'Auvergne—*Light cruiser*

Jeanne d'Arc—*Light cruiser*

Emile Bertin—*Light cruiser*

La Pomone—*Light destroyer*

Diligente—*Gunboat*

Marne—*Gunboat*

Bougainville—*Gunboat*

Requin—*Ocean-going submarine*

Naiade—*Coastal submarine*

Lion—*Destroyer*

CH. 106—*Submarine chaser*

Dubourdieu—*Gunboat*

Ancre—*Gunboat*

Granit—*Minesweeper*

Argonaute—*Coastal submarine*

Jean Bart—*Battleship. Escaped unfinished from Brest in 1940, badly damaged at Casablanca on November 9, 1942. Only completed in 1946.*

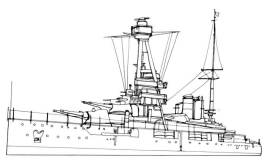

Provence—*This ship was sunk by its own crew at Toulon on November 27, 1942. It was one of the old French dreadnoughts still in service at the start of the war.*

serves mention because of its design and concept. The *Surcouf* cruiser-submarine was one of the largest submarines of World War II.

Apart from ten months of operations during the Normandy campaign, the French fleet saw little service. France signed an armistice with Italy and Germany on June 22, 1940, little more than nine months after the start of the war. Its military fleet was split up. One part managed to reach the British Channel ports and took part in the evacuation of Dunkirk. Most of the French ships that escaped took refuge at the Mers-el-Kebir base at Oran, Algeria, while another group headed for Toulon. The ships anchored in the Algerian harbor were attacked by British battleships and torpedo bombers, which sank the 22,189-ton battleship *Bretagne* and seriously damaged the battleships *Dunkerque* (26,500 tons) and *Provence*, sister ship of the *Bretagne*. The British carried out this action on July 3, 1940, for fear that the French ships might be requisitioned by the German navy. But the Toulon fleet, about 100 ships in all, showed its fidelity to the anti-Nazi cause on November 27, 1942, when it was sunk by its crews almost to the last ship. A total of about 218,984 tons of military shipping were lost.

The Union of Soviet Socialist Republics

At the outbreak of war, the Russian navy was technically and militarily inferior to those of the other powers. Its ships were limited to coastal-patrol duty. Russian Black Sea ships clashed with Italian assault vessels engaged in the blockade of the port of Sevastopol, and on August 5, 1942, the Italians sank the 6,934-ton cruiser *Krasni Krim* off Theodosia.

In June 1941 the Russian navy consisted mainly of ships built at the start of the century, like the battleships of the *Pariskaia Kommuna* class, 3 ships with a displacement of about 23,000 tons, armed with twelve 305-mm (12-in.) guns, built between 1909 and 1914 and modernized between 1931 and 1937.

A more modern type of battleship, the *Treti International*, of 34,447 tons, was under construction.

The Soviet Union had one aircraft carrier, the *Stalin*, built in 1936, a 8,858-ton vessel that could accommodate 22 planes. It had been created from a modified heavy cruiser, the *Krasnaya-Bessarabia*. Two other ships, of 11,810 tons each, were being built.

The cruiser fleet numbered 5 large ships, including the *Orjonikidse*, which was never launched. It was smashed in the shipyard so that it would not fall into German hands. Among 6 smaller cruisers was the *Avrora*, used as a training ship but still ready for combat, a vessel built in 1896 and one of the oldest ships in service. The scout cruisers of the *Leningrad* class were more modern in design and replaced the more costly 5,905-ton cruisers.

Archangelsk—*The British battleship* Royal Sovereign, *transferred to the Soviet Navy under Lease-Lend agreement, 1944.*

Courbet—*The first of the French dreadnoughts laid down by French shipyards from 1911; modernized in 1927. When France was occupied, it was taken over by the Royal Navy. It was later returned to the Free French.*

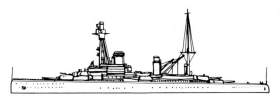

Marat—*The former* Petropavlosk, *launched in 1911. After taking part in the war against Finland, this old battleship was hit by German bombs in September 1941, in the port of Kronstadt, where it sank. It was salvaged and then demolished in 1953.*

The old destroyer fleet, ships dating to the years between 1911 and 1927, was thoroughly modernized and reinforced by ships of more advanced design, such as the 33 vessels of the *Gorki* class, of 1,575 tons, equipped with antisubmarine bombs and minelaying apparatus (100 mines). During the war the Russian shipyards turned out excellent destroyers of the *Stremitelni* class (1,400 tons), from which was developed the *Gromki* class (1,860 tons) carrying four 5.1-in. guns and six to eight 21-in. torpedoes and capable of 37 knots.

The Soviet fleet did not play a leading role in the war. The war on the Russian front was basically a land war. Later political and economic considerations led to a total reconstruction of the Russian fleet, and it is now one of the most modern in the world.

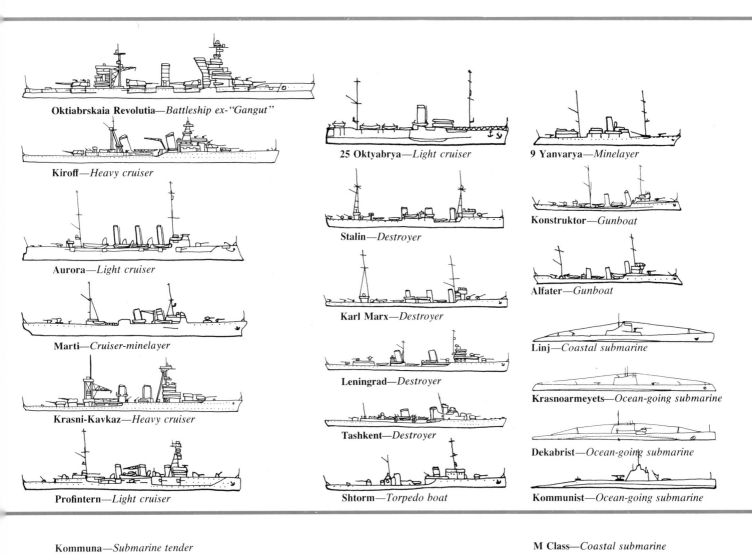

Oktiabrskaia Revolutia—*Battleship ex-"Gangut"*

Kiroff—*Heavy cruiser*

Aurora—*Light cruiser*

Marti—*Cruiser-minelayer*

Krasni-Kavkaz—*Heavy cruiser*

Profintern—*Light cruiser*

25 Oktyabrya—*Light cruiser*

Stalin—*Destroyer*

Karl Marx—*Destroyer*

Leningrad—*Destroyer*

Tashkent—*Destroyer*

Shtorm—*Torpedo boat*

9 Yanvarya—*Minelayer*

Konstruktor—*Gunboat*

Alfater—*Gunboat*

Linj—*Coastal submarine*

Krasnoarmeyets—*Ocean-going submarine*

Dekabrist—*Ocean-going submarine*

Kommunist—*Ocean-going submarine*

Kommuna—*Submarine tender*

M Class—*Coastal submarine*

Germany

When the Treaty of Versailles was signed after World War I, the new size of the German war fleet was established at 6 cruisers of the *Washington* type, 6 light cruisers of 5,905 tons each, 12 destroyers, and 12 torpedo boats. Germany was forbidden to build battleships or submarines. The Germans later refused to observe the conditions of the peace treaty and began building their so-called pocket battleships in 1929. The first of them, the *Deutschland*, illustrated quite clearly the German idea of what war at sea should be like as far as large fighting ships were concerned.

The *Deutschland* had six 280-mm (11-in.) guns as well as many smaller weapons including 8 torpedo tubes. Its speed of 26 knots easily outdistanced any other ship of its class then in service. Two other ships of the same class went into service in 1934 (the *Admiral Scheer*) and 1936 (the *Admiral Graf von Spee*).

After Adolf Hitler came to power, these three ships were joined by the *Scharnhorst* and the *Gneisenau*, the first battleships Germany built after World War I. The armament of these two ships followed a principle applied by the German navy even during World War I. They were less powerful than comparable ships in other navies, but they were much faster (27 knots). With the launching of the *Bismarck* in 1939 and its sister ship, the *Tirpitz*, the German war fleet had 7 modern, well-armed ships. Nevertheless the German surface fleet could not stand up to the com-

Gneisenau—*Launched in 1936 with its sister ship* Scharnhorst, *it represented a new type of battle cruiser. On July l, 1942, its main guns were removed, and the ship was assigned to Norwegian coastal defense. A plan for rebuilding this handsome ship was given up because of the war, and its hull was used to block the entrance to the port of Gdynia.*

Bismarck—*The most powerful battleship of its time, with excellent antitorpedo and antiaircraft armament. Launched in 1939 and put into service in 1941, it went into the North Atlantic on May 18 to attack British convoys. Intercepted by the Home Fleet, it managed to sink the battle cruiser* Hood *but was later hit by planes from the* Ark Royal. *It was finished off by salvos from the* King George V *and the* Rodney, *and was finally sunk by a torpedo from the British cruiser* Dorsetshire.

Admiral Graf von Spee—*One of the three famous German pocket battleships, launched in 1932. While raiding in the South Atlantic, it encountered the British cruisers* Exeter, Ajax, *and* Achilles *on December 13, 1939. Forced to take refuge in the neutral port of Montevideo for repairs, it was sunk outside the Uruguayan harbor on orders from its commander, Captain Langsdorff. This clash, known as the Battle of Rio de la Plata, showed up the limitations of the pocket battleships in comparison with other warships.*

XXXI-C—*The last type of ocean-going submarine in Admiral Dönitz's undersea fleet. The hull was built of prefabricated sections welded together. Thanks to its snorkel, it could sail in submersion using diesel, instead of electric, engines.*

192

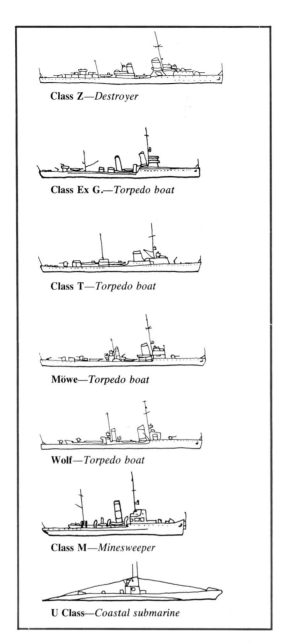

Class Z—*Destroyer*

Class Ex G.—*Torpedo boat*

Class T—*Torpedo boat*

Möwe—*Torpedo boat*

Wolf—*Torpedo boat*

Class M—*Minesweeper*

U Class—*Coastal submarine*

bined British and French fleets, and its operations were more frequently defensive than offensive.

The cruiser program of the Third Reich included the construction of 6 light, 7,677-ton ships, but they never went to sea because they were damaged by air attack while still on the stocks. Two large vessels of the *Prinz Eugen* class, of 14,566 tons and armed with eight 203-mm (8-in.) guns, also went into construction. One of these, the *Lützow*, was sold to Russia still unfinished. Among the smaller cruisers, mention should be made of the *Emden*, the first military vessel on which electric welding was used. It was built in 1925 and modernized in 1934.

As soon as war broke out, the Germans concentrated on building submarines. In 1935 Germany and Great Britain signed a bilateral pact, outside the agreements set up during the various naval conferences. One provision of this agreement was that if the international situation got worse, the German undersea fleet could be brought up to the British level. But in the next four years, the German naval industry, already highly advanced, produced 32 short-range submarines of 280 tons, 25 medium-range craft of 735 tons, and 15 ocean-going submarines of 984 tons. At the start of the conflict, 57 submarines were already at sea and ready for action, while another 63, both short- and long-range, were being built. One of the most important German innovations in submarine warfare was the development of ships that could supply attack submarines with fuel and provisions, thus eliminating long and dangerous voyages back to their bases.

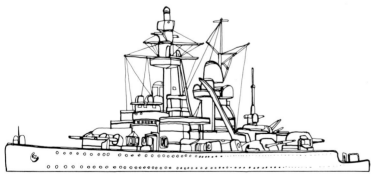

Lützow—*Formerly the* Deutschland, *the first of the series of pocket battleships with which the Germans surprised the world of naval engineering in 1929.*

The underwater offensive was an extremely important part of overall German strategy. The high technical level of the submarines and their crews became evident in 1942, when German U-boat attacks (especially during the Battle of the Atlantic) destroyed over 6 million tons of Allied shipping heading for Britain and Russia. During the war Germany put 1,105 submarines into service. A total of 635 were sunk. Improved ships were built, and technically outdated ones became training ships. The offensive tactics of German submarines consisted mainly of surface torpedo attacks followed by rapid submersion.

Aircraft carriers were regarded with some skepticism. Two ships, the *Graf Zeppelin* of 32,600 tons, begun in 1936, and a second one begun in 1938, were launched by 1939 but never went into service.

Sixteen ships of the *Maas* class (1,599 tons, five 127-mm [5-in.] guns, eight 533-mm [21-in.] torpedoes, and a speed of 36 knots) were the latest destroyers in German service on the eve of war. A total of 22 ships of this type were ready to go into action.

It was naval inferiority that stymied the invasion of England planned for September 1940. A landing fleet of 1,900 barges, 422 tugboats, 994 motorboats, and 150 troopships had been prepared, but the operation was never carried out.

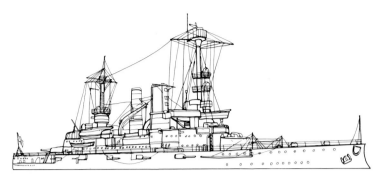

Schlesien—*An old German battleship launched in 1906. During World War II it was used as a training ship.*

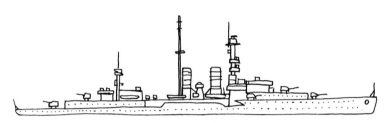

Emden—*A small German light cruiser of 1925, modernized in 1934. The first ship on which electric welding was used.*

Königsberg—*Two other ships completed this class of light cruisers: the* Karlsruhe, *sunk by a British mine, and the* Köln, *sunk by RAF planes.*

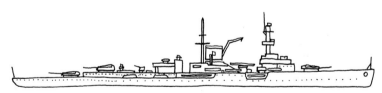

Leipzig—*A German light cruiser. It had a central propeller with variable pitch driven by 4 diesel engines with a total of 13,000 hp.*

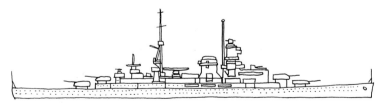

Admiral Hipper—*A German cruiser with a maximum speed of 32 knots.*

▲

Prinz Eugen—*The third heavy cruiser built by the Germans in defiance of the Treaty of Versailles. It took part in two famous episodes in the history of naval warfare: the incursion into the North Atlantic with the* Bismarck, *and the crossing of the English Channel with the* Scharnhorst *from Brest to German waters, in 1942.*

Admiral Scheer—*During a cruise of 46,000 miles, from October 1940 to March 1941, it sank 17 cargo ships for a total of 111,215 tons. In April 1945 it was hit by British planes while at anchor in the base at Kiel. It capsized in a flooded dry dock.*

Scharnhorst—*A more advanced version of the battle cruiser, it entered service in 1939. It operated in the North Atlantic for a long time, and also forced the British blockade of the Channel. On December 26, 1943, during the Battle of Bear Island, it met the* Duke of York *and was hit 3 times from a distance of over 7 miles. It sank after repeated attacks by British destroyers.*

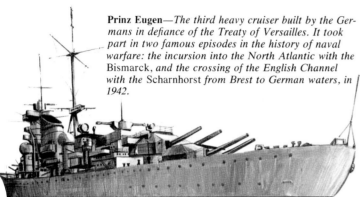

▼

Tirpitz—*Ready for action in 1941, this ship was the finest example of its type. It was assigned to the Baltic fleet, and after taking part in various war actions, anchored in the Altafjord on the coast of Norway, where it was attacked and damaged by British pocket submarines. Subjected to repeated bombing by the Royal Air Force it was sunk by 6- and 8-ton bombs on November 12, 1944.*

▼

U-boat—*Of type II-B, the most numerous when war broke out, with a total of 16 ships. Because of their limited range and light armament, these submarines operated only in the waters of the North Sea and the Baltic. Despite these limitations, German navy considered the U-boat its decisive weapon.*

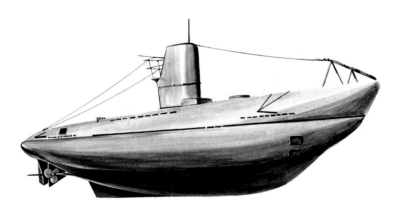

Italy

When Mussolini's government declared war on France and Great Britain on June 10, 1940, the Italian navy might well have been considered one of Europe's most modern and well trained fleets. The battleships *Littorio* and *Vittorio Veneto*, to which two others of the same class, the *Roma* and the *Impero* were added, were among the most efficient fighting ships of their day.

Noteworthy among the heavy and the light cruisers was the *Trento* of 1927, a fast and powerful ship, though too costly to be produced in large numbers. The *Washington*-class ship *Bolzano* reached a speed of 34 knots. The ships of the *Capitani Romani* class (3,747 tons), laid in 1939, were even

Duilio—*Launched in 1913 and modernized in 1937 at the same time as the construction of the* Vittorio Veneto. *This ship was assigned to the base at Taranto in 1940; there it was damaged in the bow and to starboard by a torpedo launched during a British air attack on the Italian base on September 7, 1940. After various missions as convoy escort, it reached Malta when the armistice was signed. During the war it went to sea four times to hunt enemy ships and seven times to serve as convoy escort.*

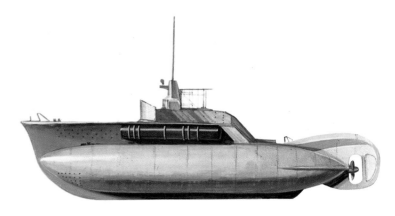

Barchino MTM—*Built in 1940; 5.40 meters (17.9 feet) long and 1.67 meters (5.5 feet) wide. Piloted by one man at a speed of 33 knots, it carried an explosive charge of 300 kg (661 lbs.).*

Olterra—*A tanker converted into a tender ship for Italian operations in the port of Algeciras. Its crew was made up of underwater-assault men, and inside the hull was a pool connected with the outside, from which the "pigs" could come and go.*

The "pig"—*Designed by Teseo Tesei using the shell of a normal 533-mm (21-in.) torpedo, 6.70 meters (22 feet) long. Two men straddled it. It had an explosive warhead holding about 300 kg (661 lbs.) of TNT. Speed: 2.5 to 2.8 knots. Endurance: 5 to 6 hours. Maximum depth in submersion: 30 meters (98.5 feet).*

Pocket submarine CB—*It displaced from 36 to 45 tons, and was 15 meters (49 feet) long and 3 meters (10 feet) wide. It held a crew of from one to 3 men. Two 450-mm (17.7-in.) torpedo tubes were set outside the hull.*

Roma—*It entered service in June 1942. After the armistice, it left La Spezia for Malta on September 9, but during the passage was hit by two rocket bombs fired from German planes. The keel split and the ship sank in two sections, with great loss of life.*

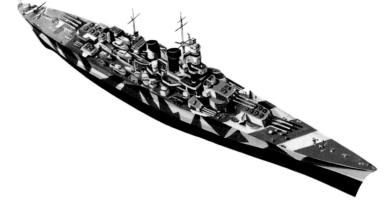

faster, and were really ocean-going scout cruisers. They could do 40 knots and were armed with eight 135-mm (5.3-in.) guns, eight 37-mm guns, eight 20-mm guns, and eight 21-in. torpedoes.

As of June 10, 1940, Italy had 8 large and 26 smaller cruisers, 14 of which were still in construction.

The lack of aircraft carriers, and the consequent lack of air protection, had a great deal to do with a series of events that saw a modern navy fighting under obvious conditions of inferiority. After the Battle of Cape Matapan (March 28, 1941), it was decided to turn two transatlantic liners into aircraft carriers, one of these the 32,533-ton motorship *Roma*, which was renamed the *Aquila*. The *Aquila* never went to sea. The second project, that of converting another transatlantic vessel into a carrier, was never begun. The Italian navy had 61 destroyers, among

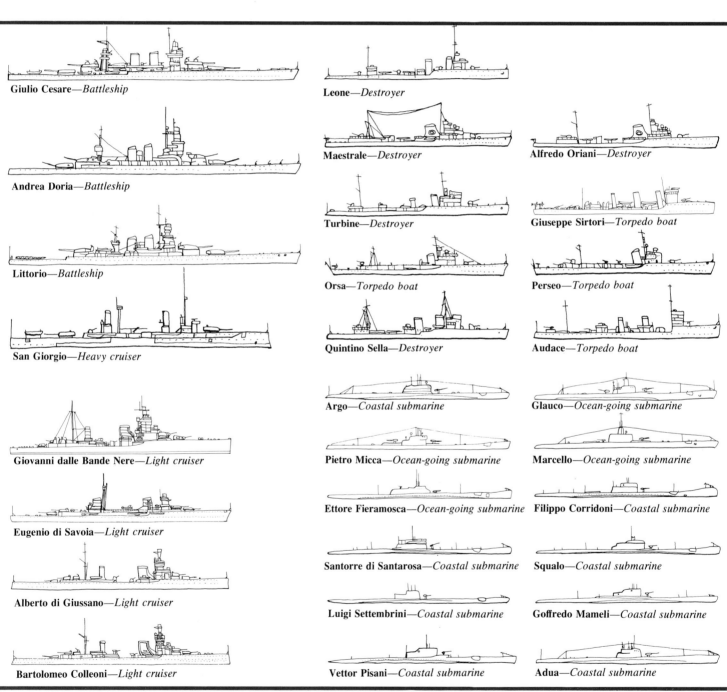

Giulio Cesare—*Battleship*

Andrea Doria—*Battleship*

Littorio—*Battleship*

San Giorgio—*Heavy cruiser*

Giovanni dalle Bande Nere—*Light cruiser*

Eugenio di Savoia—*Light cruiser*

Alberto di Giussano—*Light cruiser*

Bartolomeo Colleoni—*Light cruiser*

Leone—*Destroyer*

Maestrale—*Destroyer*

Turbine—*Destroyer*

Orsa—*Torpedo boat*

Quintino Sella—*Destroyer*

Argo—*Coastal submarine*

Pietro Micca—*Ocean-going submarine*

Ettore Fieramosca—*Ocean-going submarine*

Santorre di Santarosa—*Coastal submarine*

Luigi Settembrini—*Coastal submarine*

Vettor Pisani—*Coastal submarine*

Alfredo Oriani—*Destroyer*

Giuseppe Sirtori—*Torpedo boat*

Perseo—*Torpedo boat*

Audace—*Torpedo boat*

Glauco—*Ocean-going submarine*

Marcello—*Ocean-going submarine*

Filippo Corridoni—*Coastal submarine*

Squalo—*Coastal submarine*

Goffredo Mameli—*Coastal submarine*

Adua—*Coastal submarine*

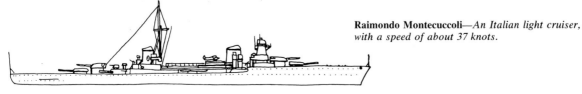

Raimondo Montecuccoli—*An Italian light cruiser, with a speed of about 37 knots.*

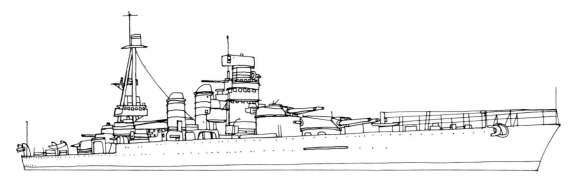

which the most modern were those of the *Soldati* class, of 2,460 tons, with four 120-mm (4.3-in.) guns and a speed of 39 knots.

In addition to the submarines built before 1926 (4 long-range and 8 medium-range ones), 10 medium-range ships were built, with 8 torpedo tubes, as well as 6 coastal prototypes of 610 tons, equipped with 6 torpedo tubes and a 100-mm (3.9-in.) gun. Surface speed was 14 knots, and underwater speed was 8.5 knots. Twenty-two submarines eventually entered service: 3 ocean-going ones of 1,378 tons, a minelayer, 6 medium-range and 12 coastal vessels, in addition to those built before 1939: 29 coastal submarines and 15 ocean-going ones, 3 of them minelayers. Finally 14 ocean-going undersea craft were put into service by the end of 1939 and another 4 during 1941. The 32 Italian submarines operating in the waters of the Atlantic Ocean destroyed more than 100 ships, for a total of 569,852 tons. The Italian navy was severely hampered by insufficient fuel supplies. There were only 1,968,500 tons of reserve fuel available at the start of the war, barely enough to last one year.

The MAS boats and the *barchini* and "pigs" carried their offensive action to bases at Malta, Gibraltar, and Alexandria, but this did not alter the course of events. As a tribute to Italian seamanship, surrendered Italian vessels were not required to lower their flags when they entered English ports.

Conte di Cavour—*One of the large Italian battleships, launched in 1911 and modernized between 1933 and 1937. Sister ship of the* Giulio Cesare.

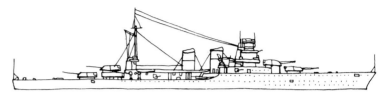

Giuseppe Garibaldi—*A light cruiser*

Trento—*Built at the same time as the* Trieste, *in 1925.*

Zara—*An Italian heavy cruiser of 1931; it was part of a class of four ships.*

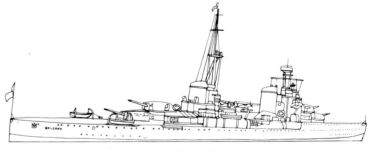

Bolzano—*One of the best examples of an Italian heavy cruiser.*

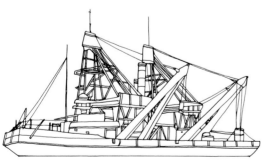

Anteo—*An Italian submarine-tender ship.*

Vittorio Veneto—*Of the same class as the* Littorio, ▶ *built by the Joint Adriatic shipyards in Trieste in the years 1934–1940. It took part in the Battle of Cape Teulada.*

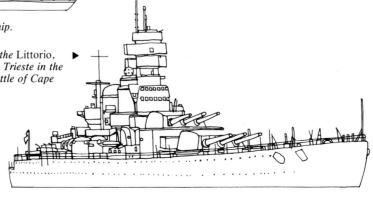

Japan

December 7, 1941, will remain one of the fundamental dates in the history of warfare. With its surprise attack on the American base at Pearl Harbor, Japan culminated the period of Pacific expansion that had begun with the Chinese and Russo-Japanese wars. Fully aware of the importance of naval air strategy, the Japanese devoted most of their industrial effort to producing aircraft carriers. In 1922, just before the British *Hermes II* was launched, they finished the *Hosyo*, the world's first ship designed as an aircraft carrier. Japanese strategists assigned a vital function in the vast war plans they were developing to the aircraft tender and the aircraft carrier. Ten years later, after the transformation of the 25,589-ton battle cruiser *Akagi* and the battleship *Kaga* into aircraft carriers, the smallest aircraft carrier then in existence was launched—the 6,988-ton *Ryuzyo*, with a completely bare flight deck and the smokestacks set to one side. The *Soryu* and the *Hiryu* appeared in the waters of the Far East shortly thereafter, with a standard tonnage of 10,391 tons. When war broke out in Europe, the Japanese naval air force was in full development, and its aircraft carrier fleet was superior to that of America, since the 13,779-ton *Koryu*, *Shokaku*, and *Zuikaku* had been added to those already in service.

At the start of the war in the Pacific, in 1941, the Japanese had 8 aircraft carriers in service. These were followed by another 24, 5 for attack and the rest for escort duty.

Yamashiro—*This large battleship of the* Huso *class, completed in 1917 and rebuilt in 1932, was not used very often during the war because of its low speed. It made a last desperate attack during the Battle of Leyte. It was destroyed by American torpedo planes during the battle in the strait of Suriago on October 25, 1944.*

Syokabu—*One of the first Japanese aircraft carriers built after the end of the restrictions on naval armament. It was launched in 1939 and had a reinforced flight deck. It had good range and high speed.*

▼

Yamato—*The largest Japanese battleship was launched in 1940 and put into action in June 1944, when it took part in the Battle of the Philippine Sea. In 1945 it went on its last mission when the Americans attacked Okinawa. On April 7 it was attacked by American planes and hit by twelve torpedoes, seven large bombs, and several 250-kg (551-lb.) ones. One of them exploded in an ammunition deposit on board, and the huge battleship went to the bottom.*

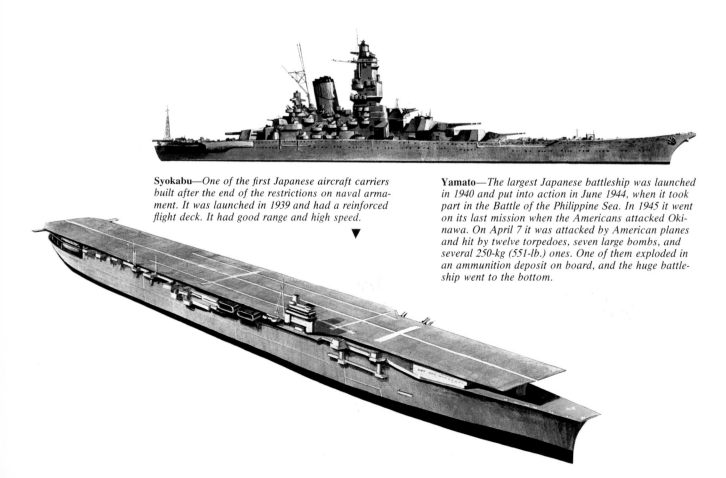

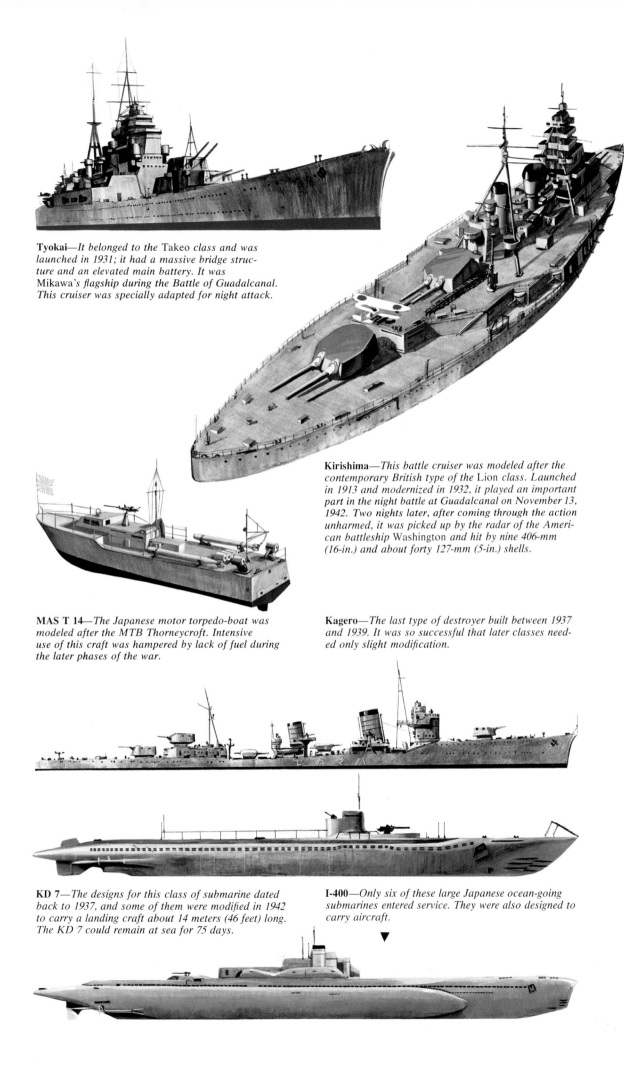

Tyokai—*It belonged to the* Takeo *class and was launched in 1931; it had a massive bridge structure and an elevated main battery. It was Mikawa's flagship during the Battle of Guadalcanal. This cruiser was specially adapted for night attack.*

Kirishima—*This battle cruiser was modeled after the contemporary British type of the* Lion *class. Launched in 1913 and modernized in 1932, it played an important part in the night battle at Guadalcanal on November 13, 1942. Two nights later, after coming through the action unharmed, it was picked up by the radar of the American battleship* Washington *and hit by nine 406-mm (16-in.) and about forty 127-mm (5-in.) shells.*

MAS T 14—*The Japanese motor torpedo-boat was modeled after the MTB Thorneycroft. Intensive use of this craft was hampered by lack of fuel during the later phases of the war.*

Kagero—*The last type of destroyer built between 1937 and 1939. It was so successful that later classes needed only slight modification.*

KD 7—*The designs for this class of submarine dated back to 1937, and some of them were modified in 1942 to carry a landing craft about 14 meters (46 feet) long. The KD 7 could remain at sea for 75 days.*

I-400—*Only six of these large Japanese ocean-going submarines entered service. They were also designed to carry aircraft.*

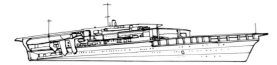

Akagi—*A 42,000-ton battle cruiser turned into an aircraft carrier. It took part in the attack of Pearl Harbor on December 7, 1941.*

Miduho—*A seaplane carrier for aiding and rescuing seaplanes.*

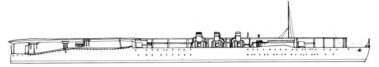

Hosyo—*The first aircraft carrier in the world, built as such in 1922.*

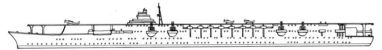

Shokaku—*One of the largest and most modern Japanese aircraft carriers, built in 1941.*

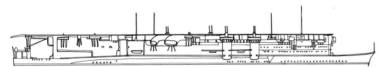

Ryuzyo—*The smallest Japanese aircraft carrier, with its smoke flues laid sideways.*

Some of these were converted cargo ships.

Only when Japan had more carriers than the United States could it face the American navy.

And just as the aircraft carrier was showing that it was the most important surface ship in a fleet, the Japanese put into active service the world's two largest battleships, the *Yamato* and the *Musashi*, extremely fast despite their impressive displacement of almost 68,894 tons. They could attain a speed of 27.7 knots. The Japanese battleship fleet also included four *Kongo*-class vessels, of 28,867 tons; two *Huso*-class ships, with the same displacement, the 29,516-ton *Ise* and *Hyuga*; and the *Nagato* and *Mutu*, of 32,203 tons.

The Japanese had agreed to observe the rules laid down by the Washington Conference, and turned out heavy cruisers within the limits assigned them. The *Kako* and *Aoba* classes, built in 1925 and 1926, respectively, had only six 203-mm (8-in.) guns, while the *Nachi* and *Atago* classes later carried 10. The Treaty of London of 1936 limited the displacement of light cruisers to 7,874 tons. Japan signed this treaty and stayed close to the limits with the 8,366 tons of the *Mogami*-class cruisers. Japanese

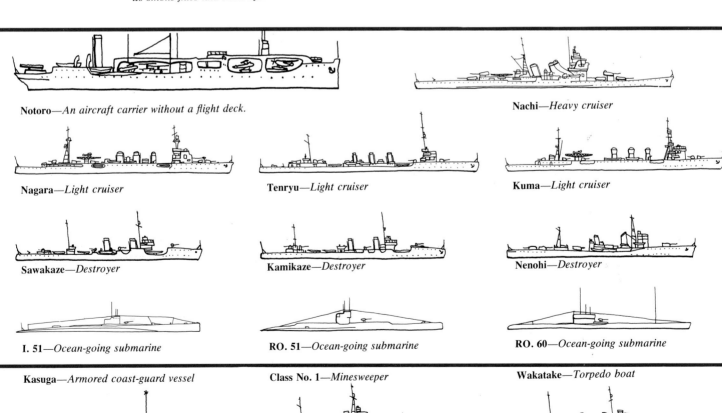

Notoro—*An aircraft carrier without a flight deck.*

Nachi—*Heavy cruiser*

Nagara—*Light cruiser*

Tenryu—*Light cruiser*

Kuma—*Light cruiser*

Sawakaze—*Destroyer*

Kamikaze—*Destroyer*

Nenohi—*Destroyer*

I. 51—*Ocean-going submarine*

RO. 51—*Ocean-going submarine*

RO. 60—*Ocean-going submarine*

Kasuga—*Armored coast-guard vessel*

Class No. 1—*Minesweeper*

Wakatake—*Torpedo boat*

cruisers, especially those of the *Kako* class, with their 6 separate turrets (three each, at bow and stern), were stubborn adversaries of American cruisers, although the Japanese only turned out four *Agano*-class ships, of 6,547 tons, with six 155-mm (6-in.) guns, as well as the *Oyodo*, of 8,035 tons, with six 155-mm (6-in.) guns. The *Mogami*, a 12,013-ton heavy cruiser, was modified to carry 11 seaplanes; and the light cruiser *Kitakami*, already modified in 1941 to carry up to forty 609-mm (24-in.) torpedo tubes, was reconverted in 1944 into an assault troop transport ship.

At the outbreak of the war, Japan had a fleet of 112 destroyers, some of them survivors of World War I, including 1,132-ton destroyers and 670-ton vessels. There were also two ships of the *Kagero* class, of 2,510 tons, with eight 127-mm (21-in.) torpedoes, able to reach a speed of about 39 knots. Twelve more ships of the same type were built subsequently.

The 66 submarines that made up the Japanese undersea fleet, as well as pocket submarines, had no chance to carry out important war operations.

An aspect of the Japanese-American war that involved carrier-based as well as land-based planes was the activity of the Japanese suicide pilots, the *Kamikazes*, who crash-dived into enemy ships. These suicide missions were the idea of Admiral Ohnishi. *Kamikaze* means "divine wind" and alluded to the wind that scattered the fleet of Kublai Khan in 1281, as it was crossing the Strait of Tsushima to invade Japan. The *Kamikaze* missions first used Zero fighters, armed with one 250-kg (551-lb.) bomb. Later, specially designed bombs were prepared, with a charge of 1,888 kg (1.8 tons). These were dropped from a bomber in flight and then directed to the enemy target by the *Kamikaze* in a gliding flight powered by a small jet engine. The Americans called this bomb the **baca**, meaning "crazy" in Japanese. It was developed in 1944 and designed expressly for suicide attacks. More than 700 of them were built. The first made its appearance in February 1945, during the Battle of Iwo Jima.

Kongo—*The four battleships of this class formed the nucleus of the Japanese war fleet. The Kongo was modernized in 1937.*

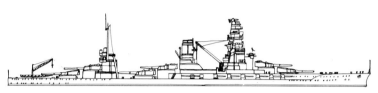

Ise—*One of the first examples of a Japanese battleship entirely built by Japanese shipyards.*

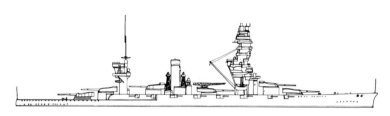

Huso—*Completed in 1915 with its sister ship* Yamashiro; *this large Japanese battleship was sunk during the Battle of Leyte.*

Aoba—*A Japanese heavy cruiser, with the classic arrangement of the guns in twin turrets.*

Yubari—*A light cruiser, equipped with light vertical and horizontal armor and completed in 1923.*

Nagato—*This battleship, sunk in April 1945, was one of the most powerful Japanese warships.*

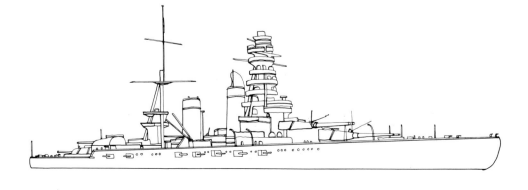

The Aircraft Carrier

CAPITAL SHIP OF THE FUTURE

Enterprise—The world's largest warship and also the largest vessel with nuclear propulsion, until the entrance into service of the new and more powerful *Nimitz*. Built at a cost of almost 450 million dollars, the *Enterprise* has a large flight deck set at a pronounced angle to the ship. Thanks to the relatively small size of nuclear engines, the ship can carry more aircraft fuel reserves. The eight nuclear reactors are Westinghouse A 2w pressurized-water cooled, and have a maximum power of 350,000 hp. Two Sea Sparrow missile systems were installed on board in 1968, and a third one in 1971. The ship's crew consists of 5,500 men: 3,100 for running the ship and 2,400 for servicing the planes.

January 18, 1911, may be considered the birth date of the aircraft carrier. On that day, an American civilian pilot, Eugene Ely, landed a plane on a wooden platform built on the forecastle of the armored cruiser *Pennsylvania*. He also took off from the ship afterward. This exploit demonstrated that planes could be carried on ships.

The forerunner of the aircraft carrier was the seaplane carrier, usually a vessel equipped with a crane for recovering seaplanes after their flights. One seaplane carrier, the *Engadine*, took part in the Battle of Jutland in 1916.

After World War I, great attention was paid to the designing and building of ships expressly planned as aircraft carriers, apart from the many adaptations and conversions that had been effected in the United States, Great Britain, and Japan. The world's first original aircraft carrier was the Japanese *Hosyo*, which entered service in 1922, shortly before the British *Hermes*. As planes became heavier and faster, more efficient blocking devices were developed to make deck landings easier, high-pressure steam catapults were introduced, and flight decks were set at an angle to the ship (a British idea). Between the two world wars only the navies of the United States, Great Britain, and Japan made use of aircraft carriers in large-scale operations. In the United States, for instance, the building of the carrier was greatly facilitated by the introduction of large-scale prefabrication. During World War II the American navy built 22 aircraft carriers of 27,000 tons each; 9 lighter ones of 11,000 tons each; 19 escort carriers of 11,400 tons each; 50 of 7,800 tons each; and 10 of 9,800 tons each; plus 26 of this last *Bogue* class, on loan to Great Britain.

Aircraft carriers, and more recently helicopter carriers, form an integral part of the fleets of the major naval powers of the globe. Many ships not specifically designed as carriers carry helicopters for antisubmarine action and for supply and rescue missions. Ships such as the Italian helicopter cruiser *Vittorio Veneto*, the British *Blake*, the French *Jeanne d'Arc*, and the Russian *Moskva*, have traditional arms or missiles in the bow section, and a large aircraft repair shop and helicopter landing platform in the stern.

After World War II, the United States and Great Britain were convinced of the future importance of the aircraft carrier, and larger and better vessels were put into service: the British *Eagle* of 36,420 tons, and the American *Forrestal*, with a flight deck more than 330.8 meters (990 feet) long and a displacement of 59,650 tons. These giants of the sea were surpassed only in 1961, by the *Enterprise*, a nuclear vessel of 89,600 tons, the naval marvel of our time. New American ships of the *Nimitz* class, of 93,400 tons, have been developed.

Aquila—The only aircraft carrier built for the Italian navy, and never put into active service. It resulted from the transformation of a requisitioned transatlantic liner, the 32,020-ton *Roma*.

The Aircraft Carrier

Formidable—British aircraft carrier with armored flight decks. It was begun in 1937. In March 1941, a "Fairy Albacore" took off from its deck and torpedoed the Italian heavy cruiser *Pola* during the Battle of Cape Matapan.

Essex—Length: 250 meters (774 feet); overall length: 276 meters (888 feet); beam: 45 meters (93 feet); speed: 32 knots; armament: twelve 127-mm (5-in.) cannons and seventy-two 40-mm guns; 82 aircraft; 2,900 men; displacement: 33,000 tons.

The cross section shows the interior of the *Essex*; from top to bottom: the plane elevator, the 20-mm (13/16-in.) and 40-mm (1 5/8-in.) antiaircraft guns on the sides, and just below them, the lifeboats. On the far left are the ventilation engines, the plane-repair workshops, and the large central maintenance shop. Below are the elevator workshop, the spare-parts depot, and the air-conditioning room. In the lower part of the ship are the cooling system, the steam ducts of the turbines, the four large turbines, the antiincendiary air cavity, and double holds for aircraft fuel. In the middle of the cross section and to the sides of the ship is the plane engine deposit area with repair shop, ammunition storage, and emergency-lighting equipment.

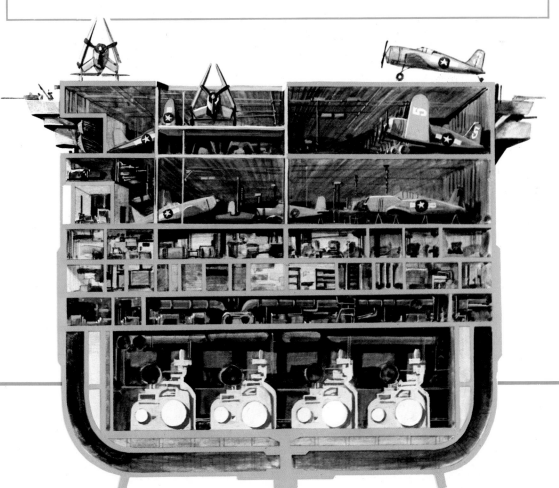

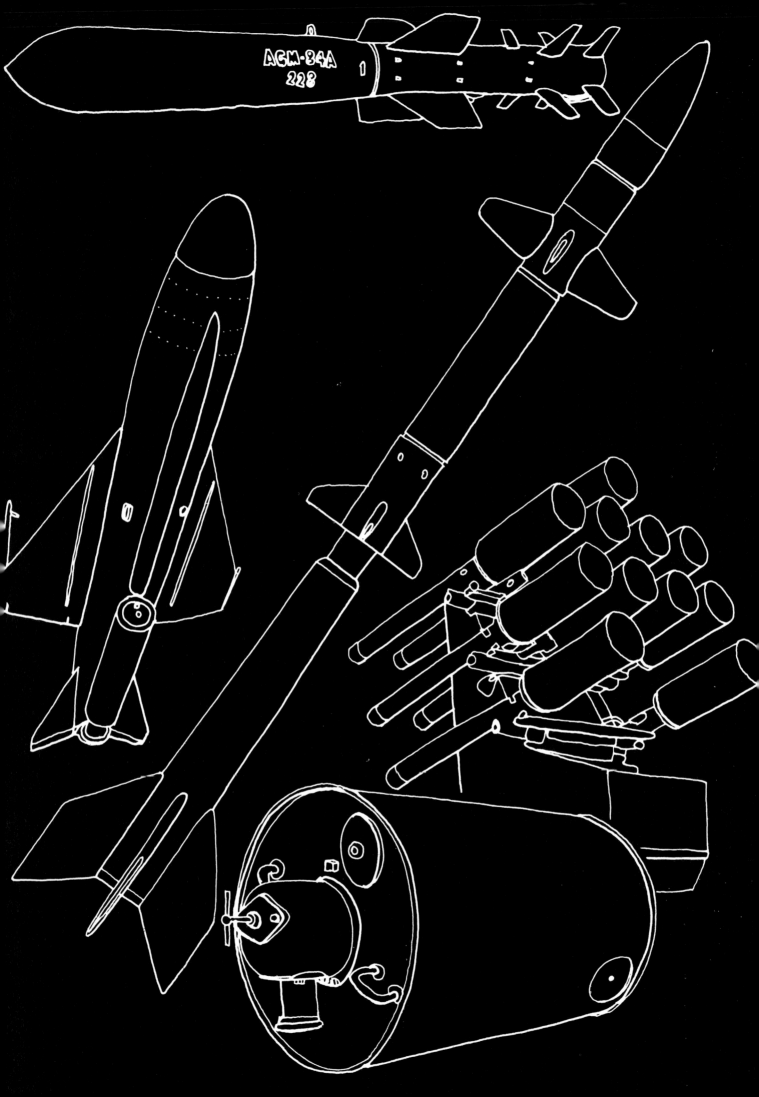

Today's Navy

The history of the world's navies in the postwar period is closely linked to changes in the international situation and naval policies. The continuing energy crisis and the drying-up of sources of raw materials are bound to have repercussions on military development generally, as new technology seeks solutions to new problems.

Only the United States has continued to build large aircraft carriers, while other countries, including the Soviet Union, have concentrated on multipurpose ships. The world's major navies have developed escort ships of from 2,460 to 4,921 tons, for antisubmarine, antiaircraft, and antiship operations, along with fast missile-launching gunboats; and hydrofoil and hovercraft vessels have been designed and built with considerable offensive capacity.

Only the four navies—those of the United States, Russia, Great Britain, and France—have built nuclear submarines, while smaller navies have greatly increased the number of their conventional submarines.

Nuclear propulsion has been applied to underseas craft, to some large aircraft carriers, and to some escort vessels. The Soviet Union has built icebreakers, and France has designed a nuclear helicopter-carrier. But the gas turbine, often paired with a diesel engine, continues to be the basic element in conventional propulsion and reaches quite high speeds. At the same time, water-jet propulsion with an intermediate gas turbine is being widely applied. It is being used on ships with displacement up to 2,000 tons, according to the American design for "surface-effect" vessels.

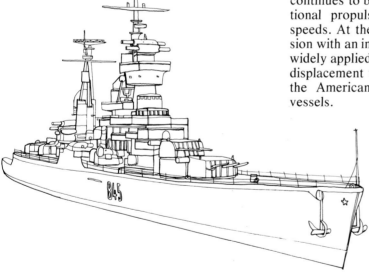

Admiral Ushakov—*A conventional Soviet cruiser, designed after the war and then turned into a naval command headquarters.*

Guided missiles are assuming greater importance. There are strategic air-to-surface, surface-to-surface, surface-to-depth, and depth-to-surface versions. The U.S. Navy has developed an exceptional surface-to-surface system for 31 of the 41 guided-

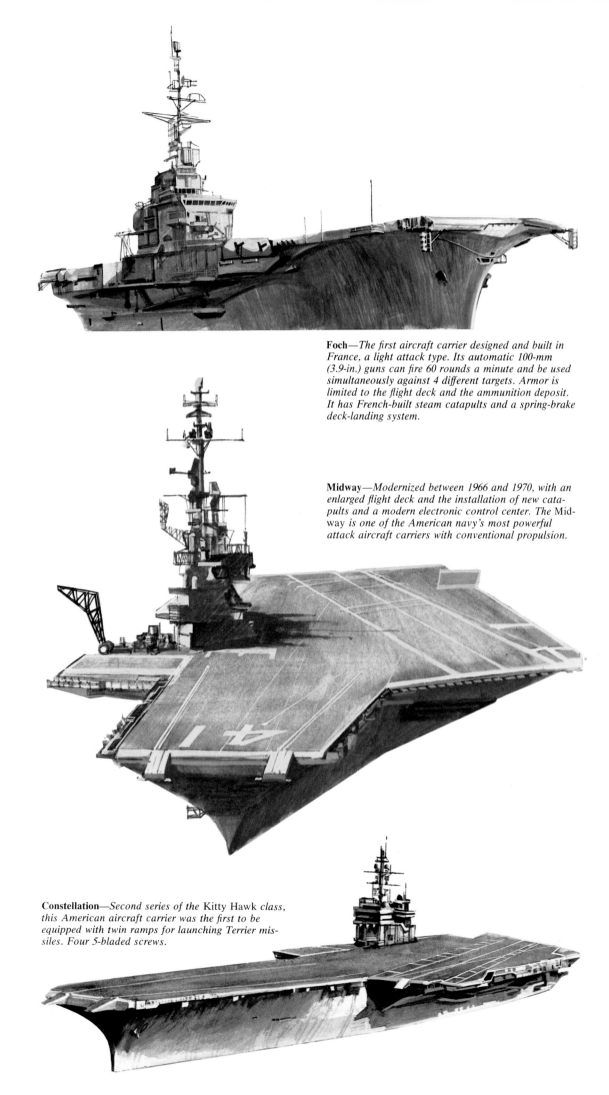

Foch—*The first aircraft carrier designed and built in France, a light attack type. Its automatic 100-mm (3.9-in.) guns can fire 60 rounds a minute and be used simultaneously against 4 different targets. Armor is limited to the flight deck and the ammunition deposit. It has French-built steam catapults and a spring-brake deck-landing system.*

Midway—*Modernized between 1966 and 1970, with an enlarged flight deck and the installation of new catapults and a modern electronic control center. The Midway is one of the American navy's most powerful attack aircraft carriers with conventional propulsion.*

Constellation—*Second series of the* Kitty Hawk *class, this American aircraft carrier was the first to be equipped with twin ramps for launching Terrier missiles. Four 5-bladed screws.*

Aircraft and Helicopter Carriers

In 1975, the second American nuclear aircraft carrier, the *Chester Nimitz*, went into its operational phase. At the same time, work continued on the third vessel, the *Dwight D. Eisenhower*, and the *Carl Winston*, fourth and last of the series, was put into construction.

The Soviet Union planned to launch the *Kiev*, its first large ship for vertical-takeoff planes and helicopters, while its sister ship, the *Minsk*, was in an advanced stage of construction in Black Sea shipyards.

Great Britain has kept its last conventional aircraft carrier, the *Ark Royal*, in service. Plans for the building of a new ship, an all-deck multipurpose vessel with all-gas propulsion have been proposed. Building of two other ships of the same class *Invincible* and conversion of two cruisers of the old *Tiger* class into helicopter carriers have been outlined. The entire program has, however, been affected by cuts in defense spending.

The French navy plans to put two aircraft carriers and two helicopter carriers into operation by 1980, according to a general program for restructuring and substantially strengthening the French armed forces.

Kiev—*Although this ship is usually described as an aircraft carrier, it is really a development of the helicopter-carrier cruiser of the* Moskva *class. Depending on its mission, it will carry helicopters or vertical-takeoff airplanes. It is more heavily armed than U.S. carriers.*

Ark Royal—*The last aircraft carrier put into service in the British navy. The military construction program foresaw the building of four large aircraft carriers to be used in the Pacific, to be followed by a three-ship class of larger-sized vessels. But the end of the war halted this plan, and only the* Ark Royal *and the* Eagle *were completed. The former went back into service in 1970, after being thoroughly modernized and equipped with a sophisticated electronic system.*

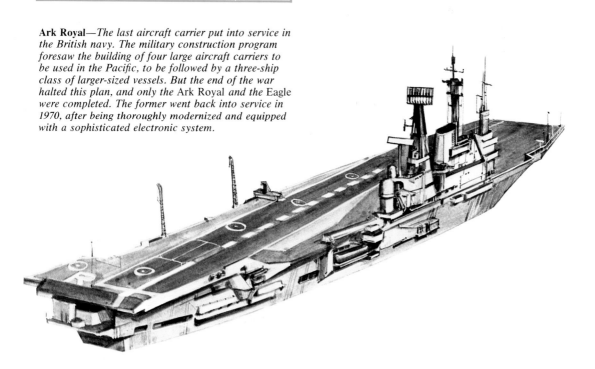

207

208

Although the various navies of the world have
their own classifications, a general classification
applicable to all has been developed.
  Ships are therefore grouped in the following
way:

R = aircraft carriers; **B** = battleships; **C** = cruisers; **D** = destroyers and flotilla leaders; **F** = frigates and corvettes; **S** = underwater vessels; **M** =
mine hunters and minesweepers; **N** = minelayers;
P = light craft; **L** = vessels for amphibious operations; **AL** = ships for logistic support; **A** = auxiliary ships.

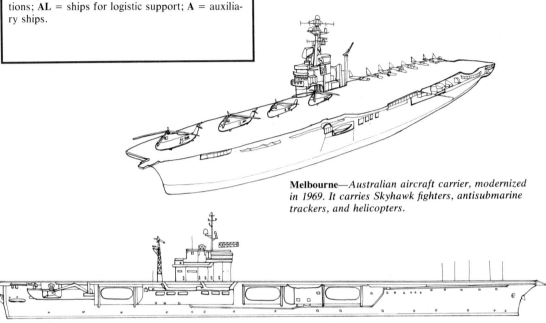

Melbourne—*Australian aircraft carrier, modernized
in 1969. It carries Skyhawk fighters, antisubmarine
trackers, and helicopters.*

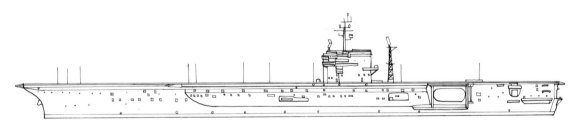

America—*Developed from the* Forrestal *class, it is a sister ship of the* Constellation *and the* Kitty Hawk. *It cost
about 230 million dollars to build and has a completely automatic landing system.*

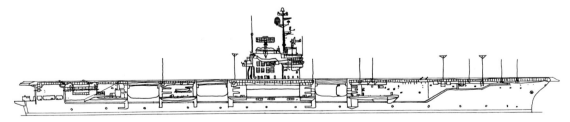

John F. Kennedy—*The last aircraft carrier with conventional propulsion built by the United States, and the natural
successor of the large postwar carriers. This was the first aircraft carrier to be equipped with a guided-missile
system.*

Forrestal—*The first major ship built by the U.S. Navy after World War II. The landing deck is heavily armored.*

Cruisers

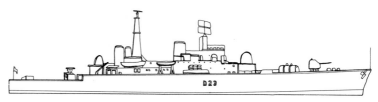

Tiger—A British helicopter cruiser that holds from two to four helicopters. An interesting step on the way to the creation of the all-deck cruiser.

Cruisers, like battleships, have less strategic and tactical importance than they did during World War II. Their place is being taken by lighter ships with more modern armament, at present called flotilla leaders. Nevertheless cruisers are still part of most of the world's major navies and now carry ballistic missiles. In 1959, the United States launched the *Long Beach*, the first American surface unit with nuclear propulsion and the first in the world to be equipped from the beginning exclusively with missiles. With its 17,350-ton displacement, it can be compared with the Russian cruisers *Moskva* and *Leningrad*, of 18,000 tons. The current tendency is to replace guns with missiles of varying potential, or to turn older vessels into headquarters ships and even into training ships. Italy has built three guided-missile cruisers, of large displacement and equipped with flexible antiaircraft and antisubmarine features.

creasingly employed for antisubmarine and antiship operations and can be equipped with air-to-surface and mine-destroying tactical missile systems.

The United States gives prime importance to the quantitative and qualitative development of its naval air force, and the extensive renewal of the American fleet has seen the almost total withdrawal from service of a large number of wartime and postwar vessels, while the efficiency of modern warships has reached higher levels.

The Soviet Union is challenging the Western powers' influence on all the seas of the world, making maximum use of its naval

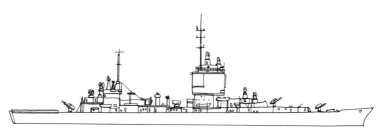

Long Beach—An American guided-missile cruiser, the first U.S. surface vessel with nuclear propulsion and the first cruiser in the world to use missiles as its exclusive armament.

missile launchers now in service, using the Poseidon ballistic missile with independent multiple warheads that guide themselves on to the target.

Conventional weapons continue to be used as well. They are of small and medium caliber and highly automated, with rapid firing speed. Italian weapons are among the finest in this field; the 76- and 127-mm (3- and 5-in.) types are used by several navies throughout the world. Short vertical-takeoff planes will make up the air-attack groups on most of the larger aircraft and mixed carriers, along with the helicopter, which is in-

Bristol—A missile-carrying light cruiser of the Royal Navy, seaworthy, fast, and highly automated.

Leningrad—The first Soviet ship to carry guided missiles and helicopters. Equipped with two sonars, one on the keel, and one that can be towed.

Kresta—A Russian class of guided-missile cruiser of 1970, an example of the efforts made by the USSR to strengthen its naval forces.

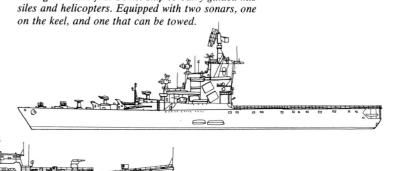

Vittorio Veneto—*The original design of the* Andrea Doria *led the Italian navy to develop a cruiser with greater possibilities for carrying helicopters and an improved* Terrier *and* Asroc *missile system.*

De Zeven Provincien—*This Dutch cruiser was turned into a guided-missile launcher in 1962–1964 and is a good example of operational flexibility combined with a high degree of automation.*

New Jersey—*One of the last four battleships of the* Iowa *class, rearmed in 1967–1968 for the Vietnam War. This large vessel was put back in the reserves in 1969.*

Battleships

The large battleship of the two world wars has been outmoded by technical progress. Only the United States still has four battleships of the *Iowa* class in reserve, each with a displacement of 57,-950 tons.

---

forces to back up its foreign policy. In recent decades, large multipurpose conventional ships and nuclear submarines have undergone intense development.

Great Britain devotes much of its attention to European waters, strengthening those forces assigned to the defense of vital lines of maritime communications. Britain has also developed amphibian vessels for special missions.

France has been building a strategic deterrent force to maintain its prestige throughout the world. The modernization of the French fleet is scheduled to be completed by 1980.

Japan has resumed its authoritative position on the seas.

Otvashnyi—*A Russian guided-missile-launching destroyer that appeared in 1964; it can be used for escorting larger vessels and operational groups, as well as for antiaircraft and antisubmarine operations. It was one of the first ships to use engine equipment mainly composed of gas turbines.*

Hampshire—*A British light cruiser, with guided-missile-launching, antiaircraft, and antisubmarine capabilities. It can operate even in radioactive areas, and all its main equipment is below deck. There is a gas turbine engine, the first of its kind used by the Royal Navy. The ship also has a reconnaissance helicopter and gyrostabilizers.* ▶

Destroyers

Better known today as flotilla leaders, these ships have gradually taken over the tactical and strategic role of cruisers and battleships. Destroyers function as escort vessels for aircraft carriers, with varied armament and flexibility of function. The U.S. Navy's *California*, a nuclear-propulsion ship, is a typical example of the modern destroyer, replacing the outdated cruiser. Its nuclear propulsion and its new weapons systems are highly advanced technologically. Its range is 700,000 miles. It has a guided-missile system and a light but effective system of 127/54-mm (5/2.1-in.) guns with a firing rate of 20 rounds a minute. The Soviet Union, Great Britain, and France are also oriented toward such powerfully armed surface units, almost all equipped with atomic propulsion or all-gas turbines.

California—*With the traditional cruiser practically obsolete, its place has been taken by this new category, the nuclear leader, with a very advanced operational system. The United States built the nuclear-powered California for many functions, but especially to protect the large aircraft carrier. Its two nuclear reactors are water-cooled and give the ship a range of 700,000 miles.* ▼

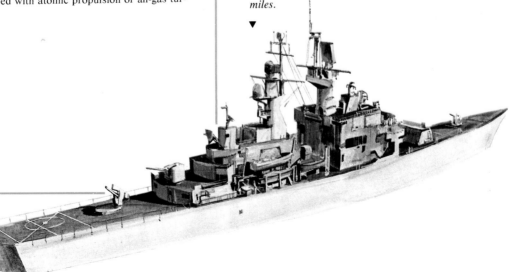

212

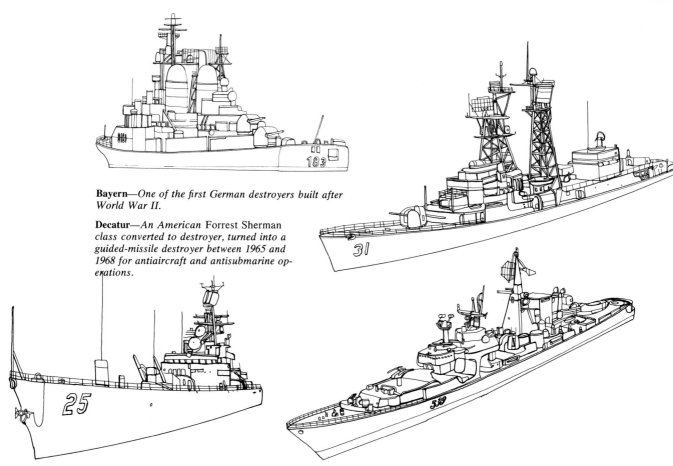

Bayern—*One of the first German destroyers built after World War II.*

Decatur—*An American* Forrest Sherman *class converted to destroyer, turned into a guided-missile destroyer between 1965 and 1968 for antiaircraft and antisubmarine operations.*

Bainbridge—*The first guided-missile cruiser with nuclear propulsion, launched on May 15, 1959, and built at a cost of 163 million dollars.*

Nikolajev—*A large Soviet cruiser, equipped with exceptional multipurpose armament and destined for long cruises with larger vessels.*

Hai Class Corvette—*An East German antisubmarine vessel.*

Sheffield—*Destroyer of the Royal Navy.*

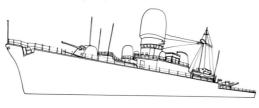

Haruna—*One of the largest ships in the modern Japanese navy, it is used for antisubmarine purposes. It can also function as a headquarters ship.*

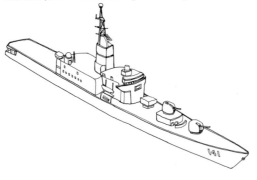

Since World War II the Italian navy has built new ships for a displacement total of about 49,210 tons. A modest naval program, already authorized, foresees the construction of about 18 new vessels by 1980, including frigates, hydrofoils, submarines, and special-purpose ships.

Other world navies—those of Canada, Australia, New Zealand, Norway, and Denmark, as well as the modernized fleets of Argentina, Brazil, West Germany, Spain, Greece and Turkey—are planning, or have already carried out, development programs incorporating the latest advances in both traditional armament and guided missiles. Italy has contributed new weapons systems, like the 127/54 (5/2.1-in.) and 76/62 (3/2.4-in.) compact cannons and the surface-to-surface tactical missile system Otomat, which has been adopted by the navy of the German Federal Republic.

Present-day fighting ships differ from those of the past in that they can carry

Frigates and Corvettes

The tendency of modern warship construction is to assimilate these two types into a single vessel, to be used as both escort and supply ships for larger vessels. Their displacement is between 2,500 and 4,000 tons. Highly advanced shipbuilding materials and techniques as well as large prefabricated modules are used in construction. Their armament generally consists of a surface-to-air missile system, although some Russian ships of this type have a great deal of light conventional armament as well.

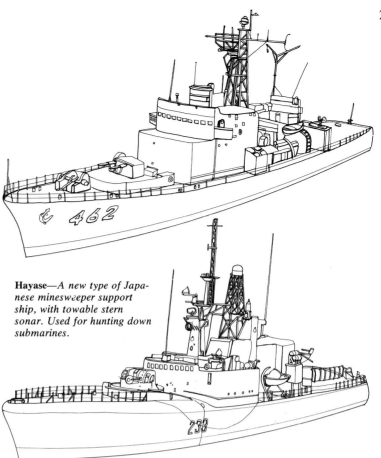

Hayase—*A new type of Japanese minesweeper support ship, with towable stern sonar. Used for hunting down submarines.*

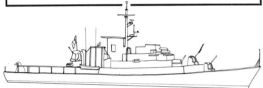

Alpino—*An Italian frigate.*

Duquesne—*A French destroyer.*

Fraser—*One of the first Canadian frigates, it was built using a modular construction technique.*

South Carolina—*An American guided-missile cruiser.*

Robert E. Peary—*A frigate of the U.S. Navy.*

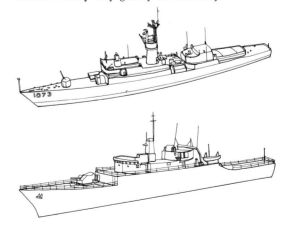

Saam—*One of the most modern frigates sailing today, built by the British Vosper shipyards for the Royal Iranian Navy. Equipped with Italian-built missiles.*

"strategic" offense far beyond limits that were considered insuperable only a few years ago. The results that can now be obtained by a single ship, or by a small group of ships, are far greater than combined air-and-naval operations could achieve not long ago. Modern fighting ships are equipped with weapons that have been designed expressly for them. These new weapons are highly automated and require a minimum of manual intervention. Much of this progress is due to the development of remote-controlled equipment, miniaturization, and electronics. A modern naval weapon combining all these characteristics is the medium-range ballistic missile with a nuclear warhead, which can be launched thousands of miles away from its target by surface or underseas ships. Modern naval guided missiles include a host of remote-controlled weapons for strategic tasks: surface-to-surface and depth-to-surface missiles; and for tactical purposes, like short-range ballistic weapons, sea-to-air,

214

Roger de Lauria—*A Spanish destroyer of the* Ensenada *class, modernized in 1967 for antisubmarine use; it closely resembles the American* Gearing.

Annapolis—*A Canadian antisubmarine ship, officially classified as a helicopter-carrying frigate.*

Baleares—*The most modern ship in the Spanish navy, based on the design of the American vessels of the* Brooke *and* Knox *classes. It has three-dimensional radar.*

Ardito—*Combined-purpose Italian destroyer derived from the* Impavido *class, with a helicopter component and antiaircraft and antiship surface-to-surface missile armament.*

Tourville—*This French ship is similar in function to the ships of the* Suffren *class, the detection and attacking of underwater craft. It can locate such craft at a depth of 65,000 feet. It has radar for air and surface detection as well, and a high degree of automation for analyzing tactical data.*

sea-to-depth, and depth-to-surface missiles.

New torpedoes have been developed with internal-combustion engines or compressed-air propulsion. The latter have systems for correcting their routes. Microphones and sonar devices electronically transmit corrections to the control mechanism of the torpedo.

Naval artillery is not as important as it used to be, but it is still used for antiship and anticoast fire. Modern naval artillery is characterized by compactness and light weight. The smaller-caliber guns can fire up to 80 to 100 rounds per minute. The modern naval arsenal also includes antiship and antisubmarine mines (moored or depth torpedoes). There are various ways of detonating these torpedoes, including direct contact (when they are struck by a passing ship), and influence contact (magnetic, acoustic, or pressure

Lupo—*Designed for various functions, this Italian frigate is an antisubmarine and antiship vessel, a convoy escort-ship, and a supply ship for amphibious operations. It has aircraft- and ship-warning radar, sonar to detect submarines, and all the varied armament and firing systems usually allied with an electronic system of elaboration of tactical data.*

Peder Skram—*A Danish-designed frigate, with antisubmarine guided-missile weapons. Variable-pitch propellers make the ship highly maneuverable. The ship has centralized equipment for engine control and electronic devices for air and surface detection.*

torpedoes). Depth charges are launched against submarines by special ships with roll-off systems and mortars. All operations concerned with the use of a ship's weapons, and particularly with the launching and remote control of missiles, as well as with the training, aiming, and firing of the ship's artillery, are coordinated by the combat-operations control room, which is equipped with automatic electronics devices. These include aircraft-warning radar, ship-warning radar, and analytical instruments that can determine in less than a second whether an object is an enemy ship or plane, its degree of danger, and its position. Other supplementary data supplied by the combat operations information center are transmitted to the target classification center, which automatically selects the kind of weapon to be used

Lynx—*A British frigate with diesel propulsion for for antiair use, built of prefabricated elements, totally welded. Radar for detection and firing direction. Seacat missile armament.*

Amatsukaze—*The only guided-missile ship in the Japanese navy. It is similar to American and Western vessels of that type and has simple lines and a reduced superstructure.*

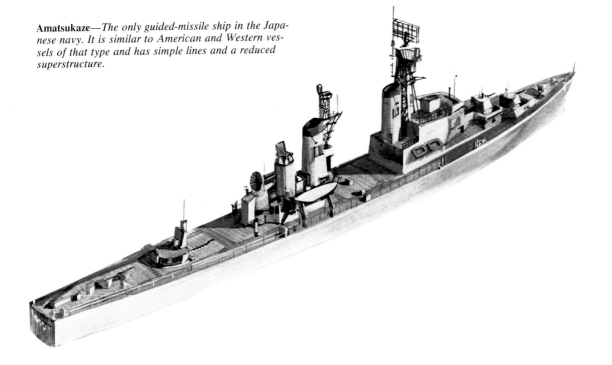

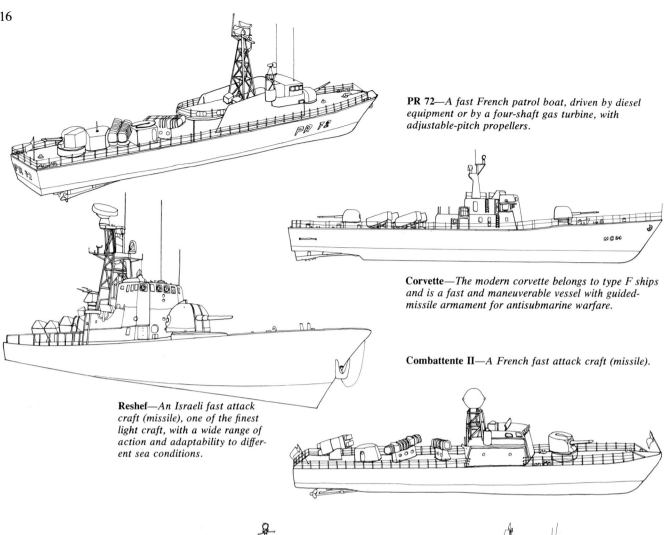

PR 72—*A fast French patrol boat, driven by diesel equipment or by a four-shaft gas turbine, with adjustable-pitch propellers.*

Corvette—*The modern corvette belongs to type F ships and is a fast and maneuverable vessel with guided-missile armament for antisubmarine warfare.*

Combattente II—*A French fast attack craft (missile).*

Reshef—*An Israeli fast attack craft (missile), one of the finest light craft, with a wide range of action and adaptability to different sea conditions.*

Tenacity—*One of the most interesting British fast attack craft (patrol), with both conventional and missile armament. Used for exercises and fishery protection.*

Lampo—*An Italian torpedo built from German designs; it is part of the light craft of type P.*

Jeanne d'Arc—*A type L ship, built for a double purpose. In peacetime it is used as a training ship, and in case of emergency it can act as a helicopter carrier, commando ship, or troop transport. It can carry eight helicopters on board and has guided missile armament.*

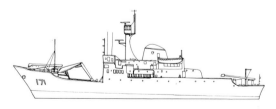

Endeavour—*A Canadian navy research ship, designed and built for antisubmarine research. The hull is reinforced for navigation through ice.*

Zinnia—*A Belgian AL type ship, designed to operate in zones made radioactive by a nuclear explosion. Assigned to minesweeper support, it carries one helicopter aboard.*

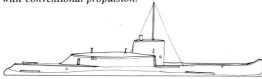

Zulu V Class submarine—*A Russian underwater craft with conventional propulsion.*

Gymnote—*An experimental French ship for testing guided-missile systems, originally designed with an atomic engine.*

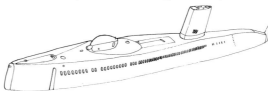

Whiskey Long Bin—*A Russian class of cruise missile submarine, another effort to create the finest possible underwater ship with all the new offensive weapons.*

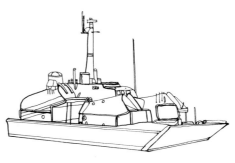

Halibut—*An American submarine.*

Conventional Submarines

Despite remarkable technical progress, the submarine was definitely in decline by the end of World War II. The great discovery of nuclear energy gave birth to the atomic submarine, while ships with conventional propulsion continue to be part of all the most important navies of the world. A submarine is an underwater vessel that can operate in temporary submersion. It is this aspect of its function that has benefited most from technological advances. Its electric engines are almost noiseless,

and the range of its underwater navigation and of its depth of submersion have been enormously increased. Its armament has remained the conventional type, although new torpedoes are highly sophisticated weapons. They can travel at a speed up to 50 knots for a distance of 2 miles. Their path correction and their automatic detection and control equipment—magnetic, thermic, sound, and sonar—have made them formidable weapons.

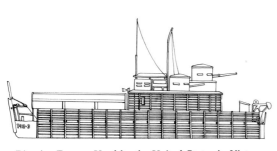

Riverine Force—*Used by the United States in Vietnam for war operations in the labyrinth of canals, swamps, and rivers there; created by adapting traditional landing craft.*

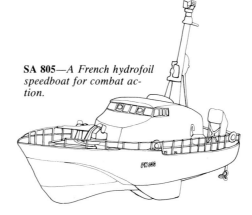

Isku—*A Finnish experimental vessel, extremely fast and able to operate in shallow water, it has missile armament.*

Hovercraft—*Part of the equipment of the Royal Marines, for the fast transportation of small troop contingents for commando action; armed with two light machine guns.*

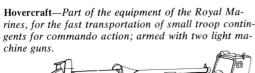
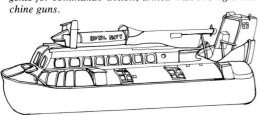

SA 805—*A French hydrofoil speedboat for combat action.*

Intrepid—*A British assault ship armed with missiles, and able to carry 15 tanks, 27 motor vehicles, or 700 men in landing units, as well as a few helicopters.*

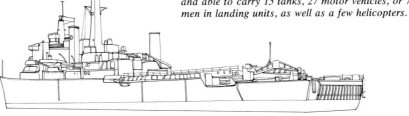

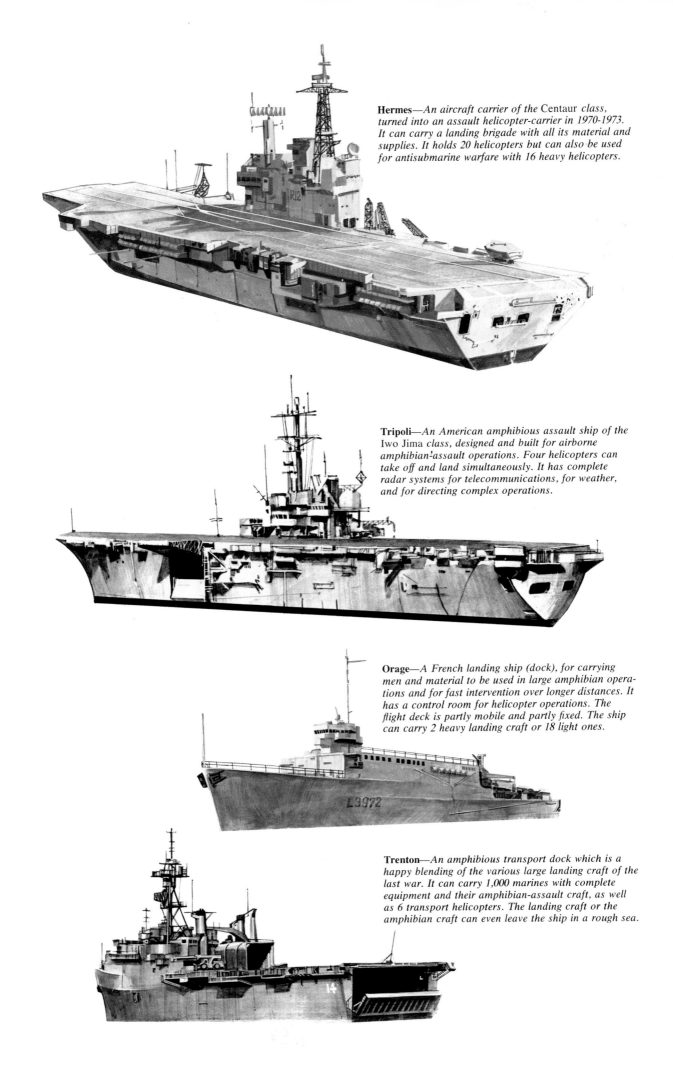

Hermes—*An aircraft carrier of the* Centaur *class, turned into an assault helicopter-carrier in 1970-1973. It can carry a landing brigade with all its material and supplies. It holds 20 helicopters but can also be used for antisubmarine warfare with 16 heavy helicopters.*

Tripoli—*An American amphibious assault ship of the* Iwo Jima *class, designed and built for airborne amphibian-assault operations. Four helicopters can take off and land simultaneously. It has complete radar systems for telecommunications, for weather, and for directing complex operations.*

Orage—*A French landing ship (dock), for carrying men and material to be used in large amphibian operations and for fast intervention over longer distances. It has a control room for helicopter operations. The flight deck is partly mobile and partly fixed. The ship can carry 2 heavy landing craft or 18 light ones.*

Trenton—*An amphibious transport dock which is a happy blending of the various large landing craft of the last war. It can carry 1,000 marines with complete equipment and their amphibian-assault craft, as well as 6 transport helicopters. The landing craft or the amphibian craft can even leave the ship in a rough sea.*

and furnishes the first approximate firing data. The "director" then recognizes and identifies the target through its own radar, determines the exact firing data, and communicates them to the weapons. By reducing weight and size, the technical conquests of miniaturization, transistors, and integrated circuits have permitted the creation of authentic electronic laboratories aboard ship.

Hayes—*One of the first American ships for oceanographic research to have a catamaran hull. This permits a large working area, lets the laboratories be housed far from the engines, and makes research equipment easier to handle.*

Kosmonaut Vladimir Komarov—*A ship built by the Russian navy for upper-atmosphere research and for control of space vehicles.*

P 420—*An Italian hydrofoil gunboat with both traditional and missile armament. The hull is built of a special aluminum alloy and has five watertight compartments. It has water-jet-propulsion equipment for fin navigation and radar for detection, navigation, and firing.*

George Washington—*An American ballistic missile submarine launched in 1959. It is armed with 16 Polaris missile tubes. The missiles can be launched when the ship is submerged and can reach targets 1,500 miles away.*

Triton—*The largest American nuclear submarine and also the largest underwater vessel ever built. The two reactors hold enough fuel to last for two years. The Triton has long-distance radar and electronic devices for controlling firing and launching. It cost 109 million dollars, and is used for detection and warning, and in cooperation with attack aircraft carriers.*

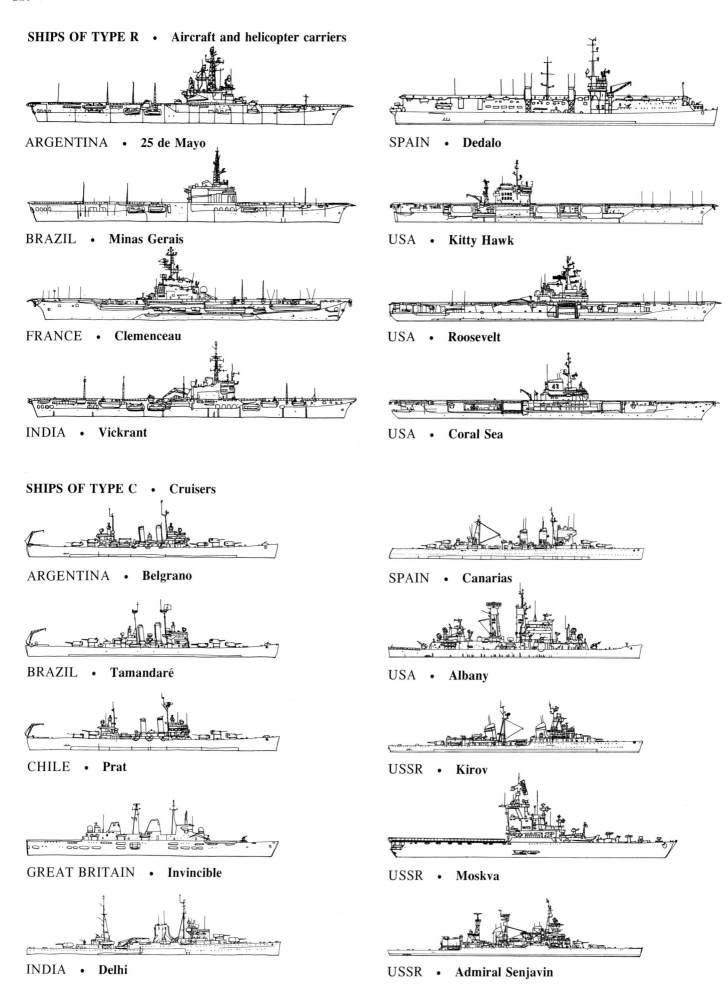

SHIPS OF TYPE R • **Aircraft and helicopter carriers**

ARGENTINA • **25 de Mayo**

SPAIN • **Dedalo**

BRAZIL • **Minas Gerais**

USA • **Kitty Hawk**

FRANCE • **Clemenceau**

USA • **Roosevelt**

INDIA • **Vickrant**

USA • **Coral Sea**

SHIPS OF TYPE C • **Cruisers**

ARGENTINA • **Belgrano**

SPAIN • **Canarias**

BRAZIL • **Tamandaré**

USA • **Albany**

CHILE • **Prat**

USSR • **Kirov**

GREAT BRITAIN • **Invincible**

USSR • **Moskva**

INDIA • **Delhi**

USSR • **Admiral Senjavin**

SHIPS OF TYPE D • Destroyers and destroyer escorts

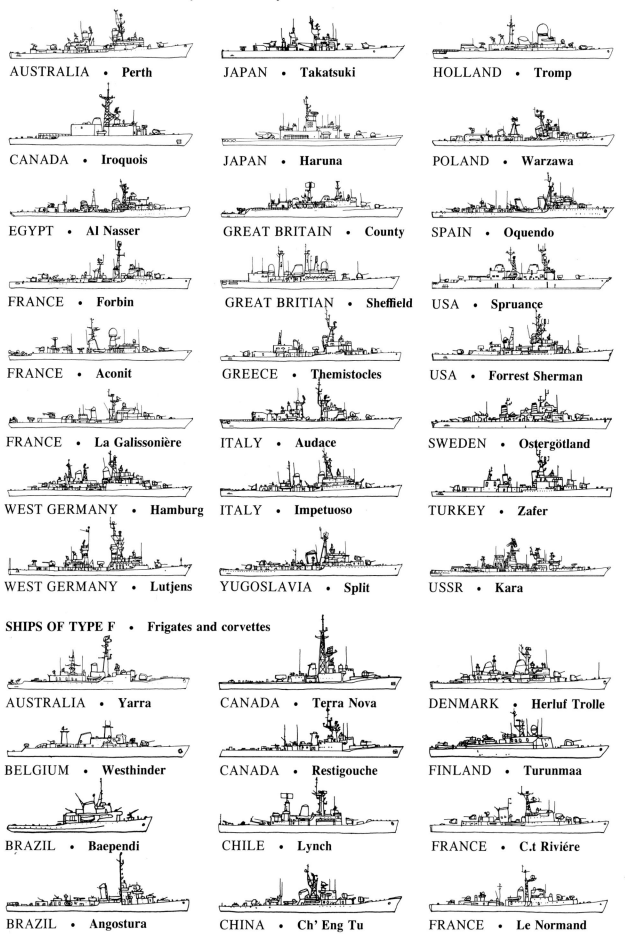

AUSTRALIA • **Perth**

JAPAN • **Takatsuki**

HOLLAND • **Tromp**

CANADA • **Iroquois**

JAPAN • **Haruna**

POLAND • **Warzawa**

EGYPT • **Al Nasser**

GREAT BRITAIN • **County**

SPAIN • **Oquendo**

FRANCE • **Forbin**

GREAT BRITIAN • **Sheffield**

USA • **Spruance**

FRANCE • **Aconit**

GREECE • **Themistocles**

USA • **Forrest Sherman**

FRANCE • **La Galissonière**

ITALY • **Audace**

SWEDEN • **Ostergötland**

WEST GERMANY • **Hamburg**

ITALY • **Impetuoso**

TURKEY • **Zafer**

WEST GERMANY • **Lutjens**

YUGOSLAVIA • **Split**

USSR • **Kara**

SHIPS OF TYPE F • Frigates and corvettes

AUSTRALIA • **Yarra**

CANADA • **Terra Nova**

DENMARK • **Herluf Trolle**

BELGIUM • **Westhinder**

CANADA • **Restigouche**

FINLAND • **Turunmaa**

BRAZIL • **Baependi**

CHILE • **Lynch**

FRANCE • **C.t Riviére**

BRAZIL • **Angostura**

CHINA • **Ch' Eng Tu**

FRANCE • **Le Normand**

SHIPS OF TYPE F • Frigates and corvettes

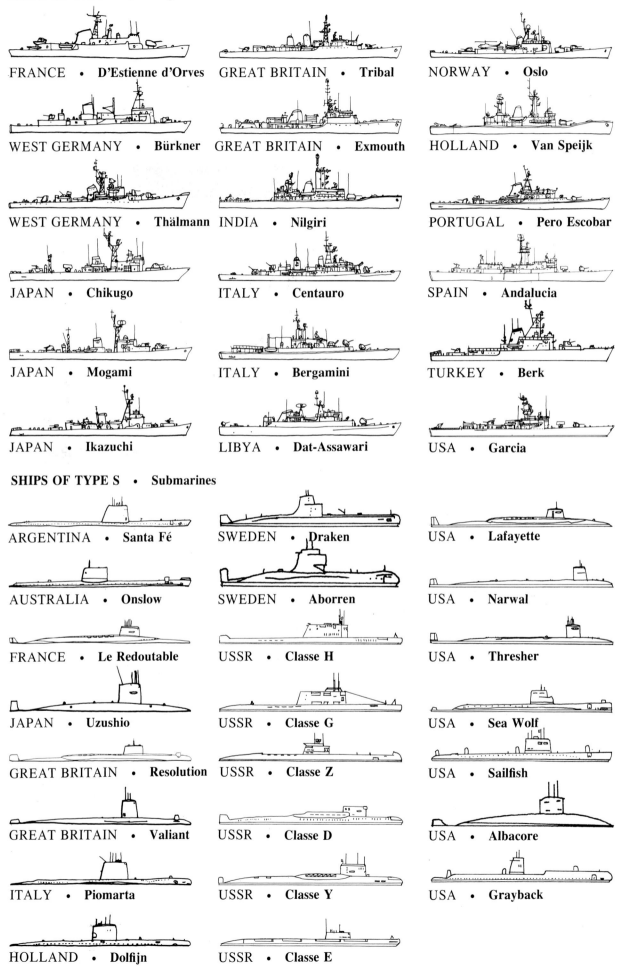

FRANCE • D'Estienne d'Orves GREAT BRITAIN • Tribal NORWAY • Oslo

WEST GERMANY • Bürkner GREAT BRITAIN • Exmouth HOLLAND • Van Speijk

WEST GERMANY • Thälmann INDIA • Nilgiri PORTUGAL • Pero Escobar

JAPAN • Chikugo ITALY • Centauro SPAIN • Andalucia

JAPAN • Mogami ITALY • Bergamini TURKEY • Berk

JAPAN • Ikazuchi LIBYA • Dat-Assawari USA • Garcia

SHIPS OF TYPE S • Submarines

ARGENTINA • Santa Fé SWEDEN • Draken USA • Lafayette

AUSTRALIA • Onslow SWEDEN • Aborren USA • Narwal

FRANCE • Le Redoutable USSR • Classe H USA • Thresher

JAPAN • Uzushio USSR • Classe G USA • Sea Wolf

GREAT BRITAIN • Resolution USSR • Classe Z USA • Sailfish

GREAT BRITAIN • Valiant USSR • Classe D USA • Albacore

ITALY • Piomarta USSR • Classe Y USA • Grayback

HOLLAND • Dolfijn USSR • Classe E

SHIPS OF TYPE L • Amphibious operations

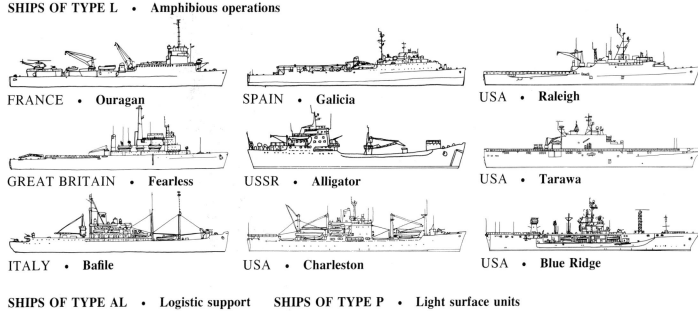

FRANCE • **Ouragan**

SPAIN • **Galicia**

USA • **Raleigh**

GREAT BRITAIN • **Fearless**

USSR • **Alligator**

USA • **Tarawa**

ITALY • **Bafile**

USA • **Charleston**

USA • **Blue Ridge**

SHIPS OF TYPE AL • Logistic support   SHIPS OF TYPE P • Light surface units

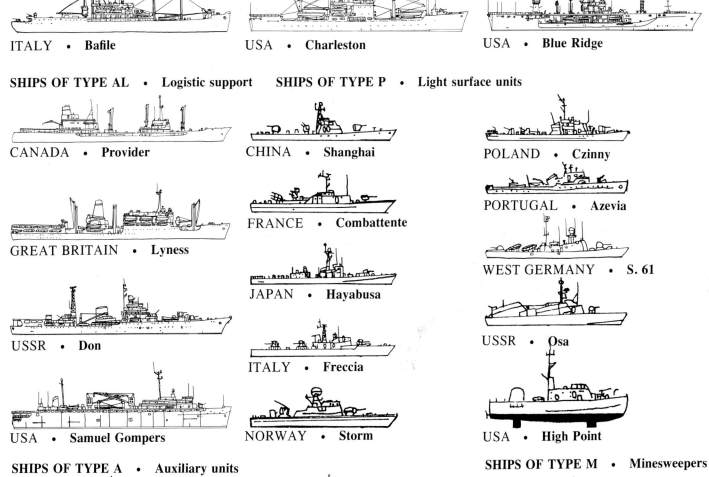

CANADA • **Provider**

CHINA • **Shanghai**

POLAND • **Czinny**

GREAT BRITAIN • **Lyness**

FRANCE • **Combattente**

PORTUGAL • **Azevia**

USSR • **Don**

JAPAN • **Hayabusa**

WEST GERMANY • **S. 61**

USA • **Samuel Gompers**

ITALY • **Freccia**

USSR • **Osa**

NORWAY • **Storm**

USA • **High Point**

SHIPS OF TYPE A • Auxiliary units

SHIPS OF TYPE M • Minesweepers

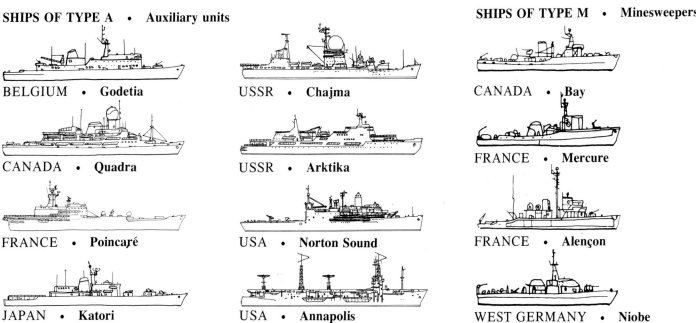

BELGIUM • **Godetia**

USSR • **Chajma**

CANADA • **Bay**

CANADA • **Quadra**

USSR • **Arktika**

FRANCE • **Mercure**

FRANCE • **Poincaré**

USA • **Norton Sound**

FRANCE • **Alençon**

JAPAN • **Katori**

USA • **Annapolis**

WEST GERMANY • **Niobe**

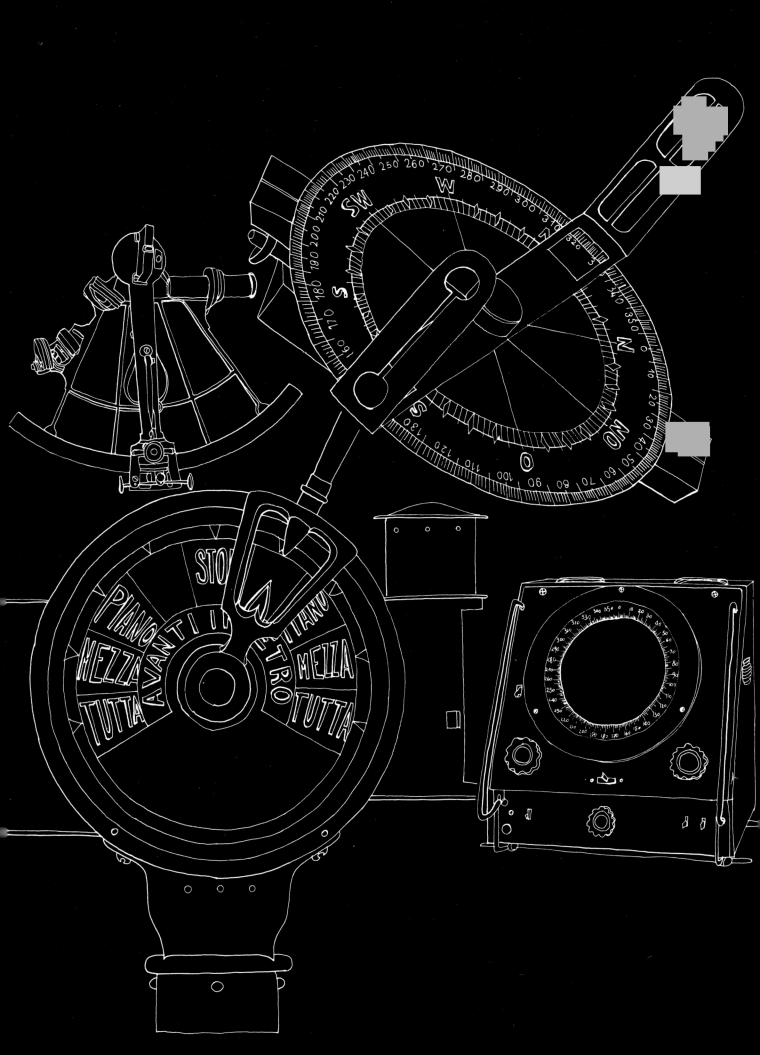

Tomorrow's Adventure

At the end of World War II, the total tonnage of the Allied merchant marine fleet was larger than it had been at the start of the conflict, thanks to the colossal effort made by heavy industry to replace all the ships that were sunk.

During the war large transatlantic liners were turned into troopships. The gigantic, 83,673-ton *Queen Elizabeth*, for instance, carried more than 15,000 American soldiers to Europe in one trip. The *Queen Mary*, the *Ile de France*, and the *Nieuw Amsterdam* were also used for troop transport.

The 25 years that followed 1945 were golden years for large transatlantic ships. Between 1920 and 1930, with the decline of immigration, which had carried an enormous number of passengers to America (2,576,000 in 1923 alone), about 650,000 people a year crossed the Atlantic, mainly for business or pleasure. But the floating cities, large and luxurious as they were, had to face the competition of the airplane.

Although the energy crisis has reduced air travel, the figures speak clearly. In 1948 transatlantic airline passengers totaled 252,000, as against the 501,000 carried by ships. In 1953 about 892,000 went by ship and 507,000 by plane. In 1955 some 964,000 went by ship and 652,000 by plane. And in 1957 about 1,036,000 traveled by ship and 968,000 by plane. Then the balance shifted. In 1963, for example, 788,000 people crossed the ocean by ship and 2,422,000 went by plane. And the percentage tends to increase steadily in favor of the airplane, despite the efforts

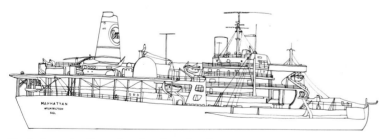

Manhattan—*An Esso oil tanker, it made a famous voyage through the Northwest Passage. It left Philadelphia on August 24, 1969, with a crew of 54 men and 72 experts, scholars, and reporters. Its structures had been reinforced; the bow was equipped with an icebreaker; and the ship had a 43,000-hp engine. It reached Prudhoe Bay on the northern coast of Alaska on September 19. The trip covered 4,500 miles and involved the collaboration of 28,000 men, plus various icebreakers and helicopters.*

of shipping lines to keep prices down and to offer maximum comfort. Speed has been increased by the use of light alloys and plastic in construction.

By 1970, the tonnage of passenger ships had gone down to five million tons, slightly more than one million accounted for by what

Queen Elizabeth I—*Launched in 1940. During World War II it transported 811,324 U.S. soldiers to Europe. In 1946 it went into passenger service on the Cunard Line, serving the Southampton–New York route. Gross tonnage: 83,673 tons; length: 1,031 feet; speed: 28.5 knots; 2,240 passengers.*

Michelangelo—*The largest postwar Italian transatlantic liner, launched in 1965. It covered the Genoa–New York route in 7 days. Load displacement: 41,330 tons; length: 276 meters (302 yards); speed: 26.5 knots; 2 geared turbines; 1,800 passengers; crew: 720 men. Its sister ship, the* Raffaello, *made its last crossing on April 30, 1975, and was then withdrawn from service.*

BLUE RIBAND				
Ship	Year	Speed in knots	Tonnage	Country
Artic	1852	13.2	2,860 t.	USA
Persia	1856	13.75	3,300	Britain
Scotia	1872	15.2	3,871	Britain
Servia	1881	17	7,400	Britain
Umbria	1881	19	8,100	Britain
City of Paris	1885	20	10,500	Britain
Teutonic	1889	20.35	9,984	Britain
Campania	1891	21.2	12,952	Britain
Lucania	1893	22	13,000	Britain
Kaiser Wilhelm der Grosse	1895	22.5	14,300	Germany
Deutschland	1897	23.3	16,500	Germany
Kaiser Wilhelm II	1900	24	19,000	Germany
Mauretania	1906	26	31,938	Britain
Mauretania	1929	26.85	31,938	Britain
Bremen	1929	27.83	51,656	Germany
Europa	1930	27.91	49,746	Germany
Bremen	1933	28.51	51,656	Germany
Rex	1933	28.92	51,062	Italy
Normandie	1935	30.31	82,799	France
Queen Mary	1936	30.63	81,237	Britain
Normandie	1937	30.99	82,779	France
Normandie	1937	31.2	82,779	France
Queen Mary	1938	31.69	81,237	Britain
United States	1952	35.59	53,329	USA

used to be the world's largest passenger fleet, that of Great Britain. To compensate for this decline, the shipping lines make greater use of their passenger vessels on tourist cruises. Vacation cruises were very popular in the 1960s in the Mediterranean, the Baltic, South Africa, and South America. Many of these ships carried only one class, and all passengers enjoyed the same activities (including gymnasiums, libraries, swimming pools, film showings, the game deck, and shore excursions). Several companies have since adopted the air-sea cruise system, carrying their passengers by air to a waiting ship, on which they cruise, and then carrying them back home by plane afterward.

The passage from the sailing ship to the steamship, which took place at the end of the last century, finds its historical counterpart in the present revolutionary changes that have come about in the merchant marine fleet of the world. These changes, still taking place, concern both the regular cargo ship owned by shipping lines, with established routes and schedules, and the tramp steamers that carry goods with no fixed itinerary. The world cargo fleet, which tripled in size between 1948 and 1970, has met new demands by division into three fundamental branches: cargo liners, bulk carriers, and

France—*One of the world's longest transatlantic liners, over 1,000 feet from bow to stern. It cost about 50 billion old francs, and went from Le Havre to New York in less than 5 days. Gross tonnage: 66,384 tons; speed: 31 knots; 4 steam turbines; 2,044 passengers; crew: 1,171 men.*

United States—*Launched in 1952 for the United States Line, this ship has held the Blue Riband Trophy since 1952, with a crossing of 3 days, 10 hours, and 40 minutes from Le Havre to New York. Cost: 72 million dollars. Gross tonnage: 51,502 tons; length: 990 feet; 4 steam turbines; speed: 30 knots; 2,008 passengers; crew: 1,100 men.*

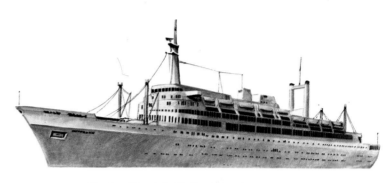

Rotterdam—*The flagship of the Holland-American Line, launched in 1959 and the first passenger ship to do away with smokestacks. It has 12 decks and all the latest technical devices, including 3 evaporators for distilling seawater. Displacement: 38,621 tons; length: 228 meters (249 yards); speed: 20.5 knots; 1,369 passengers; crew: 776 men.*

tankers, as well as specialized ships for particular types of transport.

The cargo liners touch at fixed ports on regular schedules. They often carry a few passengers, 12 at the most, all accommodated in first-class cabins.

The bulk carrier has become increasingly popular. The traditional tramp steamer has given way to the bulk carrier, which is used by mining industries throughout the world. The bulk carrier has only one large hold. At first the cargo was almost exclusively mineral, but now there are ore carriers, ore-oil carriers, and ore-bulk oil carriers transporting ore, coal, grain, maize, bauxite, aluminum, phosphates, scrap iron, or sugar.

To save time during loading and unloading operations in port, various solutions have been developed, all tending toward the pre-packing of the cargo so that it can be handled more easily; in other words, integrated transport in container ships. The container is simply a large metal box, built to measurements that are standard all over the world, in which all the cargo is placed after being divided according to type and destination, in groups of a certain fixed weight.

The use of containers and of the pallet—a loading method that makes stowage and unloading easier—has revolutionized maritime

Queen Elizabeth II—*The last of the great Cunard transatlantic liners; 57,084 tons and 3 propellers; designed for vacation cruising as well. Large passenger ships are decreasing in number all over the world.*

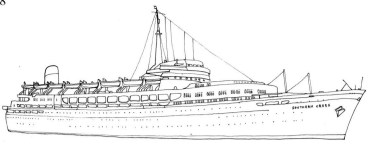

Southern Cross—*The first British passenger ship to have its engines installed at the stern. Launched in 1954 and assigned to the Australian and New Zealand routes. Gross tonnage: 20,204 tons; speed: 20 knots; 1,160 passengers.*

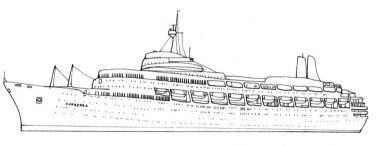

Canberra—*Launched in 1961 for the P. & O. Steam Navigation Company. Gross tonnage: 45,733 tons; speed: 27.5 knots; 2,186 passengers; crew: 938 men.*

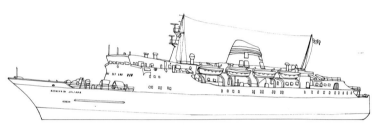

Koningin Juliana—*A medium-tonnage Dutch passenger ship. On this kind of ship, a diesel engine is more efficient than the steam turbine used by the giants of the sea.*

cargo systems, cutting time and expense in half and creating what is known as door-to-door integrated transport.

The container ship is now being flanked by the LASH ship, which need not enter port. The LASH or "lighter above ship," has an open space instead of a hold. This space is filled with barges loaded with containers. The LASH remains outside port and unloads the barges at sea. It loads new barges in the same manner and continues its voyage. Thus complex loading operations are carried out in a few hours.

A similar system is used by the Seabee, a vessel consisting of a bow containing the engines and a long axis onto which a series of self-propelled barges are attached. The Seabee saves port expenses and loss of time by detaching the barges at the entry to the port.

The good old ferryboat of 1855 has been transformed into the present-day "roll-on, roll-off" vessel that, even on transatlantic lines, lets trucks or containers go on board and roll off through openings set in the bow or the stern of the ship. This keeps costs down and saves time during port and customs operations, which are carried out in the terminal warehouse.

Leonardo da Vinci—*This ship entered service on the North America route on June 30, 1960, and was the flagship of the Italian passenger fleet. In the illustration, from top to bottom: the belvedere deck with the bridge and the chartroom; on the sun deck, the captain's and ship's officers' quarters; on the lido deck, the swimming pool, gymnasium, and first-class cabins; on the promenade deck, the first-class saloons, the bars, and the tourist-class swimming pool; on the lobby deck, the crew's quarters and the tourist-class dining room. Five other decks held the tourist-class cabins and other crew quarters, the telephone switchboard, the firemen's station, the garage, the refrigerator, the baggage room, and the automobile hold. The entire ship was air-conditioned, with infrared heating, while an independent television system completed the luxurious furnishings of this authentic floating city. Height at bridge: 45 meters (148 feet); 33,340 tons; length: 232 meters (254 yards); beam: 28 meters (92 feet); speed: 23 knots.*

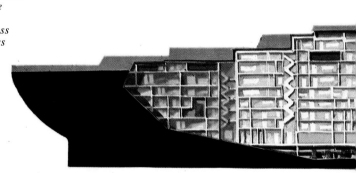

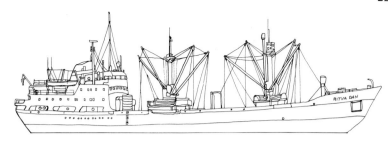

Ritva Dan—*A Swedish cargo ship used for mixed cargoes in the North Sea. The special shape of the bow helps in navigation through ice.*

Special-purpose ships have also been produced, including the LPG (meaning liquefied petroleum gas) ships for carrying gas, liquid oil, propane, butane, ammonia and butadiene, and the LNG (meaning liquefied natural gas) vessels, commonly known as natural-gas tankers. There are cement-carrying vessels, ships with refrigeration equipment for transporting bananas and tropical fruit; wine-transport ships; vessels for dry or liquid cargoes; and boats for lumber, cellulose, and liquid sulphur; as well as tankers for various oil-refining products.

The tanker is the cargo ship that bears the main burden of satisfying the world's demand for oil. Oil tankers get bigger and bigger, reaching a tonnage of 469,487 tons. Many shipyards (especially in Japan, which specializes in the building of oil tankers) have programmed a ship of half a million tons, while designs for a million-ton tanker are now ready. By June 30, 1974, the global tonnage of the tanker fleet was about 100 million tons.

The tramp steamer goes on moving from port to port, loading when and what it can. At the end of World War II the tramps represented the major part of the world's cargo *(cont'd. on p. 231)*

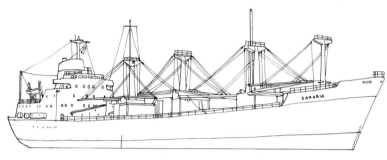

Samaria—*A multiple-use cargo ship for dry cargoes. This modern 8,858-ton vessel has a dead-weight capacity of 12,795 tons, a length of 143 meters (150 yards), a beam of 18 meters (59 feet), and a speed of about 15 knots.*

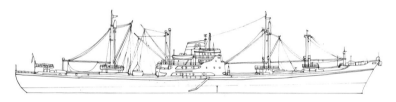

Ore cargo ship—*It has a reinforced structure, a deeper bottom than normal, and a hold that takes up half the ship. The hold is trapezoidal in shape, with walls widening toward the bottom so as to prevent dangerous shifting of the cargo.*

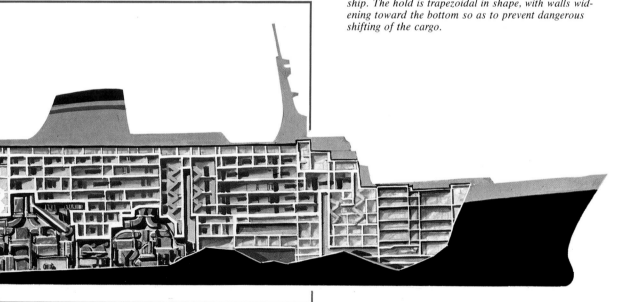

The Hovercraft

SAILING ON AIR

The hovercraft is a vehicle supported by an air cushion between its lower surface and the surface over which it moves. Over the past 100 years, many attempts have been made to apply this principle to the keels of ships. Suffice it to mention the experiments made by the Dutchman William Froude in 1875 and by Charles Gustave Patrice de Laval, who in 1883 patented a system in which a series of ducts created a layer of air between the keel and the water. It was only in the 1950s that a British electronics engineer, Christopher Cockerell, thought of using a round blast of air

around the edge of a disk, exploiting the well-known effect of the proximity of the earth's surface on wing resistance. With aid from the British Ministry of Supply and the National Council for Research and Development, the first hovercraft (the 3.8-ton SR. N1) crossed the Channel on July 25, 1959. The supporting air jet was improved by giving it a slight inward angle, and in 1967 Cockerell prepared the final form of the thrusting mechanism, containing the air cushion in a kind of apron made of neoprene-covered nylon. With this system, smaller vessels can rise 4 feet above the surface, while 156-ton vessels can rise 6 to 8 feet.

The engine apparatus, powered by gas turbines, is made up of propellers or air jets and blowers that create the cushion. The hovercraft is amphibious: it can move over land, sea, and ice; climb rivers and rapids; and cross swamps. To increase its stability on the surface of the sea a hovercraft has been developed with two rigid keels mounted on each side of the hull and permanently immersed. This model used naval propellers and rudders. An intermediate version is the semiamphibious hovercraft, while the most recent and most widely used model is the "air bubble," used only on open water.

Modern concepts of antisubmarine defense have concentrated the attention of military naval experts on the hovercraft. It is hard for a submerged submarine to locate it because of its high speed. Amphibious hovercraft are ideal for beach landings. Armed hovercraft are already used by the British and Iranian navies, while the United States has carried out successful experiments with an attack craft based on the air-bubble hovercraft called a surface-effect ship. A model of this type weighing about 12,000 tons is being studied at the D. Taylor Basin in Washington.

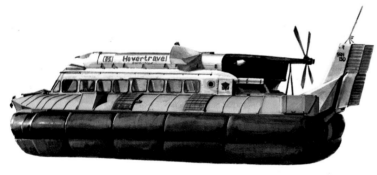

Many of the world's navies have adopted the **hovercraft** *because of its speed and its amphibian qualities.*

SR. N/3—Designed by the Westland Company in 1964 and equipped with 4 powerful Bristol Siddeley turbines. Length: 23.5 meters (77 feet); beam: 9.3 meters (30.6 feet); height above waterline: 10.3 meters (34 feet); weight: 37.5 tons. It can carry 150 passengers.

The world's largest **hovercraft**, *built by Westland, is in service between Boulogne and Dover. Length: 69.5 meters (228 feet); beam: 25.2 meters (83 feet); height above waterline: 12.4 meters (41 feet); 2 Rover turbines and 4 Bristol engines that let it reach a top speed of 77 knots; a range of 190 miles; displacement: 165 tons.*

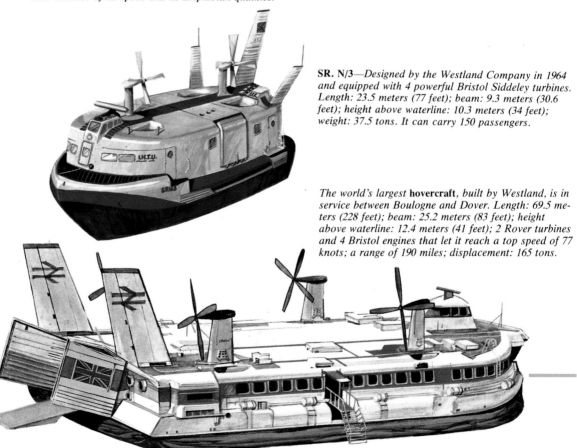

Descartes—*A French natural-gas ship of 50,000 cubic meters (65,395 cubic yards), of a type commonly referred to by the initials LNG (liquid natural gas).*

Orotava Bridge—*A bulk carrier with large cargo hatches, and no derricks. Bulk carriers tend more and more to avoid the tramp cargo system and follow regular and more profitable lines.*

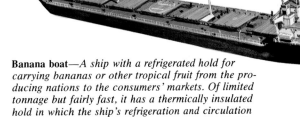

Banana boat—*A ship with a refrigerated hold for carrying bananas or other tropical fruit from the producing nations to the consumers' markets. Of limited tonnage but fairly fast, it has a thermically insulated hold in which the ship's refrigeration and circulation plant maintains the temperature between 5° and 10° centigrade.*

shipping. Many were ships built during the war as supply or troopships. Among these was the U.S. Liberty ship, built from prefabricated parts, displacing about 10,000 tons, with a speed of 11 knots. In January 1941, 40 American shipyards received orders for the Liberty ship. A total of 332 had been launched by September. The number of shipyards was doubled in the following year, and 542 Liberty ships went into active service. This figure increased to 1,253 in 1943. The Liberty ship was composed of 9,300 pieces. Since it was built of prefabricated sections, a ship could be launched in about 50 days. The record construction time for a Liberty ship was 4 days, 15 hours, and 24 minutes.

It was later joined by the Victory, a turbine-driven ship that could do 16.5 knots. Some 2,892 were built. Many Liberties and Victories became tramp steamers after the war. The present-day tramp has a gross tonnage of 5,000 to 8,000 tons.

Konan—*A Japanese whaler with a flying bridge that lets the crew reach the harpoon gun as soon as the whales are sighted.*

The tugboat, a motor ship for towing or pushing other vessels, made its official debut on the Thames River in 1832. There are 4 categories of tugs. The first includes ocean-going tugs for emergency aid and lifesaving; these are up to 250 feet long, with a displacement of some 1,000 tons, long range, and great maneuverability. Coastal tugboats are usually between 100 and 150 feet long, can tow up to 30 tons, and reach a cruising speed of 12 to 15 knots. They are powered by engines of between 1,500 and 3,000 hp. Estuary and harbor tugboats form the 2 most numerous and varied categories. They are usually 75 to 115 feet long, with 1,000 to 1,800-hp engines.

The present tendency is to automate the harbor tugboat. The tugboats of New York, a port that handles about 25,000 ships a year in its 450 berths, have a high bridge set very near the bow and fenders at the prow and along the sides for pushing.

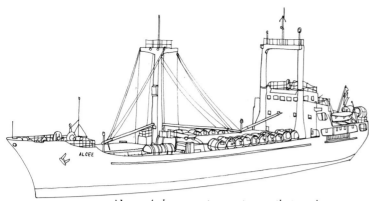

Alcee—*A dry-cargo tramp steamer that carries cargo on deck as well. Modern cargo ships are becoming more and more specialized according to the cargo they handle.*

The icebreaker is designed to open a channel through seas, lakes, and large rivers covered with ice. It is a fairly common vessel in the north, and in the Arctic and Antarctic oceans. It is a strongly built vessel with a long range (the Arctic route between the Bering Strait and the Russian port of Murmansk is 3,400 miles long) and is driven by powerful electric diesel-engines. The icebreaker's propellers have to have great power to drive the ship through ice. The propellers have three widely spaced blades made of special, highly resistant alloys. As early as 1930 the Russians, great specialists in this field, applied the principle of "mount it and split it," devised around 1865 by Britneff. The large and powerful icebreaker has a projecting wedge-shaped prow that mounts on top of the ice and breaks it by using the weight of the ship itself. Another type of icebreaker has a plow-shaped bow (invented by the Canadian Scott E. Alexander in 1968) that cuts its way through layers of ice.

Whale hunting used to be dominated by the Basques, the Dutch, the French, the English, and the North Americans. Modern whaling involves a highly complex organization. Modern whalers—displacing 500 to 900 tons, with 6-cylinder diesel engines of 2,000 to 3,500 hp—are based at deep-sea-whaling factory-ships of about 20,000 tons or more. The whales are quartered on the deck; the edible meat is frozen at once; and the oil from fatty parts is collected in special boilers. An international commission controls whale hunting, today almost exclusively carried out by Russians and Japanese, whose whalers have an ultrasonic device that frightens the whales and forces them into groups that can be attacked more easily.

By now the specialization of ships is a worldwide phenomenon, and we must of necessity limit our rapid survey of the various types of those which have come into common use.

There are the lightships with optical beacons to aid navigation. There are several cable ships, which watch over and maintain the undersea cables for long- and short-distance telephone and telegraph communications. Mention must be made of repair ships; ships for sweeping the sea bottom; and crane ships for salvage work.

Rynstroom—*A medium-tonnage container ship. The evolution of the merchant marine is undoubtedly the most interesting naval phenomenon of the 1970s.*

Jules Verne—*A tanker that carries inflammable gas, the first of its type to be built in France, for Gaz Maritime of Paris, and launched in 1964. Displacement: 21,940 tons; speed: 17 knots; 7 cylindrical gas tanks with a capacity of 900,000 cubic meters (1,177,110 cubic yards). Liquid gas tankers are now very numerous, but differ greatly in appearance.*

Etna—*An LNG (liquid natural gas) tanker. The tanker was originally designed to carry crude oil, but is now used for transporting liquids of all kinds.*

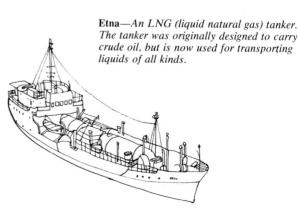

Alibut I—*A shrimp trawler used for the industrial fishing of shrimp in northern Europe, the United States, and New Zealand.* ▶

The bottom of the sea has increasingly attracted the attention of scholars and scientists in search of new food sources, oil deposits, and mining reserves. Oil is extracted from the sea bottom today from offshore platforms. The sea bottom itself is explored by bathyscaphes, self-propelled vessels that can submerge to great depths. The *Trieste* was built by Auguste Piccard, who coined the term "bathyscaphe."

In its first submersion, in August 1953, the *Trieste* reached a depth of some 3,500 feet. Seven years later, then the property of the U.S. Navy, it descended into the Philippine Trench to a depth of 36,000 feet, carrying Jacques Piccard, Auguste's son, and navy Lt. Don Walsh. The *Trieste* also took part in recovering the wreck of the atomic submarine *Thresher*, which sank mysteriously on April 10, 1963. Jacques Cousteau's *Soucoupe Plongeante* was the first really mobile bathyscaphe. Launched in 1959, it could operate at a depth of about 1,000 feet with a crew of 2 men. The construction materials used for these civilian submarines have been steel and an aluminum alloy (used for the American *Aluminaut*), an acrylic material still in the experimental stage. The United States, France, Japan, Russia, and Great Britain, to cite only the main nations interested, have a series of undersea ships in an advanced stage of construction, vessels designed for military, scientific, and commercial operations. The day is not far off when the present bathyscaphe of less than 20 tons will be replaced by specialized ships weighing 100 tons or more.

The modern fishing boat is a far cry from those colorful ships of another age with painted sails and carved hulls. Modern fishing vessels are highly specialized craft. Scandinavian and North American fishing fleets are built and organized for single types of fishing. The herring boats that fish along the east coast of the United States use compressors and perforated plastic tubes to produce an air-bubble barrier to block herring schools and make them easy to catch. Electric-current fishing is also practiced. The fishing boat uses an underwater anode to draw the fish into an electric field that stuns them. The fish are then netted and drawn aboard with water-scooping pumps. Fishing boats, and especially deep-sea ones, work from a fishing factory-ship.

Freezer ships, on the other hand, work alone. They are fishing boats with a tonnage *(cont'd. on p. 236)*

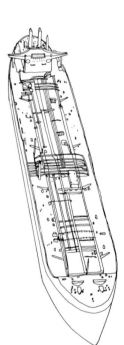

Universe Ireland—*A giant, 307,070-ton oil tanker. In recent years oil tankers have had the greatest development of all cargo ships, and their tonnage has increased enormously.*

Jacob—*A small deep-sea vessel operating in the North Sea. It has a diesel engine, perfect for fishing as regards both power and range.*

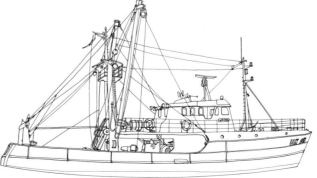

Eugene Dermott—*A modern French fishing boat from Cape Finisterre, equipped for trawling.*

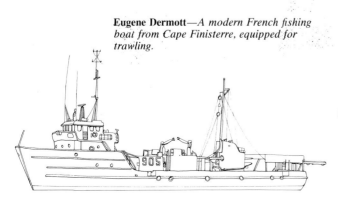

The Nuclear Propulsion Ship

20,000 LEAGUES OVER THE SEA

June 14, 1952, is a historic date in naval history. It was the day work began on the world's first atomically propelled vessel. The moment had finally arrived, thanks to the boundless energy of an American naval officer, Captain Hyman C. Rickover. After studying the principles of atomic energy, he concluded that if a small reactor were to be installed in a submarine it could remain submerged almost indefinitely. It would not require oxygen, as the diesel engine did. Less than two years later, the *Nautilus* was launched, the first ship driven by nuclear energy. Eight months later it was in active service.

Displacement: 3,470 tons on the surface; 3,975 tons in submersion. Length: 98.6 meters (323 feet); maximum beam: 8.4 meters (27.7 feet); draft: 6.7 meters (22 feet); 2 steam turbines fed by a pressurized reactor develop a power of 15,000 hp; speed: more than 20 knots. Crew: 10 officers and 95 sailors. At 11:15 P.M. on August 3, 1958, after a memorable crossing in submersion, it reached latitude 90 degrees north, below the Arctic icecap. Commander Anderson headed this mission. The *Nautilus* received its third supply of uranium in 1959 after having covered more than 91,324 miles. It was recharged again after reaching the 150,000-mile mark.

The expression "atomic or nuclear engine" means nothing, and it is a great mistake to oversimplify matters and call a nuclear-powered vessel an atomic ship. Nuclear energy acts on the generator system, and the driving machine is a steam turbine or an electric engine. A nuclear reactor has a nuclear-fuel core of enriched uranium enclosed in a zirconium container. Bars of hafnium, a metal with the same characteristics as zirconium, inserted into or withdrawn from the core of the reactor as needed, control the fission level and the heat that is transmitted to a refrigerant liquid that surrounds the core. This radio-active liquid is pumped into a steam generator which moves the ship's turbines. Both reactor and steam generator are enclosed in a lead shield, which is the heaviest piece of equipment. Nevertheless, it is not as heavy as the electric batteries used in conventional submarines.

Lenin—*The world's first surface ship to have atomic propulsion. It is used as an icebreaker by the Russian navy.*

Otto Hahn—*This atomic-propulsion cargo ship went into service in 1968 and navigated without interruption until 1973, when it was given a new charge of 20 grams of uranium. This cross section amidships shows the large nuclear reactor that supplies the turbines with 10,000 hp letting the ship reach a speed of 16 knots. Gross weight: 16,871 tons; overall length: 172 meters (188 yards); beam: 23 meters (76.92 feet); draft: 9 meters (30.19 feet). The ship is specially equipped for carrying iron ore.*

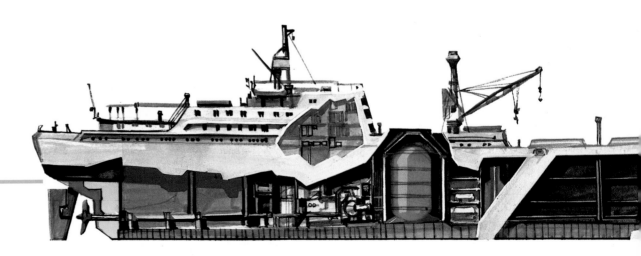

The Nuclear Propulsion Ship

The turbines are mounted directly on the tail shafts and act on them through reduction gears. The reactor reaches its critical phase on land and can function for very long periods. Thus the ship has a range of more than 100,000 miles. Since it does not need oxygen and does not produce exhaust gas, the nuclear reactor is ideal for the submarine. The latest types of nuclear-powered submarines have already reached a top speed of 45 knots. There are now more than 170 military vessels with nuclear power, including submarines and surface ships. The nuclear-powered cargo ship *Savannah* was launched in 1962 and laid up in August 1967. The ship lost 1.5 million dollars a year. Other nuclear cargo ships include the German *Otto Hahn* and the Soviet icebreaker *Lenin*, used to open up the Arctic waters to mercantile navigation. Nuclear projects are being studied around the world. Since 1966 the Italian navy has been considering the building of an auxiliary ship of 17,700 tons, the *Enrico Fermi*, to be powered by a nuclear reactor using enriched uranium.

The future of the nuclear ship has hardly begun, but there is already much talk about underwater maritime transport. A project for the construction of a nuclear-powered cargo submarine has been presented to the Geneva Committee for the Peaceful Use of Atomic Energy.

Thanks to the high propulsion power supplied by its nuclear reactor, to its speed in submersion, to its long range, to the ease with which it can reach depths of more than 650 feet, and to its powerful armament of long-range ballistic missiles, the submarine is today the most formidable warship in existence.

Savannah—*The world's first merchant ship with atomic propulsion, created by the U.S. Atomic Energy Commission and the United States Maritime Administration to demonstrate the possibilities of the peaceful use of atomic energy and its flexibility of function. After making a series of courtesy stops around the world, it was used on the USA–Mediterranean route until 1972. Because of the high cost of operation, the ship was withdrawn from service. It was launched on July 21, 1959, at the shipyards of the New York Shipbuilding Company in Camden and made its maiden voyage in August 1962. Gross tonnage: 13,890 tons; cargo capacity: 9,251 tons; length: 175.71 meters (595.5 feet); 60 passengers; crew: 110 men; a Babcock and Wilco reactor weighing 2,460 tons; speed: 20.5 knots; range: 336,000 miles, equal to 16,000 hours of navigation at top speed, that is, 700 days without refueling.*

Ethan Allen—*One of the U.S. Navy's best-equipped atomic-propulsion ships, it is part of the United States' strategic-deterrent forces. It has a range of 140,000 miles, thanks to its 30,000-hp nuclear reactor.*

of from 500 to 2,000 tons, but profitable operations cannot be carried out too far from home base. As soon as the fish are caught, they are cleaned and frozen.

Modern technology has provided the fishing industry with highly sophisticated instruments, and there is increasing concern about the rapid depletion of the ocean's fish. Underwater fishing vessels are already on the drawing board. The bow would carry a parachute-opening net, and the vessel would be led directly to schools of fish by echo sounders. The fish would be kept in seawater compartments and carried live.

The history of the ship, which began so far back in history, has not ended. Indeed, it has a long way to go.

Trade, the love of adventure, scientific research, and the exploitation of the still immense resources of the oceans still draw man to the sea. Columbus's little caravels now seem pathetically frail in comparison with the giant modern warships and cargo vessels.

Atomic energy finds its best and most advanced application in large aircraft carriers for attack; in the oceanic submarine; in guided-missile-launching cruisers; and in light escort vessels, such as frigates and corvettes. There are now 170 military ships with atomic propulsion in the world. The merchant vessel *Nuclear Ship Savannah* was put into service in 1962 and withdrawn 5 years later because of its high cost of operation.

Atomic propulsion could lead to the development of commercial submarine transportation, oil tankers, and passenger vessels. But a great deal of research and experimentation is still needed before atomic energy can bring commercial vessels up to the level of the military sector.

The future of the ship is already at hand, in the new concepts that have been applied to the hydrofoil speedboat and the air-cushion hydroplane.

The hydrofoil speedboat has four bearing wings that protrude from the hull, two to-

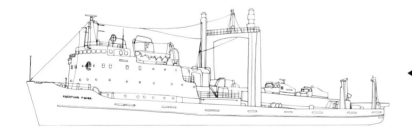

◀ **Abertham Fisher**—*A modern English Channel ferryboat for motor-vehicle transportation. The exceptional development of maritime transportation ships right after World War II led to rapid technological evolution in smaller vessels.*

Puebla—*A typical cargo ship with many derricks.*

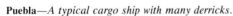

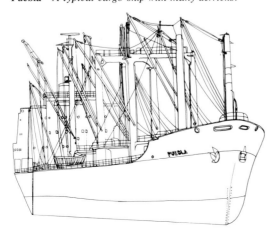

Lifeboat—*An "all-weather" boat than can take any kind of sea and is used for rescue work. Unsinkable, it measures about 40 feet in length. Its 2 engines drive it at a speed of 10 knots.*

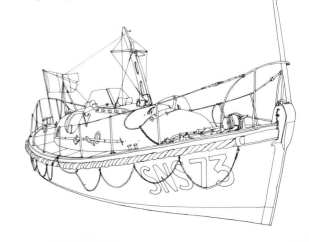

ward the bow, and two toward the stern, set transversely under the keel and shaped like a very open V. Because of its speed, and the density and resistance of the water, the hydrofoil's keel emerges completely from the water, supported by hydrodynamic thrust. The hull has no water resistance and can attain a speed of some 80 mph. The latest research carried out in the United States should lead to the construction of hydrofoils of about 1,000 tons, capable of carrying hundreds of passengers at a speed of 97 knots an hour. This means one could cover the distance between New York and Le Havre in about 30 hours, a third of the time it takes the fastest transatlantic liner.

The air-cushion hydroplane, or hovercraft, is lifted above the surface by jets of compressed air produced by powerful vertical turbines. It is moved at high speed by propellers driven by conventional engines. Hovercraft are widely used by the military for fast attack and for troop landings. It may well be the passenger ship of the future, since it can

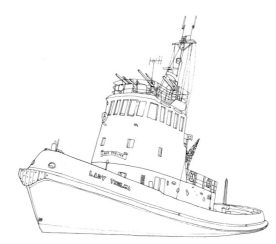

Batcombe—*A British tugboat equipped for fire-fighting duty. Every nation has rescue companies that include special tugs supplied with foam- or water-throwers to help fight fire.*

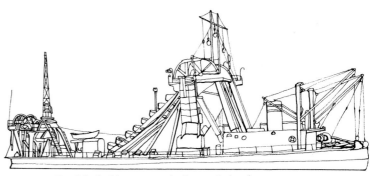

Archéonaute—*A French ship built to explore and protect undersea archaeological zones. French law is strict in its protection of anything of historical or artistic interest found or placed beneath the sea, which is legally the property of the nation.*

Scarabeo II—*A platform built in Italy and used for undersea oil research. These platforms can also be equipped with pneumatic diving bells for deep-sea divers. The Scarabeo is kept afloat by hollow columns that can be filled with air and that can also rest on a shallow bottom.*

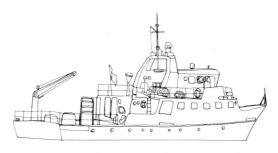

Dredge—*Furnished with a water wheel or a chain of rotating buckets for digging below the sea and on river and lake bottoms. It may be towed or have its own engine.*

Antipollution boat—*A special large pneumatic boat that is used in English waters to eliminate such pollutants as naphtha and crude oil.*

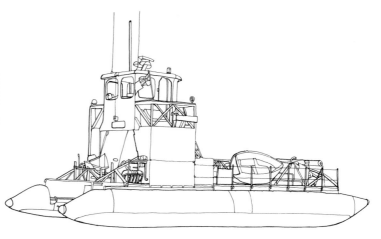

238

Calshot Spit—*An English Channel lightship. The floating lighthouse is used to signal danger on coasts where it would be impossible or too expensive to build lighthouses. It is also employed where the bottom must be carefully watched because of tide action and river mouths.*

Ragna—*A containership with three holds for containers. Containers can pass from the ship to a train or truck with very little handling, thus improving maritime transport and causing a profound transformation of harbor installation.*

Cable ship—*A ship specially equipped for the laying, recovery, and repairing of submarine cables for telecommunications. Special hold arrangements permit the transporting and unwinding of the cable, and complicated dynamometric winches assure it steady tension. The first submarine communications cable was laid in 1857, between the island of Valentia in Ireland and Trinity Bay in Newfoundland, a distance of 2,200 miles. Two ships took part in the operations, the British propeller ship* Agamemnon *of 3,691 tons, and the large American frigate* Niagara.

Ocean-going tugboat—*A British vessel, very seaworthy, extremely powerful, with long range and great maneuverability.*

Shearwater—*A British hydrofoil speedboat for fast service on the English Channel. The sustaining action developed by the bearing wings is due to the phenomenon of circulation.*

Surprise—*A sloop built of iroko and mahogany, designed by American architect Doug Petersen in 1964 and built by N. Puccinelli's Cantiere Navale 71 at Castiglion della Pescaia, Italy, in 1966. Overall length: 11.28 meters (37 feet); beam: 3.20 meters (10.6 feet); 32,000 miles covered during the one-man round-the-world voyage of the Italian Ambrogio Fogar in 1973–1974. Apart from its sails and an automatic wind-controlled rudder, the Surprise also has a small, 10-hp Fairyman diesel engine with oleodynamic transmission, set at the end of the bow.*

travel over both land and sea. A 5,000-ton hydroplane that can link the shores of California with Hawaii in 24 hours is being designed in the United States. Hovercraft are used for ferrying passengers across the English Channel. Other countries have used hovercraft as ferryboats.

But the most important result of maritime technology, from 1960 to the present day, is undoubtedly automation. A complex electronic system directs the most important operations connected with automatic control of the engine equipment on a ship. Engine-room personnel have been reduced and consist of highly specialized officers who watch over the functioning of the equipment itself.

Oceanographic research, stimulated by scientific and practical needs, was quickly modernized after World War II, and man now explores the ocean floor with electronic eyes and ears. The study of the ocean bottom has become infinitely more important than the conquest of space, given the problems of food, energy, and water pollution. Veritable submarine laboratories have been set up hundreds of feet under water. And underwater cities may not be science-fiction fantasies. The ocean floor promises rich yields, including oil, diamonds, and minerals. Exploration of the sea will transform the mate-

Soucoupe Plongeante—*The first modern oceanographic submarine, the creation of Jacques Cousteau. It weighs 3 tons and can reach a depth of 100 feet with two people aboard. Launched in 1959, the ship has an ellipsoidal hull, 2 meters (6.8 feet) wide and 1.6 meters (5.4 feet) high. It is powered by a 2-hp engine and steered by 2 adjustable hydraulic jets.*

John Biscoe—*An oceanographic ship specially equipped for research in polar seas, for the study of currents, variations in sea level, wave motion, salinity, and temperature.*

240

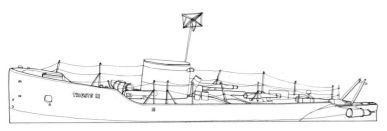

Trieste 2—*The bathyscaphe built by Jacques Piccard, son of the famous Swiss scientist, in which he descended into the Philippine Trench, off the island of Guam, to a depth of 35,000 feet in December 1959.*

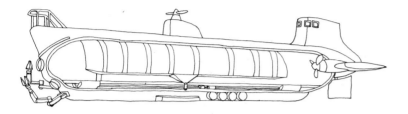

Aluminaut—*An American bathyscaphe designed to operate at a depth of 15,000 feet. The hull is made of a series of aluminum-alloy rings and was built in 1965. Cruising speed: 3 knots; weight: 80 tons.*

rials, the technical procedures, and the very life of man. It will assure him of fresh water, an ever increasing need, and of electric current with the harnessing of the tides, already carried out in France with the "sea-engine" plant on the Rance River. It should also supply him with more than 10 billion tons of gold, nickel, iron, potassium, manganese, cobalt, and copper. Fluorocarbon, the sensational discovery of the Dutch Dr. Klijstra, is a synthetic liquid that resembles water but that can store up 30 times more oxygen than water. It should make it possible for man to descend to great depths. Even now the large bathyscaphe *Auguste Piccard*, designed and built by Jacques Piccard, the son of the scientist who died on March 25, 1968, carries passengers 500 feet down to the bottom of Lake Geneva. Tomorrow may well be here sooner than we think. The ship still holds unimaginable surprises for us, and man has always found his true being and his true strength in his contact and confrontation with the sea. He owes his life, his survival, the development of his civilization, to the sea; and to the sea he owes and will continue to owe his feeling of brotherhood and communion with his fellowmen.

Sealab II—*An American undersea laboratory that can operate when fixed to the sea bottom. Internal pressure is kept equal to that on the surface to permit accurate research into undersea life.*

Hotel Atlantis—*One of the world's favorite dreams is that of* Homo aquaticus, *that is, the man who can live at the bottom of the sea. Perhaps the fantastic undersea hotels of the future may look like this.*

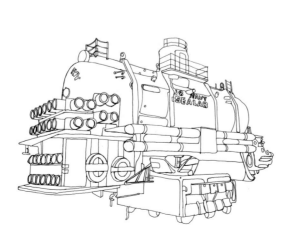

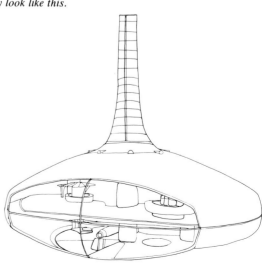

Appendixes

THE GREAT NAVIGATORS

IN THE WAKE OF
CHRISTOPHER COLUMBUS

Alonso Nino—Ignored the agreement signed by the rulers of Spain and Portugal at the time of Columbus's first voyage, and sailed along the coast of Maracaibo in 1500, bringing back a precious cargo of pearls.

Vicente Yanez Pinzon—After taking part in Columbus's first voyage as captain of the *Niña*, reached Cape Saint Roche on the coast of Brazil in 1500.

Diego de Lepe—In that same year, he reached Cape Saint Augustine, south of Cape Saint Roche.

Rodrigo de Bastidas—Sailed from the gulf of Maracaibo to the bay of Darien, completing the exploration begun by Columbus during his fourth and last voyage.

IN THE WAKE OF
VASCO DA GAMA

Giovanni da Nova—In 1501, discovered the islands of Saint Helena and Ascension in the Atlantic.

Tristan da Cunha—In 1506, discovered the small island that bears his name in the South Atlantic.

Antonio d'Abreu—Sent off to explore the East by Alfonso d'Albuquerque, in 1511 he sailed to the archipelago of the Moluccas, starting from Malacca and coasting along Sumatra and Java.

Fernando Perez d'Andrade—Reached Canton with a large fleet in 1517.

Giovanni da Empoli—Left Lisbon with four ships and in 1503 reached Malabar as agent for the Florentine firm of Gualtierotti and Frescobaldi. He sailed again in 1509 with a squadron under the command of Diego Mendèz de Vasconcéllos and took part in the conquest of Goa and Malacca. In 1518, he reached Canton from Lisbon.

IN THE WAKE OF
AMERIGO VESPUCCI

Nuno Manuel and Christovam de Haro—In 1514, reached Bahia Blanca, near Patagonia, while looking for a passage to the Indies.

Juan Diaz de Solis—After the death of Vespucci, took the latter's post as *piloto mayor* and in 1516 organized an expedition to the mouth of the Rio de la Plata, which he explored. He was killed in a battle with the natives.

Sebastian Cabot—*Piloto mayor* of Charles V after de Solis's death. He organized and led a squadron of three carracks and two caravels that left the Spanish coast for the estuary of the Rio de la Plata on April 2, 1526, following the river up to where it was joined by the Paranà and the Rio Uruguay. He built forts and set up colonies on the banks of these two rivers. On July 22, 1530, he arrived back in Spain and served at court. He later entered the service of the king of England.

Pedro de Mendoza—A navigator and soldier sent by Charles V to occupy with arms the region of Rio de la Plata, present-day Argentina, which was threatened by Portuguese raids. With 12 ships and 800 men, he explored the Rio de la Plata and its tributary, the Paranà, and not far from the point where the two rivers joined, founded a city he called Nuestra Señora de Buenos Aires. Constantly attacked by the natives and with three-quarters of his men lost through illness or combat, Pedro de Mendoza sailed back to Spain with what was left of his fleet.

IN THE WAKE OF
MAGELLAN

Alvarado de Saavedra—Went directly from Mexico to the Moluccas and New Guinea in 1528. Because of contrary winds, he accidentally discovered the eastern Carolines and the Marshall Islands.

Ruy Lopez de Villalobos—Left Mexico in 1542 and rediscovered the Saint Lazarus Islands, already found by Magellan; he called them the Philippines, in honor of Philip II of Spain.

Miguel Lopez de Legaspi—Conqueror and colonizer of the Philippines, which he reached in 1565.

Andrea de Urdaneta—The navigator who, in that same year, established the best route between the Spanish dominions in America and Asia, passing through the region of the northeast trade winds.

Alvaro de Mendana—Discovered the Solomon Islands in 1567, starting from the port of Callao on the coast of Chile. He returned to the Solomons in 1595 to start colonization, and on this second voyage discovered the Marquesa Islands and the small island of Santa Cruz, where he died of illness.

Thomas Cavendish—Sailed from England in 1586 to repeat Magellan's voyage, but for a far different purpose; he returned with rich booty taken from Spanish ships and ports.

John Davis—One of the most important navigators of the Elizabethan age. In 1592 he accidentally discovered the Falkland Islands east of Patagonia.

Jakob Mahu—A Dutch navigator, who in 1598 was driven by a storm to the Austral Shetlands and later reached Japan.

Oliver van Noort—The first Dutch navigator, whose voyages in 1598 marked the start of Dutch hegemony in the Pacific.

Pedro de Quiros—The pilot on Mendaña's last expedition. In December 1605 he sailed with two carracks to find the legendary Land of the South and discovered the Society Islands. He died in Panama while organizing a second expedition.

Luis Vaz de Torres—Quiroz's first mate, he retraced his captain's route and reached the southern coast of New Guinea, giving his name to the strait that separates that island from the Australian continent.

Francesco Carletti—The only private navigator to reach Central America and then—after coasting along Peru and New Spain—the Philippines, Japan, and Macao on the Chinese coast. He then visited India and returned to Europe through the Cape of Good Hope. He left Spain in 1594 and returned to Italy in 1606.

THE EXPLORATION OF THE
COAST OF NORTH AMERICA

John Cabot—With the backing of Henry VII of England, he left Bristol on May 2, 1497, and reached the coast of Cape Breton Island in North America, where he entered the estuary of the Saint Lawrence River. He arrived back in England on August 6 of the same year.

Gaspare Cortereal—Set foot on the east coast of Newfoundland in 1500. A year later, he and his brother Miquel reached the farthest cape of Greenland, coasting along Labrador. He never returned from this expedition.

Giovanni da Verrazzano—With only the *Delfina* (a crew of 50 men and supplies for 8 months), he sailed on January 17, 1524, with the backing of Francis I of France, and explored the North American coast from present-day Georgia to Cape Hatteras and Cape Cod. He returned to Dieppe at the end of July 1524. On March 17, 1528, he left for the Bahamas and the southern Antilles, but never returned. He was tortured and killed by the natives.

THE NORTHWEST PASSAGE

Expeditions set out along the coast from the Gulf of Darien to the north, seeking the passage that was supposed to lead from the New World to the Indies. It was clear that America was a separate continent and not part of Asia.

Juan Diaz de Solis, Vicente Yanez Pinzon, and Pedro de Ledesma—Sailed in 1508 from the island of Haiti to the Gulf of Honduras and along the coast of Yucatán.

Juan de la Cosa and Diego de Nicuesa—Reached the coast of Veragua, now French Guiana, in the same year.

Sebastiano de Ocampo—The first man to circumnavigate Cuba and establish the fact that it was an island, in 1508.

Vasco Nunez de Balboa—The last expedition organized by Vespucci as *piloto mayor* sailed on April 11, 1513, under the command of Balboa, who reached the Gulf of Darien. After a period spent colonizing the land at the mouth of the Atrato River, Balboa crossed the mountains to the west and discovered the Pacific Ocean, which he called the Southern Sea.

Diego de Velasquez—In 1517, reached the Yucatán Peninsula, discovering traces of an advanced civilization. He was seriously wounded in a battle with the natives and forced to return to Cuba.

Juan de Grijalva—In 1518 discovered traces of the Mayan civilization on the island of Cozumel, off Yucatán. He reached what is now the city of Tampico, but was unable to find the long-sought passage.

Juan Ponce de Leon—Also failed to find the passage. In 1513 he reached the peninsula between the Bahamas and Cuba, which he called *Pascua florida* (modern Florida). In 1519 he was killed by natives.

Alonso Alvarez de Pineda—Left Jamaica in 1519 and followed the entire coast of the Gulf of Mexico without finding the famous (and nonexistent) passage.

Lucas Vasquez de Ayllon—On two trips, in 1520 and 1526, tried without luck to find the passage, sailing north of what is now Georgia.

Estevam Gomez—Pushed farther north than all his predecessors in 1524, along the coast now occupied by some of America's largest cities.

Jacques Cartier—The first French navigator and explorer. With two 60-ton caravels, he left Saint Malo on April 20, 1534, and headed toward Labrador, crossing a huge gulf he thought was the passage to the Pacific. A second expedition left on May 19, 1535, and he then realized that he had come upon a broad estuary at the mouth of the river he called the Saint Lawrence. He followed it up to a native village (*Canada* in the native tongue), on the spot where the city of Quebec later rose; he went as far as the hilly zone he called Mont Royal, site of the city to be known as Montreal. He returned to France in July 1535. In 1541 he set out on his third and last voyage. Jacques Cartier laid the foundations for the vast French colonial empire in North America.

Martin Frobisher—Brought England into the competition for the discovery of a passage to the Sea of Cathay. Frobisher sailed from the Thames estuary with two carracks and reached Greenland on June 7, 1576. He went farther on to make the first contact with the Eskimos who lived in what was to be known as Baffin Land. He was convinced he had found the mythical Northwest Passage and set out again in 1577 and 1578. His voyages drew English attention to the territories in the Northwest Atlantic that, with the island of Newfoundland, were to form the basis of England's colonial empire in North America.

John Davis—Before turning his attention to the South Atlantic, went to Greenland in 1585 and down the coast of Baffin Land, thinking he had found the long-sought passage in the huge inlet of Cumberland Bay. In the two voyages that followed (1586 and 1587), he headed north and happened on what was later to prove to be a genuine Northwest Passage.

THE NORTHEAST PASSAGE

Those who did not want to challenge Portuguese claims to the Indian route that circled Africa, or to compete with the Spanish in the New World, had another possibility open to them: that of sailing north around Europe and Asia, and reaching the lands described so enticingly by Marco Polo from that direction. When Sebastian Cabot left Spain for England, he carried with him plans for an expedition to reach Cathay by way of the northern seas. In London, the Muscovy Company was set up to exploit the commercial possibilities of the new passage, and from the middle of the 16th century on, expeditions were regularly sent out.

Hugh Willoughby and Richard Chancellor—Sailed from Deptford in 1553 with three carracks for the northern coasts of Scandinavia. A storm destroyed two ships and led to Willoughby's death, but Chancellor got to the White Sea Gulf and reached Moscow, setting up the first trade relations to compete with the Hanseatic League.

Steven Burrough (or Borough, or Borrows)—In April 1556, sailed on the North Cape route along the coast of the Kola Peninsula and even beyond, up to the Vajgac Islands at the edge of the inlet of the sea of Kara. Here he met the first Samoyeds, natives for whom the reindeer is the sole source of food. The bitter winter arrived, and Burrough hastened home.

Arthur Pet and Charles Jackmann—The expedition of these two English navigators reached the islands of Navaja Zemlja in 1580. Pet was lost at sea with all his crew, and Jackmann died shortly after returning home, worn out by hardship.

Willem Barents—The Dutch sent out an expedition organized by Barents, the most famous and the most unfortunate of all the voyages made to find the Northeast Passage. In 1594, with four ships equipped by the merchants of Amsterdam, Barents reached 77 degrees north latitude, but found his path barred by the great Arctic icefields. His second expedition, in 1595, reached the strait of Kara; the third, with seven ships, left in May 1596 and sailed as far as Bear Island and the Spitsbergens, the first land discovered by Barents. The expedition was taken by surprise by the winter ice formation during the return trip and was forced to pass the winter at about 76 degrees north latitude, remaining for ten months in a hut built of logs found floating on the sea. When spring arrived, the survivors of the Arctic winter began the voyage home. They set out in May 1597 in launches, because the ship was totally blocked by ice. Barents, worn out by hardship and afflicted with scurvy, died during the trip. The sea along the Russian and Norwegian coasts in northern Europe, between the Spitsbergen Islands and Novaja Zemlja, is named for him.

EXPLORING THE OCEANS

1605–1606

The Portuguese navigator Queiros, in the service of Spain, discovered the New Hebrides and believed them to be the mythical *Terra Australis.*

1607–1611

During his three successive expeditions in search of the Northwest Passage, Henry Hudson visited Greenland, the Spitsbergens, and Chesapeake Bay on the coast of North America. He sailed past the Labrador Peninsula as far as the bay that now bears his name.

1608–1609

Diego de Prado and Torres sailed along the coast of New Guinea and crossed the strait between that island and Australia.

1616

Dutch navigators Jacob Lemaire and Cornelius Schouten discovered Cape Horn and crossed the Pacific, passing Tuamotu, Samoa, and the Solomon Islands.

1639–1643

Abel Tasman circumnavigated Australia and gave his name to Tasmania.

1683–1710

Englishman William Dampier, an excellent hydrographer and expert botanist, doubled Cape Horn and reached the coast of California, later crossing the Pacific to the Indies.

1698–1700

British astronomer Edmund Halley made a voyage from England to Saint Helena, studying the action of the winds and tides. He later went as far as 52 degrees south latitude in the Atlantic, carrying out experiments with the magnetic compass.

1721–1724

The Dutchman Roggeven circumnavigated the globe and discovered Easter Island.

1728

Bering's expedition discovered the strait between Asia and America, later named after the Danish navigator.

1764–1766

The Englishman Byron circumnavigated the globe and made important observations on the salinity and density of the sea.

1766–1768

The globe was circumnavigated by the Englishmen Wallis and Carteret, who made many scientific observations on the action of the winds and studied marine biology.

1766–1779

Louis Antoine de Bougainville sailed from the coast of Brazil through the Strait of Magellan and discovered Tahiti, Tehai, Lancier, Crocker, Melville, and Samoa. In the years that followed, he sailed along the coast of New Guinea and New Britain. His *Voyage autour du monde*, published in 1771, made him famous.

1767–1772

Scientific voyages were organized by the French navy to test the new marine chronometers of Lerov and Berthoud, thus opening the era of modern chronometric navigation.

1768–1779

The three great voyages of James Cook, the first genuinely scientific expeditions of the century. Natural sciences, winds, and currents were studied during the expeditions of the great English navigator, who was killed by natives in Hawaii on February 14, 1779.

1773

An expedition was made to study and chart the coasts of the southern lands by Frenchman Marion-Dufresne. He was killed by Maoris in New Zealand.

1785–1788

The French navigator Jean François de Galaup, Count de la Perouse sailed from Brest in 1785 to find the Northwest Passage from the Pacific side, an exploit already attempted by Cook on his second voyage. The expedition doubled Cape Horn, touched the Alaskan coast, and reached the Philippines. A year later, La Perouse reached the coast of Japan and sailed as far as present-day Vladivostok, discovering the passage called by his name, between Sakhalin and the northernmost Japanese islands. In the following year, the expedition reached the coast of Australia, carrying out accurate surveys and observations. During the return trip, La Perouse's two ships were shipwrecked off the island of Vanikoro, in the Santa Cruz archipelago.

1790

The three-masted *La Solide*, captained by Etienne Marchand, sailed from Marseilles to the Pacific coast of Canada and then to China. An example of "speed and precision, the triumph of scientific navigation."

1791–1793

Captain d'Entrecasteaux set out to look for La Perouse, who had vanished three years before. The expedition visited the coast of Tasmania, discovered that it was an island, and passed near the Santa Cruz archipelago, where La Perouse was shipwrecked. D'Entrecasteaux died of scurvy on July 21, 1793.

1791

Englishman George Vancouver completed Cook's hydrographic mission along the coast of Australia, with the two ships *Discovery* and *Chatham*. He then sailed along the Pacific coast of North America and founded the city that bears his name.

1791–1795

The Spaniard Malaspina, in command of the *Descubierta* and the *Atrevida*, made a reconnaissance voyage along the coast of South America, establishing the exact route for the Philippines and making observations on the great American glacier called by his name.

1800–1803

Twenty persons, including botanists, zoologists, astronomers, and mineralogists, took part in an expedition commanded by Nicolas Baudin, which sailed from Le Havre to study

EXPLORING THE OCEANS

the west and south coasts of Australia. Baudin died on the return trip. Important contacts were made with the aborigines of Australia and Tasmania.

1800–1804
During a French scientific expedition, François Peron made the first deep temperature measurements.

1803–1810
The first American military-scientific expedition, led by David Porter, based first on the Galápagos and then on the Marquesa islands, made important contributions to the cartography of the Pacific Ocean.

1803–1806
A Russian circumnavigation commanded by Ivan F. Kruzenstein, accompanied by physicist J. C. Horner, took measurements of deep-sea temperature in the Pacific.

1807–1822
Englishman William Scoresby, Jr., a scientist and whale hunter, made surface and deep-sea observations on the seas around Greenland and Spitsbergen.

1808–1818
J. Golovine, a commander in the Russian navy, devoted himself to the study of the Arctic Ocean and the North Pacific.

1816–1826
Russian Adm. Otto von Kotzebue circumnavigated the globe twice in this period, making important discoveries regarding surface currents at low and high latitudes.

1817
Louis de Freycinet, a ship's officer on the Baudin expedition, commanded the *Uranie* on a voyage to the glacial regions of the south, after visiting and charting Timor, New Guinea, Guam, the Marianas, and Hawaii. He brought back an important collection of scientific specimens, including more than 400 unknown plants.

1819–1821
Circumnavigation of the Arctic continent by the Russian expedition of Fabion G. van Bellingshausen.

1822–1825
Duperrey completed Freycinet's work as captain of the *Coquille*, covering more than 50,000 miles in the Pacific Ocean without losing a single man. He published his findings in seven volumes and four atlases.

1826–1836
This decade was marked by the voyages of the *Beagle*, commanded by Captain Fitzroy, along the coasts of Patagonia, Chile, and Peru. On board was Charles Darwin, the famous naturalist. His observations during these voyages provided the basis for his theory of the evolution of species.

1826–1840
Jean Sébastien Dumont d'Urville sailed in the *Coquille* (renamed the *Astrolabe*) on three circumnavigations; he charted 2,500 miles of coastline in the Pacific, located about 150 new islands, carried out oceanographic studies, and found remains of La Perouse's shipwreck on the Vanikoro atoll. On his third voyage toward the Atlantic, he discovered Adélie Land. This famous sailor-scientist died two years after his return, in one of the first railroad accidents.

1827–1876
Oceanographic research missions were carried out by the British *Challenger*, commanded by Capt. Wylie Thomson, in the Atlantic, Pacific, and Indian oceans, as far as 40 degrees south latitude.

1838–1842
A famous American scientific expedition of six ships was led by Capt. Charles Wilkes, assisted by the famous naturalist J. D. Dana, who carried out an important study of crustaceans. The Wilkes mission brought back data on the tides and currents of the Antarctic region and of the western coast of North America, as well as more than 5,000 specimens of Antarctic vegetation and extensive studies on geology and mineralogy.

1839–1843
Sir James Clark Ross, with the two ships *Erebus* and *Terror*, studied terrestrial magnetism and the temperature of deep waters. He collected botanical and biological specimens during his voyages to the southern seas and the Antarctic.

1874–1875
Capt. George E. Belken took the *Tuscarora* of the U.S. Navy on a long oceanographic research cruise to the seas east of Japan and to the North Pacific, systematically using piano wire as sounding cable.

1874–1876
The oceanographic expedition of the *Gazelle*, a German navy corvette, had as its object the study of oceanic physics.

1877–1880
Commanded first by Alexander Agassiz and then by John Elliot Pillsbury, the oceanographic ship *Blake* of the American navy carried out study and research in the Caribbean Sea, in the Gulf of Mexico, and along the Florida coast.

1885–1922
Prince Albert of Monaco's oceanographic expeditions ranged from the Cape Verde Islands to the Spitsbergen coast and from the Mediterranean to New England and Newfoundland. The results of these missions is collected in the Oceanographic Museum in the Principality of Monaco. The research ships were the *Hirondelle I* and *II* and the *Princess Alice I* and *II*.

1886–1889
Under the command of Adm. S. O. Makarov, the Russian research ship *Vitiaz* circumnavigated the globe gathering data on the temperature of the sea and on the specific gravity of the currents and tides. Makarov contributed to the foundation of the International Council for the Exploration of the Sea.

1888–1905
Agassiz again commanded a naval research ship, the *Albatross* of the U.S. Navy, which was ordered by the American Fishing Commission to carry out studies in the eastern part of the Pacific, from Easter Island to Callao in Peru, and up to the Bering Sea, as well as in Japanese waters and the Sea of Okhotsk.

1889–1926
Two ships of the Indian navy, the *Investigator I* and *II*, carry out thorough biological studies in the Arabian Sea and the Bay of Bengal.

1889
Professor Victor Hensen, discoverer of plankton, led the German oceanographic expedition on board the specially equipped ship *National*, which spent a great deal of time in the North Atlantic.

1893–1896
Fridtjof Nansen made his famous voyage on board the *Fram* adrift in the Arctic icefields, making valuable oceanographic, magnetic, astronomic, and meteorologic observations.

1897–1899
A Belgian expedition on board the *Belgica* was the first to spend a winter in the Antarctic, carrying out biological and physical research in the ocean west of the Graham Straits and south of Peter I Island.

1898–1899
The *Valdivia* was the first oceanographic ship to carry out research at great depths in the southern latitudes, under the guidance of Professor Chun Carl. The expedition studied marine biology and physics in the Antarctic, Atlantic, and Indian oceans.

1899–1900
The *Siboga*, a Dutch oceanographic ship, was the last 19th-century vessel to carry out biological and hydrographic studies of the waters of the Antilles and Malaysia.

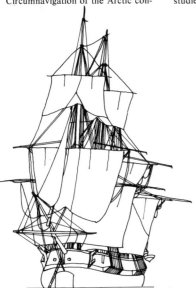

Hecle—*The ship in which William E. Parry and James Clark Ross tried to reach the North Pole in 1827. The frigate* Fury *also took part in this expedition, and the strait discovered during this Arctic mission was named for the two vessels.*

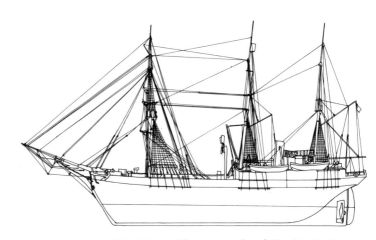

Stella Polare—*The commander of this ship, Luigi Amedeo di Savoia, tried to reach the North Pole in 1899–1900. One member of the expedition, Adm. Umberto Cagni, reached 86 degrees north latitude on April 24, 1900, a limit which was not surpassed until 1909.*

NAVAL MUSEUMS OF THE WORLD

1. ARGENTINA

Museo Naval de la Nacion, Buenos Aires

2. AUSTRALIA

Institute of Applied Sciences, Victoria

3. BELGIUM

National Scheepvaart Museum, Antwerp

4. CANADA

The Maritime Museum, Vancouver
The New Brunswick Museum—Marine Gallery, Saint John, New Brunswick

5. DENMARK

Orlogsmuseet, Copenhagen
Handels og Sofartsmuseet paa Kronborg, Helsingör
National Maritime Museum, Roskilde

6. FINLAND

Alands Sofartsmuseum, Mariehamn

7. FRANCE

Musee de la Marine (Palais de Chaillot)—Conservatoire National des Arts et Metiers, Paris
Musee de la Marine, Bordeaux
Musee de la Marine, Marseille
Musee de la Marine, Rochefort
Musee de la Marine, Toulon
Musee de la Mer, Biarritz
Musee de la Peche, Concarneau
Musee des Salorges, Nantes
Musee du Chateau, Dieppe
Musee du Chateau, Saint-Malo
Musee du long cours cap-hornier, Sainte Servan–Tour Solidor
Musee du Vieux Granville, Granville
Musee du Vieux Havre, Le Havre
Musee du Vieux Honfleur, Honfleur
Musee la Faille, la Rochelle (oceanographic)
Musee Massena, Nice
Musee Naval, Saint Tropez
Musee Place de Gaulle, Dunkirk

8. GERMANY

Altonaer Museum, Hamburg
Deutsches Museum, Munich
Museum fur Hamburgische Geschichte, Hamburg
Schiffahrts Museum, Brake-Unterweser

9. GREAT BRITAIN

Art Gallery and Museum, Glasgow
City of Liverpool Museum, Liverpool
Pickering Maritime Museum, Hull
Museum of Science and Engineering, Newcastle-on-Tyne
National Maritime Museum, Greenwich, London
New Forest Maritime Museum, Buckler's Hard-Beaulieu, Hampshire
Royal Scottish Museum, Edinburgh
Science Museum, London
Sunderland Museum, Sunderland, Durham
The Victory Museum, Portsmouth, Hants

Valhalla Maritime Museum, Scilly Isles, Cornwall
Whitby Museum, Whitby

10. HOLLAND

Maritiem Museum Prins Hendrik, Rotterdam
Nederlandsch Historisch Scheepvaart Museum, Amsterdam
Rijksmuseum, Amsterdam

11. ICELAND

National Museum, Reykjavik

12. ISRAEL

The National Maritime Museum, Haifa

13. ITALY

Museo Civico Navale, Genoa
Museo delle Scienze, Milan
Museo del Mare, Trieste
Museo Navale, La Spezia
Museo Storico Navale, Venice

14. JAPAN

Transportation Museum, Tokyo

15. MONACO

Oceanographic Museum, Monte Carlo

16. NORWAY

Bergens Sjofartmuseum, Bergen
Bygdoy Museum, Oslo
Hanseatic Museum, Bergen
Norsk Sjofartmuseum, Oslo
Norwegian National Maritime and Folk Museum, Oslo

17. PORTUGAL

Museu de Marinha, Lisbon

18. SPAIN

Museo Maritimo, Barcelona
Museo Naval, Madrid

19. SWEDEN

Marinmuseum, Karlskrona
Sjofartmuseum, Göteborg
Statens Sjohistoriska Wasa Museet, Stockholm

20. UNITED STATES

Cabrillo Beach Marine Museum, San Pedro, California
Chesapeake Bay Maritime Museum, Navy Point, Maryland
Cohasset Maritime Museum, Cohasset Village, Massachusetts
Marine Museum, Bath, Maine
Marine Historical Association, Mystic Seaport, Connecticut
Maritime Museum, Philadelphia, Pennsylvania
Museum of the City of New York, New York, New York
Museum of Science and Museum of Fine Arts, Boston, Massachusetts
Old Dartmouth Historical Society and Jonathan Bourne Whaling Museum, New Bedford, Massachusetts

Penobscot Marine Museum, Searsport, Maine
Portsmouth Naval Shipyard Museum, Portsmouth, Virginia
South Street Seaport Museum, New York, New York
Suffolk County Whaling Museum, Sag Harbor, Long Island, New York
The Mariners Museum, Newport News, Virginia
The Marine Museum, San Francisco, California
The Peabody Museum, Salem, Massachusetts
The Whaling Museum, Cold Spring Harbor, Long Island, New York
The Whaling Museum—Nantucket Historical Association, Nantucket, Massachusetts
Truxtun Decatur Naval Museum, Smithsonian Institution, Washington, D.C.
U.S. Naval Academy Museum, Annapolis, Maryland
U.S. Navy Memorial Museum, Washington, D.C.

21. USSR

National Naval Museum, Admiralty Palace, Leningrad

22. YUGOSLAVIA

Maritime Museum of the Academy of Arts and Sciences, Dubrovnik

1. BELGIUM

National Scheepvaart Museum, Antwerp
Contains a good collection of ship models, including the ships of the East Indies route, a late-18th-century Dutch frigate and the two-decker *Caesar* of 1806. There are also (one-quarter actual size) Napoleon's gala boat of 1810, an early-19th-century galleass, the Belgian war brick *Duc de Brabant*, and many examples of 19th- and 20th-century sailing ships and steamships. The museum also has models of regional boats, such as the *Pavilioenpoon*, the *Garnalknots*, the *Schokker*, the *Steenschuit*, and various pilot boats. There is a fine collection of oil and watercolor seascapes and lithographs, an important library, and a catalog in several languages.

2. CANADA

The Maritime Museum, Vancouver
The history of navigation and shipbuilding in Canada is shown in a series of models, building plans, and other documents referring to sailing ships and steamships. The museum also publishes some technical publications.

The New Brunswick Museum—Marine Gallery, Saint John, New Brunswick
The models, pictures, and naval relics preserved in this museum concern navigation in the Maritime Provinces and the Bay of Fundy, with a great deal of documentation on regional fishing boats. Among others, exceptional models of the clipper *Star of the East*, the three-master *Berteaux*, and the *Josephine Troop*.

3. DENMARK

Handels og Sofartsmuseet paa Kronborg, Helsingor
This museum is in Kronborg Castle and has important documents of Denmark's maritime activity, past and present. Along with an excellent collection of contemporary models, there are interesting collections of nautical instruments and maps, as well as a section dedicated to lifesaving at sea, shipbuilding, and coastal navigation. The museum has a well-stocked library and publishes a yearbook and many works on maritime history.

National Maritime Museum Roskilde
This town is perhaps better known for its cathedral, which contains the tombs of the Danish kings; but its museum preserves the remains of five Viking ships used between 1000 and 1500 to defend a channel of Roskilde Fjord against pirate raids. They were recovered in 1962, including a *kanrr*, a deep-sea cargo ship, as well as two "long ships" from the Viking era.

4. FRANCE

Musee de la Marine, Paris
This museum, originally part of the Louvre and now in the Palais de Chaillot, contains everything that refers to the great French maritime tradition, mercantile and military. Among the most interesting pieces are reconstructions of Columbus's *Santa Maria* and of the 120-cannon, three-decker *Ocean*. Other models show the *Soleil Royal* of 1690, the *Royale*, and the *Louis XV*. The museum also contains the stern of the *Réale* of 1700, decorated with many wooden statues attributed to Pierre Puget of Toulon. The collection of paintings by Claude Joseph Vernet (1714–1789), illustrating the ports of France, is extremely good. There are models of frigates and xebecs, and particularly interesting ones of the 1782 "steamboat" of Jouffroy d'Abbans, of the frigate *Le Murion*, on which Napoleon returned to France from Egypt, and of the famous *Belle Poule*, which carried the emperor's body back from Saint Helena. Fishing-, cargo-, and pleasure-boats are also represented. The museum publishes a monthly magazine, *Neptunia*, and sells a catalog and many maritime publications.

5. GERMANY

Altonaer Museum, Hamburg
Two important sections of this museum document the development of the fishing industry in the North Sea, the construction of wooden sailing ships, and the evolution of the merchant marine in the lower Elbe. In addition to a considerable number of ship models, there are nautical instruments, construction tools, and sailmaking implements. The archives have a rich collection of photographic material and building plans, with an impressive library of maritime works, both literary and technical. A separate collection consists of about 40 drawings of galleons and old sailing ships. The museum publishes a yearbook and sells separate catalogs for each section.

Museum fur Hamburgische Geschichte, Hamburg
A large part of this museum is dedicated to the history of local navigation. It contains about 80 ship

models, a fourth of which are of 18th- and 19th-century ships, plus a number of steamships. The collection also includes paintings and photographs.

Deutsches Museum, Munich
Several naval collections, including a section dedicated to the U-boat, from its appearance during World War I to the present.

6. GREAT BRITAIN

Royal Scottish Museum, Edinburgh
The technological section contains a fine collection of model warships and cargo ships, from Roman times to the present. There are fine reconstructions of one of the oldest Scottish warships, the *Yellow Carvel* (1480), and the *Great Michel* (1511). Almost all the models shown are fully rigged. Among the more recent are those of the *D'Bataviase Eeuw*, a Dutch East India ship of 1719, a 230-cannon ship of the line of 1794, and a three-masted armed sloop of 1830. There are small models of fishing boats and coastal boats.

Art Gallery and Museum, Glasgow
The collection of maritime models goes from the prehistoric dugout to the great transatlantic liners, cargo ships, and warships of our own time. A particularly interesting group is made up of 18th- and 19th-century sailing ships. One of most valuable models is that of the H.M.S. *Oxford* of 1727, built to the authentic plans of the British Admiralty. Steam models go from the paddle ship *Comet* (1815) to the *Empress of Britain*, while model warships cover the period from 1866 to 1942. There are also models of steamboats built for cruises on the Firth of Clyde.

National Maritime Museum, Greenwich, London
One of the world's richest and most interesting maritime museums. It has a fine collection of maritime treasures, with all kinds of paintings and antiques on the subject. There is a series of model ships made from plans used by English 17th- and 18th-century shipyards and those of the Admiralty. There are also small models of the royal yachts of the 17th and 18th century, Victorian steamboats, and English and foreign merchant ships, from the three-masters of the 1700s to the clippers of the 19th century. There is also an important collection of smaller vessels, *hoys, cotres,* transport vessels for marine troops, and lightships of the 18th and 19th centuries. The museum also contains the complete collection of the Admiralty's plans and drawings of ships built in England from the beginning of the 18th century to 1837, about 4,000 complete plans, together with the building plans of 19th-century merchant ships and coastal vessels, down to the end of sailing-ship navigation. Noteworthy too is the collection of figureheads displayed on board the *Cutty Sark,* the clipper berthed in the Greenwich basin. The museum library contains more than 10,000 manuscripts, a fine collection of books on navigation, and a complete archive of historical photographs of ships.

Science Museum, London
The naval section of the Science Museum contains an important collection of contemporary models of combat vessels of the 17th, 18th, and 19th centuries, and a special collection showing steam- and engine-powered vessels. There are also miniature ships. The museum published *Sailing Ships* (parts I and II), *British Fishery Boats and Coastal Craft,* and *Merchant Steamers and Motor-Ships.*

Sunderland Museum, Sunderland
It contains a collection of model ships built in Sunderland shipyards, including sailing ships, steamships, battleships, lifesaving launches, pilot lifeboats, etc. There is also a remarkable prehistoric canoe found in the Wear River and a collection of plans and photographs of ships built in the region.

Whitby Museum, Whitby
This collection includes about 120 models, most of them from English shipyards and showing vessels in construction. Among them are some interesting working models, including the steamships *Whitehall, Beemah, Normandy, Liverpool,* and *Bagdale,* along with models of the *Golden Hind,* H.M.S. *Endeavour,* and *Resolution,* the clipper *Cutty Sark,* and the emigrant transport ship *Columbus* of 1832. There is also a fine collection of models made of bone, including ships of the line with 50, 64, 74, and 100 cannons, and a group of models of lifeboats, coal boats, and Newfoundland schooners.

Pickering Maritime Museum, Hull
A rich collection of nautical material for whale hunting in the Arctic, including carved whale and shark bones.

New Forest Maritime Museum, Buckler's Hard-Beaulieu, Hampshire
This museum contains relics mainly from the region's shipyards, collected in the Master Builder's House: plans and drawings of most of the English warships, among them the *Agamemnon,* commanded by Nelson before he was made an admiral. This is a small but attractive museum that evokes the atmosphere of the old-time shipping industry.

Museum of Science and Engineering, Newcastle-upon-Tyne
The city of Newcastle is still famous for its shipyards, and its museum reflects this tradition. Among the models shown, one of the most interesting is the original model for the *Turbinia,* the small boat that was equipped with Charles Pearson's turbine engine in 1897, and totally changed the concept of maritime propulsion with the reciprocating engine. The visitor will also be interested in the building plans of the *Mauretania,* built on the river Tyne and holder for 22 years (1907–1929) of the Atlantic Blue Ribbon for the fastest crossing.

British Floating Museums
Aside from the *Cutty Sark,* anchored at Greenwich, one can also visit the propeller-driven steamship *Great Britain,* built by Isambard Kingdom Brunel, launched in 1843, and berthed in the port of Bristol; one can also view the most important relic of all, Nelson's *Victory,* launched at Chatham and now in drydock at Portsmouth. Its mast still flies Nelson's flag, while the history of one of the 18th century's most famous ships of the line is illustrated in the nearby shipyard, where the Battle of Trafalgar is depicted in a panoramic display from the poop deck of one of the ships that took part in the battle.

7. HOLLAND

Nederlandsch Historisch Scheepvaart Museum, Amsterdam
This museum has about 300 models of warships, merchant vessels, and smaller craft. Almost all are Dutch ships of the 17th, 18th, and 19th centuries, and 200 of them are outfitted with sails. There are also about 90 plans of 18th- and 19th-century ships, a large library, and a fine collection of building plans and historical photographs, well illustrated in the museum catalog.

Maritiem Museum Prins Hendrik, Rotterdam
An important collection of sailing-ship models from the 17th to the 19th century, with special attention to the exotic craft of the Far East. In the archives, there are about 2,000 building plans, along with paintings, drawings, prints, nautical charts, navigation instruments, spheres, and the like.

Rijksmuseum, Amsterdam
The great national museum of Holland, which had an overseas empire that survived well into the 20th century. This museum contains some of the world's best sea paintings. Among the rare items are the shield that decorated the stern of the *Royal Charles,* the enormous ship of the line, pride of the British navy, captured in the Thames in 1666 and towed to Holland.

8. ITALY

Museo Civico Navale, Genoa
This museum is housed in the 16th-century Villa Doria and has a fine collection documenting the naval history of Genoa, with its commercial traffic and its wartime exploits.

Museo Storico Navale, Venice
Along with the Arsenal dating from the Middle Ages, the Naval Museum of Venice (housed in an old grain warehouse on the Riva degli Schiavoni) provides documentation of the great ships of the Republic, as well as the construction details of the gondola and the Bucentaur.

9. NORWAY

Bygdoy Museum, Oslo
This important museum, one of the finest in the world, contains two of the world's most important vessels: Nansen's *Fram,* in which that great explorer and navigator voyaged in the seas of the North Pole from 1893 to 1896; and *Kon Tiki,* the balsa raft on which Thor Heyerdahl crossed the Pacific from South America to Polynesia in 1947.

Norwegian National Maritime and Folk Museum, Oslo
In it are preserved three Viking ships (probably burial vessels): the Tune ship, discovered in 1867 near Friedrikstad and unfinished; the Gokstad ship, the largest of those found (1880), 21 meters and 35 centimeters (69 feet and 13.8 inches) long, it too used at a funeral but apparently seaworthy; and the Oseberg ship, found in 1903 near Tonsberg, 21.5 meters (70.6 feet) long and about 5 meters (16.5 feet) wide. These three ships, dated to about the 9th century A.D., are among maritime archaeology's most important finds.

Hanseatic Museum, Bergen
Offers a broad summary of the birth and growth of the Hanseatic League.

Bergens Sjofartmuseum, Bergen
Models of lifeboats, merchant ships, and fishing vessels, along with a fine painting collection, objects used in navigation, and plans and drawings of Norwegian boats and small craft. The museum publishes a yearbook and has a catalog.

Norsk Sjofartmuseum, Oslo
The museum contains models of boats with oars, sails, and engines, as well as cutters from all the Norwegian maritime regions. There are drawings of galleons, rigging details, construction plans, and historical photographs, along with sections dedicated to polar expeditions, whale hunting, lighthouses, lifesaving at sea, and so forth. The museum publishes a yearbook and sells a catalog printed in several languages.

10. PORTUGAL

Museu de Marinha, Lisbon
A fine collection of maritime objects, housed in Jeronimos monastery on the banks of the Tagus. The museum includes a large planetarium and a large collection of Portuguese ships, building plans, and models. There is a fine royal launch, built in 1785, in excellent condition and still seaworthy. It is flanked by the tiny sloop *Santa Cruz*, in which Gago Coutinho and Sacadura Cabral made their Atlantic crossing in 1922.

11. SPAIN

Museo Naval, Madrid
This collection is housed in the Spanish Admiralty Building and includes model ships, paintings, and portraits of famous commanders. The banner of the Captain General of the Galleys, from the 17th century, covers an entire wall in one of the large rooms of the museum.

Museo Maritimo, Barcelona
The objects in this collection are displayed in the rooms that held the national "Naval and Artillery Works" in the Middle Ages. It is devoted chiefly to the products of Spanish shipyards. Among the shipyard models is one that may have been a royal vessel, a ship of the line with 74 cannons, built in Cartagena in the 18th century.

12. SWEDEN

Sjofartmuseum, Goteborg
The large amount of material gathered in this collection illustrates the evolution of Swedish maritime life, from the beginnings to our own time; and fishing, lighthouses, port organization, and oceanography are all represented in it. This museum publishes a yearbook and occasional volumes. There is a complete catalog.

Statens Sjohistoriska Wasa Museet, Stockholm
There are ship models, paintings, drawings, and plans of large merchant ships, forming an interesting and homogeneous collection described in a thorough catalog and illustrated in the museum yearbook and in numerous specialized publications. In a specially built enclosure, one can visit the *Vasa*, the large warship built in 1628 by Henrik Hybertson, which sank during its maiden voyage.

Marinamuseum, Karlskrona
Karlskrona, Charles XI's naval base in 1679, preserves the building plans and charts of Frederick Chapman (1721–1808), the great naval architect of English origin who reorganized the Swedish navy and was the author of the *Architecture Navalis Mercatoria*, an important treatise on the construction of sailing ships. The collection also includes some fine models collected by King Adolph Frederick in 1752, as well as a fine collection of carved figureheads assembled between 1781 and 1828.

13. UNITED STATES

Marine Historical Association, Mystic Seaport, Connecticut
A collection of American sailing vessels, steamships, and seal-fishing boats, along with typical local vessels. The museum also has work by the French painter Roux.

Old Dartmouth Historical Society and Jonathan Bourne Whaling Museum, New Bedford, Massachusetts
A superb collection of material dealing with New England whaling. There are models of whaling boats, fishing instruments, sounding logs, whalebone sculptures, and other objects collected or made by the fishermen themselves. Among the models are an English cutter and a schooner-clipper. A large room holds a model on a scale of 1 to 50 of the whaler *Laconda*. The museum publishes some technical works.

The Mariners Museum, Newport News, Virginia
This museum has gathered important and varied maritime material from all over the world. Its archives include one of the most important photographic collections on the subject, and there are displays of paintings, prints, small models, and fine Indian canoes. The museum publishes some technical works and a catalog.

The Peabody Museum, Salem, Massachusetts
This collection is mainly concerned with the sailing ships of Salem and of New England in general. There are models of cutters and merchant ships, along with instruments for whaling, nautical instruments and maps, building plans and works by Roux, the French painter of marine subjects. The museum puts out occasional publications and issues *The American Neptune*, a quarterly of maritime history.

The Maritime Museum, San Francisco, California
This museum's collection is mostly concerned with the tradition and history of modern navigation, especially that of the Pacific Ocean. It has models of large square-rigged ships, completely and perfectly outfitted with sails. Among these is the five-masted *Preussen*, built in Hamburg. There are paintings, navigation instruments, prints and building plans, an excellent library, and a large collection of photographs. The completely restored iron vessel, the three-masted *Balklutha*, is anchored in San Francisco Bay near the museum. The museum publishes the magazine *Sea Letters*.

Penobscot Marine Museum, Searsport, Maine
It contains a small but superb collection of marine views by the painter Roux and others, and also has models and plans of craft used on the coast of Maine.

Truxtun Decatur Naval Museum, Smithsonian Institution, Washington, D.C.
The naval section has a large collection of American ship models, including small boats, fishing schooners, pilot boats, and clippers. There is also a fine collection of plans and layouts of merchant ships. A very complete catalog, *The National Watercraft Collection*, gives a detailed picture of this museum's collection, which include the first Viking ships to reach the Atlantic coast of the United States and a reconstruction of Columbus's *Santa Maria*.

United States Naval Academy Museum, Annapolis, Maryland
This museum has more than 20,000 objects concerning the history of the U.S. Navy, including the Rogers collection of admiralty models. It also contains the table of the cruiser *Missouri* on which Japan's surrender was signed at the end of World War II, and a good collection of figureheads. John Paul Jones, the naval hero of the American Revolution, is buried in the crypt of the Academy chapel.

United States Navy Memorial Museum, Washington, D.C.
Once the breechblock warehouse in the Navy Yard, this museum houses a large collection of nautical models and objects illustrating the story of the American navy from its foundation to the present time. One diorama depicts John Paul Jones's battle with the English frigate *Serapis*. Also on display is the submarine *Turtle*, used during the Civil War.

American Floating Museums
At Mystic Seaport in Connecticut, in a setting still reminiscent of early American fishing days, the whaler *Charles W. Morgan* is on view with 7 other ships. The port of Plymouth has the reconstruction of the *Mayflower* that Capt. Alan Villiers and 33 volunteers used to repeat the journey made by the Pilgrim Fathers in the 17th century.

Jamestown, Virginia, has three totally reconstructed sailing ships, the *Susan Constant*, the *Godspeed*, and the *Discovery*, which carried the first permanent settlers to the United States in 1607. Boston has the famous frigate *Constitution*, built in 1794. Other famous vessels of the past are anchored at Baltimore: the *Constellation*, from the same period as *Old Ironsides* (as the *Constitution* was called), and the brigantine *Niagara*, commanded by Oliver Hazard Perry on Lake Erie on September 10, 1813. America also preserves modern vessels, including the 45,000-ton battleship *Massachusetts*, anchored at State Pier in Norfolk, Virginia; the *North Carolina*, another important World War II ship, now at Wilmington; the battleship *Texas*, launched in 1914 and anchored in the Houston Ship Canal; and all that remains of the hull of the battleship *Arizona*, which was sunk at Pearl Harbor on December 7, 1941.

14. USSR

National Naval Museum, Admiralty Palace, Leningrad
The Soviet Naval Museum is located in this building, with its 230-foot tower ending in a point and banderole shaped like a ship. The museum contains the collection of Peter the Great, a great lover of things naval. Includes a fine sailing ship used by the tsar and the complete hull of a 19th-century experimental submarine. The cruiser *Aurora*, which bombed the tsar's palace during the Bolshevik Revolution, is anchored on the Neva River and is visited by thousands of persons each year.

THE LAST LARGE SAILING SHIPS AFLOAT

Nationality	Name	Type	Displacement or Tonnage	Year and Place Launched	Last Sailed	Function
ARGENTINA	Libertad Presidente Sarmiento	full-rigged ship full-rigged ship	3,765 tons 2,860 tons	1956 Rio Santiago 1897 Birkenhead	still sailing 1961	training ship museum ship
BELGIUM	Mercator	schooner	770 tons	1932 Leith	1963	training ship
BRAZIL	Albatros Almirante Saldanka Custodio de Mello	3-masted schooner 4-masted topsail schooner schooner	100 tons 3,189 tons —	1920 USA 1933 Barrow — USA	still sailing 1964 —	training ship unrigged m.v. used for oceanographic research training ship
BULGARIA	Assen Burgas Kamcia	schooner schooner schooner	240 tons 240 tons 240 tons	1912 — — — — —	still sailing still sailing still sailing	training ship training ship training ship
CANADA	Bluenose II Harelda St. Lawrence II	2-masted gaff schooner 3-masted schooner brigantine	285 tons 30 tons 34 tons	1963 Canada — — 1953 Canada	still sailing still sailing still sailing	training ship training ship training ship
CHILE	Esmeralda General Baquedano	4-masted schooner 3-master	3,500 tons 2,500 tons	1952 Cadiz 1898 England	still sailing 1951	training ship training ship
COLOMBIA	La Atrevida	ketch	—	— —	still sailing	training ship
DENMARK	Arken Danmark Georg Stage Jylland Lilla Dan	2-masted topsail schooner full-rigged ship full-rigged ship 3-master full-rigged steam frigate	120 tons 790 tons 298 tons 2,450 tons 95 tons	1908 Brittany 1932 Denmark 1935 Frederikshavn 1862 Copenhagen 1950 Svendborg	1939 still sailing — 1892 still sailing	stationary school ship training ship training ship floating museum training ship
DOMINICAN REPUBLIC	Duarte Patria	schooner 4-master	170 tons 3,077 tons	1943 — 1931 Kiel	still sailing still sailing	training ship training ship
FINLAND	Pommern Suomen Joutsen	4-masted bark full-rigged ship	2,376 tons 2,266 tons	1903 Glasgow 1902 St. Nazaire	1939 1955	museum ship stationary school ship
FRANCE	Duchesse Anna La Belle Poule Le Dauphin Le Mutin L'Etoile La Zélée	full-rigged ship 2-masted topsail schooner ketch schooner 2-masted topsail schooner —	1,260 tons 227 tons — 227 tons	Geestemünde 1932 Fécamp 1954 — — — 1932 Fécamp — —	1939 still sailing — — still sailing still sailing	naval barracks training ship training ship training ship training ship
GERMAN DEMOCRATIC REPUBLIC	Wilhelm Piek	brigantine	290 tons	1950 Warnemunde	still sailing	training ship
GERMAN FEDERAL REPUBLIC	Gorch Fock II Norwind Passat Schulschiff Deutschland Seute Deern Seute Deern II	3-masted bark ketch 4-masted bark full-rigged ship 3-masted bark ketch	1,760 tons 112 tons 3,182 tons 1,257 tons 767 tons 425 tons	1958 Hamburg 1944 Bremen 1911 Hamburg 1927 Bremerhaven 1919 Gulfport 1939 Svendborg	still sailing still sailing 1957 1944 1944 still sailing	training ship training ship museum & stationary ship stationary school ship museum ship & restaurant training ship
GREAT BRITAIN	Arethusa Cutty Sark Prince Louis II Victory Sir Winston Churchill Worcester	4-masted bark full-rigged clipper 3-masted schooner 3-masted 1st-rate ship of the line 3-masted topsail schooner 1st-rate ship of the line	3,100 tons 963 tons 160 tons 281 tons 5,480 tons	1911 Hamburg 1869 Dumbarton 1944 Svendborg 1765 Chatham 1966 Hessle 1904 Barrow	1932 1922 still sailing 1813 still sailing still sailing	stationary school ship floating museum training ship museum training ship built as stationary school ship
GREECE	Eugene Eugenides	3-masted topsail schooner	636 tons	1929 Dumbarton	still sailing	training ship
HOLLAND	Albatros Pollux Urania	schooner 3-masted bark ketch	93 tons 747 tons 38 tons	1920 Holland 1940 Amsterdam 1928 Haarlem	still sailing — — still sailing	training ship built as stationary school ship training ship
INDONESIA	Dawarutji	barkentine	886 tons	1953 Hamburg	still sailing	training ship

THE LAST LARGE SAILING SHIPS AFLOAT

Nationality	Name	Type	Displacement or Tonnage	Year and Place Launched	Last Sailed	Function
ITALY	Amerigo Vespucci	full-rigged frigate	3,550 tons	1931 Castellammare	still sailing	training ship
	Ebe	ketch	100 tons	1924 —	still sailing	training ship
	Giorgio Cini	barkentine	562 tons	1896 Nantes	still sailing	training ship
	Palinuro	barkentine	858 tons	1934 Nantes	still sailing	training ship
	San Giorgio	3-masted schooner	90 tons	— —	—	—
JAPAN	Kaiwo Maru	4-masted bark	2,286 tons	1930 Kobe	still sailing	training ship
	Meji Maru	full-rigged ship	1,038 tons	1874 Glasgow	1897	museum ship
	Nippon Maru	4-masted bark	2,286 tons	1930 Kobe	still sailing	training ship
	Unyo Maru	3-masted bark	448 tons	1909 Japan	c1930	museum ship
NORWAY	Christina Radich	full-rigged ship	696 tons	1937 Sandefjord	still sailing	training ship
	Sorlandet	full-rigged ship	568 tons	1927 Kristiansand	still sailing	training ship
	Statsraad Lehmkuhl	3-masted bark	1,701 tons	1914 Bremerhaven	still sailing	school ship
PANAMA	Wandia	3-masted schooner	—	—	1966	laid up
POLAND	Dar Pomorza	full-rigged ship	1,561 tons	1909 Hamburg	still sailing	training ship
	Henryk Rutkowski	ketch	70 tons	1944 Germany	still sailing	training ship
	Iskra	3-masted gaff schooner	500 tons	1917 Holland	still sailing	training ship
	Janek Krasicki	2-masted gaff schooner	70 tons	1945 Newg Warpno	still sailing	training ship
	Lwow	full-rigged ship	1,200 tons	1869 Birkenhead	1929	training ship
	Marius Zaruski	ketch	71 tons	1939 —	still sailing	training ship
	Zawisza Czarny II	3-masted staysail schooner	164 tons	1952 Gdansk	still sailing	training ship
	Mloda Gwardia	3-masted schooner	120 tons	1939 —	still sailing	training ship
	Zwe Morza	2-masted gaff schooner	70 tons	1945 Dziwnów	still sailing	training ship
PORTUGAL	F. de Gloria	full-rigged ship	1,600 tons	1857 India	—	training ship
	Sagres II	3-masted bark	1,869 tons	1937 Hamburg	still sailing	training ship
	Santo Andre	3-masted bark	3,067 tons	1896 Bremerhaven	1962	depot ship
RUMANIA	Mircea	3-masted bark	1,760 tons	1938 Hamburg	still sailing	training ship
SPAIN	Baleares	brigantine	607 tons	1919 Majorca	—	training ship
	Cruz del Sur	3-masted schooner	220 tons	1945 Spain	still sailing	training ship
	Estrella Polar	schooner	144 tons	1939 Denmark	still sailing	training ship
	Galatea	3-masted bark	2,800 tons	1896 Glasgow	still sailing	training ship
	Juan Sebastian d'Elcano	4-masted topsail schooner	3,750 tons	1927 Cadiz	still sailing	training ship
SWEDEN	Af Chapman	full-rigged ship	1,425 tons	1888 Whitehaven	1937	youth hostel
	Albatros	4-masted motor schooner	1,049 tons	1942 Sweden	still sailing	training ship
	Elida	ketch	80 tons	— Sweden	still sailing	—
	Falken	2-masted gaff schooner	220 tons	1946 Sweden	still sailing	training ship
	Gerda	brick	234 tons	1869 Gävle	1931	floating museum
	Gladan	2-masted gaff schooner	220 tons	1947 Sweden	still sailing	training ship
	Jarramas	full-rigged ship	350 tons	1900 Karlskrona	1946	museum ship
	Lys	ketch	—	— Sweden	still sailing	training ship
	Naiaden	3-master	350 tons	1897 Karlskrona	1939	floating museum
	Viking	4-master	2,952 tons	1906 Copenhagen	1947	training ship
UNITED ARAB REPUBLIC	El Faroukieh	3-masted bark	930 tons	1874 Glasgow	1929	stationary school ship
UNITED STATES	Balclutha	full-rigged ship	1,689 tons	1886 Glasgow	1933	floating museum
	Black Pearl	barkentine	27 tons	1951 Wickford	still sailing	training ship
	Brilliant	schooner	30 tons	1932 USA	still sailing	training ship
	Charles W. Morgan	full-rigged ship	313 tons	1841 New Bedford	1921	floating museum
	Eagle	3-masted bark	1,809 tons	1936 Hamburg	still sailing	training ship
	Emery Rice	3-master	1,261 tons	1876 USA	1944	floating museum
	Falls of Clyde	full-rigged ship	1,741 tons	1878 Glasgow	1922	floating museum
	Freedom	3-masted schooner	100 tons	1931 USA	still sailing	training ship
	Joseph Conrad	full-rigged ship	203 tons	1882 Copenhagen	1945	floating museum
	L. A. Dunton	3-masted schooner	—	— —	—	floating museum
	Mariner	yawl	30 tons	1950 USA	still sailing	training ship
	Royono	yawl	30 tons	1936 USA	still sailing	training ship
URUGUAY	Aspirante	3-masted schooner	250 tons	1919 —	—	training ship
USSR	Krusenstern	4-masted bark	3,545 tons	1926 Wesermünde	still sailing	training ship
	Sedov	4-masted bark	3,476 tons	1921 Kiel	still sailing	training ship
	Johnsen	3-master	1,510 tons	1933 Hamburg	still sailing	training ship
	Tovarich	3-masted bark	1,392 tons	1933 Hamburg	still sailing	training ship
	Alpha	barkentine	322 tons	1948 Finland	still sailing	training ship
	Kapella	barkentine	322 tons	1948 Finland	still sailing	training ship
	Junga	brigantine	300 tons	1948 Finland	still sailing	training ship
	Kodor	3-masted schooner	339 tons	1951 Holland	still sailing	training ship
	Sekstan	barkentine	322 tons	1948 Finland	still sailing	training ship
	Tropic	barkentine	322 tons	1948 Finland	still sailing	training ship
	Vega	brigantine	300 tons	1948 Finland	still sailing	training ship
	Zenith	brigantine*	300 tons	1948 Finland	still sailing	training ship
	Praktika	schooner	300 tons	1948 Finland	still sailing	training ship
	Utscheba	schooner	300 tons	1948 Finland	still sailing	training ship
	Zaritza	schooner†	300 tons	1948 Finland	still sailing	training ship
	Ex-Cristoforo Colombo	3-master	2,787 tons	1928 Castellammare	still sailing	training ship
YUGOSLAVIA	Jadran	3-masted topsail schooner	700 tons	1931 Kiel	still sailing	training ship
	Villa Velebita	brigantine	257 tons	1908 Kiel	—	training ship

*Two other ships with the same characteristics are still sailing but their names are not known.

TRAINING SHIPS

In the age of the sailing ship, seamen learned their trade on board. But technological evolution, from the use of steam down to our own time, has brought about a radical change in professional training, which now takes place first in schools on land and only later on board training ships. Sailing experience is still considered an essential part of training.

Almost all of the world's great navies have sailing ships for training. Great Britain, despite her long sailing tradition, is the only exception. The Russian navy, which never built a sailing ship for training, possesses some of the finest training ships in the world. They were part of World War II reparations and include the *Tovarich* (the former *Gorch Fock*), the Italian *Colombo*, the four-masted *Kruzestern*, and the *Sedov*.

Libertad—*Argentina. A full-rigged ship of 3,765 tons launched in 1956. Length: 94.2 meters (338 feet); speed under power: 13.5 knots. She carries one 76-mm and four 40-mm antiaircraft guns.*

Dar Pomorza—*Poland. Full-rigged ship of 1,561 tons, launched in 1909. Length: 74 meters (298.5 feet). Equipped with an auxiliary engine.*

Amerigo Vespucci—*Italy. Launched in 1931. Iron-hulled full-rigged frigate of 3,550 tons. Length: 83 meters (331.5 feet); sail area: 2,100 m² (22,600 square feet); speed under power: 10.5 knots.*

Gorch Fock II—*West Germany. Three-masted bark of 1,760 tons, launched in 1958. Length: 81.3 meters (293 feet); sail area: 1,964 m² (21,011 square feet); speed under power: 10 knots.*

Sagres II—*Portugal. Ex-German sail training ship Horst Wessel of 1,869 tons, launched in 1937.*

Juan Sebastian d'Elcano—*Spain. Launched in 1927. A 4-masted topsail schooner of 3,750 tons. Length: 94.1 meters (350.5 feet); speed under power: approximately 9 knots.*

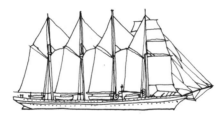

Esmeralda—*Chile. Four-masted schooner of 3,500 tons, launched in 1952. Length: 94 meters (371 feet); speed under power: 12 knots.*

Almirante Saldanha—*Brazil. Four-masted topsail schooner of 3,189 tons, launched in 1933. Length: 94 meters (351.16 feet); speed under power: 11 knots. She carried four 102-mm (4.5 in.) guns.*

Oka—*USSR. Ex-Imperial Yacht, launched in 1896 and refitted in 1937. Of 5,980 tons. Length: 124 meters (406.7 feet). Converted to a training ship (minelayer).*

Alvsnabben—*Sweden. Launched in 1943. Displacement: 4,250 tons; length: 102 meters (334.5 feet); armament: two 152-mm (6-in.) guns and secondary armament; speed: 14 knots.*

Deutschland—*West Germany. A gunnery training ship of 4,880 tons, launched in 1960. Length: 138 meters (452.75 feet); armament: four 100-mm (3.9 in.) guns and four torpedo-tubes; speed: 22 knots.*

YACHTING

The term "yacht" comes from the Dutch *jacht*, "pursuit ship," derived from *jaght*, "a hunt." Originally the Dutch *jachtschip* was used to hunt down pirates. Yachting as a sporting activity may have begun when the city of Amsterdam bought the *Mary*, a typical Dutch yacht of about 100 tons, from the East India Company as a gift for King Charles II of England. The *Mary* was followed a year later (in 1661) by a smaller vessel—the *Bezan*, a fore-and-aft yacht. When Charles II was restored to the throne, he lost no time in satisfying his passion for the sea and set his shipwrights to work. When he tired of a yacht, he handed it over to the Royal Navy as a coast-guard vessel. One of his yachts, the *Jamie*, a 25-ton boat, won history's first regatta. In 1662 it raced a Dutch-built yacht belonging to the king's brother James, duke of York.

Other yachting fans were Peter the Great of Russia and Louis XIV of France. Aristocrats and wealthy men set up the first "yacht clubs," including the Cumberland Fleet, founded by the Duke of Cumberland in 1775. The first nautical club was the Water Club, inaugurated in Cork in 1720. But the nautical group that served as the model for world yacht clubs was the Royal Yacht Squadron—later to become the Royal Yacht Club—founded in 1812 at Cowes on the Isle of Wight.

Pleasure-yacht construction was modified after the United States schooner *America* won the regatta around the Isle of Wight in 1851. The American schooner's hull became the model for new and faster vessels, and its rig was epoch-making. Although yachting was still a rich man's sport, it became popular in the United States, in the Mediterranean, in the Baltic, and in Australia and New Zealand.

Britannia—*The British royal yacht that was built for the future King Edward VII in 1890.*

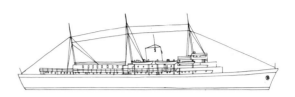

Britannia—*Built in 1954, the official yacht of the British royal family.*

With the arrival of steam, yachts were equipped with auxiliary engines. Cutters also became popular sporting vessels. The most important cutter was the *Britannia*, designed by G. L. Watson in 1890 for the future King Edward VII of England. The *Britannia* was handed on to George V and took part in 624 regattas, winning 360 prizes. The royal cutter was sunk off Cowes when he died in 1936. The end of the *Britannia* marked the end of the cutter as a regatta boat. The new sailing vessels—the sloop, the ketch, and the yawl—found increasing favor with yachtsmen. Motorboating also became popular in the United States, France, and Italy.

Yachting took on its present form with the creation of different classes of racing vessels. Modern sailboats have highly advanced features and complex rigging. The most elaborate sporting boats are the 40-foot International Tonnage boats that race for the America's Cup today.

Sailing as a sport is becoming more and more popular, as is motorboating. New materials, such as fiberglass for hulls and synthetic fibers for sails, have been introduced, and the double hulls of catamarans and trimarans have also become popular. There are many international deep-sea regattas, and some of them have taken on an importance and interest that was inconceivable a few decades ago.

Special mention must be made of the one-man sailing races. They demand great courage and meticulous technical preparation. The forerunner of solitary navigation was J. M. Crenston. In 1849 he sailed from New Bedford, Massachusetts, to San Francisco in a 40-foot cutter called the *Tocca*. He was followed by Johnson; by B. Gilboy, and by the most famous single sailor of his time, Joshua Slocum. At the age of fifty-one Slocum was the first man to go around the world alone, on board the *Spray*, a vessel about 35 feet long. An old tin alarm clock was his only navigation instrument. The *London Observer* now sponsors a Single-handed Transatlantic Race. Single-handed navigation almost always uses modified mass-produced boats. The great tradition of the sailing ship is kept alive by sportsmen.

Shamrock IV—*It belonged to the famous English tea magnate Sir William Lipton, Britain's competitor in the 1920 America's Cup Race.*

America—*An American schooner built in 1851 for Commodore Stevens, founder of the New York Yacht Club, to race in the regatta called The One Hundred Guinea Cup organized by British yachtsmen around the Isle of Wight. The* America *won the race, and today the America's Cup is still run by the 40-foot International Tonnage boats; it is considered the world's most important yachting race.*

17th-century Dutch yacht—*The fast "yacht," a small, elegant, and easily handled vessel, with a small sail surface and lateral stabilizers that could be raised, was born in Holland; first used as a commercial boat for domestic navigation along the canals or near the coast, it then became a luxury craft.*

Romantica—*An American motor yacht, a small cruise ship in miniature, with all comforts and superb seagoing qualities.*

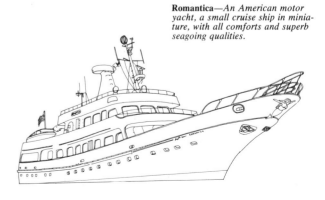

Twelve-meter international series— *The modern regatta yachts used in the America's Cup Race today. Overall length: 19.50 meters (64 feet); beam: 3.65 meters (12 feet); sail area: 172 square meters (206 square yards); displacement: 26.1 tons.*

Triton—*A monotypic cruise yacht with cabin.*

Folkboat—*A monotypic Swedish yacht for pleasure sailing.*

Ketch—*A type of cruise and regatta yacht, which takes its name from its sail plan and the arrangement of the rudder, set abaft the mizzenmast.*

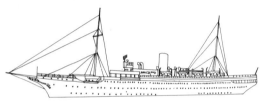

Victoria and Albert—*The British royal yacht, built in 1899. It is reminiscent of the last great sailing ships.*

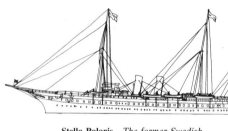

Stella Polaris—*The former Swedish royal yacht. It is now a passenger cruise ship in the northern seas.*

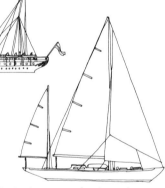

Yawl—*A regatta and cruise yacht like the ketch, with the wheelhouse set between the two masts.*

THE SINGLEHANDED NAVIGATORS

Spray—*Joshua Slocum was the first man to sail single-handed around the world. His boat, the Spray, was a yawl 37 feet long.*

Islander—*This pleasure craft, 10.50 meters (34.5 feet) long, was the first of its kind to go around the world twice, in 1921–1925 and 1932–1937, with American Harry Pidgeon as its solitary crewman. Route: Los Angeles–Torres–Cape of Good Hope–Panama–Los Angeles.*

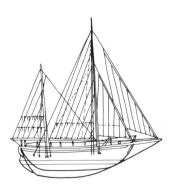

Lehg II—*With Argentine Vito Dumas aboard, this vessel made the first trip around the world via Cape Horn to be carried out by a pleasure craft with sails.*

Trekka—*John Guzzwell, one of the youngest of all single-handed navigators, sailed this small, 6.25-meter (20.6-feet) yawl in 1956–1959. Route: Victoria–San Francisco–Honolulu–Samoa–New Zealand–Sydney–Durban–Panama–Galápagos–Hawaii–Vancouver, with a 2-year stopover in New Zealand.*

THE SINGLEHANDED NAVIGATORS

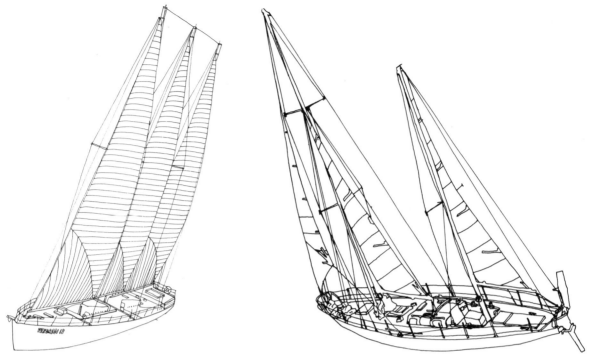

Vendredi 13—*One of the largest pleasure craft ever manned by a single person during a race. In the fourth OSTAR (Observer Single-handed Transatlantic Race), Jean Yves Terlain came in second in this unusual 3-masted schooner equipped with 3 boomed jibs for a total of 360 square meters (430 square yards). Built of fiberglass in 1972, it is 39.10 meters (128 feet) long and 5.80 meters (19 feet) wide. Draft: 3.50 meters (11.5 feet); mast length: 25 meters (82 feet).*

Gipsy Moth IV—*Sir Francis Chichester sailed this 56-foot ketch around the world in 1966–1967. He sailed from Plymouth around Cape Horn, with a single stopover at Sydney, Australia.*

Manureva I—*The largest racing yacht, built by Michel Bigoin for the Observer Single-handed Transatlantic Race. It was sailed in 1976 under its original name, Club Méditerranée, by the Frenchman Alain Colas, who won the 1974 edition of the race. Its characteristics are compared with those of the Cutty Sark (in parenthesis): Length: 75.50 meters (64.70 meters); beam: 11 meters (11 meters); draft: 6.60 meters (6.40 meters); displacement: 180 tons (960 tons); sail surface: 1,240 square meters (1,250 square meters); speed: 20 knots (15 knots); crew: 1 (55).*

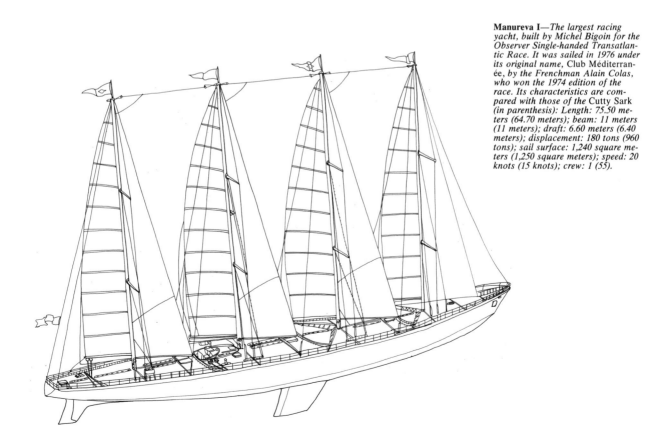

Olympic Classes

Finn—*centerboard*
Designer: R. Sarby (1952)
4.50 × 1.47 × 0.17 (14 ft 9 in × 4 ft 10 in × 7 in); kg: 145 (319 lbs.)
Olympic class

Flying Dutchman—*centerboard*
Designer: U. Van Essen (1951)
6.04 × 1.70 × 1.17 (9 ft 10 in × 5 ft 6 in × 5 ft 7 in); kg: 165 (364 lbs.)
SA: 36.2 m² (390 sq ft); crew: 2
Olympic class

470—*one-design; centerboard*
Designer: A. Cornu
4.72 × 1.68 × 0.15 (15 ft 6 in × 5 ft 6 in × 6 in); kg: 115 (254 lbs.)
SA: mq 12.7 m² (137 sq ft); crew: 2
French national class and IYRU B

Dragon—*keelboat*
Designer: J. Anker (1928)
8.89 × 1.92 × 1.2 (29 ft 2 in × 6 ft 5 in × 3 ft 11 in); kg: 1,698 (3,740 lbs.)
SA: 26.6 m² (286 sq ft); crew: 3
Olympic class until 1972

5.5 Internazionale—*regatta yacht*
IYRU (1949)
9.50 × 1.90 (31 × 6.3 ft); kg: 1.742 (3.840 lbs.)
SA: mq 29 (312 sq ft); crew: 3
Olympic class until 1968

Tempest—*retractable keelboat*
Designer: Ian Proctor
6.71 × 1.93 × 1.09 (22 × 6 ft 4 in × 3 ft 7 in); kg: 499.4 (1100 lbs.)
SA: mq 23 m² (247 sq ft); crew: 2
Olympic class

Tornado—*centerboard catamaran*
Designer: Rodney March
6.09 × 3.02 × 0.17 (20 ft × 10 ft × 7 in); kg: 127 (280 lbs.)
SA: mq 20.4 (220 sq ft); crew 2
Olympic class in 1976

Soling—*keelboat*
Designer: J. Linge (1966)
8.15 × 1.91 × 1.3 (26 ft 9 in × 6 ft 3 in × 4 ft 3 in); kg: 999 (2,200 lbs.)
SA: 21.7 (233 sq ft); crew: 3
No longer Olympic in 1976

International Classes

Zef Junior—*centerboard*
Designer: Nivelt
3.20 × 1.45 × 0.11 (10.5 × 4.8 × 0.4 ft); kg: 60 (132 lbs.)
SA: mq 5.50 (59 sq ft); crew: 3
French national class

Cadet—*centerboard*
Designer: J. Holt (1947)
3.22 × 1.26 × 0.17 (10.7 in × 4 ft 2 in × 7 in); kg: 54.43 (120 lbs.)
SA: mq 5.2 m² (56 sq ft); crew: 2
Class: IYRU B

Dinghy *(12-foot) centerboard*
Designer: G. Cosckott (1912)
3.66 × 1.42 × 0.48 (12 × 4.7 × 1.6 ft); kg: 115 (253 lbs.)
SA: 9.30 (100 sq ft); crew: 1
Olympic class in 1920 and 1928
International class and national FIV class

Zef—*centerboard*
Designer: Nivelt
3.68 × 1.55 × 0.74 (12 ft 1 in × 5 ft 1 in × 2 ft 5 in); kg: 91 (200 lbs.)
SA: 8.9 m² (96 sq ft); crew: 4
French national class

Fox—*one-design; centerboard*
Designer: Y Marechal
3.70 × 1.50 × 0.15/0.95 (12 × 5 × 0.5/3 ft); kg: 90 (198 lbs.)
SA: mq 8.50 (91.5 sq ft); crew: 2–3
French national class

Fennec—*one-design; centerboard*
Designer: Y. Marechal
3.51 × 1.45 × 0.15 (11 ft 6 in × 4 ft 9 in × 6 in); kg: 90 (198 lbs.)
SA: mq 8.50 (92 sq ft); crew: 2
French national class

O.K. International—*one-design; centerboard*
Designer: Knud Olsen
4.01 × 1.42 × 0.18 (13 ft 2 in × 4 ft 8 in × 7 in); kg: 72 (159 lbs.)
SA: 8.4 m² (90 sq ft); crew: 1
International class IYRU B

Flying Junior—*one-design; centerboard*
Designer: U. Van Essen (1956)
4 × 1.6 × 0.15 (13 ft 2 in × 5 ft 3 in × 6 in); kg: 91 (200 lbs.)
SA: 9.30 (100 sq ft); crew: 2
International class and FIV national class.

Vaurien—one-design; centerboard
Designer: J. J. Herbulot
4.04 × 1.45 × 0.08 (13 ft 3 in × 4
ft 9 in × 3 in); kg: 95 (209 lbs.)
SA: 8 (86 sq ft); crew: 2
National class IYRU B

420—one-design; centerboard
Designer: C. Maury (1960)
4.19 × 1.66 × 0.15 (13 ft 9 in × 5
ft 5 in × 6 in); kg: 98 (216 lbs.)
SA: 10.2 (110 sq ft); crew: 2
International class

Classe S 1966—centerboard
U.S.V.I. 1949
4.75 × 1.75 × 0.55 (15.6 × 5.8 ×
1.8 ft); kg: 100 (220 lbs.)
SA: 12.40 (133.5 sq ft); crew: 2
Italian national class

Star—keelboat
Designer: W. Gardner (1911)
6.91 × 1.73 × 1.01 (22 ft 8 in × 5
ft 8 in × 3 ft 4 in); kg: 409 (1,460
lbs.)
SA: 26.5 (285 sq ft); crew: 2
Olympic class until 1972

Snipe—one-design; centerboard
Designer: W. Crosby (1931)
4.72 × 1.52 × 0.15 (15 ft 6 in × 5
ft × 6 in); kg: 182 (400 lbs.)
SA: 11.9 m² (128 sq ft); crew: 2
National class IYRU B

Windy Junior—one-design; centerboard
Designer: L. Bruckner
4.80 × 1.76 × 1.10 (15.8 × 5.8 ×
3.7 ft); kg: 125 (275 lbs.)
SA: 13.60 (146 sq ft); crew: 2
French national class

Filibustier—one-design; centerboard
Designer: J. J. Herbulot (1957)
4.80 × 1.65 × 0.15 (15.8 × 5.5 ×
0.5 ft); kg: 110 (242 lbs.)
SA: 13.25 (142.6 sq ft); crew: 2
French national class

Fireball—one-design; centerboard
Designer: P. Milne (1962)
4.93 × 1.45 × 0.17 (16 ft 2 in × 4
ft 9 in × 7 in); kg: 79 (175 lbs.)
SA: 11.4 m² (123 sq ft); crew: 2
British national class

Strale—one-design; centerboard
Designer: E. Santarelli (1968)
4.90 × 1.58 × 0.15 (16 ft 1 in × 5
ft 2 in × 6 in); kg: 120 (265 lbs.)
SA: 13.50 (145 sq ft); crew: 2
National class FIV

Raz—one-design; fin keel
5.20 × 1.92 × 0.38 × 0.84 (17 ×
6.4 × 1.3 × 2.8 ft); kg: 280 (617
lbs.)
SA: 16.90 (182 sq ft); crew: 3
French national class

Le Ponant—one-design; centerboard
Designer: Deschamps
5.25 × 1.98 × 0.13 (17.3 × 6.5 ×
0.5/4.3 ft); kg: 170 (375 lbs.)
SA: 16.21 (174.5 sq ft); crew: 2
French national class

Windy—one-design; centerboard
Designer: L. Bruckner
5.28 × 1.96 × 1.22 (17.4 × 6.5 ×
4 ft); kg: 160 (353 lbs.)
SA: 16.21 (174.5 sq ft); crew: 2
French national class

Note: The first measurements refer to the boat's
overall length, beam, and draft, with the centerboard raised. This is followed by the boat's
empty weight. "SA" indicates the sail area.
"Crew" refers to the number of men who man
the vessel during a regatta.

Lightning—one-design; centerboard
Designer: Sparkman & Stephen
(1938)
5.79 × 1.98 × 0.44 (19 ft × 6 ft 6
in × 1 ft 5 in)
SA: 16.5 (178 sq ft); crew: 3
International class
IYRU B

Scimitar—one-design; keelboat
Designer: L. Giles & Partners
6.17 × 1.91 (20 ft 3 in × 6 ft 3 in
× 3 ft)
SA: 17.9 m² (193 sq ft); crew: 2
British national class

GLOSSARY

A—"Alfa," letter of the alphabet designated in the International Code by a blue and white broad pennant divided vertically. Hoisted on its own it means: "I am undergoing a speed trial."

aback—A ship is taken aback when the sails are forced flat against the mast, either by a sudden change of wind or in course of backing the ship (*see* BACK).

abaft—On board ship an object is abaft of another when it is situated toward the stern in relation to it.

abandon—An anchor is abandoned when it becomes fouled and left on the bottom together with part of its chain or rope.

abeam—On the side of and to midships of a vessel.

accommodation ladder—The ladder or portable steps set against the side of a vessel when she is at anchor or HEAVES TO to allow access to and from boats coming alongside.

adrazo—A word of Spanish origin applied to the rough-and-ready system of distilling salt water used aboard Spanish ships in their 16th and 17th-century ocean voyages.

alidade—A movable ring provided with verniers round the edge and fitted to compasses or other navigational instruments to facilitate reading from them.

almanac—Nautical almanacs are issued a year ahead and contain, inter alia, star tables showing their variables at regular intervals throughout the year in question and valid for that year only.

aloft—Overhead; on the yards or in the rigging.

anchor—A piece of metal equipment provided with two or more arms which bite into the seabed thereby ensuring that the vessel has a fixed position to which it can moor by means of the rope or chain attached to the anchor. It comprises the *shank*, the main beam with the *eye* at the head to take the *anchor ring*, and the *arms* at the foot. The *arms* usually branch from the foot of the shank at an angle of about 50° to it. They end in hooks or flattened points called *flukes*. They ensure that the anchor BITES into the GROUND. From the eye hangs the *anchor ring* to which the anchor rope is bent or to which the anchor chain is secured by a large SHACKLE known as the *anchor shackle*.

Below the eye, the *stocks* run out at right angles to the shank so that when viewed from above or below stocks and arms form a cross. Iron was substituted for the original stout oak of the stocks, but nowadays stockless anchors are widely used (*see* DANFORTH; HALL).

When a vessel comes to anchor she is said to drop, cast, or let go her anchor. She *backs* her anchor when she drops a smaller anchor ahead of her main anchor in order to reinforce the holding powers of the latter.

The anchor is *weighed* when it is lifted from the ground; it is *catted* when it is hoisted from the water to the CAT-HEAD, and *fished* when it is brought into the horizontal position and secured to the BILLBOARD.

anchorage—A stretch of water protected from wind and waves, of sufficient depth and with a clean bottom into which the anchor will bite, which will provide a vessel with safe moorings.

astern—Behind; in the wake of a vessel.

awning—A canvas roof provided to screen the upper deck from sun or rain.

B—"Bravo," second letter of the alphabet indicated in the International Code by a completely red broad pennant. When hoisted on its own it means: "I am taking in *or* discharging explosives." When hoisted by a yacht competing in a regatta it means: "I intend to lodge a protest."

back—To haul the sails over to windward (*see also* ABACK). To *back water* when rowing is to stop the run by holding the blade vertical in the water and then reverse direction by pushing on the oars rather than pulling (*see also under* ANCHOR; VEER AND BACK).

back-rope—The rope which stays the DOLPHIN-STRIKER.

back-stay—Standing rigging with the task of keeping the masts steady against going forward. They take their name from the mast which they support. Topmast back-stays are so arranged that they can be slackened when the boom swings over.

bale—To bale is to throw over the side any water which may have gotten into a vessel. A *baler*, a large wooden or plastic scoop with a handle and a deep bowl, is used.

ballast keel—Instead of carrying ballast in the boat, modern racing yachts carry the lead as a cigar-shaped bulge on the foot of the keel.

barepoles—The masts and yards of a vessel when not carrying sail (*see* SCUD).

battens—Narrow wooden or plastic strips fitted into the appropriate slots in the sail to improve its drawing powers by flattening it.

beacon—Guiding mark embedded on land or in shallows to help vessels find a safe passage through shoals, etc. Beacons serve the same purpose as BUOYS and are topped by correspondingly shaped and colored markers as guides to navigation; but in contrast to the floating buoy, beacons are fixed to the seabed.

beam—In shipbuilding the timbers that connect one side with the other and support the deck. Beams are set one above the other in the sheer plan of the vessel and each is arranged in succession across its longitudinal axis. Where they are interrupted by the presence of hatchways or other openings in the deck, the shortened beam which results is called a *half-beam*. The upper surface of the beam is shaped to take the deck camber and its extremities to follow the lines of the vessel.

Because they run from side to side beams give their name to the *beam* or width of the vessel, which is taken from the longest beam, that is the widest part. However, this measurement should be specified as being either internal or external, at waterline or at deck level, or overall.

bear away—A deliberate maneuver whereby the helm of a vessel sailing CLOSE-HAULED is put up (that is brought to the windward side) so that the vessel turns to run before the wind.

beat—See TACK.

Beaufort Scale—A scale of wind forces named for its inventor, the British Admiral Sir Francis Beaufort (1774–1857) and adopted by the International Meteorological Committee in 1874. It runs from 0 (dead calm) to Force 12 (hurricane).

belay—To belay is to secure a rope in a figure eight and without knotting it to a suitable projection such as a *belaying-pin*. The latter, once much used on the big square-riggers, were turned and polished wooden or

metal pins set on PIN-RAILS close to the shrouds or forward of the mast.

bell—Once used on board ship to express time, being struck every half hour, the strokes regulating the change of watch. Bells were also used to sound warnings in cases of danger or emergency. Nowadays their functions have been superseded by the "intercom" and ship's siren.

bend—To secure anything, such as one rope to another, an anchor to its cable, or a sail to a stay, boom, yard, or mast. Jib-sails are bent to stays; while the modern triangular Bermuda sails are bent by means of metal slides which run on tracking attached to the mast or part of it, or else they are equipped with a bolt-rope which slides into a groove running the length of the mast. The same system applies to booms, while gaff-sails are bent on a series of mast-rings. Square sails are bent to metal jack-stays on the aftermost side of the yard, while the lateen sail is bent to its yard by lacing.

Bermuda sail—A triangular mainsail very generally carried nowadays by racing and cruising yachts. Outside the English-speaking world it is incorrectly called a "Marconi," this term properly applying not to the sail, but only to the mast and rigging, from their resemblance from height and cordage to the early transmitter-masts used by Marconi (*see also under* BEND).

berth—A ship's berth is the place at which she anchors or ties up to discharge and load passengers and freight. A seaman's berth is his cabin, bedspace, or place where he swings his hammock.

bight—A rope bent upon itself to form a U-shape, a basic element in all knots and HITCHES.

bilge—The portion of the ship's hull below the load waterline, from the second FUTTOCK to the keel. It comprises all the internal timbers and is used to support the outer planking. Internally all the water which cannot pass overboard through the scuppers collects here and therefore the bilges even of small boats must constantly be kept dry. Larger vessels use a system of pipes to pump the water out through the scuppers.

bill-board—Reinforced plate fitted to the decks of vessels using a stocked-anchor. The billboard supports the flukes of the anchor after it has been catted and fished.

binnacle—The housing, wooden or demagnetized metal, in which a ship's steering compass is fixed on Cardanic suspension.

bite—An anchor is said to bite when its flukes hold the ground.

bitt—"To bitt" is to secure a rope or a chain to a bitt—small posts made of wood or of such metals as steel, cast iron, brass, or aluminum and generally fixed through the deck around the bowsprit to support the anchor cable. This cable is bitted to prevent it from running out too fast, particularly when the ground concerned is in deep water or unfamiliar.

block—The seaman's word for "pulley." The block comprises a slim oval SHELL of wood, metal, or synthetic resin. Inside one or more shells *sheaves* (pulley-wheels) are fitted, around which the ropes run. The shells are bound by a piece of rope called a *strop*, with loops at either end from which the block may be hung. Nowadays the strop has been superseded by a closed metal bracket. Blocks may be single, double-sheaved, or triple-sheaved, according to the number of pulley-wheels. Special types of blocks are the SNATCH-BLOCK and the FIDDLE-BLOCK.

bluff—A bluff-bowed vessel is one with broad bows rising almost straight from the water.

board—The act of going aboard another vessel; consequently the word has come to be used for attacking a ship by boarding it. A "board" is also used to describe the distance sailed between tacks.

boat—An undecked vessel, propelled by engine, sail, or oars. This is perhaps too strict an interpretation, the distinction between "boat" and "ship" being one of size; decked yachts, fishing boats, and other small craft are generally in the first rather than the second category.

boat-hook—Stout wooden pole with one or two hooks on the end used to pick up the buoy during mooring maneuvers or to hold a boat against or alongside a wharf or another vessel.

bobstay—The stay which runs from the cutwater to the end of the bowsprit and counteracts

the upward pressure of the topmast forestay.

bollard—Stout wooden or metal posts, the latter often with mushroom-shaped heads, set in the dockside to take the mooring cables of a ship.

bolt—The name given to the length of cloth (canvas or man-made fiber) from which the sail is made. Width tends to vary according to purpose as does the weight of the cloth.

bolt-ropes—The ropes inserted along the edges of sails to strengthen them. Those at the head and foot are called the head- and foot-rope respectively, those along the sides, the leech-ropes.

bomb—A warship conceived by the French which first saw action in the last quarter of the 17th century and was employed until well into the 19th century. A mainmast stepped almost amidships carried a square sail, with a jigger-mast in the stern setting a lateen or gaff-sail, while the absence of the foremast enabled a number of jib-sails to be hoisted. With ample deckroom forward for the main-mast, very heavy pieces of ordnance could be mounted—mortars with a bore of up to 13 in.—capable of destroying the most elaborate coastal defense works. The mortars, which were without trunnions and fired at a fixed angle, were mounted in a forehold and discharged through a wide hatchway. The heaviest bombs had a loaded weight of around 150 tons.

boom—A spar of wood or metal of varying crosssection to which is bent the foot-rope and hence the foot, or lower side of the sail; or else either slotted into a groove or shackled by metal slides running along the track provided. The boom is fixed horizontally to the after side of the foot of the mast round which its jaw turns by means of parrels, while at the other end of the boom are fixed the halyards and a grommet for the topping lift to support it. The boom may also be attached to the mast by GOOSENECK.

bosun—The chief subordinate officer on a merchant ship who directs all working parties aboard ship. In the past this was done by means of his *whistle*, a small silver instrument, which signalled to the crew which sheets to hoist, pay out, or secure. In addition the watch was called on deck by whistle, while on warships officers are still "piped on board" by the bosun's whistle.

bosun's chair—A short plank slung by a rope to provide a seat while working aloft or over the side.

bower anchors—The principal anchors of a vessel held ready for use one on either side of the bow.

bowline—On square-rigged ships the bowline was a rope attached to the leech of the sail and used to keep the weather edge steady so that the ship could point as close to the wind as possible. Hence to sail with a taut bowline is to sail close-hauled.

bowsprit—A stout spar protruding from the bow of a vessel at an angle of approximately 20° above the waterline, this angle being known as the *steave*. The bowsprit may be prolonged by the jib boom and the flying jib boom. The bowsprit is supported laterally by the bowsprit shrouds and vertically by the BOBSTAY and the forestays to which the jib-middle-jib and flying-jib-sails are bent. Additional support for the bobstay is provided by the DOLPHIN-STRIKER.

brace—Rope running to the yardarm of a square-rigged ship which allows the yards to be swung round in the horizontal plane. The brace takes its name from the yard to which it is attached, e.g., fore-royal, main-sky, etc. Yards were braced square to run before the wind, braced in so that the yards formed the smallest angle with the centerline of the vessel to sail against the wind. To brace back is to haul the yards over to windward so as to stop the run of the ship; to brace round, to traverse the yards when running before the wind, to increase constantly the angle of the yards to the centerline so as to reduce leeway.

brail—Rope encircling a sail so as to gather it to a mast or yard.

breaming—Applying heat to melt the old pitch out of the seams of a boat preparatory to re-caulking her.

breast-hook—See STEM.

breeze—Defined on the Beaufort Scale as winds from Force 2 (Light Breeze 4–7 mph) to Force 6 (Strong Breeze 25–31 mph). On the coast they are liable morning and evening, blowing from land to sea and vice versa respectively.

bridge—Superstructure and deck which houses all the gear

and equipment for navigating the ship and from which she is steered. It is located in different positions according to the type of vessel concerned and contains wheel-house, chart-room, and radio-room plus all their equipment, the captain's cabin, and a cabin for the pilot when he is aboard. The navigating-bridge runs the full width of the ship, has a clear lookout, and is equipped with gyro-compass, signaling gear, etc. This area is known as the wings and is particularly useful when maneuvering the ship.

brig—Two-masted vessel, square-rigged except for the mainsail which was gaff-sail. From this developed the *hermaphrodite brig* on which the foremast remained square-rigged but with the mainmast now completely schooner-rigged, i.e., carrying fore-and-aft sails. Hermaphrodite brigs are also known as *brigantines.*

broach—The action of a vessel running before the wind which through mishandling or through the action of the elements slews round to lie beam on to wind and waves.

bulwarks—The side-planking which extends above decklevel to provide a parapet all round the vessel. The bulwarks of the old ship-of-the-line were particularly lofty and her seamen would stow their HAMMOCKS in nets along the bulwarks thus providing protection against enemy musketry.

bunk—A bed on board ship of whatever shape or form, but essentially fixed, as opposed to the hammock which is swung.

bunt—The main body of a sail, the central area within the head, foot, luff, and leech.

buntlines—Lines for gathering a square sail to its yard.

buoy—Floating object moored to the seabed and made of wood, cork, metal, or resin principally used to assist safe navigation at sea. They may be conical, spherical, or cylindrical; and their shape and coloring are standardized to indicate the particular hazard to navigation and the course to be steered to avoid it. Such buoys may also carry lights and homing devices.

Buoys are also used to indicate moorings.

burgee—Small pointed flag flown at the masthead of yachts and dinghies in the colors of and bearing the devices of the yacht or sailing club to which they belong. Apart from identification, the flag preeminently acts as a DOG-VANE, indicating the direction of the wind.

C—"Charlie," third letter of the alphabet designated in the International Code by a square flag with five horizontal stripes—blue, white, red, white, blue. When hoisted in isolation it means: "Yes (affirmative)."

cabin—A suitably fitted compartment on board ship for lodging crew or passengers.

cabin-cruiser—A description generally applied to a medium-to-small-sized yacht, particularly engine-driven and especially designed for inland waterways rather than the open sea. It indicates that the vessel is completely decked and provided with a roundhouse. The space thus gained below decks is used to provide accommodation, depending upon the size of the vessel, for from 2 to 6 persons, with bunks, galley, and separate toilet facilities.

cable—The rope or chain attached to the ship's anchor. A cable's length is one-tenth of a nautical mile, or approximately 200 yards.

cable-laid—A rope made of three large strands which themselves each comprise three small strands twisted left-handed. Cable-laid rope has the advantage of not becoming snarled and is often used as a mooring rope or warp.

cable-lifter—A wheel, provided with five or six large teeth set round the rim which engage in the links of the anchor-chain ensuring that it does not slip as it is being hauled in by the capstan and providing sufficient traction to weigh the anchor and cat it.

camber—The curve of the sail when it is drawing; also the downward curve of the deck from the centerline to the scuppers. A rounded keel is said, too, to be cambered.

cap—A ring at the extremity of a spar. The *upper* and *lower* caps are the fittings at the head of a lower mast through which an upper mast passes (*see* YOKE). A rope is said to have been *capped* when the end which may be subjected to wear has been covered by a piece of tarred canvas, leather, or plastic and whipped with yarn or twine.

capsize—To HEEL completely over until the vessel floats bottom-up. In DINGHIES this is caused by an insufficiency of centerboard (KEEL) and righting them is a normal and not very difficult operation.

capstan—Mechanism employed on board ship for a variety of duties: raising the anchor, lowering lifeboats, hoisting cargo, etc. The capstan can be worked manually although it enjoys the power provided by internal combustion engines, steam, electricity, and even hydraulic power. The working part of the capstan comprises the axle, that is, a drum suitably fashioned to take the bight of the cable which it is to haul. Under the drum of the anchor-capstan a chain lifter is fitted—a toothed wheel—which keeps the anchor-chain clear and taut. Capstans are manually operated by means of long levers fitted to holes in the wheel. Capstans of this sort have pawls fixed to the axle, that is, projections which engage in a toothed wheel and prevent the axle from running backward in the absence of pressure from the levers.

careen—To careen a vessel is to haul a vessel over onto her side (by exerting a strong purchase on her masts) so that the bilges emerge and maintenance or repairs may be effected without placing her in dry dock. Maintenance of the hull, which may involve cleaning the fouling, BREAMING, and CAULKING, may be described as *careening.*

carlines—An important element in shipbuilding, being the longitudinal beams which run between the deck beams and support the deck.

carvel build—In wooden ships when the hull-planking is joined edge to edge.

cat—To cat the anchor is to hoist it, once it has been weighed, and to bring it up until it hangs vertically from the *cat-heads.* These are beams projecting from the sides of the bows to which the anchor is secured by the *cat-block,* the lower block of a stout tackle which carries a hook which is engaged in the anchor ring.

caulking—An operation to stop the seams of both hull and deck planking and thus prevent water leaking through. In wooden ships caulking consisted in driving OAKUM into the seams with the help of special *caulking-irons* and wooden mallets, the largest of which is known as the *reeving-beetle.* Then the seams were *payed* with boiling pitch to preserve both timbers and oakum from rotting, thus keeping the hull in good condition. Caulking the decks, too, was completed by paying the seams with pitch, for which a resin seal has been substituted nowadays.

center of effort—The point at which is concentrated the aerodynamic force exerted by the wind upon the sails of a vessel or yacht.

centerboard—See KEEL.

certificate—All maritime nations have systems whereby certificates of competence are issued following the examination of candidates. Only officers so qualified may hold commands. The certificates are generally known as "tickets," "master's tickets," etc.

chain—These came to be used at sea for ships' anchors and for anchoring buoys, DEADHEADS, lightships, etc. On old-time square-riggers chains came to be used in the standing-rigging, being gradually superseded by steel- and galvanized-wire ropes. Large chains, such as anchor-chains, use *stud-links,* that is, links with a crossbar to strengthen them. Incidentally you should speak of an anchor-cable not an anchor-chain, since all chains are cables, although all cables need not necessarily be chains! A chain length is $12\frac{1}{2}$ fathoms or 75 feet.

chain cable compressor—Apparatus made of metal and set beside the path followed by the cable from the chain-locker to the capstan on the port and starboard quarters of the bows. By moving a lever on the compressor a mesh engages in the links of the chain which is then securely shackled. By this means the cable can be held without the need to use the power of the capstan to which it is attached, when for one reason or another the original operation has to be interrupted.

chain-grab—See CABLE-LIFTER.

chain-locker—The vertical hold lying under the decking of the bows in which the anchor-cable is stored when the anchor has been fished.

chain-plate—Flat metal bars securely fastened to the vessel—sometimes to her sides, sometimes to her deck—to which the shrouds are kept taut by means of rigging screws. Chain-plates are generally made of stainless steel or bronze.

channels—Served the same purpose on large sailing ships as chain-plates on modern yachts, being wooden platforms projecting from the sides of the ship over which the shrouds passed and under which they were secured. This increased the angle between the mast and its supporting shrouds and consequently made that support all the more firm.

charter-party—In law a contract between the owner of a ship and a person hiring the whole or any part of it for a specific purpose and on agreed terms. Although of long standing in freight shipping, it is becoming increasingly common practice where yachts are concerned.

check—Can not only mean stop the run of a rope or cable, but also when applied to a sheet have the opposite meaning of letting it out slightly.

cheeks—See HOUNDS.

chine—Another name for BILGES. *Hard-chine* construction, employed in building yachts and dinghies, describes the hull-shape in which the sides meet the bilges at an angle, instead of being rounded or CAMBERED.

chock-a-block—When the blocks of a working tackle are brought into contact the one with the other before their task is completed. In order to obtain the necessary purchase to complete the task they have to be pulled apart or *overhauled.*

chronometer—Accurate timekeeping at sea is an essential of navigation since, without it, is impossible accurately to determine a vessel's longitudinal position. The invention of an accurate and reliable marine chronometer in the mid-18th century by John Harrison opened an era of greatly improved safety at sea and made possible the great voyages of exploration which followed.

class—The division into which yachts and dinghies are placed according to their RATING. More generally the category to which a ship belongs—schooner, clipper, frigate, cruiser, etc.—while among warships a class of battleship, cruiser, destroyer, etc., may take its name from the first of a number of similar vessels to be laid down, or from the generic name given to such vessels as, for example, the Royal Navy's World War II destroyers of the "Tribal Class" such as H.M.S. *Ashanti, Afridi, Zulu,* et al.

clear—A rope or a chain is *clear* when it can run freely, and it is *cleared* when it is unsnarled or when any kinks are removed from it. A vessel *clears customs* when she passes examination by customs officers; she *clears harbor* when she leaves it and she *sails clear* of an obstacle or a danger.

cleat or cavil—A kind of hook that generally has two horizontal arms fixed to the deck or to any other appropriate place on the boat to which a rope may be secured by winding it round without knotting. They are used particularly for securing sheets and halyards.

clew—The lower corner of a sail and in fore-and-aft sails the after corner, since it it is always to leeward, the forward corner being the *weather-clew* or *tack*. Which lower corner of a square sail is the tack and which is the clew depends on the direction of the wind in relation to the sail.

clew-lines—Ropes employed on square sails, running from the lower corners to the yard and used to draw the sails up for furling.

clinker build—The system of wooden boatbuilding in which the hull-planking (STRAKES) overlap.

close-hauled—To sail close-hauled is to sail with the bows pointing as closely as possible in the direction from which the wind is blowing.

clove hitch—The knot most generally used to join two lengths of rope.

coaming—The raised wooden or metal edge round a hatchway so fashioned in relation to the deck as to prevent water getting below.

coaster—A small merchant vessel engaged in the coasting trade, that is, carrying goods from one port to another (generally) in the same country. Most nations try to confine this trade to their own ships, subject to the control of various international agreements.

cockpit—On decked racing and cruising yachts, particularly sailboats, the well, protected by WEATHER-BOARDS (or their modern equivalents), which contains the steering gear and to which the principal pieces of running rigging lead. Access to the cabin is from the cockpit, which is usually self-draining.

coil—The turns of a rope circling in a clockwise direction one on top of the other in order to save space and particularly to prevent the rope from becoming snarled when used. One complete circle is known as a *fake* and the hole in the middle after the rope has been coiled is the *tier*. In commercial terms a coil of rope is 113 fathoms (678 feet).

come—To *come alongside* is to bring the side of a vessel up against the side of another vessel or against a wharf or jetty; an anchor is said to *come home* when it drags; a sailing vessel *comes round* or *comes about* when tacking, *comes to* when she luffs right into the wind, and *comes up* with another ship or piece of shoreline when she overtakes or passes it. However, to *come up* a fall or capstan is to slacken it off.

companionway—The well down which the companions (ladders or stairs) lead from one deck to another in a ship.

compass—A basic piece of navigational equipment in any vessel since it gives continuous indication of the direction in which the bows of the vessel are pointing when she is under way, no matter where she may be, by measuring the angle formed by the centerline of the vessel with the direction of the magnetic meridian.

conning tower—To con is an old word for "to steer" and the navigational bridge on 19th- and early 20th-century ironclads was from its shape sometimes called the conning tower. The usage is now applied solely to submarines.

core—The core of a rope made of vegetable or synthetic fibres is the strand round which the other small strands are wound. The core gives the rope a rounded cicumference and helps to keep it pliable. On the other hand all wire ropes have a hemp or manila strand round which the wires are wound.

course—Obviously, the direction in which a ship travels, so that when a ship alters course, she changes direction. But on a square-rigged vessel, the courses are the lowest sails bent to each mast and take their name from the mast on which they are carried, e. g., fore-course, main-course, and mizzen-course.

corvette—A small sailing warship of the 18th and early 19th centuries. In World War II the name was revived and applied to vessels smaller than frigates; these were used very extensively for convoy protection and submarine hunting and armed and equipped for such duties.

coxswain—The steersman and therefore the person in charge of an oared-boat and particularly of the ship's boat. The commander of a shore-based lifeboat is still called the coxswain although oars have long given way to engines.

cradle—The stout framework and strutting which supports the hull of a ship during launching as she is traveling down the slipway and into the water. Smaller versions are used to support smaller vessels, particularly yachts, in drydock.

crane—Lifting apparatus usually comprising cargo-cranes found on most freighters and used for a variety of purposes. Cranes may be fixed turret cranes with a wide field of traverse or mobile cranes operating on rails running the length of the ship and close to her sides. Cranes were also used for raising anchors, particularly the type with stocks; these were of two sorts, one to raise the bower anchors and one placed in the stern.

crank—The handle used to operate hand-winches on board yachts and larger sailboats.

cringles—A small ring or grommet of rope or metal fastened to the edge of a sail (*see* REEF-BANDS).

cross-jack yard—See YARD.

crosstrees—Wooden or metal arms extending sideways from the mast. On square-rigged ships the topmast shrouds were attached to the ends of these arms to give the mast lateral stability. On modern sailboats the crosstrees are set on the upper half or third of the mast and are there to keep the upper shrouds clear of the mast and to impart greater rigidity to them.

crow's foot—The larger rope terminating in a block, eyelet, shackle, or plate from which radiate a number of smaller ropes to different points. This larger rope takes the total strain imposed upon the smaller ropes and in practical terms the crow's foot can be a means of suspension to support awnings, ship's boats, etc.

crutch—An X-shaped wooden trestle used to support the boom when the sail is furled. It can also be an adjustable X-shaped trestle which can be secured to the deck, or it can apply to the crossbeam and supports with slot to take the boom.

cutter—The small single-masted, gaff-rigged sailboat used by customs officers and pilots in the 18th and 19th centuries, which is in many ways the ancestor of the modern racing and cruising yacht from its speed and seaworthiness.

D—"Delta," fourth letter of the alphabet designated in the International Code by a square flag with a broad blue horizontal stripe flanked by narrower yellow stripes. Hoisted in isolation it means: "Keep clear of me, I am maneuvering with difficulty."

Dacron—Registered trade-name of an American man-made fiber; one of the polyesters much used nowadays in the manufacture of sails and ropes, particularly sheets and halyards.

Danforth—A type of stockless anchor first manufactured in 1939. It has movable triangular flukes.

davit—A light crane used for lowering and hoisting boats—particularly the lifeboats—over the ship's side.

deadeye—Stout disk of hard wood, grooved round the edges and pierced by two or three holes through which lanyards were passed joining two deadeyes to form a kind of block. Once this was used to hold the shrouds firm. Nowadays rigging-screws serve the same purpose, but deadeyes may still be found occasionally on the fishingboat.

deadhead—Large lumps of concrete, probably reinforced, pigs of cast iron, or even riveted or welded steel caissons heavily weighted. Such objects of considerable weight would be sunk and fitted with chains and sometimes even with anchors as well. Their presence on the seabed was indicated by a buoy moored to them by a chain or wire rope. Deadheads were sunk in anchorages, bays, or shallows to provide moorings for large vessels, which tied up directly to the deadhead. In addition to indicating its whereabouts the buoy also supported the mooring cable which was picked up and made fast to the vessel. Deadheads also came into use wherever a marker buoy was needed, as to warn of shoals or wrecks, or to buoy channels.

deadlights—Wooden or metal covers for skylights and portholes.

deck—The decks of merchant vessels are numbered down-

GLOSSARY

wards; the lowest deck of all is known as the *orlop-deck.* The upper deck is the topmost deck completely planked from stem to stern and from one side of the ship to the other and exposed in whole or in part to the elements. The upper deck is generally provided with stout BULWARKS, GANGWAY, SCUPPERS which allow whatever water may collect there to run off, as well as the windlasses, winches, and cranes which make up the deck gear.

The decks themselves are supported transversely by BEAMS and longitudinally by CARLINES. The freight on cargo decks is always shored to prevent movement. Decks are nearly always cambered to increase their strength and to allow the water used to wash them down, as well as any other that may have come inboard, to run off through the scuppers.

derrick—Apparatus used for hoisting and lowering weights comprising a boom secured at the foot of a mast from which runs the block and tackle controlling the elevation and traverse of the boom.

diagonal build—A method of wooden shipbuilding in which the hull-planks are laid diagonally across the timbers. Sometimes, for extra strength a second casing is laid in the opposite direction.

dinghy—The small open boat carried on yachts as ship's boats which has developed into an inshore racing sailboat in its own right. There are various one-design boats, single-masted and with centerboard.

dismast—A vessel becomes dismasted when its mast and rigging are brought down by stress of weather or from any other cause. When masts are deliberately taken down (for refitting, etc.), they are said to be *struck.*

displacement—The weight of the vessel based upon Archimedes' principle that it equals the weight of water displaced by its own hull. In countries using the Metric System, displacement is expressed in metric tons equalling 1,000 kilograms; in countries using the Imperial System displacement is expressed in English "long tons," each of 2,240 lbs., the equivalent of approximately 1.016 metric tons.

distress—The flying upside down of the ship's ENSIGN is a signal that the vessel is in distress, that fighting has broken out on board, or that she requests assistance.

dock—An artificial basin built to receive vessels for the loading and discharge of their cargo and passengers or for refitting and repairs. The latter are performed in a *dry dock,* with a lock-gate to shut off the sea or estuary and facilities for pumping itself dry when the vessel to be repaired is moored in it. There are also floating docks for this purpose.

dodgers—Canvas screens set round the rails or on the BRIDGE to act as WEATHER-BOARDS in protecting the crew of a vessel from water coming over her side.

dog-vane—Small flag or strip of light canvas which does not fray, raised to the mast-truck to show the direction of the apparent wind, that is that of the true wind plus that of the vessel's motion.

dogwatch—Watch on board ship from 4 to 6 P.M. (1st Dogwatch) and from 6 to 8 P.M. (2nd Dogwatch). A dogwatch is a two-hour instead of a four-hour spell introduced so that the same watch does not have the same turn of duty day in and day out.

dolphin-striker—A small spar rigged beneath the BOWSPRIT of large sailing vessels at right angles to it and used for extra staying of the bowsprit and JIB BOOMS.

down by the head—A depression of a vessel towards its bows due to such various causes as the shifting of ballast or cargo or that she has sprung a leak forward. The opposite phenomenon is when the vessel is *down by the stern* or *heel.*

downhaul—The name given to any rope which is used to haul-down or lower any sail or spar or other object on board ship.

drag—A vessel drags her anchor when, because of the effects of wind or tide or because insufficient cable has been paid out, the anchor ceases to *bite* and *comes home.* However, to *drag for an anchor* is to search for a lost anchor by sweeping the seabed with a length of rope or chain carried between two boats.

drift—The lateral distance which a vessel is driven from her course by the tide or current. It should not be confused with LEEWAY, the same phenomenon caused by the action of the wind on sails, hull, and rigging.

draw—A sail *draws* when it is inflated and the lee sheets are

taut. A vessel is said to *draw* so many feet of water, being the distance between her loaded waterline and the bottom of her keel (loaded draught), She *draws away* from another vessel or from a point on the shore when she leaves them behind.

dunnage—Pallets, frames, or balks of timber on which the cargo rests when for any reason it is impractical for it to lie directly on the decking.

duralumin—An industrial light alloy composed of copper, magnesium, silicon, and manganese on an aluminum base which is beginning to be used in shipbuilding. Besides being used for the construction of a small number of racing yachts, the "light alloy," as duralumin is called, has proved a substitute for wood in building masts and booms, which are protected from corrosion by anodization.

E—"Echo," fifth letter of the alphabet designated in the International Code by a square flag divided horizontally, the upper half being blue, the lower red. Hoisted in isolation it means: "I am directing my course to starboard."

earings—These are the small ropes attached to the CRINGLES in the BOLT-ROPE at the head of sails.

ease—To *ease away* is to reduce the tension on a rope by letting it out.

echo-sounders—These are now widely used, even on pleasure boats, to determine the depth of water. They are ultrasonic instruments which bounce their information back from the seabed or from any obstacle which they encounter on the way. This information is shown on a screen (similar to a TV screen) as a bulge in a vertical light beam. Apart from their use in "taking soundings" they are widely employed by fishing vessels to detect shoals of fish.

ensign—The national flag flown at the stern of vessels between sunrise and sunset. Many countries produce a special variant of their national flag for their shipping, with differences between the ensigns for warships and those for merchant vessels.

eye—A small hole, loop, or ring such as an *eye-bolt,* a screw with a ringhead fixed in the deck to secure blocks or ropes (*see also* FAIRLEAD).

eye-splice—An *eye* made in a rope or wire by turning the end back and splicing it upon itself.

eyelet holes—Any hole made in the body of a sail, normally protected by a rustproof metal ring. Some sorts of GAFF-sail, for example, are not provided with REEF-CRINGLES, but simply reef-eyes, through which the REEF-PENDANTS are passed.

F—"Foxtrot," sixth letter of the alphabet designated in the International Code by a square white flag with a red diamond in the center, its points touching the middle of each of the four edges. Hoisted in isolation it means: "I am disabled, communicate with me."

fairlead—Any eye, ring, bolt, or loop fixed to the deck of a vessel and used to guide a rope in a required direction.

fake—A fake of rope is one complete ring or course in a coil of rope.

fall—That part of the rope or sheet which is pulled.

fall off—A sailing ship or boat is said to fall off if, when the helm is held steady, it has a tendency to run away from the wind. A vessel will tend to fall off if the center of effort is too far forward of the center of leeway, or even if the aerodynamic thrust produced by the foresails is greater that that produced by the mainsails.

fathom—Measure of length of 6 feet.

felucca—Small two-masted lateen-rigged Mediterranean sailing vessel, used for cargo carrying and, in the 18th and early 19th centuries, as a warship and privateer.

fender—Anything which serves to *fend off* the impact of one body with another as may occur when one vessel ties up against a wharf or quay or alongside another vessel. Fixed fenders may be carried round the sides in the shape of a band or rope or rubber, or portable ones may be lowered over the side at likely points of impact. The latter may be *pudding-fenders* made of old rope, or of rope woven into cylinders or balls, of cork covered with tarred canvas, of rubber, or of plastic. Frequently they are nothing more than old automobile tires, which may not look very pretty, but which work very well and cost very little!

ferro-concrete—First used by the Italian, P. L. Nervi, in boatbuilding. The technique consists in creating a thin concrete shell on a very small-mesh metal frame and has been successfully applied to the construction of sail- and motor-yachts of some size.

fid—The bolt (of wood or metal) used to secure the heel of a TOPMAST or BOWSPRIT.

fiddle-block—A block with two SHEAVES of different width and different diameter mounted on separate pins. It can therefore take two different sizes of rope and is used in restricted spaces.

figure-head—Sculptured wooden figure decorating the prow of wooden ships, generally representing the subject of the ship's name.

fish—See ANCHOR.

fitting out—The phase in the life of a ship which follows her launch when the machinery, wiring, internal fittings, etc., are installed and the painting done. Fitting out generally takes place in a dock away from the slipway and where the necessary warehouses and workshops are to be found. Fitting out a sailing ship involves setting up the masts and rigging, stowing the holds, etc.

fleet—All the ships comprised under one command or allotted to one particular duty, as a navy's Atlantic Fleet, Pacific Fleet, or Mediterranean Fleet. In the merchant service the name can be applied to all the shipping either under a national flag or the flag of a specific shipping company, or engaged in a particular operation, such as a tanker fleet or a fishing fleet.

flood—When fire develops aboard ship it may be brought under control by *flooding* the site through special saltwater valves called Kingston Valves. They may also be used to right the list in a ship which has sprung a leak by flooding a compartment in the ship which will balance the effect of the water taken on board through the leak.

flotilla—Operational grouping for destroyers and lighter warships, cruisers, battle cruisers, and battleships being grouped in SQUADRONS. Destroyers designated as *flotilla-leaders* were normally slightly larger than similar ships of their CLASS, to accommodate the officer commanding the flotilla, his staff, signaling equipment, etc.

flush-deck—Type of upper deck which is flat and free of all obstruction found on many racing and cruising yachts, small-scale heirs of the 19th-century wind-jammers which adopted the flush-deck, almost completely exposed to the elements though it was, to simplify their sail handling.

fly—The fly of the flag is its length, as opposed to the hoist which is its height. However, the free end can also be called the fly.

foghorn—Siren for signaling in fog which takes its name from the instrument used for the same purpose on board sailing ships in antiquity—a cow's horn with the end cut off.

foot—The lowest part of any object, the lowest end of a mast or spar, or the lower edge of a sail.

foot-rope—The BOLT-ROPE running along the lower edge of a sail: another name given to the HORSE.

foot-timbers—Traditional elements of wooden boatbuilding: transverse short ribs set in the spaces between the FUTTOCKS to reinforce the lower STRAKES.

fore-and-aft—The term applied to GAFF, BERMUDA, and such rigs in which the principal sails are set on booms on the longitudinal axis of the vessel, as opposed to square-rig where the sails are set on yards at right angles to it.

forecastle—The forward deck and somewhat raised above the main deck. On old sailingships it ran from the STEM to the foremast and was particularly handy for working the foresails and the anchor. Earlier still, when its height above the main deck was even greater, it was used as a fighting "castle" by the soldiers carried on board the ship.

foremast—On ships of three or more masts the mast nearest the STEM is always the foremast, and this is nearly always true of two-masted vessels as well. However, in the cases of KETCHES, yawls, and some other categories, where the foremast of the two masts is considerably higher, this mast is termed the MAINMAST and the after mast the MIZZEN (*see also* MAST).

fore-peak—A space in the bows of a vessel forward of the FORECASTLE.

foresail—On square-rigged ships generally called the fore-COURSE; in fore-and-aft rig, the foremast gaff-sail; while on cutters and yawls it is the triangular sail set on the stay which runs from the lower FOREMAST to the STEM head.

forward—On board ship one object is forward of another when it is closer to the bows in relation to it.

foul—Chains, ropes, anchors, etc., *foul* one another when they become mutually entangled.

fouling—Weed and other vegetable organisms, but particularly barnacles which live on the ship's hull below the waterline. The normal antidote is to paint the hull with an antifouling paint containing copper and mercury to form a poisonous shield against marine organisms.

In tropical waters a calcareous concretion like stalactites forms below the waterline reducing the speed of the vessel and making it necessary for her to go regularly into dry dock for CAREENING.

foundering—The entry of water into the ship, causing her to lose buoyancy and sink.

frames—The entire set of timbers and the planks that cover them, which make up the skeleton of the ship. The frames give the vessel the shape designed for her by the architect; provide the most important and delicate element in the shell of the hull, the necessary resistance to localized stresses; and jointly contribute to the overall strength of the vessel.

fray—To tear at the edges (sails) or untwist at the ends (ropes).

freeboard—The part of the ship "free" of the water, measured from the loaded waterline to the deck, excluding the superstructure. The old name was "quick works" in contradistinction to "dead works."

full-rigged ship—A three-masted ship with a full complement of sails, that is, a ship with ROYAL MASTS.

furl—To roll up a sail and secure it to its yard so that it will take up as little room as possible by means of the ropes provided known as GASKETS and ties.

futtock—One of the constituent parts of the rib of the old-fashioned wooden ship. They were four in number: 1st Futtock (ground futtock or floor timber) which secured the garboard STRAKES to the KEEL; the 2nd Futtock; 3rd (middle) Futtock; and 4th Futtock (top timber) which was supported internally by the deck BEAMS.

futtock-plate—Circular or semicircular platform set at the head of the lower mast of square-rigged ships and used both as a support for the topmast foot, and to provide additional purchase for the topmast SHROUDS, as well as a base for the seamen working aloft and even a lookout post. On modern ships the futtock-plate generally carries the radar scanner.

G—"Golf," sixth letter of the alphabet designated in the International Code by a square flag divided vertically into six stripes (from the jack): yellow, blue, yellow, blue, yellow, and blue. Hoisted in isolation it means: "I require a pilot."

gaff—A tapering spar, provided with JAWS at the thicker end which enable it to engage on the after side of the mast, to which is bent the LUFF of the gaff-sail. The gaff is hoisted by a HALYARD close to the jaws called the *throat-halyard* and its angle is controlled by the *peak-halyard* at the outer end. The *gaff-sail* has an irregular trapezoid shape, the head being laced to the gaff, the luff to the mast, and the foot to the boom. The gaff-TOPSAIL is a triangle or irregular trapezoid set above the gaff-sail with the luff bent to the mast and the foot to the gaff. This type of FORE-AND-AFT rig was carried by SCHOONERS and on the MIZZENmasts of square-rigged ships and then spread to those famous racing CUTTERS of the 19th century; but it has now fallen almost completely into disuse.

gammon—Gammoning is securing the BOWSPRIT by fastening it down with thick lashings.

gangway—Strictly speaking, this is that part of the BULWARKS of a vessel which can be removed to allow a plank or *gang-board* to be extended for passage of persons or goods from ship to ship or from ship to shore. It has, however, come to be applied to the board itself, and gangways are the platforms with handrails and wheels at one end used to land passengers and cargo when a vessel is moored alongside a quay.

garboard—The lowest part of the vessel. See STRAKES.

garland—A collar woven from rope of appropriate thickness and placed round the ANCHOR ring when the anchor-cable is of rope, not chain. The garland is used to prevent the cable from wearing on the anchor ring. Also a similar collar wound round the head of a mast to prevent the SHROUDS from galling.

gaskets—Short lengths of rope bent to the yards and used for securing square sails when they have been furled. They are also known as *ties* and *furling-lines*.

gear—All the working apparatus of a vessel, sails, rigging, cordage, navigational instruments, etc., or any part thereof, such as *steering gear*, etc.

genoa—A large jib-sail, which on modern racing yachts has an area greater than that of the mainsail. It is a fairly flat sail and normally has a foot 1.8 times longer than the base of the bow-triangle, that is to say, the triangle formed by the foredeck, mast, and forestay. Genoas are cut to different shapes and weights to suit different weather conditions.

gimbals—A system of ring mounting to prevent the pitching or rolling motion of a vessel from being imparted to such precision instruments as compass, barometer, or chronometer. The system is sometimes applied to the galley-stoves of yachts as well.

girth-bands—Also known as *belly-bands*, these are strips of canvas sewn across large sails to prevent them from bellying or stretching.

go about—Come round head to wind.

gooseneck—A method of securing a BOOM to a mast by means of a pin (called a "gooseneck") at the heel of the boom which fits ino a ring round the mast called a *shaffle*.

goosewing—Also known as *wing-and-wing*, this was a trim adopted by fore-and-aft rigged craft for running before the wind with the sail of one mast boomed out on one side of the vessel and the sail of the other boomed out on the other side.

grapnel—A small stockless anchor with three or (generally) four arms carried on small vessels. In the days of fighting sail it was fastened to a rope and thrown from the attacking vessel to hook on the enemy's bulwarks or rigging so that the two could be drawn and held together, thus allowing the attacker to send over a boarding party. It was an of equipment much used in the days when boarding was one of the regular tactics of naval warfare. The grapnels so used were known as *grappling irons*.

gratings—Wood or metal grilles used as DEADLIGHTS to cover ports and hatchways without stopping the circulation of air below decks. Similar wooden reticulataions are used as head-and stern SHEETS in open boats and are sometimes placed in the well of the COCKPIT.

grommet—A ring or loop made by splicing the end of a rope back upon itself.

ground—The seabed; "grounding" is when by accident or design the keel of a vessel comes in contact with the seabed.

GRP—Glass reinforced plastic, the material commonly used in the molding of the hulls and other parts of yachts and smaller craft.

gudgeons—Metal bands mounted either on the rudder or on the sternpost or on both to take the PINTLES.

guy—Rope or system of ropes which serves to keep the rigging in trim.

H—"Hotel," eighth letter of the alphabet designated in the International Code by a square flag divided vertically white to the jack and red to the FLY. Hoisted in isolation it means: "I have a pilot on board."

hall—A type of steel stockles ANCHOR.

halyard—As the name implies, a part of the running rigging which is used to raise or haul an object, particularly a sail. Halyards take their names from the sail on which they are employed and thus we have jib-halyards, mainsail-halyards, and, in the case of GAFF-sails, throat- and peak-halyards. A halyard is generally a TACKLE, and the part between the object being hauled and the block is called the *pendant* and the part between the block and the end hauled upon the *fall*.

hammocks—Swinging canvas sheets used as beds on board ship. In the days of fighting sail the crew rolled their hammocks each morning and stowed them in *hammock-nettings* along the BULWARKS where they afforded some protection against enemy musketry.

handy—Adjective applied to a vessel which handles well.

hanks—Metal or wooden rings or snap-hooks fitted to the foot of the sail by which it may be set on a stay. Hanks, for example, enable the jibs to be set on the jib-stays. Mainsails of modern yachts are fitted with hanks, or rather with metal slides which run on tracking fixed to the mast, or else slot into a groove in it allowing the mainsail to be bent in this way.

hardtack—The basic food of seamen in the days of sail. In damp or hot weather the biscuits bred weevils (hence their nickname, "weevils' delight"); they were not, however, thrown away but rebaked and then banged against some hard object to get rid of the weevils. This was generally done after dark to avoid the distasteful sight of the weevils dropping out. In distinction to biscuit, bread is known as *soft-tack*.

hatchway—An opening cut in the deck of a vessel to allow the loading or unloading of freight in or from the hold. Hatchways are equipped with wood, metal, or canvas covers called *hatches* with which they may be closed. Hatchways include the openings in the deck for the passage of passengers and crew as well as freight (*See also* COMPANION-WAY; PORT; SCUTTLE).

haul—To pull a rope, cable, or chain manually, as opposed to heaving it, when mechanical means are used. Such sailing terms as *close-hauling*, *hauling off* (sailing to windward to avoid something), or *hauling out of line* or *out of action* all imply the action of hauling on the SHEETS. The word however is more loosely used in the term *hauling up*, when a vessel is dragged out of the water and up a slipway by powerful electric winches for work on her hull.

hawse—This is the distance between the point in the water immediately above the anchor and the bows of the ship riding at that anchor. The anchor is, however, attached to the vessel by her CABLE; it emerges from either side of the bows of the vessel through the *hawse-holes* to which it is led by the *hawse-pipes*, short iron or steel tubes running downward from under the foredeck.

hawser—A vessel's mooring ropes and chains and WARPS. A rope is said to be *hawser-laid* when the three or four strands of which it is composed are twisted left-handed.

head—The upper part of any object. The head of a ship is the fore part. The head of the mast is that part of the mast upward from the HOUNDS; the head of the BOWSPRIT runs forward form the BITTS.

head-rope—The BOLT-ROPE at the head of the sail.

head-sheets—The flooring in the bows of an open boat.

heave—To pull a rope, cable, or chain with mechanical help. To *heave taut* is to pull any rope or chain as tight as it should be and is applied in particular to tightening the standing RIGGING—the SHROUDS and STAYS which support the masts.

heave-to—To bring a sailing vessel to a stop. This is done by bringing her head to the wind and bracing her yards so that she is taken ABACK.

heel—A tilting or inclining to one side of a vessel caused by the lateral pressure of the wind on the rigging. If she fails to right herself, she *heels over* on her beam-ends and may well capsize.

heel—The lower end of anything; thus the *heel of the mast* is the lower end of it.

heliograph—A signaling instrument which uses the rays of the sun reflected in a system of mirrors to transmit visual signals in Morse code. It is used by warships especially, when they do not wish to break radio silence for intercommunication over short distances.

helm—The steering apparatus of a vessel. To put the *helm hard over* is to turn it rapidly to the angle opposite to the one previously maintained, with the effect of stopping the forward motion of the vessel. A vessel which carries a *weather helm* is one with a tendency to come up to the wind, while one that carries a *lee helm* has a tendency to fall off from the wind of its own accord.

high seas—The open sea beyond the three-mile limit, a limit which in a happier age was all that nations claimed as their territorial waters.

hitch—Any of the twists and knots made in ropes which may be easily loosened. These hitches are made to mooring posts which keep a vessel alongside the quay while the anchor is being hoisted and the hawsers heaved in. The hitch can easily be freed and the rope hauled in without assistance from the shore. Such hitches are the running bowline (which does not loose under tension, but which unknots once the tension is relaxed) and the timber hitch used to fasten a rope to an upright.

hogging—The fall of the head and stern of a vessel due to a weakening of her keel caused by action of the sea.

hoist—To raise an object with or without mechanical aid. Signal flags are *hoisted* and the vertical length of the flag is termed the *hoist*.

hold—The space within a vessel where cargo is stowed: in shipbuilding *hold-beams* are the traverse beams which support the floor of the hold.

horse—A word with two meanings: (1) On square-riggers it was a rope (sometimes called the *foot-rope*) running below and behind the yards to provide a footing for seamen working her sails. It was attached to the yard by lengths of rope called *stirrups*. Their length could be adjusted so that the seamen standing on the horse could rest their chests on the yard and have both hands free to work the sails. (2) The horse was a piece of gear used on old-fashioned sailboats, an iron bar on which the sheet-tackle of a fore-and-aft sail could travel. On modern yachts it takes the form of metal tracking running athwart the deck just ahead of the cockpit or on the deck house roof on which runs a slide for the sheet-tackle, with the necessary SHEET-CLIPS to hold the sail in the required position.

hounds—The projections at the head of the mast (also called *cheeks*) which support the TRESTLE-TREES and to which the SHROUDS and STAYS are attached. The *hounding* is the portion of the mast below the hounds.

hour-glass—A sand or water-clock used in bygone days to regulate watches aboard ship.

hug—To keep close to: hug the wind or hug the coast, for example.

hull—The body of the vessel, excluding masts and rigging, upper works, etc. The LINES of the *wetted surface*, that is, the portion of the hull below the waterline, determine the qualities and performance of the vessel, its buoyancy, lateral and longitudinal stability, its resistance, behavior in heavy seas, and potential speed.

hydrofoil—The name now given to the whole of a special type of boat equipped with hydrofoils—open, V-shaped planes or wings—fitted below the bows and stern. The thrust of the vessel's seaward acceleration is

sufficient to lift the hull from the water and she planes on her wings or hydrofoils. They support her with hydrodynamic thrust, not hydrostatic balance.

hydrojet—A system of jet propulsion applied to outboard and inboard engines using the thrust of water sucked into the engine from ahead and below the boat and expelled at high pressure astern.

hydroplane—Another name for HYDROFOIL.

I—"Indo," ninth letter of the alphabet, designated in the International Code by a square yellow flag with a black ball in the center. Hoisted in isolation it means: "I am directing my course to port".

International Code—The code of signals regulating all visual, voice, radiotelephonic, or radiotelegraphic signals from ship to ship or from ship to shore of whatever nationality they may be.

J—"Juliet," tenth letter of the alphabet, designated in the International Code by a square flag divided horizontally into three stripes, blue, white, blue. Hoisted in isolation it means: "I am going to send a message by semaphore."

jack—The jack-staff is the pole upon which the ENSIGN is hoisted.

jack-stay—Metal bar passing along the rear of a yard to provide a hold for seamen working aloft.

jaw—The metal horns fitted to the end of a BOOM so that it can engage upon the mast and swivel upon it both horizontally and vertically.

jib—The *jib boom* is a wooden spar used to lengthen the BOWSPRIT to which the fore-TOP-GALLANT stay is attached, the BOBSTAY being secured to the bowsprit. The *flying-jib-boom* is a further extension of the jib boom to which the fore-ROYAL stay is secured. *Jib-sails* are the sails bent to the FOREMAST stays (sails carried on the stays of other masts being known as STAY-SAILS), the *flying-jib* to the fore-royal stay, the *middle-jib* to the fore-top-gallant stay, and the *inner-jib* to the TOPMAST stay. The forestay sail is set on the stay running between the stem-head and the HOUNDS on the lowest section of the mast. The sails themselves are triangular, the corner at the head of

the sail to which the HALYARD is attached being known as the PEAK, while of the two lower corners, the foremost is called the TACK, the aftermost, to which the SHEETS will be attached, the CLEW. The "hypotenuse," that is, the leading edge of the sail generally strengthened by a wire rope sheathed along the edge, is called the LUFF and usually has the HANKS which will secure it to the stay already fitted. The after edge is called the LEECH and the bottom the FOOT of the sail. Jibs are made from cloths of varying cuts and sizes and can have varying shapes. Two sheets are attached to the clew, one for either side of the vessel. Jibs are used when RUNNING to supplement the main sails and to counteract their tendency to bring the vessel into the wind when REACHING. On modern yachts jibs are given various names according to their shape and the material from which they are made; thus we have the "Bolero," "Drifter," GENOA, "Reacher," "Spanker," TALL-BOY, "Yankee," etc.

jibe—The (violent) swing of the boom from one side of the vessel to the other when running before the wind due to the variation of the angle of the wind to the course of the vessel. A jibe may be a deliberate maneuver or may be caused by a shift of the wind or the helm unnoticed by the helmsman. In the latter case it may sometimes be so violent as to dismast the vessel concerned.

jigger—An extra mast fitted to some types of small craft which can be taken down. At the head it carries a tackle for the HALYARDS and the sail is usually FORE-AND-AFT. The name is also given to the fourth mast (from bow to stern) of four- and five-masted ships to which fore-and-aft sails are set in contrast with the square sails carried on the other masts.

jumper—The highest sail of a square-rigged ship very exceptionally set above the ROYALS and MOONRAKERS.

jury rig—Term applied to all items of rig of a temporary nature used to take the place of damaged gear, such as a *jury-mast* or *jury-rudder* rigged when the permanent mast or rudder has been carried away by stress of weather or other damage.

K—"Kilo," eleventh letter of the alphabet, designated in the International Code by a square flag divided vertically into two

halves, the yellow half nearest the JACK, the blue nearest the FLY. Hoisted in isolation it means: "You should stop your vessel instantly."

kedge—Small anchor carried by yachts. On ships it is used in conjunction with the main anchor.

keel—The main timber of a vessel running along the bottom with stem- and stern-posts at either end and, like a backbone, supporting the ribs. In wooden ships, if the length allows, the keel is made of a single timber, otherwise of several pieces of the right size joined the one to the other according to various systems. The keel of a yacht is a *false-keel*, attached to and descending below the true keel. Its purpose is to provide stability and to counteract LEEWAY, keeping the vessel on course. Such keels are of various shapes, such as the *fin-keel*, and may be single (mounted centrally) or double. When they carry the ballast at the foot they are known as BALLAST-KEELS. A similar purpose is served by the movable keel of a DINGHY called the *centerboard*, which can be raised into a housing in the boat and dropped through a slot cut in the keel. A somewhat similar arrangement applied to yachts is called a *drop-keel*.

keel-hauling—A punishment much inflicted in the old sailing navy which involves dropping the culprit from the yardarm on one side of the ship, dragging him under the keel, and hauling him up again on the other side.

keelson—A square-section timber in wooden ships running along the upper face of the keel so as to protect it from shock and damage.

ketch—A classification of contemporary racing and cruising yachts. They carry two masts, the mainmast being forward and the MIZZEN slightly ahead of the STERN-POST with BERMUDA sails and jibs. Historically, ketches were small, two-masted coasting vessels with a wide variety of rigs mixing square and fore-and-aft sails.

knees—Term used in shipbuilding to describe the wooden or metal angled members used to connect the beams with the sides of a vessel.

knightheads—In shipbuilding the name given to the two posts on either side of the STEM-POST between which the BOWSPRIT runs.

knot—The unit by which the speed of a vessel is measured; it equals the number of nautical MILES traveled in one hour. Thus a vessel sailing at six knots covers six nautical miles in one hour.

L—"Lima," twelfth letter of the alphabet, designated in the International Code by a square flag quartered black and yellow, the upper quarter at the FLY being black and the lower yellow. Hoisted in isolation it means: "You should stop: I have something important to communicate."

lacing—Thin rope for "lacing," that is attaching, a sail to a boom, yard, or stay.

lanyards—Short pieces of rope used particularly for making the SHROUDS taut at the DEADEYES.

lashing—Length of rope or chain used to secure any movable object on board ship in a predetermined position. Lashings may be provided with expanding springs or snap-hooks.

lateen—A type of triangular sail, developed in the Mediterranean area, of which the LUFF, or leading edge, is bent to a long yard.

launch—Originally a square-sterned boat, some 30 to 36 feet long, propelled by eight or ten oars; nowadays, however, a fairly large motorboat, for river or harbor work, or else a large motor lifeboat or ship's boat carried on merchant vessels.

lay—The *lay of a rope* is the direction in which the threads, strands, or yarns are twisted, as CABLE-LAID.

lay up—To lay up a vessel is to prepare it for a period when it will not be used and involves either total or partial removal of rigging, gear, and internal fittings. When pleasure boats are laid up at the end of the season the procedure will involve, HAULING up the vessel, unshipping the mast, stowing the sails, cleaning down the deck, hull, and rigging to prevent corrosion, coiling and stowing all ropes, stripping the auxiliary engine (if any), etc.

lead—A lead weight at the end of a line used to discover the depth of water (measured by the amount of line used) and the nature of the ground below the vessel ascertained by a sample (sand, mud, etc.) brought up in the cup hollowed in the lead itself for that purpose.

lee—This term designates the side of a vessel and the area beyond, which is away from the direction from which the wind is blowing, the latter being particularly important in relation to the rule of the road at sea and to rules governing sail racing which concern vessels crossing one another's tracks.

leech—The leeward edge of a sail. With GAFF or triangular sails it will always be the edge which is not attached to the mast or stay; with square sails it will alter since it will be the side away from the direction from which the wind is blowing.

leech-lines—Ropes running from the CLEW of a square sail to its YARD.

leeway—The lateral movement of a vessel through the water caused by the action of the wind. It should not be confused with DRIFT, an identical motion, but caused by the action of waves, tide, or current.

length—The measurement of a vessel on her longitudinal axis. *Length overall* is the length measured along a line between the two most distant extremities of her hull. *Waterline length* is the length along the vessel's loaded waterline. *Length between perpendiculars* is the distance between two lines drawn perpendicularly from the waterline to the inner faces of the STEM- and STERN-POSTS of a vessel.

lie to—To remain without motion when under sail.

lifeboat—All merchant ships, passenger liners, and freighters alike, are compelled by law to carry enough lifeboats to hold the full ship's complement of passengers and crew. They should be unsinkable and equipped with engine, oars, or mast and sail.

life-jacket—A development of the *life-belt*, a ring of a buoyant material such as cork, was the horse-shoe of the same substance designed to keep its wearer's head and chest above water, with a line to attach him to the vessel and a light to assist his recovery. Most modern life-jackets are of the self-inflating "Mae West" type.

life-line—Safety device used on racing and cruising yachts in rough weather so that the normal operations of boat-handling can be carried out on deck without danger. It comprises a belt with two shoulder-straps made of leather or man-made fiber

fitted with a stout rope, at the other end of which is a snap-hook. The latter may be secured to some firm piece of rigging or boat, allowing the person at the end of the life-line to move around on deck and to be hauled back on the vessel should he be washed overboard.

life-raft—Originally a float made of any buoyant material to provide immediate succor to persons in the water. Nowadays made of rubber with a self-inflating device, which goes into action when the raft is thrown into the water, and often provided with a protective hood as well.

lighter—Flat-bottomed, powered steel barge used for harbor duties and the carriage of cargo, fuel-oil, water, or refuse.

line—A small rope.

lines—An exceedingly common word in different maritime contexts. A *line* is a small rope; a *shipping line* is a shipping company, which includes personnel ships and shore installations and service. The *line of battle* was the fighting formation of warships, first employed in the latter part of the 17th century, in which all steered on the same course and in the same alignment; in *line abreast*, side by side, in *line ahead*, in front of, or in *line astern*, behind the flagship.

More important is the use of the word in naval architecture where the shape of a vessel's hull is indicated by her lines, the *lines of flotation* or *waterlines* and the *buttock line* which shows the convexity of the stern.

lining—Canvas strengthening stitched to those parts of the sail subject to the greatest strains.

link—Constituent of a chain. *Open link*, an elongated ring, *closed link*, an oval ring, and *stud-link*, an oval ring with a supporting crossbar, are all employed. The *end ring* is a circular metal ring set at the end of the chain to take the anchor SHACKLE.

loaded weight—In reference to a merchant ship this is the weight in tons of the freight, passengers, their baggage, and of the provisions, as well as of the crew and its gear.

load-lines—Lines marked on the side of the vessel to indicate the loaded waterline. They vary according to the ocean in which the ship operates and summer and winter. Clearly the Atlantic

winter load-line will permit of far less freight being carried than the tropical summer load-line of the same vessel.

locker—Storage space on board ship for stores and equipment. The most important is the *chain-locker*, the hold in the bows of a ship in which the anchor-cable is stored. Small sailboats also keep their anchors there. Their other lockers can be found under the floor of the COCKPIT or below the bunks in the cabin, or in other suitable locations.

log—Instrument used to measure the speed of a vessel. Originally a log or piece of wood thrown overboard on the end of a line knotted at fixed distances along its length (hence KNOT), their recurrence being timed as the line was paid out over the stern, it developed into more or less sophisticated devices incorporating a screw rotated by the waterflow past the hull and a recording device. Since the readings from the old *log-line* were recorded in a book, the word *log-book* is used for the document in which all the day-to-day details of a vessel's voyage are recorded. Log-books are also kept for the engine-room and wireless-room.

long-boat—The largest of the ship's boats carried in the days of sail.

loof—Both sides of a vessel's FREEBOARD curving in toward the prow.

loom—The part of the oar between the handle, or grip, and the blade.

lubber's hole—The aperture in the FUTTOCK-PLATE by which access may be gained to the TOPMAST from the SHROUDS.

luff—*The luff* of the sail is the weather edge, that is, the edge in the direction from which the wind is blowing. With square sails it obviously varies, but with FORE-AND-AFT sails it is always the edge which is bent to the mast or stay. The fact that the luff is the weather side explains why *to luff* is to bring a vessel's head closer to the wind.

lug—A four-sided sail bent, not to the mast, but to a yard which hangs from it.

lull—A drop in the wind and waves even for a brief period. Sometimes the prelude to a more intense storm.

M—"Mike," thirteenth letter of the alphabet, designated in the

International Code by a square flag bearing a white saltire (St. Andrew's cross) on a blue ground. Hoisted in isolation it means: "I have a doctor on board."

mainmast—On three-masted vessels it is the central and highest mast. On two-masted vessels the position of the mast varies with the type of vessel. On BRIGS and SCHOONERS, for example, it is the sternmost mast, while on ketches it is the foremost. It gives its name to the SHROUDS and STAYS which support it (and to the sail the latter carries) and to the yard and sail which it carries. It also gives its name to the masts and rigging which it supports, that is to the main TOPMAST, main TOP-GALLANT mast and main ROYAL MAST (*see* MAST).

mainsail—The sail carried on the MAINMAST, known on square-rigged ships as the main-COURSE.

man-ropes—Wire or hemp rope covered with canvas and used as a hand rail on boarding ladders. Also applied to ropes used in climbing the ship's side or her hatchways and to those used for support when working on the yards, etc.

marina—Modern name given to a harbor for yachts and pleasure craft with moorings, slipway, stores for the purchase of food and fuel, and facilities for maintenance and repair.

maritime law—The body of law which regulates seafaring and seafarers. Maritime law is characterized by being essentially case-law, by its close interconnection of public with private law and by its uniformity throughout the world.

marline—Small line composed of two strands loosely twisted. It is used for various tasks, particularly PARCELING, and for securing the BOLT-ROPES of large sails

marline-spike—A pointed instrument of wood or metal used to unpick the strands of rope when splicing.

martingale—A rope running from the end of the JIB BOOM to the DOLPHIN-STRIKER, staying the former as the BOBSTAY supports the BOWSPRIT.

mast—On sailing boats the upright, either fashioned from a single piece or a number of pieces joined together, which carries the yards or booms from which the sails are suspended. On

power-driven ships they support the cargo-derricks and carry signaling and navigational equipment (wireless masts, radar scanners, etc.). The parts of the mast of a sailing vessel are as follows: the HEEL is fitted into the STEP on the keelson. The portion of the mast below decks, enclosed in the *mast-case*, is called the *housing*. It is supported as it emerges from the deck by the PARTNERS. The length of the mast from the deck to the HOUNDS is known as *the hounding* and from the hounds to the cap as the *mast-head*. Collectively this is termed "the mast" (qualified by its position as FOREMAST, MAINMAST, MIZ-ZEN mast, etc.) and further pieces may be added in succession, TOPMAST, TOP-GALLANT mast and ROYAL MAST, each qualified in the same way as the mast itself. These separate pieces are attached to the mast below by a system using CAP, YOKE, FID, TRESTLE-TREES, and cheeks. The masts are maintained in their upright position by a system of lateral supports called SHROUDS and longitudinal supports called STAYS and BACK-STAYS. These items of standing RIGGING are qualified by the masts which they support.

messenger—A small rope used to haul in a cable too large for the capstan drum.

mile—The nautical mile, the unit by which distance at sea is measured, varies slightly from country to country. The Nautical Mile (also known as the Geographical or Air Mile), adopted by Great Britain, Eire, Canada, Argentina, and other countries, is calculated as one-sixtieth of a degree on the earth's equator and equals 6,080 feet or 1,853.18 meters; the United States Nautical Mile equals 6,080.27 feet or 1,853.248 meters; and the International Nautical Mile equals 6,076.103 feet or 1,852 meters, established by the International Hydrographic Conference of 1929 and adopted by most countries, including Italy.

mizzen—The aftermost mast of a three-masted ship, the third mast (from bow to stern) of four- and five-masted ships, and the aftermost mast of two-masted vessels such as KETCHES, but not of BRIGS and SCHOONERS (if two-masted). It qualifies the pieces of mast which it carries and their standing and running RIGGING and the yards and sails they carry.

moderate—A gale is said to moderate when it begins to die down.

mold—To make a drawing of the parts of a given vessel in their actual size for the builder.

moon-rakers—Square sails occasionally set above the SKY-SAILS.

moor—To moor is to hold a ship in a fixed position in a harbor or anchorage by one or more devices designed to prevent the wind or tide from moving her. A ship may be moored by dropping one or more anchors, or by shackling her anchor-cable to a buoy, or by bitting her cable or hawsers either to the bollards or to the mooring rings set in the quayside or to another ship which is already moored. In this event, if the ship is sideways to the quay or to the other ship she is said to *moor alongside*.

mooring ring—A metal ring set in the quayside to which a vessel secures her HAWSER.

moorings—The BUOY or DEAD-HEAD to which a ship ties or the ground over which she lies at anchor. The area of quayside at which she moors is generally known as her BERTH.

N—"November," fourteenth letter of the alphabet, designated in the International Code by a square flag checkered blue and white with 16 squares, the upper line of them running blue, white, blue, white to the FLY. Hoisted in isolation it means: "No (negative)."

nock—The upper corner at the LUFF of a GAFF-sail.

O—"Oscar," fifteenth letter of the alphabet, designated in the International Code by a square flag divided diagonally, the upper half being red, the lower half yellow, with the division running downward from the JACK to the FLY. Hoisted in isolation it means: "Man overboard."

oakum—The pickings of hemp rope used to CAULK the seams of wooden vessels.

oilskins—Waterproofed or plastic clothing worn by seamen when on deck in wet or rough weather. The name derives from the fact that such protective clothing was originally produced by steeping the garments in linseed-oil.

outboard motor—Engine of which the driving shaft does not pass through any part of the vessel's hull.

overhaul—See CHOCK-A-BLOCK.

P—"Papa," sixteenth letter of the alphabet, designated in the International Code by a square blue flag with a white oblong in the center. Hoisted in isolation it means: (*in harbor*) "All persons are to repair on board as the vessel is about to proceed to sea." (*at sea*) "Your lights are out *or* burning badly."

painter—The rope or ropes attached to the bows or stern of an open boat and used to moor it.

palm—The device used in sailmaking to protect the thumb and palm of the hand when driving the needle through canvas.

parceling—See SERVE.

parrel—A length of rope on which are strung hard wooden beads known as *trucks*. Extending from the ends of the JAWS of a GAFF or BOOM, so that together they encircle the mast, the parrel enables the gaff or boom to traverse freely without excessive friction on the mast. On old square-riggers the system of *rib and truck parrels* was used to TRAVERSE the yards. Short strings of trucks were held vertically between ribs or narrow battens secured to the yard so as to embrace the mast.

partners—The stout casing supporting the MAST where it emerges from the deck.

pawl—Metal stop or catch which acts on the rack-wheel of a capstan to stop it from running back.

pay out—To loose or slacken a rope or cable (*pay away* can be used in this sense) with the particular sense of letting it go slowly, bit by bit and under control.

peak—The upper end of a GAFF and the upper corner of a gaff-sail. It is also the name given to the upper end of the triangular BERMUDA SAIL to which the HALYARD is stitched. *To peak a yard* is to raise one end of it above the horizontal.

pilot—Originally the pilot was the officer embarked on board ship to take charge of the helm and be responsible for steering her on both coasting voyages and ocean passages. However, the meaning of the word has long been confined to the officer (he must carry a master's TICK-ET) with first-rate local knowledge of ports, rivers, canals, straits, and shoals needed to take vessels in and out and through them.

pin—The axle of a BLOCK.

266

pinrack—A stout frame securely fixed to the deck around or forward of each mast of a sailing vessel and designed to take the strain of the greater part of the running RIGGING of each mast by which it was qualified, as *fore-pinrack*, etc. Naturally it was provided with a proper complement of CLEATS, BLOCKS, and FAIRLEADS.

pitch—One of the six motions to which a vessel may be subjected; it is an oscillation in the vertical and horizontal plane with the alternate dipping of bow and stern in the water.

planksheer—The outermost deck plank, that is, the plank running along the side of the vessel.

plug—Also called the *bung*, this is the stopper for the hole cut in the bottom of an open boat to allow any water shipped to drain out when the boat is beached or hauled out.

poop—The after part of a vessel, or more precisely an extra deck there.

port—The left-hand side of a vessel when facing toward the bows.

ports *or* **portholes**—Openings in the sides of vessels, such as the *gun-ports* of sailing warships or the ports, equipped with watertight doors, in the sides of vessels above the waterline to allow the embarking and disembarking of passengers and freight. *Portholes* are the traditional round openings cut in the ship's side and superstructure to provide light and fresh air to the cabins. They are closed by thick glass lights in solid brass rims with screws to shut them tight and often a metal DEADLIGHT as well for safety during rough weather.

pram—DINGHY with square bow section carried on board yachts and used as a ship's boat. Driven by oars, sail, or outboard motor, it is a small dinghy of Norwegian origin.

preventer—An extra rope to support another rope, as for example a *preventer brace* or a *preventer sheet.*

puddening—A ring or wreath of rope or oakum set round the mast to support a yard, or round some piece of rigging particularly subject to friction to prevent wear.

purchase—*To purchase* is to raise a weight, hence the name applied to the TACKLE employed for the task.

Q—"Quebec," seventeenth letter of the alphabet, designated in the International Code by a square yellow flag. Hoisted in isolation it means: "My vessel is healthy and I request free pratique."

quarter-deck—The raised deck running from the stern of a sailing vessel to her MIZZENmast, raised above the level of her main deck, and, as the name implies, housing the officers' accommodation.

quarters—A vessel's quarters are the portions of her sides midway between the stern and beam.

quick works—The part of a vessel's hull immersed in the water when she is fully loaded.

R—"Romeo," eighteenth letter of the alphabet, designated in the International Code by a square flag with a yellow cross on a red ground. Hoisted in isolation it means: "The way is off my ship: you may feel your way past me."

rabbet—The triangular grooving cut in one piece of timber to receive the edge of another piece of timber.

railings—Run round the edge of the main deck and of any open upper or lower decks of vessels. They may form a solid metal or wooden parapet or be composed of STANCHIONS, upright metal tubes, linked by one or more levels of chain or wire rope.

rake—*The rake* of the bows is their angle to the water. A vessel with raking bows is one whose bows cut the water at a pronounced angle.

range—*To range* the CABLE is to lay it out before dropping anchor to ensure that it runs freely. The term is applied to all ropes prepared for use in this way. The *cruising range* of a powered vessel is the distance which it will travel at a given speed without replenishing its fuel supplies.

rate—A vessel is *rated* for insurance purposes when she is judged impartially on fixed criteria by an expert who pronounces on the technical efficiency and the degree of confidence which may be reposed in her seaworthiness. Similarly yachts are rated for racing purposes, these *ratings* being based on different formulae to produce handicaps for different events.

ratlines—Lengths of tarred

rope, or occasionally metal bars, fixed horizontally and at short intervals to the SHROUDS so as to form a ladder enabling the seamen to go aloft with great speed.

reaching—Sailing with the wind on, but slightly ahead of the beam. When the angle of the wind to the vessel's course is broad, she may be said to be *broad reaching*, as the angle narrows, the vessel is *close reaching*, until she is sailing CLOSE-HAULED.

reef—To reef is to take in a portion of a sail so as to reduce the area exposed to the wind. Square sails are reefed at the head by gathering them up under the yard. GAFF-sails are reefed at the foot, round the boom, and jib and stay-sails are also reefed at the foot. LATEEN sails are reefed to the yard. The portion of the sail to be reefed is confined by *reef-points*, short lengths of rope, which on the triangular BERMUDA SAIL are often attached in pairs to the *reef-eyes*, the holes in the *reef-bands*, strips of canvas stitched across the BUNT of the sail for the purpose and for reinforcement. In this case, when reefing, the sail is lowered and the portion to be reefed is wrapped round the boom and secured by reef-pendants passing through the *reef-cringles* on the LEECH of the sail, as when reefing a gaff-sail.

reef-knot—Knot used for joining two lengths of rope.

reeve—*To reeve* is to pass anything through a hole or aperture; thus to *reeve a block* is to pass a rope through it, while to *reeve a tackle* is to prepare it for use by reeving the blocks which comprise it.
Reeving also means opening the seams of a wooden vessel for CAULKING which is done with special *reeving-irons*. The largest hammer or mallet used by caulkers is known as a *reeving-beetle.*

refloat—To free a vessel from the bottom on which she has grounded. How this is done depends upon the means available, the nature of the ground, the state of the sea, the type and size of vessel, and the state of her hull, etc.

registration—All vessels are registered with the country whose flag they fly, which issues the certificate of seaworthiness which allows them to operate.

retire—Yachts signal their re-

tirement from a race by hoisting their national ENSIGN at the stern.

ribs—The timbers which shape the hull. In large wooden ships they are composed of several pieces called FUTTOCKS.

ride—*To ride* is to lie at anchor. When doing so the vessel will, at night, show the appropriate *riding-lights.*

rig—See FORE-AND-AFT and SQUARE-RIGGED.

rigging—All the ropes, of wire, natural and man-made fiber, which support the masts and yards of a sailing vessel and which are used to work her sails. In this sense *upper rigging* is applied to the cordage of the topmasts and *lower rigging* to that of the lower masts. However, the fundamental division is into *running rigging* and *standing rigging*. When any rope is used to brace, hoist, lower or strike, haul or reef, it is part of the running rigging; such are the sheets to trim the sail, the halyards to hoist it, the braces which support the yards, the clew-lines, preventers (*qq v*), etc. Standing rigging, on the other hand, is all those ropes, usually wire-ropes, which are used to support the masts, such as the shrouds, stays, backstays, and martingale (*qq v*).

rigging-screw—Metal device used to tighten standing rigging as desired. The rigging-screw, which replaced the use of DEADEYES employed on the old square-riggers, comprises a hollow cylindrical body, threaded at both ends and made of stainless steel or chromium-plated bronze, into which two bolts screw. The bolts, with left-hand and right-hand threads to match the ends of the central body, have rings on their ends. By turning the body in one direction or the other the length of the whole can be altered, and since it is attached to the standing rigging the latter may be tightened or slackened as required.

ring-tail—See STUDDING-SAILS.

rivet—A metal pin clenched at both ends and used when hot to join the plates of a steel ship. This process has been superseded largely by welding.

roach—The curve in the foot and sides of a square sail.

rocket apparatus—The equipment, ranging from a hand-held pistol to a mortar, which when the distance is more than throwing-range projects from shore to ship or from ship to ship a rocket to which is attached a light line acting as a MESSENGER to a heavier rope. This allows first contact to be made and the heavier warp to be passed for mooring, salvage, towing, sending men or supplies across, or lifesaving operations.

rolling—The oscillation of a vessel in the lateral plane.

rope—Technically, cordage of more than one inch in circumference. It can be made of such natural fibers as hemp, manila (fiber of wild bananas); or coir (coconut husks); or of steel or galvanized iron wires. Nowadays such synthetic fibres as nylon and DACRON are being widely used in rope-making.

rope-guard—The ring of oil-impregnated rope or rags which prevents water from seeping into the tunnel where the propeller shaft extrudes from the stern of a vessel.

roundhouse—Cabin roof emerging above deck and neither so long nor so broad as the deck from which it emerges.

rowlocks—Metal forks or pins set in the gunwales of a rowing boat which act as the fulcrums for the oars which propel her.

royal mast—The uppermost of the four pieces or masts which compose the mast of a full square-rigged ship. It is qualified by its position, i.e., FORE-, MAIN-, or MIZZEN-royal-mast, and in turn qualifies all the rigging, yards, and sails which it carries. Above the *royal-sails* the mast carries the SKY-SAILS and vary occasionally MOON-RAKERS and JUMPERS.

rubbing strake—See WALES.

rudder-chains—The ropes or chains which transmit the movements of a vessel's helm or wheel to the rudder, causing the blade to move in the required direction.

rudder-pintles—The pins attached to the stern of the vessel and to the rudder which engage in the GUDGEONS with which each is provided and enable the rudder to turn freely.

run—*To run* is to sail with the wind astern, from abaft of the beam to dead astern, when the vessel is said to be *running before the wind*. A vessel may also *run* for safety from storms and other dangers to some port or other refuge. The *run* of a vessel is also its uninterrupted

motion through the water, and a *run* is the distance traveled or *run* by a vessel during a given period of time.

runners—See SINGLE-WHIP.

running bowline—A special knot which resists tension but is easily untied when that tension is relaxed.

S—"Sierra," nineteenth letter of the alphabet, designated in the International Code by a square white flag with a blue oblong in the center. Hoisted in isolation, it means: "My engine is going full astern."

saddle—The rest for any BOOM or SPAR, such as a ring or bracket on a mast, etc.

sagging—The opposite of HOGGING and therefore the tendency of the KEEL to droop in the middle.

sail—The *sail-plan* of a vessel is the total number of sails carried and the manner in which they are set. To *reduce sail* or *take in sail* is to reduce the sail-area by REEFING or STRIKING some of the sails.

sailmaker's needle—The thick needle used in conjunction with the PALM to stitch the canvas of the sails.

sail-trimmer—The name once given on board sailing vessels to the seamen who worked aloft.

samson-post—A metal or stout wooden post which supports the DERRICK-boom.

saxboard—The uppermost STRAKE in an open boat.

schooner—A FORE-AND-AFT rigged sailing vessel of from two to four masts. The two-masted schooner carries fore- and mainmasts (unlike the KETCH). A *topsail-schooner* is fore-and-aft rigged on her mainmast and her foresail, but carries square TOPSAILS on her foremast.

scoop—See BALER.

scotchman—Piece of wood or metal placed over those parts of a yard or mast which show signs of cracking. Similar pieces of wood or stiff leather are attached to standing RIGGING to prevent chafing on metal parts.

screw-race—The framework within which the main propeller of a screw-driven ship is lodged.

scroll-work—The carving, often

gilded, which adorned the sterns of old-time sailing vessels.

scud—To RUN before a gale or tempest under BAREPOLES.

scull—To propel a small boat with a pair of oars, A boat may also be sculled with a single oar over the stern. The loom of the oar engages in a recess in the TRANSOM and a rotary movement of the blade propels the boat.

scuppers—Apertures in the BULWARKS to carry off the deck water.

scuttle—Any hole cut in the side or deck of a vessel; from the verb *to scuttle*, that is, to cut a hole. Thus to *scuttle a ship* is quite literally to sink her by cutting a hole in her bottom. Scuttles are generally comparatively small PORTS provided with covers.

seize—To secure, that is, to bind together, two ropes or different parts of the same rope with a thinner rope or line which is called *seizing*.

self-steering gear—Broadly speaking this comprises a vane mounted over the stern of a yacht that acts independently or with the assistance of an electric motor either directly upon the vessel's rudder or indirectly through a tab fixed to it via a system of gears and shafts. When a particular course has been set, the gear is "locked on" to the rudder. Any change in the direction of the wind will be felt by the vane and transmitted to the rudder which will automatically adjust to keep the vessel on course. Self-steering gear is carried by all SINGLE-HANDERS and enables them to sleep, prepare and eat meals, and carry out all other duties below decks without the constant need to come up on deck to adjust the helm, for the vessel steers herself. The principle was rediscovered by Sir Francis Chichester, who designed and built his *Miranda* gear, and has been subsequently refined and improved. In fact, in the days of sail, fishing boats shipped a small mast and sail on the rudder for precisely the same purpose—to keep their vessel on course while all hands went about their fishing duties.

serve—To bind or cover anything. *To serve a rope* is to complete the last process in *worming, parceling,* and *serving,* a method of protecting rope liable to chafing. First the *worms*, thin strands of rope, were inserted

between the strands of the rope to be served; next they were *parceled*, that is to say, a strip of tarred canvas was wrapped round the worming; finally the rope was served when the whole was bound tightly with thin rope or yarn.

shackle—A U-shaped metal link with one end open and drilled to allow a pin to pass through and close it. Shackles are used to join lengths of chain (*see* ANCHOR shackles) and small shackles are used for a variety of purposes by yachtsmen. The word is both noun and verb.

shank-painters—Two lengths of chain attached to the sides or deck of a vessel below the CAT-tackle and employed to secure the shank of an ANCHOR on the BILL-BOARD after it has been catted and FISHED.

sheave—The wheel of a BLOCK.

sheepshank—The name of a knot used to shorten a rope without cutting it.

sheer—When a vessel is viewed from the side, the line of the deck from bow to stern can describe a curve called the *sheer*. If it does not curve it is known as a *straight sheer*.

sheer-legs—Stout beams used as a makeshift crane for hoisting heavy weights.

sheer-strakes—The line of planks immediately below the *sheer* along the side of a vessel (*see also* STRAKE).

sheet—Rope attached to the CLEW of a sail and used to work it according to the direction of the wind. It is therefore part of the running RIGGING.

sheet-clips—Yacht fittings which take the place of CLEATS and either hold the sheet until released, or else, by use of PAWLS, allow the sheet to run in one direction but prevent it from running back in the other.

sheet-home—To haul in a sheet as taut as possible and BELAY it, as when sailing CLOSE-HAULED.

shells—The sides of a BLOCK in which the SHEAVES revolve on their PINS.

ship—A broad term used to indicate a large vessel whether sail- or engine-powered. Strictly speaking a ship is a FULL-RIGGED ship. *To ship* has the sense of to prepare for sea, such as *shipping oars, shipping the rudder,* etc., while to *ship a cargo* is to get it on board.

shipping forecast—Radio transmissions from the different Weather Bureaus and Meteorological Offices advising shipping of weather conditions and in particular warning navigation of the imminence of storms and gales.

ship's boat—Any smaller boat carried on another vessel for whatever purpose, from the PRAM or rubber dinghy of a yacht to a ship's LAUNCH.

ship's papers—The whole range of documents and certificates carried on board a ship, including bills of lading and cargo manifests, musters of the ship's company, passenger lists, and the LOGS of the engine-room, wireless-room, etc.

ship's stores—Food, water, fuel, spares, etc., required on a voyage.

shipwright—The skilled craftsman employed in shipbuilding.

shiver—The reaction of the sails when the wind is taken out of them. An action preparatory to FURLING or STRIKING the sails.

shroud-plates—Plates fitted to the sides of smaller sailboats that perform the function of CHANNELS.

shrouds—A basic item of the standing RIGGING since they provide the lateral supports to the masts from which they take their name, e.g., FORE-, MAIN-, and MIZZENmast shrouds. These names apply to the lower masts. The shrouds of the upper masts have the additional qualification of *topmast-shrouds*.

side-ladder—Portable rope-ladder let down over the side of a vessel or from a davit on her deck.

signal flags—These are used, particularly by warships, to transmit visual signals and are regulated by the International Code. *See pages 162–163.*

single-hander—A yachtsman who sails single-handed. Since World War II single-handed sailing has enjoyed a great vogue and produced some very notable practitioners. Single-handed races have been organized round the world and across the Pacific, but perhaps the most famous of all are the Transatlantic Single-handed Races, originally organized by the London newspaper *The Observer* and held every four years from 1960 onward.

single-whip—System employed to hoist weights whereby a rope is attached to one end and passes through the SHEAVES of a BLOCK which is itself attached to the weight (*see also* WHIP).

skeg—A timber that connects the keel and the stern-post of a ship.

skipper—The master of a merchant ship and whoever is in charge of a racing or cruising yacht.

skylight—Wooden framework provided with glass lights set at an angle to allow rainwater and seawater to drain off and which can be opened and shut, used to cover an aperture in the deck and to allow light and air below. Old-fashioned skylights are very stout and strengthened with metal grilles. It is sound practice for skylights in the bows of smaller vessels to be opened only against the wind.

sky-sails—In general terms the topmost sails of a SQUARE-RIGGED ship (occasionally MOON-RAKERS and JUMPERS were set above them). Set on the ROYALMAST above the royal-sails, they take their name from the mast on which they are carried, e.g., FORE-, MAIN-, MIZZEN-sky-sails.

slack—The length of a rope or chain in excess of that required to perform its duty, that is, the loose part. Hence the slack must be taken in before that duty can be performed, or the rope or chain must be *slacked away* when it is no longer required to perform it.

sling—The ropes, chains, canvas or leather bands in their entirety which are swathed round or under an object preparatory to hoisting it. Netting is used for the same purpose so that an object may be hung, hoisted, or supported and still retain a certain amount of freedom.

slip—To let go a rope or cable purposely.

smoke-flare—Comprises a small quantity of calcium carbide which, on contact with water, emits flame and a considerable quantity of smoke. In case of shipwreck it helps rescuers to pinpoint the person or persons to be saved, and such flares are therefore carried on LIFE-JACKETS, life-rafts, and life-boats.

snarled—A rope or chain becomes *snarled* when it tangles and twists and will not run freely.

snatch-block—Special block with a single SHEAVE, which can be opened from the side so that the rope does not have to be REEVED.

sou'wester—Waterproof hat worn in bad weather.

spanker—GAFF-sail on the MIZZENmast of a ship. Also the sternmost mast of a five-masted ship.

spar—A vessel's spars are her GAFFS, BOOMS, and YARDS taken collectively. A spar, however, is any one of these disunited from the rest.

spell—A period of time, not necessarily a turn of duty, although it may be applied to such. See also TRICK; WATCH.

spider-hoop—A metal band round the mast of yachts and other smaller craft to hold the shaffles of the GOOSENECK; on SQUARE-RIGGED ships, it is a mast-ring below the FUTTOCK-PLATES which holds the SHROUDS.

spill—Maneuver on SQUARE-RIGGED ships to cause the lower sails to cease their action by letting go the sheets and tacks.

spinnaker—A large light FORE-SAIL generally made of nylon. Originally it was only set when RUNNING, but new synthetic materials and modern sailshapes allow it to be carried when REACHING.

splice—To join two lengths of rope by interweaving the strands of each. The ropes themselves are unpicked with a pointed tool called a *splicing-fid* and the splices are termed *long-* or *short-splices* depending on the amount unpicked and interwoven at the end of each rope.

sponge—The long wooden pole with a piece of fleece at the end used to *sponge-out*, or clean, the barrel of a muzzle-loading gun after each shot.

spring—Generally the name given to the lighter ropes used in mooring and berthing operations for which heavier cables are substituted when those operations are completed.

sprit—A pole set diagonally across a FORE-AND-AFT sail (consequently called a *spritsail*) to extend that sail at the PEAK. It should be clearly distinguished from the *sprit-sail*, a square sail carried by 16th- and 17th-century vessels on a yard below the BOWSPRIT.

sprung—A mast or yard is said to be *sprung* when through warping or twisting it loses its strength and elasticity with damage to the wood or material from which it is made.

square-rigged—Vessels setting square sails on yards set at right-angles to that vessel's centerline are said to be square-rigged.

stabilizers—Appendages fitted to the hulls of ships, but not extending below the keel nor beyond the beam, which considerably reduce the angle of a vessel's ROLL, increase the length of time between rolls, and accelerate recovery from rolling.

stanchions—Iron or stainless steel posts set along the edges of open decks. They are normally movable and support awnings or the one or more strands of wire-rope or chain which together comprise the *railings*.

standing—The *standing end* or *part* of a rope is the part made fast to something as opposed to the running part which is the part hauled upon. For *standing rigging* see RIGGING.

starboard—The right-hand side of a vessel when facing toward the bows, so called because this was the steer-board or side on which steering oar was placed before the "invention" of the rudder.

station—A vessel's station is her position in relation to another, with particular reference to the formation adopted by warships, which may *take station* ahead or astern or abeam of another vessel.

stay—In general any support to a MAST, YARD, or SPAR but specifically the longitudinal support running forward from each mast. (The lateral supports are known as SHROUDS; the longitudinal supports running aft are the BACK-STAYS.) One end of the stay is attached to the HOUNDS of the mast it supports, the other to the deck, or to the mast immediately forward, or to the STEM-post, the BOWSPRIT, and the JIB BOOM. The stays themselves are generally made of wire-rope and take their name from the mast and section of mast which they support.

stay-sails—These sails take their name from the stay to which they are bent (*see also* JIB). The *forestay-sail* is, of course, lower and aft of the jib-sails since it is bent to the forestay which is attached to the STEM-post.

Nowadays cruising and racing yachts hoist it when RUNNING behind the SPINNAKER and it is known as a "bolero." Twin stay-sails bent to each of the forestays are also carried, especially by SINGLE-HANDERS instead of a spinnaker. Besides providing a greater sail area and being easier to handle, they can also be used to provide a sort of SELF-STEERING GEAR by running their SHEETS back to the TILLER.

steering gear—The equipment needed to impart the movements of the wheel to the ruddern when the latter is not subject to direct manual operation because of its size or for any other reason.

steeve—The angle which the BOWSPRIT makes with the horizontal plane.

stem—The foremost part of a vessel, also known as the prow. The essential structural element is the *stem-post*, joined externally to the KEEL by the *stembands*, while the STRAKES are firmly attached to it by the *breast-hook*. The shape of the stem and the way in which it is constructed have, however, varied over the years from the beak of the galley to the bulbous prow, and from the BLUFF to the RAKING.

step—The stout wooden block mounted on the KEELSON with a hole in it to take the HEEL of the mast. Thus *to step* a mast is to set it up. See also TABERNACLE.

stern—The aftermost part of the vessel from which it was controlled in the days of sail. The *stern-post* is the timber at the stern of the vessel held in place by the TRANSOM; it supports the rudder. The phrase "from STEM to stern" indicates the whole of the vessel.

stern-frame—The advent of screw-propulsion meant that the *stern-post* had to be duplicated into a *screw-post* and a *rudderpost* so that the screw could revolve freely in the space between them, the SCREW-RACE. Both posts and their associated structural elements are known as the *stern-frame*.

stern-post—See STERN.

stern-walk—A kind of railed balcony at the sterns of old-fashioned sailing vessels, particularly warships.

stirrup—See HORSE.

stock—See ANCHOR.

stop—*To stop* is to tie up temporarily with ropes or chains known as *stops*. (They are also known as *ties*, and when used to stop sails, as GASKETS and *furling-lines*.) Sometimes stops have hooks at one end which can be inserted in an EYE-BOLT while the other stops the piece of gear.

stores—Supplies of food, drink, fuel, and spares taken on board a vessel for a voyage.

storm-sails—Small sails of very stout canvas carried in bad weather, such as TRYSAILS, storm-STAY-SAILS, storm-JIBS. The latter, in particular are nowadays hoisted on racing and cruising yachts when bad weather forces the vessel to LIE-TO, to act in conjunction with the TILLER to keep her head to the wind.

strain-band—An extra band of canvas sewn on large square sails to reinforce them.

strakes—A strake is a single line of planking along the vessel's side. The uppermost is known as the SHEER-STRAKE, the lowermost as the *garboard-strake*.

strand—A strand is composed of a number of YARNS twisted together to form it in the same way as the strands themselves are twisted together to form a rope. A rope is said to be *stranded* when one or more of the strands become broken or worn.

A vessel, however, is *stranded* when she is left high and dry by the falling of the tide (*see* GROUND).

strike—To strike is to lower. Thus to *strike sail* is to lower sail; to *strike a mast* or *yard* is to take it down, for example for maintenance or repair, or when laying the vessel up for the winter if it is a yacht; and of course a topmast may be struck without taking down the lower mast as well. However, to *strike a flag* is to lower it permanently, the sign of surrender in navel warfare and of a merchant vessel's passing from one national register to another.

studding-sails—Four-sided sails set outboard and on either side of the regular sails of a SQUARE-RIGGED ship in fine weather to increase her speed before a favorable wind.

studsail—Also known as a *ringtail*, this is the extra strip of canvas carried at the LEECH of a FORE-AND-AFT sail to act as a STUDDING-SAIL.

surge—To slacken a rope suddenly.

sway—To HOIST.

swell in—To become watertight. A wooden boat which has been laid up for any length of time needs to be placed in the water to allow her planks to *swell in*.

swifters—Extra STAYS generally forward of those which they reinforce.

swivel—Links comprising two rings joined by a pin round which both may revolve. They prevent the anchor-cable from SNARLING when a vessel swings at anchor through stress of wind or sea or through some maneuver.

T—"Tango," twentieth letter of the alphabet, designated in the International Code by a square flag divided into three equal vertical bands running red, white, and blue from JACK to FLY. Hoisted in isolation it means: "Do not pass ahead of me."

tabernacle—Case, often of metal, for the foot of a mast, set on the centerline of a vessel and secured for strength to the deck beams rather than to the roof of the deck house. A pair of bolts prevents the mast from coming out of the tabernacle, and this method of setting up a mast is particularly handy for craft which have to navigate inland waterways and need to lower the mast constantly to pass under bridges.

tabs—Extra canvas (and sometimes, as at the PEAK of a GAFF-sail, wood or metal) triangular or square reinforcements at the corners of sails or along their edges.

tack—The *tack of a sail* is the leading lower corner of a FORE-AND-AFT sail or the windward corner of a square sail and is sometimes more comprehensibly called the weather-CLEW. The *tack* is also the name given to the rope attached to the tack of the sail and used to work it.

(*2*) *To tack* is to make progress against the wind by frequent changes of course so that the wind strikes now on one side of the bows and now on the other.

(*3*) *To pass on opposite tacks* is when two vessels pass close to one another on parallel but opposite courses.

tackle—The PURCHASE created by the combination of ropes and BLOCKS used for hoisting, as for example the HALYARDS or the CAT-tackle.

taffrail—The rail round the stern of a vessel.

tallboy—Very light nylon STAY-SAIL set behind the SPINNAKER to increase sail thrust and lessen the pitching motion resulting from RUNNING before the wind.

tar—A distillation of wood or coal employed from the earliest times to waterproof wood, textiles, and the yarns of ropes.

tender—A small vessel used to ferry persons and goods to a larger one.

thimble—Metal or wooden rings or ovals grooved on the outside to prevent wear on the eyesplice of the rope into which they are inserted, or rather which is spliced round them.

tholes—Pegs fitted to the gunwales of open boats to serve as ROWLOCKS.

throat—The part immediately behind the JAWS of a GAFF to which the *throat-halyards* are attached. Hence the leading upper corner of a gaff-sail is called the throat.

thrumming—Working a mass of tarred YARN on a sail-cloth round the hull of a vessel and securing it by chains or ropes to cover a leak and to prevent water from entering the vessel.

ticket—CERTIFICATE of competence awarded to a ship's officer with the required practical experience in terms of service and theoretical knowledge proved by examination. As a *master's ticket*, or *a mate's ticket*.

tie—See STOP.

tier—Hollow space in a coil of rope.

tiller—The wooden or metal bar inserted in the head of a rudder which works manually or mechanically to impart the necessary angle to the rudder which will enable the vessel to sail her desired course.

timber hitch—Knot employed to secure a rope to an upright.

timbers—The various members employed in building a wooden vessel are referred to collectively as her *timbers*, with particular reference to her ribs.

toggle and becket—Length of thin rope with a loop (the *becket*) at one end and wooden pin (the *toggle*) at the other. Used for temporary lashings on sails, standing RIGGING, the TILLER, etc.

tonnage—The measurement of the internal capacity of a vessel from which the relation between its internal volume and the amount of cargo it can carry may be established.

top—(*1*) The part of the masts from the HOUNDS upward. In sailing warships this was crowned by the *fighting-top*, a platform in which marksmen were posted to shoot down on the enemy's decks. Nelson was mortally wounded by a marksman in the *tops* of the *Redoubtable.*

(*2*) *To top* the yards of a SQUARE-RIGGED ship is to raise one end of the yard as near vertical as possible in relation to the plane of the deck to allow it to TRAVERSE without interruption by the STAYS. This is done by means of a *topping-lift*, a rope running through a block with the STANDING end attached to the end of the yard or boom to be topped.

top-gallant—The third section of mast from the deck upward, between the TOPMAST and the ROYAL and giving its name to all rigging, sails, yards, etc., which it carries.

top-hamper—Collectively, all the gear carried above decks by a vessel—masts, rigging, yards, sails, etc.

topmast—The second section of a mast from the deck upward, qualified by the mast from which it rises, i.e., FORE, MAIN, or MIZZEN.

topsails—On square-rigged ships the sails carried on the TOPMASTS immediately above the COURSES and which take their name from the mast on which they are set, i.e., FORE-, MAIN-, MIZZEN-topsails. Because of their size they were sometimes divided into *upper* and *middle* (or *lower*) topsails. In FORE-AND-AFT rigged vessels the *main topsail* is set immediately above the mainsail; the *jib-topsail* is a JIB set on the topmast fore-STAY. A *gaff-topsail* is a topsail set on a GAFF and if triangular is called a *jib-headed topsail*; while a *jack-topsail* is a triangular sail set on a yard called a *jack* which is hoisted close to the mast and extends above it.

topsides—The dead works, that is, that part of the hull above the waterline.

toss oars—To raise the oars of a boat and hold them vertical in the air, their blades parallel with the keel of the boat.

transom—Transoms are the crossbeams attached to the STERN-post. In small boats they may be a single piece. The lowest are the *wing-transoms*; above them the *helm-transoms* are attached to the head of the STERN-post, while the deck-planking is recessed into the highest of all, the *deck-transoms*. Transoms are connected to the sides of the vessel by the transom-KNEES.

traveler—Rings made of wood, metal, or other materials used to bend sails or stays or spars along which they *travel* by means of hooks or catches. They have been superseded nowadays by metal slides fitted to the sails.

traverse—*To traverse* the yards of a square-rigged ship is to swing them round the axis of the mast by BRACING them.

treenail—Wooden bolt used to connect the planking of a wooden vessel with her timbers.

trestle-trees—On square-rigged ships with masts made of more than one section, the trestle-trees were two pieces of timber running fore and aft supported by the HOUNDS of the lower mast and supporting the CROSS-TREES in their turn. The foot of the upper mast passed between them and was secured by the FID which passed through both.

triatic stay—The stay from the mainmast to the foremast head in a SCHOONER.

trice—*To trice* is to draw up a rope or sail by means of *tricing-lines.*

trick—The period during which a man is on duty at the wheel or elsewhere: a SPELL of duty.

trim—*To trim* a boat is to dispose her load, masts, and sails so that her centers of gravity and of buoyancy are in the same vertical plane and she is stable and answers the helm. A vessel with a permanent HEEL is said to be *out of trim*. To *trim the sails* is to brace the YARDS and SHEET the sails so that they take full advantage of the wind and produce the best performance of which the vessel is capable in those conditions. A vessel will have a particular *trim* for specific weather conditions.

tripping—Tripping a topmast is raising it with *tripping-lines* so that the FID may be removed when the mast is struck.

truck—(*1*) The round wooden cap on the ends of masts and

JACKS.

(*2*) See PARREL.

trysail—(*1*) A small STORM-SAIL bent on old square-riggers to the *trysail-mast*, a spar abaft the foremast and mainmast.

(*2*) In FORE-AND-AFT rigs, a trysail is a GAFF-sail without a BOOM.

tunnel—Watertight tunnels are used in steel shipbuilding to house the shaft of the screw, electric wiring, etc.

turn—A turn is one loop of a rope around a CLEAT, for example. To *turn in* a rope is to turn the end of a rope back upon itself, forming a loop or eye.

turning room—The circumference in which a vessel can revolve, its center being the anchor, when the latter has been dropped. It will depend upon the length of the anchor-CABLE and the depth of water over the GROUND.

U—"Uniform," twenty-first letter of the alphabet, designated in the International Code by a square flag quartered red and white, the white quarter being the upper quarter at the FLY and the red the lower at the JACK. Hoisted in isolation it means: "You are standing into danger."

unbend—To take off, as a sail from its yard.

unbitt—To free a rope or chain from the BITT to which it has been secured.

unrig—To remove the rigging from a vessel.

unship—To remove anything from its working location.

upper works—Obsolete term for FREEBOARD.

V—"Victor," twenty-second letter of the alphabet, designated in the International Code by a square white flag bearing a red saltire (St. Patrick's cross). Hoisted in isolation it means: "I require assistance."

vang—Tackle fixed to a BOOM so that it my be pulled down, thus flattening the sail and exposing a greater area to the wind.

veer—*To veer* a rope is to let it out.

veer and back—The wind *veers* when it changes its direction with the sun, that is, from east through south and west, and *backs* when it changes in the opposite direction.

very light—red, white, and green flares fired as distress signals at sea from a Very pistol.

W—"Whiskey," twenty-third letter of the alphabet, designated in the International Code by a square white flag with a broad blue border and a red oblong in the center. Hoisted in isolation it means: "I require medical assistance."

waist—On vessels with POOPS or QUARTER-DECKS, the waist was that part of the upper deck immediately forward of them.

wales *or* **waling**—In boat building these are strengthening planks or battens laid to protect the skin. The *outer wale* or *rubber strake* is a STRAKE running below and supporting the *gunwale* with tapering ends. On some vessels, especially yachts, it does duty as a FENDER as well.

warp—A lighter HAWSER by which a vessel is moved. In the days of sail, when tugs were not available, a vessel was *warped* to sea. That is, her warp was secured to a buoy, to a point on shore, or to another vessel at anchor. Her crew then hauled on the warps to get the vessel under WAY. A modern warp is a HAWSER-laid wire or hemp rope of from 6 to 11 in. in circumference used in mooring operations.

watch—A period of duty served by officers and men aboard ship at their different posts. Watches are changed every four hours day and night except at the DOG-WATCHES.

water-sail—A triangular or four-sided sail sometimes set below the lowest STUDDING-SAILS and very close to the water, hence its name.

waterways—The line of deck-planking nearest the side of the vessel, generally grooved so as to carry away surface water.

waterline—See LINES.

way—The momentum achieved by a vessel from the thrust of its means of propulsion, or the residual momentum once that propulsion has ceased. A vessel makes *fresh way* or *gathers way* when it accelerates; it *loses way* when it decelerates; *headway* is forward motion, *sternway* the reverse, while *steerage-way* is sufficient momemtum to permit the rudder to act.

wear—To bring a vessel onto a different TACK by bringing her round stern to wind (the opposite to *tacking*). To *wear round* is to pass something to LEEward.

weather—The *weather side* is the windward side and *to weather* another vessel or a cape or headland is to pass it to windward.

weather-boards—Boards erected in the bows and forward of the COCKPIT of larger sailing vessels to protect the decks from water coming over the side or into the cockpit.

weather-cocking—When a boat runs up to the wind and refuses to pay off in either direction.

weather-helm—See HELM.

weather-ship—Vessels belonging to the Meteorological Offices and Weather Bureaus of various nations and stationed at sea to record continuously weather conditions within their observation. Their function has largely been taken over by *weather satellites*.

well—Another name for the COCKPIT of yachts.

wetted surface—See HULL.

whip—A BLOCK fixed aloft, through which a rope runs, thus forming a simple lifting system. Two blocks, one fixed, the other movable, are known as a *double whip*.

whipping—The thin rope used to *whip* another piece of rope, that is, bind the end tightly to prevent its fraying. Whipping is generally tarred.

whiskers—The CROSSTREES of the BOWSPRIT and JIB BOOM, standing at right angles to them and giving increased support to them by the pressure they exert on the bowsprit SHROUDS.

width—See BEAM.

winch—A small capstan turned by a CRANK. On cruising and racing yachts these are manually operated and are used to work the HALYARDS and SHEETS. These are of two types, the *capstan-winch* with a vertical axis, and the *coffee-mill* with a horizontal axis. Larger horizontally and vertically powered winches are employed on freighters and other ships to hoist loads, etc.

wind force—The speed and pressure of the wind on the BEAUFORT SCALE.

windlass—Lifting gear operating on precisely the same principles as the CAPSTAN and like it used to haul in the chain. Smaller than a capstan and larger than a WINCH, it operates on a vertical axis.

windward—The WEATHER side. *Plying to windward* is another term for close REACHING.

wing and wing—See GOOSEWING.

wings—Another name for STUDDING-SAILS; also for the lateral extremities of the BRIDGE.

woolding—Rope or metal strengthening round a mast or yard.

worming—See SEIZE.

X—"Xray," twenty-fourth letter of the alphabet, designated in the International Code by a square white flag bearing a blue cross. Hoisted in isolation it means: "Stop carrying out your intentions and watch my signals."

Y—"Yankee," twenty-fifth letter of the alphabet, designated in the International Code by a yellow flag bearing six diagonal stripes running downward from the FLY to the JACK. Hoisted in isolation it means: "I am carrying mail."

yard—Wooden spar made of a single timber or of a number of pieces, cylindrical or polyhedral (traditionally octagonal) in the middle and tapering to conical tips called *yardarms*. The yards are raised on the mast by HALYARDS and in SQUARE-RIGGED ships they run at right angles to the centerline of the vessel on the forward side of the mast round which they are enabled to TRAVERSE freely by means of PARRELS. Sails are BENT to the yards, which are TRIMMED by BRACES. In order to avoid the STAYS the yardarm may have to be raised during trimming. This is to TOP the yard and is done by means of the topping-lift. Sails take their name from the yard to which they are bent and the yards from the mast on which they are hoisted, e.g., MIZZEN-ROYAL-yard, etc. The exception is the lowest yard of the MIZZENmast which is known as the *cross-jack yard*. Vessels in the 16th and 17th centuries carried a yard on the BOWSPRIT on which was set the SPRIT-sail. In addition to the blocks through which their SHEETS are REEVED, yards may also carry *yard-tackle* for hoisting weights. Their other rigging includes TRICING-lines and BRAILS, and the HORSE on which the seamen stand when working the sail.

yarn—The fibrous threads twisted together to form the strands of a rope. When the rope is too old for service, the yarn may be unpicked and used to CAULK seams, etc., which is known as OAKUM.

yoke—The *yoke of a mast* is the oval ring (made of metal or hard wood) which secures the foot of an upper mast to the HOUNDING of a lower mast. A similar ring, called the *cap*, secures the head of the lower mast to the hounding of the upper mast. Thus the pieces of a mast have a triple binding—at the cap, the CROSSTREES, at the FUTTOCK-PLATE and TRESTLE-TREES (the HOUNDS), and at the yoke.

Z—"Zulu," twenty-sixth letter of the alphabet, designated in the International Code by a square flag bearing four triangles (black at the JACK, yellow at the head, blue at the FLY, and red at the foot), their points meeting in the center. It is reserved for communication with the shore.

TECHNICAL DATA

Battleships	Aircraft carriers	Heavy cruisers	Light cruisers	Destroyers and Torpedo boats	Submarines	Total tonnage
17	7	15	73	241	56	1,692,302

British naval forces at the outbreak of the Second World War

The war on the seas. The British war: principal marine classes cited in this chapter

Page	Class	Shipyard	Date: ld c r	Displacement (full load)	Length o.a. meters	Length o.a. feet	Beam meters	Beam feet	Draft (mean) meters	Draft (mean) feet
	Battleships									
180	**Resolution** (5 ships)	Palmers	1913/1916/1930	33,000	187·1	620½ ft.	31·1	102½ ft.	9·4	28½ ft.
178	**Revenge** (same class)	Vickers	1913/1916/1937			624½ ft.				
180	**Ramillies**	Beardmore	1913/1917/1927							
	Repulse (2 ships)	John Brown	1915/1916/1936	37,400	242	794 ft. 2½ in.	31·3	102 ft. 8 in.	9·6	27 ft. 31¾ ft. (max.)
180	**Renown**	Fairfield	1915/1916/1939							
175	**Hood**	John Brown	1916/1918/1920	46,200	262·2	860 ft. 7 in.	31·7	105 ft. 2½ in.	8·7	28½ ft. 31½ ft. (max.)
176	**Nelson** (2 ships)	Armstrong	1922/1927	38,000	216·4	660 ft. (wl)	32·3	106 ft.	9·1	30 ft.
178	**Rodney**	Cammell Laird	1922/1927							
176	**Queen Elizabeth** (5 ships)	Portsmouth Dockyard	1912/1915/1940	36,000	195	643¾ ft.	31·7	104 ft.	9·7	30 ft. 8 in. 33½ ft. (max.)
175	**Warspite**	Devonport Dockyard	1912/1915/1938	35,000						
180	**Valiant**	Fairfield	1913/1916/1939	36,000						
180	**Malaya** (same class)	Elswick	1913/1916/1929	35,100						
178	**King George V** (4 ships)	Vickers	1937/1940	45,000	227·1	739 ft. 8 in.	31·4	103 ft.	10·9	27 ft. 8 in.
175	**Prince of Wales**	Cammell Laird	1937/1941							
177	**Duke of York** (same class)	John Brown	1937/1941							
	Aircraft carriers									
181	**Argus** (ex-**Conte Rosso**)	Beardmore	1914/1918/1937	14,450	172·2	565 ft.	20·7	68 ft.	6	21 ft.
177	**Eagle**	Armstrong Whitworth	1913/1924/1932	26,400	203·3	667 ft.	31·6	105½ ft.	8·2	24 ft. 27 ft. (max.)
177	**Courageous** (2 ships)	Armstrong	1915/1917/1930	26,500	239·6	786¼ ft.	24·7	100 ft.	7·9	22 ft. 2 in. 28 ft. 4 in. (max.)

ABBREVIATIONS — **Date: ld** = laid down **c** = completed **r** = refit **length o.a.** = length over all **mg** = machine gun mounting **mmg** = multi-machine gun mounting **dct** = depth charge thrower **pdr** = pounder **aa** = anti-aircraft **a/s** = anti-submarine **4-bar** = 4-barrelled **T** = tonnage **hp** = horsepower **sub** = speed when submerged **tt** = torpedo tube **cal** = caliber **wl** = water level **d** = deck **fd** = flight deck **ct** = control or conning tower **t** = turret **b** = barbette **tb** = turret base **bt** = battery

Armaments	Armor	Machinery	Speed (knots)	Range (miles)	Complement	Page
8/381 mm – 42 cal 12/152 mm – 50 cal 8/102 mm aa 4/3 pdr 1/12 pdr 5 mg 10 Lewis 1 catapult 1 aircraft	**Vertical** max 330 mm **Horizontal** d 102 mm ct 279 mm tb 330 mm bt 152 mm external bulges below wl	4 Parsons geared turbines 18 Babcock or Yarrow boilers (oil) 40,000 hp 4 screws Fuel 3,230 T	22	4,200	1,009 1,146	180 178 180
6/381 mm – 42 cal 12/102 mm – 40 cal 8/114 mm aa 4/3 pdr 1/12 pdr 5 mg 8 tt 1 catapult 4 aircraft	**Vertical** max 229 mm **Horizontal** d 76 mm ct 254 mm t 279 mm external bulges below wl	4 Parsons-Curtis geared turbines 8 Admiralty boilers (oil) 42 Babcock & Wilcox boilers 112,000 hp 4 screws Fuel 4,250 T	29	3,600	1,181 1,205	180
8/381 mm – 42 cal 12/140 mm – 50 cal 8/102 mm aa – 45 cal 4/3 pdr 5 mg 10 Lewis 4/533 mm tt 1 aircraft	**Vertical** max 305 mm **Horizontal** 2d 38–76 mm ct 305 mm t 381 mm b 305 mm external bulges below wl	4 Brown-Curtis geared turbines 24 Yarrow boilers (oil) 150,000 hp 4 screws Fuel 4,000 T	31	4,000	1,341 1,400	175
9/406 mm – 45 cal 12/152 mm – 50 cal 6/120 mm aa 4/3 pdr 1/12 pdr 5 mg 2/533 mm tt 1 catapult 2 aircraft	**Vertical** max 355 mm **Horizontal** d 159 mm t 406 mm b 381 mm bulkheads below wl	2 Brown-Curtis geared turbines 8 Admiralty boilers (oil) 46,000 hp 2 screws Fuel 4,000 T	23	5,000	1,314 1,361	176 178
8/381 mm – 42 cal 8/152 mm – 50 cal 4/3 pdr 5 mg 10 Lewis 1 catapult 4 aircraft	**Vertical** max 330 mm **Horizontal** d 76 mm ct 356 mm tb 279 mm bt 152 mm external bulges	4 Parsons geared turbines 8 Admiralty boilers (oil) 82,000 hp 4 screws Fuel 3,800 T	25	4,400 5,000	1,124 1,184	176 175 180 180
10/356 mm 16/133 mm aa 6 mmg aa 1 catapult 4 aircraft	**Vertical** max 356 mm **Horizontal** d 159 mm tb 406 mm multiple bulkheads	4 Parsons geared turbines 8 Admiralty boilers (oil) 152,000 hp 4 screws Fuel 3,900 T	29	6,300	1,600	178 175 177
18 mg 1 catapult 14 aircraft		Parsons turbines 12 Yarrow boilers (oil) 20,000 hp 4 screws Fuel 2,000 T	20	4,000	373	181
9/152 mm – 50 cal 4/102 mm aa 131 mg aa 21 aircraft		Brown-Curtis turbines 32 Yarrow boilers 50,000 hp 4 screws Fuel 3,750 T	24	4,200	750	177
16/120 mm – 40 cal 4/3 pdr 24/40 mm aa 18 mg 2 catapults 48 aircraft	**Vertical** max 76 mm **Horizontal** fd 76 mm external bulges below wl	4 Parsons geared turbines 18 Yarrow boilers (oil) 90,000 hp 4 screws Fuel 3,940 T	30·5	3,200	750 1,216	177

TECHNICAL DATA

Page	Class	Shipyard	Date: ld c r	Displacement (full load)	Length o.a. meters	Length o.a. feet	Beam meters	Beam feet	Draft (mean) meters	Draft (mean) feet
177	**Hermes**	Armstrong Whitworth	1918/1923/1933	12,900	182·3	598 ft.	21·3	90 ft.	6·4	18¾ ft.
203	**Formidable** (Illustrious class, 6 ships)	Harland & Wolff	1937/1940	23,000	229·5	753 ft.	29·2	96 ft.	7·3	24 ft.
179	**Indomitable** (same class)	Vickers-Armstrong	1937/1940							
181	**Furious**	Armstrong Whitworth	1915/1917/1925	22,450	239·6	786¼ ft.	27·5	89¾ ft.	7·6	21 ft. 8 in. 25 ft. (max.)
	Heavy cruisers									
181	**London** (4 ships)	Portsmouth Dockyard	1925/1929	9,850	192·9	633 ft.	20·1	66 ft.	5·2	17 ft.
181	**York** (2 ships)	Palmers	1927/1930	8,250 (standard)	175·2	575 ft.	17·4	57 ft.	5·2	17 ft.
181	**Kent** (5 ships)	Chatham Dockyard	1924/1928	10,000	192	630 ft.	20·9	68 ft. 4 in.	5	16¼ ft.
	Light cruisers									
181	**Caledon** (3 ships)	Cammell Laird	1916/1917	4,180	137·2	450 ft.	13·2	42¾ ft.	4·3	14 ft. 1 in. 16¼ ft. (max.)
181	**Ceres** (4 ships)	John Brown	1916/1917	4,290	137·2	450 ft.	13·2	43½ ft.	4·3	14 ft. 1 in. 16¼ ft. (max.)
181	**Hawkins** (3 ships)	Chatham Dockyard	1916/1919	9,800	184·4	605 ft.	19·8	58 ft. 65 ft.	5·3	17¼ ft. 20½ ft. (max.)
181	**Dauntless** (8 ships)	Palmers	1918/1922	4,850	144	472½ ft.	14·8	46½ ft.	5	14¼ ft. 16½ ft.
181	**Emerald** (2 ships)	Armstrong	1918/1926	7,550	173·7	570 ft.	16·6	54½ ft.	5	16½ ft.
181	**Adventure** (minelayer)	Devonport Dockyard	1922/1924	6,740	158·5	520 ft.	18	59 ft.	5·9	19¼ ft.

Armaments	Armor	Machinery	Speed (knots)	Range (miles)	Complement	Page
6/140 mm – 50 cal 3/102 mm aa 4/47 mm 8/40 mm aa 14 mg aa 20 aircraft	**Vertical** max 76 mm **Horizontal** fd 25 mm external bulges below wl	2 Parsons all geared turbines 12 Yarrow boilers (oil) 40,000 hp 2 screws Fuel 2,000 T	25	3,000	664	177
16/114 mm dual-purpose aa 32/40 mm aa 32/4-bar mg aa 2 catapults 40 aircraft		3 Parsons geared turbines 6 Yarrow boilers (oil) 110,000 hp 3 screws Fuel 4,500 T	30·5	4,000	1,600	203 179
10/140 mm – 50 cal 2/102 mm aa – 45 cal 4/47 mm 24/40 mm 8-bar aa 14 mg 33 aircraft	**Vertical** max 76 mm **Horizontal** d 76 mm external bulges	Brown-Curtis all geared turbines 18 Yarrow boilers (oil) 90,000 hp 4 screws Fuel 4,010 T	30	3,200	750 1,200	181
8/203 mm – 50 cal 8/102 mm aa 4/3 pdr 4/40 mm aa 14 mg 8/533 mm tt 1 catapult 1 aircraft	**Horizontal** d 76 mm bulkheads below wl	4 Parsons geared turbines 8 Admiralty boilers 80,000 hp 4 screws Fuel 3,200 T	32·2	10,000	650	181
6/203 mm – 50 cal 8/102 mm – 45 cal 4/3 pdr 8/40 mm 6 mg aa 6/533 mm tt 1 catapult 1 aircraft	**Vertical** max 76 mm **Horizontal** d 51 mm ct 76 mm tb 51 mm bulges	Parsons geared turbines 8 Admiralty boilers 80,000 hp 4 screws Fuel 1,900 T	32·5	10,000	650 600	181
8/203 mm – 50 cal 8/102 mm aa 4/47 mm 20 mg aa 1 catapult 3 aircraft	**Vertical** max 91 mm **Horizontal** d 76 mm bulges	Parsons turbines 8 Admiralty boilers (super- heated) 80,000 hp 4 screws Fuel 3,400 T	32	10,000	680	181
5/152 mm – 50 cal 2/76 mm – 45 cal 4/47 mm 2/40 mm aa 9 mg aa 8/533 mm tt	**Vertical** max 76 mm **Horizontal** d 25 mm ct 52 mm	Parsons all geared turbines 8 Yarrow boilers 40,000 hp 2 screws Fuel 935 T	29	2,000	400 437	181
5/152 mm – 50 cal 2/76 mm – 45 cal 4/3 pdr 2/40 mm aa 9 mg aa 8/533 mm tt	**Vertical** max 76 mm **Horizontal** d 25 mm ct 52 mm	Brown-Curtis all geared turbines 8 Yarrow boilers 40,000 hp 2 screws Fuel 950 T	29	2,000	400 437	181
9/152 mm – 50 cal 4/102 mm aa 4/3 pdr 8/40 mm aa 12 mg aa 4/533 mm tt 1 catapult 2 aircraft	**Vertical** max 76 mm **Horizontal** d 38 mm ct 76 mm external bulges below wl	4 Parsons turbines 8 Yarrow boilers 55,000 hp 4 screws Fuel 2,600 T	29·5	5,400	712 750	181
6/152 mm – 50 cal 3/102 mm – 45 cal 4/3 pdr 4/40 mm 8 mg aa 12/533 mm tt	**Vertical** max 76 mm **Horizontal** d 25 mm ct 152 mm	2 Brown-Curtis geared turbines 6 Yarrow boilers (small tube) 40,000 hp 2 screws Fuel 1,050 T	29	2,300	450 469	181
7/152 mm – 50 cal 5/102 mm – 45 cal 4/3 pdr 2/40 mm aa 10 mg aa 16/533 mm tt 1 catapult 1 aircraft	**Vertical** max 76 mm **Horizontal** d 25 mm ct 152 mm	4 Brown-Curtis geared turbines 8 Yarrow boilers (small tube) 80,000 hp 4 screws Fuel 1,746 T	33	3,800	572	181 181

TECHNICAL DATA

Page	Class	Shipyard	Date: ld c r	Displacement (full load)	Length o.a.		Beam		Draft (mean)	
					meters	feet	meters	feet	meters	feet
181	**Southampton** (8 ships)	John Brown	1934/1937	9,100	178	591 ft. 6 in.	19	61 ft. 8 in.	5·2	17 ft. 20 ft. (max.)
181	**Dido** (10 ships)	Cammell Laird	1937/1940	5,450	154·2	506 ft.	15·7	51½ ft.	4·3	14 ft. 1 in.
181	**Neptune** (Leander class, 5 ships)	Portsmouth Dockyard	1931/1934	7.175	169	554½ ft.	16·8	55 ft. 2 in.	4·9	16 ft.
181	**Arethusa** (4 ships)	Chatham Dockyard	1933/1935	5,220	152·4	500 ft. (wl)	15·5	51 ft.	4·2	13 ft. 10 in.
181	**Fiji** (13 ships)	John Brown	1938/1939	8,000	167·6	550 ft.	18·9	61 ft. 8 in.	5	61 ft. 8 in.
181	**Destroyers** **Vanoc** (Admiralty V class, 12 ships)	John Brown	1916/1917	1,090	95·1	312 ft.	9	29½ ft.	3·4	10 ft. 10 in. 11¾ ft. (max.)
181	**Acasta**	John Brown	1928/1930	1,350	98·4	323 ft.	9·8	32¼ ft.	2·5	8½ ft. 12 ft. (max.)
181	**Beagle** (8 ships)	John Brown	1929/1931	1,360	98·4	323 ft.	9·8	32¼ ft.	2·5	8½ ft.
181	**Exmouth**	Portsmouth Dockyard	1933/1934	1,475	104·5	343 ft.	10·3	33¾ ft.	2·7	8 ft. 8 in.
181	**Greyhound** (8 ships)	Vickers-Armstrong	1934/1936	1,335	98·4	323 ft.	10	33 ft.	2·6	8½ ft.
181	**Jervis** (Javelin class, 24 ships)	Hawthorn Leslie	1937/1939	1,695	106·4	348 ft.	10·9	35 ft.	2·9	9 ft.
181	**Escort vessels** **Belmont** (14 ships, ex-**Saterlee** USN)	Various US shipyards	1916/1921	1,190 (standard)	94·7	314 ft. 4 in.	9	30 ft. 8 in.	2·7	9¼ ft.

Armaments	Armor	Machinery	Speed (knots)	Range (miles)	Complement	Page
12/152 mm – 50 cal 8/102 mm – 45 cal 4/3 pdr 16/40 mm 8-bar aa 6/533 mm tt 1 catapult 3 aircraft	**Vertical** max 127 mm **Horizontal** d 51 mm ct 102 mm t 50 mm	Parsons geared turbines 8 Admiralty boilers 75,000 hp 4 screws Fuel 1,970 T	32·5	—	700	181
10/133 mm 16/40 mm 8-bar 6/533 mm tt 1 catapult 1 aircraft	**Vertical** max 76 mm **Horizontal** d 51 mm	Parsons geared turbines 4 Yarrow boilers (oil) 62,000 hp 4 screws	32·25	—	—	181
8/152 mm – 50 cal 8/102 mm – 45 cal 4/3 pdr 12/4-bar mg aa 8/533 mm tt 1 catapult 2 aircraft	**Vertical** max 102 mm **Horizontal** d 50 mm ct 102 mm	Parsons geared turbines 4 Admiralty boilers 72,000 hp 4 screws Fuel 1,800 T	32·5	12,000	550	181
6/152 mm – 50 cal 8/102 mm aa 2/3 pdr 8/4-bar mg aa 6/533 mm tt 1 catapult 1 aircraft	**Vertical** max 51 mm **Horizontal** d 51 mm ct 102 mm	Parsons geared turbines 4 Admiralty boilers 64,000 hp 4 screws Fuel 1,200 T	32·5	12,000	450	181
12/152 mm – 50 cal 8/102 mm aa 16/40 mm 8-bar aa 6/533 mm tt 1 catapult 3 aircraft	**Vertical** max 53 mm **Horizontal** d 51 mm tb 102 mm	4 Clydebank turbines 4 Yarrow boilers (oil) 80,000 hp 4 screws Fuel 2,000 T	33	12,000	580	181
4/102 mm – 45 cal 1/2 pdr 6 mg aa 6/533 mm tt 20 mines		Brown-Curtis geared turbines 3 Yarrow boilers 27,000 hp 2 screws Fuel 370 T	34	4,000	182 134	181
4/120 mm – 50 cal 2/40 mm aa 5 mg aa 8/533 mm tt		Brown-Curtis high-pressure turbines 3 Admiralty boilers 34,000 hp 2 screws Fuel 380 T	35	5,000	138	181
4/120 mm – 50 cal 2/40 mm aa 5 mg aa 8/533 mm tt		Brown-Curtis high-pressure turbines 3 Admiralty boilers 34,000 hp 2 screws Fuel 380 T	35	5,000	139	181
5/120 mm – 50 cal 8/40 mm aa 8/533 mm tt		Parsons geared turbines 4 Admiralty boilers 38,000 hp 2 screws Fuel 490 T	36	6,000	175	181
4/120 mm – 50 cal 8/40 mm aa 8/533 mm tt		Parsons geared turbines 3 Admiralty boilers 34,000 hp 2 screws Fuel 480 T	35·5	6,000	145	181
6/120 mm – 50 cal 4/40 mm aa 8 mg aa 10/533 mm tt		Parsons geared turbines 2 Admiralty boilers 40,000 hp 2 screws Fuel 500 T	36	6,000	183	181
4/102 mm – 50 cal 1/76 mm aa – 23 cal 12/533 mm tt		2 Curtis turbines 4 White boilers (oil) 26,000 hp 2 screws Fuel 375 T	35	5,000	122	181

TECHNICAL DATA

Page	Class	Shipyard	Date: ld c r	Displacement (full load)	Length o.a. meters	Length o.a. feet	Beam meters	Beam feet	Draft (mean) meters	Draft (mean) feet
179	**Minesweepers** **Bangor** (20 ships)	Harland & Wolff	1939/1940	817	75	247½ ft.	10·2	33½ ft.	2·2	9 ft. 10 in.
181	**Submarines** **Oberon** (3 ships)	Chatham Dockyard	1924/1927	1,311/1,831	82·3	270 ft.	8·5	28 ft.	4·1	13¼ ft.
181	**Thames** (3 ships)	Vickers-Armstrong	1931/1932	1,850/2,723	99·1	325 ft.	8·5	28 ft.	4·2	13½ ft.
181	**Porpoise** (6 ships)	Vickers-Armstrong	1931/1933	1,500/2,053	82·6	267 ft.	7·8	29 ft. 10 in.	4·6	13¾ ft.
181	**Triton** (15 ships)	Vickers-Armstrong	1937/1938	1,095/1,579	80·6	265 ft.	8·1	26½ ft.	3·6	12 ft.
181	**Patrol vessels** **Foxglove** (Flower class, 3 ships)	Barclay, Curle	1914/1915	1,165	80	262½ ft.	10	33 ft.	3·6	11 ft.
181	**Falmouth** (3 ships)	Devonport Dockyard	1929/1932	1,060	81·1	266 ft.	10·4	34 ft.	2·7	8¾ ft.
181	**Depot ship** **Cyclops**	Laing	1905	11,300	145	477 ft.	16·8	55 ft.	6·4	21 ft. 1 in.
179	**Torpedo boats** **M.T.B.** (13 BPB type)	British Power Boats	1936/1938	18	18·3	60 ft.	4·3	13¼ ft.	0·8	2 ft. 10 in.
181	**M.T.B. 102** (2 Vosper)	Vosper	1937/1938	28	20·1	68 ft.	4·8	14¾ ft.	0·96	3 ft. 2 in.
179	**Special assault craft** Midget submarine (class "X")	Varley Marine	1940/1943		16	52 ft.	1·65	3 ft. 7½ in.	1·55	3¹³⁄₁₆ ft.
179	**Chariot**			1·7	7·6	22¹³⁄₁₆ ft.				

Armaments	Armor	Machinery	Speed (knots)	Range (miles)	Comple-ment	Page
1/102 mm – 45 cal 1/102 mm aa – 45 cal 5 mg aa 4/7·7 mm mg		Parsons triple expansion 2 Yarrow boilers (oil) 1,770 hp 2 screws Fuel 220 T	16·5		80	179
1/102 mm – 40 cal 2 mg aa 8/533 mm tt		Diesel 2,950 hp Electric motors 1,350 hp Fuel 200 T	sub 9 15·5		54	181
1/102 mm – 40 cal 2 mg 6/533 mm tt		Diesel 10,000 hp Electric motors 2,500 hp Fuel 224 T	sub 10 22·5		60	181
1/102 mm – 40 cal 2 mg aa 6/533 mm tt 120 mines		Diesel 3,300 hp Electric motors 1,630 hp Fuel 136 T	sub 8·75 15		54	181
1/102 mm – 40 cal 2 mg aa 10/533 mm tt		Diesel 2,500 hp Electric motors 1,450 hp	sub 9 15·25		53	181
2/102 mm – 45 cal 4/47 mm 12/40 mm aa 12 mg		1 set triple expansion 2-cylinder boilers (coal) 2,000 hp 1 screw Fuel 200 T of coal	16·5	2,000	98	181
1/102 mm – 45 cal 1/102 mm aa 2/47 mm 8 mg aa		2 Parsons impulse reaction turbines 2 Admiralty boilers (oil) 2,000 hp 2 screws Fuel 275 T	16·5	2,000	100	181
2/102 mm – 45 cal		Triple expansion 3-cylinder boilers (coal) 3,500 hp 2 screws Fuel 1,595 T of coal	13		266	181
2/456 mm tt 8 mg aa		3 Napier Sealion engines 1,500 hp 3 screws	35	500	7	179
2/533 mm tt 2/20 mm mg aa		3 Isotta-Fraschini engines 3,000 hp 3 screws	47·8	450	10	181

2 releasable high explosive
  charges carried externally
		Surface, diesel motor
		Submerged, battery-driven
		  electric motors
			sub 4
			7
				1,200	3	179

320 kg of TNT in torpedo head		Battery-driven electric motor	3·5	20	2	179

TECHNICAL DATA

American naval forces at the outbreak of the Second World War						
Battleships	Aircraft carriers	Heavy cruisers	Light cruisers	Destroyers and Torpedo boats	Submarines	Total tonnage
15	7	18	18	220	100	1,344,870

American naval forces at the end of the Second World War						
Battleships	Aircraft carriers	Heavy cruisers	Light cruisers	Destroyers and Torpedo boats	Submarines	Total tonnage
21	102	26	45	745	205	—

The war on the seas. The American war: principal marine classes cited in this chapter

Page	Class	Shipyard	Date: ld c r	Displacement (full load)	Length o.a.		Beam		Draft (mean)	
					meters	feet	meters	feet	meters	feet
182	**Battleships** Arkansas	New York Shipbuilding	1910/1912/1927	29,000	170·3	562 ft.	32·3	106 ft.	9·7	26 ft. 32 ft. (max.)
185	Texas (2 ships)	Newport News	1911/1914/1927	30,000	174·7	573 ft.	32·3	106 ft.	9·6	26 ft. 31½ ft.
184	Nevada (2 ships)	Fore River	1912/1916/1929	34,000	177·8	583 ft.	32·9	107 ft. 11 in.	9·9	27½ ft. 32½ ft. (max.)
184	Pennsylvania (2 ships)	Newport News	1913/1916/1931	36,500	185·3	608 ft.	32·4	106 ft. 3 in.	10·2	28 ft. 33½ft. (max.)
184	Mississippi (New Mexico class, 3 ships)	Newport News	1915/1917/1932	35,100	190·7	624 ft.	32·4	106¼ ft.	10·4	29¼ ft. 34 ft. (max.)
185	Idaho	New York Shipbuilding	1915/1919/1935							
182	California (2 ships)	Mare Island Navy Yard	1916/1921/1943	35,190	190·2	624 ft.	29·7	97½ ft.	10·7	30¼ ft. 35½ ft. (max.)
184	Maryland (3 ships)	Newport News	1917/1921	33,590	190·2	624 ft.	29·7	97½ ft.	10·7	29 ft. 8 in. 35 ft. (max.)

ABBREVIATIONS — Date: ld = laid down **c** = completed **r** = refit **length o.a.** = length over all **mg** = machine gun mounting **mmg** = multi-machine gun mounting **dct** = depth charge thrower **pdr** = pounder **aa** = anti-aircraft **a/s** = anti-submarine **4-bar** = 4-barrelled **T** = tonnage **hp** = horsepower **sub** = speed when submerged **tt** = torpedo tube **cal** = caliber **wl** = water level **d** = deck **fd** = flight deck **ct** = control or conning tower **t** = turret **b** = barbette **tb** = turret base **bt** = battery

Armaments	Armor	Machinery	Speed (knots)	Range (miles)	Complement	Page
12/305 mm – 50 cal 16/127 mm – 51 cal 10/76 mm – 32 cal 36/40 mm – 56 cal 8/76 mm aa – 50 cal 4/3 pdr (saluting) 4/40 mm mg aa 1 catapult 3 aircraft	**Vertical** max 279 mm **Horizontal** d 76 mm ct 305 mm t 305 mm b 279 mm bt 165 mm bulges below wl	4 Parsons turbines 4 White-Forster boilers (oil) 28,000 hp 4 screws Fuel 5,100 T	20·5 19·2 (present)	8,000	1,330	182
10/356 mm – 45 cal 6/127 mm – 51 cal 8/76 mm aa – 50 cal 36/40 mm – 56 cal 30/20 mm 4/3 pdr (saluting) 8/40 mm mg aa 1 catapult 3 aircraft	**Vertical** max 305 mm **Horizontal** d 95 mm ct 305 mm b 305 mm bt 152 mm	Vertical triple expansion 4-cylinder 6 Bureau Express boilers (oil) 28,100 hp 2 screws Fuel 5,200 T	21	9,000	1,314	185
10/356 mm – 45 cal 16/127 mm – 38 cal 36/40 mm – 56 cal 38/20 mm 8/127 mm aa – 25 cal 4/6 pdr 8/40 mm mg aa 2 catapults 3 aircraft	**Vertical** max 343 mm **Horizontal** 2d 76–51 mm ct 406 mm t 457–406 mm b 342 mm external bulges below wl	Parsons turbines with reduction gears 6 Bureau Express boilers (oil) 26,500 hp 2 screws Fuel 2,000 T	20·5	10,000	1,301	184
12/356 mm – 45 cal 16/127 mm – 38 cal 45/40 mm – 56 cal 12/127 mm – 51 cal 8/127 mm aa – 25 cal 50/20 mm 4/3 pdr (saluting) 8/40 mm aa 2 catapults 3 aircraft	**Vertical** max 356 mm **Horizontal** 2d 102–51 mm ct 406 mm t 457 mm b 356 mm external bulges below wl	Curtis turbines Westinghouse geared turbines 1 Bureau Express boiler (oil) 5 White-Forster boilers 31,500 hp 4 screws Fuel 2,322 T	21	8,000	1,358	184
12/356 mm – 50 cal 10/127 mm – 25 cal 56/40 mm – 56 cal 8/127 mm aa – 25 cal 4/6 pdr 15/20 mm 12/40 mm mg aa 2 catapults 3 aircraft	**Vertical** max 356 mm **Horizontal** 2d 102–51 mm ct 406 mm t 457 mm b 356 mm external bulges below wl	Westinghouse turbines 6 Bureau Express boilers (oil) 40,000 hp 4 screws Fuel 2,200 T	21·5	9,000	1,323	184 185
12/356 mm – 50 cal 16/127 mm – 38 cal 8/127 mm aa – 25 cal 4/6 pdr (saluting) 30/20 mm 56/40 mm – 56 cal 11/40 mm mg aa 2 catapults 3 aircraft	**Vertical** max 356 mm **Horizontal** 2d 127 mm ct 406 mm t 457 mm b 356 mm external bulges below wl	General Electric turbines and electric drive 8 Bureau Express boilers 26,800 hp 4 screws Fuel 3,328 T (max.)	21	10,000	1,480	182
8/406 mm – 45 cal 16/127 mm – 38 cal 32/40 mm – 56 cal 37/20 mm 8/127 mm aa – 25 cal 11/40 mm aa 2 catapults 3 aircraft	**Vertical** max 406 mm **Horizontal** 2d 102–51 mm ct 406 mm t 457 mm b 406 mm multiple bulkheads below wl	General Electric turbines and electric drive 8 Babcock & Wilcox boilers (oil) 27,300 hp 4 screws Fuel 4,000 T (max.)	21	8,000	1,407	184

TECHNICAL DATA

Page	Class	Shipyard	Date: ld c r	Displacement (full load)	Length o.a.		Beam		Draft (mean)	
					meters	feet	meters	feet	meters	feet
185	**Iowa** (2 ships)	New York Navy Yard	1940/1943	57,500	270·5	880 ft.	33	108 ft.	11	36 ft. (max.)
182	**Missouri** (same class)	New York Navy Yard	1944							
	Aircraft carriers									
186	**Saratoga** (2 ships) Originally authorized as a battlecruiser of 35,000 T. Transformed in 1922	New York Shipbuilding	1920/1927	40,000	270·6	888 ft.	32·2	105½ ft. (extreme)	7·4	24 ft. 2 in. 32 ft. (max.)
182	**Lexington**	Fore River	1921/1927		271	889 ft.	32·4	106 ft. 3 in.	7·4	24 ft. 2 in. 32 ft. (max.)
186	**Ranger**	Newport News	1931/1934	14,500	234·4	769 ft.	24·5	80 ft. 1 in.	6	19 ft. 8 in.
186	**Enterprise** (Yorktown class, (4 ships)	Newport News	1934/1938	19,900	246·6	809½ ft.	25·4 fd 33	83¼ ft.	6·6	21 ft. 8 in.
186	**Wasp**	Bethlehem Shipbuilding	1936/1940	14,700	225	739 ft.	33·5	80 ft. 9½ in.	6	20 ft.
	Aircraft carriers									
186	**Long Island**	Sun Shipbuilding	1939/1942	12,800	193·6	612 1/16 ft.	21·3	69 ft.	6·6	21 ft. 8 in.
	Heavy cruisers									
184	**Chester** (Northampton class, 6 ships)	New York Shipbuilding	1928/1930	9,200	182·9	600¼ ft.	20·1	66 ft.	5	16½ ft.
184	**Augusta** (same class)	Newport News	1928/1931							
184	**Portland** (2 ships)	Bethlehem Shipbuilding	1930/1933	9,800 (standard)	186	610¼ ft.	20·1	66 ft.	5·3	17½ ft.
184	**Pensacola** (2 ships)	New York Navy Yard	1926/1930	9,100	177·5	585½ ft.	19·9	65¼ ft.	4·9	16 ft. 2 in. 22 ft.
184	**Minneapolis** (7 ships)	Philadelphia Navy Yard	1931/1934	9,950	179·2	588 ft.	18·8	61¾ ft.	5·9	19 ft. 5 in.

Armaments	Armor	Machinery	Speed (knots)	Range (miles)	Comple- ment	Page
9/406 mm – 50 cal 20/127 mm – 38 cal 64/40 mm – 56 cal 49/20 mm 2 catapults 4 aircraft	**Vertical** max 310 mm **Horizontal** d 142 mm t 496 mm b 439 mm ct 445 mm multiple bulkheads below wl	Geared turbines 8 Babcock & Wilcox boilers (oil) 212,000 hp 4 screws Fuel 7,250 T	33	15,000	2.900	185 186
8/203 mm – 55 cal 12/127 mm aa – 25 cal 4/6 pdr (saluting) 8/40 mm mg aa 1 catapult 79 aircraft (*Saratoga*) 90 aircraft (*Lexington*)	**Vertical** max 152 mm **Horizontal** fd 76 mm external bulges below wl	General Electric turbines and electric drive 16 White-Forster boilers (*Saratoga*) 16 Yarrow boilers (*Lexington*) 180,000 hp 4 screws Fuel 5,400/7,000 T	33·25	12,000	1,401 1,899 3,300	182 182
8/127 mm aa – 25 cal 40/40 mm 8-bar aa 72/120 aircraft		Geared turbines (high-pressure Curtis; low-pressure Parsons) 6 Babcock & Wilcox sectional Express boilers 53,000 hp 2 screws	29·2		1,016 1,788	186
8/127 mm aa – 38 cal 16/127 mm aa 16 mg 83/100 aircraft	**Vertical** max 152 mm **Horizontal** max 76 mm external bulges below wl	4 Parsons geared turbines 9 Babcock & Wilcox Express boilers 120,000 hp 4 screws Fuel 3,500 T	34	8,000	2,072	186
as for *Enterprise*	as for *Enterprise*	4 Parsons geared turbines 6 Yarrow boilers 55,000 hp 2 screws	30	6,000	1,600	186
8/127 mm aa – 38 cal 16/27 mm aa 16 mg aa 30 aircraft	**Vertical** max 125 mm **Horizontal** max 56 mm	Geared turbines 4 Yarrow boilers (oil) 85,000 hp Fuel 4,500 T	28	6,500	980	186
9/203 mm – 53 cal 4/127 mm aa – 25 cal 2/3 pdr 8/40 mm aa 2 catapults 4 aircraft	**Vertical** max 76 mm **Horizontal** 2d 51–25 mm t 63 mm b 38 mm	Parsons geared turbines 8 White-Forster boilers 107,000 hp 4 screws Fuel 1,500 T	32·7	13,000	611	184 184
9/203 mm – 55 cal 8/127 mm aa – 25 cal 2/3 pdr 10/40 mm aa 2 catapults 4 aircraft	**Vertical** max 102 mm **Horizontal** 2d 51 t 76 mm	Parsons geared turbines 4 Yarrow boilers (oil) 107,000 hp 4 screws Fuel 1,500 T	32·7	14,000	551	184
10/203 mm – 55 cal 4/127 mm – 25 cal 2/3 pdr 4/40 mm aa 2 catapults 4 aircraft	**Vertical** max 76 mm **Horizontal** 2d 51/25 mm t 63 mm b 38 mm	4 Parsons geared turbines 8 White-Forster boilers 107,000 hp 4 screws Fuel 1,500 T	32·7	13,000	710	184
9/203 mm – 55 cal 8/127 mm – 25 cal 2/3 pdr 8/40 mm aa 2 catapults 4 aircraft	**Vertical** max 127 mm **Horizontal** 2d 76–51 mm tb 152–76 mm ct 203 mm	Westinghouse geared turbines 8 Babcock & Wilcox boilers 107,000 hp 4 screws Fuel 1,650 T	32·7	14,000	551	184

TECHNICAL DATA

Page	Class	Shipyard	Date: ld c r	Displacement (full load)	Length o.a.		Beam		Draft (mean)	
					meters	feet	meters	feet	meters	feet
184	**Concord** (Omaha class, 10 ships)	William Cramp	1920/1923	7,050	169·3	555½ ft. 4 in.	16·9	55 ft.	4·1	13½ ft. 20 ft.
184	**Light cruisers** **Savannah** (Brooklyn class, 9 ships)	New York Shipbuilding	1934/1938	9,475	182·9	600 ft.	18·8	61½ ft.	5·8	19¾ ft.
183	**Boise** (same class)	Newport News	1935/1939							
184	**Atlanta** (4 ships)	Federal Shipbuilding, Kearny	1939/1941	6,000	161·2	521 ft.	16·6	52 ft.	5	15 ft.
184	**Destroyers** Flush Deck (153 ships)	Various	1918/1919/1921	1,020/1,090	94·7	314½ ft.	9	30½ ft.	2·7	8½ ft. 13½ ft.
184	**Farragut** (8 ships)	Bethlehem Shipbuilding	1932/1934	1,365	104	330 ft.	10·4	34 ft. 2 in.	2·6	8 ft. 8 in.
184	**Porter** (8 ships)	New York Shipbuilding	1934/1937	1,850	113	381 ft.	11·3	36 ft. 2 in.	3	10 ft. 5 in.
184	**Mahan** (16 ships)	United Dry Docks	1934/1936	1,450	101·8	341¼ ft.	10·6	34 ft. 8 in.	3·1	9 ft. 8 in. 17 ft.
184	**Henley** (Craven class, 22 ships)	Mare Island Navy Yard	1935/1938	1,500	101·8	341¼ ft.	10·6	34 ft. 8 in.	3	9 ft. 6 in.
184	**Sims** (12 ships)	Bath Iron Works	1937/1939	1,570	101·9	341½ ft.	10·6	34 ft. 8 in.	3·1	9 ft. 1 in.
182	**Fletcher** (115 ships)	Bath Iron Works	1940/1942	2,050	114	374 ft.	12	39 ft.	5·4	18 ft.
184	**Submarines** Class **O** (7 ships)	Puget Sound Navy Yard	1917/1918	480/624	52·5	172 ft. 4 in.	5·5	18 ft.	4·4	14½ ft.
184	Class **R** (18 ships)	Fore River Union Iron Works	1917/1918	530/680	56·7	186 ft.	5·5	18 ft.	4·4	14½ ft.

Armaments	Armor	Machinery	Speed (knots)	Range (miles)	Complement	Page
10/152 mm – 53 cal 4/76 mm aa – 50 cal 2/3 pdr 8/40 mm aa 6/533 mm tt 2 catapults 4 aircraft 30 mines	**Vertical** max 76 mm **Horizontal** max 38 mm	Westinghouse turbines with reduction gears 12 White-Forster boilers (oil) 90,000 hp 4 screws Fuel 2,000 T	34·7	10,000	458 560	184
15/152 mm – 47 cal 8/127 mm aa – 25 cal 4/3 pdr 5/40 mm aa 2 catapults 4/8 aircraft	**Vertical** max 76 mm **Horizontal** 2d 51–76 mm ct 203 mm tb 127 mm internal bulges below wl	Parsons geared turbines 12 Babcock & Wilcox Express boilers (oil) 100,000 hp 4 screws Fuel 2,100 T	32·7	13,000	540 868	184 183
16/127 mm aa – 38 cal 12/27 mm aa 6/533 mm tt 1 catapult 2/3 aircraft	**Vertical** max 76 mm **Horizontal** d 55–75 mm	Curtis geared turbines 6 Babcock & Wilcox boilers (oil) 75,000 hp 4 screws Fuel 1,600 T	37	10,000	532	184

4/102 or 127 mm – 50 cal
1/76 mm aa – 23 cal
12/533 mm tt
		Westinghouse, Parsons or
		  Curtis geared turbines
		4 Yarrow or White-Forster
		  boilers (oil)
		26,000 hp
		2 screws
		Fuel 370 T
			35	5,000	122	184

5/127 mm aa – 38 cal 4/40 mm aa 8/533 mm tt		Parsons geared turbines 4 Yarrow boilers (oil) 42,800 hp 2 screws Fuel 400 T	36·5	6,000	162 188	184
8/127 mm aa – 38 cal 8/1 pdr 2 mg 8/533 mm tt		Parsons geared turbines 4 Babcock & Wilcox boilers (oil) 50,000 hp 2 screws Fuel 300 T	37	8,000	175	184
5/127 mm aa – 38 cal 4 mg aa 12/533 mm tt		Curtis geared turbines 4 Express boilers (oil) 42,800 hp 2 screws Fuel 400 T	36·5	6,000	172	184
4/127 mm aa – 38 cal 4 mg aa 16/533 mm tt		Parsons geared turbines 4 Express boilers (oil) 42,800 hp 2 screws Fuel 400 T	36·5	6,000	172	184
5/127 mm – 38 cal 4/40 mm aa 8 mg 12/533 mm tt		Parsons geared turbines 4 Express boilers (oil) 44,000 hp 2 screws Fuel 400 T	36·5	6,000	166	184
5/127 mm aa 10/40 mm 10/20 mm mg 10/533 mm tt						182
1/76 mm aa – 23 cal 4/475 mm tt		2 sets Nelseco diesel engines 880 hp 2 electric motors 740 hp 2 screws Fuel 78 T	sub 11 14·5	3,000 3,500	30	184
1/76 mm aa – 50 cal 4/457 mm tt		2 sets Nelseco diesel engines 880 hp 2 electric motors 934 hp 2 screws Fuel 56 T	sub 10·5 3·6	3,500	31	184

TECHNICAL DATA

Page	Class	Shipyard	Date: ld c r	Displacement (full load)	Length o.a. meters	feet	Beam meters	feet	Draft (mean) meters	feet
183	**Gato** (Fleet type, 75 ships)	Electric Boat and others	1939/1940	1,525/2,400	93·5	307 ft.	8·2	26½ ft.	4·2	13¾ ft.
183	**Landing craft** **L.S.T.** (Landing ship tank)	Various	1941/1943	7,600	76·4	261 ft.	6·3	20¾ ft.	4·6	15½ ft.
183	**L.C.M.** (Landing craft mechanized)	Various	1941/1943	18	34·6	111 ft.	3·2	9¾ ft.	2	6¼ ft.
183	**Motor torpedo boats** **Elco**	Higgins	1942/1943	38	24·4	81¾ ft.	6·3	20½ ft.	1·5	5¾ ft.
184	**P.T. 12** (44 ships)	Electric Boat	1940	32	22	72¼ ft.	6·65	21¾ ft.	1·2	4 ft.

French naval forces at the outbreak of the Second World War

Battleships	Aircraft carriers	Heavy cruisers	Light cruisers	Destroyers and Torpedo boats	Submarines	Total tonnage
8	1	7	11	71	78	564,108

The war on the seas. The French war: principal marine classes cited in this chapter

Page	Class	Shipyard	Date: ld c r	Displacement (full load)	Length o.a. meters	feet	Beam meters	feet	Draft (mean) meters	feet
189	**Battleships** **Courbet** (2 ships)	Lorient Navy Yard	1910/1913/1927	25,850	168	551 ft.	28·2	92½ ft.	9·9	32½ ft.
188	**Paris**	La Seyne	1911/1914/1929							
189	**Provence**	Lorient Navy Yard	1912/1915/1933	22,189 (standard)	166	544½ ft.	27	88½ ft.	9·8	32 ft.
187	**Dunkerque** (2 ships)	Brest Navy Yard	1932/1938	26,500 (standard)	214	702 ft.	31·1	101¾ ft.	8·6	28 ft.
187	**Strasbourg**	Penhoët	1936							

Armaments	Armor	Machinery	Speed (knots)	Range (miles)	Comple- ment	Page
1/76 mm aa 2 mg aa 10/533 mm tt		GM diesels 6,500 hp	sub 14 21	16,000	65	183
2 smoke mortars 2/102 mm 4/40 mm aa 6/20 mm mg aa 12 tanks of 25 T or 18 tanks of 18 T or 33 lorries of 3 T 217 soldiers or 2 L.C.M.		White turbines 4 Express boilers (oil) 40,000 hp 2 screws Fuel 450 T	12	6,000	98	183
2/8 mm Lewis mg 100 soldiers or 1 tank of 18 T or 1 lorry of 16 T		MAN diesel 1,600 hp 2 screws	7·5		6	183
1/20 mm aa 4/12·7 mm mg 8 a/s bombs 2/533 mm tt		Nelseco diesel 2 screws	40		14	183
4 mg 4/456 mm tt depth charges		3 Packard V12 motors 4,050 hp	40	3,000		184

ABBREVIATIONS — Date: ld = laid down **c** = completed **r** = refit **length o.a.** = length over all **mg** = machine gun mounting **mmg** = multi-machine gun mounting **dct** = depth charge thrower **pdr** = pounder **aa** = anti-aircraft **a/s** = anti-submarine **4-bar** = 4-barrelled **T** = tonnage **hp** = horsepower **sub** = speed when submerged **tt** = torpedo tube **cal** = caliber **wl** = water level **d** = deck **fd** = flight deck **ct** = control or conning tower **t** = turret **b** = barbette **tb** = turret base **bt** = battery

Armaments	Armor	Machinery	Speed (knots)	Range (miles)	Comple- ment	Page
12/305 mm – 45 cal 22/138 mm – 55 cal 7/75 mm aa – 60 cal 2/47 mm aa 4/450 mm tt	**Vertical** max 270 mm **Horizontal** d 30–45–75 mm ct 300 mm tb 300 mm b 180 mm	Parsons turbines 24 Belleville boilers (mixed firing) 43,000 hp 4 screws Fuel 3,000 T (coal and oil)	20	8,400	1,118 1,070	189 188
10/340 mm – 45 cal 14/138 mm – 55 cal 8/75 mm aa – 60 cal 7/47 mm aa 1 catapult 4 aircraft	**Vertical** max 270 mm **Horizontal** 3d 30–45–75 mm ct 314 mm tb 400 mm b 180 mm	Parsons turbines 6 Indret boilers (oil) 29,000 hp 4 screws Fuel 2,600 T	20	9,000	1,135	189
8/330 mm – 52 cal 16/130 mm aa 8/37 mm aa 32/13·5 mm 4-bar mmg aa 1 catapult 4 aircraft	**Vertical** max 280 mm **Horizontal** 2d 125–50 mm ct 356 mm tb 356 mm internal bulges 33 mm	Parsons geared turbines 6 Indret boilers (oil) 100,000 hp 4 screws	31·5	7,500	1,381 1,431	187 187

TECHNICAL DATA

Page	Class	Shipyard	Date: ld c r	Displacement (full load)	Length o.a.		Beam		Draft (mean)	
					meters	feet	meters	feet	meters	feet
187	**Richelieu** (4 ships)	Brest Navy Yard	1935/1940	35,000	242	794 ft.	33·1	108¼ ft.	8·2	26½ ft.
188	**Jean Bart**	Penhoët	1937							
	Aircraft carriers									
187	**Béarn**	La Seyne	1914/1920/1935	25,000	182·6 fd 183	599 ft.	32·2 fd 31	89 ft. 115½ ft. (ex-treme)	9·3	30½ ft. (max.)
	Seaplane carriers									
188	**Commandant Teste**	Ch. de la Gironde	1929/1932	11,500	167	558 ft.	21·8	71½ ft. 88½ ft. (ex-treme)	6·9	22¾ ft.
	Heavy cruisers									
188	**Tourville** (2 ships)	Lorient Navy Yard	1925/1928	11.900	191	626 ft. 8 in.	19	62 ft. 4 in.	6·3	23 ft. (max.)
188	**Suffren** (4 ships)	Brest Navy Yard	1926/1930	10,000	196	643 ft.	20	65 ft. 8 in.	6·1	24½ in. (max.)
	Light cruisers									
188	**Duguay-Trouin** (3 ships)	Brest Navy Yard	1922/1926	9,350	181·2	594¾ ft.	17·5	57½ ft.	5·3	17¼ ft. 20 ft. 8 in.
188	**Jeanne d'Arc**	Penhoët	1928/1931	6,496 (standard)	170	557¾ ft.	17·5	57½ ft.	5	20 ft. 8 in.
188	**Emile Bertin**	Penhoët	1931/1934	5,886	177	580¾ ft.	15·8	51¾ ft.	5·4	17¾ ft. (max.)
188	**La Galissonière** (6 ships)	Brest Navy Yard	1931/1935	9,120	178·9	580¾ ft.	17·5	57 ft. 4 in.	5·2	17 ft. 4 in.
188	**La Tour d'Auvergne**	Lorient Navy Yard	1928/1931	4,773	152·5	500 ft. 4 in.	15·6	51 ft.	5·8	17 ft. 20 ft.

Armaments	Armor	Machinery	Speed (knots)	Range (miles)	Comple-ment	Page
8/381 mm 15/152 mm 10/100 mm aa 12/37 mm aa 20/37 mm aa 2 catapults 4 aircraft	**Vertical** max 400 mm **Horizontal** 2d 200 mm internal bulges	Parsons geared turbines 6 Indret boilers (oil) 1 Babcock auxiliary boiler 150,000 hp 4 screws	31·5		1.500	187 188
8/155 mm – 55 cal 6/100 mm aa – 60 cal 8/37 mm aa 4/550 mm tt 40 aircraft	**Vertical** max 83 mm **Horizontal** 3d 25–70–25 mm gunnery shield 70 mm	2 turbines on inner screws 2 sets reciprocating engines on other screws 12 Du Temple Normand small tube boilers 37,000 hp 4 screws Fuel 2,160 T	21·5	6,000	875	187
12/100 mm – 60 cal 8/3 pdr 12 mg aa 4 catapults 26 aircraft	**Vertical** max 50 mm **Horizontal** d 36 mm	2 Schneider-Zoelly turbines 4 Yarrow-Loire boilers (mixed firing) 21,000 hp 2 screws Fuel 1,010 T	20·5	6,000	648 686	188
8/203 mm – 50 cal 8/75 mm aa – 60 cal 8/37 mm aa 12 mg aa 6/550 mm tt 1 catapult 2 aircraft	virtually none	4 Rateau-Chantiers geared turbines 9 Guyot boilers (oil) 120,000 hp 4 screws Fuel 1,800 T	33·7	5,000	605	188
8/203 mm – 50 cal 8/90 mm aa – 50 cal 8/75 mm aa – 60 cal 8/37 mm aa 12 mg aa 6/533 mm tt 2 catapults 2 aircraft	**Vertical** max 60 mm internal bulges below wl	3 Rateau-Chantiers geared turbines 9 Guyot boilers (mixed firing) 90,000 hp 3 screws Fuel 1,800 T	32·5	5,000	605	188
8/155 mm – 55 cal 4/75 mm – 60 cal 2/3 pdr (saluting) 4 mg aa 12/550 mm tt 1 catapult 2 aircraft		4 Parsons geared turbines 8 Guyot boilers (oil) 102,000 hp 4 screws Fuel 1.500 T	33	4.500	578	188
8/155 mm – 55 cal 4/75 mm – 60 cal 4/37 mm aa 12 mg aa 2/550 mm tt 1 catapult 2 aircraft	**Horizontal** d 76 mm	Parsons geared turbines 4 Penhoët boilers (oil) 32,500 hp 2 screws Fuel 1,400 T	26	5,000	506	188
9/152 mm – 50 cal 4/90 mm aa – 50 cal 8/37 mm aa 6/550 mm tt 1 catapult 2 aircraft 200 mines	**Horizontal** d 50 mm	Parsons geared turbines 6 Penhoët boilers (oil) 4 screws Fuel 1,400 T	34	6,000	567	188
9/152 mm – 50 cal 8/90 mm – 50 cal 8/13 mm mg aa 4/550 mm tt 1 catapult 3 aircraft	**Vertical** max 120 mm **Horizontal** d 68 mm ct 95 mm tb 140 mm	2 Rateau-Chantiers geared turbines 4 Indret small tube boilers 84,000 hp 2 screws Fuel 1,500 t	31	6,000	540 608	188
4/138 mm – 40 cal 4/75 mm aa – 60 cal 2/37 mm aa 12 mg aa 200 mines		2 Bréguet geared turbines 4 small tube boilers 57,000 hp 2 screws Fuel 1,200 T	30		397	188

TECHNICAL DATA

Page	Class	Shipyard	Date: ld c r	Displacement (full load)	Length o.a.		Beam		Draft (mean)	
					meters	feet	meters	feet	meters	feet
188	**Destroyers** **Lion** (Guépard class, 6 ships)	Ch. France	1926/1931	3,080	130·2	427 ft.	11·8	38¾ ft.	3·6	15¾ ft.
188	**Torpedo boats** **La Pomone** (12 ships)	Ch. de la Loire	1933/1936	700	80·7	264¾ ft.	7·9	26 ft.	2·8	9¼ ft.
188	**Submarines** **Requin** (9 ships)	Cherbourg	1922/1926	974/1,441	78·6	257½ ft.	7	23 ft.	5·4	17¾ ft.
187	**Surcouf**	Cherbourg	1927/1929/1934	2,880/4,300	110	361 ft.	9	29½ ft.	7·2	23½ ft.
188	**Naïade** (Sirène class, (10 ships)	Ch. de la Loire	1923/1927	548/744	66	210 ft.	6·5	21 ft.	4·5	14¾ ft.
188	**Argonaute** (Diane class, 22 ships)	Schneider-Crensot	1927/1932	565/800	63·4	208 ft.	6·4	21 ft.	4·2	13¾ ft.
188	**Patrol vessels** **Bougainville** (8 ships)	Ch. de la Gironde	1929/1932	2,156	103·7	340 ft.	12·7	41 ft. 8 in.	4·5	14¾ ft.
188	**Marne** (2 ships)	Lorient Navy Yard	1916/1917	601	78	256 ft.	8·4	29¼ ft.	3·4	11 ft.
187	**Ancre** (2 ships)	Lorient Navy Yard	1917/1918	604	77·6	250 ft.	8·4	28½ ft.	3·2	10¾ ft.
188	**Dubourdieu** (2 ships)	Brest Navy Yard	1918/1920	453 (standard)	65	213¼ ft.	6·6	27 ft.	3·1	10 ft. (max.)
188	**Diligente** (3 ships)	Brest Navy Yard	1916/1917	315	66	217¾ ft.	7	23 ft.	2·8	9¼ ft.
188	**Submarine chasers** **CH. 106** (3 ships)	Nounand	1919/1920	128	43	142 ft.	5·2	17 ft. 2 in.	2	8¼ ft. (max.)
188	**Minesweepers** **Granit** (2 ships)	Lorient Navy Yard	1918/1919	354	56	189 ft.	7·5	26 ft.	1·9	7½ ft.

Armaments	Armor	Machinery	Speed (knots)	Range (miles)	Complement	Page
5/138 mm – 50 cal 4/37 mm aa 4 mg aa 6/550 mm tt equipped for minelaying		Zoelly-Fives-Lille turbines 6 Indret boilers 64,000 hp 2 screws Fuel 600 T	36	3,000	209 238	188
2/750 mm – 60 cal 2/37 mm aa 4 mg aa 2/550 mm tt		Parsons geared turbines or Rateau-Bretagne type 2 boilers (oil) 22,000 hp 2 screws Fuel 90 T	34·5	1,800	92 170	188
1/100 mm – 40 cal 2 mg aa 10/550 mm tt		Sulzer diesels (or Schneider- Carel) 2,900 hp Electric motors 1,800 hp	sub 10 16	7,000	54	188
2·203 mm 2/37 mm aa 4 mg aa 10/550 mm tt 4/450 mm tt 1 seaplane		Sulzer diesels 7,600 hp Electric motors 3,400 hp 2 screws	sub 10 18	12,000	109 150	187
1/75 mm – 35 cal 2 mg aa 7/550 mm tt		Sulzer diesels or Vickers- Normand) 1,300/1,250/ 1,200 hp Schneider-Carel electric motors 1,000 hp	sub 7·5 14	2,000	40	188
1/75 mm aa – 35 cal 1 mg aa 7/550 mm tt 2/450 mm tt		Schneider-Sulzer diesels 1,350 hp Electric motors 1,000 hp	sub 9 14	3,000	43 48	188
3/138 mm – 40 cal 4/37 mm aa 6 mg aa 1 seaplane 50 mines		Schneider Burmeister diesels 3,200 hp 2 screws Fuel 280 T	15·5	9,000	135	188
4/100 mm – 40 cal 2/65 mm 1/47 mm		2 sets geared turbines 2 Guyot boilers 5,000 hp 2 screws Fuel 145 T	21	4,000	103	188
4/100 mm – 40 cal 6/47 mm aa 2/65 mm		2 sets geared turbines 2 Du Temple boilers 5,000 hp 2 screws Fuel 142 T	20	4,000	107	188
1/138 mm – 55 cal 1/100 mm – 40 cal		2 sets Bréguet turbines 2 Guyot boilers 2,000 hp 2 screws Fuel 143 T	17	2,000	74	188
2/100 mm – 40 cal		Sulzer diesels 900 hp 2 screws Fuel 30 T	14·5	3,000	57	188
1/75 mm 2 mg aa depth charges		Triple expansion 2 Normand boilers 1,300 hp Fuel 28 T of coal	16·5		31	188
1/65 mm		Triple expansion 550 hp 2 screws Fuel 90 T of coal	12·5		63	188

TECHNICAL DATA

Russian naval forces at the outbreak of the Second World War						
Battleships	**Aircraft carriers**	**Heavy cruisers**	**Light cruisers**	**Destroyers and Torpedo boats**	**Submarines**	**Total tonnage**
8	—	**4**	**4**	**46**	**156**	**270,489**

The war on the seas. The Russian war: principal marine classes cited in this chapter

Page	Class	Shipyard	Date: ld c r	Displacement (full load)	Length o.a. meters	feet	Beam meters	feet	Draft (mean) meters	feet
	Battleships									
189	**Archangelsk** (Sovereign class) On loan from Great Britain)	Portsmouth Dockyard	1914/1916	33.500	189·1	620½ ft.	31·1	102½ ft.	9·4	28½ ft.
190	**Marat** (Pariskaya Kommuna class, 3 ships)	Baltic Works	1909/1914	26.000	188·7	619 ft.	26·5	87 ft.	8·4	27½ ft.
190	**Oktiabrskaia Revolutia** (same class)	Galernu	1909/1914/1933							
	Heavy cruisers									
190	**Krasni-Kavkaz**	Nikolaiev	1913/1932	8.030	158	530 ft.	15·4	50½ ft.	6·2	20 ft. 4 in.
190	**Kiroff** (3 ships)	Baltic Works	1936	10,000	192·8	600 ft.	18	60 ft.	6·4	21 ft. (max.)
	Light cruisers									
190	**Aurora**	Baltic Works	1896/1903/1917	5,662	127	420½ ft.	16·8	53¼ ft.	6·5	21 ft.
190	**Profintern**	Böker, Reval	1915/1917	6,600	158·5	507¾ ft.	15·3	50 ft. 4 in.	5·6	18 ft. 4 in.
190	**25 Oktyabrya**	Baltic Works	1875/1936	4,250	86·6	284 ft.	14·6	48 ft.	6·7	22 ft.
190	**Marti**	Burmeister, Sweden	1893/1896/1936	4,600	124	370 ft.	15·4	52½ ft.	6·7	22 ft.

ABBREVIATIONS — Date: ld = laid down **c** = completed **r** = refit **length o.a.** = length over all **mg** = machine gun mounting **mmg** = multi-machine gun mounting **dct** = depth charge thrower **pdr** = pounder **aa** = anti-aircraft **a/s** = anti-submarine **4-bar** = 4-barrelled **T** = tonnage **hp** = horsepower **sub** = speed when submerged **tt** = torpedo tube **cal** = caliber **wl** = water level **d** = deck **fd** = flight deck **ct** = control or conning tower **t** = turret **b** = barbette **tb** = turret base **bt** = battery

Armaments	Armor	Machinery	Speed (knots)	Range (miles)	Comple-ment	Page
8/381 mm – 42 cal 12/152 mm – 50 cal 8/102 mm – 45 cal 4/3 pdr 2/40 mm 8-bar mmg aa 2/20 mm 4-bar 10 mg aa 1 catapult 1 aircraft 4/533 mm tt	**Vertical** max 330 mm **Horizontal** d 102 mm ct 279 mm tb 330 mm bt 152 mm external bulges below wl	Parsons turbines 18 Babcock boilers (oil) 40,000 hp 4 screws Fuel 3,230 T	22	4,200	1,010 1,146	189
12/305 mm – 52 cal 16/120 mm – 50 cal 6/75 mm – 30 cal 8 mg aa 4/450 mm tt 1 aircraft	**Vertical** max 225 mm **Horizontal** d 75 mm ct 250 mm t 305 mm b 203 mm tb 152 mm	Parsons turbines 25 Yarrow boilers (mixed firing) 42,000 hp 4 screws Fuel 3,000 T	23	4,000	1,125 1,230	190 190
4/180 mm – 55 cal 8/127 mm aa 4/102 mm – 45 cal 4/37 mm aa 5 mg aa 12/533 mm tt 100 mines 1 catapult 1 aircraft 4 dct		Parsons turbines 14 Yarrow boilers 55,000 hp 4 screws Fuel 1,230 T	30	3,700	624	190
6/180 mm – 55 cal 4/102 mm aa 4/37 mm aa 4 mg aa 6/533 mm tt 1 catapult 2 aircraft 60 mines	**Vertical** max 76 mm **Horizontal** d 60 mm ct 76 mm tb 76 mm	Geared turbines and diesels 100,000 hp 4 screws	35		624	190
10/130 mm – 55 cal 4/75 mm 2/75 mm aa – 30 cal 2/47 mm 4 mg aa 125 mines	**Horizontal** max 76 mm ct 152 mm b 76 mm	Triple expansion 24 Belleville boilers 11,600 hp 3 screws Fuel 960 T of coal	17	2,000	598	190
15/130 mm – 55 cal 8/102 mm aa – 45 cal 6/75 mm aa – 50 cal 10 mg aa 12/533 mm tt 100 mines 2 aircraft		Parsons turbines 12 Yarrow boilers (mixed firing) 55,000 hp 4 screws Fuel 1,230 T	29	3,700	630	190
2/75 mm aa 2/75 mm – 50 cal 4 mg aa 500 mines		Triple expansion 12 coal-burning boilers 4,500 hp 2 screws Fuel 950 T	11	5,900	262	190
4/130 mm – 55 cal 3/75 mm aa – 30 cal 250 mines		Parsons geared turbines 2 screws	25	4,500	198	190

TECHNICAL DATA

Page	Class	Shipyard	Date: ld c r	Displacement (full load)	Length o.a.		Beam		Draft (mean)	
					meters	feet	meters	feet	meters	feet
190	**Destroyers** **Leningrad** (18 ships)	Baltic Yard	1935/1938	3,500	134	459 ft. 4 in.	13·7	40 ft.	3.7	14 ft.
190	**Tashkent**	Odero-Terni-Orlando	1936/1939	2,895	132	457 ft. 8 in.	13	45 ft.	3·7	11 ft. 4 in.
190	**Stalin**	Leningrad Metal Works	1914/1915	1,280	96	321½ ft. (max.)	9·3	30½ ft.	3	9¾ ft.
190	**Karl Marx** (2 ships)	Böker, Reval	1912/1917	1,354	105	344½ ft.	9·5	31¼ ft.	3	9¾ ft.
190	**Torpedo boats** **Shtorm** (18 ships)	Baltic Yard	1932/1935	740	72	238¾ ft.	7·3	24 ft.	3	9¾ ft.
190	**Patrol vessels** **Konstruktor**	Sandwiken-Helsinki	1906	750	74·97	246 ft.	8·2	27½ ft.	2·4	8¼ ft.
190	**Alfater** (Markin class, 3 ships)	Lange's Yard, Riga	1911	710	73·15	240 ft.	7·2	23¾ ft.	2·2	7½ ft.
190	**Submarines** **Krasnoarmeyetz** (Bolshevik class, 2 ships)	Nobel & Lessner, Reval	1914/1917/1936	650/780	68	223 ft.	4·8	14 ft. 8 in.	3·8	12 ft. 8 in.
190	**Dekabrist** (22 ships)	Baltic Yard	1931	896/1,318	73	279 ft.	7	23 ft.	4·9	16½ ft.
190	**Kommunist** (Metallist class, 4 ships)		1916/1924	375/467	46·8	150½ ft.	4·6	15¾ ft.	3·6	15¼ ft.
190	**Linj** (46 ships)	Baltic Yard	1938	600/735	60	198 ft.	6·8	22½ ft.	4·6	15 ft. 2 in.
190	Class **M** (50 ships)	Baltic Yard		200/350	35	115 ft.	4	13¾ ft.	3	9¾ ft.
190	**Minelayer** **Deviatoye Yanvarya** (ex-**Volga** 1905)	Black Sea Yard	1906/1909	1,711	65	229 ft.	11·9	45 ft.	4·8	13 ft.
190	**Depot ship submarine** **Kommuna**	Kiev	1913/1917	2,400	68	315 ft.	10·2	69 ft.	3·6	11¾ ft.

TECHNICAL DATA

Armaments	Armor	Machinery	Speed (knots)	Range (miles)	Comple-ment	Page
5/130 mm – 55 cal 2/75 mm aa – 30 cal 4/37 mm aa 8/22 mm mg 6/533 mm tt equipped for minelaying		Geared turbines 4 boilers (oil) 90,000 hp 2 screws Fuel 450 T	36	3,500	146	190
6/130 mm – 55 cal 6/45 mm aa 6 mg aa 9/533 mm tt 4 dct		Turbines 95,000 hp 2 screws	39		176	190
4/102 mm – 60 cal 1/75 mm – 30 cal 1/37 mm aa 2 mg aa 9/450 mm tt 60 mines		Turbines 4 Thornycroft boilers 30,000 hp 2 screws Fuel 400 T	30	2,800	160	190
5/100 mm – 60 cal 1/75 mm aa – 30 cal 1/37 mm aa 2 mg aa 6/450 mm tt 60 mines		Parsons turbines 4 Normand boilers 32,700 hp 2 screws Fuel 450 T	28	2,000	167 180	190
2/100 mm – 60 cal 2/37 mm aa 2 mg aa 3/450 mm tt 40 mines 2 dct		Geared turbines 13,200 hp 2 screws	29		72	190
3/75 mm – 50 cal 2/47 mm aa 2 mg aa 2/450 mm tt 40 mines		Triple expansion 7,300 hp 2 screws Fuel 215 T	25	700	101	190
3/100 mm – 60 cal 1/1 pdr 2 mg aa 2/450 mm tt 16 mines		Triple expansion 6,200 hp 2 screws Fuel 135 T	25	700	88 100	190
2/75 mm – 50 cal 1/37 mm aa 4/450 mm tt 8 mines		Diesel 1,200 hp Electric motors 900 hp 2 screws Fuel 40 T	sub 8 10	3,000	33	190
1/102 mm aa – 45 cal 1/37 mm aa 8/533 mm tt 8 mines		Diesel 2,500 hp Electric motors 1,200 hp 2 screws Fuel 78 T	sub 8 15	7,000	44	190
1/6 pdr 1 mg aa 4/450 mm tt		Diesel 500 hp Electric motors 320 hp 2 screws Fuel 60 T	sub 8 12	1,500	28	190
2/1 pdr 4/533 mm tt 45 mines		Diesel 750 hp Electric motors 600 hp 2 screws	sub 8 18	2,500	38	190
1/37 mm aa 2/450 mm tt		Diesel 500 hp Electric motors 320 hp 2 screws	sub 8·5 13	1,600	42	190
2/75 mm – 50 cal 2/75 mm aa – 50 cal 1/47 mm aa 2 mg aa 236 mines		Babcock boilers 1,200 hp 2 screws Fuel 160 T of coal	10	3,200	190	190
2/75 mm aa 8 mg aa		Diesel 1,200 hp 2 screws Fuel 800 T	10	3,600	135	190

TECHNICAL DATA

German naval forces at the outbreak of the Second World War						
Battleships	**Aircraft carriers**	**Heavy cruisers**	**Light cruisers**	**Destroyers and Torpedo boats**	**Submarines**	**Total tonnage**
5	—	2	6	42	56	225,000

The war on the seas. The German war: principal marine classes cited in this chapter

Page	Class	Shipyard	Date: ld c r	Displacement (full load)	Length o.a. meters	feet	Beam meters	feet	Draft (mean) meters	feet
	Battleships									
194	**Scharnhorst** (2 ships)	Wilhelmshaven	1934/1938	38,900	234·9	787 ft.	30	98½ ft.	9·9	24 ft. 8 in.
191	**Gneisenau**	Deutsche Werke, Kiel	1934/1938							
191	**Bismarck** (4 ships)	Blohm & Voss	1935/1940	50,900	251	823¼ ft.	36	118 ft.	10·2	33½ ft.
194	**Tirpitz**	Wilhelmshaven	1936/1941	56,000	251	823¼ ft.	36	118 ft.	11·3	37 ft.
193	**Schlesien** (2 ships)	Schichau, Danzig	1904/1908 1936	13,200	127·7	419 ft.	22·2	72 ft. 10 in.	7·7	25¼ ft.
	Heavy cruisers									
192	**Lützow** (3 ships)	Deutsche Werke, Kiel	1922/1933	10,000	182	609¼ ft.	21·7	67½ ft.	5	21 ft. 8 in.
194	**Admiral Scheer**	Wilhelmshaven	1931/1934					69½ ft.		
191	**Admiral Graf Spee**	Wilhelmshaven	1932/1936					70 ft. 10 in.		
193	**Admiral Hipper** (2 ships)	Blohm & Voss	1935/1939	10,000	195	639¾ ft.	21·3	69¾ ft.	4·7	15½ ft.
194	**Prinz Eugen**			13,900	198·3	654½ ft.	21·6	71 ft.	4·5	15 ft.
	Light cruisers									
193	**Emden**	Wilhelmshaven	1921/1925/1934	5,400	156	508½ ft.	14·3	47 ft.	5·8	17½ ft.
193	**Königsberg** (3 ships)	Wilhelmshaven	1926/1929	6,000 (standard)	173·7	570 ft.	15·2	49 ft. 10½ in.	5·4	17¾ ft.

ABBREVIATIONS — Date: ld = laid down **c** = completed **r** = refit **length o.a.** = length over all **mg** = machine gun mounting **mmg** = multi-machine gun mounting **dct** = depth charge thrower **pdr** = pounder **aa** = anti-aircraft **a/s** = anti-submarine **4-bar** = 4-barrelled **T** = tonnage **hp** = horsepower **sub** = speed when submerged **tt** = torpedo tube **cal** = caliber **wl** = water level **d** = deck **fd** = flight deck **ct** = control or conning tower **t** = turret **b** = barbette **tb** = turret base **bt** = battery

Armaments	Armor	Machinery	Speed (knots)	Range (miles)	Comple-ment	Page
9/280 mm – 54 cal 12/150 mm – 55 cal 14/105 mm aa 16/37 mm aa 2 catapults 4 aircraft	**Vertical** max 350 mm **Horizontal** d 56 mm t 360/200/150 mm ct 350/200 mm	3 geared turbines + diesels 12 Wagner high-pressure boilers 165,000 hp 3 screws Fuel 6,300 T	32	10,000	1,461	194 191
9/380 mm – 47 cal 12/150 mm – 55 cal 16/105 mm – 65 cal 16/37 mm 12/20 mm 46/20 mm 1 catapult 6 aircraft	**Vertical** max 320 mm **Horizontal** d 50/60 mm t 360 mm b 340 mm ct 350/200 mm	3 geared turbines 12 Wagner boilers 150,000 hp 3 screws Fuel 7,900 T	30·1	9,300	2,400	191
8/380 mm – 47 cal 12/150 mm – 55 cal 16/105 mm aa 16/20 mm mmg aa 16/37 mm aa 2/533 mm quadruple tt 4 seaplanes type 196 2 catapults	as for *Bismarck*	3 geared turbines 12 Wagner boilers 144,000 hp 3 screws Fuel 8,700 t	30·8	9,000	2,370	194
4/260 mm – 40 cal 10/150 mm – 45 cal 4/88 mm aa – 45 cal 4 mg aa 10/40 mm 22/20 mm	**Vertical** max 240 mm **Horizontal** d 67 mm ct 300 mm tb 280 mm	3 sets 3-cylinder triple expansion 8 oil-fired boilers 4 coal-fired boilers 17,000 hp 3 screws Fuel 1,130 T of oil 436 T of coal	16	5,900	725	193
6/280 mm 8/150 mm 6/105 mm aa 8/3 pdr 10 mg aa 8/533 mm tt 1 catapult 2 aircraft	**Vertical** max 60 mm **Horizontal** d 40 mm t 140 mm b 100 mm ct 150 mm	8 sets MAN diesels 54,000 hp 2 screws Fuel 1,200 T	26	10,000	965 1,150	192 194 191
8/203 mm 12/105 mm 12/37 mm aa 12/533 mm tt 1 catapult 3 aircraft	**Vertical** max 120 mm	3 geared turbines 8 high-pressure boilers 80,000 hp 3 screws	32		980 1,600	193 194
8/150 mm – 45 cal 3/88 mm aa 4 mg aa 4/500 mm tt	**Vertical** max 101 mm **Horizontal** t 50 mm ct 76 mm	Geared turbines 10 Schulz-Thornycroft boilers 46,500 hp Fuel 1,260 T	29	5,200	630	193
9/150 mm 6/88 mm aa 4 mg aa 12/533 mm tt 1 catapult 2 aircraft	**Vertical** max 101 mm **Horizontal** t 50 mm ct 76 mm	Geared turbines 6 Marine boilers 65,000 hp 2 diesel 2,000 hp 2 screws Fuel 1,200 T of oil 300 T for diesels	32	9,800	592	193

TECHNICAL DATA

Page	Class	Shipyard	Date: ld c r	Displacement (full load)	Length o.a. meters	feet	Beam meters	feet	Draft (mean) meters	feet
193	**Leipzig** (2 ships)	Wilhelmshaven	1928/1931	6,000 (standard)	165·8	580 ft.	16·3	53¼ ft.	4·8	15¾ ft.
192	**Destroyers** Class **Z** (20 ships)	Deutsche Werke. Kiel	1934/1937	1,625	114	374 ft.	11·3	37 ft.	2·8	9 ft. 4 in.
192	**Torpedo boats** Class **Ex G** (4 ships)	Krupp, Kiel	1911/1912	760	75	247¼ ft.	7·5	25 ft.	3·2	10½ ft.
192	**Möwe** (6 ships)	Wilhelmshaven	1925/1926	960	85	277¾ ft.	8·4	27½ ft.	2·8	9 ft. 2 in.
192	**Wolf** (6 ships)	Wilhelmshaven	1927/1929	800 (standard)	89	304 ft.	8·6	28 ft.	2·6	9 ft.
192	Class **T** (8 ships from T.1 to T.2)	Wilhelmshaven	1936/1939	600	81	267 ft.	8·6	28 ft.	1·9	6¼ ft.
192	**Submarines** Class **U** (25 ships)	Deutsche Werke. Kiel	1935/1936	250/330	41·6	136½ ft.	4	13 ft.	3·8	12 ft. 8 in.
191	**XX1-C** (40 ships)	Deutsche Werke. Kiel	1937/1940	1,600/1,800	86·4	283½ ft.	5	16 ft.	4·3	14½ ft.
192	**Minesweepers** Class **M** (19 ships)	Duetsche Werke. Kiel	1917/1920	525	56	192 ft.	7·4	24¼ ft.	2·2	7¼ ft.

Armaments	Armor	Machinery	Speed (knots)	Range (miles)	Complement	Page
9/150 mm 6/88 mm aa 8/37 mm aa 4 mg aa 12/533 mm tt 1 catapult 2 aircraft		Geared turbines 6 Marine type boilers 60,000 hp 4 MAN diesels 12,000 hp 3 screws Fuel 1,205 T of oil 378 T for diesels	32	7.000	632	193
5/127 mm 4/37 mm aa 8/533 mm tt		Geared turbines 3 oil-fired boilers	36		283	192
1/105 mm – 45 cal 2 mg aa 3/533 mm tt 1/500 mm tt		2 Krupp Germania turbines 3 Schultz-Thornycroft boilers (oil) 16,000 hp 2 screws Fuel 173 T	25	1.055	85	192
3/105 mm 2 mg aa 6/533 mm tt		Geared turbines 3 Schultz-Thornycroft boilers 24,000 hp 2 screws Fuel 321 T	33	2.000	120	192
3/105 mm 2/37 mm mg aa 6/533 mm tt		Geared turbines 3 Schultz-Thornycroft boilers (oil) 25,000 hp 2 screws Fuel 338 T	34		125	192
1/105 mm 2/37 mm aa 6/533 mm tt		Geared turbines 3 Schultz-Thornycroft boilers (oil) 24,000 hp 2 screws Fuel 345 T	36		86	192
1/1 pdr 3/533 mm tt		Diesel 700 hp Electric motors 1.300 hp	7 13		23	192
4/30 mm aa 18/533 mm tt		Diesel 1,800 hp Electric motors 2.300 hp Fuel 100 T	9·8 16	11.150	57	191
1/105 mm – 45 cal 1 mg aa		2 sets triple expansion 2 boilers (coal) 1,850 hp 2 screws Fuel 160 T of coal	16	2.000	51	192

TECHNICAL DATA

Italian naval forces at the outbreak of the Second World War						
Battleships	**Aircraft carriers**	**Heavy cruisers**	**Light cruisers**	**Destroyers and Torpedo boats**	**Submarines**	**Total tonnage**
6		8	14	160	100	672,750

The war on the seas. The Italian war: principal marine classes cited in this chapter

Page	Class	Shipyard	Date: ld c r	Displacement (full load)	Length o.a. meters	feet	Beam meters	feet	Draft (mean) meters	feet
	Battleships									
197	**Conte di Cavour** (2 ships)	La Spezia	1911/1915/1937	29,100	186·4	611¼ ft.	28	92 ft.	10·4	33 ft.
196	**Giulio Cesare**	Ansaldo, Genoa	1911/1937							
195	**Duilio** (2 ships)	Castellammare	1912/1915/1940	29,000	186·9	613¼ ft.	28	92 ft.	10·4	33 ft.
196	**Andrea Doria**	La Spezia, Trieste	1912/1916/1940							
197	**Vittorio Veneto** (4 ships)	CRDA San Marco, Trieste	1934/1940	45,752	237·8	775 ft.	32·4	106½ ft.	10·5	33¼ ft.
196	**Littorio**	Ansaldo, Genoa	1934/1940	43,835						
195	**Roma**	CRDA San Marco, Trieste	1938/1942	44,050						
	Aircraft carriers									
202	**Aquila** (ex-battleship **Roma** 32,533 T). Transformed but never entered into service	Ansaldo, Genoa	1941	27,800	232	761 ft.	30	99 ft.	7·3	24 ft.
	Heavy cruisers									
196	**San Giorgio**	Castellammare	1905/1910	9,232	140·9	462¼ ft.	21	69 ft.	6·9	22¾ ft. 24 ft. (max.)
197	**Trento** (3 ships)	Orlando, Leghorn	1925/1929	10,000	196·6	645 ft.	20·6	67¼ ft.	5·4	19 ft.
197	**Bolzano**	Ansaldo, Genoa	1930/1933							
197	**Zara** (4 ships)	Odero-Terni-Orlando	1929/1931	10,000	182·8	599½ ft.	20·6	67 ft. 8 in.	5·9	19½ ft.
	Light cruisers									
196	**A. da Gussano** (Condottieri class, 5 ships)	Ansaldo, Genoa	1928/1931	5,069	169·3	555½ ft.	15·5	50 ft. 5 in.	4·3	14¼ ft.
196	**B. Colleoni**	Ansaldo, Genoa	1928/1931							
196	**Giovanni dalle Bande Nere**	Castellammare	1928/1931							

ABBREVIATIONS — **Date:** **ld** = laid down **c** = completed **r** = refit **length o.a.** = length over all **mg** = machine gun mounting **mmg** = multi-machine gun mounting **dct** = depth charge thrower **pdr** = pounder **aa** = anti-aircraft **a/s** = anti-submarine **4-bar** = 4-barrelled **T** = tonnage **hp** = horsepower **sub** = speed when submerged **tt** = torpedo tube **cal** = caliber **wl** = water level **d** = deck **fd** = flight deck **ct** = control or conning tower **t** = turret **b** = barbette **tb** = turret base **bt** = battery

Armaments	Armor	Machinery	Speed (knots)	Range (miles)	Complement	Page
10/320 mm – 44 cal 12/120 mm – 50 cal 8/100 mm aa – 47 cal 8/37 mm – 54 cal 12/20 mm – 65 cal 36 mg aa	**Vertical** max 250 mm **Horizontal** d 80–20 mm tb 280 mm ct 260 mm	2 Belluzzo geared turbines 8 Yarrow boilers (oil) 93,000 hp 2 screws Fuel 2,500 T	28	3.100	1.198 1.240	197 196
10/320 mm – 44 cal 12/135 mm – 45 cal 10/90 mm aa – 50 cal 19/37 mm – 54 cal 12/20 mm – 65 cal 39 mg 4 aircraft 2 catapults	**Vertical** max 250 mm **Horizontal** d 80 mm t 280 mm ct 260 mm b 290 mm	2 Belluzzo geared turbines 8 Yarrow boilers (oil) 87,000 hp 2 screws Fuel 2,550 T	27	3.390	1.500	195 196
9/381 mm – 50 cal 12/152 mm – 55 cal 12/90 mm – 50 cal 20/37 mm – 54 cal 30/20 – 65 cal 4/120 mm – 40 cal 40 mg 1 catapult 3 aircraft	**Vertical** max 350 mm **Horizontal** d 100 mm 2 tb 350–135 mm b 100 mm ct 260 mm 130 mm	4 Belluzzo geared turbines 8 Yarrow boilers (oil) 140,000 hp 4 screws Fuel 4,000 T	30	4.580	1.920	197 196 195
8/135 mm – 45 cal 12/65 mm – 54 cal 132/20 mm – 65 cal 2 catapults 51 aircraft		4 Belluzzo geared turbines 8 Yarrow boilers (oil) 140,000 hp 4 screws Fuel 4,200 T	30	5.500	1.400	202
4/254 mm – 45 cal 8/190 mm – 45 cal 8/100 mm aa – 47 cal 11 mg aa	**Vertical** max 203 mm **Horizontal** d 44 mm ct 248 mm tb 203 mm	2 sets 4-cylinder triple expansion 8 Yarrow boilers (oil) 18,000 hp 2 screws Fuel 4,000 T	22	6.300	726 860	196
8/203 mm – 53 cal 12/100 mm aa – 47 cal 16 mg aa 8/533 mm tt 1 catapult 2 aircraft	**Vertical** max 75 mm **Horizontal** d 50 mm	4 Parsons geared turbines 12 Yarrow boilers (oil) 150,000 hp 4 screws Fuel 3,000 T	35		723	197 197
8/203 mm – 53 cal 12/100 mm aa – 47 cal 16 mg aa 1 catapult 2 aircraft	**Vertical** max 150 mm **Horizontal** d 70 mm	2 Parsons geared turbines 8 Yarrow boilers (oil) 95,000 hp 2 screws Fuel 2,200 T	32	3.200	705	197
8/152 mm – 53 cal 6/100 mm aa – 47 cal 16 mg aa 4/533 mm tt 1 catapult 2 aircraft		2 Belluzzo geared turbines 6 boilers 95,000 hp 2 screws Fuel 1.000 T	37	2.500	500	196 196 196

TECHNICAL DATA

Page	Class	Shipyard	Date: ld c r	Displacement (full load)	Length o.a.		Beam		Draft (mean)	
					meters	feet	meters	feet	meters	feet
196	**Eugenio di Savoia** (Condottieri class D type, 2 ships)	Ansaldo. Genoa	1932 1936	7.283	186	610¼ ft.	17·5	57 ft. 4 in.	5	16 ft. 4 in.
197	**Giuseppe Garibaldi** (2 ships)	CRDA. Trieste	1933 1937	9.000	187·1	613¾ ft.	18·6	61 ft.	5·2	17 ft.
196	**Raimondo Montecuccoli** (2 ships)	Ansaldo. Genoa	1931 1935	8.000	182·2	597¾ ft.	16·5	54½ ft.	5·04	14¾ ft.
196	**Destroyers** **Leone** (3 ships)	Ansaldo. Genoa	1921 1924	2.283	113·4	375 ft.	10·4	34 ft.	2·7	15 ft. 5 in.
196	**Q. Sella** (4 ships)	Pattison. Naples	1922 1926	935 (standard)	84·9	275½ ft.	8·6	27 ft.	2·6	9¾ ft.
196	**Turbine** (8 ships)	Orlando. Genoa	1925 1927	1.092	93·6	307½ ft.	9·2	30½ ft.	2·9	10¾ ft.
196	**Maestrale** (Grecale class. 4 ships)	Ancona	1931/1934	1.449	106·7	350 ft.	10·2	33 ft. 4 in.	3	10 ft.
196	**A. Oriani** (4 ships)	Orlando. Leghorn	1935 1937	1.950	106·8	350 ft. 4 in.	10·2	33 ft. 4 in.	3·4	11¼ ft.
196	**Torpedo boats** **Audace**	Yarrow, Glasgow	1913 1916	1.000	87·6	283 ft.	8·4	27½ ft.	1·9	9½ ft.
196	**G. Sirtori** (11 ships)	Odero. Sestri	1916 1917	670 (standard)	73	240 ft.	7·3	24 ft.	2·45	9 ft. 2 in.
196	**Perseo** (Spica class. 30 ships)	Quarnaro. Fiume	1934 1936	642 (standard)	81·9	267 ft.	8·2	27 ft.	2·2	7½ ft.
196	**Orsa** (4 ships)	Palermo	1936 1938	855 (standard)	89·2	292¾ ft.	9·5	31 ft.	2·4	11½ ft. (max.)
196	**Submarines** **E. Fieramosca**	Tosi. Taranto	1926 1931	1,340/1,760	82·4	270¼ ft.	8·4	27½ ft.	4·9	14¾ ft.

TECHNICAL DATA

Armaments	Armor	Machinery	Speed (knots)	Range (miles)	Comple- ment	Page
8/152 mm – 53 cal 6/100 mm aa – 47 cal 16 mg aa 6/533 mm tt 1 catapult 3 aircraft equipped for minelaying	**Vertical** max 150 mm **Horizontal** d 70 mm t 250 mm ct 240 mm	2 Belluzzo geared turbines 6 boilers (oil) 110.000 hp 2 screws Fuel 1.200 T	36·5		551	196
10/152 mm – 55 cal 8/100 mm aa – 47 cal 16 mg aa 6/533 mm tt 2 dct 2 catapults 4 aircraft equipped for minelaying	**Horizontal** d 70 mm t 250 mm ct 240 mm	Parsons geared turbines 8 boilers (oil) 100.000 hp 2 screws Fuel 1.200 T	35		600	197
8/152 mm – 53 cal 6/100 mm – 47 cal 16 mg aa 4/533 mm tt 2 dct 1 catapult 3 aircraft equipped for minelaying		Belluzzo geared turbines 6 boilers (oil) 106.000 hp 2 screws Fuel 500/1.200 T	37		522	196
8/120 mm – 45 cal 6 mg aa (2/40 mm) 4/533 mm tt 60/100 mines		2 Parsons turbines 4 Yarrow boilers (oil) 40.000 hp 2 screws Fuel 400 T	34		118	196
4/120 mm – 45 cal 4/40 mm mg aa 4/533 mm tt equipped for minelaying		2 Parsons turbines 3 boilers (oil) 36.000 hp 2 screws	35	2.750	120	196
4/120 mm – 45 cal 4 mg aa 6/533 mm tt equipped for minelaying		2 Parsons turbines 3 boilers (oil) 40.000 hp 2 screws Fuel 270 T	36		142	196
4/120 mm – 50 cal 2/120 mm mortars – 15 cal 12 mg aa 6/533 mm tt equipped for minelaying		2 Parsons turbines 3 boilers (oil) 44.000 hp 2 screws Fuel 250 T	38		153	196
4/120 mm – 50 cal 2/120 mm mortars – 15 cal 10 mg aa 6/533 mm tt 2 dct equipped for minelaying		2 Parsons turbines 3 boilers (oil) 48.000 hp 2 screws Fuel 250 T	39		157	196
7/102 mm – 35 cal 4/450 mm tt 2/40 mm aa 4 mg		2 Curtis turbines 3 Yarrow boilers (oil) 22.000 hp 2 screws Fuel 252 T	31	2.180	113	196
6/102 mm – 35 cal 6 mg aa (2/40 mm) 4/450 mm tt		2 Tosi turbines 4 boilers (oil) 15.000 hp 2 screws Fuel 150 T	30	1.700	100	196
3/100 mm – 47 cal 8 mg aa (2/13 mm) 4/450 mm tt 2 dct equipped for minelaying		2 Tosi turbines 2 boilers (oil) 19.000 hp 2 screws	34		94	196
2/100 mm – 47 cal 8 mg aa 4/450 mm tt 6 dct equipped for minelaying		2 turbines 2 boilers (oil) 16.000 hp 2 screws	28			196
1/120 mm – 45 cal 4/13 mm mg aa 8/533 mm tt		2 Tosi diesels 5.500 hp Electric motors 2.000 hp	sub 10 19		64	196

TECHNICAL DATA

Page	Class	Shipyard	Date: ld c r	Displacement (full load)	Length o.a. meters	Length o.a. feet	Beam meters	Beam feet	Draft (mean) meters	Draft (mean) feet
196	**Glauco** (2 ships)	Monfalcone	1931/1935	863/1,167	73	239½ ft.	7·2	23½ ft.	4·5	14½ ft.
196	**Pietro Micca**	Tosi, Taranto	1931/1935	1,371/1,883	90·3	296½ ft.	7·7	25¼ ft.	5·3	17½ ft.
196	**Marcello** (9 ships)	Monfalcone	1937/1938	941/1,300	73	239½ ft.	7·2	23½ ft.	4·7	15½ ft.
196	**G. Mameli** (4 ships)	Tosi, Taranto	1925/1929	770/994	64·6	213¼ ft.	6·5	21¼ ft.	4·1	13 ft.
196	**V. Pisani** (4 ships)	Monfalcone	1925/1929	791/1,040	68·2	223 ft.	5·7	19 ft.	4·2	14 ft.
196	**F. Corridoni** (2 ships)	Tosi, Taranto	1927/1931	803/1,051	71·5	234½ ft.	6·2	20 ft.	4·7	13½ ft.
196	**S. di Santarosa** (4 ships)	Orlando, La Spezia	1928/1930	8·5/1,078	69·8	229 ft.	7·2	23 ft. 8 in.	4·8	13 ft. 4 in.
196	**Squalo** (4 ships)	Monfalcone	1928/1930	810/1,077	69·8	229 ft.	7·2	23 ft. 8 in.	4·8	13 ft. 4 in.
196	**L. Settembrini** (2 ships)	Tosi, Taranto	1928/1932	797/1,134	69·1	226¾ ft.	7·7	25 ft. 4 in.	3·9	11½ ft.
196	**Argo** (2 ships)	Monfalcone	1935/1937	689/901	63·1	206¾ ft.	6·9	22½ ft.	4	10½ ft.
196	**Adua** (Perla class, 16 ships)	Monfalcone	1936/1937	615/855	60·2	197½ ft.	6·5	21 ft.	4·4	13 ft.
	Depot ship submarine (Special salvage ship for submarines)									
197	**Anteo**	Smulders, Holland	1911/1913	1,243	50	164 ft.	24	78¾ ft.	2	6¾ ft.
	Special assault craft									
195	Long-distance torpedo (Pig)		1935	1,300 kg	6·7	22 ft.			0·533	1¾ ft.
195	**Modified Turistic Motorboat (M.T.M.)**	Cattaneo Applicazione Cantieri Baglietto	1941	1,400 kg	5·4	18 ft.	1·67	5¾ ft.		
195	Midget submarine (Class **CB**)			36/45	15	49¼ ft.	3	10 ft.		

Armaments	Armor	Machinery	Speed (knots)	Range (miles)	Comple-ment	Page
2/100 mm – 47 cal 2/13 mm mg aa 8/533 mm tt		2 Fiat diesels 3,000 hp Electric motors 1,400 hp 2 screws	sub 8·5 17		48	196
2/120 mm – 45 cal 4/13 mm mg aa 6/533 mm tt equipped for minelaying		2 Tosi diesels 3,000 hp Electric motors 1,300 hp 2 screws	sub 8·5 15·5		66	196
2/100 – 47 cal 4/13 mm mg aa 8/533 mm tt		2 Sulzer CRDA diesels 3,000 hp Electric motors 1,300 hp 2 screws	sub 8·5 17		68	196
1/102 – 35 cal 2/13 mm mg aa 6/533 mm tt		2 Tosi diesels 3,000 hp Electric motors 1,000 hp 2 screws	sub 9 17		46	196
1/102 mm – 35 cal 2/13 mm mg aa 6 533 mm tt		2 Tosi diesels 3,000 hp Electric motors 1,300 hp 2 screws	sub 9 17·5		46	196
1/102 mm – 35 cal 2/13 mm mg aa 4/533 mm tt 2 mine launching chutes 24 mines		2 Tosi diesels 1,500 hp Electric motors 1,000 hp 2 screws	sub 8 14		47	196
1/102 mm – 35 cal 3/13 mm mg aa 8/533 mm tt		2 Fiat diesels 3,000 hp Electric motors 1,300 hp 2 screws	sub 9 17·5		48	196
1/102 mm – 35 cal 2/13 mm mg aa 8/533 mm tt		2 Fiat diesels 3,000 hp Electric motors 1,400 hp 2 screws	sub 9 16·5		48	196
1/102 mm – 35 cal 2/13 mm mg aa 8/533 mm tt		2 Tosi diesels 3,000 hp Electric motors 1,400 hp 2 screws	sub 9 17·5	9,000	48	196
1/100 mm – 47 cal 2 mg aa 6/533 mm tt		2 Fiat diesels 1,350 hp Electric motors 800 hp 2 screws	sub 8 14·8			196
1/100 mm – 47 cal 2 mg aa 6/533 mm tt		2 Fiat diesels 1,350 hp Electric motors 800 hp 2 screws	sub 8·5 14			196
		Triple expansion 2-cylinder coal-burning boilers 720 hp	8			197
Detachable head with 300 kg of TNT		Continuous current electric generator 1·6 hp 150 amp/hours 60 volt batteries	2·8	5/6 hours		195
300 kg charge of TNT		Cattaneo inboard/outboard propulsion system	32			195
2/450 tt mounted externally						195

TECHNICAL DATA

Japanese naval forces at the outbreak of the Second World War

Battleships	Aircraft carriers	Heavy cruisers	Light cruisers	Destroyers and Torpedo boats	Submarines	Total tonnage
10	8	18	20	134	66	1,015,975

The war on the seas. The Japanese war: principle marine classes cited in this chapter

Page	Class	Shipyard	Date: ld c r	Displacement (full load)	Length o.a. meters	feet	Beam meters	feet	Draft (mean) meters	feet
	Battleships									
201	**Kongo** (4 ships)	Vickers	1911/1913	36,600	222	704 ft.	31	92 ft.	9·6	20¾ ft. 27½ ft.
199	**Kirishima**	Mitsubishi, Nagasaki	1913/1915			704 ft.		95 ft.		
201	**Fuso** (2 ships)	Kure	1914/1915	39,150	212·9	673 ft.	33·1	94 ft.	9·7	28½ ft. (max.)
198	**Yamashiro**	Yokosuka								
201	**Ise** (2 ships). Transformed in 1943 into an aircraft carrier with two cata-pults and 22 aircraft	Kawasaki, Kobe	1915/1917/1937	42,700	215·8	683 ft.	33·8	94 ft.	9·8	28 ft. 8 in. (max.)
201	**Nagato** (2 ships)	Kure	1917/1920/1936	46,350	224·9	729 ft.	34·6	95 ft.	9·5	31¾ ft. (max.)
198	**Yamato** (2 ships)	Kure	1940/1941	72,800	263	865 ft.	38·9	127¾ ft.	10·9	36 ft.
	Aircraft carriers									
200	**Hosyo**	Asano, Tsurumi	1919/1922/1935	7,470	163	535 ft.	14·7	60 ft.	4·6	20¼ ft.
200	**Akagi**	Kure	1920/1927/1937	26,900	232·6	763¼ ft.	28	92 ft.	6·5	21¼ ft.
200	**Ryuzyo**	Yokosuka	1929/1933	7,100	172	548 ft.	18·2	60½ ft.	4·4	15 ft. 4 in.
200	**Syokaku** (2 ships)	Kawasaki, Kobe	1939/1941	14,000	210	689 ft.	20·8	66 ft.	5	16¼ ft.
198	**Zuikaku**	Kawasaki, Kobe	1938/1940	14,000	216·7	711 ft.	24·8	81¾ ft.	5·5	18 ft.

TECHNICAL DATA

ABBREVIATIONS — **Date: ld** = laid down **c** = completed **r** = refit **length o.a.** = length over all **mg** = machine gun mounting **mmg** = multi-machine gun mounting **dct** = depth charge thrower **pdr** = pounder **aa** = anti-aircraft **a/s** = anti-submarine **4-bar** = 4-barrelled **T** = tonnage **hp** = horsepower **sub** = speed when submerged **tt** = torpedo tube **cal** = caliber **wl** = water level **d** = deck **fd** = flight deck **ct** = control or conning tower **t** = turret **b** = barbette **tb** = turret base **bt** = battery

Armaments	Armor	Machinery	Speed (knots)	Range (miles)	Comple-ment	Page
8/356 mm – 45 cal 16/152 mm – 50 cal 8/127 – 50 cal 7 mg aa 4/533 mm tt 1 catapult 3 aircraft	**Vertical** max 203 mm **Horizontal** d 70 mm ct 254 mm t 229 mm b 254 mm bt 152 mm external bulges below wl	4 Kanpon turbines 10 Kanpon boilers (oil) 136,000 hp 4 screws Fuel 4,500 T	30·3	10,000	980 1,437	201 199
12/356 mm – 45 cal 16/152 mm – 50 cal 8/127 mm aa – 50 cal 26 mg aa 2/533 mm tt 1 catapult 3 aircraft	**Vertical** max 305 mm **Horizontal** 2d 51–32 mm ct 305 mm tb 305 mm bt 152 mm	4 Kanpon turbines 24 Kanpon boilers (oil) 75,000 hp 4 screws Fuel 5,100 T	24·7	11,800	1,243 1,400 198	201
12/356 mm – 45 cal 18/140 mm – 50 cal 8/127 mm aa 7 mg aa 4/533 mm tt 1 catapult 3 aircraft	**Vertical** max 305 mm **Horizontal** 2d 63–32 mm ct 305 mm tb 305 mm bt 152 mm	4 Kanpon turbines 24 Kanpon boilers (oil) 45,000 hp 4 screws Fuel 5,100 T	25·3	8,500	1,376	210
8/406 mm – 45 cal 20/140 mm – 50 cal 8/127 mm – 50 cal 7 mg aa 6/533 mm tt 1 catapult 3 aircraft	**Vertical** max 330 mm **Horizontal** d 180 mm ct 305 mm tb 356 mm external bulges below wl	4 Kanpon turbines 21 Kanpon boilers 82,000 hp 4 screws Fuel 5,600 T	23	8,600	1,370	201
9/460 mm – 45 cal 6/155 mm – 60 cal 24/127 mm – 50 cal 150/25 mm aa 2 catapults 6 aircraft	**Vertical** max 410 mm **Horizontal** d 200 mm ct 500 mm tb 650/550 mm external bulges below wl	4 Kanpon turbines 12 Kanpon boilers (oil) 150,000 hp 4 screws Fuel 6,300 T	27	7,200	2,500	198
4/140 mm – 50 cal 2/76 mm aa – 40 cal 2 mg aa 26 aircraft	external bulges below wl	2 Kanpon geared turbines 8 Kanpon boilers (oil) 30,000 hp 2 screws Fuel 550 T	25	5,500	550	200
10/203 mm – 50 cal 12/120 mm aa – 50 cal 22 mg aa 1 catapult 60 aircraft	**Horizontal** fd 135 mm	2 Kanpon geared turbines 19 Kanpon boilers (mixed firing) 131,200 hp 4 screws Fuel 6,000 T	28·5	9,000	875	200
12/127 mm aa – 50 cal 24 mg aa 40 aircraft		Kanpon geared turbines 8 Kanpon boilers (oil) 40,000 hp 2 screws Fuel 500 T	24	5,000	530	200
12/127 mm aa – 50 cal 24 mg aa 40 aircraft		Kanpon geared turbines 8 boilers (oil) 60,000 hp 4 screws Fuel 5,300 T	30	6,000	650	200
10/203 mm – 50 cal 12/120 mm aa – 50 cal 22 mg aa 80 aircraft	**Vertical** max 120 mm **Horizontal** fd 250 mm external bulges below wl	Brown-Curtis geared turbines 12 Kanpon boilers (oil) 91,000 hp 4 screws Fuel 5,600 T	26	6,000	800	198

TECHNICAL DATA

Page	Class	Shipyard	Date: ld c r	Displacement (full load)	Length o.a. meters	Length o.a. feet	Beam meters	Beam feet	Draft (mean) meters	Draft (mean) feet
200	**Seaplane carriers** **Notoro** Converted from a tanker into a seaplane carrier	Kawasaki, Kobe	1919/1920	14,050	143·5	470¾ ft.	17·7	58 ft.	8	26½ ft.
200	**Mizuho**	Kawasaki, Kobe	1937/1939	9.000	176	577½ ft.	18·8	61½ ft.	5·8	19 ft. 2 in.
200	**Coast defense ships** **Kasuga**	Ansaldo, Genoa	1902/1904	7,080	108·8	357 ft.	18·9	61 ft.	7·3	24 ft.
201	**Heavy cruisers** **Aoba** (Kako class, 4 ships)	Mitsubishi, Nagasaki	1924/1927/1939	7,100 (standard)	181·3	595 ft.	15·5	50¾ ft.	4·5	14¾ ft.
200	**Nati** (4 ships)	Kure	1924/1928/1936	10,000	195	640 ft.	19	62 ft. 4 in.	5	16½ ft.
199	**Tyokai** (Atago class, 4 ships)	Mitsubishi, Nagasaki	1928/1932	9,850 (standard)	198·1	650 ft.	19	62 ft. 4 in.	5	16 ft. 5 in.
200	**Light cruisers** **Tenryu** (2 ships)	Yokosuka	1917/1919/1937	3,230	142·6	468 ft.	12·4	40¾ ft.	4	13 ft.
200	**Kuma** (5 ships)	Sasebo	1919/1921/1927	5,100 (standard)	163·1	535 ft.	14·4	40¾ ft.	4·8	15¾ ft.
200	**Nagara** (Natori class, 6 ships)	Sasebo	1920/1922	5,170 (standard)	163·1	535 ft.	14·4	40¾ ft.	4·8	15¾ ft.
201	**Yubari** (Nagara class, 6 ships)	Sasebo	1922/1923	2,890 (standard)	132·6	435 ft.	12	39½ ft.	3·6	11¾ ft.

Armaments	Armor	Machinery	Speed (knots)	Range (miles)	Comple-ment	Page
2/120 mm – 50 cal 2/76 mm aa – 40 cal 16 aircraft		Reciprocating engines Oil-burning boilers 5,850 hp 2 screws Fuel 1,000 T	12		155	200
6/127 mm aa – 50 cal		Geared turbines 15,000 hp 2 screws	20		130	200
1/254 mm – 45 cal 2/203 mm – 45 cal 14/152 mm – 45 cal 4/76 mm – 40 cal 1/76 mm aa – 40 cal 2/37 mm aa 4/456 mm tt	**Vertical** max 152 mm **Horizontal** d 40 mm ct 150 mm t 150 mm	2 sets 3-cylinder vertical triple expansion 12 Kanpon boilers 13,500 hp 2 screws Fuel 1,200 T	20	9,000 •	600	200
6/203 mm – 50 cal 4/120 mm aa – 50 cal 10 mg aa 12/533 mm tt 1 catapult 2 aircraft	**Vertical** max 51 mm **Horizontal** d 51 mm t 37 mm external bulges below wl	Geared turbines 10 Kanpon boilers (oil) 2 boilers (mixed firing) 95,000 hp 4 screws Fuel 2,250 T	33	12,000	604 625	201
10/203 mm – 50 cal 8/120 mm aa – 50 cal 8/40 mm aa 2 mg 8/533 mm tt 2 catapults 4 aircraft	**Vertical** max 102 mm **Horizontal** d 45 mm t 76 mm external bulges below wl	Geared turbines 12 Kanpon boilers (oil) 100,000 hp 2 screws Fuel 2,000 T	33	14,000	692 773	200
10/203 mm – 50 cal 4/120 mm aa – 50 cal 4 mg 8/47 mm aa 8/533 mm tt 2 catapults 4 aircraft	**Vertical** max 102 mm **Horizontal** d 76 mm t 76 mm triple sweepings	Geared turbines 12 Kanpon boilers (oil) 100,000 hp 4 screws Fuel 4,000 T	33	14,000	773	199
4/140 mm – 50 cal 1/76 mm – 40 cal 2 mg 6/533 mm tt 34 mines	**Vertical** max 50 mm	Parsons turbines 10 Kanpon boilers 51,000 hp 3 screws Fuel 900 T	33	6,000	330	200
7/140 mm – 50 cal 2/76 mm aa – 40 cal 6 mg 8/533 mm tt 1 catapult 1 aircraft 80 mines	**Vertical** max 51 mm **Horizontal** d 51 mm ct 51 mm	Parsons or Curtis geared turbines 10 oil-fired Kanpon boilers 2 boilers (mixed firing) 70,000 hp 4 screws Fuel 1,500 T	33	9,000	440	200
as for Kuma class	as for Kuma class	Parsons or Curtis geared turbines 8 oil-fired Kanpon boilers 4 coal-burning boilers 70,000 hp 4 screws Fuel 1,500 T	33	9,000	440	200
6/140 mm – 50 cal 1/76 mm aa – 30 cal 2 mg 4/533 mm tt 2 minelaying chutes 34 mines	**Vertical** max 51 mm	Geared turbines 8 Kanpon boilers (oil) 57,000 hp 3 screws Fuel 820 T	33	7,500	328 360	201

TECHNICAL DATA

Page	Class	Shipyard	Date: ld c r	Displacement (full load)	Length o.a. meters	Length o.a. feet	Beam meters	Beam feet	Draft (mean) meters	Draft (mean) feet
200	**Destroyers** **Sawakaze** (Akikaze class, 15 ships)	Mitsubishi, Nagasaki	1918/1920	1,215	102·6	336½ ft.	8·9	29¼ ft.	2·9	9½ ft.
200	**Kamikaze** (9 ships)	Mitsubishi, Nagasaki	1921/1922	1,270	97·5	320 ft.	9·1	30 ft.	2·9	9 ft. 7 in. (max.)
200	**Nenohi** (Hatuharu class, 7 ships)	Uraga	1931/1933	1,368 (standard)	103	337¾ ft.	9·9	32½ ft.	2·7	8¾ ft.
199	**Kagero** (12 ships)	Maiduru	1937/1940	2,000	108·6	361 ft.	10·2	33 ft. 4 in.	2·7	8¾ ft.
200	**Torpedo boats** **Wakatake** (7 ships)	Kawasaki, Kobe	1921/1922	820	83·8	275 ft.	8·1	26½ ft.	2·5	8¼ ft.
200	**Submarines** **RO. 51** (3 ships)	Mitsubishi, Kobe	1918/1920	893/1,082	70·6	232 ft.	7·2	23½ ft.	3·8	13 ft.
200	**RO. 60** (Mitsubishi class, 7 ships)	Mitsubishi, Kobe	1921/1923	988/1,300	76·2	258 ft.	7·4	24 ft.	3·8	13 ft.
200	**I. 51** (2 ships)	Kure	1921/1924	1,390/2,000	91·4	300 ft.	8·8	29 ft.	4·6	15 ft.
200	**Minesweepers** Class **N. 1**	Harima Shipping	1922/1923	615	71·6	235 ft.	8	26 ft. 4 in.	2·3	7½ ft.

Armaments	Armor	Machinery	Speed (knots)	Range (miles)	Complement	Page
4/120 mm – 45 cal 2/37 mm aa 6/533 mm tt equipped for minelaying		4 Parsons turbines 4 Kanpon boilers (oil) 38,500 hp 2 screws Fuel 315 T	34	4,000	148	200
4/120 mm – 50 cal 2/37 mm aa 6/533 mm tt		4 Parsons turbines 4 Kanpon boilers (oil) 38,500 hp 4 screws Fuel 350 T	34	4,000	148	200
5/127 mm – 50 cal 2 mg aa 6/533 mm tt		Parsons geared turbines 3 Kanpon boilers (oil) 37,000 hp 2 screws Fuel 400 T	34		200	200
6/127 mm – 50 cal 2 mg aa 8/533 mm tt		Geared turbines 3 Kanpon boilers (oil) 45,000 hp 2 screws Fuel 400 T	36		200	199
3/120 mm – 45 cal 2 mg aa 4/533 mm tt		Parsons turbines 3 Kanpon boilers 21,500 hp 2 screws	31·5	3,000	115	200
1/76 mm – 40 cal 1 mg aa 6/476 mm tt		Vickers diesel 2,400 hp Electric motors 1,200 hp Fuel 65 T	sub 10·5 17	7,500	48	200
1/76 mm aa – 40 cal 1 mg aa 6/533 mm tt		Vickers diesel 2,400 hp Electric motors 1,800 hp Fuel 75 T	sub 10 16	11,000	47	200
1/120 mm – 40 cal 1 mg aa 8/533 mm tt		Sulzer diesel 5,200 hp Electric motors 1,800 hp Fuel 100 T	sub 9·5 17	10,000	60	200
2/120 mm – 50 cal 1/76 mm aa – 40 cal 2 dct		Triple expansion 3 Kanpon boilers (coal) 4,000 hp 2 screws Fuel 60 T	20		87	200

TECHNICAL DATA

Naval forces today. Principal marine classes of the world cited in this chapter

SHIPS IN CATEGORY R = Aircraft carriers
SHIPS IN CATEGORY B = Battleships
SHIPS IN CATEGORY C = Missile cruisers
SHIPS IN CATEGORY D = Destroyers
SHIPS IN CATEGORY F = Frigates and Corvettes
SHIPS IN CATEGORY S = Submarines and underwater craft

SHIPS IN CATEGORY AL = Stores support ships
SHIPS IN CATEGORY A = Auxiliary ships
SHIPS IN CATEGORY M = Minesweepers
SHIPS IN CATEGORY P = Light and fast attack craft
SHIPS IN CATEGORY L = Amphibious warfare forces

SHIPS IN CATEGORY R: Aircraft carriers

Page	Nation	Name of Ship	Shipyard	Date ld l c r	Displacement (full load)	Length o.a. meters	Length o.a. feet
220	ARGENTINA	**25th De Mayo** (1 ship)	Cammell Laird	1942/43/45 1955/58	19,896	212·7	693·2
208	AUSTRALIA	**Melbourne** (1 ship)	Vickers-Armstrong	1943/45/45 1957/72	20,000	213·8	705·1
220	BRAZIL	**Minas Gerais** (1 ship)	Swan Hunter	1942/44/45 1957/60	19,890	211·8	695
206	FRANCE	**Foch**	Chantiers de l'Atlantique	1957/60/63	32,780	265	869·4
220		**Clemenceau**	Brest Dockyard	1955/57/61			
216		**Jeanne d'Arc** (1 ship) Helicopter carrier	Brest Dockyard	1960/61/64	12,380	182	597·1
207	GREAT BRITAIN	**Ark Royal** (1 ship) ex-**Irresistible**	Cammell Laird	1943/50/55 1964/65	50,786	258	845
218		**Hermes** Helicopter carrier	Vickers-Armstrong	1944/53/59	28,700	226·8	744·3
220	INDIA	**Vickrant** (1 ship) ex-**Hercules**	Vickers-Armstrong	1943/45/61 1957/61	19,550	213·4	700
203	UNITED STATES OF AMERICA	**Essex** (withdrawn)	Newport News	1939/40/43	40,600	271·3	888
202		**Enterprise** (1 ship)	Newport News	1958/60/61	89,600	341·3	1,123
208		**America** (3 ships)	Newport News	1961/64/65	80,800	319·3	1,047
220		**Kitty Hawk**	New York Shipbuilding	1956/60/61	80,800	323·9	1,062·5
206		**Constellation**	New York Navy Yard	1957/60/62	80,800	326·9	1,072
208		**J. F. Kennedy** (1 ship)	Newport News	1964/66/68	87,000	319·3	1,047
208		**Forrestal** (4 ships)	Newport News	1952/54/55	78,000	316·7	1,039
206		**Midway** (3 ships)	Newport News	1943/45/45	64,000	298·4	979
220		**Roosevelt**	New York Navy Yard	1943/45/45	62,472	297	968
220		**Coral Sea**	Newport News	1944/46/47	63,400		

ABBREVIATIONS — **Date: ld** = laid down **l** = launched **c** = commissioned **r** = refit **length o.a.** = length over all **dc** = depth charge **dct** = depth charge thrower **aa** = anti-aircraft **a/s** = anti-submarine **tt** = torpedo tube **4-bar** = 4-barrelled **ml** = missile launcher **rl** = rocket launcher **cal** = caliber **T** = tonnage

sub = speed when submerged **bpdms** = basic point defense missile system **mg** = machine gun **fd** = flight deck **b** = boiler **gt** = geared turbine **gas t** = gas turbine **d** = diesel engine **de** = diesel electric motor **e** = electric motor **nr** = nuclear reactor **te** = turbo-electric motor

Beam		Draft		Principal armaments	Engine equipment	Speed (knots)	Range (miles)	Complement	Page
meters	feet	meters	feet						
20·4 fd 40·7	80 fd 131·6	7·6	25	9/40 mm aa 14 helicopters	2 b – 2 gt 40,000 hp Oil fuel 3,300 T	24	12,000	1,500	220
24·4 fd 23	80·2 fd 80	7·3	25·5	12/40 mm aa 8 Skyhawk aircraft 10 Wessex helicopters 1 catapult	4 b – 2 gt 42,000 hp Oil fuel 3,200 T	23	12,000	1,070 1,335	208
24·4 fd 37	80 fd 121	7·5	24·5	10/40 mm 2/47 mm aa 20 aircraft 1 catapult	4 b – 2 gt 40,000 hp Oil fuel 3,200 T	24	12,000	1,000 1,300	220
31·7 fd 51·2	104·1	7·5	24·6	8/100 mm 40 aircraft 2 catapults	6 b – 4 gt 126,000 hp 2 screws Oil fuel 3,720 T	32	7,500	2,239	206 220
24	78·7	7·3	24	4/100 mm aa 4 Exocet ml 8 helicopters 700 marines	4 b – 2 gt 40,000 hp Oil fuel 1,360 T	26·5	6,000	809	216
34·3 fd 50·2	112·8 fd 166	10·9	36	Fitted for Seacat ml 30 aircraft 6 helicopters 2 catapults	8 b – 4 gt 152,000 hp Oil fuel 5,500 T	31·5		2,380	207
27·4 fd 48·8	90 fd 160	8·5	29	2 quadruple Seacat launchers 20 helicopters 750 commandos	4 b – 2 gt 76,000 hp Oil fuel 3,900 T Diesel fuel 320 T	28		980	218
39 fd 24·4	128 fd 72·9	7·3	24	4 mg 15/40 mm aa 22 aircraft	4 b – 2 gt 100,000 hp Oil fuel 3,200 T	24·5	12,000	1,343	220
31 fd 59·7	94·3 fd 170·3	9·4	31	100 aircraft 2 catapults 8/127 mm – 38 cal	8 b – 4 gt 150,000 hp 4 screws Oil fuel 6,000 T	30	18,000	3,230	203
40·5 fd 78·5	133 fd 257	10·8	35·8	2 bpdms launchers with Sea Sparrow missiles 90 aircraft 4 catapults	8 nr – 4 gt 300,000 hp	35	400,000	3,100 5,500	202
39·6 fd 76	130 fd 249	10·9	35·9	2 twin Terrier launchers 90 aircraft 4 catapults	8 b – 4 gt 280,000 hp Oil fuel 7,800 T	35	8,000	2,795 4,950	208 220
38·5	129·5								206
39·6 fd 76·9	130 fd 252	10·9	35·9	3 bpdms launchers with Sea Sparrow missiles 90 aircraft 4 catapults	8 b – 4 gt 280,000 hp Oil fuel 7,800 T	33	8,000	2,795 4,950	208
38·5 fd 76·8	129·5 fd 252	11·3	37	2 bpdms launchers with Sea Sparrow missiles 4/127 mm – 54 cal 4 catapults 90 aircraft	8 b – 4 gt 260,000 hp Oil fuel 7,800 T	33	8,000	4,940	208
36·9 fd 72·5	121 fd 238	10·9	35·3	4/127 mm – 54 cal 75 aircraft 2 catapults	12 b – 4 gt 213,000 hp	33	15,000	2,710 4,500	206
36·9 fd 72·5	121 fd 238	10·8	35·3	3 catapults 4/127 mm aa – 54 cal 80 aircraft	12 b – 4 gt 212,000 hp	33	15,000	2,615 4,400	220 220

TECHNICAL DATA

Page	Nation	Name of Ship	Shipyard	Date ld l c r	Displacement (full load)	Length o.a. meters	feet
220	SPAIN	**Dedalo** (1 ship) Helicopter carrier	New York Shipbuilding	1942/43/43	16,416	190	623
207	USSR	**Kiev** (1 ship)	Nikolaiev	1971/73/76	40,000	282	925
	SHIPS IN CATEGORY B: Battleships						
210	UNITED STATES OF AMERICA	**New Jersey** (Iowa class, 4 ships)	Philadelphia Navy Yard	1940/42/43	59,000	270·4	887·2
	SHIPS IN CATEGORY C: Missile cruisers						
220	ARGENTINA	**Belgrano** (2 ships) ex-USN Brooklyn class	Camden, New York	1935/38/39	13,645	185·4	608·3
220	BRAZIL	**Tamandaré** (1 ship) ex-USN St. Louis class	Newport News	1936/38/39	13,500	185·5	608·5
220	CHILE	**Prat** (1 ship) ex-**Nashville,** Brooklyn class	New York Shipbuilding	1935/37/38 1957/58	13,500	185·3	608·3
220	GREAT BRITAIN	**Invincible** (3 ships)	Vickers	1974/75	20,000	207	650
209		**Tiger** (2 ships)	John Brown	1941/45/59	12,080	169·3	555
220	INDIA	**Delhi** (1 ship) ex-**Achilles,** Leander class	Cammell Laird	1931/32/33 1955	9,740	166	544·5
210	ITALY	**Vittorio Veneto** (1 ship) Guided missile cruiser, Doria class	Castellammare	1965/67/69	8,850	179·6	589
210	NETHERLANDS	**De Zeven Provincien** (1 ship)	Rotterdamse Droogdok	1949/50/53	11,850	190·3	614·5
220	SPAIN	**Canarias**	Ferrol	1928/31/36	13,969	193·9	636·5
209	UNITED STATES OF AMERICA	**Long Beach** (1 ship) Guided missile cruiser	Bethlehem Shipbuilding	1957/59/61	17,350	219·7	721
220		**Albany** (3 ships) Guided missile cruiser	Bethlehem Shipbuilding	1944/45/46	17,800	205·3	673
209	USSR	**Leningrad** (2 ships) Guided missile cruiser and helicopter carrier	Nikolaiev	1965/67/69	18,000	196·6	644·8
220		**Moskva**	Nikolaiev	1965/67/68			

| Beam | | Draft | | Principal armaments | Engine equipment | Speed (knots) | Range (miles) | Comple- ment | Page |
meters	feet	meters	feet						
21·8 fd 33·2	71·5 fd 109	7·2	26	26/40 mm 20 helicopters	8 b – 4 gt 100,000 hp Oil fuel 1,800 T	32	7,200	1.112	220
61	200	—	—	2 twin SAN-3 ml 4 SAN-4 ml 4/76 mm 2/12-bar MBU 2500A launchers 50 aircraft incl. 25 helicopters		30			207
32·9	108·2	10·6	38	9/406 mm – 50 cal 20/127 mm – 38 cal 2 helicopters	8 b – 4 gt 212,000 hp	33	15,000	1,612	210
20·7	69	7·3	24	15/152 mm – 47 cal 8/127 mm – 25 cal 2 twin 40 mm 4/47 mm saluting 2 helicopters 2 quadruple Seacat launchers	8 b – 4 gt 100,000 hp Oil fuel 2,200 T	25	7,600	1,200	220
21	69	7·3	24	15/152 mm – 47 cal 8/127 – 38 cal 28/40 – 56 cal 8/20 mm aa 1 helicopter	8 b – 4 gt 100,000 hp Oil fuel 2,100 T	29	14,500	975	220
21	69	7·3	24	15/152 mm – 47 cal 8/127 mm – 25 cal 28/40 mm – 56 cal 24/20 mm – 70 cal 2 helicopters	8 b – 4 gt 100,000 hp Oil fuel 2,100 T	32·5	14,500	888 975	220
25·6	84	7·3	24	1 twin Sea Dart ml 9 helicopters 6 aircraft	4 Olympus gt 112,000 hp	30	—	1,200	220
19·5	63·6	6·4	21	2/152 mm – 47 cal 2 twin 76 mm 2 quadruple Seacat ml 4 helicopters	4 b – 4 gt 80,000 hp Oil fuel 1,850 T	31·5	4,000	885	209
16·8	55·2	6·1	20	6/152 mm – 47 cal 8/102 mm 14/40 mm	4 b – 4 gt 72,000 hp Oil fuel 1,800 T	23	7,000	800	220
19·4	63·6	6	19·7	1 twin Aster ml 8/76 mm – 62 cal 2 a/s tt 9 helicopters	4 b – 2 gt 73,000 hp Oil fuel 1,200 T	32	6,000	530	210
17·3	56·7	6·7	22	1 twin Terrier ml 4/152 – 47 cal 6/57 mm aa 4/40 mm aa	4 b – 2 gt 85,000 hp	32		940	210
19·5	64	6·5	21·3	8/203 mm – 50 cal 8/120 mm – 45 cal 12/37 mm 3/20 mm – 70 cal	8 b – 2 gt 90,000 hp Oil fuel 2,794 T	31	8,000	1,000	220
22·3	73·2	8·8	29	1 twin Talos ml 2 twin Terrier ml 2/127 mm – 38 cal 1 8-bar Asroc launcher 6 a/s tt 1 helicopter	2 Westinghouse nr 2 gt 80,000 hp	35	—	1,000	209
21·6	70	8·2	27	2 twin Talos ml 2 twin Tartar ml 2/127 mm – 38 cal 1 8-bar Asroc launcher 6 a/s tt 2 helicopters	4 b – 4 gt 120,000 hp Oil fuel 1,500 T	33	9,000	1,000	220
35 fd 90	115 fd 295·3	7·6	24·9	2 twin SAN-3 ml 1 a/s twin ml 4/57 mm 2/533 mm tt 18 helicopters	4 b – 2 gt 100,000 hp	30	7,000	800	209 220

TECHNICAL DATA

Page	Nation	Name of Ship	Shipyard	Date ld l c r	Displacement (full load)	Length o.a. meters	Length o.a. feet
220	USSR	**Admiral Senyavin** (Sverdlov class, 13 ships)	Komsom Amur	1952/54	19,600	210	689
205		**Admiral Ushakov** (same class)	Nikolaiev	1951/52/54	19,600	210	689
220		**Kirov** (2 ships)	Leningrad	1936/37/40	9,060	191	626·7
209		**Kresta** class (10 ships)	Nikolaiev		7,500	158	519·8

SHIPS IN CATEGORY D: Destroyers

Page	Nation	Name of Ship	Shipyard	Date ld l c r	Displacement (full load)	Length o.a. meters	Length o.a. feet
221	AUSTRALIA	**Perth** (3 ships)	Defoe Shipbuilding	1962/63/65 1972/74	4,618	132·2	437
221	CANADA	**Iroquois** (4 ships)	Marine, Sorel	1969/70/72	4,200	129·9	426
221	EGYPT	**Al Zaffer** (4 ships) ex-**Al Nasser**	USSR	1949/51/52	3,500	120·5	395·2
214	FRANCE	**Tourville** (3 ships)	Lorient Dockyard	1970/72/73	5,745	152·7	510/3
221		**Aconit** (1 ship)	Lorient Dockyard	1967/70/73	3,800	127	416·7
221		**La Galissonière** (1 ship)	Lorient Dockyard	1958/60/61	3,750	132·8	435·7
221		**Forbin** (4 ships)	Brest Dockyard	1954/55/58	3,750	128·4	421·3
212	GERMANY, FEDERAL REPUBLIC OF	**Bayern**	Stülken, Hamburg	1962/62/65	4,400	134	439·7
221		**Hamburg**	Stülken, Hamburg	1958/60/64	4,400	134	439·7
221		**Lutjens** (Adams class, 3 ships)	Bath Iron Works	1966/67/69	4,500	134·1	440
212	JAPAN	**Haruna** (4 ships) Anti-submarine helicopter carrier	Mitsubishi, Nagasaki	1970/72/73	4,700	153	502

TECHNICAL DATA

| Beam | | Draft | | Principal armaments | Engine equipment | Speed (knots) | Range (miles) | Comple-ment | Page |
meters	feet	meters	feet						
22	72·2	7·5	24·5	6/152 mm 2 twin SAN-4 launchers 12/100 mm 16/37 mm 8 helicopters	6 b – 2 gt 150,000 hp Oil fuel 4,000 T	34	8,000	1,000	220
22	72·2	7·5	24·5	12/152 mm 12/100 mm 32/37 mm 10/533 mm tt 150 mines	6 b – 2 gt 150,000 hp Oil fuel 4,000 T	34	8,700	1,000	205
18	58	6·3	20	9/180 mm 8/100 mm 27/37 mm 180 mines	6 b – 2 gt + d 110,000 hp Oil fuel 1,280 T	34	3,500	734	220
17	55·1	6	19·7	1 aircraft 4 SAN-3 ml 8 SSN-10 ml 4/57 mm 8/30 mm 2/12-bar MBU 2500A launchers 2/6-bar dct 10/533 mm tt	4 b – 4 gt 100,000 hp	33	5,000	500	209
14·3	47·1	6·1	20·1	1 single Tartar launcher 2/127 mm – 54 cal 6 a/s tt 2 a/s Ikara launchers	4 b – 2 gt 70,000 hp Oil fuel 900 T	35	6,000	333	221
15·2	50	4·4	14·5	1/127 mm – 54 cal 2 Sea Sparrow ml 6 a/s tt 1 Mk 10 Limbo mortar 2 helicopters	2 + 2 b – 2 gt 50,000 hp + 7,400 hp	29	4,500	245	221
11·8	38·7	4·5	15·1	4/130 mm – 50 cal 2/76 mm 8/37 mm 4/57 mm 10/533 mm tt 2 a/s dct 2 a/s MBU 2500 80 mines	3 b – 2 gt 60,000 hp	35	4,000	260	221
15·3	50·2	5·7	18·7	6 MM 38 Exocet ml 1 twin Crotale SAM ml 1 a/s Malafon ml 3/100 mm aa 2 helicopters	4 b – 2 gt 54,400 hp	31	5,000	303	214
13·4	44	5·8	18·9	2/100 mm aa 4 MM 38 Exocet missiles 1 a/s Malafon ml 1 quadruple 305 m a/s mortar 2 a/s tt 4 MM 33 missiles	2 b – 1 gt 28,650 hp	27	5,000	215	221
12·7	41·7	5·5	18	2/100 mm aa 1 a/s Malafon tl 1 rl 6 a/s tt 1 helicopter	4 b – 2 gt 63,000 hp Oil fuel 725 T	34	5,000	333	221
12·7	41·7	5·4	17·7	4/127 mm 6/57 mm 2/20 mm 6/550 mm a/s tt 1 a/s tt	4 b – 2 gt 63,000 hp Oil fuel 800 T	34	5,000	274	221
13·4	44	5·2	17	4/100 mm – 54 cal 8/40 mm aa – 70 cal 5/533 mm tt	4 b – 2 gt 68,000 hp	35·8	6,000	280	212
13·4	44	5·2	17	2 a/s mortars 1 dct 4 MM 38 Exocet ml					221
14·3	47	6·1	20	1 single Tartar ml 2/127 mm – 54 cal 1 Asroc launcher 5 a/s tt 1 dct	4 b – 2 gt 70,000 hp Oil fuel 900 T	35	4,500	340	221
17·5	57·4	5·1	16·7	2/127 mm – 54 cal 1 Asroc launcher 6 a/s tt 3 helicopters	2 b – 2 gt 70,000 hp	32	7,000	364	212

TECHNICAL DATA

Page	Nation	Name of Ship	Shipyard	Date ld l c r	Displacement (full load)	Length o.a. meters	feet
215	JAPAN	**Amatsukaze** (1 ship)	Mitsubishi, Nagasaki	1962/63/65	4,000	131	429·8
221		**Takatsuki** (4 ships)	Ishikawajima, Tokyo	1964/66/67	4,000	136	446·2
221	GREAT BRITAIN	County class (7 ships)	Cammell Laird and others	1959/60/62	6,200	158·7	520·5
211		**Hampshire** (same class) Also classed as light cruiser	John Brown	1959/61/63			
221		**Sheffield** (6 ships)	Vickers	1970/71/74	3,675	125	410
221	GREECE	**Themistocles** (4 ships)	Bath Iron Works	1944/45/71	3,550	119·2	390·5
214	ITALY	**Ardito** (2 ships)	Castellammare	1968/71/73	4,400	136·6	446·4
221		**Audace**	Riva Trigoso	1968/71/72			
221		**Impetuoso** (2 ships)	Riva Trigoso	1959/62/64	3,851	131·3	429·5
221	YUGOSLAVIA	**Split** (1 ship)	Brodograd, Rileka	1939/40/58	3,000	120	393·7
221	NETHERLANDS	**Tromp** (2 ships)	Schelde, Flushing	1971/73/76	5,400	138·4	454·1
221	POLAND	**Warzawa** (1 ship) ex-Russian **Kotlin**	USSR	1958	3,885	126·5	415
214	SPAIN	**Roger de Lauria** (2 ships)	Ferrol	1951/58/69	3,785	119·3	391·5
221		**Oquendo** (1 ship)	Ferrol	1951/56/61	3,005	116·4	382
211	UNITED STATES OF AMERICA	**California** (2 ships)	Newport News	1970/71/74	10,150	181·7	596
213		**South Carolina**					
212		**Bainbridge** (1 ship)	Bethlehem Shipbuilding	1959/61/62	8,580	172·5	565
221		**Spruance** (30 ships)	Litton Ship Systems, Mississippi	1972/73/75	7,800	171·1	563·3

Beam		Draft		Principal armaments	Engine equipment	Speed (knots)	Range (miles)	Complement	Page
meters	feet	meters	feet						
13·4	44	4·2	13·8	1 Tartar ml 4/76 mm – 50 cal 1 Asroc launcher 6 a/s tt	2 b – 2 gt 60,000 hp Oil fuel 900 T	33	7,000	290	215
13·4	44	4·4	14·5	2/127 mm – 54 cal 1 Asroc launcher 6 a/s tt 3 helicopters	2 b – 2 gt 60,000 hp Oil fuel 900 T	32	7,000	270	221
16·5	54	6·1	20	1 twin Seaslug ml 2 quadruple Seacat ml 4 Exocet ml 4/114 mm 1 helicopter	2 b – 2 gt – 4 gas t 60,000 hp Oil fuel 600 T	32·5	3,500	471	221 211
14·3	47	6·7	22	1 twin Seadart ml 1/114 mm 2/20 mm 1 helicopter	2 b – 2 gt 54,000 + 8,200 hp	30	4,500	280	221
12·4	40·9	5·8	19	6/127 mm – 38 cal 1 Asroc launcher 6 a/s tt	4 b – 2 gt 60,000 hp Oil fuel 650 T	34	4,800	269	221
14·23	47·1	4·6	15	1 Tartar ml 2/127 mm – 54 cal 4/76 mm – 62 cal 6 a/s tt 2 helicopters	4 b – 2 gt 73,000 hp	33	—	395	214 221
13·6	44·7	4·5	14·8	1 Tartar ml 4/127 mm – 38 cal 16/40 mm – 56 cal 6 a/s tt 1 a/s mortar 4 helicopters	4 b – 2 gt 65,000 hp Oil fuel 650 T	34	3,450	344	221
11·1	36·5	3·8	12·3	4/127 mm – 38 cal 12/40 mm – 56 cal 5/533 mm tt 2 a/s Squids 6 dct 2 dc racks 40 mines	2 b – 2 gt 50,000 hp Oil fuel 590 T	31	—	240	221
14·8	48·6	4·6	15·1	1 Tartar ml 1/8-bar Seacat ml 2/120 mm 6 a/s tt 1 helicopter	2 + 2 gas t 44,000 + 10,000 hp	30	4,000	306	221
12·9	42·3	4·9	16·1	1 twin Goa ml 2/130 mm 4/47 mm 4/30 mm 5/533 mm tt 2/12-bar MBU	4 b – 2 gt 80,000 hp Oil fuel 300 T	36	5,500	285	221
13	42·7	5·6	18·4	6/127 mm – 38 cal 2/533 mm tt 6 a/s tt 1 helicopter	3 b – 2 gt 60,000 hp Oil fuel 673 T	30	4,500	318	214
11·1	36·5	3·8	12·5	4/120 mm – 50 cal 6/40 mm – 70 cal 2 a/s Hedgehogs 2 Mk 4 tt	3 b – 2 gt 60,000 hp Oil fuel 659 T	32·4	5,000	250	221
18·6	61	9·6	31·5	2 Tartar ml 2/127 mm – 54 cal 1 Asroc launcher 6 a/s tt	2 nr – 2 gt 140,000 hp	35	—	540	211 213
17·6	57·9	7·9	29	2 Terrier SAM ml 4/76 mm – 50 cal 1 Asroc launcher 6 a/s tt	2 nr – 2 gt 100,000 hp	35	150,000	450	212
17·6	57·9	8·8	29	2/127 mm – 54 cal 1/8-bar Sea Sparrow ml 1/8-bar Asroc launcher 2 a/s tt 2 helicopters	4 gas t 80,000 hp 2 screws	30	6,000	250	221

TECHNICAL DATA

Page	Nation	Name of Ship	Shipyard	Date ld l c r	Displacement (full load)	Length o.a. meters	feet
212	UNITED STATES OF AMERICA	**Decatur** (4 ships)	Bethlehem Shipbuilding	1954/55/67	4,450	127·6	418·4
221		**Forrest Sherman** (14 ships)	Bath Iron Works	1953/55/55	4,050 (standard)	127·6	418·4
221	SWEDEN	**Ostergotland** (4 ships) Frigate also classed as light cruiser	Götaverken, Göteborg	1955/56/58 1962/64	2,600	112	367·5
221	TURKEY	**Zafer** (1 ship)	Federal Shipbuilding	1944/44/45	3,320	114·8	376·5
212	USSR	**Nikolaiev** (4 ships)	Nikolaiev	1969/71/73	9,500	173·8	570
221		**Kara** (same class) Frigate also classed as light cruiser	Nikolaiev	1969/71/73			
211		**Otrazhny** (Kashin class, 19 ships) Frigate also classed as destroyer	Leningrad	1961/68/70	5,200	146·5	481
	SHIPS IN CATEGORY F: Frigates and Corvettes						
221	AUSTRALIA	**Yarra** (Yarra class, 6 ships) Frigate	Williamstown Naval Dockyard	1957/58/61	2,700	112·8	370
221	BELGIUM	**Westhinder** (E-71 class, 4 ships)	Cockerill, Hoboken	1974/75/78	1,828	96·6	317
221	BRAZIL	**Angostura** (10 ships) Corvette minelayer	Netherlands	1955/56	911	56	184
221	CANADA	Improved **Restigouche** class (14 ships)	Vickers, Montreal	1953/54/58/73	3,000	113·1	371
221		**Terra Nova** (same class)	Vickers, Montreal	1953/54/58/68	2,880		
213		**Fraser** (St. Laurent class, 6 ships)	Yarrows, British Columbia	1951/53/57/66	2,800	111·5	366
221	CHILE	**Lynch** (British Leander class, 2 ships)	Yarrow, Glasgow	1971/72/75	2.962	113·4	372
221	CHINA	**Ch' Eng Tu** (Russian Riga class, 4 ships) Corvette	Hutang, Shanghai	1955/57/60	1,600	91	298/8

Beam		Draft		Principal armaments	Engine equipment	Speed (knots)	Range (miles)	Complement	Page
meters	feet	meters	feet						
13·8	45·2	6·1	20	1 single Tartar SAM ml 1/127 mm – 54 cal 1 Asroc launcher 4 a/s tt	4 b – 2 gt 70,000 hp	33		335	212
13·8	45·2	6·1	20	3/127 mm – 54 cal 4/76 mm – 50 cal 2 Hedgehogs 6 a/s tt 1/8-bar Asroc launcher	4 b – 2 gt 70,000 hp	33	—	292	221
11·2	36·8	3·7	12	4/120 mm 4/40 mm aa 1 quadruple Seacat ml 6/533 mm tt 1 a/s Squid 60 mines	2 b – 2 gt 40,000 hp Oil fuel 330 T	35	2,200	244	221
12·4	40·9	5·8	19	6/127 mm – 38 cal 2 a/s Hedgehogs 2 triple a/s tt 2 Mk 25 a/s tt	4 b – 2 gt 60,000 hp Oil fuel 650 T	34	4,600	275	221
18·3	60	6·2	20	8 SS 10 ml 2 SAN-3 ml 2 SAN-4 ml 4/76 mm 8/30 mm 2 dct 10/533 mm tt 1 helicopter	b + gas t 120,000 hp 2 screws	33	—	686	212 221
15·9	52·5	5·8	19	2 twin SAN-1 ml 4/76 mm 5/533 mm tt 2 MBU 2500A launchers 2 dct	4 gas t 95,000 hp 2 screws	35	—	535	211
12·5	41	5·3	17·2	2/114 mm 1 quadruple Seacat ml 1 Ikara a/s launcher 1/3-bar Limbo a/s mortar	2 b – 2 gt 34,000 hp Oil fuel 400 T	30	4,500	250	221
11·8	38·6	5·3	17·2	1/100 mm 1/8-bar Sea Sparrow ml 4 Exocet ml 2/40 mm 2 rl 6 a/s rl 1 helicopter	2 d – 1 gas t 33,500 hp 2 screws Oil fuel 190 T	28	3,000	160	221
9·6	30·5	3·5	11·7	1/76 mm – 50 cal 4/20 mm aa	3 d 2,160 hp Oil fuel 135 T	16	—	60	221
12·8	42	4·4	14·4	2/76 mm 1 Mk 10 Limbo a/s launcher 2 triple a/s tt 2/76 mm 1/8-bar Sea Sparrow ml 1 Asroc launcher	2 b – 2 gt 30,000 hp	28	4,750	246	221 221
12·8	42	4	13·2	2/76 mm – 50 cal 1 Mk 10 Limbo a/s launcher 6 a/s tt 1 helicopter	2 b – 2 gt 30,000 hp	28·5	4,570	250	213
13·1	43	5·5	18	2/114 mm 4 Exocet ml 1 quadruple Seacat ml 2/20 mm 1 helicopter	2 b – 2 gt 30,000 hp	30	4,500	263	221
10·2	33·7	3	10	1 SSN-2 ml 3/100 mm 4/37 mm 3/533 mm tt 4 dct 50 mines	2 b – 2 gt 25,000 hp	28	2,500	150	221

TECHNICAL DATA

Page	Nation	Name of Ship	Shipyard	Date ld l c r	Displacement (full load)	Length o.a. meters	feet
215	DENMARK	**Peder Skram** (2 ships)	Helsingörs	1965/65/66	2,720	112·5	396·5
221		**Herluf Trolle** Frigate					
221	FINLAND	**Turunmaa** (2 ships) Corvette	Helsinki	1967/67/68	770	74·1	243·1
221	FRANCE	**Commandant Rivière** (9 ships) Frigate	Lorient Dockyard	1957/58/62	2,250	103	338
221		**Le Normand** (14 ships) Frigate	F.Ch. de la Medit	1953/54/56	1,702	99·8	325·8
222		**D'Estienne d'Orves** (14 ships) Corvette	Lorient Dockyard	1972/73/75	1,170	80	262·5
222	GERMANY	**Thälmann** (Russian Riga class, 2 ships)	USSR	1954/56	1,600	98	298·8
222	JAPAN	**Chikugo** (12 ships) Frigate	Mitsui, Tamano	1968/70/70	1,750	93	305·5
222		**Mogami** (Isuzu class, 4 ships) Frigate	Mitsui, Tamano	1960/61/61	1,700	94	308·5
222		**Ikazuchi** (2 ships) Frigate	Kawasaki, Kobe	1954/55/56	1,300	88	288·7
222	GREAT BRITAIN	**Tribal** (7 ships)	Yarrow, Scotstown	1958/59/61	2,700	109·7	360
222		**Exmouth** (Blackwood class, 6 ships)	White, Cowes	1952/53/56	1,456	94·5	310
215		**Lynx** (Leopard class, 3 ships)	John Brown	1953/55/57	2,520	103·6	339·8
222	INDIA	**Nilgiri** (6 ships) Frigate	Bombay	1967/68/71	2,800	113·4	372
213	IRAN	**Saam** (4 ships) Frigate	Vosper Thornycroft, Woolston	1967/68/71	1,290	94·5	310
215	ITALY	**Lupo** (4 ships) Frigate	Riva Trigoso	1975/79	2,500	106	330
213		**Alpino** (2 ships) Frigate	Riva Trigoso	1963/67/68	2,689	113·3	371·7

Beam		Draft		Principal armaments	Engine equipment	Speed (knots)	Range (miles)	Complement	Page
meters	feet	meters	feet						
12	39·5	3·6	11·8	4/127 mm 4/40 mm 2 dct 1 Sea Sparrow ml	2 d – 2 gas t 44,000 + 4,800 hp	30	—	112	215 221
7·8	25·6	2·6	7·9	1/120 mm 2/40 mm 2/30 mm 2 dct	3 d – 1 gas t 22,000 + 3,900 hp Oil fuel 300 T	33	—	70	221
11·5	37·8	3·8	12·5	1 quadruple a/s mortar 2/30 mm 4 Exocet ml 6 tt 1 helicopter	4 d 16,000 hp 2 screws Oil fuel 210 T	25	4,500	215	221
10·3	33·8	3·4	11·2	6/57 mm 2/20 mm 12 a/s tt 1/6-bar mortar 2 dct 1 dc rack	2 b – 2 gt 20,000 hp Oil fuel 310 T	27	4,500	205	221
10·3	33·8	2·8	9·8	2/20 mm aa 1/100 mm 2 MM 38 missiles 4 a/s tt 1 rl	2 d 11,000 hp	24	4,500	62	222
9·5	33·7	3	11	3/100 mm 4/37 mm 2/533 mm tt 4 dct 50 mines	2 b – 2 gt 25,000 Oil fuel 300 T	28	—	—	222
10·8	35·5	3·5	11·5	2/76 mm – 50 cal 2/40 – 56 cal 1/8-bar Asroc launcher 6/533 mm tt	4 d 16,000 hp 2 screws	25	—	165	222
10·4	34·2	3·5	11·5	4/76 mm – 50 cal 4/533 mm a/s tt 1 rl 2 dc racks	4 d 16,000 hp 2 screws	25	—	180	222
8·7	28·5	3·1	10·2	2·76 mm – 50 cal 2/40 mm – 56 cal 1 a/s Hedgehog 8 K guns 2 dc racks	2 d 12,000 hp	25	6,500	160	222
12·9	42·3	5·3	17·5	2 quadruple Seacat ml 2/114 mm 1/3-bar a/s Limbo mortar 1 helicopter	2 b – 1 gt + 1 gas t 20,000 + 7,500 hp Oil fuel 400 T	28	4,500	—	222
10·1	33	4·7	15·5	2/40 mm 2/3-bar a/s Limbo mortars	2 b – 1 gt 25,000 hp Oil fuel 275 T	27·8	4,000	275	222
12·2	40	4·9	16	4/114 mm 1/40 mm 1/3-bar a/s Squid mortar	8 d 14,400 hp 2 screws Oil fuel 230 T	24	4,500	235	215
13·1	43	5·5	18	2/40 mm 2/114 mm 2 quadruple Seacat ml 1/3-bar a/s Limbo mortar 1 helicopter	2 b – 2 gt 30,000 hp	30	—	—	222
10·4	34	3·4	11·2	1/114 1 quintuple Seakiller ml 1 triple Seacat ml 1/3-bar a/s Limbo mortar	2 d + 2 gas t 46,400 + 3,800 hp	40	5,000	125	213
12	40	3·7	12	1/127 mm – 54 cal 8 Otomat missiles 1/8-bar Sea Sparrow ml 6 a/s tt 1 helicopter	2 d + 2 gas t 50,000 hp + 7,800 hp	33	—	—	215
13·3	43·6	3·9	12·7	6/76 mm – 62 cal 1 dct 6 a/s tt 1 helicopter	4 d – 2 gas t 31,800 + 15,000 hp Oil fuel 275 T	29	—	254	213

TECHNICAL DATA

Page	Nation	Name of Ship	Shipyard	Date ld l c r	Displacement (full load)	Length o.a. meters	feet
222	ITALY	**Bergamini** (4 ships) Frigate	CRDA, Trieste	1959/60/62	1.650	96	311·7
222		**Centauro** (4 ships) Frigate	Ansaldo, Leghorn	1952/54/57	2.250	103·3	338·4
222	LIBYA	**Dat-Assawari** (1 ship) Frigate	Vosper Thornycroft, Woolston	1968/69/73	1.625	100·6	330
222	NORWAY	**Oslo** class (5 ships) Frigate	Marinens Hovedverft Horten	1963/64/66	1.745	96·6	317
222	NETHERLANDS	**Van Speijk** class (6 ships) Frigate	Amsterdam	1963/65	2.850	113	372
214	SPAIN	**Baleares** (Andalucia class, 5 ships)	Bazan, Cartagena	1968/70/73	4.177	135·5	438
222		**Andalucia**	Bazan, Cartagena	1969/71/74			
222	TURKEY	**Berk** (2 ships)	Gölcük Naval Yard	1967/71/73	1.950	95·2	311·7
213	UNITED STATES OF AMERICA	**R. E. Peary** (Knox class, 46 ships)	Todd, Seattle	1966/66/69	4.100	133·5	438
222		**Garcia** (10 ships)	Bethlehem Shipbuilding	1962/63/64	3.490	126·6	414·5
SHIPS IN CATEGORY S: Submarines and underwater craft							
222	ARGENTINA	**Santa Fè** (USN Balao class, 2 ships)	General Dynamics	1944/44/45 1972	1.840/2.425	93·8	307·5
222	AUSTRALIA	**Onslow** (6 ships)	Scotts' Shipbuilding, Greenock	1967/68/70	1.610/2.196	90·1	295·5
217	FRANCE	**Gymnote** (1 ship)	Cherbourg Dockyard	1963/64/66	3.000/3.250	84	275·6
222		**Le Redoutable** (5 ships) Nuclear-powered	Cherbourg Dockyard	1964/67/71	7.500/9.000	128	420
222	JAPAN	**Uzushio** (8 ships)	Kawasaki, Kobe	1968/70/71	1.850 (standard)	72	236·2
222	GREAT BRITAIN	**Resolution** (4 ships)	Vickers, Barrow	1964/67/68	7.500/8.400	129·5	425
222		**Valiant** (5 ships) Nuclear-powered	Vickers, Barrow	1962/63/66	3.500/4.500	86·9	285
222	ITALY	**Piomarta** (2 ships) ex-**Trigger**	General Dynamics	1949/51/52	1.970/2.700	87·4	287

| Beam | | Draft | | Principal armaments | Engine equipment | Speed (knots) | Range (miles) | Comple- ment | Page |
meters	feet	meters	feet						
11·3	37·4	3·2	10·5	2/76 mm – 62 cal 1 dct 6 a/s tt 1 helicopter	4 d 15,000 hp	24	4,000	160	222
12	39·5	3·8	12·6	3/76 mm – 62 cal 1 dct 6 a/s tt	2 b – 2 gt 22,000 hp Oil fuel 400 T	25	3,660	255	222
11	36	3·4	11·2	1/114 mm 2/40 mm 2 triple Seacat ml 1 dct	2 d – 2 gas t 26,000 hp	37	5,700	—	222
11·3	36·7	5·3	17·4	4/76 mm – 50 cal 2 a/s Terne launchers Penguin or Sea Sparrow ml 1 helicopter	2 b – 1 gt 20,000 hp	25	4,500	151	222
12·5	41	4·2	18	2/114 mm 2 quadruple Seacat ml 1 a/s Limbo mortar 1 helicopter	2 b – 2 gt 30,000 hp	28·5	4,500	254	222
14·3	46·9	7·9	25·9	1 Standard ml 1/127 mm – 38 cal 1/8-bar Asroc launcher 6 a/s tt	2 b – 1 gt 35,000 hp	28	4,000	256	214 222
11·8	38·7	5·5	18·1	4/76 mm 6 a/s tt 1 rl 1 dct 1 helicopter	4 d 24,000 hp 2 screws	25	—	—	222
14·3	46·9	7·6	24·75	1/127 mm – 54 cal 1/8-bar Sea Sparrow ml 1/8-bar Asroc launcher 4 a/s tt 2 helicopters	2 b – 1 gt 35,000 hp	27	4,000	245	213
13·4	44·2	7·3	24	2/127 mm – 38 cal 1/8-bar Asroc launcher 2 triple a/s tt 1 helicopter	2 b – 1 gt 35,000 hp	27	—	247	222
8·2	27·2	5·2	17	10/533 mm tt	3 d – 4,800 hp 2 e – 5,400 hp	sub 15 18	12,000	82 84	222
8·1	26·5	5·5	18	8/533 mm tt	2 d 3,600 hp Oil fuel 300 T	sub 16 18	12,000	—	222
10·6	34·7	7·6	25	4 MSBS tubes	4 d/2 e 2,600 hp	sub 10 11	—	78	217
10·6	34·7	10	32·8	16 Polaris missiles 4/550 mm tt	1 nr/2 gt – 15,000 hp 1 e 1 d	sub 19 25	—	135	222
9·9	32·5	7·4	24·6	6/533 mm tt	2 d – 3,400 hp 1 e – 7,200 hp	sub 20 12	—	80	222
10·1	33·2	9·1	30	16 Polaris missiles 6/533 mm tt	1 nr/1 gt – 1 de 20,000 hp	sub 25 20	—	141	222
10·1	33·2	8·2	27	6/533 mm tt	1 nr/1 gt 20,000 hp	sub 30	—	103	222
8·3	27·3	6·2	19	8/533 mm tt	3 d – 4,500 hp 2 e – 5,600 hp	sub 18 20	14,000	83	222

TECHNICAL DATA

Page	Nation	Name of Ship	Shipyard	Date ld l c r	Displacement (full load)	Length o.a. meters	feet
222	NETHERLANDS	**Dolfijn** (2 ships)	Rotterdamse Droogdok	1954/59/60	1,140/1,494	78	260·9
222	UNITED STATES OF AMERICA	**Lafayette** (31 ships)	General Dynamics	1961/62/63	6,650/7,320	129·5	425
235		**Ethan Allan** (5 ships)	General Dynamics	1959/60/61	6,900/7,900	125	410·5
222		**Narwal** (1 ship)	General Dynamics	1966/67/69	4,450/5,350	95·7	314
222		**Tresher** (6 ships) Nuclear-powered	Ingalls Shipbuilding	1960/62/64	3,526/4,310	84·9	276·4
217		**Halibut** (1 ship)	Mare Island Navy Shipyard	1957/59/60	3,845/5,000	106·7	350
222		**Sea Wolf** (1 ship) Nuclear-powered	General Dynamics	1953/55/57	3,720/4,280	102	337·5
219		**G. Washington** (5 ships) Nuclear-powered	General Dynamics	1957/59/59	5,900/6,700	115·8	381·7
219		**Triton** (1 ship) Nuclear-powered	General Dynamics	1956/58/59	5,940/7,780	136·3	447·5
222		**Sailfish** (2 ships)	Portsmouth Dockyard	1954/55/56	2,625/3,168	106·8	350·4
222		**Albacore** (1 ship)	Portsmouth Dockyard	1952/53/53	1,517/1,847	63·6	210·5
222		**Grayback** (1 ship)	Mare Island Navy Shipyard	1957/58/69	2,671/3,652	101·8	334
222	SWEDEN	**Draken** (6 ships)	Kockums	1957/60/62	835/1,100	69·2	226·4
222		**Abborren** (3 ships)	Kockums	1944/45/62 1964	430/460	50	164
222	USSR	Class **D** (8 ships) Nuclear-powered	USSR	1972/75	8,000/9,000	130	426·5
222		Class **Y** (30 ships)	USSR	1967/72	8,000/9,000	130	426·5
222		Class **E** (25 ships) Nuclear-powered	USSR	1960/64	5,000/5,600	118	387·4
222		Class **H** (9 ships) Nuclear-powered	USSR	1959/64	3,700/4,100	116	377·2
222		Class **G** (6 ships)	USSR	1962	1,250/1,700	82·5	269·6
222		Class **Z** (20 ships)	USSR	1951/55	2,100/2,700	90	295·3
217		**Long Bin** (Class **W.** 120 ships)	USSR	1962	1,300/1,800	83	272·3
217		Class **ZV** (2 ships)	USSR	1954/58	2,150/2,750	90	295·3

SHIPS IN CATEGORY AL: Stores support ships

Page	Nation	Name of Ship	Shipyard	Date ld l c r	Displacement (full load)	Length o.a. meters	feet
216	BELGIUM	**Zinnia** (1 ship)	Cockerill, Hoboken	1966/67/68	2,435	99·5	326·4
223	CANADA	**Provider** (1 ship) Superceded by **Preserver** and **Protecteur**	Davie Shipbuilding	1961/62/63	24,000	167·9	546

| Beam | | Draft | | Principal armaments | Engine equipment | Speed (knots) | Range (miles) | Complement | Page |
meters	feet	meters	feet						
7·8	25·8	4·8	15·8	8/533 mm tt	3 d – 3,100 hp 2 e – 4,200 hp	sub 16 19	—	64	222
10·1	33	19·6	31·5	16 Poseidon missiles 4/533 mm tt	1 nr 1 gt – 30,000 hp	sub 20 30	200,000	147	222
10·1	33	9·4	30	16 Polaris missiles 4/533 mm tt	1 nr 1 gt – 30,000 hp	sub 20 30	140,000	139	235
11·5	38	7·9	26	4/533 mm tt Subroc missiles	1 nr 2 gt – 34,000 hp	sub 30 20	—	107	222
9·7	32	8·8	29	4/533 mm tt Subroc missiles	1 nr 1 gt – 30,000 hp	sub 20 30	60,000	—	222
8·9	29·5	6·5	21·5	6/533 mm tt	1 nr 2 gt – 7,000 hp	sub 15 18	—	97	217
8·5	27·7	6·7	22	6/533 mm tt	1 nr 2 gt – 16,700 hp	sub 19 20	70,000	105	222
10·1	33	8·8	29	16 Polaris missiles 6/533 mm tt	1 nr 1 gt – 30,000 hp	sub 20 30	140,000	140	219
11·3	37	7·3	24	6/533 mm tt	2 nr 2 gt – 34,000 hp	sub 22 27	—	172	219
8·8	28·4	5·5	18	6/533 mm tt	4 d – 6,000 hp 4 e – 8,200 hp	sub 14 19·5	—	95	222
8·3	27·5	5·6	18·5		2 d – 2 e 15,000 hp	sub 25 35	—	52	222
9·1	30	5·8	19	8/533 mm tt	3 d – 4,500 hp 2 e – 5,600 hp	sub 15 18	—	87 67 (soldiers)	222
5·1	16·7	5·3	17·4	4/533 mm tt	de – 1,900 hp	sub 17 20	—	36	222
4·3	14·1	3·8	12·5	4/533 mm tt	2 d – 1,500 hp 1 e – 750 hp	sub 9 14	—	23	222
10·6	34·8	10	32·8	12 SSN-8 ballistic missiles 8/533 mm tt	1 nr – 2 gt 24,000 hp	25	—	120	222
10·6	34·8	10	32·8	16 SSN-6 ballistic missiles 8/533 mm tt	1 nr – 2 gt 24,000 hp	sub 22 30	—	120	222
8·6	28·4	7·9	25·9	6 SSN-3 missiles 8 SSN-3/E2 missiles 6/533 mm tt 4/406 mm tt	1 nr – 1 gt 22,500 hp	sub 20 25	—	100	222
8·6	28·2	7·5	25	3 SSN missiles 6/533 mm tt 2/450 mm tt	1 nr – 2 gt 22,500 hp	sub 20 25	—	90	220
8·5	28	4·7	15	4 SSN-3 missiles 4/533 mm tt	2 d – 4,000 hp 2 e – 2,500 hp	sub 15 17	—	86	222
7·3	24·1	5·8	19	2 SSN-4 missiles 10/533 mm tt 40 mines	2 d – 10,000 hp 2 e – 3,500 hp	sub 15 18	13,000	85	222
6·4	19·8	4·8	15·7	6/533 mm tt 4 SSN-3 missiles 40 mines	2 d – 4,000 hp 2 e – 2,800 hp	sub 15 17	13,000		217
7·3	24·1	5·8	19	2 SSN-4 missiles 10/533 mm tt	2 d – 10,000 hp 2 e – 3,500 hp	sub 15 18	25,000		217
14	49·9	3·6	11·8	3/40 mm 1 helicopter	2 d 5,000 hp Oil fuel 500 T	18	4,400 10,000	125	216
23·2	76·6	9·1	30	2/76 mm 3 helicopters	2 b – 1 gt 21,000 hp Oil fuel 1,200 T	20	7,500	227	223

TECHNICAL DATA

Page	Nation	Name of Ship	Shipyard	Date ld l c r	Displacement (full load)	Length o.a. meters	feet
223	GREAT BRITAIN	**Lyness** (3 ships)	Swan Hunter	1965/66/66	16,500	158·7	524
223	UNITED STATES OF AMERICA	**Samuel Gompers** (4 ships)	Puget Sound Navy Yard	1964/66/67	21,600	196	643
223	USSR	Don class (6 ships)	USSR	1959/61	9,500	140·5	461
	SHIPS IN CATEGORY A: Auxiliary ships						
216	CANADA	**Endeavour** (1 ship)	Farrows, British Columbia	1962/63/65	1,564	77·2	236
223		**Quadra** (2 ships)	Burrard, British Columbia	1965/66/67	5,600	123	404·2
223	FRANCE	**Poincaré** (1 ship)	CRDA	1960	24,000	180	590·6
223	JAPAN	**Katori** (1 ship)	Ishikawajima Harima, Tokyo	1967/68/69	4,000	127·5	418·5
223	UNITED STATES OF AMERICA	**Norton Sound** (1 ship)	Los Angeles Shipbuilding	1942/43/44	15,092	165·2	543·25
214		**Annapolis**	Todd, Tacoma	1962/64	11,373	171·6	563
219		**Hayes** (1 ship)	Todd, Seattle	1968/70/72	3,080	75·1	246·5
219	USSR	**Kosmonaut Vladimir Komarov**	USSR	1967/68	17,500	156	510·8
223		**Chajma** (2 ships)	USSR	1956	5,000	145	440·8
223		**Arktika** (1 ship)	USSR	1961	25,000	160	524·9
	SHIPS IN CATEGORY M: Minesweepers						
223	CANADA	**Bay** (1 ship)	USA	1968/70/71	510	46·5	148
223	FRANCE	**Alencon** (14 ships)	USA	1955/56	780	50·3	171
223		**Mercure** (1 ship)	CMN, Cherbourg	1955/57/58	400	45	145·5
223	GERMANY, FEDERAL REPUBLIC OF	**Niobe** (10 ships)	Krögerwerft, Rendsburg	1956/57/58	180	37·9	115·2
	SHIPS IN CATEGORY P: Light and fast attack craft						
223	CHINA	Shanghai (220 ships)	USSR	1974/75	130		
217	FINLAND	**Isku** (1 ship)		1969/70	115	26·3	86·5
216	FRANCE	**La Combattante**	CMN, Cherbourg	1962/64	202	45	147·8
216		**P.R. 72**	SFCN	1970/74	420	57	200
217		**S.A. 805**	SNIAS	1971/74	78	—	—
223	GERMANY	**S. 61**	Lurssen	1973/76	378	57	200

TECHNICAL DATA

Beam		Draft		Principal armaments	Engine equipment	Speed (knots)	Range (miles)	Complement	Page
meters	feet	meters	feet						
21·9	72	7·8	25·5	2/40 mm helicopter deck	1 d 12,000 hp	17	—	105	223
26	85	9	22·5	1/127 mm – 38 cal 1 Sea Sparrow ml	de 20,000 hp	19	—	1,806	223
19·2	63	7·3	24	4/100 mm 8/57 mm 1 helicopter	4 d 14,000 hp 2 screws	20	—	—	223
12·8	38·5	4·6	13	1 helicopter	2 de – 2,960 hp 2 screws	16	10,000	58	216
18·2	50	6·4	17·5	1 helicopter	2 b – 2 te 7,500 hp	18	8,400	96	223
22·2	72·8	9·5	28·9	1 helicopter 1/20 mm aa	2 b – 1 gt 8,000 hp	14	11,800	305	223
15	49·3	4·3	14·6	4/76 mm 6 a/s tt 1 rl 2 helicopters	b – 2 gt 20,000 hp	25	7,000	460	223
21·5	71·6	7·15	23·5	1/127 mm – 54 cal 1 Sea Sparrow ml	4 b – 2 gt 12,000 hp	19	—	292	223
22·9	75	9·3	30·6	8/76 mm aa – 50 cal	4 b – 2 gt 16,000 hp	18	—	710	214
24·4	75	5·8	18·8	Oceanographic survey ship	2 d 5,400 hp	15	—	74	219
21	75/5	9	29·5	Atmospheric research ship	2 d 24,000 hp	22	—	162	219
17	51·6	6	18·2	1 helicopter	d 18,000 hp	18	—	108	223
25	82	8·8	33·5	8 helicopters	1 nr – gt 26,000 hp	25	—	126	223
8·9	29·3	2·5	6·5	1/20 mm aa	1 d 1,800 hp	15	3,000	59	223
10·7	35	3·2	10·3	1/40 mm aa	2 d 1,600 hp	14	3,000	56	223
8·3	27	4	18·5	2/20 mm aa	2 d 4,000 hp	15	3,000	48	223
7·8	21·3	2	5·9	1/40 mm aa	2 d 2,000 hp	14	740	22	223
—	—	—	—	4/37 mm 2/25 mm 2 tt 1/57 mm	4 d 4,800 hp	28	—	—	223
8·7	28·6	2	6·6	4 SSN-2 system launchers 2/30 mm	4 d 4,800 hp	25	—	17	217
7·35	24·2	2·45	6·5	1/30 mm aa 1 quadruple SS-11 ml	2 d 3,200 hp	23	2,000	25	216
8·5	26·2	2·5	6·6	4 Exocet ml 2/35 mm aa 1/57 mm	4 d 18,000 hp	37·5	—	64	216
—	—	—	—	2 Exocet ml 2/30 mm	4 d 16,000 hp	47	—	7	217
7·8	24·6	2·4	8·5	4 Exocet ml 2/76 mm – 62 cal 2 a/s tt	4 d 18,000 hp	38	1,300	40	223

TECHNICAL DATA

Page	Nation	Name of Ship	Shipyard	Date ld l c r	Displacement (full load)	Length o.a. meters	feet
223	JAPAN	**Hayabusa**	Mitsubishi, Nagasaki	1956/57	380	58	190·2
216	GREAT BRITAIN	**Tenacity**	Vosper Thornycroft	1968/69	220	44	144·5
216	ISRAEL	**Reshef**	Haifa Shipyard	1972/73	415	58·1	190·6
223	ITALY	**Freccia**	Riva Trigoso	1963/65	205	46·1	150
216		**Lampo**	Arsenale MM, Taranto	1957/60/63	196	43	131·5
219		**P. 420**	Oto Melara, La Spezia	1973/74	62·5	22	75
212	NORWAY	**Hai**	Båtservois, Mandal	1958/66	82	24·5	80·3
223		**Storm**	Bergens MV	1962/69	125	36·5	120
223	POLAND	**Czuiny**	USSR	1957/60	370	51	172·8
223	PORTUGAL	**Azevia** (4 ships)	Arsenal do Alfeite	1951/52	275	41	139·8

SHIPS IN CATEGORY L: Amphibious warfare forces

Page	Nation	Name of Ship	Shipyard	Date ld l c r	Displacement (full load)	Length o.a. meters	feet
218	FRANCE	**Orage** (2 ships)	Brest Dockyard	1966/67/68	8,500	149	488·9
223		**Ouragan**	Brest Dockyard	1962/63/65			
223	GREAT BRITAIN	**Fearless** (2 ships)	Harland & Woolf	1962/63/65	12,500	158·5	520
217		**Intrepid**	John Brown	1962/64/66			
223	SPAIN	**Galicia** (1 ship) ex-**San Marcos**	Philadelphia Navy Yard	1944/45	9,375	139	475·4
218	UNITED STATES OF AMERICA	**Tripoli** (Iwo Jima class, 7 ships)	Ingalls Shipbuilding, Mississippi	1964/65/66	18,300	182·8	592
223		**Tarawa** (5 ships)	Ingalls Shipbuilding, Mississippi	1971/73/75	39,300	250·1	820
223		**Blue Ridge** (2 ships)	Philadelphia Navy Yard	1965/69/70	19,290	189	620
223		**Charleston** (5 ships)	Newport News	1966/67/68	20,700	176·8	575·5
223		**Raleigh** (2 ships)	New York Navy Shipyard	1960/62/62	13,900	158·4	521·8
218		**Trenton** (12 ships)	Lockheed Shipbuilding, Trenton	1966/68/70	16,900	174	570
223	USSR	**Alligator** (10 ships)	USSR	1964/66	5,800	114	374
223		**Osa**	USSR	1969/70	200	40·1	128·7

Beam		Draft		Principal armaments	Engine equipment	Speed (knots)	Range (miles)	Complement	Page
meters	feet	meters	feet						
7·8	25·7	2·1	7	2/40 mm 1 a/s Hedgehog 2 Y guns 2 dc racks	2 d – 1 gas t 5,000 + 4,000 hp	26	2,000	75	223
8·1	26·6	2·4	7·8	2 mg	2 d – 3 gas t 12,750 hp	39	2,500	32	216
7·6	25	2·4	8	7 Gabriel missiles 2/76 mm – 62 cal 2 tt	4 d 10,700 hp	32	1,500	45	216
7·2	23·8	1·5	5·5	3/40 mm – 70 cal 2/533 mm tt	2 d – 1 gas t 11,700 hp	40	—	36	223
6·3	21	1·5	5	3/40 mm – 70 cal 2/40 mm – 70 cal 2/533 mm tt	2 d – 1 gas t 11,700 hp	39	—	36	216
7	36·5	—	—	1/76 mm – 62 cal 2 Sea Killer missiles	4 d – gas t 19,000 hp	50	400–1,200	10	219
7·5	24·5	1·9	6·8	1/40 mm aa 1/20 mm 4/533 mm tt	2 d 6,200 hp	45	450	18	212
6·2	20·5	1·5	5	6 Penguin missiles 1/76 mm – 50 cal 1/40 mm – 70 cal	2 d 7,200 hp	33	600	28	223
6	19·6	2·7	7·3	1/85 mm 2/37 mm 4/25 mm mg aa	2 d	24	—	39	223
6·5	21·3	2·6	7	2/20 mm aa	2 d 2,400 hp	17	3,584	30	223
21·5	70·5	4·7	16·1	6/30 mm 2/120 mm 4 helicopters	2 d 8,640 hp	17	4,000	239	218 223
24·4	80	6·1	20·5	4 Seacat ml 2/40 mm 5 helicopters 4 landing craft 700 marines	2 b – 2 gt 22,000 hp	22	5,000	580	223 217
21·9	76·2	4·9	18	12/40 mm aa – 60 cal 8/40 mm – 56 cal 3 helicopters 3/18 landing craft	2 b – 2 gt 7,000 hp	15	8,000	265	223
25·6 fd 32	84 fd 104	7·6	26	4/76 mm aa – 50 cal 2 Sea Sparrow ml 24 helicopters 2,000 marines	4 b – 1 gt 28,000 hp	22	—	528	218
32·3 fd 29·9	106 fd 92·8	8·4	27·5	3/127 mm – 54 cal 2 Sea Sparrow ml 6/20 mm aa 8 VTOL Harrier aircraft 20 helicopters	2 b – 2 gt 140,000 hp	25	10,000	1,825	223
25·2	82	8·2	27	2 Sea Sparrow ml 4/76 mm – 50 cal 3 helicopters	2 b – 2 gt 22,000 hp	20	—	720	223
25	82	8·5	25·5	8/76 – 50 cal helicopter deck landing craft 300 marines	2 b – 1 gt 22,000 hp	20	—	334	223
25·6	84	6·4	21	8/76 mm – 50 cal 6 helicopters landing craft 1,000 marines	2 b – 2 gt 24,000 hp	23	—	490	223
25·6	84	7	23	8/76 mm aa – 50 cal 6 helicopters landing craft	2 b – 2 gt 24,000 hp	20	—	490	218
15·6	50·9	3·5	12·1	2/57 mm aa landing craft	d 8,000 hp	16	6,000	—	223
7	25·1	2	5·9	4/30 mm 4 SS-N 2A ml	3 d 15,000 hp	35	800	25	223

INDEX

[Page numbers in italics (*123*) refer to locations of illustrations.]